INVITATION TO World Religions

INVITATION TO World Religions

JEFFREY BRODD
California State University, Sacramento

LAYNE LITTLE
University of California, Berkeley

BRADLEY NYSTROM
California State University, Sacramento

ROBERT PLATZNER
California State University, Sacramento

RICHARD SHEK
California State University, Sacramento

ERIN STILES
University of Nevada, Reno

Oxford   New York
Oxford University Press

Oxford University Press is a department of the University of Oxford. It furthers
the University's objective of excellence in research, scholarship, and education by
publishing worldwide.

Oxford New York
Auckland   Cape Town   Dar es Salaam   Hong Kong   Karachi
Kuala Lumpur   Madrid   Melbourne   Mexico City   Nairobi
New Delhi   Shanghai   Taipei   Toronto

With offices in
Argentina   Austria   Brazil   Chile   Czech Republic   France   Greece
Guatemala   Hungary   Italy   Japan   Poland   Portugal   Singapore
South Korea   Switzerland   Thailand   Turkey   Ukraine   Vietnam

For titles covered by Section 112 of the US Higher Education Opportunity
Act, please visit www.oup.com/us/he for the latest information about
pricing and alternate formats.

Published by Oxford University Press
198 Madison Avenue, New York, New York 10016
http://www.oup.com

Oxford is a registered trademark of Oxford University Press.

Library of Congress Cataloging-in-Publication Data
Invitation to world religions / Jeffrey Brodd, Layne Little, Bradley Nystrom,
Robert Platzner, Richard Shek, Erin Stiles. — First [edition].
      pages cm
   Includes bibliographical references and index.
   ISBN 978-0-19-973843-4 (pbk.)
   1. Religions.
   BL80.3.I595 2012
   200—dc23

                                                              2012018179

Printing number: 9 8 7 6 5 4 3 2

Printed in the United States of America
on acid-free paper

BRIEF CONTENTS

CONTENTS

5   Buddhism 145

6   Jainism 211

PREFACE

THE WORLD'S RELIGIOUS TRADITIONS have offered answers to the weightiest questions of human existence, contributed to the formation of political and social institutions, inspired masterpieces of art and literature, and provided many of the cultural values and ideals on which entire civilizations have been based. Today, religions continue to play a powerful role in shaping the ways in which people understand themselves, the world they live in, and how they should live.

Invitation to World Religions welcomes all students who may come to this course with concerns such as these. In these pages, we open the doors and invite the reader to explore with wonder and respect. We describe the essential features of the world's great religions and show how they have responded to basic human needs and to the cultural settings in which they developed. We also compare the answers religions have offered us regarding some of the most essential human questions—Why are we here? What is the nature of the universe? How should we live? Our aim has been to balance concision and substance in an introductory text that is accessible as well as challenging.

A team of authors cooperated in writing this book, each one of us bringing our particular scholarly expertise—as well as years of teaching experience—to our respective chapters. We wrote with important learning goals in mind. We want students to gain an objective understanding of the beliefs and practices associated with the world's religions, but we also encourage an empathetic appreciation of what their beliefs and actions actually *mean* to adherents. By emphasizing the connections between religious traditions and their cultural contexts, we seek to heighten awareness of the extent to which religions have influenced, and been influenced by, politics and society, literature, the arts, and philosophy. We also examine the role of religions in our contemporary world, particularly the frequently uneasy boundaries between religion and science, urbanization, and globalization. A thoughtful reading of this book will provide a clear understanding of the characteristics that are unique to individual religions and highlight many of their shared qualities and concerns. Finally, we trust that every reader will find here a means of making sense of other ways of believing and living and of finding a solid basis for the tolerance and respect that are so critically important in times like ours.

Religions are multidimensional. Accordingly, each chapter examines three primary aspects of each religion: teachings, way of life (practices and experiences), and historical development. The text does not, however, strive in all chapters to maintain this same order, nor does it strive to devote equal attention to each category. To do so would be to ignore the varying nature of the religious traditions and to force an inappropriately rigid structure. Judaism, for example, naturally calls for extensive attention to historical development; Jainism, for which an early historical record barely exists, does not. In each case, we structure our approach in the way that seems most natural given the characteristics of the tradition under discussion.

Teachings. Commonly found in scriptures, myths, creeds, and ethical codes, the basic teachings of a religious tradition convey its answers to fundamental questions, such as: What is the human condition? How can the human condition be improved or transcended? What is the nature of the world? What is ultimate reality, and how is it revealed? The authority on which a religion answers questions like these is also important. Are its truths revealed? Are they the products of intellectual effort? Are they insights gained in moments of profound psychological experience? Or are they simply traditional ways of looking at reality and our place within it that have been passed down from generation to generation?

Way of Life. By way of life we mean practices—the things people *do* in making practical application of their beliefs, such as engaging in prayer, meditation, communal worship, or various other forms of ritual. Closely related to practices are modes of experience, the ways in which a religion's adherents actually experience the consequences of applying its teachings. These might include a sense of inner peace, a more acute sense of community with others, a greater awareness of the divine, or a state of profound enlightenment.

Historical Development. Finally, every religious tradition has a history that reveals how and why it developed its distinctive features, including its system of beliefs, leadership and governance structures, social institutions, and forms of artistic expression. Sometimes the forces that generate change arise largely from within a tradition, as in the case of conflict between opposing sects or schools of thought. At other times they operate from the outside, as with the influence exerted by Western powers on foreign colonies and spheres of influence or through the expansion of a tradition into a new cultural milieu. A religion's history also functions to unite the individual with others in a shared memory of the past that helps to explain the present.

ORGANIZATION

Our survey begins with an introductory essay on the academic study of religions found in Chapter 1. After considering what religion *is*, Chapter 1 identifies some of the other important questions scholars ask: What do religions do? What issues of universal concern do they address? What do scholars mean when they speak of mystical experience or of transcendence? What are the constituent parts of religious traditions? How are religions today being affected by the forces of modernization, urbanization, globalization, and science? Finally, the chapter explains why a multidisciplinary approach is necessary in any serious attempt to understand the world's religions.

Chapter 1 is followed by two chapters on indigenous traditions. The book concludes with a chapter on new religions. The nine chapters in the middle are organized according to geographical and (roughly) chronological order, as follows: first, the religions of South Asian origin (Hinduism, Buddhism, Jainism, Sikhism); next, those of East Asian origin (Chinese religions, Japanese religions); and finally, those of West Asian (or Middle Eastern) origin (Judaism, Christianity, Islam). By studying the indigenous traditions first, students will gain an appreciation not only for the many living traditions that continue to thrive but also for certain ways of being religious (such as emphasis on oral transference of myths and other sacred lore) that at one time were predominant in most of today's major world religions. By studying new religions last, students will likewise gain appreciation for living traditions, along with glimpsing the sorts of innovations that occur within the old traditions, too, as religions respond to the cultural, technological, social, and cultural changes and challenges of the world around them.

FEATURES

The study of religions can be daunting to newcomers, who must plunge into a sea of unfamiliar words, concepts, and cultures. For this reason, we have provided a variety of ways for students to engage with important ideas, personalities, and visuals, such as:

- Voices: In personal, candid interviews, a diverse array of people share the ways they live their faith.
- Visual Guide: A key to important religious symbols provided in an easy-to-read table for quick reference and comparison is included in each "Way of Life" section.
- Maps and Timelines: Each chapter begins with a map to provide geographical context for a religion's development. Key features and places mentioned in the chapter are called out on the map. A Timeline in the History section of each chapter further helps students trace the development of each religion within a larger social and political context.
- Seeking Answers: After each chapter's Conclusion, we revisit three essential questions that religions strive to answer. This feature helps students to review the chapter's key concepts and informs their ability to compare constructively the ways in which different religions address the same fundamental human questions:

    1. What is ultimate reality?
    2. How should we live in this world?
    3. What is our ultimate purpose?

PEDAGOGY

Because the concepts and contexts of the world's religions are immeasurably complex, we have worked to present a clear and accessible introductory text. Our tone throughout, while deeply informed by scholarship, is both accessible and appropriate for a wide range of undergraduate students. Consistent chapter structure also helps students to focus on *content* rather than trying to renavigate each chapter anew. With the exception of Chapters 1 and 13, every chapter in the book includes three core modules: the teachings of the religion, the religion as a way of life, and the history of the religion. This modular and predictable structure is also highly flexible, allowing instructors to easily create a syllabus that best reflects their own scholarly interests as well as their students' learning needs.

Other elements that facilitate teaching and learning include:

- Glossary: Important terms are printed in **bold type** at their first occurrence and are explained in the **Glossary** that follows each chapter. In addition, a glossary at the back of the book includes all of the key terms from the entire text.
- End-of-Chapter Questions: Each chapter concludes with two sets of questions to help students review, retain, and reflect upon chapter content. For Review questions prompt students to recall and rehearse key chapter concepts; For Further Reflection questions require students to think critically about the chapter's nuances and encourage both discussion and personal response by inviting students to engage in a more penetrating analysis of a tradition or taking a comparative approach.
- Suggestions for Further Reading: These annotated lists of some of the best and most recent works on each tradition, as well as online resources, encourage students to pursue their exploration of the world's religions.
- Rich, robust, and relevant visuals: Finally, we have filled the pages of *Invitation to World Religions* with an abundance of color photographs and illustrations that add visual experience to our verbal descriptions of sacred objects, buildings, art, and other material aspects of religious life.

SUPPLEMENTS

A rich set of supplemental resources is available to support teaching and learning in this course. These supplements include an **Instructor's Manual with Computerized Test Bank on CD**, downloadable **Learning Management System Cartridges**, and a **Companion Website** for instructors and students available online at oup.com/us/brodd.

The **Instructor's Manual with Computerized Test Bank on CD** includes:
- Instructor's guide
- Chapter overviews
- Chapter summaries
- Chapter goals

- Customizable lecture outlines in PowerPoint® format
- Key terms and definitions
- Web links and other media resources
- A customizable Computerized Test Bank featuring:
  - Multiple choice, true/false, and fill-in-the-blank questions and answer key for each chapter
  - Essay and discussion questions for each chapter

The **Learning Management System Cartridges** include:
- Instructor's Manual and Computerized Test Bank, as well as student material from the companion website, in a fully downloadable format for instructors using a learning management system in their courses.

The **Companion Website** includes the following material:
- Introduction to Book/Authors
  - Table of Contents
  - About the Authors
- Instructor's Resources (password protected)
  - A downloadable version of the Instructor's Manual and Test Bank
- Student Study Guide website
  - Practice quizzes featuring select questions from the Test Bank
  - Interactive flashcards of key terms and definitions
  - Web links and other media resources
  - Chapter Goals

ACKNOWLEDGMENTS

This book has been a long time in the making. Along the way, family members, friends, and colleagues have supported us with love, patience, insights, and suggestions. While there is no way we can adequately thank them here, we can at least acknowledge them: Edward Allen, Dr. Onkar Bindra, Rabbi Brad Bloom, Jill Brodd, Ms. Mary Chapman, Rev. Dr. Christopher Flesoras, George and Kausalya Hart, Kathleen Kelly, Hari Krishnan, Ray and Marilyn Little, Terrie McGraw, Annie Post, Mia Sasaki, Girish Shah, Kitty Shek, Davesh Soneji, Archana Venkatesan, Krishna and Jayashree Venkatesan, and Fr. Art Wehr, S.J.

We have also benefited immensely from the hard work and good suggestions of colleagues across the country. In particular, we would like to thank:

Asad Q. Ahmed, Washington University in St. Louis

Todd M. Brenneman, University of Central Florida

John Baumann, University of Oregon

Robert E. Brown, James Madison University

Dexter E. Callender, Jr., University of Miami

Philip R. Drey, Kirkwood Community College–Cedar Rapids

James Ford, Rogers State University

Kathleen Hladky, Florida State University

Jon Inglett, Oklahoma City Community College

Jeffrey Kaplan, University of Wisconsin Oshkosh

Brad Karelius, Saddleback College

Erik Larson, Florida International University

Mirna Lattouf, Arizona State University

Peter David Lee, Columbia College

Wade Maki, University of Toledo

Isabel Mukonyora, Western Kentucky University

Samuel Murrell, University of North Carolina, Wilmington

Benjamin Murphy, Florida State University–Panama City

Tom Norris, Florida International University

Robert Y. Owusu, Clark Atlanta University

Marialuce Ronconi, Marist College

Claudia Schippert, University of Central Florida

Paul G. Schneider, University of South Florida

Theresa S. Smith, Indiana University of Pennsylvania

Hugh B. Urban, Ohio State University

James W. Ward, James Madison University

Keith Welsh, Webster University

Mlen-Too Wesley, Pennsylvania State University–Altoona

David Wisdo, Columbus State University

Finally, we owe a debt of gratitude to the editorial staff at Oxford University Press. Our thanks go to Robert Miller, executive editor for philosophy and religion, who read our proposal and invited us to publish with Oxford. Robert then put us in the excellent care of two development editors, Frederick Speers and Meg Botteon, whose professionalism and skill were indispensible in making this book a reality. Our thanks also go to Christina Mancuso, who helpfully managed reviews and other editorial tasks, and to Kristin Maffei, for her work with art and images and with the development and production of supplements for the book.

INVITATION TO World
Religions

An INVITATION to the STUDY of WORLD RELIGIONS

ON AMERICAN COLLEGE CAMPUSES, the world's religions are often highly visible. Bulletin boards bear fliers announcing upcoming events pertaining to Buddhist meditation or Hindu sacred art or the Islamic observance of Ramadan. Campus religious groups engage in outreach activities at tables alongside walkways or in student unions, oftentimes with posters quoting scripture or displaying religious icons. Religious elements abound in the subject matter of a wide variety of courses. For example, no culture's history can be explored without at least some reference to its religious traditions. An introduction to philosophy course inevitably involves questions about the nature of ultimate reality, of the soul, and of human destiny. And classes in the appreciation of art or music invite consideration of the typically pronounced influence of religious traditions.

The world's religions are readily apparent well beyond the campus, too. Many people have friends or family members who adhere to a religious tradition different from their own. Driving through many American cities, one is bound to see not only Christian churches and Jewish synagogues, but also Muslim mosques and Hindu and Buddhist temples. Internationally, the religions of the world play a fundamental role in shaping events, from the sustenance of peace movements, charitable causes, and educational institutions to the destructive chaos of terrorist attacks and wars.

On many campuses, people of different religious perspectives gather for candlelight vigils to observe times of sorrow as well as celebration.

A study of the world's religions affords an enhanced understanding of the traditions themselves, of their interrelationship, and of their effects on events, both globally and at home. This chapter introduces the study by first attempting to define "religion," and then explaining appropriate strategies for the academic exploration of religion. First we turn to a basic question that has no easy answers: What exactly *is* a religion? ☀

"RELIGION" AND THE STUDY OF WORLD RELIGIONS

For more than a century, scholars from various academic disciplines have struggled to define the term "religion," without ever having produced a single definition that pleases everyone. Wilfred Cantwell Smith (1916–2000), an important scholar of Islam and philosopher of religion, went so far as to argue in his influential book *The Meaning and End of Religion* (1964)[1] that use of the term by theorists should be abandoned altogether, due to its ambiguity and misleading inferences. Some theorists today maintain a similar stance, asserting that it is impossible to formulate a definition of "religion" that suitably applies to all of its diverse manifestations throughout the ages and around the globe.

Since this entire book is about world religions, we take seriously the insights of Smith and others who have taken on the challenges of clarifying the meaning of the term. The importance of agreeing from the outset on a definition of "religion" can be understood through an analogy that compares religions to houses. Embarking on our study without a shared definition of *what*, exactly, we are studying would be akin to setting off for foreign places to explore the nature of houses without first agreeing on what counts as a house. Would we include apartments? Vacation cabins? Palaces? Defining terms helps us draw clear boundaries around the subject of study. Another challenge involves our preconceived notions of things. We might assume that everyone shares a common idea of a typical "house" (like the kind we learned to draw in grade school), but such an assumption is mainly the result of preconceptions based on our own culture's norms. People from other cultures might dwell in structures that have little in common with our standard notion of a house.

Let's consider some notable attempts at conceptualizing "religion," while keeping in mind our "house" analogy. In fact, when exploring the more specific category "world religion," it will be useful to think of a similarly more specific category of house: a mansion, and more specifically, an old mansion that has undergone a long process of refurbishing. While certainly considered a type of house, a mansion has many rooms that serve a wide variety of functions and styles. Imagine an old mansion that has kept the same foundation and basic structure over the years, but to which various inhabitants have made changes that have enabled the structure to survive into modern times. Our study of the world's religions is an invitation to explore several extraordinary "old mansions." Our tools of study—beginning with considerations of definition—are designed to help us make the most of our explorations, to take in fully the histories, the teachings, and the practices of the world's religions.

Defining "Religion"

The attempt to define "religion"—indeed, the entire enterprise of religious studies—is a relatively recent phenomenon. Prior to the European Enlightenment of the eighteenth century, it rarely occurred to anyone to think of a religion as an entity that could be separated from other aspects of culture, and therefore as something that could be defined as a distinct category. Enlightenment thinkers, most influentially the German philosopher Immanuel Kant (1724–1804), conceived of religion as something separate from the various phenomena the human mind is capable of perceiving.[2] This impulse toward categorically separating religion, coupled with European exploration of distant lands and their unfamiliar "religions," launched efforts to define religion that have continued to the present day.

The world's religions, in other words, have come to be seen as distinctive "houses" (or "mansions") on the cultural landscape. This shift means that we modern observers need to be cautious when appraising the religious aspects of traditional cultures, lest we make the error of assuming that traditional peoples recognized religion as a distinctive category. In no way, however, does this mean that our attempts to study the religions of traditional people are inappropriate. To use a stark example, while Neolithic cave-dwellers might not have thought of their places of shelter as "houses" distinct from other aspects of their surroundings, from our modern perspective, it is perfectly legitimate—and interesting—to categorize caves as such and to analyze Neolithic culture in this light.

Portrait painting of Immanuel Kant (1805) by Joachim Guenin. Deutsches Historisches Museum, Berlin.

The history of the attempt to formulate suitable definitions of "religion" is an intriguing one. In many instances, definitions reveal as much about the age and about the intentions of the theorist as they do about the nature of religion.

The following well-known definitions of "religion" were set forth by notable theorists in several different fields:

> A religion is a unified system of beliefs and practices relative to sacred things, that is to say, things set apart and forbidden—beliefs and practices which unite into one single moral community called a Church, all those who adhere to them.[3]
>
> —Émile Durkheim

> [Religion is] . . . the feelings, acts and experiences of individual men in their solitude, so far as they apprehend themselves to stand in relation to whatever they may consider the divine.[4]
>
> —William James

> [T]he religious aspect points to that which is ultimate, infinite, uncon-
> ditional in man's spiritual life. Religion, in the largest and most basic
> sense of the word, is ultimate concern.[5]
>
> — *Paul Tillich*

French sociologist Émile Durkheim (1858–1917), a founding figure of the sociological study of religion, emphasizes in his definition the *social* nature of religion. He insists on the unification brought about by "beliefs and practices," culminating in a "moral community called a Church." Durkheim surely hits on some central functions of religion, but most scholars contend that he overemphasizes this social orientation. On the other hand, American psychologist William James (1842–1910) emphasizes the *individual* nature of religion. While this aspect is also clearly important, his definition omits any mention of religion's social nature. The definitions put forth by Durkheim and James, while provocative, are therefore problematically limiting.

Paul Tillich (1886–1965), a Protestant theologian, naturally connects religion to a focus on "man's spiritual life." His notion of religion as "ultimate concern" has been quite influential over the past several decades, probably in part because many find it true to their own experiences. But the definition is very broad, and it says nothing regarding the specific content of religious traditions. In emphasizing the existential concerns of religion, it neglects the social and institutional components of the traditions. This is akin to defining "house" as "the place at which an individual feels most at home"—a meaningful perspective for the individual, but problematically vague for outsiders. Furthermore, an individual might claim to feel quite sufficiently "at home" without dwelling in a house. Likewise, people commonly claim to be "spiritual" while also denying that they belong to a religion. A sound definition needs to accommodate this distinction.

Let us now consider four promising definitions of religion that avoid these sorts of shortcomings. According to cultural anthropologist Melford Spiro (b. 1920), religion is "an institution consisting of culturally patterned interaction with culturally postulated superhuman beings."[6] Spiro's definition encompasses a suitably wide array of cultural phenomena, while at the same time restricting the category, most especially with the concept "superhuman beings." First published in 1966, Spiro's definition continues to enjoy the favor of many theorists. The *HarperCollins Dictionary of Religion* offers a similar formulation: "One may clarify the term religion by defining it as a system of beliefs and practices that are relative to superhuman beings."[7]

Spiro's (and the *Dictionary*'s) focus on "superhuman beings," although a broad category that is not restricted only to God or "gods," leads some to reject the definition as too narrow. As Spiro readily acknowledges, it does not, for example, include within the boundaries of "religion" some forms of Buddhism. The definition of another cultural anthropologist, Clifford Geertz (1926–2006) (first published in the same volume as that of Spiro), avoids this specificity:

> Religion is (1) a system of symbols which acts to (2) establish power-
> ful, pervasive, and long-lasting moods and motivations in men by
> (3) formulating conceptions of a general order of existence and (4)
> clothing these conceptions with such an aura of factuality that (5) the
> moods and motivations seem uniquely realistic.[8]

Throughout the closing decades of the twentieth century, Geertz's definition was highly esteemed by many scholars of religion. With its open-ended reference to "a system of symbols," this definition encompasses a suitably broad range of phenomena. Such a system could include anything we normally think of as "religious": sets of beliefs or creeds, patterns of ritual practice, diverse forms of sacred art, and so forth. The other features of Geertz's definition address various aspects that set religion apart from other forms of human behavior and perspective.

Recently, however, Geertz's definition has been the subject of much criticism, due in large part to its emphasis on the private or internal thoughts and feelings—in a word, the interiority—of the religious person. Some see this as reflecting a Protestant Christian, faith-based bias. On another front, critics see the interiority of "long-lasting moods and motivations" as problematically private, inaccessible to the objective observer. Like the "at home" approach to defining "house," or Tillich's definition of religion as being "ultimate concern," Geertz's alleged dependence on interiority is considered to be too subjectively based.

By contrast, consider how *observable* are the aspects of religion according to this definition set forth by religious scholar Gerald James Larson:

> A Religion . . . is a network of cultural symbols (or what semioticians
> call "secondary modeling systems") used by people (individuals,
> families, societies, nations and so forth) to talk about (through myth,
> prayer, exhortations, ideological discourse), act out (through liturgy,
> cultic reenactment, ritual performance, dance, patterned behavior) and
> mediate (through architecture, plastic art, festival gatherings, silent
> meditation) their apprehensions or experience of transcendence.[9]

Larson refers to "a network of cultural symbols." For Geertz, religion is a "cultural system." Both definitions therefore emphasize the inseparable link between religion and *culture*. They also both emphasize the role of symbols (and, in Larson's definition, of semiotics, the academic discipline that studies the nature and function of symbols). These similarities notwithstanding, however, Larson's definition differs from that of Geertz in notable ways. As already noted, Larson offers a description of religion that more readily facilitates observation. Whereas Geertz asserts that the "system of symbols" itself "acts to establish" the rest, Larson asserts instead that the "network of cultural symbols" is "used by people." Larson's definition thus much more explicitly acknowledges the active role of human beings in religion.

Another difference lies in Larson's use of the term "transcendence." People use the network of symbols, he states, "to talk about . . . act out . . . and mediate . . . their apprehensions or experience of transcendence." On one hand, centering a definition of religion on "transcendence" is helpful; religion can thus more readily be separated from other cultural phenomena. Geertz's definition, with its references to "general order of existence" and "aura of factuality," goes some ways toward providing this helpful separating of religious phenomena, but Larson's "transcendence" goes further by suggesting a supra-ordinary realm or experience. On the other hand, the concept of "transcendence" is itself difficult to define and to apply with conceptual clarity.

Bruce Lincoln (b. 1948), another prominent theorist of religion, offers a definition that also incorporates the concept of transcendence and emphasizes the observable. Lincoln asserts that a religion always consists of four "domains"—discourse, practice, community, and institution:

1. A discourse whose concerns transcend the human, temporal, and contingent, and that claims for itself a similarly transcendent status. . . .
2. A set of practices whose purpose is to produce a proper world and/or proper human subjects, as defined by a religious discourse to which these practices are connected. . . .
3. A community whose members construct their identity with reference to a religious discourse and its attendant practices. . . .
4. An institution that regulates religious discourse, practices, and community, reproducing them over time and modifying them as necessary, while asserting their eternal validity and transcendent value.[10]

Obviously, the definitions of Larson and Lincoln are considerably more laden with technical terms than is Spiro's definition. But they are both impressively precise, without going so far as to limit the boundaries of our subject of study. This is not to say that they state more accurately what religion "truly" is. In the words of sociologist Peter Berger (b. 1929), commenting on the challenge of defining religion, "a definition is not more or less true, only more or less useful."[11] Employing the insights born of various attempts at definition will prove useful in our study of the world's religions.

In keeping with Spiro, Geertz, and Larson, for the purposes of this book we emphasize that a religion is a *cultural system*. Along with highlighting the inseparability of religious traditions from their cultural settings, this approach acknowledges that the same religion often manifests itself quite differently in varying cultural settings. For example, as Geertz himself showed in his book *Islam Observed*,[12] Islam in Indonesia is distinct in many ways from Islam in Morocco. Agreeing with Larson and Lincoln, we understand that religion involves relating to the *transcendent*. As already noted, the concept of "transcendence" is conceptually challenging. But in the absence of *something* of this sort, it is difficult to distinguish religion as a specific type of cultural system. Furthermore, many religions quite readily do recognize some entity or experience that can helpfully be identified as transcendence. Finally, we acknowledge that religions involve a wide variety of phenomena. Let us agree, then, on a working definition for purposes of our study: **religion is a cultural system integrating teachings, practices, modes of experience, institutions, and artistic expressions that relates people to what they perceive to be transcendent**. We will revisit this definition later in this chapter when we describe the book's organizational approach to setting forth these various phenomena.

Having briefly surveyed various descriptions of what religions *are* in order to arrive at our own working definition of "religion," we now adjust our focus to consider what religions *do*. In our description of religion as a specific type of cultural system, we have already stated what religions do in a basic sense: religions relate people to whatever they perceive as being transcendent. In the next section, we explore further the possible forms of transcendence by analyzing various functions of religion, concentrating especially on the fundamental questions to which religious traditions provide answers.

WHAT RELIGIONS DO

Whatever one thinks a religion *is*, this much remains certain: a religion *does*. This fact is closely related to the challenge of defining religion. Drawing on our "house" analogy, perhaps the act of *dwelling in* should be enough to qualify a structure as a house. In other words, perhaps an entity should be defined based on its *function*, not just its substantive qualities (e.g., the presence of enclosing walls and a roof or the number and type of rooms).

Some theorists have emphasized this functional side of religion in their explanations. Underlying Durkheim's definition, for example, is a theory that reduces religion to being an effect of societal forces. Religion, in turn, serves to promote social unity. Here is a clear case in point that definitions reveal as much about the intentions of the theorist as they do about the nature of religion. As we have already noted, Durkheim is regarded as a founder of sociology; it is not surprising that he emphasizes

Sigmund Freud.   Karl Marx.   Émile Durkheim.

the social aspects of religion. Consider also this assertion from psychologist Sigmund Freud (1856–1939):

> Religion would thus be the universal obsessional neurosis of humanity; like the obsessional neurosis of children, it arose out of the Oedipus complex, out of the relation to the father.[13]

Freud was an atheist whose psychological theory held religion to be undesirable. Political philosopher Karl Marx (1818–1883), likewise an atheist, offers a similarly negative assessment, which is even more antagonistic toward religion:

> *Man makes religion*, religion does not make man. In other words, religion is the self-consciousness and self-feeling of man who has either not yet found himself or has already lost himself again. But *man* is no abstract being squatting outside the world. Man is the *world of man*, the state, society. . . . Religion is the sigh of the oppressed creature, the heart of a heartless world, just as it is the spirit of a spiritless situation. It is the *opium* of the people.[14]

Marx, strongly affected by what he perceived as the economic disparities of the Industrial Revolution, was a thoroughgoing materialist who dismissed all forms of ideology as being abstractions and, to some extent, obstacles to the pursuit of true well-being. Freud similarly regarded religion as an effect of other forces, regarding it as a byproduct of psychological forces. According to Freud, religion functions as an unhealthy (but to some extent necessary) buffer against the inner terrors of the psyche. For Marx, religion functions in a similarly unhealthy manner, as an "opiate" that deters the suffering individual from attending to the true cause of affliction.

These functionalist explanations, while provocative and at least somewhat insightful, are largely regarded now by scholars as being severely limited in their perspectives. Perhaps religions *do* function in these ways at certain times in certain situations; but surely religions do much more. In fact, neither Freud nor Marx ever tried actually to define religion; rather, they tried to explain it away. This does not diminish, however, the enduring relevance of these theorists for purposes of striving to understand the "big picture" of the role of religion in the lives of individuals and societies.

We can widen our vantage point on the functions of religion and produce a fairer and more accurate depiction by considering the variety of life's challenges that these traditions help people to face and to overcome.

Religious Questions and Challenges

It might seem disrespectful or even blasphemous to ask: Why do religions exist? But in fact this is a perfectly legitimate and instructive question. To a large extent, the academic study of religion—being based, like most other academic pursuits, in an approach to knowledge that depends on analysis of empirical data—must by its very nature regard religions as *human* enterprises. Human beings and their ways can be observed and studied through normal means of academic inquiry; empirical evidence can be gathered, and through rational argumentation hypotheses can be formulated and supported. Supernatural beings and events normally are held to be beyond the reach of academic inquiry. *Doing* religion, or *being* religious, naturally invites consideration of the supernatural and of the "truth" of religious claims. Theology, the field of inquiry that focuses on considering the nature of the divine, is an important example of *doing* and *being* religious. The academic study of religion, as understood by the authors of this book, is not theology, however much we might admire theologians and enjoy studying their work, which is itself an important human enterprise and a major component of religion.

As human enterprises, religions naturally respond to human needs, and readily acknowledge reasons for their doctrines and rituals. A typical reason has to do with some kind of perceived separation from the sacred or estrangement from a state of perfection or fulfillment. The human condition, as ordinarily experienced, is regarded as being disconnected from the fulfillment that lies at the end of a spiritual path. Various related questions and challenges are addressed by religions, with these three prominent questions recurring in some form in nearly every system:

1. What Is Ultimate Reality?
2. How Should We Live in This World?
3. What Is Our Ultimate Purpose?

The rest of this book's chapters explore the ways major religions answer these questions. For now, let's consider these questions more broadly.

What Is Ultimate Reality? It is difficult to imagine a religion that has nothing to say about ultimate reality—even if this involves asserting that "ultimate" reality consists of no more than the natural world and we human beings who inhabit it. Confucius (551–479 B.C.E.) (Chapter 8), in fact, seems to have asserted basically this very thing, although he did make reference to "Heaven" and "Dao."

Usually explanation of the nature and role of the divine takes center stage in a religion's belief system. But the "divine" is not necessarily thought of as God or gods. When it is, we refer to that religion as a **theistic** (from Greek *theos*, or god) belief system. When it is not, the religion is said to be **nontheistic**. For reasons we have just mentioned, Confucianism is an example of a nontheistic religion.

Theistic religions can be further categorized. **Polytheism** (from Greek *polys*, or many) is the belief in many gods ("gods" is considered a gender-neutral term and can—and often does—include goddesses). **Monotheism** (from Greek *monos*, or only one) is the belief in only one god (and hence the term is normally capitalized—God—a proper noun referring to a specific being).

A kind of middle ground comes in the form of **henotheism** (from Greek *hen*, the number one), which acknowledges a plurality of gods but elevates one of them to

This painting, produced in 1810, depicts the Hindu deities Shiva and Parvati with their children, Ganesha and Kartikeya. Hindus believe in many gods and goddesses, these four—and especially Shiva—being among the most popular.

special status. Some forms of Hindu devotion to a particular god such as Vishnu or Shiva are henotheistic. **Pantheism** (from Greek *pan*, or all) is the belief that the divine is identical to nature or the material world. Although not one of the world's living religions, the ancient Greek and Roman religious philosophy known as **Stoicism** is an example. It is important to bear in mind, too, that the world's religions often feature entities that are supernatural and yet not necessarily gods. These quasi-divine figures, such as angels, demons, and the monstrous characters that feature prominently in myths, are typically difficult to categorize, but are important elements of religion nonetheless. To complicate matters further, scholars of non-Western religions have commonly used the term "god" to refer to supernatural beings that are more similar to angels, or even to the saints of Catholic tradition. The *theos* in the "polytheism" of such non-Western religions therefore often refers to a very different type of being than does the *theos* in "monotheism." Simplistic application of such terms is misleading.

Nontheistic belief systems include those that uphold **atheism**, which explicitly denies the existence of a divine entity. Depending on how one defines "religion," atheism could be counted as a religion, or at least as a doctrinal aspect of a religion. Some scholars of religion, and in fact, some self-proclaimed atheists, contend that the type of understanding of self, others, and world based in atheism can indeed best be understood as being religious. Like so much else in academic study, it depends on the definitions of terms.

Nontheistic religions (and here the term is on surer footing) also include those that conceive of the divine as an impersonal force or substratum of existence. Some nontheistic religions, such as various forms of Buddhism (Chapter 5) and Hinduism (Chapter 4), even assume the existence of divine beings while rejecting the notion that such beings can truly help humans find spiritual fulfillment. Some Hindus, for example, while believing in many gods and goddesses, hold that Brahman, impersonal and ultimately indescribable, is the essence of all. Those Hindus therefore embrace **monism** because of this primary belief that all reality is ultimately one. Monism is also described as nondualistic, since there is no distinction between the divine reality, on one hand, and the rest of reality, including human individuals, on the other.

Such a categorizing scheme admits to some complications. Some Hindus are monistic because they understand all reality ultimately to be one thing: Brahman. But some of those same monistic Hindus also pay homage to a variety of supernatural and divine beings, and thus might also be described as polytheists.

Along with asserting the existence of ultimate reality, religions describe how this reality is revealed to human beings. The foundational moments of **revelation** are frequently recorded in sacred texts, or scriptures. In the case of theistic religions, scriptures set forth narratives describing the role of God or the gods in history, and also include pronouncements directly attributed to the divine. In the Jewish and Christian Bible, for example, God's will regarding ethical behavior is expressed directly in the Ten Commandments. The giving of the Ten Commandments is described in the long narrative about the Exodus of the Israelites from Egypt, in which God is said to have played a central role.

Among nontheistic religions in particular—but also among the mystical traditions that form part of every religious tradition—revelation usually combines textual transmission with a direct experience of revelation. Revelation is usually experienced by a founding figure of the religion, whose experiences are later written about; subsequent believers can then experience similar types of revelation, which requires their own participation. Buddhists, for example, have scriptural records that describe the Buddha's experience of "unbinding" or release, as well as pronouncements by various deities praising the ultimate value of that experience. Followers must then connect to such revelation through practices such as meditation.

Another helpful way of thinking about revelation is offered by historian of religions Mircea Eliade (1907–1986), who makes much descriptive use of the phenomenon he calls "hierophany," or "the *act of manifestation* of the sacred," which helps a people to establish its cosmology, or religious understanding of the order of the world.[15] Eliade emphasizes how this concept applies to indigenous or small-scale traditions (those of "archaic man" in Eliade's terminology). But the phenomenon of the hierophany is readily apparent within the world's major religions, often, but not always, as a theophany, a manifestation of God or of gods. The role of hierophanies in establishing places of special significance can be observed in many of the sites related to the founding figures and events of the major religions: Christianity's Church of the Nativity (and other sacred sites related to the life of Christ); Islam's sacred city of Mecca; Buddhism's Bodh Gaya, site of Gautama's foundational experience of Enlightenment; and so on. Sacred moments establish sacred spatial monuments, thus establishing a sense of centrality and spatial order.

Along with often referring to other worlds, religions have much to say about *this* world. Human beings have always asked searching questions about the origin and status of our planet and of the universe. Typically these two issues—origin and status—are intertwined. If our world was intentionally fashioned by a creator god, for instance, then it bears the stamp of divine affirmation. Thus the early chapters of the Book of Genesis in the Hebrew Bible (the Christian Old Testament) describe the measured, creative activity of God, including the creation of humankind. In contrast, the creation stories of

Ka'ba, Mecca.

some religious traditions deemphasize the role of the divine will in bringing about the world, sometimes (as in the religion of the ancient Greeks) describing the advent of the principal deities *after* the universe itself has been created. The gods, like humans, come into a world that is already established; gods and humans are depicted as sharing the world, which naturally affects the relationship between human and divine. In other religions, notably those same South Asian traditions that embrace liberation as the ultimate religious objective, this world is depicted as a kind of illusion, somehow not altogether real or permanently abiding. It is thus not so surprising that liberation involves being completely freed from the confines of this world.

These are but a few examples of religious understanding of the nature of the world, a general category known as **cosmology** (from *kosmos*, the Greek term for world or universe). Along with clarifying the origin and sacred status of the world, cosmology also explains how the world is ordered. Many traditions attribute the order of the universe to the doings of the divine being(s) or forces. Yet in certain respects, modern scientific explanations set forth cosmologies that are intriguingly similar to some religious cosmologies taught by religious personages of the distant past, such as Gautama the Buddha or Epicurus, a Greek philosopher who espoused a theory of atomism, arguing that reality is composed entirely of a very large number of very small particles.

Of course, a particular religion's cosmology strongly influences the degree to which its adherents are involved in caring for the world. Religions that are indifferent or hostile toward the natural world are not apt to encourage anything akin to environmentalism. On the other hand, a religion that teaches that the world is inherently sacred naturally encourages a sense of stewardship toward the natural world. Native American traditions, for example, are notably environmentally oriented.

The Andromeda galaxy.

How Should We Live in This World? Many religions have much to say about God or other superhuman beings and phenomena, and yet all religions are human enterprises. Their teachings are communicated in human languages, their rituals are practiced by human participants, and their histories are entwined with the development of human societies and cultures. Religions also explain what it is to be a human being.

Explanations regarding what it is to be human also figure largely into ethical or moral considerations. Are we by nature good, evil, or somewhere in between? Religions tend to recognize that human beings do not always do the right thing, and they commonly offer teachings and disciplines directed toward moral or ethical improvement. To say that we are by nature good, and at the same time to recognize moral failings, is to infer that some cause external to our nature is causing the shortcoming. If we are by nature evil, on the other hand, or at least naturally prone to doing wrong, then the moral challenge lies within and the means of improvement would need to be directed inwardly.

Religions typically prescribe what is right behavior and what is wrong, based on a set of ethical tenets, such as the Jewish and Christian Ten Commandments. In fact, the very prospects of improving upon the human condition and of faring well in an afterlife quite commonly are deemed to depend in some way upon right ethical behavior. The ethical teachings of many religions are notably similar. The so-called Golden Rule ("Do unto others what you would have them do unto you"[16]) set forth in the Christian New Testament is pronounced in similar forms in the scriptures of virtually all of the world's major traditions.

The religions differ, however, over the issue of the source of ethical truth. Some emphasize **revealed ethics**, asserting that God, or some other supernatural force such as Hindu *dharma* (ethical duty), has established what constitutes right behavior, and has in some manner revealed this to human beings. The divine will might be conceived of as God (or gods), or it might take the form of an impersonal principle, such as *dharma*. Another common approach, in some forms of Buddhism, for example, emphasizes the role of conscience in the moral deliberations of each individual. These two emphases are not necessarily mutually exclusive. Some religions, Christianity among them, teach that both revealed ethics and individual conscience work together as means of distinguishing right from wrong.

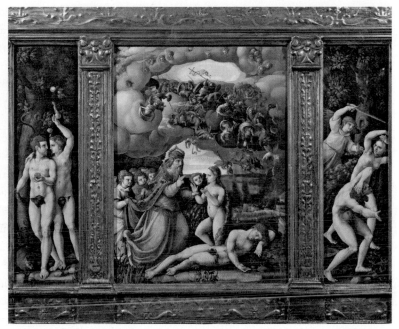

Sixteenth-century triptych (altar painting) depicting the creation of Eve (center), the eating of the forbidden fruit (left), and the expulsion from the Garden of Eden (right). This story of humankind's first sin sets forth basic biblical perspectives on the human condition.

What Is Our Ultimate Purpose? The challenge of mortality—the fact that we are destined to die—is sometimes cited as the primary motivating force behind religion. And although it is true that all religions have at least something to say about death, the wide diversity of perspectives is quite astounding. For example, while Christianity, with its focus on the resurrection of Christ and the hope of eternal life, can be said to make mortality a central concern, Zen Buddhism, drawing inspiration from the classic Daoist texts, refuses to make much at all of death beyond acknowledging its natural place in the order of things.

Both the challenge of mortality and the issue of our moral nature relate to questions regarding the human condition—and what can be done about it. In many faiths, how we conduct ourselves in this world will determine our fates after we die. Most religions readily acknowledge that human beings are destined to die (although some, such as Daoism, have at times aspired to discover means of inducing physical immortality). As we have noted, some religions have little to say about the prospects of life beyond death. But most religions do provide explanations regarding the fate of the individual after death, and their explanations vary widely.

Hinduism, Buddhism, Jainism, and Sikhism all maintain belief in *samsara*, the "wheel of life" that implies a series of lives, deaths, and rebirths for every individual. The ultimate aim of each of these religions is liberation from *samsara*. Buddhist *nirvana*, which we have seen is an example of transcendence of the human condition, is one such form of liberation. But most of the adherents of Buddhism and these other religions anticipate that death will lead to rebirth into another life form (not necessarily human), one in a long series of rebirths. Furthermore, the reborn are destined for any one among multiple realms, including a variety of hells and heavens.

Other religions, notably Christianity and Islam, teach that individuals are destined for some sort of afterlife, usually a version of heaven or of hell. Sometimes the teachings are more complicated. The traditional Catholic doctrine of purgatory, for example, anticipates an intermediary destiny somewhere between the perfect bliss of heaven and the horrible agony of hell, where an individual can gradually be purified from sin, ultimately achieving salvation and entry to heaven.

Given what a religion says about the human condition, what ultimate purpose is the religious life intended to achieve? Is there a state of existence to which the religious person can hope to aspire that perfectly completes or even transcends the human condition, overcoming entirely its cares and shortcomings?

Our working definition of religion, drawing on ideas set forth in the definitions of religion provided by Larson and Lincoln, highlights the relevance of **transcendence**. But "transcendence" seems to defy any easy explanation or description. One influential attempt is Rudolf Otto's *The Idea of the Holy* (1923). Otto (1869–1937), a Protestant theologian and a philosopher of religion, describes the encounter with "the Holy" as "numinous," a term he coined from the Latin *numen*, meaning spirit or divinity (plural, *numina*). A genuine **numinous experience**, Otto asserts, is characterized by two powerful and contending forces: ***mysterium tremendum* and *fascinans*. *Mysterium tremendum*,** which in Latin means "awe-inspiring mystery," is the feeling of awe that overwhelms a person who experiences the majestic presence of the "wholly other."[17] *Fascinans* (Latin, "fascinating"), is the contrasting feeling of overwhelming attraction. The encounter with the Holy is thus alluring (*fascinans*) even as it is fearful on account of the awe-inspiring mystery (*mysterium tremendum*). The biblical phenomenon of the "fear of God" fits this description, as the God who is being feared is at the same time recognized as the source of life and the hope for salvation.

Otto's insightful analysis of the numinous experience suffers from a significant limitation: based in his Protestant Christian outlook, it may ring true to a Protestant; from a global perspective, however, the analysis is rather limiting. For example, Otto discounts the **mystical experience**, a category that includes such phenomena as Buddhist *nirvana*, the complete dissolution of an individual's sense of selfhood said by Buddhists to be a state of perfect bliss and ultimate fulfillment. According to Otto, *nirvana* involves too much *fascinans* without enough *mysterium tremendum*.

Otto's analysis of the numinous experience nevertheless remains a major contribution to religious studies, despite its shortcomings. To be fair to Otto, and to make an important cautionary point, religious studies itself is rooted to a large extent in Christian—especially Protestant Christian—theological studies, and therefore some of the prominent terms, categories, and perspectives have been beset in one way or another with a Christian bias.

Moses & the Burning Bush (1990), charcoal and pastel on paper by Hans Feibusch. The event is told in Exodus, the second book of the Hebrew Bible (Old Testament).

It is important to clarify that transcendence, or that which is beyond the normal or mundane sphere of things, is not necessarily perceived by all cultures and religions as being *above* or *outside of* the individual or of the world as normally experienced. In other words, perceiving transcendence does not depend upon believing in God or some form of ultimate reality external to oneself. One can perceive transcendence as being in-dwelling or immanent. Buddhist *nirvana*, for example, is said to be an experience that is clearly beyond the normal sphere of things, and yet it does not depend on an external reality.

Most world religions do assert the possibility of such a state of transcendence, an ultimate objective of the religious life that brings complete fulfillment of all spiritual longings. For a Buddhist who has experienced *nirvana*, for example, there is, paradoxically, no longer a need for Buddhism. The religious life has been lived to its fullest extent, and the ultimate objective has been reached. Because *nirvana* involves the complete extinction of individual existence, it is truly transcendent of the human condition. Other religions, in widely varying ways, also set forth ultimate objectives, whether or not implying the complete transcendence of the human condition. In some cases spiritual fulfillment can be said to consist of living in harmony with nature. Others readily acknowledge the supernatural—usually God (or gods)—and the need for human beings to live in perfect relationship with it. Christianity, for example, offers salvation from the effects of sin, which otherwise estrange the individual from God. Sometimes spiritual fulfillment is thought to be achievable in this lifetime; other times it is projected into the distant future, after many lifetimes of striving and development.

Of course, improving upon the human condition does not have to involve complete transcendence or anything close to it. Day to day the world over, religious people

Meditating Buddha, sixth century C.E. (Thai). Sculptures of the Buddha typically depict the serene calm of the enlightened state.

improve upon the human condition in all sorts of ways. Belief in a loving God gives hope and fortitude in the face of life's uncertainties. Meditation and prayer bring an enhanced sense of tranquility. Religious motivations often lie behind charitable acts. Belonging to a religious group offers social benefits that can be deeply fulfilling. Even for individuals who do not participate directly in a religious tradition, sacred art, architecture, and music can bring joy to life.

BASIC COMPONENTS OF RELIGIONS

Sound definitions, whether of a religion or of a house, strive to be universal in scope. Along with a sound definition, a means of categorizing the common, though not necessarily universal, components of a subject of study can often prove beneficial. When setting out on a cross-cultural study of houses we might insist that every structure we study have enclosing walls and a roof. But we might also wish to record descriptions of a list of components present in only some of the houses, for example, the type of basement, front porch, attic, and so forth.

Recall our working definition of religion, which includes a basic list of main components: religion is a cultural system integrating teachings, practices, modes of experience, institutions, and artistic expressions that relates people to what they perceive to be transcendent. We now explore some other possibilities for identifying religious phenomena, in part to bring home the important point that there is no "right" or "wrong" way to go about categorizing them. Instead, we seek the most useful means given the task at hand. This will lead naturally to clarifying how this book goes about organizing its presentation of material.

Some scholarly approaches to the world's religions feature specific categories of phenomena as the primary means of organizing information. Religious scholar Ninian Smart's (1927–2001) "dimensional" scheme, for example, divides the various aspects of religious traditions into seven dimensions:

- The mythic (or sacred narrative)
- The doctrinal (or philosophical)
- The ethical (or legal)
- The ritual (or practical)
- The experiential (or emotional)
- The social
- The material[18]

Such an approach to the content of religious traditions is very useful, especially if one focuses on a comparative analysis that emphasizes particular motifs (that is, "dimensions" or aspects thereof).

It is also helpful to recall the elements noted in Larson's definition of religion: "myth, prayer, exhortations, ideological discourse . . . liturgy, cultic reenactment, ritual performance, dance, patterned behavior . . . architecture, plastic art, festival gatherings, silent meditation."[19] These many elements, while spelling out in more detail the content of religious traditions, fit fairly well among Smart's "dimensions" and, for that matter, with the phenomena listed in our working definition. In this book, we organize things into three main categories: teachings, way of life, and historical development. The order in which we present our three categories is not meant to imply any sort of hierarchical ordering by importance or anything else. Likewise, while each chapter of this book is organized around these three main categories, we do not strive in all chapters to devote equal attention to each category. To do so would be to ignore the varying nature of the religious traditions and to force an inappropriately rigid structure. Judaism, for example, calls for extensive attention to historical development in order to best understand the context of its teachings and practices; Jainism, for which an early historical record barely exists, does not.

Teachings

Obviously, religions tend to involve beliefs. But as long as they remain private to the individual, beliefs are problematic for the student of religion. As public elements of a religion's teachings, however, beliefs can be observed and interpreted. Such public beliefs are manifested as doctrines or creeds—sets of concepts that are *believed in*. (The term "creed" derives from the Latin verb *credo*, or "I believe.") Among the world's major religions, Christianity most emphasizes doctrines. Most Christians, for example, regularly acknowledge belief in the statements of the Nicene Creed.

Religious teachings include another significant category, often referred to as **myth** (as noted in Larson's definition and in Smart's "mythic" dimension). Quite in contrast to the modern connotation of myth as a falsehood, myth as understood by the academic field of religious studies is a powerful source of sacred truth. Set forth in narrative form and originally conveyed orally, myths do not depend on empirical verifiability or rational coherence for their power. They are simply accepted by believers as true accounts, often involving events of primordial time that describe the origin of things.

As we have noted previously, religions typically include ethical instructions, whether doctrinal or mythic, among their teachings. And as Smart readily acknowledges, the various dimensions are closely interrelated; the ethical dimension, for example, extends into the doctrinal and the mythic, and so forth.

Way of Life

This main category tends to feature two types of religious phenomena listed in our working definition: practices and modes of experience. Recall that Smart includes the ritual (or practical) and the experiential (or emotional) among his seven dimensions of religion. Larson cites several examples—"prayer . . . liturgy, cultic re-enactment, ritual performance, dance, patterned behavior . . . silent meditation"—and he connects all of this to "apprehensions or experience of transcendence."[20] Some such elements are tangible and readily observable and describable, such as a **ritual** like the exchange of marriage vows or the procession of pilgrims to a shrine. Others are highly personal and therefore hidden from the outsider's view. One of the great challenges of studying religions rests precisely in this personal, private quality. Modes of experience such as Buddhist *nirvana* are by definition beyond the reach of empirical observation and of description. Rudolf Otto, throughout his analysis of the "numinous" experience, emphasizes the impossibility of describing it fully. Even common practices like prayer and meditation tend to involve an inner aspect that is highly personal and quite inaccessible to anyone who is not sharing the experience. A book such as this one can do its best to illustrate and to explain these experiential phenomena but cannot be expected to provide a full disclosure at certain points. Such is the nature of religion.

Historical Development

It almost goes without saying that the world's major religions—all of which are many centuries, even millennia, old—have long and intricate histories. Thus, the historical development of religious traditions incorporates a vast sweep of social, artistic, and other cultural phenomena.

Devils Tower, located in northeastern Wyoming, is regarded as a sacred place by many Native Americans.

In his list of the various cultural phenomena that make up a religion, Larson includes "architecture" and "plastic art." The vast array of artistic, architectural, and other aspects of material culture generated within religious traditions is of course

obvious to anyone who has studied art history. The ornate Hindu temple sculptures, the majestic statues of Jain *tirthankaras*, the mathematically ordered architectural features of Islamic arabesque décor—these, among countless other examples, attest to the extensive role of religion in the nurturing of material culture. Other forms of artistic creation, most prominently music and theater, also are common and significant features of religions. And, as Smart helpfully clarifies when discussing the material dimension of religion, natural entities (mountains, rivers, wooded groves) are designated as sacred by some traditions.

Social institutions and phenomena of various sorts—economic activities, politics, social class structures and hierarchies—have typically played highly influential roles in the historical development of religious traditions. As we have observed, Marx and Durkheim went as far as to reduce religion to being entirely the effect of economic and societal forces, respectively. Even for theorists who opt not to go nearly as far as this, the relevance of such phenomena is obvious.

RELIGIONS IN THE MODERN WORLD

A sound analysis of the world's religions must pay heed to the rapid changes that characterize the modern world. Historical transformations, accelerated during the past several centuries by such diverse and powerful factors as colonialism, the scientific revolution, and economic globalization, have reshaped religious traditions. This book takes into account such factors whenever appropriate. Here we introduce four specific phenomena that will reappear frequently in the pages that follow: modernization, urbanization, globalization, and multiculturalism, and the encounter of religion and science.

Modernization

Modernization is the general process through which societies transform economically, socially, and culturally to keep pace with an increasingly competitive global marketplace. Its net effects include increased literacy, improved education, enhanced technologies, self-sustaining economies, increased role of women in various aspects of society, and greater involvement of the general populace in government (as in democracies). All these effects involve corresponding changes within religious traditions. Higher literacy rates and improved education, for example, facilitate increased access to religious texts that previously were controlled by and confined to the religious elite. Technological advances, strengthened economies, and increased participation in government all nurture greater equality for and empowerment of the common people. A general feature of modernity, moreover, is its tendency to deny the authority of tradition and the past. Traditional patriarchal modes, for example, have tended over time to be diminished. Around the globe, we are witnessing a general erosion of longstanding power structures within religions. Obviously this is not the case in all circumstances; changes have tended to occur in different societies at different times, and some religious institutions are better equipped to ward off change. But over the long haul, modernization clearly has influenced the reshaping of religious traditions.

Trinity Church, built in 1846, sits amidst the skyscrapers of Wall Street in New York City.

Urbanization

A significant demographic effect of modernization is **urbanization**, the shift of population centers from rural, agricultural settings to cities. A century ago, only about 10 percent of the global population lived in cities; today, more than half of us are urbanites. Many religious traditions developed within primarily rural settings, patterning their calendars of holy days and rituals around agricultural cycles. Such patterns have far less relevance today for most religious people.

Globalization

Globalization is the linking and intermixing of cultures. It accelerated quickly during the centuries of exploration and colonization and has been nurtured considerably by the advanced technologies brought about by modernization. The extent of this linking and intermixing is evinced in the very term "World Wide Web," and the pronounced and rapidly evolving effects of the Internet and other technologies are extraordinary. The almost instantaneous exchange of information that this technology allows is more or less paralleled by enhanced forms of affordable transportation. In sum, we now live in a global community that could hardly have been imagined a few decades ago.

Multiculturalism

The most pronounced religious effects of globalization pertain to the closely related phenomenon of **multiculturalism**, the coexistence of different peoples and their cultural ways in one time and place. Many people today live in religiously pluralistic societies, no longer sheltered from the presence of religious ways of life other than their own. This plurality increases the degree of influence exerted by one tradition on another, making it difficult for many individuals to regard any one religious worldview as the *only* viable one. This, in turn, fosters general questioning and critical assessment of religion. To some extent, such questioning and critical assessment erodes the authority traditionally attributed to religion. Globalization, then, like modernization, has nurtured the notably modern process of **secularization**, the general turning away from traditional religious authority and institutions.

Religion and Science

Perhaps no single phenomenon has been more challenging to traditional religious ways—and more nurturing of secularization—than the encounter of religion with science. One need only think of the impact of Charles Darwin's *Origin of Species* (1859) and its theory of evolution to note the potential for conflict between scientific and traditional religious worldviews. The question of whether the biblical account of creation should be taught alongside the theory of evolution in schools is a divisive issue in some predominantly

Christian societies today. In the domain of cosmology, too, science has tended to overwhelm traditional perspectives, such as the idea that the Earth is somehow the center of the cosmos, as implied in the Bible and in the creation myths of many traditions. But current theories regarding the Big Bang and other issues of astrophysics continue to be challenged by religious points of view. Of course, religions are not always hostile to science. In fact, as we have already noted, sometimes modern scientific theories seem almost to converge with ancient religious outlooks.

AN ACADEMIC APPROACH TO THE STUDY OF RELIGIONS

Scholars approach the study of religion in a variety of ways. And although there is no such thing as *the* correct approach, it is helpful to keep some basic concepts in mind.

Balance

One concept is the maintenance of a healthy balance between the perspective of an insider (one who practices a given religion) and the perspective of an outsider (one who studies the religion without practicing it). For while an insider arguably has the best vantage point on the lived realities of the religion, presumably the insider is primarily concerned with *being* religious, and not in explaining the religion in a manner most effective for those who hold other religious (or nonreligious) perspectives. It is quite natural for an insider to feel bias in favor of his or her own religion. The outsider, on the other hand, would have no reason to feel such bias. But the outsider would not have the benefit of experiencing the religion firsthand. It is analogous to trying to understand a goldfish in a pond. An outsider can describe the fish's color, its movements, its eating habits. But the outsider can say very little about what it is actually like to be a goldfish.[21]

The academic approach to the study of religions attempts to balance the perspectives of insider and outsider, thereby drawing upon the benefits of each. It is not an intentionally religious enterprise. As we have noted previously, it is not *doing* religion or *being* religious, unlike theology. Instead, it strives to analyze and describe religions in a way that is accurate and fair for all concerned—insiders and outsiders alike. An instructive parallel can be drawn from the discipline of political science. Rather than advocating a particular political point of view, and rather than *being* a politician, a political scientist strives to analyze and describe political viewpoints and phenomena in a fair, neutral manner. A good political scientist could, for instance, belong to the Democratic party, but still produce a fair article about a Republican politician—without ever betraying personal Democratic convictions. A good scholar of religion, of whatever religious (or nonreligious) persuasion, attends to religious matters with a similarly neutral stance.

A miniature illustration from the "Automata of al-Jaziri" a Muslim scholar, inventor, engineer, mathematician, and astronomer who lived from 1136 to 1206.

Empathy

Another basic concept for the academic approach to religion is **empathy**, the capacity for seeing things from another's perspective. Empathy works in tandem with the usual tools of scholarship—the observation and rational assessment of empirical data—to yield an effective academic approach to the study of religions. The sometimes cold, impersonal procedures of scholarship are enlivened by the personal insights afforded by empathy. On this point our "house" analogy is highly apt. Even if our primary purpose was to study another's house, we would naturally show respect to the inhabitants, honoring their right to privacy by not being disruptive toward the house or its belongings. A similar attitude is expected of the student of religion upon entering into another's tradition.

Comparative Approaches

A sound study of the world's religions also features a comparative approach. The chief benefit of this was emphasized by the nineteenth-century scholar Friedrich Max Müller (1823–1900), who is generally regarded as the founder of the modern field of religious studies. He frequently asserted that to know just one religion is to know none. In other words, in order to understand the phenomena of any given tradition, it is necessary to study many traditions, observing such phenomena as they occur in a wide variety of situations. This naturally requires that the study of world religions be cross-cultural in scope. As we proceed from chapter to chapter, the usefulness of comparison will become more and more evident.

Along with being cross-cultural, religious studies is multidisciplinary, or polymethodic, drawing on the contributions of anthropology, history, sociology, psychology, philosophy, feminist theory, and other disciplines and fields of study.

As a "cultural system," each religion obviously is situated within a culture or within various cultures, the study of which is the domain of anthropology. Geertz, who among anthropologists has exerted the greatest influence on religious studies in the past several decades, insists on painstakingly analyzing a religion's cultural setting. (Recall, too, that Larson defines religion as "a network of cultural systems.") All students of religion would do well to be so careful and to consider closely the relationship between religion and culture, that is, how religious ideals have been expressed in such things as literature, art, architecture, and festivals and how culture has influenced religion (e.g., how the spirit of growth and innovation in nineteenth-century American culture encouraged the emergence of new forms of Christianity).

The need for involvement of the other disciplines should be likewise apparent. Given their historical and social aspects, the appropriateness of the disciplines of history and sociology for the study of religions is to be expected. And especially when trying to make sense of the modes of religious experience, psychology offers important inroads to understanding that the other disciplines are not equipped to provide. Along with Freud and James, whose definitions we have considered, Swiss psychologist Carl Jung (1875–1961) deserves mention for his vital contributions to the study of religious symbolism and of the general role of the unconscious mind in the religious life. The philosophy of religion, in certain respects the closest to actually *doing* religion (or theology), endeavors to assess critically the truth claims and arguments set forth by religions. Questions involving the existence of God, for example, are among those taken up by philosophers. Feminist theory, which informs the work of scholars in many disciplines, helps to expose the unexamined assumptions of religious studies about gender that can hinder the aim of a neutral and unbiased approach to subject matter. Other, related approaches also contribute to the polymethodic makeup of religious studies as a modern academic field.

Suffice it to say that the multidisciplinary nature of religious studies accounts for its very *existence* as an academic discipline. Without the involvement and contributions of its many subdisciplines, there could be no academic field of religious studies.

CONCLUSION

In this chapter, we have explored the nature of religion and how to study it from an academic perspective. The main objective is to prepare for the study that follows, a chapter-by-chapter examination of the major religions of the world. But the relatively theoretical and methodological content of this introductory chapter is relevant and challenging in its own right. Indeed, some readers might be surprised to learn that the search for an adequate definition of such a common term as "religion" has proven to be so daunting over the years or that the study of religion requires special means of approach. Hopefully these same readers have come to recognize the complexity of the ideas and the challenge of the task, even while not feeling daunted about going forward with our study.

We have noted that the rest of this book's chapters feature a threefold organizational scheme, of teachings, way of life, and historical development. While these chapters, with their focus on the religious traditions themselves, naturally are quite different from this introduction, it is worth noticing that in this chapter, too, we have featured historical development—of both the attempts to explain or define religion and the approaches to studying it—and teachings, most especially the theories of various notable contributors to religious studies. The "way of life" aspect perhaps has been less obvious, but in fact it is important and deserves consideration as we end the chapter. On more than one occasion we have drawn a distinction between the academic study of religion and *doing* religion or *being* religious. Where, then, does this leave the individual who wants to do (and be) both? Ultimately, this is a question to be left for the individual reader to ponder. But it might prove helpful to know that the degree of *being* religious among scholars of religion spans the spectrum of possibilities, from not religious at all to highly devout. Either way (or someplace in between), one thing is true for all who venture forth to study the world's religions: we are investigating important and enduring aspects of human cultures, down through the millennia and around the globe. Our understanding of things that matter is sure to be enriched.

REVIEW QUESTIONS

For Review

1. Who is Émile Durkheim, and what is notable about his definition of religion?
2. Bruce Lincoln, in his definition of religion, identifies four "domains." What are they?
3. What is "revelation," and how is it pertinent for the question: What is ultimate reality?
4. Identify and briefly describe Ninian Smart's seven "dimensions" of religion.
5. What is "empathy," and how is it relevant for the academic study of religion?

For Further Reflection

1. Sigmund Freud and Karl Marx, while tending to be dismissive of the enduring importance of religion, asserted explanations that continue to provoke and to enrich academic consideration of the role of religion. Based on their statements included in this chapter, how might their perspectives be provocative and enriching in this respect?
2. This chapter and book pose three prominent questions with regard to the challenges addressed by the world's religions: What is ultimate reality? How should we live in this world? What is our ultimate purpose? Drawing on examples and ideas presented in this chapter, discuss to what extent and in what ways these three questions are interrelated.
3. Explore the interrelationship of these features of religions in the modern world: globalization, secularization, and multiculturalism.

GLOSSARY

atheism The belief that there is no God or gods.

cosmology Understanding of the nature of the world that typically explains its origin and how it is ordered.

empathy The capacity for seeing things from another's perspective, and an important methodological approach for studying religions.

globalization The linking and intermixing of cultures.

henotheism The belief that acknowledges a plurality of gods but elevates one of them to special status.

modernization The general process through which societies transform economically, socially, and culturally to become more in keeping with the standards set by industrialized Europe.

monism The belief that all reality is ultimately one.

monotheism The belief in only one god.

multiculturalism The coexistence of different peoples and their cultural ways in one time and place.

mysterium tremendum **and** *fascinans* The contrasting feelings of awe-inspiring mystery and of overwhelming attraction that are said by Rudolf Otto to characterize the numinous experience.

mystical experience A general category of religious experience characterized in various ways, for example, as the uniting with the divine through inward contemplation or as the dissolution of the sense of individual selfhood.

myth A story or narrative, originally conveyed orally, that sets forth basic truths of a religious tradition; myths often involve events of primordial time that describe the origin of things.

nontheistic Term denoting a religion that does not maintain belief in God or gods.

numinous experience Rudolf Otto's term for describing an encounter with "the Holy"; it is characterized by the two powerful and contending forces, *mysterium tremendum* and *fascinans*.

pantheism The belief that the divine reality is identical to nature or the material world.

polytheism The belief in many gods.

revealed ethics Truth regarding right behavior believed to be divinely established and intentionally made known to human beings.

revelation The expression of the divine will, commonly recorded in sacred texts.

ritual Formal worship practice.

secularization The general turning away from traditional religious authority and institutions.

Stoicism Ancient Greek and Roman pantheistic religious philosophy.

theistic Term denoting a religion that maintains belief in God or gods.

transcendence General category for whatever is perceived as being beyond the normal or mundane sphere of things, whether understood as external or as within the individual or world.

urbanization The shift of population centers from rural, agricultural settings to cities.

SUGGESTIONS FOR FURTHER READING

Berger, Peter L. *The Sacred Canopy: Elements of a Sociological Theory of Religion.* Garden City, New York: Anchor, 1969. An engaging and influential work in the sociological approach to the study of religion.

Eliade, Mircea. *The Sacred and the Profane: The Nature of Religion.* Translated by Willard R. Trask. New York: Harper and Row, 1961. Eliade's most accessible work, offering a rich analysis of sacred space and time.

Pals, Daniel. *Eight Theories of Religion.* 2nd ed. New York: Oxford University Press, 2006. The best introduction to the history of religious studies as an academic field, including chapters on Karl Marx, Sigmund Freud, Émile Durkheim, Max Weber, Mircea Eliade, and Clifford Geertz.

Smart, Ninian. *Worldviews: Crosscultural Explanations of Human Belief.* New York: Scribner's, 1983. An engaging introduction to Smart's "dimensions," along with his approach to analyzing "worldviews"—a category that includes along with traditional religions such secular phenomena as humanism and Marxism.

Smith, Jonathan Z. *Imagining Religion: From Babylon to Jonestown.* Chicago Studies in the History of Judaism. Chicago and London: Chicago University Press, 1982. A collection of essays that exemplify Smith's impressively wide-ranging and astute approach to the study of religion.

Taylor, Mark C., ed. *Critical Terms for Religious Studies.* Chicago: University of Chicago Press, 1998. Articles on various central topics for the study of religions, written by leading scholars in the field.

ONLINE RESOURCES

American Academy of Religion
aarweb.org
The largest and most influential North American academic society for the study of religion.

The Pluralism Project at Harvard University
pluralism.org
Offers an impressive array of helpful resources, especially with regard to the world's religions in North America.

INDIGENOUS RELIGIONS of NORTH AMERICA

THE HOT AFTERNOON SUN beats down on the eighteen men and women who dance in patterned formation in the midst of a circular enclosure. Caleb, a 26-year-old medical technician from Rapid City, South Dakota, is one of the Eagle Dancers. Caleb and the others dance to the rhythmic beating of a large drum, their faces turned upward to the eastern sky. This is the sixth time this day that the group has danced, each time for forty minutes, each time gradually shifting formation in order to face all four directions, honoring the spirit beings of the east, the south, the west, and the north. One more session of dancing, later this afternoon, will bring to an end this year's annual **Sun Dance**. The Sun Dance is a midsummer Native American ritual that spans nearly two weeks, culminating in four days of dancing. This Sun Dance, in the wilderness of the Pacific Northwest, is open to all participants—from all Native American nations and even non–Native Americans.

In the center of the circular enclosure stands a remarkable tree. Perhaps a hundred bundles of colorful cloth hang from its boughs. Its central limbs hold a branch of chokecherry, from which hang effigies of a buffalo and of a man. The cottonwood tree was carefully selected months in advance for this purpose, then ceremoniously felled the day before the dancing began and carried many miles to be positioned at the enclosure's center.

This photo from 1910 shows several Cheyenne people gathered in preparation for a Sun Dance ceremony.

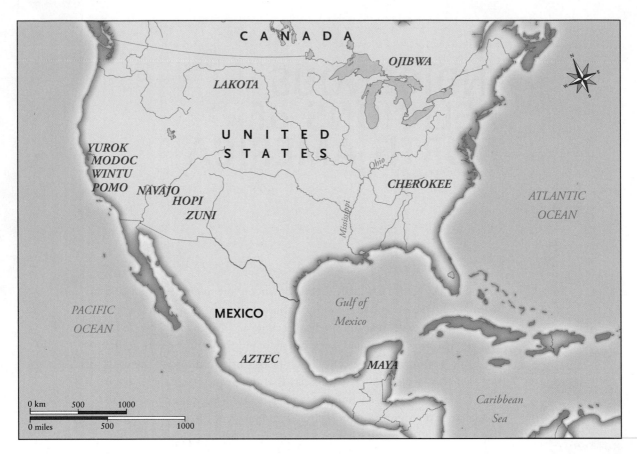

Indigenous peoples of North America.

The tree's significance for all those gathered at the Sun Dance can hardly be over-stated. Due to the ritual of the dancing, the circle for these four days is sacred space. The tree stands at the center and marks the most sacred space of all. In fact, it is the tree that *establishes* the circle and defines the sacred space. Added to this is the significance of its verticality. By reaching upward the tree is thought to be the point of contact with the spirit world that connects the sacred expanse of the sky to the sacred space of the circle and to Caleb and the dancers. In every respect, the cottonwood tree is a kind of *axis mundi* (Latin, "the center of the world"), a symbol that scholars of religious studies and mythology have recognized in cultures and traditions globally. Planted in the earth, reaching skyward, and establishing the sacred enclosure of the Sun Dance, the tree is perceived by the participants as being the center of the world—and of reality itself.

Caleb is a member of the Lakota Nation, a people of the Northern Plains. Caleb is a very special type of dancer known as an Eagle Dancer. He and the two other Eagle Dancers dance attached to ropes that are strung from the tree's trunk and looped around skewers that were pierced through the skin of their chests on the first day of dancing. At the end of the fourth day, they will fall back on their ropes, pulling the skewers free from their flesh. This act is considered a sacrifice to the Great Spirit, or

God, a gift of the one thing that is truly one's own to give—one's being. The Eagle Dancers spend almost the entire four days in the midst of the sacred circle, enduring the days' heat and the nights' chill, and taking neither food nor drink. Though he is a young man, Caleb has spent several years preparing for this Sun Dance, the first summer of three in which he will be an Eagle Dancer. Training under the guidance of a Lakota healer, Caleb has practiced the difficult arts of fasting and enduring the heat.

As the temperature hovers near 100 degrees, the dancers gradually complete this round. The challenges of the fast and the hot sun are especially daunting for the three Eagle Dancers. As the youngest and least experienced of the Eagle dancers, Caleb has difficulty enduring the harsh conditions and the rigors of the dance. He nearly faints on several occasions.

The Sun Dance incorporates many ritual features: the sounds of the beating drum, often accompanied by chanting of sacred words; the sights of the tree and the dancers; the smell of cedar smoke used to ritually purify the grounds and participants; and, for the Eagle dancers, the experiences of fasting and the acts of sacrifice. The cumulative effects of these features are self-evident to Caleb and the others involved. The perception of sacred space, with the tree as *axis mundi*, is complemented and enhanced by the perception of sacred *time*. The usual partitioning of everyday life is superseded by the ritualized stages of the dancing and of the ceremony at large. For Native Americans like Caleb, these effects tend to induce a state of heightened awareness of the spirit world—and of the Great Spirit, or God.

The Sun Dance has been practiced for centuries by many Native American tribes of the Northern Plains. Details have varied, depending on particular tribal traditions. The Sun Dance retains its importance today and is becoming more popular as Native peoples strive to rediscover and to nurture traditions rooted in the past. No one ritual, however important or popular, can exemplify the religious practices of all Native Americans. Still, the Sun Dance features certain elements—such as the *axis mundi*, the perception of sacred space and sacred time, and the communing with the spirit world—that are quite common to the religions of North America. ☼

I n this chapter, we will explore indigenous religions of North America. Because these religions are so numerous, we will not attempt to discuss them all but, rather, will select examples from a few. It is important to observe that these religions are not relics of the past. Although they are practiced on a smaller scale, they are not simpler or more basic than large religions like Christianity, Buddhism, or Islam. Therefore, they should not be considered evidence of a "primitive" or less developed religious mentality. Rather, Native American religions are highly complex belief systems, with sophisticated cosmologies and firm ethical principles. Although followers, like Caleb, certainly inherit ideas and practices from their ancestors, the religions are not simply copies of ancient religions. They have changed—and continue to change—in response to interaction with other belief systems, other cultures, and technological advances.

Although we explore these religions together in a single chapter, it is important to note that there is much diversity in the indigenous religions of North America. Today, over 700 tribal nations are recognized in the United States alone. In the past, there were many more. The human landscape of North America changed dramatically with the arrival of Europeans. Prior to European contact, the population of the Americas as a whole was estimated to be as high as 100 million. However, due to disease and conquest, the Native population throughout the Americas was decimated, and it is likely that some religious traditions were lost forever.

There is much diversity in Native American religious traditions, but there are also some common patterns in Native American religious practice, teachings, and historical development. Ritual practices like the Sun Dance are found in many Native American religions. Also, many religions share the belief that the sacred coexists with and infuses everyday life. Similarly, many share a belief in the interconnectedness of all things in the natural world. Many religions therefore emphasize the importance of reciprocal relationships between humans and other elements of the natural world. Also, although these religions each have individual histories, they have faced similar issues and events in modern times, particularly with the European conquest of the Americas.

THE TEACHINGS OF NATIVE AMERICAN INDIGENOUS RELIGIONS

We will begin our exploration of Native American religions by looking at the belief systems and teachings of some of these religions. Because they are complex and varied, we will focus our attention primarily on elements of belief that are common in many Native religions. We will look particularly closely at beliefs about creation and human origins, the interrelationship of humanity and other elements of the world, and the nature of sacred language.

Most Native American religions do not have a specific creed or statement of belief. Rather, essential teachings are revealed in mythic narratives and shared and enacted through religious practice. As we learned in Chapter 1, all religions have a mythic component. The religions of North America have especially rich and detailed sacred narratives. Myths contain sacred knowledge about the world, humanity, and the meaning of existence. It is through hearing and retelling myths that people commit this knowledge to heart and pass it on to the next generation. In most Native religions, religious knowledge is highly valued, and those people who have it are greatly respected. With their intriguing characters and compelling stories, myths are a powerful way for people everywhere to learn about their origins, the supernatural, and ethics and morality. As in other religions, the myths of Native American religions also provide guidelines for human behavior, relationships, and ritual practice.

Creation and Origins

Creation stories abound in the myths of native North America, and there is a remarkable variety in types of creation narratives. Some myths focus on the creation of the earth and the origins of humans in general, and others simply account for the origins of one particular people. Some myths tell of people coming to the surface of the earth from deep underground, and others tell of humans being fashioned from corn by creator gods. Despite this diversity, most Native American mythologies regard the Americas as the original ancestral home. Although there is a great deal of diversity in creation accounts, these myths do share some common elements, as we will explore next.

The Creators and Sacred Power In Native American myths, acts of creation are most often attributed to superhuman beings, often referred to simply as "creators." Because of the vast differences between Native religions, it is difficult to make generalizations about Native conceptions of superhuman beings. Some Native religions, like those of the Great Plains tribes, hold a belief in a supreme being, sometimes known as the Great Spirit. Such religions, like the religion of the Lakota, may also teach that all elements of creation, both animate and inanimate, contain the spiritual essence of the Great Spirit. Sometimes, the supreme being is thought to be somewhat removed from the day-to-day lives of human beings. Spirits or lesser deities, however, may be more active in everyday human affairs.

Many Native American religions also share a belief in a supreme force or sacred power. This sacred power may be manifest in different ways. It may be inherent in parts of the natural world or may be an important quality of gods or other supernatural beings. The Navajo of the southwestern United States teach of a **Holy Wind**, which is a spiritual force that inhabits every element of creation. The Holy Wind enters living beings through their own breath and directs their actions and thoughts. In this way, the Holy Wind connects all living things.

The Aztecs of central Mexico recognized a sacred power that infused elements of everyday life and supernatural beings. Aztecs also recognized many different deities, who possessed different aspects of sacred power. Some deities were associated with the power of creation and fertility, and others with the sun. The god **Quetzalcoatl**, who is often depicted as a feathered serpent, was thought to possess the sacred power of creation. Many mythic narratives surround Quetzalcoatl. One myth teaches that he assisted with creation by providing food and nourishment for the Aztec people. As a result, he is regarded as an important cultural hero in Mexico.[1]

Human Origins and Human Ancestors The creation narratives of indigenous North American religions differ significantly from each other in their accounts of the origin of humans. Some myths describe how humans were created, and others focus on how they came to live in a particular geographic locale. Despite such differences, however, North American Native myths often teach that human beings and human ancestors originated in the Americas. This belief contradicts anthropological theories that the Americas were settled by people from Asia tens of thousands of years ago.

The Mayan people of Central America have very complex creation narratives. Mayan cultural roots go back thousands of years. Although most myths of the Americas have been transmitted orally, the Maya have an ancient written language and texts that contain their mythic heritage. The Quiché Maya, one of several Mayan eth-nic groups, are from the highlands of Guatemala. The Quiché creation epic, known as the ***Popol Vuh***, contains stories about creation, the exploits of the gods, and the first humans. The written text of *Popol Vuh* in the Quiché language dates back several centuries.

The *Popol Vuh* contains a dramatic account of the creation of the first humans. The creator gods attempted to make humans several times, and failed in their first three attempts. The first time, the gods succeeding in creating animals, but they could only squawk and chatter—they could not speak. This disappointed the gods, who wanted humans to be able to worship them with spoken language. The second time, the creators made humans out of mud, but the clumsy figures just melted away. The third time, the gods fashioned wooden manikins. The manikins looked human and could talk, but they were cruel and heartless. The *Popol Vuh* tells that these manikins became the first monkeys. Finally, the creators mixed cornmeal with water to fashion human beings. This attempt was successful, and the humans could talk, think, and worship the gods.[2]

Other Native American myths do not describe the creation of humans, but instead account for their emergence on the surface of the earth. The Zuni are a people who live in the southwestern United States. In Zuni mythology, a god called Awaonawilona created the world from his own breath and body. At the time of creation, the ancestors of the Zuni lived underground in dark and unpleasant conditions. Eventually, two warrior gods were created. They led the ancestors out from under the earth to live on its surface in the sun. Zuni mythology teaches that the Zuni were the first people on the surface of the earth, but every few years the earth would open again and another people would emerge. The Zuni regard the other Southwest peoples who followed them, like the Navajo and the Hopi, as their younger siblings.[3]

Navajo creation myths similarly describe the ancestors of humans, sometimes known as **Holy People**, emerging from under the surface of the earth. The myths tell that ancestors of the Navajo lived a stressful and conflict-ridden life underground. This unpleasantness was due to the inherent chaos of their environment—there was neither order nor purpose to life under the earth, and people behaved badly toward one another. To escape the turmoil, the ancestors traveled through many subterranean worlds in search of one in which order would prevail. They finally emerged on the surface of the earth. First Man and First Woman were born, and it was their responsibility to help create this world.

The ancestors prepared the world for humans through specific rituals using special objects. The

This 7th or 8th century vase from Guatemala depicts scenes from the *Popol Vuh*.

rituals established order and served as the foundation for Navajo religious practice, even as practiced today. In one ritual, the ancestors created a painting on the ground, in which they depicted all that was going to exist in the world. Then, through prayer and song, the real world came to be from this wonderful painting. In stark contrast to the chaos underground, the world was perfectly balanced and ordered. Eventually, an important figure known as **Changing Woman** was born. She gave birth to heroic twins, who prepared the way for humanity by vanquishing monsters that roamed the earth. Then, Changing Woman created the first Navajo people from her own body.[4]

In some religions, ancestors are the spiritual representations of what humans can hope to become. The Pueblo peoples are cultures of the Four Corners region of the American southwest that include the Hopi and the Zuni. Among the Pueblo peoples, ancestral spirits are known as **kachinas**. Kachinas, which may take the form of animals, plants, or humans, represent the spiritually perfect beings that humans become after they die. The Hopi believe that in this life, humans are spiritually imperfect. But in the afterlife, the Hopi leave their human nature behind and become unsullied spirits. Humanity's spiritual imperfection is represented in public dances and ceremonies by clowns. This is because in Hopi mythology, a clown led human beings as they emerged from the ground. In some of these ceremonies, masked dancers portraying the kachina spirits tell the clowns to mend their imperfect ways and strive to be better human beings. When the dancers don the masks, the kachina spirits inhabit and inspire them.[5]

Life Lessons in Myths

Native American mythologies contain teachings about how to live properly in the world. From myths, people learn to live respectfully with others in society, to make a living off of the land, and to understand the meaning of life. In many Native myths, these lessons are taught through the exploits of a character known as a **trickster**. The trickster figure is often an animal who has adventures and engages in all manner of mischief. In many myths, the trickster suffers repercussions because of his failure to follow established rules about social behavior. Because of this, those hearing the myth are warned about the importance of proper behavior.

One trickster tale featuring Coyote comes from the Pima of Arizona. In the past, Bluebird was an unattractive color. The bird decided to bathe in a special blue lake every morning for four days. After the fourth dip in the lake, the bird grew beautiful blue feathers. Coyote, who was green at the time, saw the beautiful color and asked Bluebird how he could become beautiful, too. The bird explained his method, and Coyote turned a beautiful blue. Coyote was very proud, and he looked around arrogantly as he walked to make sure he was being admired. But he did not watch where he was going, and he tripped and fell in the dirt. When he got up, he was the color of dirt, and now all coyotes are dirt-colored.[6] This short tale teaches an important lesson about the dangers of arrogance.

Myths of North America may also account for the origins of subsistence activities, like hunting and farming. Often, the subsistence practices of a people are said to have been determined by the gods. This divine origin of daily activity casts everyday life and everyday activities, like planting crops or preparing food, in a sacred dimension.[7]

Consider, for example, the many diverse myths about the origins of corn. Corn, or maize, has been a staple crop of great importance throughout North America. Some myths explain that human beings have a special duty to raise corn. Myths may tell of a particular god who is responsible for providing the crop or for protecting the fertility of the earth. The Cherokee, historically of the southeastern United States, tell a myth in which the goddess Corn Woman produced corn through the treachery of her son and his playmate. In the myth, Corn Woman rubbed her body to produce food. One day, the two boys saw her doing this. They thought she was practicing witchcraft and so decided to kill her. After they attacked her, she instructed the boys to drag her injured body over the ground. Wherever her blood fell, corn grew. This myth teaches about the relationship between life and death: the blood that causes death can also produce life.[8]

Many other myths teach about life and death. The following passage from the *Popol Vuh* is a moving speech made by the heroic twin gods to the maiden Blood Moon. At this point in the myth, the lords of the underworld have defeated the twins. The severed head of one of the twins has been placed in a tree, and his skull impregnates the maiden with his spittle when she holds out her hand. Blood Moon will eventually bear the next generation of hero twins who avenge their fathers' deaths and prepare the world for the arrival of humans. In the twins' poignant speech to the maiden, we learn something about the Mayan view of the meaning of life: even after death, we live on in our children.

> And then the bone spit out its saliva, which landed squarely in the hand of the maiden. . . .
>
> "It's just a sign I have given you, my saliva, my spittle. This, my head, has nothing on it—just bone, nothing of meat. It's just the same with the head of a great lord: It's just the flesh that makes his face look good. And when he dies, people get frightened by his bones. After that, his son is like his saliva, his spittle, in his being whether it be the son of a lord of the son of a craftsman, an orator. The father does not disappear, but goes on being fulfilled. Neither dimmed nor destroyed is the face of a lord, a warrior, a craftsman, orator. Rather, he will leave his daughters and sons. So it is that I have done likewise through you. Now go up there on the face of the earth; you will not die. Keep the word. So be it."[9]

Stories of heroic twins are also common in other indigenous American mythologies. This shows an important degree of continuity between traditions throughout regions of North America. As you recall, Navajo mythology includes a similar tale of heroic twins preparing the world for humanity. The Apache, also of the southwestern United States, share a similar tale.

The Importance of Balance:
Humanity and the Natural World

Many indigenous North American religions emphasize the interrelationship of all things. As we saw earlier, the elements of creation, humans included, are often thought to share a common spiritual energy or sacred power. This may be understood as a life force or as the presence of the Supreme Being. This idea is beautifully captured by the words of **Black Elk** (1863–1950), a famous Lakota religious leader. In a book titled *Black Elk Speaks* (1932), he tells of his life and of a great vision. He opens by saying: "It is the story of all life that is holy and is good to tell, and of us two-leggeds sharing in it with the four-leggeds and the wings of the air and all green things; for these are the children of one mother and their father is one spirit."[10]

This interconnectedness often extends to humanity's relationship with animals. In some teachings, humanity is created as the companion of other creatures—not as their master. In other traditions, humans are thought to be descended from animal or animal-like ancestors. A myth of the Modoc of Northern California tells of the special relationship between humans and grizzly bears. The Sky God created all creatures and also created Mt. Shasta, a 14,000-foot volcanic peak, which served as the home for the Sky God's family. One day, his daughter fell to earth from the top of the mountain. She was adopted and raised by a family of grizzly bears, who could talk and walk on two feet. Eventually, she married one of the bears, and from this union were born the first people. When the Sky God eventually found his daughter, he was angry that a new race was born that he had not created. He then cursed the grizzly bears to forever go about on all fours.[11]

Mt. Shasta, in northern California, is regarded as sacred by many tribes in the region.

As a result of this interconnectedness, many Native American religions emphasize the importance of maintaining balance among all things. Often, this is viewed as the primary responsibility of humanity. A critical part of religious practice is therefore focused on developing and preserving harmonious relationships between humans and other elements of the world. As we have learned, Navajo myths tell that the ancestors learned to maintain this balance as an example to later generations. The myths of the Yurok of Northern California similarly describe a time when the Immortals inhabited the earth. The Immortals knew how to maintain balance, but humans did not. Thus, the Immortals taught the Yurok people ceremonies that they could use to restore the balance of the earth.[12]

Sacred Places and Spaces The focus on balance extends to the physical landscape. According to Native American religious traditions, humanity is often thought to live in a reciprocal relationship with the land: each relies on and must care for the other, and all are part of a sacred whole. Certain geographical features, like rivers, mountains, and rocks, may be permeated with sacred power. Such places often feature prominently in mythology and are infused with power because of what happened there in the mythic past. One such place is Mt. Shasta. Many tribes of the region regard the mountain as sacred because of its importance in mythology. Myths tell that the Creator made the mountain so he could reach the earth from the heavens. (As we saw in the Modoc myth, the Creator resided in the mountain with his family.) Because of its sacred history, areas of Mt. Shasta are powerful places where Native religious experts can make contact with the spirit world. To this day, leaders from several tribes use the area for religious ceremonies.

Among the White Mountain Apache of Arizona, the significance of certain places comes alive in the stories people tell about them. Tales about the local landscape are an important part of Apache cultural and religious knowledge, and they convey important moral teachings. The landscape is thus imbued with life lessons. An Apache woman named Annie Peaches told the anthropologist Keith Basso (b. 1940) about a place called "Big Cottonwood Trees Stand Here and There." In the tale, the Apaches and the neighboring Pima were fighting at the place of the big cottonwood trees. The fighting awakened a sleeping old woman, but she thought the noise was simply her son-in-law cursing her daughter. She yelled at him and told him to stop picking on the young woman. The Pima heard her yell, rushed in, and killed her. The tale illustrates the danger of disregarding appropriate behavior in certain types of relationships: in Apache culture, a woman should not criticize her son-in-law unless her daughter asks her to intervene. The old woman suffered dire consequences from interfering, and when Apache people pass the place known as Big Cottonwood Trees Stand Here and There, they are reminded of this social rule.[13]

Myths that cast the land in a sacred light may also teach people how to build their communities. Thus, even architecture has a sacred dimension. Among the Navajo, the guidelines for building the sacred dwelling known as a **hogan** are found in myth. The Holy People taught that a *hogan* should be built as representation of Navajo lands and the cosmos. Four posts, which represent four sacred mountains that surround the Navajo homeland, support the *hogan*. The roof represents Father Sky and the floor is Mother Earth. The **tipi**, a typical structure of the tribes of the Great Plains, has a similar sacred blueprint. Each *tipi* is an image of the universe. The perimeter of the *tipi* is the edge of the universe, and the lit fire in the center represents the center of all existence. Joseph Epes Brown, a scholar of Native religions, writes that the smoke from the

The *tipi*, a typical structure of the tribes of the Great Plains, has a sacred blueprint. Each *tipi* can be understood as an image of the universe.

fire, which escapes the *tipi* through a hole in the ceiling, can carry messages to the spirit world.[14] The *tipi* is thus another *axis mundi*, connecting different planes of existence.

Sacred Language and Sacred Time

In many Native American cultures, time is regarded as circular, not linear. Thus, events that happened at one point on the circle of time are not simply past; they will be experienced again. Beliefs about death further illustrate this concept. In many Native American religions, death is considered to be an important spiritual transition. During old age, death may be welcomed and prepared for, and funeral rituals ease the transition of the deceased

Navajo *hogans* are built to represent the Navajo lands and the cosmos.

into the next stage in the afterlife. In many cultures, the transition of a person from birth to death is thought to be comparable to the cyclical nature of the seasons of the year.[15] Thus, just as winter precedes spring, human death is connected to the reemergence of life. Recall the Cherokee myth about the origins of corn, which emphasizes the necessity of death to produce life. As you read the next passage, think about cyclical time and the nature of death. Joseph Epes Brown tells us how Black Elk explained this to him:

> This cyclical reality was beautifully expressed . . . when I noticed how the dignified old Lakota man Black Elk would relate to little children. He would get down on his hands and knees and pretend he was a horse, and the children would squeal with joy. . . . There obviously was no generation gap; he fully connected with children. I once asked him how it was that he could so relate to the children, and he replied "I who am an old man am about to return to the Great Mysterious and a young child is a being who has just come from the Great Mysterious, so it is that we are very close together."[16]

The words of Black Elk illustrate the important relationship between the elderly and the very young. In many Native religions, elders teach youngsters about their religious heritage through myths. Often, the telling of myths is regarded as sacred speech. Because of the cyclical nature of time, the events related in myths are not thought to be a part of a distant and irrecoverable past but, rather, are representative of another place on the circle of time. Recounting a myth re-creates the events of the myth, transporting listeners into mythic time.[17]

Earlier in this chapter, we learned how the ancestors of the Navajo sang and painted the world into existence. Thus, words and language were the building blocks of creation. The rituals of the ancestors provide the foundation for Navajo ceremonial practice, which is focused on maintaining order in the world. This is primarily done through practices known as **chantways**. Chantways involve ritualized singing and chants and may take place over several days. The songs and chants retell the stories of creation, and thus through language bring the power of the time of creation into the present. Chantways are used in many contexts, like marriages, births, and puberty rites, and are thought to have the power to bring great benefit. The chantways are used for healing by aiming to bring afflicted individuals into harmony with their surroundings. Normally, the ceremonies take place in *hogans*.

VOICES: An Interview with Lin Estes

Lin Estes

Lin Estes is a woman of Shawnee, Choctaw, and Welsh descent. She is a student who is pursuing a degree in American Indian Studies at Black Hills State University.

What is your religious background?

I grew up in an atmosphere where religion was not forced on me. This was a good thing because I never bought the concept that sitting in a building one day a week made me a good person. I preferred to be outside absorbing the world.

In your view, what is the nature of the world? What is humanity's place in it?

I think that we are all connected. I believe that there is a Creator and that we have many paths to the Creator. I believe that people share a desire to be content, safe, and have food, shelter, and comfort for their families. Our core beliefs allow us to function and to find meaning when unfortunate events impact our lives. There are always some people who through ignorance, greed, or fear will cause unrest. It is then that we either reach inside for an answer or accept that matters are out of our control. We all want freedom from the oppression of our beliefs. In the United States, many policies have been enacted to keep Natives from expressing their spirituality.

Could you describe your religious practice and your personal spirituality?

Even though I did not have a structured religious upbringing, I knew from a young age that I was part of something greater. I knew Connection of Spirit early on. I believe that we are a part of Mother Earth—we are connected to every living thing. In my thirties, some of my uncles, who were Episcopalian ministers, told me that I was like my great grandmother Eudora. She had been called Prophetess by her community and her "ways" were not Christian. They advised me that I had gifts of insight that she had. However, they thought that I should be more "Christian" and turn away from Eudora's ways. Because of assimilation, my uncles didn't consider themselves Native. Certain events during their military careers in the 1940s and 1950s led them to hide behind their lighter Shawnee complexions. They did not want to be Indian. But I knew who I was. I lived from the inside out instead of trying to be who others told me I should want to be or instead of practicing a religion that did not work for me. I live in Spirit, connected to the Native Spirit that is Creator. I have also embraced Buddhism because it has similar qualities.

What opportunities and challenges do you face as a member of a native community in the United States today?

I believe that the indigenous people of the United States have been and are still the targets of genocide. While some of the overt policies of the past are no longer in place, Native people still lack freedom to express spirituality. Bear Butte in South Dakota comes to mind. Bear Butte is a sacred place where Native peoples travel to pray, to prepare for Sun Dance, and to cleanse. One will find prayer ties and tobacco ties offered to Creator for the passing of a loved one. Just near Bear Butte there is a town called Sturgis, where roughly a half million people gather for a biker rally every August. Natives praying at the Butte are subjected to the stadium type lights, loud music, and the nonsacred atmosphere of the many bars built to accommodate the bikers. Strip clubs, wet t-shirt contests, and drunkenness offend those who travel to the Butte for ceremony. The state of South Dakota and Sturgis are more concerned with money than they are with "those Indians" on the Butte. Today, I think Native spiritual practice is still viewed as "primitive." I hope there will be a time when there is equality for Natives. I have been called a "witch," a "psychic," and also a "Lamanite" *(see Chapter 13)*. But I am a Native woman who has been blessed with the strength to know who I am. I am not troubled by those who call me anything else or tell me I can't practice the way that is right for me.

NATIVE AMERICAN INDIGENOUS RELIGIONS AS A WAY OF LIFE

Now that we have examined some prevalent beliefs of Native American religions, we can explore how these beliefs relate to religious practice. Followers of Native American religions do not usually make stark distinctions between what is "religious" and what is "secular." As we have seen, myths instill everyday life with a sacred quality by providing explanations even for seemingly mundane activities like planting or preparing food. Therefore, many actions have a religious dimension.

Healing

In Native American religions, healing the sick is often part of religious practice. Healers may use religious knowledge to cure physical and mental illnesses. In addition, healers are frequently well-known for their understanding of local plant remedies. Because of this, the term "medicine man" has often been used for healers. Some healers undergo years of training to acquire great depths of religious knowledge. Others are considered specialists not because of particular training but because they have an inherent ability to interact with the spirit world or have been selected by a spirit to become a healer. In many Native traditions, healers are also religious leaders.

A well-known twentieth-century spiritual healer was **Mabel McKay** (1907–1993), a Pomo woman of Northern California. As a young woman, Mabel was called to be a liaison between her people and the spirit world. Spirit guides told her that she would develop a special gift of healing. Here, Mabel McKay's close friend Greg Sarris describes how she was called by a spirit to be a healer.

> The spirit talked to her constantly now. . . . Sometimes it felt as if her own tongue were moving, shaping the words she was hearing. This happened when she sang the songs that came loud and clear. "Am I going crazy?" she asked once. . . . "No," the spirit said, "it's me. And what is happening is that you have an extra tongue. Your throat has been fixed for singing and sucking out the diseases I've been teaching you about. It's talking. It's me in you." "Well, how am I to suck?" Mabel asked. "You'll know when you get to that point. You will have a basket to spit out the disease. All your baskets will come from me. Like I told you. Watch how things turn out." The spirit explained each of the songs that Mabel could hear and sing clearly now. "This is your setting-down song, for when you're calling me. This song is for putting the sickness to sleep. You will have many more songs."[18]

In addition to the chantways we learned about earlier in this chapter, Navajo healing ceremonies also use an art form known as **sand painting**. The Holy People gave the paintings to the Navajo people. As the name suggests, sand paintings are created using vivid colors of sand and other dry materials like pollen. The paintings are created on the floors of *hogans* and treat illnesses by bringing individuals into alignment with nature. A healer, or singer, selects the subjects of the painting in consultation with the family of the person being treated; these may include animals, plants, and mythic figures.

During the ceremony, the afflicted person is seated in the center of the painting, which tells one of the creation stories. As sand is applied to his body, he identifies with the Holy People depicted in the painting. During the treatment, the painted figures are thought to come to life to aid in the healing of the patient. After the ceremony is complete, the painting is destroyed and the sand is removed. In the past, Navajo people never kept permanent copies of the paintings because it was thought that it would diminish their healing power. Although today small paintings are produced for sale, ideally these permanent paintings should not represent or depict the important figures and symbols used in healing practice.

Rites of Passage

Like other religions around the world, Native American traditions use rituals to recognize important changes in a person's social status. Such rituals are known as **rites of passage**. Often, rites of passage mark the transition from childhood to adulthood. Many Native cultures have elaborate rites marking this transition for young women

Navajo man preparing a sand painting.

and men. In this section, we will examine two rites of passage. First, we will look at the **Kinaalda**, which marks a Navajo girl's transition to adulthood. Then, we will examine a spiritual rite of passage known as a **Vision Quest**.

The Kinaalda The Navajo puberty rite for girls is known as the *Kinaalda*. It takes place soon after a girl begins menstruating. Each girl undergoing *Kinaalda* has a sponsor. This is an older woman who serves as a guide and role model and teaches her about the expectations of her as a Navajo woman. The ceremonial activities last several days and are part of the chantways. Thus, the ritual has its foundation in mythology. Changing Woman experienced the first *Kinaalda*, which is the model ritual for all girls. Indeed, girls are believed to take on the identity and spiritual qualities of Changing Woman during the ritual. Because she takes on the identity of Changing Woman, a girl going through the rites is thought to have special healing powers. People may visit her to request healing for their ailments.

One important *Kinaalda* activity is baking a giant cake of cornmeal. The initiate prepares the cake with the assistance of her family. She grinds the corn and prepares the batter carefully, since it is believed that if a cake turns out well, she will have a full and productive life. A poorly made cake bodes ill for her future.

Vision Quests A rite of passage common to many North American religions is the Vision Quest. This is the attempt by an individual to communicate with the spirit world. It is especially well known among peoples of the Great Plains and Great Lakes regions, like the Sioux and the Ojibwa. The quest may be undertaken by men or women, depending on the culture, and may occur once or at several points in an individual's life. In some cultures, the vision quest marks the transition from childhood to adulthood.

Usually, the goal of the vision quest is for an individual to make contact with the spirit world. This is frequently accomplished through contact with a spirit guide. Often, the spirit guide takes an animal form, which may be revealed during the quest. Sometimes, individuals report that the spirit guide appeared to them directly. Others learned the identity of the guide by spotting a particular animal during the quest. In other vision quests, the focus is not on a spirit guide but, rather, on accessing a spiritual power more generally.

In most quests, the initiate will remove himself from normal society by spending several days alone in the wilderness. The vision quest can be both mentally and physically demanding, as it may require long periods of isolation and fasting. A vision quest teaches a person about the importance of seeking and following guidance from the spirit world and has the potential to cultivate a mental and physical hardiness that will serve the individual throughout his or her life.[19] Among the Ojibwa, boys normally undertook the vision quest at puberty. After a period of preparation, a boy was taken deep in the wood where he would remain by himself, fasting, until he received a vision. For many boys, visions were journeys into the spirit world, and spirit guides would help the boy figure out his life's path. Boys who were not able to endure the fast could try again at a later time.[20]

Rites of Renewal and Rites of Purification

As we learned earlier in this chapter, many Native American religions focus on humanity's important role in maintaining balance with other elements of creation. This goal forms the foundation of many kinds of ritual practice, specifically those ceremonies known as **rites of renewal**. Like the term suggests, rites of renewal seek to renew the sacred balance of all things. Such rites are often seasonal because they are designed to correspond with the cycle of planting and harvesting or moving herd animals for grazing. They may aim to enhance natural processes like rainfall or the growth of crops.

As you recall, the Yurok tell of the knowledge given to human beings by the Immortals, who lived on earth before humans. The Immortals taught human beings a ritual known as the **Jump Dance**, which restores the balance of the earth and renews the harmony that was present in the time of the Immortals. Along with a number of other rituals, the Jump Dance is performed during the World Renewal Ceremonial Cycle. This is a cycle of ceremonies that are performed by many Northern California Indians at various times of the year, and their purpose is to maintain the balance of all living things on earth. In the Jump Dance, men march to a special place that has been sanctified by a priest, where they dance. By engaging in this religious practice, which imitates and repeats the words and actions that the Immortals taught humans, the mythic time is called into the present and the earth is renewed. In addition, because an entire community may participate in rites of renewal, they have the ability to enhance group solidarity.[21]

In North American religions from Mexico to Alaska, **sweat lodge** ceremonies are used to ritually purify and cleanse the body. They are rites of purification. In these ceremonies, participants build an enclosed structure that is filled with heated stones. Pouring water over the stones generates steam. The steam has the power to cleanse the body and clear the mind of anything that might distract an individual from focusing on the divine. A sweat bath may be used to prepare for other ritual activities, like the Sun Dance described in the opening part of this chapter. The ritual use of the sweat lodge encourages a bond between all those who bathe in it. And sometimes, the cleansing power extends even beyond the inhabitants of the lodge to other elements of creation.[22] In this way, this rite of purification also serves as a rite of renewal. The ritual use of the sweat bath is such an important part of religious practice that some states have been ordered by federal judges to provide Native prisoners access to sweat lodges.[23]

Among Pueblo peoples like the Hopi and Zuni, kachina dances are a type of renewal rite. As we discussed earlier in this chapter, when dancers wear the masks of the kachinas, they are thought to become imbued with the spirit of the kachina. Kachinas have the power to bring rain and enhance fertility. Among the Hopi, who recognize over 200 kachina spirits, several dances take place during the part of the year between the winter solstice and the summer solstice. The songs used with

This Hopi kachina doll from the twentieth century might be used to remind children of the qualities the kachinas possess.

the dances often call for fertility of the land, for rainfall, and for the flourishing of crops. Rites of renewal also often have significance beyond these material aims. The Hopi dance for rain calls not just for nourishment of crops but also for nourishment of the cosmos. In the Hopi belief system, the spiritual qualities of rain underlie all of existence. The world, in a sense, rests on rain. Thus, rain dances rejuvenate the entire cosmos, not just the crops in a particular locale.[24]

The kachina dances also teach young people about ethics and morality. Children are not allowed to see the dancers without their masks. This is so the children will have a strong association of the dancers with the kachinas and think of them only as representing the idealized qualities the kachinas possess. However, when they are old enough, children learn that their parents or other relatives are behind the masks. This disillusionment is part of their religious development, as children learn that the world is not always as it seems.[25]

VISUAL GUIDE
North American Religions

Among Pueblo peoples like the Hopi and Zuni, kachina dances are a type of renewal rite. When dancers wear the masks of the kachinas, they are thought to become imbued with the spirit of the kachina. Kachinas have the power to bring rain and enhance fertility. This is a Hopi kachina doll, representing a kachina, from Arizona. The doll dates to before 1901, and is made of painted wood, feathers, and pine needles.

In North American religions from Mexico to Alaska, sweat lodge ceremonies ritually purify and cleanse the body. In these ceremonies, participants build an enclosed structure that is filled with heated stones.

The *tipi* is a typical structure of the tribes of the Great Plains that has religious significance. Each *tipi* is an image of the universe. The perimeter of the *tipi* is the edge of the universe, and the lit fire in the center represents the center of all existence.

THE HISTORY OF NATIVE AMERICAN INDIGENOUS RELIGIONS

As we have seen throughout this chapter, the indigenous religions of North and Central America are complex and multifaceted. Just like other major world religions, these traditions have developed historically and have both resisted and accommodated cultural changes. In this section of the chapter, we will look at how Native North American religions have responded to the social and political changes in the modern world. As you read this section, think about how indigenous American religions have adapted and endured despite colonialism, encroaching Christianity, and culture change.

Conquest, Colonization, and Christianity

The expansion of European imperialism from the sixteenth through the early twentieth century ravaged and radically influenced indigenous religious traditions in the Americas. Throughout North America, the effects of colonialism on indigenous peoples were disastrous: indigenous populations were devastated by disease and warfare, forced to move far away from their ancestral homelands, and sometimes enslaved or indentured to work for the colonists. In the "Voices" interview earlier in this chapter, Lin refers to these events as the ongoing genocide of Native peoples.

Spanish, British, and French colonial powers sent Christian missionaries to their imperial holdings (and beyond) in North and Central America with the aim of "saving" indigenous peoples from what were viewed as their "pagan" ways. As a result, many indigenous peoples converted (forcibly or by choice) to the Christianity of the colonizers. Some colonizers like the Spanish also believed that they could bring about the second coming of Christ by completing the work of taking the gospel to the ends of the earth.

More recently, in the nineteenth and twentieth centuries Native American children in the United States were forcibly removed from their homes and sent to boarding schools, where they were taught the "errors" of their cultural and religious ways. The 1819 Civilization Fund Act, which aimed to educate native children in an effort to "civilize" them, led to the development of many of these boarding schools. In the interview earlier in the chapter, recall that Lin's uncles were ashamed of their Indian heritage. As another example, in the southwestern United States, Navajo children were adopted by white families and raised in Mormon or other Christian traditions.

However, indigenous religious traditions were never entirely eradicated, even when Native peoples identified as Christians. When the Spanish conquistadors arrived in Mesoamerica, the indigenous religion of the Mayan peoples was banned, written versions of holy texts were burned, and the Maya were often forcibly converted to Roman Catholicism. Although many Mayan people today identify as Catholic, elements of indigenous religion remain. Catholic saints may be equated with Mayan gods, and some Maya have equated Jesus and Mary with the sun and the moon in Mayan cosmology. Today, many Mayan people may draw on both elements of Catholic and Mayan religion in their beliefs and practice.

In the United States today, many Native Americans identify as Catholics, Protestants, or nondenominational Christians. However, as with the Maya, this does not necessarily mean that the beliefs and practices of Native religions are no longer relevant. Furthermore, Christianity is sometimes understood as an indigenous American religion by Native Christians. Among the White Mountain Apache of Arizona, some religious leaders make the claim that they "have always had the Bible."[26] As with the Navajo, an important part of Apache girls' initiation is the assumption of the powers of Changing Woman. In Apache mythology, Changing Woman was distressed about the difficulty of life on earth and prayed to God to change it. God answered her prayers by impregnating her with the rays of the sun, and she gave birth to a heroic son,

TIMELINE
North American Religions

20,000 years ago Anthropologists believe humans migrated to the Americas from Asia.

300–900 C.E. The Mayan culture is flourishing; elements of *Popol Vuh* seen in hieroglyphic script.

700–1400 The city of Cahokia inhabited in Illinois.

900–1519 The Mayan cities decline; major urban centers are deserted.

1050 The first pueblos are built in the American Southwest.

1100–1519 The Aztec civilization thrives.

1492 Columbus arrives in Americas.

1513 The Spanish arrive in Florida.

1519 The Spanish arrive in Mexico; Hernan Cortes.

1540s The Spanish arrive in southwestern United States.

1550s First written copy of the *Popol Vuh*.

1565 The Spanish establish St. Augustine in Florida.

1560s First French colony in Florida.

1607 The English establish Jamestown

1700s The *Popol Vuh* written in Quiché Mayan language in Roman script.

1857 The *Popol Vuh* published in Spanish language.

1819 The Civilization Fund Act passed.

1870 The First Ghost Dance.

1889 Wovoka's vision.

1890 The Second Ghost Dance.

December 29, 1890 Tragic battle at Wounded Knee ends the Ghost Dance.

1904 The Sun Dance banned in United States.

1918 The Native American Church is founded.

1978 The American Indian Religious Freedom Act is passed.

1995 The use of peyote is made legal for religious purposes.

who made the earth safe for humans. Some Apache religious leaders interchange the names of Jesus and Mary for Changing Woman and her son. Furthermore, at the girls' puberty ceremony, participants draw parallels between other sacred Apache narratives and the stories of Genesis. It is in such contexts that practitioners argue that Christianity is indeed an indigenous American religion that predated colonization.[27] For other

In Chichicastengo, Guatemala, Mayan men take part in a religious ceremony where saints are taken to the streets by members of religious brotherhoods.

Apache Christians, however, traditional religion is viewed not as a complement to Christianity but as a relic of the past that good Christians should reject.

Resistance Movements

Many resistance movements developed in Native communities in response to European-American encroachment throughout North America. Such movements often had an overtly religious dimension, and indigenous religious leaders were frequently at the forefront of resistance movements. Many movements had influence far and wide and can therefore be understood as pan-Indian religious movements.

One such movement was the **Ghost Dance**. In the mid-nineteenth century, a religious leader of the Northern Paiute claimed to have had a vision that taught him that the white occupiers would leave if the Indians performed a special dance described by the spirits. This event was called the Ghost Dance because of the belief that it would usher in the destruction and rebirth of the world and that dead ancestors would return. Versions of the dance spread rapidly throughout the western United States in 1870 because many Native people embraced the possibility that the dance not only could allow them to communicate with deceased ancestors but also could revive the Native cultures in the face of European domination.

In 1890, another Paiute man of Nevada named **Wovoka**, who had studied Paiute religion and participated in the first Ghost Dance, founded a second Ghost Dance. In 1889, Wovoka experienced a powerful vision in which the Creator told him the ancestors would rise up. If people demonstrated their belief through dances, human misery and death would come to an end. The dances spread quickly across the Great Basin and to the Sioux of the northern Midwest and other Plains peoples.

Regrettably, many white Americans feared the dances, and the U.S. government interpreted the widespread dances as an armed resistance movement. The Ghost Dance came to a tragic end on December 29, 1890, at Wounded Knee, South Dakota. American troops killed hundreds of Lakota people, including women and children, who had gathered for a dance. The Ghost Dance came at a critical time in the history of Native American peoples and was seen by many participants as a final attempt to revive the ways of the past. Although the second Ghost Dance ended in catastrophe, the movement brought together people of different Native backgrounds and contributed to creating a shared sense of identity, history, and purpose among peoples of diverse origins.

Although the massacre at Wounded Knee is perhaps the most well known of U.S. attempts to control Native religious practice, government suspicions of religious practice continued well into the twentieth century. In 1904, the Sun Dance was officially banned because it was considered chaotic and dangerous. And as we have learned, for much of the nineteenth and twentieth centuries, the U.S. government backed a program in which young Native American children were taken from their homes and relocated to specially built boarding schools, where they were forced to leave behind their religious beliefs, languages, and other cultural practices while adopting the ways of European-Americans.

The **Native American Church** can be considered another resistance movement. In the early twentieth century, followers of **Peyote Religion** formed this church to protect their religious practice. The hallucinogenic peyote cactus has been used for thousands of years in indigenous religions of northern Mexico. In the late nineteenth and early twentieth century, the use of the plant spread to Native communities in the United States, particularly in the Plains. Around 1890, a Comanche chief called **Quanah Parker** (1845–1911) spread the call for American Indians to embrace peyote religion. He had been introduced to peyote use in the 1890s when he was treated with peyote for an injury, and he became an important defender of the use of peyote against detractors. Peyote is not habit-forming and is primarily used for healing purposes and to encourage encounters with the spirit world. However, Christian missionaries and other activists in the United States preached against peyote use, and federal and state governments eventually outlawed its use. (Centuries earlier, the Spanish colonizers also prohibited the use of peyote in religious practice as a result of a decree of the Spanish Inquisition.) In 1918, followers of Peyote Religion incorporated as the Native American Church to request legal protection for practicing religion.

A photograph of Wovoka seated.

In 1978, the **American Indian Religious Freedom Act** was passed in an effort to give Native peoples the right to express and practice their beliefs, according to the First Amendment of the U.S. Constitution. However, Native peoples have not always been able to protect their rights to religious freedom by referencing the act. Some practices, like the use of peyote for religious purposes, continued to face challenges from the government for years. Since 1995, however, the use of peyote has been legally permissible.

Native Religions and Non-Native Practitioners

Despite the history of antagonism toward Native religions in North America, many non–Native Americans are interested in learning about Native religious traditions. Today, people in the United States and elsewhere are attracted to what they view as the nature-centered focus of Native religions. In recent decades, some non–Native Americans have started following religious practices, rituals, and beliefs of Native religions as an alternative to what they perceive as drawbacks of Western religious traditions like Christianity and Judaism.

In the 1960s, many people, particularly those involved in the so-called counter-cultural movement, began to develop an interest in the teachings and practices of Native religions. Some were attracted to teachings about the interconnectedness of all things and found what they thought to be an appealing lack of materialism in Native religions. Others were particularly interested in practices that involved the use of hallucinogenic plants like peyote.

Some Native Americans appreciate the growing interest of non-Natives in indigenous religions. However, non-Native interest in Native religious practices has also been criticized by Native thinkers. Critics argue that selective adoption of certain practices, like peyote use, removes the activity from the cultural and historical context in which it developed. Sometimes, conflicts arise over the use of sacred places. In recent years, for example, non–Native Americans have felt the pull of Mt. Shasta. Their interest has not always been welcomed by American Indians—primarily because of a perception that non-Natives are appropriating Native spirituality without proper understanding or proper training. Among the Native people of the region, the springs and meadows of Mt. Shasta are treated with great reverence, and they believe a person should not approach these places without proper guidance from an expert or elder with great religious knowledge. Non-Native spiritual seekers, however, often bathe in sacred springs or play music in sacred groves and meadows without the advice or permission of religious leaders in the area, which offends some Native practitioners. Native views of the sacred nature of the land often conflict with the aims and goals of non–Native Americans, many of whom see the potential for development on the very lands that Indians consider sacred.[28]

CONCLUSION

As we have seen in this chapter, Native American religions are not relics of the past but are living traditions that continue to develop and change. One of the major challenges Native American religions have faced is the spread of Christianity, particularly through European colonialism of the Americas. However, even in those areas that have seen widespread conversion to other religions, elements of indigenous religions have often been maintained and even incorporated into the practice of the colonizing religions. In North America, many non-Native peoples have found Native American religions attractive because they offer a compelling and seemingly earth-centered spiritual alternative to other religions. However, American Indians respond to such interest from non-Native spiritual explorers in different ways. Some Native Americans welcome this interest, and others reject what they view as an inappropriate appropriation of Native religious ideas by non-Native peoples.

What does the future hold for the religions of Native North America? It is likely that Native and even non-Native peoples will continue to find great spiritual meaning and religious fulfillment in the teachings and practices of indigenous religions, many of which have roots several generations back. Although many Native Americans are Christians today, as we have seen, Native religious ideas often coexist harmoniously with Christian teachings and practices. In many communities, Native Americans are advocating a resurgence of indigenous religious ways, and, as we saw with the Ghost Dance and the Native American Church, pan-Indian or intertribal interest in certain types of religious practice will likely continue. Although throughout this chapter we have emphasized the importance of recognizing the diversity of Native American religious traditions, it is also essential to acknowledge that pan-tribal movements and ceremonies can be an important means of fostering a collective Native American identity.

SEEKING ANSWERS

What Is Ultimate Reality?

Myths contain sacred knowledge about ultimate reality and the nature of the world. In Native American religions, the world is believed to have been created by creator deities. The entire world, and the many elements within it—including human beings—may be believed to be infused by the spiritual essence of a Supreme Being, or Great Spirit.

How Should We Live in This World?

In most Native American religions, myths provide the foundations for the way people should live their lives. Humans are one part of the general order of existence and live in a reciprocal relationship with the land, plants, and other animals. Myths teach that it is the responsibility of humans to maintain balance, order, and right relationships with other elements of creation.

What Is Our Ultimate Purpose?

Native American religions differ in terms of humanity's ultimate purpose. Some religions focus on humanity's role in maintaining balance with the natural world, and certain religious practices like the Jump Dance aim to do this. Maintaining this balance can improve the human condition, and upsetting the balance can have terrible consequences. Many Native American religions conceive of life and death as cyclical in nature. In Native religions, the transition of a person from birth to death is thought to be comparable to the cyclical nature of the seasons of the year. In some religions, the deceased transitions to the land of the dead, which may resemble this life.

REVIEW QUESTIONS

For Review

1. Why is it difficult to make generalizations about Native American religions?
2. Many Native American religions emphasize the interconnectedness of all things. How does this play out in religious practice?
3. What are some common themes in Native American mythology? What do these themes teach the listeners?
4. What was the significance of the Ghost Dance?

For Further Reflection

1. Think about the nature of sacred narratives, or myths, in Native American and other religious traditions. Does myth play a similar or different role? How so?
2. How do Native American traditions answer some of the Great Questions that many religions address? What is unique to Native traditions? What do they share with other traditions?

GLOSSARY

American Indian Religious Freedom Act 1978 U.S. law to guarantee freedom of religious practice for Native Americans.

axis mundi (ax-is mun-di; Latin) An academic term for the center of the world, which connects the earth with the heavens.

Black Elk Famous Lakota religious leader.

Changing Woman Mythic ancestor of the Navajo people who created the first humans.

chantway The basis of Navajo ceremonial practice; includes chants, prayers, songs and other ritual practice.

Ghost Dance Religious resistance movements in 1870 and 1890 that originated in Nevada among Paiute peoples.

hogan (ho-gan; Pueblo) A sacred structure of Pueblo peoples.

Holy People Ancestors to the Navajo people, described in mythic narratives.

Holy Wind Navajo conception of a spiritual force that inhabits every element of creation.

Jump Dance Renewal dance of Yurok people.

kachina (ka-chee-na; Hopi) Pueblo spiritual beings.

Kinaalda (kee-nal-dah) Rite of passage for young Navajo women.

McKay, Mabel A Pomo woman who was well known as healer and basket-weaver.

Native American Church A church founded in early twentieth century based on Peyote Religion.

peyote Hallucinogenic cactus used in many Native American religions.

Popol Vuh (po-pol voo; Quiché Mayan, "council book") The Quiché Mayan book of creation.

Quanah Parker Comanche man who called for embrace of Peyote religion.

Quetzalcoatl (ket-zal-ko-at'-l; Aztec) Aztec God and important culture hero in Mexico.

rites of passage Rituals that mark the transition from one social stage to another.

rites of renewal Rituals that seek to enhance natural processes, like rain or fertility, or enhance the solidarity of a group.

sand painting A painting made with sand used by Navajo healers to treat ailments.

Sun Dance Midsummer ritual common to many Native American religions; details vary across cultures.

sweat lodge A structure built for ritually cleansing and purifying the body.

tipi A typical conical structure of the tribes of the Great Plains which is often constructed with a sacred blueprint.

trickster A common figure in North American mythologies; trickster tales often teach important moral lessons.

vision quest A ritual attempt by an individual to communicate with the spirit world.

Wovoka A Paiute man whose visions started the Ghost Dance of 1890.

SUGGESTIONS FOR FURTHER READING

Brown, Joseph Epes. *Teaching Spirits: Understanding Native American Religious Tradition.* Oxford University Press, 2001. A comprehensive look at Native American religions including topics like geography, creativity, and ritual.

DeLoria, Vine Jr. *God Is Red: A Native View of Religion.* New York: Dell Publishing Company, 2003. A seminal work on Native American spirituality from a Native perspective.

Gill, Sam. *Native American Religions: An Introduction.* Boston: Thomson Wadsworth, 2005.

Hirschfelder, Arlene, and Paulette Molin. *An Encyclopedia of Native American Religions.* New York: Facts on File Ltd., 1992. A useful encyclopedia with detailed entries on many aspects of Native American religious belief and practice.

Kehoe, Alice Beck. *The Ghost Dance: Ethnohistory and Revitalization.* Long Grove, IL: Waveland Press, 2006. A detailed look at the Ghost Dance in its cultural and historical context.

Neihardt, John G., and Black Elk. *Black Elk Speaks: Being the Life Story of a Holy Man of the Oglala Sioux.* Omaha: University of Nebraska Press, 1961. An intimate account of the religious visions and worldview of the Lakota religious leader Black Elk.

ONLINE SOURCES

National Museum of the American Indian
nmai.si.edu
This museum, part of the Smithsonian Institution, has many materials about the research collection online.

National Archives
archives.gov/research/alic/reference/native-americans.html
This portal page at the website of the National Archives leads to the Archives' research materials on federally recognized tribes.

INDIGENOUS RELIGIONS of AFRICA

TEPILIT OLE SAITOTI is a Maasai man from Tanzania, a country in East Africa. The Maasai are a cattle-herding people, most of whom live in Kenya and Tanzania. As a promising young student, Tepilit eventually studied in the United States and Europe. In 1988, he published his autobiography, *The Worlds of a Maasai Warrior*. In the book, he describes the initiation ceremony that transformed him from a young boy into a warrior.

When Maasai boys reach adolescence, they are circumcised in a public ritual to mark their transition to the status of warriors. Different ceremonies mark the transition of Maasai girls into womanhood. In the Maasai culture, warriors are known as **moran**. The *moran* are a special group of young men who have particular responsibilities. They are usually between the ages of 15 and 35 and are traditionally responsible for protecting the community and for herding the cattle and other animals. Boys who become *moran* together form a special bond that continues throughout their lives. But first, a young man must survive his circumcision. For Tepilit, undergoing the circumcision ceremony was an intense and transformational experience:

> Three days before the ceremony my head was shaved and I discarded all of my belongings such as my necklaces, garments, spear, and sword. I even had to shave my pubic hair.

Competitive jumping can be part of the young Maasai warriors' rite of passage ceremonies.

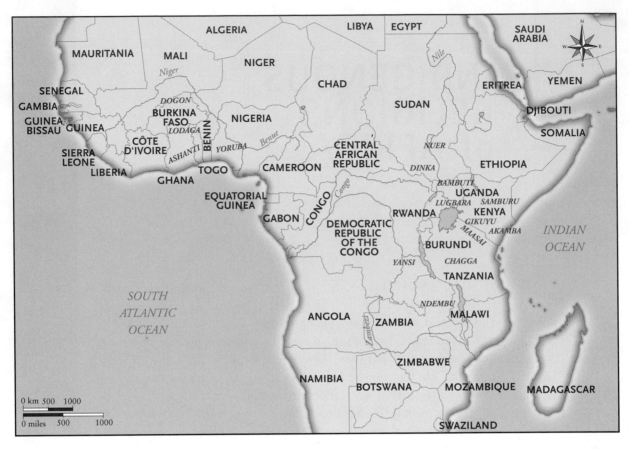

Indigenous peoples
of Africa.

Circumcision in many ways is similar to Christian baptism. You must put all
the sins you have committed during childhood behind and embark as a new
person with a different outlook on life.[1]

Tepilit describes the apprehension he felt as the day approached. The circumcision
was important not just for Tepilit but for his entire family. His father and brothers
warned him that he must not cry, scream, or kick the knife away when the circumciser
removed his foreskin because that would embarrass his family. It could even jeopardize his future. Bravery is highly valued in the Maasai culture, and people would lose
respect for Tepilit if he showed himself to be a coward. He would never be considered
for a position of leadership if he became known as a "knife-kicker."

The circumciser appeared, his knives at the ready. He spread my legs and said
"One cut," a pronouncement necessary to prevent an initiate from claiming
that he had been taken by surprise. He splashed a white liquid, a ceremonial
paint called *enturoto*, across my face. Almost immediately I felt a spark of pain
under my belly as the knife cut through my penis' foreskin.[2]

Tepilit made it through the ceremony bravely and was congratulated by his friends and family. His head was shaved to mark his new status as a man, and a warrior.

> As long as I live, I will never forget the day my head was shaved and I emerged a man, a Maasai warrior. I felt a sense of control over my destiny so great that no words can accurately describe it.[3] ☀

Like the Maasai, most African cultures (and cultures everywhere) have rituals that mark the transition of young people into adulthood. Although details of the ceremonies vary from culture to culture, they share the public recognition that a young person has entered a new phase of life. Often, this new phase of life is understood through a religious worldview. In African religions, other phases of life are also marked through specific ceremonies. For example, birth marks the journey of an individual soul from the spirit world to the human world, and death is the transition back to the spirit world.

In this chapter, we will explore the indigenous, small-scale religious traditions of Africa today and in recent history. Although many Africans are Muslims, Christians, or followers of other large-scale religions with roots elsewhere, we will concern ourselves here with small-scale religions that originated in Africa. Since North Africa (Egypt, Libya, Algeria, Morocco, Tunisia) has been predominantly Muslim for about 1,000 years, this chapter explores Africa south of the Sahara, where indigenous religions have remained more prominent until the present.

Today, about 1 billion people live on the African continent. There are thousands of different African cultural, ethnic, and linguistic groups. This cultural diversity is reflected in the religious diversity of the continent. There is not one single "African culture" or "African religion." Because African religions are so numerous, we will not attempt to discuss them all in this chapter. Instead, we will explore examples from a few religions that reflect African cultural and geographic diversity. And although we address them together in a single chapter, it is important to remember that all African religions are not the same. Because of this diversity, it is not easy to generalize about them in a textbook chapter.

And yet, despite this diversity, it is possible to identify some common characteristics in the realms of practice, teaching and beliefs, and historical development. The story of Tepilit's initiation explores one of these characteristics: many African religions have specific ceremonies that mark the transition from one social state of being to another. Many African religions also share some elements of belief and worldview. For example, many religions share the belief in a supreme deity, or creator God. Also, many African religions are primarily concerned with life in the here and now, rather than with what comes after death.

African religions also share a great deal in terms of historical development. Most African religions originated in small-scale communities, and thus may be intimately connected with a particular culture in a particular place. And although some followers of African religions still live in small-scale societies today, many more have been incorporated into large political systems and market economies in the modern, global era. Furthermore, in the nineteenth and twentieth centuries, African religions faced the reality of widespread European colonialism on the continent. In addition, the influence of African religions has spread far beyond their places of origin. This was primarily a result of the Atlantic slave trade, which lasted from the 1500s to the 1800s. As we will learn in this chapter, certain religions of the Americas, like **Vodou** and **Santeria**, were derived from and share a great deal with African religions.

THE TEACHINGS OF INDIGENOUS AFRICAN RELIGIONS

For followers of indigenous African religions, "religion" is not considered to be separate from everyday existence. Religious practice is not relegated to particular times, places, or spaces. Instead, religious beliefs and practices infuse and inform daily life and everyday concerns. We will begin our discussion of African religions by considering their beliefs and teachings. Although the religions of Africa differ significantly, certain ideas about the supernatural, the natural world, and humanity's place within it are common to many of the continent's religions.

Myths

The beliefs of African religions are found primarily in mythic narratives, which contain essential teachings. All religions, as we learned in Chapter 1, have a mythic component. African religions are no exception, and most have a very rich mythic heritage. Myths are not falsehoods; rather, they are narratives that we humans tell about our origins and ourselves. In religions the world over, myths relate compelling stories about gods, spirits, heroic figures, or human ancestors. Because of these intriguing narratives, myths have the ability to teach the listener about the origins of humanity, about supernatural beings, and about morality and ethics in a powerful and memorable way.

In most African religions, myths have been part of an oral tradition and have been passed from one generation to the next through the spoken word. Today, however, many myths also exist in written form. In many African cultures, it is elders or religious leaders who are responsible for maintaining and disseminating the teachings of myths to others. Although all members of a culture may be familiar with basic mythic narratives, elders and religious specialists often know greater details and deeper meanings.

The myths of many African religions are most often concerned with this world—the world of humanity—rather than the greater universe. Myths most often tell stories about the origins of the earth and of human beings and about human social life and social organization. Myths often convey moral lessons. When African myths contain stories of gods and other supernatural beings, the stories frequently focus on the way in which these beings interact with or relate to humanity.

Among the Dogon people of Mali and Burkina Faso, in West Africa, myth has been part of the oral tradition for generations. The Dogon are primarily farmers, and although some Dogon are Christians or Muslims, most still follow traditional Dogon religion. Dogon religious experts know far more about myths than the average person and are therefore responsible for preserving, understanding, and passing on the myths. Dogon mythology is intimately related to religious and social life. It involves complex explanations of the origins of the world and human beings and the way in which human beings should live on the earth, such as explanations for farming practices. Throughout this section of the chapter, we will consider various myths from different African religions, including the Dogon, as we learn about beliefs and teachings of African religions.

Supernatural Beings: Gods and Spirits

Many African religions teach that everyday human life is influenced or even controlled by gods or other supernatural beings. African religions are therefore *theistic*, a term you will recall from Chapter 1. Most also share the belief in a supreme deity, or High God. In African religions, the High God is normally believed to be all-knowing, all-powerful, and the creator of the world and of humanity. This supreme deity is often associated with the sky and may be more specifically connected to the sun or the rain because both of these have life-giving powers. Most African religions regard the High God as eternal. And although the High God is generally not thought to be human-like, the supreme deity may be described as having human-like attributes, such as mercy, goodness, and a concern for justice.

In many African religions, the High God is considered to be transcendent and removed from the lives of humans. As a result, there are rarely temples, churches, or shrines devoted to the High God. Because the High God is removed from everyday life, most religious practice focuses on communicating with spirits or lesser gods. In the religion of the Dogon, the High God **Amma** is an example of a deity who is distant from the lives of ordinary humans. The Dogon creation myth tells that Amma made the earth out of mud and clay. Although he was active in creation, Amma eventually retired from the earth and left lesser deities to manage earthly affairs and attend to human interests. Other African mythologies explain the transcendence of the High God as the result of a transgression committed by humans or animals that upset the High God, who then left this world for a supernatural realm. We will examine some of these myths later in this chapter.

In some African religions, the High God is associated with the qualities of both a father and a mother. In others, the High God is not gendered. The Samburu people of Kenya believe that God, known as Nkai, is flexible in gender and in form. In the Samburu language, the word "Nkai" is feminine. God is associated with procreation and is considered to have many female characteristics. Interestingly, some Samburu people who claim to have been taken to the divine home of Nkai have reported that the deity is not one individual at all but is actually a family group.[4]

Sammy Letoole, a young Samburu man from Kenya, is a student at Friends Theological College in Kaimosi, Kenya. Although he is studying Christianity, he was raised in the Samburu religion and finds that it does not conflict with his Christian faith. The Samburu people live in northern Kenya, and Samburu culture and religion share some elements with Maasai culture and religion. Festus Ogunbitan is a scholar of religion from Nigeria whose ancestry is Yoruban. Festus was raised in a Christian home, but he explored his ancestral religion as he matured. An author, he has written several books on Yoruba religion.

What is your religious background?

Sammy: My religious background is Samburu and now I am a Christian. I was raised in a pure Samburu family who believed in traditional Samburu religion. Every day, my father woke up very early in the morning to go out and pray for everything—including the animals and the children. As a result, my faith in God became very strong because I saw my dad praying without stopping. And this makes my Christian foundation strong.

Sammy Letoole

Festus: I am from the Yoruba nation of the southwestern part of Nigeria. I was born into a Christian family who were biased about the values and virtues of their ancestors' culture. This happened to many Africans, since Christianity and Islam declared their religion as the universal religion. When I grew up, I started to read books about the religion of my ancestors, and I discovered that religion is a social process—it is like a plant growing up to bring forth fruits. Therefore, my Yoruba religion does not need to be suppressed by any foreign religion.

Sammy, you don't seem to see much conflict between Christianity and Samburu religion. Could you explain their similarities and differences? How does your religious practice draw on both traditions?

The Samburu religion and Christianity have a similar conception of God. In both traditions, God is a creator, provider, and protector and is caring and loving. The Samburu people believe that God is found in the mountains, so they name their gods after those big mountains. During the time of the Old Testament, Moses climbed Mt. Sinai to pray, and he was given the commandments; similarly, the Samburu pray to their God to give them direction.

There are many things that Samburu religion shares with the Bible, especially the Old Testament. During that time, the Israelites were not supposed to eat all grey animals without divided hooves and who did not chew the cud. Even now, the Samburu do not eat those animals. Also, the people in the time of the Old Testament offered sacrifices to their God; the Samburu also offer sacrifices to their God.

Festus, could you explain your view of the nature of the world and humanity's place in it and how this developed through learning about the religion of your ancestors?

> I believe that the universe is created by God, and the universe is part of God through nature. I believe in the ancient Yoruban concept of God which says that nature is part of God—plants, animals, outer space, and human nature. As a result, they worship nature and human nature by reinforcing them with praise singing. I believe that nature is divine, and a sincere and ingenious person is divine, and we should respect them. If we treat nature and creativity in humans as divine, we shall be able to get lots of good things from them—such as the invention of products and services for the needs of mankind.

Could you both describe your worship and religious practice?

> Sammy: My worshiping styles and praises are influenced by Samburu religion. Samburu prayers and Christian prayers differ because the Samburu believe that God is found in mountains, rivers, and good springs. Therefore, when performing prayers a person must face a certain mountain like Mt. Kenya or Mt. Nyiro. Christians forward their prayers to God through Jesus Christ, our savior. Although people pray to God in different ways, they all seek protection, guidance, love, and satisfaction.

Festus Ogunbitan

> Festus: I am not a Christian, and I don't really practice Yoruba traditional religion in a shrine. But I have faith in the religion of my ancestors, most especially Ogun—the Yoruba god of Iron—which is half of the pronunciation of my last name. My last name, Ogunbitan, means "a child through whom Ogun the god of Iron shall create history." By writing a book called *Lyric Poems on Creation Story of the Yorubas*, I have fulfilled this promise.

In addition to the belief in a High God, most African religions also recognize other supernatural beings that are lower in status than the High God, but still powerful. As you learned in Chapter 1, a belief system in which many supernatural beings (including gods and spirits) are recognized, but one of these beings is elevated to a higher status, is known as henotheism. In African religions, gods or spirits interact with human beings and are sometimes thought to be mutually interdependent with humans. Because of this, much religious practice focuses on these beings. Therefore, unlike the High God, these lesser gods and spirits often have temples, shrines, and rituals devoted to them.

In many African religions, including the Dogon, the Ashanti, and the Igbo, the earth is an important female deity. She is often understood to be the consort or daughter of the High God, who is typically associated with the sky, the sun, or the heavens in general. In Dogon mythology, the earth was created by Amma, who then forcibly took her as his mate. A jackal was born from this union. The Dogon consider the birth of the jackal to be unfavorable because it was a single birth, not a twin. In Dogon culture, as we will learn later in this chapter, twin birth is considered ideal. This misfortune of the jackal's birth is attributed to Amma's unjust rape of the earth.[5]

Dogon religion provides another example of lesser deities. Although the original union of Amma and the earth was problematic, Dogon myths tell that there was a second union. This was favorable and produced twins—an ideal birth. The twins took the form of a supernatural being, or lesser god, called the Nummo. The Nummo twins represent the balance of male and female elements. The Nummo plays an important role in Dogon myths about the origins of humans and the development of human social structure. The Nummo is active in the affairs of humans, while Amma is not.

Some African religions have large and complex **pantheons**, or groups of deities. One example of a pantheon is in the religion of the Yoruba people, a large ethnic group in West Africa. Although many Yoruba have converted to Islam and Christianity, indigenous beliefs are still prominent, even among the converts. In Yoruba religion, the High God, known as Olodumare, is accompanied by other categories of deities. One such category is the **Odu**, who were the original prophets gifted with the ability to look into the future. Another category is the *orisa*, who are believed to inhabit an otherworldly realm called *orun*. The *orisa* live in a hierarchical social order that closely reflects Yoruba social organization. Yoruba mythology teaches that the hundreds of *orisa* were the first inhabitants of the earth. The *orisa* were sent to earth by the High God to create land from the water, and each was given a specific duty. Yoruba people believe that the High God ultimately determines their destiny, although they serve different *orisas* as their personal deities.

One of the foremost *orisas* is a goddess known as **Oshun**. Oshun is merciful, beautiful, and loving, and she is associated with fertility and the life-giving properties of water. Because of this, Yoruba people may call on her to help them with matters pertaining to childbirth and family. She is also known as the "hair-braider" or "hair-plaiter" and is powerful in this ability to make people beautiful. In Yoruba mythology, Oshun was present at the time of creation, but she was the only female, and the *Odu* ignored her. However, Olodumare reproached them and explained how important Oshun was. The following passage from a Yoruba myth relates how the *Odu* appealed to Oshun for forgiveness. In the myth, Oshun eventually bears a son who joins the other Odu.

> They returned to Oshun
> And addressed her: "Mother, the pre-eminent hair-plaiter with the
>   coral beaded comb.
> We have been to the Creator
> And it was discovered that all Odu were derived from you.
> And that our suffering in the world would continue
> If we failed to recognize and obey you."
> So, on their return to earth from the Creator,
> All the remaining Odu wanted to pacify and please Oshun.[6]

In some African religions, like that of the Nuer people of Sudan, the High God may manifest as multiple deities. The anthropologist E. E. Evans-Pritchard (1902–1973) lived with the Nuer in the 1930s and made a detailed study of their religion.[7] He argued that the Nuer belief system should be considered both monotheistic *and* polytheistic because the different deities recognized were simply reflections of the High God. Although many Nuer people are Christian today, some elements of Nuer religion remain important. The Ashanti people of West Africa similarly regard the many gods in their belief system as the way in which the High God manifests.

In African religions, spirits are often considered to be a part of God's creation, like humanity. Most often, spirits are thought to live alongside human beings in a shared world. As a result, in many African cultures, spirits are a part of normal daily life. Spirits are commonly believed to be immortal and invisible. In many African religions, spirits are associated with elements of the natural world, like mountains and trees, and forces of the natural world, like rain and lightning. However, they are able to interact with human beings in various ways. Like human beings, spirits are neither entirely good nor entirely evil. They are typically thought to be more powerful than human beings, but humans can learn to interact with and even manipulate them to some degree. Religious experts or leaders may even call upon the spirits to act as messengers between humans and God.

This picture of a Nuer homestead was taken by anthropologist E. E. Evans-Pritchard in the 1930s.

Spirits of the Dead   In many African religions, the spirits of deceased humans are very important. In fact, in most African religions, death is not regarded as a final state of oblivion. Instead, death is a change to another spiritual state. As birth is believed to be a transition from the world of the spirits to the world of the living, death is a transition back to the spirit world. This belief often has a basis in mythology. In Dogon myths, the original human ancestors became spirits, who then paved the way for later generations to enter the spirit realm after their death. Although the spirits of the dead are sometimes called "ancestor spirits," scholars of African religions argue that this term is not very accurate. This is because the category includes the spirits of many people who have died—not just those who bore children and have living descendants to whom they are ancestors.[8] Therefore, children or people who died childless can also become spirits.

The spirits of the dead are often active in the lives of their relatives and descendants for several generations. These spirits may also be concerned with upholding cultural values and family unity from beyond the grave. They are also frequently believed to be the most effective intermediaries between the High God and humans. Because of this, living people engage in specific practices to maintain positive relations with these spirits. And the spirits are dependent to some extent on humans. The living may symbolically care for the spirits by offering food and drink or making sacrifices to them. Like other supernatural beings of African religions, ancestor spirits are not necessarily good or bad, and they can both help and hurt their living relatives. If spirits are neglected, they may become angry and cause problems for the living. It is therefore very important for the living to respect their elderly relatives, who are close to transitioning to the spirit world. It is also essential to remember and pay respect to the deceased.

The Gikuyu people of Kenya (also known as the Kikuyu) recognize several categories of spirits of the dead. One category consists of deceased members of the immediate family, and another category includes the deceased members of the extended family group, or clan. The former are active in the day-to-day life of the living immediate family, and the latter spirits maintain an interest in the welfare of the clan. Living people may consult with the spirits of the dead for advice or guidance in their own affairs.[9] Therefore, in African cultures like the Gikuyu, a person's family is considered to include not just his living relatives, but also those who have passed on. The Gikuyu believe that if the spirits of the dead are neglected, they can harm the living as a form of punishment for such bad behavior. They may cause illnesses or bring about other misfortunes on their negligent descendants. Usually, the living make an effort to care for the spirits of the dead until the last person who knew the deceased during his life has died. At this point, the deceased moves into a different spiritual category where he will have less active involvement in the lives of the living, or none at all.[10]

Humanity and the Human Condition

Most African religions are anthropocentric, which means that they recognize humanity as the center of the cosmos.[11] Because of this, African belief systems understand the cosmos and elements within it, like supernatural beings, in terms of their relationship to humanity. Unlike many other religions, most African religions do not teach about the possibility of salvation or punishment in an afterlife. Rather, teachings generally focus on the importance of the present world.

This anthropocentrism is reflected in the many African mythologies that begin with the creation of human beings instead of the creation of the world. As we have seen, a High God is often the creator of human beings. In many African myths, God creates humanity from clay or mud. The Dogon creation narrative tells that after the birth of the Nummo twins, Amma decided to create eight human beings from clay. The Dogon recognize these eight beings as the original human ancestors. In myths from other African traditions, God brings forth humanity from beneath the earth or out of a rock or tree. In still others, human beings come to this world from another one. The myths of the Chagga people of Tanzania explain that humanity descended to earth from heaven by the gossamer thread of a spider's web.

In some creation narratives, lesser gods are responsible for creating human beings. In a Yoruba narrative, the deity Obatala, son of the High God, was assigned by his father to make human beings from clay. Once the beings were made, the High God breathed life into them. One version of the myth tells that Obatala got very thirsty during his work of making humans. To quench his thirst, he started to drink beer. He became so drunk that he fashioned some people who were missing limbs, had crooked backs, or had other physical problems. When he sobered up, Obatala was so distraught at what he had done that he vowed to always watch over the disabled people he had made. This myth accounts for people who are born with disabilities and for Obatala's special concern for them.

Many African religions teach that humans were created in a male-female pair as either husband and wife or (less often) as brother and sister. Dogon myths explain that the first eight humans each had a dual soul—they were both male and female. As a result, all humans are born with a dual soul. Through circumcision, this dual soul is reduced to one soul—male or female. Other African cultures also regard humans as having a dual nature. Sometimes this is understood to be a physical body and an immaterial essence, like a spirit. The Lugbara people of Uganda believe that human beings have multiple souls. Each soul is associated with a different part of the body, like the heart or the lungs.

As we discussed earlier in this chapter, African religions often teach that the High God is removed from everyday human life. However, many teach that the High God was not always distant, but originally lived with humans in a time of complete happiness, when God provided people with all they needed. However, God and humanity became separated. In some religions, this separation from God introduced death and toil into the lives of humans. These religions tend to emphasize the past—when humans coexisted with God—as an ideal, paradise-like existence.

In myths, the separation from the High God often was the result of humans breaking one of God's rules. In a myth of the Dinka people, who are cattle herders in southern Sudan, death is explained as the result of the anger of the first woman. In the beginning, the High God gave one grain of millet to the first woman and her husband. The woman was greedy and decided to plant more than a single grain. In her eagerness to plant, she hit God with her hoe. God was so angry he withdrew from humanity and severed the rope that connected heaven and earth. Because of this, the Dinka believe that humans are doomed to work hard throughout life and then die. The myth also teaches an important moral lesson: humans should avoid being prideful and greedy.

Sometimes, human mortality results from the actions of animals who deliberately or unintentionally betrayed humans. The religion of the Nuer people teaches that a rope originally connected earth to heaven; this is similar to the Dinka myth. If someone climbed the rope to heaven, Kwoth, the High God, would make that person young again. One day, a hyena and a bird climbed the rope. Kwoth said they were not allowed to return to earth because they would cause trouble there. However, they escaped and returned to earth. Then, the hyena cut the rope. Because of this, humans could no longer get to heaven, and now grow old and die.

Many African religions also teach that the High God created human social organization, customs, and rules of conduct. Ethical and moral teachings often focus on the importance of maintaining agreeable relationships within human society and the spirit world. Sometimes, this extends to the proper relationship between humanity and the earth. Dogon mythology teaches that after they were created, the Nummo twins taught human beings how to farm. In many African cultures, farming is an important activity not only for subsistence but also in terms of religion. As we read, Dogon myths explain that the first child of the unfortunate union between Amma and the earth was a jackal. The jackal defiled its mother, the earth, by attempting to rape her. Humans, however, have the ability to correct this defilement and purify the earth through farming.

INDIGENOUS AFRICAN RELIGIONS AS A WAY OF LIFE

For followers of African religions, religion is something that infuses everyday life. It is not reserved for just one day of the week or for certain times of the year. Instead, religious practice is a daily activity. As we have learned, most African religions do not focus on reward or punishment in the afterlife, so religious practice does not normally center on preparing for an afterlife. Instead, rituals and ceremonies focus on improving life in this world. Thus, religious practice might address vital material needs, like a good harvest, or social needs, like a harmonious family life. Also, because the High God is often believed to be remote from day-to-day human life, most African religions do not emphasize worshiping a supreme deity. Instead, religious practice normally focuses on communication with other supernatural beings.

Communicating with the Spirit World

In African religions, the world of the spirits and the world of humans are believed to be closely intertwined. Spirits live near human beings in the same communities and often exist in a reciprocal relationship with them. Because spirits can interact and interfere with the lives of humans, religious rituals and ceremonies often focus on communicating with spirits or accessing their power. People may ask spirits to intervene with God on their behalf or assist with particular problems in family or work life. In this section, we will discuss three practices associated with communicating with the spirit world: sacrifice, divination, and spirit possession.

Sacrifice In African religions, the primary way people communicate with supernatural beings is through sacrifice. In many religions the world over, the dedication of something valuable to a spirit—a sacrifice—has the power to influence that spirit. A sacrifice can be relatively small, like a prayer, or a portion of one's daily food or drink. In some religions, like the Yoruba, individuals may have a special relationship with one or more spirits or gods, and small offerings like this might be made every day to maintain their goodwill. Yoruba families often have household shrines where similar offerings are made to the spirits of the dead.

In other African contexts, larger sacrifices, like an animal, are necessary. In some religions, there has traditionally been a close relationship between practices of healing and sacrifice. Illnesses may be attributed to a spirit's punishment of a person's bad behavior. In such cases, an animal may be sacrificed as a form of repentance and as a request for forgiveness from the aggrieved spirit. Among the Nuer, for example, animals were typically sacrificed as a substitute for the person who was afflicted with an illness. The animal was offered to the spirits in exchange for the health of the person. However, in recent years, as Nuer people have begun attributing illness to biological causes instead of angry spirits, and, as more have adopted Christianity, the use of animal sacrifice in healing has diminished.[12]

Divination In some African religions, a practice called **divination** is used to communicate with spirits. Divination is the attempt to predict the future through supernatural agents or powers. Among the Yoruba, a divination system called *Ifa* is used to communicate with the spirit world. A person called a diviner performs the divination. Yoruba religion teaches that *Ifa* was developed when the High God removed himself from the earthly world. His children remained behind, and he gave them a divinatory system to communicate with him. They shared this system with human beings. Through *Ifa*, humans are able to communicate with and make requests of the gods and the spirits of the dead.

Yoruba diviners also use *Ifa* to predict the destinies and future of individuals. The diviners use a special collection of poetic verses and palm nuts to foresee future events and converse with supernatural beings. Most of the verses are from sacred Yoruba texts, and they tell of the time of the gods and ancestors. Diviners select specific verses because they contain the solution to problems that faced the ancestors and are thus helpful in solving current problems.

Spirit Possession Another way people communicate with the spirit world is through spirit possession. A belief in spirit possession is prevalent throughout Africa, and in many places this sort of interaction with spirits is a normal part of daily life. People communicate with spirits through a **medium**—an individual who has become possessed. Although women and men may both become possessed, in many cultures women are far more likely to do so. The possessed individual is called a medium because she *mediates* between the human world and the spirit world. The spirit is thought to take over the medium's body, and the medium then acts according to the will of the spirit while she is possessed. Because spirit possession usually takes place in public, many people

Palm nuts with a blue cloth bag, used by the Yoruba people for divination.

can witness the possession and interact with the spirit through the medium. When a spirit possesses a person, she enters a state of trance. Others may then talk to or make requests of the spirit through her.

Throughout Africa, people ascribe different meanings to possession. In some traditions, possession is viewed negatively. It might be thought to cause illness or to cause the medium to harm others. In such cases, a spiritual healer may be called upon to drive the spirit away. Elsewhere, people may encourage possession in order to communicate with the spirit world. Individuals may use special dancing, music, and drumming to entice a spirit. In such contexts, some people, such as women, may be more prone to spirit possession than others. Sometimes, people who have the ability to become possessed achieve a special religious status.

In West Africa, there is a widespread belief in spirits known as **bori** who have the power to possess people. There are many different *bori*, and they have individual personalities. Among the Mawri people of Niger, spirits like Maria, a flirtatious young prostitute, regularly possess mediums.[13] In northeast Africa, the **zar** spirits are similar to the *bori* and prominent throughout the region. Possession beliefs are also prevalent among Muslims and Christians in Africa. As these religions gained adherents in sub-Saharan Africa, many elements of preexisting religious practice remained. For example, Mawri people began converting to Islam in the mid-twentieth century, but the *bori* spirits remain. In northeast Africa, the *zar* spirits possess both Muslims and Christians.

Why do people become possessed? What does it mean for those who become possessed? Many scholars have tried to answer these questions. Some have argued that spirit possession is therapeutic for those who have mental or physical illness. Others suggest that spirit possession is a way for people to deal with rapid cultural change and the problems of modernity. For example, when the spirit Maria possesses Mawri women, they might be expressing an internal conflict between their desire to be traditional wives and mothers and the temptations of urban life and consumer culture, which Maria loves.[14]

As noted earlier, women are more likely to become possessed than men. When possessed, a woman becomes a powerful representative of the spirit world. Some scholars have argued that this allows women to achieve a temporarily high status in male-dominated societies and in religions in which men control mainstream religious practice.[15] However, women's spirit possession practices are frequently at the center of religious life, not relegated to the margins. In Nigeria, Edo women participate in the worship of the god Olokun, who is at the heart of Edo religion. In Edo cosmology, Olokun is a very important god who has authority over

Two Orixás, or orisas, who possess the women, dance in their finery at a Candomblé festival in Brazil held in their honor.

fertility and wealth. By participating in the possession cult, Edo women gain permanent high status in the community. And although women who serve Olokun as priestesses do not have political authority in the same way men do, they can exert a great deal of power through settling disputes and acting as medical advisors.[16]

Using Supernatural Powers

In African religions, some people are believed to have the ability to manipulate the supernatural for their own ends. Western scholars have traditionally used the term **witchcraft** to explain the use of supernatural powers to cause illness or other misfortune. (It is important to note that in other religions, like Wicca, the term "witchcraft" does not have negative connotations.) In African languages, many different terms are used to denote witchcraft, although the idea that one can use supernatural powers to cause harm is fairly widespread. Often, witchcraft pervades everyday life and is understood as a normal part of existence. However, the use of witchcraft is not always thought to be intentional. In fact, in some cultures, people may be "witches" without even knowing it. As a result, they may cause harm to others unintentionally.

One of the most well-known examples of witchcraft is from the Azande people, who live in Sudan and the Central African Republic. The Azande believe that witchcraft is a physical substance that is present in some people's bodies. Evans-Pritchard, who conducted research among the Azande in the 1930s, showed that witchcraft beliefs were part of the Azande theory of causation. Witchcraft is a way of explaining why certain things happen to certain people. For example, if a man happened to be killed because he was sitting under a granary when it collapsed, the Azande would attribute this to witchcraft. Even if it was known that the granary collapsed because termites had destroyed the supporting wooden posts, there remained the question of *why* it collapsed when a particular individual was sitting underneath it. The Azande would argue that this was an instance of witchcraft: the termites explained how it collapsed, but this explanation did not answer the question of why it collapsed when it did and killed the man sitting under it. Only witchcraft could answer the "why" question.[17]

Sometimes, people use supernatural powers or call on supernatural beings to facilitate healing. Healers may use special divination methods to determine what has caused an illness. Although illness might be attributed to biomedical causes, a healer normally looks for an ultimate cause, which might be witchcraft or the malicious actions of spirits. Then, the healer can take special ritual action to try to cure it. A cure may involve repairing damaged social relationships that have caused jealousy. Or, a cure may involve a sacrifice to appease an angry spirit who caused the illness. Among the Ndembu of Zambia, some illnesses are believed to be caused by a particular spirit who is attracted to social conflicts. The spirit eats at the flesh of quarreling people with a sharp "tooth." To get rid of the spirit, Ndembu religious priests encourage the afflicted people to air their grievances against one another. During this discussion, the priest will use a special cup to extract the tooth that has been causing the illness.[18]

Life Cycle Rituals

Most African religions emphasize the life cycle. Celebrations and ceremonies that mark the transitions from one phase of existence to another are an important part of religious practice. It is through these ceremonies that individuals are defined as new members of the human community, as adults with full responsibilities and privileges of adulthood, or as having departed the living for the world of the spirits. In African religions, the life cycle is frequently believed to begin before birth and to continue after death. Rituals (Chapter 1) are formal religious practice. They are repetitive and rule-bound and are often enacted with a specific goal in mind. The goal could be pleasing a deity, encouraging a good crop, or smoothing the transition between phases of the life cycle. Rituals that facilitate this transition are called **rites of passage**. These rituals may be performed after a birth, during the transition from childhood to adulthood, or at death, when the deceased moves to the world of the spirits.

Birth: The Transition to the Human World

In many African religions, birth is the first important spiritual transition in a person's life. It is when a new individual enters the living community of humans. Preparing for a birth and welcoming a child is a process that often begins long before the child is born. Among the Bambuti people of the central African rainforest, a pregnant woman will offer food to a god as thanks for the pregnancy. In other African cultures, pregnant women are expected to observe certain rules and restrictions as a means of protecting herself and the child. For example, a woman may avoid certain foods or sexual relations with her husband while pregnant.

Practices surrounding the birth of a child vary tremendously from culture to culture in Africa. However, there are some common beliefs surrounding birth. One of these is the belief that birth marks the transition of the newborn from the world of spirits to the world of the living. Ceremonies after birth designate the child as belonging to the entire community, not just the mother. In many cultures, the placenta symbolizes the link between the child and its mother in its dependent state in the womb, and special care may be taken with its disposal after the child is born. The disposal of the placenta can symbolize the necessary separation of the child from its mother. Among the Yansi people of the Democratic Republic of Congo, the placenta is thrown in a river. This act symbolizes that the child no longer belongs only to his or her mother, but now belongs to the entire community.[19] A rite with a similar meaning is practiced among the Gikuyu of Kenya. After she has given birth, a mother's head is shaved. This represents

Bambuti woman and children in Uganda.

the severing of the exclusive tie between her and the child and also represents renewal: the mother is now ready to bear another child. Like the Yansi, the Gikuyu child is then recognized as a member of the wider society.[20]

Many African cultures have special naming ceremonies for children to mark their transition from the spirit world to the human world. Among the Akamba people of Kenya, a child is named on the third day after he or she is born. The next day, the child's father presents it with a special necklace, and the parents have ritual intercourse. Together, these events mark the transition of the child from the spirit world to the world of living humans.[21] The Yoruba name their children after a special birth ritual called "stepping into the world." The ritual teaches parents how to raise their new child. At the request of the new parents, a diviner uses the *Ifa* divination system (discussed earlier in this chapter) to determine the baby's future. Using special tools, foods, and texts, the Yoruba diviner will try to determine the nature of the infant and will select a name based on what is found out. One of the most important parts of the ritual is when the diviner holds the baby's feet in the center of a special divination tray, which represents the entire world. This act places the baby symbolically in the center of the world and lets the diviner understand the baby's nature.[22]

Initiation Rites: The Transition to Adulthood Rites of passage marking the transition from childhood to adulthood are extremely important in African religious traditions. Although they differ significantly in the details, rites of passage focus on successfully initiating a young person into adulthood and setting him or her on the path to becoming a complete member of the community. The new adult will have new privileges and responsibilities and will be expected to behave with maturity and wisdom appropriate to this new status. Often, it is rites of passage at adolescence that create a fully gendered adult. In many cultures, young people are able to marry only if they have been initiated. Sometimes, young people acquire special religious knowledge during initiation. Rites of passage also form important bonds for young people who go through them together. Among the Ndembu people of Zambia, for example, boys going through initiation are secluded for circumcision rites. Their mothers bring them food, which is shared among all the boys. The boys spend all their time together and develop close friendships, which are intended to last their entire lives.

Young Maasai men (like Tepilit, whose story begins this chapter) become warriors when they go through initiation. Much later, when men are in their thirties, they will be initiated as elders and be allowed to marry. Maasai girls are also circumcised when they reach adolescence. However, they do not transition into an intermediate warrior stage, but become ready for marriage. Young women change the way they dress, and they spend much time preparing beautifully beaded necklaces and head ornaments to wear. Many of these young women marry soon after they are circumcised, and they most often move away from their homes to the villages of their husbands. As with the young men, girls become fully socially mature when they transition through these

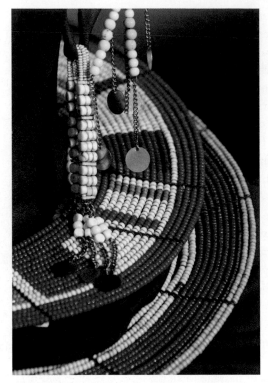

Maasai women often wear intricately beaded necklaces.

important rituals. For both, the coming of age rituals express important community values, such as strength, responsibility, and maturity.

In recent years, there has been much controversy surrounding female circumcision. Although it is often described as having a religious basis, it is not practiced solely within one religious community. In Africa, followers of many different religions practice female circumcision. This includes Christians and Muslims in addition to followers of indigenous religions. Circumcision can take many forms. It can range from a simple incision on the clitoris to draw blood to what is known as infibulation. In infibulation, most of the external female genitalia is removed and the incision is then sewn together. Because the more extensive types of circumcision like infibulation can endanger the health of young girls, many people have called for an end to the practice. Some countries, like Uganda, have banned it. However, reaction to these calls is mixed. Many women in Africa argue that circumcision is an essential part of their cultural identity.[23] They stress that a girl would never be considered a marriageable adult without undergoing the procedure during initiation. Others resent what they see as a movement spearheaded by Western activists, who remain silent about male circumcision because it is also prevalent in the West. Still others have succeeded in replacing circumcision with different kinds of rituals to mark the transition from girlhood to adulthood.

Death: The Transition to the Spirit World   Many African religions understand death not as an end to existence but as the transition to the spirit world. Funerals and other rituals surrounding death are important because they have the ability to ease the transition of the deceased from one state of being to another. In many cultures, the spirits of the dead cannot make the transition to the spirit world without the proper rituals. Normally, it is the living relatives of the deceased who must facilitate the performance of these rituals. The LoDagaa people of Ghana hold complex funeral rites to facilitate this transition. The LoDagaa carve a special tree branch that represents the deceased. Ideally, a son cares for the branch as a representation of his late parent. While the symbolic branch is being cared for, the soul of the dead person is believed to travel to the world of the dead. The ritual is very important. If the living relatives do not perform it properly, then the soul of the deceased will be trapped in his or her village instead of moving to the realm of the dead.[24]

Among the Dogon, a rite of passage for young men also helps the recently deceased enter the state of being ancestors. This rite is known as the *dama*, and the basis for it is laid out in myths. In the *dama*, which happens only once every several years, masked participants dance to usher the recently deceased into the world of the spirits.

The masks prepared for the *dama* are elaborately carved and represent animals and the mythical ancestors. The *dama* is also important for the living. If the dead do not enter the world of the spirits, they can cause problems for the living. Therefore, a successful *dama* frees the living from misfortune caused by the spirits of the dead and restores the normal balance of life and death. Today, these masked dances not only are used for ritual purposes but are also performed to entertain tourists; versions of the masks are produced for the tourist trade.

The rituals surrounding death are not always sad, and they may even be joyful. Among the Yoruba, for example, if a person over 40 years old dies of natural causes, then the death is regarded as an important and happy transition to the world of the spirits and gods. This world is called *orun*, and the spirit of the deceased person will remain there and be called upon to assist in the affairs of her living relatives. However, if someone is under age 40 at the time of death or dies of unnatural causes, the Yoruba consider it to be a great tragedy. Their spirits cannot enter *orun*, but are rather doomed to wander the earth unhappily forever.[25]

A Dogon masked dancer.

THE HISTORY OF INDIGENOUS AFRICAN RELIGIONS

African belief systems and religious practices are highly complex and multifaceted. Just like large-scale world religions, African religions have developed historically and accommodated cultural changes. Individual African religious traditions have unique histories that would be impossible to fully explore in a single chapter. Furthermore, the task is made more difficult because there are few surviving written records documenting the histories of these religions before the modern period. However, African religions have faced some common challenges and concerns in modern history that we can address together. We can also examine how indigenous African religions and their adherents have responded to the increasing influence of large-scale world religions, colonialism, and globalization.

The Spread of Islam

Large-scale world religions, especially Christianity and Islam, have been prevalent in Africa for centuries. More Africans convert to Islam and Christianity every day. However, even when people become Christians or Muslims, the influence of indigenous religious traditions remains, and these traditions have shaped the form that these world religions take in Africa. In much of Africa, indigenous religious ideas, narratives, and practice coexist with Christianity and Islam. Africans often combine elements of many religions in their own worldviews and practice.

Islam has been present in Africa since the seventh century c.e. By the eighth century, Arab Muslims controlled North Africa from Egypt to Morocco, and Islam has been the dominant religion in North Africa for several centuries. Islam spread more

VISUAL GUIDE
African Religions

Among the Dogon, the *dama* is a rite of passage for young men, which also helps the recently deceased enter the state of being ancestors. The rite happens only once every several years, and masked participants dance to usher the recently deceased into the world of the spirits. The masks prepared for the dama are elaborately carved and represent animals and the mythical ancestors.

This early twentieth century wooden tray is used to determine future events with the Ifa divination system, a part of Yoruba religion.

These nineteenth-century Yoruba sculptures from Nigeria commemorate twins who died. Twins are of great significance in many African religions, as among the Dogon, discussed in this chapter.

slowly throughout sub-Saharan Africa. The number of Muslims in sub-Saharan Africa increased as Islam spread throughout West Africa and along the East African coast from the eleventh century until the present. Today, in addition to North Africa, the populations of much of West Africa, Northeast Africa, and the East African coast are predominantly Muslim.

In most cases, Islam spread through trade and through the teachings of traveling scholars. Often, elite Africans adopted Islam as a means to facilitate trade connections because Muslim traders from North Africa were more likely to trade with other Muslims than with non-Muslims. As Africans became Muslims, they often retained elements of indigenous religious practice. For example, in Northeast and East Africa, the spirits known as *zar* are part of the religious worldview and practice of Muslims and Christians, as well as followers of indigenous religions. This is similar to the persistent belief in *bori* spirits in West Africa among Muslims and non-Muslims alike. Possession by *zar* and *bori* spirits preexisted the arrival of Islam and has been incorporated into the religious practice of African Muslims.

Christianity and Colonialism

Christianity has also been present in Africa for centuries and is very widespread in Africa today. The Ethiopian Coptic church is an indigenous African church that dates to the fourth century C.E. However, Christianity did not become widespread outside of Northeast Africa until much more recently. In fact, much of African Christianity today is the result of missionary efforts and European imperialism in the nineteenth and twentieth centuries. Missionary movements and proselytizing often went hand in hand with imperialism, and almost all of Africa was colonized by European powers—primarily Britain, France, and Portugal. Ethiopia is a notable exception.

The colonial powers sent missionaries to convert Africans to Christianity, and the Christian Bible was translated into numerous African languages. Often, the process of converting Africans included cultural indoctrination. African people were taught not only that their indigenous religions were false but also that their cultures were inferior to Western ways of life. Therefore, when Africans became Christians, they sometimes left behind their own cultural practices and cultural identities. Often, the new Christians were incorporated in the colonial bureaucracies as government officials. African Christians were also sometimes put in charge of missions and were charged with furthering European aims by converting their own people.[26]

Reform and Resistance

Both today and in the past, African Muslim and Christian communities have debated whether practices derived from indigenous religions are an appropriate part of Muslim or Christian religious practice. In some cases, disapproval of indigenous practices and customs has led to major reform movements. Such criticisms of indigenous religions have largely been based on the idea that the beliefs, teachings, and practices of indigenous religions are at best "primitive" deviations from Christianity or Islam and at worst heretical and sinful.

Beginning in 1804, Usman dan Fodio (1754–1817), a West African Muslim reformer and religious leader, waged a campaign in northern Nigeria to rid Islamic practice of what he thought were inappropriate indigenous elements. One of the practices that he specifically criticized was spirit possession by the *bori* spirits, which was

> ### TIMELINE
> ### African Religions
>
> **300s C.E.** King of Axum (Ethiopia) converts to Christianity.
>
> **700s** Arab Muslims extend control across North Africa.
>
> **1000s** Islam begins to spread throughout West Africa and coastal East Africa.
>
> **600–1100** The empire of Ghana rises.
>
> **800–1400** The rise of great cities and empires of Mali.
>
> **1500–1800s** Muslim Swahili city-states thrive on the East African coast.
>
> **1500s–1800s** Atlantic slave trade; African religions begin to spread to the Americas.
>
> **1884** Berlin Conference; European colonial powers divide Africa.
>
> **1800–1900s** European colonization and Christian missionary work in Africa.
>
> **1804–1809** Usman dan Fodio leads campaigns in northern Nigeria to rid Islamic practice of indigenous religious elements.
>
> **1905** Kinjikeltele organizes Maji Maji revolt against German colonizers in Tanganyika (today's Tanzania).
>
> **Early 1900s** Several new African Christian churches founded.
>
> **1920s** Josiah Oshitelu founds an independent Yoruba Christian church, known as the Aladura church.
>
> **1950s–1990s** Decolonization: sub-Saharan African countries gain independence.
>
> **1962–1965** Vatican II permits local church leaders around the world to be more accepting of local practice.

widespread at the time among both Muslims and non-Muslims. For over two decades, Usman dan Fodio and his followers tried to rid Muslim religious practice of what they viewed as inappropriate "African" elements such as this.

Similar campaigns have also been launched more recently. Christian and Muslim religious leaders have often targeted initiation rites such as those discussed earlier in this chapter. The rites have sometimes been described as "backward," "un-Christian," and "un-Islamic" or have simply been condemned as relics of a past best left behind. In some cases, Muslims and Christians have been receptive to the criticism and have stopped performing initiation rites or have replaced them with ceremonies that are deemed more appropriate by Muslim and Christian religious leaders. However, elsewhere, Muslims and Christians have continued to participate in the rites, despite the condemnation. Advocates argue that the rites are important means of achieving adulthood and are not in conflict with Christianity or Islam.

Occasionally, religious leaders who criticized the rites in the past have changed their approach. For example, at one time the Catholic church in Zambia strongly restricted female initiation rites in some Zambian cultures. However, in the 1960s, Vatican II (a meeting of Roman Catholic church leaders to address issues facing the church at the time) permitted church leaders to be more accepting of local practices. As a result, Zambian Catholic leaders changed their point of view. They argued that the initiation rites could be used to instill Catholic teachings about marriage and family in the young women.[27]

In the first decades of the twentieth century, African Christian leaders began to develop new Christian churches that spun off from the long-established mission churches, like the Anglican and Catholic churches. African Christian leaders were often frustrated with their inferior status in the mission churches. Their new churches aimed to make Christianity more accessible and appropriate in African cultural contexts. The new independent churches became very popular, and today there are thousands of independent churches in Africa.[28]

In the 1920s, a man called Josiah Oshitelu (1902–1966) founded an independent Yoruba Christian church, known as the Aladura church. As a young man, he thought witches plagued him. However, a Christian healer explained that it was God testing him and that if he prayed, he could chase away the evil. Oshitelu began praying. He received visions, and he tried to convince others that the old African religions were disappearing and that they should all become Christians. His teachings focused on the power of prayer and fasting to influence the will of God. Interestingly, many indigenous Yoruba religious beliefs and practices still held relevance for Aladura Christians. For example, most of the practitioners maintained beliefs in witchcraft and powerful spirits. The emphasis on prayer is also reminiscent of Yoruba ideas of harnessing spiritual power. Furthermore, the Aladura church focused on improving life in this world in much the same way as Yoruba religion.[29]

The Maji Maji Revolt Throughout Africa, religious groups spearheaded anti-colonial movements, and indigenous religious leaders were at the forefront of some of the most important of these. In 1905, a religious leader called **Kinjiketele** organized a rebellion against the German colonizers in Tanganyika (later called Tanzania). The revolt was known as the **Maji Maji** (Water Water) rebellion. Kinjiketele, a diviner, was believed to receive communications from the spirit world. One well-known story about him reports that a spirit took him into a river pool. Later, he emerged completely dry and carried a message to his people that their dead ancestors would all come back. Many people came to see him and to take the sacred water, which they believed would make them impervious to the bullets of the Europeans.

Kinjiketele attracted a large multiethnic following that supported his call for rebellion against the German colonizers. His message was compelling because it drew on indigenous religious beliefs in the power of spirits and the power of sacred waters. (The revolt takes its name from this sacred water.) Eventually, a group of Kinjiketele's followers, impatient with waiting for him to signal the proper time, began the revolt against the Germans without him. The uprising lasted two years and was eventually defeated by the Germans.[30]

African Religions in the Americas

The influence of African religions has spread far beyond the continent. In fact, many religious traditions of the Americas are derived from African religions. During the Atlantic slave trade, the religion of the Yoruba and other West African peoples like the Dahome and the Fon spread far beyond the shores of their homelands. Most of the millions of African people who were enslaved and brought to the Americas followed indigenous religions. And although the religious traditions and practices of Africans were most often suppressed or even forbidden by white slave owners, indigenous beliefs often survived and sometimes flourished.

The worship of Yoruba *orisa* remains popular to this day in communities of African descent throughout the Americas. The religious tradition known as **Candomblé** owes much to the Yoruba slaves who were brought to South America; Candomblé has been particularly prominent in northeastern Brazil. African slaves managed to keep worshiping Yoruba deities in the face of conversion pressure from the European slave master by cloaking the *orisa* in the guise of Catholic saints. Many of the divination practices of *Ifa* have been incorporated within Candomblé. **Santeria** is a Cuban religion that bears similarity to Candomblé and also incorporates the *orisas*. The Cuban diaspora has spread the religion throughout the Caribbean region, including northern South America, and the United States. Today, it is likely that there are hundreds of thousands of practitioners of Santeria in the United States alone.

A Benzedeira, or Brazilian traditional healer, tends to an altar in the temple that is also her home.

Another example from the Caribbean is the **Vodou** religion, which originated in Haiti and then spread elsewhere in the Caribbean and southern United States. Also known as *voodoo*, this religious tradition owes much to both Catholicism and religions of West Africa, especially the religions of Yoruba, Fon, and Kongo peoples. The term "vodou" comes from the Fon word "vudon," which means spirit. Practitioners of vodou recognize many different spirits. The spirits are called *loa* and have origins in West Africa. As in Santeria, the spirits are also sometimes identified with Catholic saints. Today, the majority of Haitians claim vodou as their primary religious affiliation, although earlier in the twentieth century the Catholic church denounced it as heretical.

SEEKING ANSWERS

What Is the Nature of Ultimate Reality?

In most African traditions, the world is understood to have been created by a High God. The natural world, the supernatural world, and the social world of human beings are not separate and distinct realms but are often considered to be interlinked. Dogon creation narratives illustrate this idea. Most African religions are *anthropocentric*, or human-centered; they teach that God created humans and that creation and the universe revolve around humanity. Often, it is believed humans and God once coexisted in an idealized past, but that something happened to separate humanity from God. African religions differ in terms of how ultimate reality is revealed to human beings: humans communicate with the divine through possession, sacrifice, and divination.

What Is Our Ultimate Purpose?

African religions do not tend to focus on salvation or the goal of transcending the human condition but, rather, seek to emulate an idealized past in this life. However, many traditions hold that after death, people may transition to a spiritual state and may continue to interact with living humans. There are some exceptions to this. The Dogon and the Yoruba, for example, conceive of the possibility of a grand afterlife.

How Should We Live in This World?

Many African religions emphasize the importance of caring for and respecting the living and deceased members of one's family, the necessity of maintaining beneficial relationships with the beings of the spirit world, and the importance of harmony with the natural world. Because most African religions do not focus on reward or punishment in the afterlife, religious practice does not normally center on preparing for an afterlife. Instead, rituals and ceremonies focus on improving life in this world.

CONCLUSION

What does the future hold for the indigenous religions of Africa? Will these religious traditions maintain relevance in the face of ever-expanding world religions and in an increasingly globalized world?

The challenges of colonialism and growing world religions in the last few centuries have vastly increased the numbers of Africans following large-scale religions like Islam and Christianity. Although the majority of Africans today profess one of these two faiths, their prevalence has certainly not eradicated traditional African religions. As we have seen in this chapter, people throughout Africa have incorporated beliefs and practices from indigenous religions into large-scale religions. As a result, Islam and Christianity have taken on distinctly African forms and have essentially *become* indigenous African religions. We have learned that African religions tend to focus on the present, and much African religious practice looks for ways to improve one's immediate circumstances. These concerns have remained meaningful to many people in Africa, even when they become followers of salvation-oriented religions like Christianity and Islam.[31]

Furthermore, religions like Santeria and Vodou that are derived from African traditions are flourishing in much of the Americas. Through increasing migration and mobility, practitioners of these religions make them significant and relevant in diverse cultural contexts and introduce others to their teachings and practices. Today, you can find practitioners of Santeria and Vodou who have no ancestral ties to Africa. As a result, these religions will likely continue to thrive and even grow in the Americas. And as more Africans move to parts of Europe and Asia for work or schooling, their religious practices will likely go with them and will adjust to new contexts.

In sum, we can assume that African religions will continue to change and adapt to wider social environments both in Africa and the African diaspora. Although their forms and modes of practice will change from one generation to the next, this only continues processes of change that are characteristic to all religions. African religions are not relics of the past; rather, they are meaningful living traditions that will continue to thrive in the future.

REVIEW QUESTIONS

For Review

1. What is the relationship between humanity and gods in African religions? Give specific examples from religions.
2. Describe the spirits of the dead. What role do they have in the lives of the living in particular religions? How are the beliefs about the dead reflected in religious practice?
3. What are the three main ways African religions communicate with the supernatural? Describe each.
4. What influence have African religions had on American religions? How did this happen?

For Further Reflection

1. Do you see any similarities between the religions of Africa and the religions of Native America? How do conceptions of the supernatural differ? Do they share similarities?
2. What parallels can you draw between Native American and African religious resistance movements? What motivated these movements, and how were they carried out?
3. Why is it difficult to describe some African religions as simply "monotheistic" or "polytheistic"? Do you see this in any other religions you have studied so far?

GLOSSARY

Amma (ah-ma; Dogon) The High God of the Dogon people.

bori (boh-ree; various languages) A term for West African spirits.

Candomblé New World religion with roots in West Africa—particularly Yoruba culture—which is prominent in Brazil.

dama (dah-ma; Dogon) A Dogon rite of passage marking the transition to adulthood and to the afterlife.

divination The attempt to learn about events that will happen in the future through supernatural means.

Ifa (ee-fah; Yoruba) The divination system of the Yoruba religion, believed to be revealed to humanity by the gods.

Kinjiketele (kin-jee-ke-te-le) The leader of the Maji Maji rebellion in Tanganyika (today's Tanzania).

Maji Maji (mah-jee mah-jee; Swahili) A 1905 rebellion against German colonizers in Tanganyika (today's Tanzania).

medium A person who is possessed by a spirit, and thus mediates between the human and spirit world.

moran (mor-an; Samburu and Maasai) A young man in Samburu or Maasai culture who has been circumcised and thus has special cultural and religious duties.

Odu (oh-doo; Yoruba) The original prophets in Yoruba religion.

orisa (oh-ree-sha; Yoruba) Term for lesser deities in Yoruba religion.

Oshun (oh-shoon; Yoruba) A Yoruba goddess.

pantheon A group of deities or spirits.

rites of passage Rituals that mark the transition from one stage to another.

Santeria (san-teh-ree-a; Spanish) New World religion with roots in West Africa; prominent in Cuba.

Vodou (voo-doo; Fon and French) New World religion with roots in West Africa; prominent in Haiti and the Haitian diaspora.

witchcraft A term used by Western scholars to describe the use of supernatural powers to harm others.

zar (zahr; various languages) A term for spirits in East Africa.

SUGGESTIONS FOR FURTHER READING

Abimbola, Wande. *Ifa: An Exposition of Ifa Literary Corpus*. Oxford University Press, 1976. Scholarly look at Yoruba religious text and beliefs.

Evans-Pritchard, Edward E. *Witchcraft, Oracles and Magic among the Azande*. Oxford University Press, 1976. Classic anthropological account of beliefs about witchcraft and magic among the Azande people of southern Sudan.

Griaule, Marcel. *Conversations with Ogotemmeli*. Oxford University Press, 1965. A firsthand description of Dogon cosmology based on conversations with a Dogon elder.

Mbiti, John S. *African Religions & Philosophy*. New York: Doubleday, 1992. Useful introduction to African belief systems and religions.

McCarthy Brown, Karen. *Mama Lola: A Vodou Priestess in Brooklyn*. University of California Press, 1998. Engrossing ethnographic account of a modern day Vodou priestess.

Olupona, Jacob K. *African Traditional Religions in Contemporary Society*. St. Paul, MN: Paragon House, 1998. Useful look at African religions in the present day.

Ray, Benjamin C. *African Religions: Symbol, Ritual, and Community*. Upper Saddle River, NJ: Prentice Hall, 2000. Introduction to African religions aimed at students focusing on religious practice.

ONLINE SOURCES

National Museum of African Art

africa.si.edu

The National Museum of African Art, part of the Smithsonian Institution, offers abundant useful resources for African religion and material culture.

African Voices

mnh.si.edu/africanvoices

The Smithsonian's "African Voices" site explores the diversity of African cultures and their connections to the global world.

HINDUISM

ON A SPRING MORNING in the Salt Lake Valley, the air is crisp with expectation. Indra Neelameggham straightens the pleats of her silk sari as her husband Neale nods to indicate the gaily dressed crowd filing into the temple, clutching offerings of flowers, fresh fruits, and coconuts in their hands. Bells ring out joyfully from inside a temple whose doors are opening for the first time after eight years of hard work and waiting.

Indra and Neale have watched friends and community pour their hearts and souls into creating a divine palace—a place for worship—in this stark, dry part of Utah. Volunteers have offered up their weekends as acts of devotion, carrying stones, pushing wheelbarrows, and installing heating ducts and insulation.

Today is the third of three days of rituals celebrating the temple's opening. Nearly 1,000 people have passed the temple threshold, gathering to attend the consecration ceremony. Ritually, this is a complex process whose intricacies Indra and Neale are watching for the first time in their lives.

After everything that has transpired in these past few days, Indra is profoundly aware of the gravity of change. A week ago a three-foot-tall, 575-pound icon of Ganesha had been moved from her home in the suburbs, where she had hosted him as an honored guest, to his new temple.

Ganesha appears adorned for worship in the sanctum of the Sri Ganesha Hindu Temple of Utah. Because Hindu deities are often associated with the land in which they are worshiped, he is affectionately called "Uppu Vinayaka" or the "Salt" Ganesha by some of the local devotees.

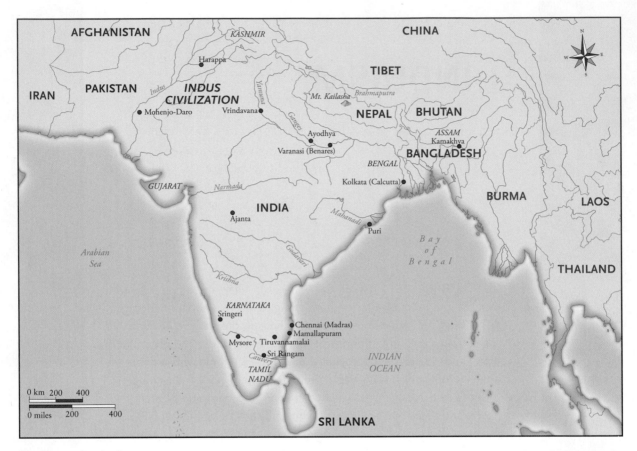

Significant sites in the history of Hinduism.

With the head of an elephant atop a human body, Ganesha, the God Who Removes All Obstacles, is one of Hinduism's most easily recognized deities. He is the patron deity of arts and sciences, and the god of wisdom, new beginnings, and commerce. He is a god who conveys warmth and a sense of humor and is especially venerated by students, writers, travelers, and businessmen. He is propitiated at the beginning of every new undertaking and is the first deity invoked in almost any Hindu ritual context. In his four arms he carries objects (including an axe, a noose, and an elephant goad) that he uses to destroy, subdue, or control the obstacles of life. He also often holds a bowl of sweets to denote his benevolent and loving nature.

The sacred image of Ganesha being installed today at this new temple in the southern part of the Salt Lake Valley had been under the care of Neale and Indra for eight years. While they never imagined themselves the sort of people to house a makeshift Ganesha temple in their basement, when the icon arrived from India—with the dream of an actual temple still so far away—it just seemed natural for them to offer to serve as hosts.

The previous day, at midnight, the deity had been permanently affixed to its base in the temple's innermost sanctum. Now, the final rites of consecration have begun. In a ritual called *prana pratishtha* (Sanskrit, "establishing the vital breath"), the priest invites the actual divine spirit into the icon, transforming a simple stone image into a deity. The final step of the *prana pratishtha* ritual requires that the priest awaken the gaze of the deity. While the priest outlines the icon's eyes with a golden needle, a sculptor pierces the pupils with a diamond-tipped chisel. The deity is now awake, and Ganesha's initial powerful gaze must first fall on auspicious things: a cow with its calf, young children, mounds of rice, and vast offerings of food that will be distributed to the devotees.

Like the other devotees gathered at the temple, Indra is overcome by the reverence and exuberance of the assembly. She steps forward to have **darshan** (Sanskrit, "to see and to be seen by the divine") and feels that she is in the presence of a living being.

Glancing about, Indra understands now. They had all thought they were just building a temple. But they were building a community and a refuge for families and lasting friendships. And at the center of it all is their Ganesha of Salt Lake. ☀

What does it mean to speak of Hindu teachings or practice, given that (unlike many other religions discussed in this book) Hinduism has no single founder or single sacred book, nor a single historical event that marks its birth? Rather, Hinduism is made up of many sects with a variety of belief systems. Yet, as we will learn, these many sects share common traits that link them together under the umbrella of "Hinduism."

Although many look to India as Hinduism's home, it has been, for the majority of its history, a transregional religion. Today, the largest population percentage of Hindus is not found in India (79%) but in Nepal (89%). Other parts of South Asia such as Bangladesh, Sri Lanka, and Bhutan also have significant numbers. It might surprise many that at least a quarter of the population of Guyana (40%), Surinam (30%), Fiji (38%), and Trinidad and Tobago (24%) is Hindu. In addition, there are considerable populations in Malaysia and South Africa.[1] Beyond this, there have been notable population increases in America, Canada, and throughout Europe in the past few decades (as we saw in Neale and Indra's story). Hinduism is not an "Eastern" religion anymore. A truly global religion, it is the third largest religion in the world after Christianity and Islam.

How can a religion nurtured by and reflected in so many diverse cultural contexts still be recognizable as a single entity? Part of the answer may lie in the fact that Hinduism has a history that embodies both continuity and dynamic change. Having never had a sole central authority—in the form of either a founder, a text, a doctrine, or an institution—its fluid character has always allowed it to adapt to a variety of

A photograph taken of a Hindu temple in Trinidad in 1931.

social and cultural contexts. Such extraordinary diversity has led many scholars to argue that Hinduism is not one religion at all, but a constellation of many religious sects that have some commonality. Still others have suggested that it is precisely the assimilative tendency of Hinduism that distinguishes it as an autonomous religious tradition. In this chapter, we will explore the ways in which Hinduism has managed to accommodate a variety of beliefs, practices, and traditions and seek to understand what unites a religious tradition whose roots go back almost 4,000 years.[2]

THE TEACHINGS OF HINDUISM

Historically, Hindus have not used the word "Hinduism" to describe their system of teachings and practice. Prior to the nineteenth century, most "Hindus" identified themselves by their sectarian orientation and their social status. The word *Hindu* was initially an ethnogeographic term used by the ancient Persians to denote the people who lived beyond the Indus River (Sanskrit *Sindhu*), in the northwestern corner of the Indian subcontinent. By 325 B.C.E., Alexander the Great had crossed the Indus; the Greek conquerors adopted the Persian convention of calling the river the "Indos" and the land beyond it "India." In the centuries that followed, the term "Indu" or "Hindu" became a territorial as well as a racial, social, and cultural designation for the people of India. After the sixteenth century C.E., the word appeared occasionally in Indian literature to distinguish "Hindus" from Muslims or other "foreigners." By about 1830, the "-ism" was added to Hindu to denote a single, cohesive religious tradition, and toward the end of the nineteenth century "Hinduism" began to be used frequently by its own adherents to describe their faith.

Today, "Hinduism" is a word that refers to diverse systems of belief, each of which is composed of a range of theological variables. Along with having no single founder or sacred text, Hinduism does not have just one creation myth or one belief about how the world will end. And most significantly, its understanding of our purpose in life and what happens afterward is complex and varied. Unlike many other religious traditions, Hinduism does not offer just one path to enlightenment and liberation, or indeed just one answer to what happens to us when we die. Using the single, homogenous term "Hinduism" can be especially problematic when we try to specify just what it is that Hindus believe.

Some Hindus look to the authority of a group of texts known as the **Vedas** (Sanskrit, "sacred books") and may rely on **brahmin** priests to officiate at ceremonies of worship and rites of passage; others, however, reject the central place of the *Vedas* and *brahmins*. Some Hindus participate in organizations built around certain teachers or saints or take part in sectarian forms of communal worship, while others seek solitude and associate religious life with contemplation, yoga, or meditation. Some Hindus believe that God is a divine person with specific identifiable attributes. In contrast, other Hindus believe that God defies description and is an all-pervading being that extends beyond all concepts. In order to acknowledge this plurality of practice and belief, it is perhaps more appropriate to speak of "Hinduisms" rather than a singular Hindu tradition and to recognize that this very plurality is one of the religion's distinguishing features.

Despite Hinduism's overwhelming diversity, it is possible to discern patterns of similarity and cohesion. One significant pattern is that most Hindus believe in the law of **karma** (that all actions produce effects), **samsara** (reincarnation, where the fruition of *karmic* reactions keeps one bound in an endless cycle of death and rebirth), and **moksha** (enlightenment; complete liberation from the bonds of *karma* and *samsara*).

For the sake of simplicity and accessibility, we have organized Hinduism's main beliefs in this chapter under four large categories. First, we examine Hindu beliefs about God. Next, we explore Hinduism's key philosophical and social concepts. We then take up a discussion of Hinduism's foundational texts, and we finally conclude with a brief survey of Hinduism's three major sects. But we must keep in mind that these four categories are not mutually exclusive; rather, as you will soon discover, their boundaries are very permeable.

Hindu Beliefs about God

Hindu beliefs about God and God's nature are wide and varied. In this section, we will seek to answer the most fundamental questions asked about Hinduism: Why are there so many gods? Why do Hindus worship images? What is an *avatar?* And, do Hindus worship cows?

God Is One and Many   In a famous passage from the *Upanishads* (a group of early philosophical texts), a questioner asks the great sage Yajnavalkya:

> "Just how many gods are there?"
> In response he cites a sacred hymn, singing
> "Three and three hundred, and three and three thousand!"
> But then he asked Yajnavalkya again, "But how many are there really?"
> He said: "Thirty-three."
> But the man persisted, "But how many are there really?"
> "Six."
> "But how many are there really?"
> "Three."

"But how many are there really?"
"Two."
"But how many are there really?"
"One and a half."
"But how many are there really?"
"One." [3]

In this famous discourse, the sage Yajnavalkya explains that the various powers of the divine manifest as many deities. He later adds that the entire universe is grounded in the "Divine Self," called *Brahman*. This ultimate reality pervades all existence. Although *Brahman* is the true nature of all that exists, this Divine Self, commonly called God, is unfathomable and can only be described in terms of "Not this! Not that!" [4] This is monism (see p. 12), the belief that all reality is ultimately one.

Yajnavalkya's ancient utterance in the *Upanishads* carries great weight in how later Hinduism forms its understanding of the mystery and majesty of God's being. Most Hindus believe that God is simultaneously one and many. Since God is all-pervasive, all things can be seen as being God's forms. For Hindus, the multiplicity of the universe is paradoxically also an expression of the unity of God. Thus, Hindus worship many deities while also affirming the singularity of the divine. Each of these deities is regarded as a manifestation of some aspect, facet, or expression of God.

Hindu worship of multiple deities is a form of polytheism. But, unlike polytheistic religions that see the various gods as limited, Hinduism regards each god as an embodiment of ultimate reality. This is a form of henotheism, which, as was noted in the introductory chapter (see pp. 11–12), acknowledges a plurality of gods but elevates one of them to special status. On any given occasion, Hindus can recognize ultimate reality in any particular god.

God and the Soul There are countless names for God in Hinduism. However, since the time of the *Upanishads* (900–600 B.C.E.), *Brahman* has been the most commonly used. The word is derived from the Sanskrit *brh* ("to grow") and thus connotes *Brahman*'s all-pervasive nature that subsumes within itself the multiplicity of the entire universe. *Brahman* is characterized by three qualities: *sat* (being, existence), *cit* (consciousness), and *ananda* (bliss). It is both the source of all things and their final destination. As the later sects of Hinduism developed, deities such as Vishnu, Shiva, and the Great Goddess (whom we will soon meet) came to be identified with *Brahman*.

All Hindus also believe in an eternal, undying soul or self, called the **atman**. Its nature is not limited by the attributes of the physical body or defined by its relationship to the world and others. It exists in the body but is rarely directly perceived, as it is obscured by the mind's imperfections. Like *Brahman*, the *atman* is pure consciousness. It is the *atman* that moves from body to body through the process of reincarnation until it finally recognizes its true nature. Many Hindu philosophical systems assert that release from the endless cycle of birth, death, and rebirth is achieved when one recognizes the absolute unity of *atman* with *Brahman*.

God as Sound (*Om*)

Om, the primordial sound, is constituted of three phonemes (sounds) of the Sanskrit language: "*A*" the first vowel, "*U*" the second vowel, and "*M*" the final consonant. As such, *Om* is said to encapsulate the entire universe. Some *Upanishads* also identify it with four states of consciousness: *A* is waking consciousness, *U* is dreaming consciousness, *M* is deep sleep, and *AUM* in its entirety is the fourth and final state of consciousness itself, which is one with Brahman. In later Hinduism, the phonemes are identified with the gods Brahma, Vishnu, and Shiva respectively, expressing the deities' functions of creating, preserving, and dissolving the universe. *Om* is also identified as the primordial, essential sound through which the universe is created, and thus is the very expression of *Brahman*. Every ritual in Hinduism begins with the intonation of this sacred syllable.

God as Image

Even while Hinduism has a speculative side that often asserts the impossibility of fathoming *Brahman*'s nature, it is also an intensely imagistic religious tradition. Images of gods, celestials, and mythical beasts decorate temples and homes alike. Such love and relish for the divine form emerge from Hindu notions of the simultaneous immanence and transcendence of God. Thus, it is through images that God manifests and is accessible to devotees and pilgrims in sacred sites as well as in personal shrines at home. Yet, ultimately God is without attribute or form, a transcendent being that exists beyond thought and conception. It is this paradoxical duality that images of God represent. On one level, an image is merely a symbolic representation meant to aid the devotee in his or her spiritual quest. On another level, an image of a god is fully divine, suffused with the divine presence, as we saw in the opening narrative about the Ganesha temple. From this perspective, an image of a god **is** God. While all things are expressions of the divine, any image that receives worship is regarded as a particularly potent vessel of the divine presence.

Images of God take a number of forms, as they may be created from any number of sacred substances. They can be formed by nature or man-made. They can be abstract or anthropomorphized with multiple arms and faces. Images can be the richly adorned stationary icons enshrined found in temples or the beautifully crafted bronze icons carried in religious processions. Many Hindus also have small icons

A *sannyasi* or Hindu ascetic. His sectarian affiliation is indicated by his forehead marking, which demonstrates that he is a worshiper of Vishnu.

in personal shrines in their homes. In modern times, with the proliferation of print and online images of the divine, Hindus revere these as God as well. Because of this emphasis on divine images and their worship, Hindus sometimes have been falsely characterized by non-Hindus as worshiping mere images. For Hindus, however, images of God are imbued with the divine essence. It is this essence that is worshiped and invoked through ritual action. For Hindus, the image in worship *is* God and has been made God by means of worship and prayer.

God in Nature If God is everywhere and everything, it follows that the natural world is the most immediate and obvious expression of the divine. Thus, it is no surprise that the worship of rivers, the earth, mountains, and the sun, as well as a reverence for certain trees and animals, can be traced back to Hinduism's earliest emergence. Many of the sacred sites in Hinduism arose in conjunction with the worship of rivers and mountains. Rivers in particular are worshiped for embodying the divine, creative, female energy that generates the universe. Furthermore, rivers are also revered as powerful places of crossing, as they represent the confluence of the divine and terrestrial worlds. It is for all of these reasons that many Hindus bathe in rivers—of which the Ganges (or *Ganga*) in India is the most important—believing that they wash away one's transgressions and sins.

A Hindu devotee performs rituals dedicated to the Sun God as he takes a holy dip in Allahabad, India, at the confluence of the Ganges and Yamuna rivers, one of Hinduism's important centers.

Many examples of nature worship in Hinduism do not have corollaries in Hindu texts or formalized doctrine. Instead, they are found only in popular everyday practices. A good example is the diagrams made with rice flour that Hindu women draw at the thresholds of their homes every morning and evening. These beautiful but impermanent images have many functions: they acknowledge the earth for supporting humanity; they indicate that the home is in a state of auspiciousness; and they are invitations to Lakshmi, the goddess of fortune and wealth. Finally, as these ephemeral works of art are made of rice flour, a sacrificial food offering made to the small creatures of the world, they are meant to be eaten by ants and other tiny animals.

Although Hinduism has a long history of reverence for the natural world, this has not always translated into ecological awareness and activism. The worship of rivers does not mean that India's sacred waterways are pristine. Since a river is divine, it is said to be able to absorb the transgressions of worshipers and still remain unaffected.

Thus for many Hindus, the river remains pure even if it is polluted from both organic and inorganic waste. While this has long been the dominant position in Hinduism, recent Hindu environmental activists are beginning to challenge these assumptions and are employing Hindu beliefs about the divinity of the natural world to champion a more informed ecological awareness.

Do Hindus Really Worship Cows? To Hindus all existence is pervaded by the divine presence and all beings are sacred. But the cow holds a special place in Hindu society because when a child is weaned from its mother's breast it is thereafter given cow's milk. The cow, therefore, is revered as a second mother. But formal rites of worship of the cow are rare. Two instances of the worship of cows occur on the first day of the *Diwali* festival, in a rite called *Vasu Baras*, and during the harvest festival, *Pongal*, which is celebrated in South India.

During British colonial rule, British scholars and administrators exaggerated the prominence of cow worship in Hinduism, partly to assert the preeminence of Christianity. In doing so, they referred to the scene in the Old Testament that describes Moses returning from the mountain with the Ten Commandments, only to be disgusted by the Hebrews worshiping a golden calf. For Judeo-Christians, cow worship was the definitive symbol of degenerate idolatry, while for Hindus it was (and continues to be) an expression of respect for the creatures that help humanity.

God Comes Down: *Avatara* Hinduism teaches that God is made manifest in the world in various ways. We have already encountered two major ways: the image and the natural world. Another crucial way in which God is made manifest is in the form of an **avatara.** An *avatara* is a manifestation of God on earth in a physical form with the specific goal of aiding the world. *Avatara* (or *avatar*) is a Sanskrit word derived from the prefix *ava* ("down") and the Sanskrit verbal root *tr* ("to cross"). This meaning of "to cross downwards" denotes the descent of a deity into material form for the purpose of intervening in the world. The *avatara* (commonly translated as "incarnation") is a divine manifestation, and as such is understood to fully embody divinity.

Avatara is most often used to describe the divine interventions of Vishnu, who is believed to have assumed ten such forms, of which nine have already appeared. The most popular of the *avataras* are Rama, Vishnu's seventh form, and Krishna, his eighth. Legend has it that Vishnu's final *avatara*, **Kalki**, will arrive at the end of this age, sword aloft and riding a white horse, and that his wrathful intervention will usher in an age of peace. It must be remembered that although some *avataras* may have a human or even animal form, for Hindus they are in no way inferior to the unknowable, supreme being of which they are manifestations. This point is made repeatedly in

The Hampi Bazaar in Karnataka, India, a sacred town where doorsteps and houses are decorated by *rangoli* or *kolam* ritual protective drawings.

a number of texts, but nowhere more eloquently than in the famous second-century B.C.E. philosophical text, the *Bhagavad Gita* (*The Song of God*).

In the *Bhagavad Gita*, Krishna discusses the concept of *avatara*, asserting the principle that, although God's essential nature is unchangeable, God chooses to intervene in the world at a time when intervention is necessary and in the form of an *avatara* that is completely God. Krishna says:

> Though myself unborn, undying, the lord of creatures, I fashion nature, which
> is mine, and I come into being through my own magic.
> Whenever sacred duty decays and chaos prevails, then, I create myself, Arjuna.
> To protect men of virtue and destroy men who do evil, to set the standard
> of sacred duty, I appear in age after age. (*Bhagavad Gita*, 4:6–8)

We will learn more about the *Bhagavad Gita* later in this chapter.

Hindu Philosophical and Social Concepts

We can find continuity within the variety of Hindu traditions in some shared, central philosophical and social concepts. Many of the philosophical concepts, such as *samsara* and *karma*, are shared by other Indic religions (such as Buddhism, Jainism, and Sikhism), although each treats these concepts in subtly different ways. As in many other religious traditions, several of Hinduism's philosophical ideas also have social dimensions and applications. In this section we consider these ideas, pointing out ways in which they are interrelated and foundational to Hinduism as a lived reality.

Karma   Hinduism's understanding of existential and cosmological issues is linked to the concept of *karma*. While the Sanskrit term means "action," in Hindu philosophy *karma* refers to the Law of Causation, of cause and effect. It is a term that has entered into common usage in the English language and popular culture, where it is not always used correctly. For instance, when something bad happens to a person because of their previous actions, people might say "Bad *karma*!" But this is an incorrect representation of how *karma* works because *karma* refers to the action or cause—not the result—of that action.

Karma encompasses all action: physical, mental, emotional, psychological, and ritual. The result of any action is the **phala** (Sanskrit, "fruit"). Taking action is compared to planting a seed, and the result of that action is the "fruit" it bears. This fruit is considered as either a positive merit or a negative result. When one acts according to prescribed religious and ritual laws and obligations (*dharma*), then one usually accrues merit. Violating individual obligation or the social order invariably earns one a negative result.

The law of *karma* is intimately connected to the notion of *samsara* (Sanskrit, "whirling" or "cycling"). *Samsara* refers both to this earthly, "real" world, as well as to the endless cycle of birth, death, and rebirth in which all living things are caught up. People are bound to *samsara* because of *karma* and its results. Earning merit over lifetimes ensures favorable rebirths, while accruing negative results leads to the opposite. Favorable rebirth increases the possibility of breaking out of *samsara*. This process of continuous birth and death occurs through the self's transmigration. The self (*atman*) is itself eternal, but when the physical body it inhabits decays and dies, it moves on to another body, repeating this cycle until its true nature is recognized. The *atman's* move from body to body is termed "transmigration" or, in popular parlance, reincarnation.

The law of causation is very subtle. Sometimes the fruits of actions appear almost immediately. At other times the full "ripening" of *karma* may spread from one lifetime to the next or through a chain of recurrent events spread over many lifetimes, until the cycle is eventually broken and the momentum of causation runs out. Most Hindus believe that the grace and mercy of God can subvert the mechanics of *karma*, transform one's destiny, and halt the endless cycle of birth and death. Liberation from *samsara* is called *moksha*.

Moksha The ultimate goal for Hindus is found beyond *samsara*. Human beings are caught up in *samsara*, in which the nature of each new existence is wholly determined by his or her previous action. Identifying with the limited self as the agent of action binds the fruit of those acts to the soul. Liberation, or *moksha*, is achieved only when consciousness is radically transformed by relinquishing identification with the limited, temporal self and seeing that it is God or Brahman who is the true agent of all activity. At that moment, one perceives ultimate reality. When one recognizes the true nature of *atman* and apprehends its relationship to God, then *moksha* is achieved. Some philosophical schools suggest that *moksha* is to recognize the *atman's* true nature and thus apprehend that all beings are pervaded by *Brahman*, the one supreme consciousness. To some devotional sects, *moksha* means that one no longer transmigrates and is forever in the presence of the divine.

Hinduism provides a number of paths out of *samsara*. All of these paths seek some way of mitigating or neutralizing the effects of *karma*, which is what keeps one bound in *samsara*. One can renounce the world, limiting one's actions in it and thereby curtailing the results, or *phala*. A person can also simply surrender to God. Meditation and ritual action are other means some Hindus pursue in order to escape the binds of *samsara*.

Renunciation Hinduism sees renunciation as the preeminent tool cultivating the detachment needed to transcend the limits of ego and achieve *moksha*. Attachment to material objects and the fruits obtained through action bind one to the wheel of *samsara*. Giving up clinging to the material world through renunciation and ascetic practice is akin to a sacrifice that earns the renouncer spiritual power. By not indulging one's desires, the very self becomes the sacrificial fire in which the ego is destroyed, replaced by the purifying heat of austerity.

Typically, the renouncer is a celibate wanderer attached to no single place. The renouncer (generally, male) usually gives up his previous social self and with it all its attendant attachments and obligations. Thus, when a man takes formal monastic vows, he is required symbolically to perform his own funeral rites, signifying the social and symbolic death of his previous persona. With this socio-symbolic death, the ascetic is expected to relinquish all social obligations.

Hinduism places equal importance on renunciation and on participation in worldly life. As we shall see, Hinduism gives renunciation a place in a Hindu's life-cycle and makes *moksha* one of the four principal goals of a good life. In doing so, Hinduism reconciles the two opposing impulses of renunciation and the worldly life.

Dharma   While the term ***dharma*** is sometimes used by Hindus to denote "religion" itself, its multiple layers of meaning make it one of the trickiest concepts to define in Hinduism. The word *dharma* is derived from the Sanskrit root *dhr*, which means "to uphold." It can refer to religious prescriptions and ordinances, sacred duty, law, moral virtue, and social or caste obligation. One important Sanskrit text defines *dharma* as that which brings about well-being both in this life and in the hereafter. In Hinduism, *dharma* links the spiritual with the material dimension through harmonizing one's inner life with life in the external world.

Dharma can be seen as the order that upholds the universe by dictating the duties, prescriptions, and obligations of all beings. *Dharma* is universal, but it is also particular in that it applies to individuals in their particular situations. The *dharma* that informs the role of ethical action and engagement in a universal sense is called *sadharana dharma*. But when *dharma* refers to the individual's duties that are informed by class, gender, and social position the term used is *sva-dharma*—literally, one's own *dharma*.

Two ancient and enormously influential Indian epic poems, the *Ramayana* and *Mahabharata*, can be read as profound meditations on these dual meanings of *dharma*. Both texts depict situations in which epic heroes experience a clash between social or filial obligation and their own personal sense of what cosmic duty demands from them. Apart from mythic narratives like the *Ramayana* and *Mahabharata*, other textual sources known as the *Dharmashastras* (*Dharma* Treatises) have sought to clarify the concept of *dharma*. The *Dharmashastras* explain *dharma* through both individual and societal order. It is to such societal aspects of *dharma* that we turn next.

Varnashrama Dharma   The concept of *varnashrama dharma* is an ideal that was traditionally observed by the upper echelons of Hindu society. The phrase refers to honoring one's duty (*dharma*) in terms of caste or station (Sanskrit *varna*) and stage in life (Sanskrit *ashrama*). This system marries the individual's duties to the obligations of society as a whole, reflecting an ideal that was particularly important to upper-caste male Hindus. The traditional influence of *varnashrama dharma* has diminished in modern times.

Let us begin by considering *ashrama*, which posits that there are "Four Stages of Life":

1. The celibate student
2. The householder
3. The forest-dwelling hermit
4. The wandering renouncer

Fulfilling the duties of these stages is said to repay the "Three Debts of Life," which are:

1. To the ancient seers (by studying the revealed texts known as the *Vedas* as a student)
2. To the gods (by making offerings as a householder)
3. To the ancestors (by having a son—again, as a householder—who will continue to perform ancestral rites)

It is the duty of the householder to support those in the other three stages of life. The last two stages are concerned with seeking *moksha* or liberation, first by remaining at a hermitage surrounded by spiritually like-minded people, and then by entering the fourth stage by becoming a wandering renouncer (Sanskrit **sannyasi**). These four *ashramas* define the ideal life stages for men. Women participate primarily in vaguely defined supporting roles through the last three stages, and thereby assist in repaying the three debts.

The *Varna* and *Jati* Systems   While the *ashrama* system is concerned with organizing the life of the individual, the *varna* system is concerned with ordering society itself. The word *varna* refers to a system of hierarchical social organization. *Varna* is determined by birth and is propagated through endogamy, or marriage only within a particular group. While *varna* is often translated as "caste," a word derived from the Portuguese *casta* ("lineage, breed, race"), the literal meaning of the term is "color." A more accurate way of expressing its meaning in this context is through the English term "class."

We encounter the first mention of *varna* in a poem known as the *Purusha Sukta*, an early Sanskrit poem found in the tenth book of the *Rig Veda* (c. 1500–1200 B.C.E.). The poem describes the primordial sacrifice of the cosmic man, thereby ascribing a mythical origin to the *varna* system. From the various parts of the cosmic man emerge the component parts of the universe—the sun, the moon, the breath, and fire among them. At the very end, people emerge. From his mouth emerge the priests (*brahmins*); from his arms, the warriors and kings (Sanskrit *kshatriya*); from his thighs, the commoner (Sanskrit *vaishya*, "merchant or agriculturalist class"); and from his feet, the servants (Sanskrit *shudra*).

The *varnas* are organized along a continuum of purity and pollution, with the purest (the priests) occupying the head of the hierarchy. A person's state of purity or pollution is determined by his or her relative contact with substances that are considered polluting. Those who constantly handle polluting items such as hair, blood, excrement, and leather occupy the lowest position. Thus, leatherworkers and sweepers, who are among the *shudras*, were considered to be among the most polluted. On the other hand, priests and warriors enjoyed a higher status because their contact with polluting substances was intermittent, and they could negate the contact through ritual actions, like bathing.

The organizational principle of purity and pollution is expressed in the *Purusha Sukta*, where the *brahmins* emerge from the mouth, while the servants emerge from the feet, the lowest and lowliest part of the body. Although it might appear from the *varna* schema and from the *Purusha Sukta* that *brahmins* are authoritatively at the top of the hierarchy, we know that from the earliest period *brahmins* and *kshatriyas* (and to some extent *vaishyas* as well) existed in a close, mutually dependent relationship. The *brahmins*, with their ritual knowledge, legitimated kings and ambitious warriors and chieftains who might come to power. In turn, kings supported the priestly class with gifts of wealth and land, while merchants and landlords paid taxes and sponsored priestly activities.

In addition to these four major classes, a fifth group below the *shudras*, called the "untouchables," was later added. Today, this lowest group constitutes nearly 20 percent of the population of India. During the Indian Independence movement of the early twentieth century, M. K. Gandhi (whom we will discuss later in the chapter) sought to uplift this class socially, referring to them as *harijans*, or "Children of God." However, many of this class rejected the label as demeaning and patronizing and now refer to themselves as **Dalit**, a word that means "oppressed." In modern India, educational institutions and government jobs have been opened to the *Dalit* and have helped many with social and economic mobility. Nevertheless, *Dalits* continue to suffer terrible oppression, especially in rural communities in India.

In addition to the *varna* system, there is an additional classificatory system called *jati*. The Sanskrit word *jati* means "birth," denoting an existence into which you are born. The term is often used to describe different orders of plants and animals, implying that the difference between human groups is similar to that between different species. While there are traditionally only four *varnas* (plus the added class of untouchables), there are literally thousands of *jatis* in India.

A few basic principles can help you to understand better the subtle nuances of *jati* in India. For the sake of simplicity, consider *jati* as a subset of *varna*. That is, each of the four *varnas* may have any number of *jatis* under it. Usually, a *jati* is composed of an endogamous group. One can marry within *jati* communities that are equal in social and ritual status, but not into a *jati* above or below one's own position. Marriage across *jati* is usually undertaken to widen communal alliances. The basic rationale behind the hierarchical system of caste is the measure of ritual purity, with certain *brahmin jatis* at the top, *Dalit* groups at the bottom, and in between a shifting list of other groups that may be perceived differently from region to region. The ranking of *jati* groups depends in part on the level of pollution involved in the work they do.

Coming in contact with death and bodily substances ensures a low place in the caste hierarchy, as is the case with leatherworkers or laundrymen. Not only does *jati* status dictate whom one can marry, but it can also dictate the people with whom one can eat or share water. In some *jatis*, one can only eat and share water with those whose *jati* is commensurate with one's own. Finally, and most importantly, the hierarchies of *jati* not only vary from region to region, but are also constantly in flux.

The *jati* system probably arose over time as new subgroupings of different endogamous communities began to proliferate and overwhelm the more narrowly defined hierarchy of the *varna* structure. It made social hierarchy more fluid, as some castes could actually shift in relative rank over time in specific regions. Sometimes a positive, upward shift in *jati* rank could be cultivated simply by perpetuating a myth of "purer" origins for a particular community or by adopting higher-caste practices, such as vegetarianism.

In the modern context, many strictures of caste have broken down. Many Hindus have embraced a more utilitarian and even egalitarian outlook formulated by nineteenth-century Hindu reformers. These reformers regarded inter-caste marriage as essential to bringing about social equality and the development of the Indian nation. In urban areas, caste status has often given way to a modern class-based system in which one's marriageability is based on education, current employment, and financial status, rather than solely on caste.

The Four Aims of Life

If the purpose of the stages of life (*ashramas*) is to organize an individual's life, then the system of the four *purusharthas*, or "Aims of Life," orients the individual to the purposes and goals of life. Classical Hindu sources describe four *purusharthas*, which can be understood as the four purposes of human existence: *dharma*, *kama*, *artha*, and *moksha*. A Hindu is meant to diligently pursue all four of these goals. As we have already seen, *dharma* is a complex term that encompasses not only ethics and duty but also living in harmony with life's unfolding. To apprehend the application of *dharma* in everyday life, some Hindus draw inspiration from the lives of the heroes and heroines of such epics as the *Ramayana*. Some Hindus take vows to practice complete nonviolence (Sanskrit *ahimsa*) and often maintain a vegetarian diet as part of that goal. Some vow never to tell a lie. Still others have strict rules for maintaining ritual purity or observe a complex ritual regimen each day to ensure the harmony and well-being of their household and family members.

The next two goals of life—*kama* and *artha*—are those of the householder. *Kama* (Sanskrit, "desire") is directed at the fulfillment of desire. It encourages Hindus to relish the human experience and celebrate the sensual aspects of life. *Artha* is wealth and abundance. It is a Hindu's duty to provide security for loved ones but also to savor and share life's bounty. *Moksha*, liberation or enlightenment, is (as we have seen) the ultimate goal.

The four aims of life in Hinduism can be regarded as reconciling the tension between the life of a renouncer and that of the worldly person. Just as the *ashrama* system finds a place for renunciation, the aims of life accommodate the impulse within the

Hindu traditions toward ascetic practice. Both the four stages and the four goals of life imply that within the life of a Hindu there is a proper time for everything. One's *dharma* is to study, to participate in the world and its delights, to accrue wealth, and to have children. It is only after one fulfills these worldly duties and obligations that one is ready to pursue the final and ultimate goal of *moksha*.

The systems of *varnashrama* and the goals of life represent ideals. They were both intended primarily for upper-caste men. We do not know the extent to which the prescriptions of the goals and stages of life have been followed in the long history of Hinduism. We do know that it is filled with stories of men and women of all castes who violated the prescriptions and yet managed to attain *moksha*.

VOICES: An Interview with Saraswati Krishnan

Saraswati Krishnan is a Western-educated *brahmin* wife and mother. She lives with her family and three cats in Sacramento, California.

As a Hindu, what is the most important part of human existence? What should Hindus do or focus on in life?

To me, as a Hindu, the most important aspect of life is to live ethically. That means, I try to cultivate compassion in all situations, have respect for everyone that I meet, and always live with humility, knowing that I might work hard, but that god in his infinite compassion will carry you through the toughest times of life. Also, at the center of this ethical life for me is a love for animals and a commitment to nonviolence. I practice this by being a vegetarian, adopting stray animals, and supporting animal welfare organizations.

What aspect of your day-to-day life as a Hindu would you characterize as being most spiritually gratifying?

The few moments in the morning, when I light the lamp in front of my image of Krishna and speak to him as my dearest friend. I spend those moments confiding my deepest fears and my smallest anxieties. During these quiet moments, I feel the presence of Krishna right beside me.

What is your favorite Hindu holiday? Can you describe what is most special about that day?

Without a question, it's Krishna Janmastami, the festival that celebrates Krishna's birth. In South India, where I am from, we offer all kinds of sweets to Krishna and await the midnight hour. That is when Krishna is said to have been born. We draw small feet on the floors of the home with rice flour, imagining a small child running around, searching for all the yummy treats. Ever since I was a child, I've loved this festival because I always imagine that I can see a young boy running around the house, and I was his cherished companion, joining in all of his mischief-making antics.

Texts in Hinduism

The great diversity within Hinduism emerges from its many different sects, each of which reveres different sets of texts. While some texts are common across sectarian affiliations, others are not. As we will see, Hindu texts are closely tied to Hindu beliefs, as they enable believers to assert new ideas, overturn old ones, or reassert the dominance of fading traditions. Hindu texts, which are composed in a range of languages and dialects, have been transmitted both in written and in oral form. Many texts are brought alive even in contemporary practice through music and dance, as they are recited and sung in temples and homes as a part of daily worship. In a very real sense, to learn from the many texts of Hinduism is to enter into the religion's complex heart. In this next section, we undertake a brief survey of Hinduism's main texts and their continued relevance in articulating the full range of Hindu beliefs.

Hindu priests perform *arati*, waving a lamp of burning camphor before an image of Hanuman (the monkey god of the *Ramyana*) at a temple in Kuala Lumpur, Malaysia, during the festival of Diwali.

The Vedas and Upanishads The earliest Hindu texts are known as the *Vedas*. Composed in Sanskrit between 1500 and 600 B.C.E., these texts are regarded by the orthodox Hindu tradition as revealed. That is, they are believed not to have been composed by man, but rather "heard" by the sages of ancient times. The *Vedas* comprise a set of four texts of hymns as well as ancillary speculative treatises, known as the *Upanishads*. While some hymns of the *Vedas* are used in ritual, most Hindus do not read the Vedic texts, which play a largely iconic role within the tradition. We will explore the role of the *Vedas* in the evolution of Hinduism later in this chapter.

For most Hindus, belief, tradition, ethics, and practice are all largely informed by and disseminated through the vast ocean of Hindu storytelling traditions and narrative texts. Two of the most significant of these are the twin Sanskrit epics, the *Ramayana* and the *Mahabharata*.

Ramayana The *Ramayana* (200 B.C.E.–200 C.E.) is one of the most important sources of Hindu notions of social and filial duty (*dharma*). Its relevance is demonstrated by the innumerable versions in different languages that have proliferated across the Indian subcontinent and beyond. The earliest of these many versions is composed in Sanskrit and is attributed to the poet Valmiki. The *Ramayana* ("The Journey of Rama") consists of seven books, which weave a compelling tale of political intrigue, romance, and philosophical speculation.

The *Ramayana* recounts that long ago the ten-headed demon King Ravana, having performed fierce austerities, was rewarded with the granting of a wish by Brahma the Creator. Ravana asks for protection from other members of his own demon race, titans, snake people, gods, and celestial or mystical creatures. Protected in this way, he and his demon hordes dominate the earth and eventually even enslave the gods of heaven. But in his arrogance Ravana neglects to ask for protection from humans and animals.

In the meantime, King Dasharatha of Ayodhya and his three queens, hoping for an heir, perform a sacrifice in hopes that the gods will grant their wish. The king is blessed with four sons—Rama, Lakshmana, Bharata, and Shatrughna. After many fantastic adventures with his brother Lakshmana, Rama eventually marries a princess, Sita. Rama is beloved by all for his adherence to righteousness and virtue, and so King Dasharatha, wishing to step down from the throne, announces that Rama's coronation will soon be held. Then, Kaikeyi, Dasharatha's favorite wife, suddenly calls in two wishes that the king had once granted her. She demands that Rama be banished to the forest for fourteen years and that her own son Bharata ascend the throne of Ayodhya in his stead. The distraught King Dasharatha cannot break his word, though seeing Rama dutifully carry out his father's command causes the king to die of a broken heart.

Rama accepts his exile without protest and is accompanied by his faithful brother Lakshmana and faultless wife Sita into the forest. They spend many blissful years in the forest until one day the demoness Surpanakha, sister to Ravana, attempts to seduce Rama. When she fails, she tries to attack Sita, but Lakshmana steps in and cuts off her nose and ears. Surpanakha runs to Ravana and, to avenge herself, incites his lust by describing Sita's beauty. Ravana kidnaps Sita and carries her off to his demon stronghold on the island of Lanka.

Rama and Lakshmana with their army of monkeys and bears are camped outside the palace of the demon king Ravana on the isle of Lanka, while the demons try to rouse Kumbhakarna, the giant brother of Ravana. India, Mughal period, c. 1595–1605.

A despairing Rama and Lakshmana wander in search of Sita. They eventually meet Hanuman, the trusty messenger of Sugriva, the recently deposed King of the Vanaras (a sophisticated race of magical monkeys). An alliance is quickly formed and Rama helps reinstate Sugriva on the throne of the Vanaras. After also gaining the support of the Bear-king Jambavan, platoons of monkeys and bears are sent out to the north, south, east, and west to search for Sita. The southern contingent, led by Hanuman, travels to the sea, from the shore of which Hanuman makes a wondrous leap across to Lanka to continue his search alone among the palaces and pleasure groves within the demon city. At the citadel of Ravana Hanuman sees Sita held prisoner in a garden. He tells her to not lose hope, promising that Rama will soon come to free her.

Upon Hanuman's return, Rama and his army march to Lanka, and a fierce battle ensues. At last Ravana's heart is pierced by Rama's arrow and the demon king is slain. Rama and Sita are reunited, but after spending a year in another man's house Sita must publicly prove her chastity through a trial by fire. With the fire-god Agni as her witness she passes through the flames and into Rama's embrace. Their exile concluded, Rama, Sita, and Lakshmana return to Ayodhya, where Bharata eagerly returns the kingdom and Rama is reinstated as Ayodhya's king. All are happy for a time, but later, because of rumors circulating about Sita spending so much time in another man's house, Rama is compelled to abandon Sita in the forest. He doesn't know she is pregnant with their two sons, who are raised by the hermit Valmiki. Valmiki, who has seen all that has come to pass while meditating, composes the *Ramayana* and teaches it to the two boys, who eventually sing it before their father. Rama dies shortly thereafter, sadly pining for Sita.

For many Hindus, the characters in the *Ramayana* serve as exemplary social role models. Sita is the faithful wife, Rama is the ideal man and perfect king, Lakshmana is the best of brothers, and Hanuman is the selfless devotee. Ultimately, the *Ramayana* is a story about loss and separation, and Rama can be seen as a tragic hero who feels the despair of losing the love of his life—whom he had fought so hard to rescue. The text grapples with the question of *dharma*, both in the public, political realm as well as in the private, familial realm. It constantly sets up difficult situations that force the characters to reflect on their individual duties and obligations. Yet, the characters of the *Ramayana* are also understood to be divine: Rama is after all the *avatara* of Vishnu. Thus, the *Ramayana* is as much a text that imparts religious and ethical knowledge as one that reiterates Hindu beliefs about the accessibility and immanence of God.

Mahabharata The other great Hindu epic, the *Mahabharata*, the longest work of epic poetry in the world, is composed of over 100,000 verses. Like the *Ramayana*, this work is deeply concerned with issues of *dharma*.

The main storyline of the *Mahabharata* concerns a dynastic conflict between two groups of royal cousins. These are the *Pandavas* (the five sons of King Pandu), the heroes of the epic who are all sired by gods, and their antagonists, the *Kauravas* (the hundred sons of the blind king, Dhritarashtra). Their dispute ultimately results in a terrible war so immense that it marks the end of an epoch for humanity.

On the eve of the great battle, the two vast armies are arrayed on each side of the battlefield. It is at this moment that Arjuna, the greatest of the Pandava warriors, experiences crippling doubt. Arjuna asks Krishna, an *avatara* of Vishnu who is acting as his charioteer, to pull the chariot out into the middle of the field so that he can survey it. He sees on both sides his friends, relatives, and loved ones clamoring for war, and he is loath to incur the sin of helping to hasten them toward it. Overcome with sorrow, his bow slips from his hands and he refuses to fight. It is at this key point in the story that the profound philosophical discourse known as the *Bhagavad Gita* ("Song of God") begins. Many Hindus regard this conversation between Krishna and his devotee Arjuna as the most significant philosophical work in Hinduism. It is such an important text that it is studied and recited independent of the larger epic.

Mischievously, Krishna steals the clothes of *gopis* or cowherd maidens who love him. He makes them emerge naked from their bath as a metaphor for how the soul must approach God.

The *Bhagavad Gita* (The Song of God) The *Bhagavad Gita*, the conversation between Krishna and Arjuna, was probably composed around the first century C.E.. The text seeks to reconcile the tension between renunciation and worldly life, and also presents radical new ideas about the pursuit of *moksha*. This pioneering text has achieved such influential status in part because of the deft manner in which it synthesizes multiple strands of philosophical enquiry.

The *Gita* begins with Arjuna refusing to act as his *dharma* as a warrior demands, out of fear of the consequences of killing his kinsmen. Krishna responds to his dilemma by revealing that one does not need to give up action to achieve *moksha*. Rather, one gives up the *fruit* of action. That is, one cultivates "desireless action," or acting without attachment to the fruit or benefit of the action. The *Gita* offers three yogas or disciplines to achieve desireless action: the path of action, the path of knowledge, and the path of devotion. It is in offering this final path of devotion, or **bhakti**, that the *Gita* charts new ground. Through *bhakti*, one surrenders the fruit of action to Krishna (God) as a sacrifice. By offering up the fruits of all action (or even the expectation of a specific result) to Krishna, one is no longer weighed down by the effects of the fruit of action.

The *Gita* amplifies the concept of *bhakti* (devotion), which to a large extent comes to dominate Hindu practice and belief. The *Gita* suggests that the path of *bhakti* is available to anyone, regardless of caste or gender, as all it requires is a singular devotion to Krishna. *Bhakti* allows people to live in this world, adhering to their *dharma*, and offers an alternate course to *moksha*. In other words, the *Gita* teaches that it is possible to achieve *moksha* by being active in the world, provided that one acts without the intention of reaping the fruits of action. Other philosophical systems had advocated the control of the senses and the cultivation of detachment as means for escaping *samsara*. In addition to teaching these ideas, the *Gita* advocates total surrender and selfless devotion to God as effective means of liberation from the cycle of birth, death, and rebirth.

The concept of *bhakti* influences the development of the theistic Hindu traditions. *Bhakti* is intimately connected to the rise of Hinduism's various sectarian affiliations and the growth of temple cultures. Put simply, *bhakti* means "devotion," but it is a subtle term. The word derives from the Sanskrit root *bhaj*, which means (among other things) "to serve, honor, love, adore, to share with, partake of, and to enjoy (also carnally)."

Bhakti advocates a deep, abiding love for God and encourages the devotee to cultivate an intimate and personal relationship with the divine. In some forms of *bhakti*, God is imagined as a friend, a confidante, a lover, a child, or as a master. The devotee may also choose a favored, personal deity, toward whom all the devotee's devotion is directed. The concept of the personal deity can be linked to the development of the many sectarian orientations in Hinduism. In this type of *bhakti*, God is worshiped through a celebration of his or her attributes. Devotion may also be directed to the abstract, transcendent, and attributeless form of God. Adherents to this subschool of *bhakti* assert God's unknowable yet accessible qualities. A poem by the South Indian female poet Mahadeviyakka (fl. 1130 C.E.) expresses the idea beautifully:

> People,
> male and female,
> blush when a cloth covering their shame
> comes loose.
>> When the lord of lives
> lives drowned without a face
> in the world, how can you be modest?
>
> When all the world is the eye of the lord,
> onlooking everywhere, what can you
> cover and conceal?[5]

For many Hindus, *bhakti* is both a belief and a practice. That is, they believe *bhakti* is the easiest and most effective way out of *samsara* and they cultivate *bhakti* through ecstatic singing and dancing, storytelling, and temple worship. As we have seen, *bhakti* is usually directed toward a favored deity, who is perceived as the supreme entity. With this understanding of *bhakti*, let us now turn our attention to Hinduism's main sects.

The Sects of Hinduism

From the time of the great Gupta empire (320–550 C.E.) in India there have been three primary sects in Hinduism. Each sect venerates one of the major deities that are at the center of Hindu cosmology. The development of the main sects of Hinduism was influenced by *bhakti*, an ideology articulated at length for the first time in the *Bhagavad Gita*.

The three main sectarian groups of Hinduism are **Vaishnavas** (devotees of Vishnu and his *avataras*), **Shaivas** (devotees of Shiva), and **Shaktas** (devotees of the Great Goddess, Devi). Beneath the umbrella of these three orientations are numerous individual subsectarian orders that differ in the sacred texts and saints they revere, their modes of worship, and their philosophical orientation.

A contemporary painting of the inner sanctum of the famous temple at Sri Rangam. Sri Ranganatha ("Lord of the Stage") is a cosmic form of Vishnu lying on the serpent, Ananta ("Infinity"), as he floats on the Cosmic Sea of Milk. This signifies the place of primordial essence from whence he emanates all of the universe.

Vaishnavism *Vaishnavas* worship Vishnu and his consort Lakshmi as supreme. Vishnu is a worldly deity, continuously intervening in the world through his *avataras* and inseparable from his beloved Lakshmi. He resides in the highest heaven in his cosmic and unknowable form. For *Vaishnavas*, Vishnu is the beginning and end of the world, its cause and its meaning. These ideas about Vishnu's fundamental nature are expressed in myths and poems that invoke him as the lord who measured the universe in a primordial act of creation.

Hindus worship Vishnu in a number of different forms. He is often depicted reclining with Lakshmi on a thousand-headed serpent that floats on the cosmic ocean. From his navel rises a lotus, upon which Brahma the Creator God is seated. Visually, this image asserts that the world is born from Vishnu and he is its sole originator and sustainer.

Vishnu can be identified by the objects he holds in his four hands. In his upper right hand, he holds a flaming discus (the sun), while his upper left hand bears a white conch shell. In his lower right hand he holds a mace, and in his lower left hand he holds a lotus. Many *Vaishnavas* also worship Vishnu's *avataras*, Rama and Krishna.

Shaivism Shiva is a more abstract deity who reconciles the tension between renunciation and involvement in the world. Often called the erotic ascetic, he embodies both the ideal of ascetic renunciation as well as a worldly, full-bodied sensuality. One of the most famous myths about Shiva tells of his seduction of the chaste wives of hermit sages as he wandered the world as a naked beggar.

Shiva is usually depicted sitting in deep meditation on Mount Kailasha in the high Himalayas. He is clad in ashes with a tiger skin wrapped about his waist and with serpents for jewelry. His third eye is turned inward and his matted locks are adorned by the crescent moon and the holy river Ganges. He is often accompanied by his beautiful consort, Parvati, whom *Shaivas* understand to represent the latent creative potential of the universe. Another symbol of Shiva is the *linga*, an abstract phallic symbol meant to denote the latent potentiality of his consciousness that is the axis of all existence.

Most *Shaivas* worship Shiva as a god with no beginning or end. But Shiva is also a family man, to be venerated with his divine queen Parvati and their two sons, Ganesha and Skanda, as princely deities.

Shaktism One of the most striking features of Hinduism is its exuberant worship of the Goddess in her many forms. While in the *Vaishnava* and *Shaiva* traditions the

Goddess is subordinated (to the great gods Vishnu and Shiva), the cults of the Great Goddess venerate her as the supreme cause and end of the universe. Although she has many names and many forms, the Great Goddess is most often referred to as Devi, Mahadevi, or Shakti. Devotees of the Goddess are referred to as *Shaktas.*

The primacy of Devi is definitively asserted in a fifth-century C.E. Sanskrit text called the *Devi Mahatmya* (*The Greatness of Devi*). It posits for the first time in textual form that the supreme cause of the universe is feminine. The *Devi Mahatmya* is the most significant text for Devi's devotees, who memorize and recite it even today.

The *Devi Mahatmya* argues for Devi's greatness through three main myths, the most important of which tells how she killed the buffalo-headed demon, Mahishasura. Mahishasura, who had been promised that he could not be killed by a man, was rampaging on the earth. The gods, unable to stop Mahishasura, despaired, but suddenly from within their bodies their latent energies emerged and coalesced into the form of a beautiful woman. This was Devi.

The fierce goddess downed a cup of wine and prepared for battle, arming herself with a trident and a discus. She gave Mahishasura a mighty kick, trampled him underfoot, and pierced him through his breast with her trident. When his humanoid form emerged from his buffalo body, she hacked off his head with her discus. As the gods sang Devi's praise, she simply vanished, much to their astonishment and wonder.

Mahishasura had assumed that femininity was synonymous with meekness, but to *Shaktas* the goddess is all-powerful and pervades the entire universe. She is the one who creates, preserves, and destroys the universe in harmony with the rhythms of cosmic time. The *Devi Mahatmya* teaches that the goddess is eternal and that she manifests herself over and over again in order to protect the universe as a mother would her child.

Shaivas and *Shaktas* tend to share a common mythological universe, as Shiva and Devi are said to be married. So, the difference between Shaivism and Shaktism is a matter of emphasis regarding the importance of each of these two primal gendered forces. For *Shaivas*, Shiva is pure consciousness that pervades all existence, and Devi is his creative, albeit subordinate, power. On the other hand, *Shaktas* believe Shiva is entirely passive. It is Shakti (the creative energy, the Great Goddess) that constitutes and governs the whole immensity of existence. Thus, the *Shaktas* say that "Shiva without Shakti is *shava*" (Sanskrit, "a corpse"). This idea is iconographically represented in the form of the goddess dancing upon the inert body of Shiva.

Accompanied by a legion of other goddesses and fierce dwarves (*ganas*), the goddess Durga, mounted on her lion, protects the world by battling the buffalo demon Mahishasura. (The buffalo is associated with Yama, the God of Death.) Pallava period, seventh century, Mahishasura Mardini Cave, Mamallapuram Tamilnadu, India.

A modern painting of the goddess Kali, a manifestation of feminine power, dancing on the body of Shiva from the Indian state of Orissa.

Her foot rests on his heart and he is drunk with bliss, enraptured by her performance.

HINDUISM AS A WAY OF LIFE

Hindus often insist that Hinduism is more a "way of life" than a system of beliefs. It is for this reason that many scholars have argued that Hinduism is a religion that values orthopraxy (i.e., correct action) over orthodoxy, or correct belief. In other words, Hinduism in all its many guises places a greater emphasis on what one *does* rather than what one *believes*. This might account not only for the range of Hindu beliefs but also for Hinduism's ability to accommodate apparently opposing positions within a single belief system. The stress on *doing* rather than *believing* might also explain the disconnect between textual injunction and actual practice that one often encounters in Hinduism. Hindu texts provide many prescriptions for how to live (e.g., the aims of life or the *ashrama* system), but these do not always translate into actual lived practice. In this section we will explore Hinduismas a way of life.

Seeing the Divine Image: Temples and Icons

Hinduism nurtures a sensory religious experience in its adherents. This experiential aspect is nowhere more clearly visible than when a Hindu goes to a temple. As religion scholar Diana Eck observes, the devotee doesn't say, "I am going for worship." Rather, the devotee asserts, "I am going for *darshan*." What constitutes *darshan*? The Sanksrit word means "to see," but in the Hindu context it specifically refers to the interlocking gaze shared by the deity and the devotee. That is, *darshan* is the intimate act of both seeing the deity and being looked upon by the divine, an act in which there is a loving relationship between devotee and God.[6]

As we learned earlier in this chapter, the image of a god in a temple or a personal shrine at home is not just a representation; it is imbued with a divine presence. Thus, for a devotee to catch sight of the image in the innermost sanctum of a temple is to have a glimpse of the divine body. In turn, the deity's powerful gaze is believed to confer grace on every person who comes into its presence. In many ways, the act of *darshan* is perhaps the most meaningful experience in theistic Hinduism.

Most Hindus go to a local temple or on pilgrimage to a sacred site for *darshan*. It is an act of worship framed by the ethos of *bhakti*. For this reason, the temple is a central religious and cultural institution in Hindu religious practice. Temple building and the veneration of images probably developed under the patronage of the Gupta empire until the two became inextricably linked to the rest of Hindu practice.

Temples generally house two different kinds of icons. The first type is the main image (or images), which resides at the center of the temple in a room called the *garbha griha* (Sanskrit, "womb-chamber"). Referred to as the *mula vigraha* (Sanskrit, "first/primordial, causal form"), it is generally made of stone and is permanently fixed in the shrine. This image is never moved, and Hindus conceive of it as the axial center of the cosmos. The second type of icon, found in most temples, are processional images, which are typically cast from an amalgam of five metals. These processional icons are smaller and mobile, and they are brought out on temple palanquins and chariots for temple festivals. They are usually adorned in fabulous costumes and jewels, and Hindus gather for a vision (*darshan*) of the divine form they embody. Although both types of icons are made by human hands and are constituted of earthly substances, once the icon is in worship it is understood to be permeated with a kind of divine super-matter. It is no longer *just* stone or metal, but the very body of God.

Clouds of incense smoke billow upward from a blazing terracotta censer as devotees pray solemnly before a multi-armed clay icon of Durga (upper center), Ganesha (lower left), and other divine attendants. This is the final opportunity for *darshan* as the icon is about to be dissolved by immersion into the Ganges River at the conclusion of the festival of Durga Puja. Kolkata, India.

All Hindu temples function as a stylized representation of the mythical Mount Meru that stands at the center of the world. Many temples are also built on a design that represents the Cosmic Man (*Purusha*) whose divine body was divided up to fashion all the components of the universe. This creation myth is hidden in the architecture of the temple.

As temples probably developed during the Gupta empire as a way of connecting earthly kings to the gods, many of the courtly rites associated with the veneration of the king were adapted to the worship of the deities. In temple rites, the deities are treated as a royal guest. Temple services usually involve 16 different offerings. Of these, the most significant is the eighth offering, a ritual that involves pouring various types of auspicious substances over the icon. These might include scented water, milk, and sandalwood paste. After the ritual, the deity is adorned in beautiful ornaments, textiles, and flowers. The elaborate temple rituals climax with the ***arati***, a waving of lamps before the image. For Hindus, this is the ideal moment for *darshan*.

Such ritual activity, both in temples and in homes, confirms that for Hindus the icon is a fully divine presence. However, icons not only function as vessels that embody the divine but are also sources of complex symbolism for the worshiper to contemplate. They can even directly convey doctrine. For instance, Nataraja, "The Lord of the Dance," is one of the most beautiful forms of Shiva. In this form he physically embodies the unending cycle of creation as destruction, representing what *Shaivas* call

The majestic towering gate of a South Indian Shiva temple is reflected in one of the two ritual bathing tanks found within its precincts. These towers are erected in the four directions and are often covered in sculptural imagery that refers to the sacred myths of the god(s) venerated within. Arunachaleswar Temple, Tiruvannamalai, India, eleventh century.

"The Five Activities" of Shiva: creation, preservation, destruction, obscuration, and liberation.

Forms of Worship

The Sanskrit word *puja* is most commonly used to describe worship in Hinduism. In its most simple form, *puja* involves making some offering to the deity (such as fruit, incense, or flowers). The deity is then believed to partake of the devotion inherent in the offering. The material aspect of the offerings left behind is now infused with the deity's blessing.

Puja can be simple or elaborate. It can be offered almost anywhere—before a home shrine, at a temple, at pilgrimage sites, by sacred trees or rivers, at roadside shrines, or within temporary structures specially made for a specific rite. Rituals may be carried out as an expression of love for the deity, as a rite of passage, to celebrate a holiday or festival, to ask for blessings, to create an atmosphere of peace and harmony, or to propitiate the gods in times of trouble. Ritual occasions are ideal for maintaining and strengthening community ties, as we learned at the beginning of the chapter with the construction and consecration of the Sri Ganesha Hindu Temple of Utah.

While Hinduism is particularly difficult to define in terms of theology or doctrine, ritual and practice have more continuity. Some might argue that the story of Hinduism is primarily a long and ongoing contemplation of the nature of ritual action and sacrifice. Let's explore Hinduism's most common modes of ritual worship.

Arati Arati, or "worship with light," is perhaps the most common form of Hindu worship. A lamp fueled with *ghee* (clarified butter) or camphor is lit and waved in a clockwise direction in front of the deity. The five flames used in *arati* symbolize the five elements (earth, water, fire, air, and aether) as well as the totality of the universe. This waving of the lamp is thought to remove evil influences and to return the object or recipient of the offering to an auspicious state, regardless of any negative thoughts or desires that might have been projected onto it.

Mantra Nearly all rituals in Hinduism are accompanied by the recitation of **mantras**. These are ritual formulas used to produce a spiritual effect. They can be used for a variety of reasons: to aid in the efficacy of an offering, for protection, to invoke auspiciousness and harmony, to produce a magical effect, to focus the mind, to induce trance, or to alter one's state of consciousness. *Mantras* are usually—but not always—in the Sanskrit language.

Mantras sometimes encapsulate an entire worldview. The most important *mantra* for *Vaishnavas* is *"Om Namo Narayanaya"* ("obeisance to Narayana;" Narayana is another name for Vishnu). For *Vaishnavas*, this *mantra* articulates the relationship between God and devotee while also asserting the fullness and unity of Vishnu. Reciting and contemplating the *mantra* is thus an act of devotion that brings the devotee closer to Vishnu. But not all *mantras* have a literal meaning. Some semantically empty mantras are regarded as the most powerful. These *mantras* are called *bija*, or "seed." A *bija* like "HUM" is thought to have a consistent magical effect, while one like "GLAUM" invokes and embodies Ganesha. *Mantras* are a key ingredient in the practice of Hinduism, whether one is exploring formal ritual practice or ascetic traditions of contemplation.

Sacrifice   Even from its earliest period, fire sacrifice was an essential component of Hinduism. A sacrifice usually involves building an altar, kindling a fire, feeding it with ghee (clarified butter), and casting various offerings into the fire to the accompaniment of *mantras*. Although fire sacrifice is usually performed by a *brahmin* priest, these rites can be performed by any married upper-caste man. A fire sacrifice is a crucial component of all important life-cycle and temple rituals.

In the Vedic period, sacrifice was seen as essential to maintaining cosmic order. This is why one of the most important Vedic myths describes the universe as being born from the sacrifice of the cosmic man. However, the later *Upanishads* rejected sacrifice as an effective means out of *samsara*. These texts argued that the true sacrifice takes place internally, with the breath itself fueling the sacrificial fire that awakens one to knowledge. The *Bhagavad Gita* also addresses sacrifice, but says that it is the surrender of the fruit of action (through *bhakti*) that is the true meaning and purpose of sacrifice.

In the earliest period, the sacrifice of animals was an important aspect of Hindu ritual. However, over time (and particularly under the influence of Jainism and Buddhism), animal sacrifice ceased to play a role in upper-caste sacrificial rituals. In these sacrifices, coconuts and pumpkins came to act as substitutes for the animal. Nonetheless, animal sacrifice continues to play a significant role in folk Hinduism and is offered to village deities and fierce forms of the Goddess, such as Kali. In animal sacrifice the ritual consecrates the meat but does not mitigate the *karmic* repercussion of the act of killing. Though some Hindus are vegetarian and are committed to non-violence, it continues to be an important ritual for many Hindus.

Yoga Traditions and Asceticism

The origins of **yoga** are obscure, although we can say with certainty that by the time of the *Upanishads* (900–600 B.C.E.) yoga had become an integral part of early Hinduism. Yoga is much more than just a system of physical exercise that promotes flexibility and good circulation. The physical postures of *hatha* (Sanskrit, "forceful") yoga are just one small facet of a comprehensive system of practices

Ringed by cosmic time represented by a fiery ring of flashing moments arising and passing away, Shiva as Lord of Dance (Nataraja) enacts his Five Activities: creation (represented by the drum in his upper right hand), preservation (his two lower right hands in the gesture of protection and lower left in the grasping elephant trunk or *gajahasta* gesture that points toward his upraised foot), dissolution (the fire in his upraised left hand), obscuration (personified by the tiny Demon of Forgetfulness being crushed beneath his right leg), and liberation (offered by surrendering to his upraised left foot). Chola period, c. eleventh century. India, Tamil Nadu.

geared to purifying mind and body and expanding consciousness to a point where one can fully apprehend ultimate reality.

Yoga, which means "union," is derived from the Sanskrit root *yuj* ("to yoke" or "to join"). Yoga is thus understood by many practitioners as a means to transcend the individual consciousness and to unite with the absolute. Perhaps the most practical definition of yoga is found in the sage Patanjali's *Yoga Sutras* (400–500 C.E.), an early, authoritative text on yoga. It declares: "Yoga is the cessation of the oscillations of the mind,"[7] emphasizing that yoga is primarily a return to one's natural state of consciousness.

The practice of yoga is central to the development of Hinduism. *Upanisadic* philosophers and even the heroes of the *Ramayana* and *Mahabharata* perform yogic austerities. Even daily *pujas* employ yogic techniques such as breath control as a purification before worship. Meditation, an integral part of any yogic practice, is also a basic fixture in formal rites of worship. The *Bhagavad Gita* itself gives detailed instructions on the practice of meditation. Indeed, the whole teaching of this essential Hindu scripture is ultimately organized around presenting the various forms of yoga as paths leading to *moksha* or enlightenment.

The *Gita* makes it abundantly clear that one's **sadhana** ("spiritual discipline or practice") need not be based solely on the performance of meditation and austerities but might also take the form of contemplative inquiry (the yoga of knowledge), simple ways of expressing one's love for God (the yoga of devotion), or even working to further the spiritual or physical well-being of others (the yoga of action). Each of these yogas is an effective means to enlightenment and the *Gita* suggests that anyone can find a path to freedom through a yoga that suits one's own nature.

Another form of asceticism is *vratas*, temporary vows of self-denial that are usually undertaken by women and often involve a short period of fasting. But a *vrata* can also be a vow of silence or a renunciation for a certain length of time of anything to which one is attached. A woman usually undertakes *vratas* for a specific purpose, such as to ensure the health and well-being of her husband and family. There are many special *vratas* observed at specific times throughout the calendar year. One of the most popular *vratas*, which is observed by married women all over South India, always falls on a Friday in early August. This *vrata* involves a period of purification and fasting after which the woman invites the goddess Lakshmi into her home. At the conclusion of a special *puja* the woman's husband ties a yellow thread with nine knots on his wife's right wrist for protection. The nine knots correspond to the nine strands of the sacred thread worn by twice-born men.

Rites of Passage

Hindu rites of passage are called **samskaras** (Sanskrit, "put together" or "constructed"). These rituals are intended to invoke blessings and divine favor and to put the individual in harmony with the universe during important times of transition. In addition, they help socialize individuals, assisting their shift into new roles that life asks them to assume.

While *brahmins* observe several *samskaras*, particularly in early childhood, there are a number of rites of passage common to most Hindus. These are:

Blessing a pregnancy The "parting of the hair" rite blesses a newly expectant mother.

Naming a child The naming ceremony of a child is observed on the tenth or twelfth day after birth.

Weaning a child The first feeding of solid food to a child celebrates the process of weaning.

A child's first haircut The tonsure ceremony marks the child's first haircut, which can be performed anytime between the first and third year.

A child's ear-piercing The ear-piercing ceremony is performed for both boys and girls between five months and five years.

A boy's initiation The sacred thread ceremony is an initiatory rite for any male *brahmin, kshatriya,* or *vaishya.* However, today it is mostly performed for *brahmin* boys around the age of eight. Beginning with a fire sacrifice, the culmination of the rite transforms the initiate into a *dvija* or "twice born." The initiate is given a sacred thread that symbolizes a kind of umbilical cord linking the boy to the sun, the source of all light and knowledge. The sacred thread lies across the chest, resting over the left shoulder and under the right arm. It consists of three strands of cotton that are knotted together at one place. As part of the rite, boys learn the *Gayatri mantra.* Three times a day—at dawn, midday, and dusk—*brahmins* and other initiated "twice-born" hold the knot of their sacred thread and recite the *Gayatri mantra* twenty-one times:

> *Om bhur bhuvah svah tat savitur varenyam bhargo devasya dhimahi*
> *dhiyo yonah prachodayat!* ("Let us meditate upon that longed-for divine
> splendor of [the sun-god] Savitur, which when contemplated propels
> us onward!")

Today, the sacred thread is the most visible sign of caste status. It is worn throughout one's life and is discarded only if a man renounces the world. In pre-Gupta times girls could also be invested with the sacred thread if they pursued study of the *Vedas.*

A girl's first period If the *upanayana* functions as a coming of age ritual for boys, the rituals used to celebrate a girl's first menstruation have a similar function in a girl's life, regardless of caste. These rites are not formally laid out in sacred texts and have great regional variations. Sometimes these observances include spending the first three days of their first period secluded in a dimly lit room (although friends can visit). She takes a ritual bath on the fourth day, and a feast is held in her honor. This transition is a very public affair because it announces her availability for marriage. Often the girl is taken to the local temple to receive a special blessing from an older married woman in her community, who will perform an *arati* ceremony to honor her new potential to bear children. Her life radically changes afterward and, for many communities, her freedom to have unsupervised interaction with boys may be greatly curtailed.

Marriage   For many Hindus marriage is considered the most important *samskara*. It is through marriage that one enters the householder *ashrama* that provides the main support for society as a whole. Marriage was traditionally arranged by the parents between a bride or groom of the same *jati* after consulting an astrologer, who determined the couple's compatibility. In the last few decades caste strictures have eased somewhat, allowing for marriages based more on social class (compatibility of education, occupation, or income, for example). As a result, marriages for love have become more commonplace.

The marriage ceremony is sanctified through a fire sacrifice, in which the gods are invoked for blessings and offerings are poured into the fire. A thread is tied around the bride's wrist and she is asked to step three times on a grinding stone from the groom's family as a demonstration of her fidelity to the new household she is joining. At the high point of the rite, the bride and groom walk together around the sacred fire seven times. The bride's family then provides a sumptuous meal for everyone in attendance, and the festivities often culminate in the evening with the bride and groom looking up at the sky and the bride vowing to be as constant as the North Star. After the last day of celebration the bride goes to the home of her husband and begins her new life.

Death   The funerary ritual, as the final *samskara*, is known as "the last sacrifice." Cremation is the principal means of funerary practice, and the cremation fire is often likened to a fire sacrifice. Earth burial is practiced for babies and among some low caste communities. Holy men and ascetics are also buried. Their bodies are placed in a special tomb called a *samadhi*, around which shrines are sometimes erected and worship performed. But for ordinary men and women, their final sacrifice is to offer up their own bodies into the fire of cremation.

Generally, cremation takes place on the same day as the death. The body is washed, smeared with sandalwood paste, wrapped in a cloth and then carried on a litter by male relatives, who chant a holy name or phrase as they bear the body to the cremation ground. The body is placed on the pyre with the head pointing to the north (the realm of Kubera, Lord of Wealth) and the feet to the south (the realm of Yama, Lord of Death). It is usually the duty of the eldest son of the deceased to conduct the last rites and light the pyre. An ancient practice that is still often observed involves releasing the soul from the body by cracking the skull of the deceased, a daunting task for a son to perform.

Following the funeral, the family and home are considered to be in a heightened state of pollution and the bereaved are expected to keep to themselves until the rites of ancestral offerings are completed. For ten days after the funeral, the deceased is offered balls of rice with which they are believed to be able to construct a body in the spirit world or intermediate realm. This rite, which reflects the gestation of a human embryo for ten lunar months, may very well predate the formulation of a belief in reincarnation that was developed by the time of the *Upanishads*.

Pilgrimage

In Hinduism, pilgrimage sites are called *tirthas* (Sanskrit, "fords" or "crossing points"). Worship, ritual offerings, and the performance of austerities at these sacred places allow worshipers to more easily "cross over" the ocean of *samsara* because these sacred sites are held to be contiguous with the divine world. Many of the earliest pilgrimage sites were located at sacred rivers and pools, and pilgrimage specifically involved ritual bathing as a means of purification. Pilgrimage sites are also places where one may obtain *darshan*. Some revered sites, marked by a shrine or temple, commemorate a sacred event or the life of a holy person. For pilgrims, these sites allow immediate, tangible access to the sacred.

One of the most important Hindu pilgrimage sites is the sacred city of Varanasi, on the banks of the Ganges. Many Hindus believe that to die in Varanasi is to be immediately released from *samsara*. For this reason, many old and sick people travel to Varanasi to die. However, since the Ganges is held to be the most sacred river in India,

Hindu pilgrimage routes in India.

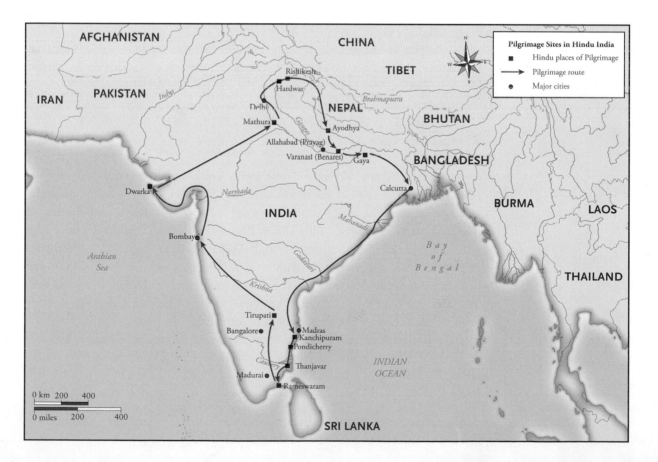

people who are unable to make it to Varanasi to die arrange to have their ashes scattered in the river. In this way, the sacred river is believed to carry the dead from this life into the divine realm.

The largest pilgrimage in India is to the sacred city of Prayag (Allahabad), where the Ganges and Yamuna, as well as a third, mythic river, the Sarasvati, come together. To bathe at the confluence of these three rivers is considered especially auspicious. Every twelve years, the *Kumbha Mela* festival takes place at Prayag. During the *Kumbha Mela*, hundreds of thousands of pilgrims converge to take a dip in the holy waters in the hope that all their transgressions will be washed away.

There are many important pilgrimage sites in India. Some are dedicated to the goddess Devi and are referred to as *Shakti Peethas* ("Seats of Power"). Still others, like the city of Vrindavan in North India, attract Krishna devotees who believe that it is not only the site of the god's birth and childhood, but the place where he continues to live.

Festivals and Holidays

Hindus employ both solar and lunar calendars, as well as a calendar based on twenty-seven different constellations. All three calendars are consulted to determine when festivals and holidays will be observed. Many Hindu festivals link mythic events to the agricultural cycle.

In addition to the festivals described earlier, temples celebrate annual festivals. Very often these festivals are a means to increase the revenue of a temple, as pilgrims from neighboring towns and villages visit the site for the special occasion. There are also countless regional holidays and observances.

Let's take a closer look at three Hindu festivals that are celebrated with great pomp and with many regional variations.

Navaratri or *Dashera* *Navaratri* ("nine nights") or *Dashera* ("ten days") is a holiday cycle celebrating the end of the monsoon season in India. In some regions of India, *Dashera* celebrates the conclusion of the great war between Rama and Ravana. In other regions, such as South India and in Bengal, the festival celebrates Devi's great battle and eventual victory against the buffalo-demon, Mahishasura. To commemorate this conquest, altars are set up with images of the Goddess. For the first three days of the festival, devotees worship Devi in her manifestation as Durga. From the third to the sixth day, they worship her as Lakshmi. On the concluding three days, she is worshiped as Sarasvati, the embodiment of knowledge. In Bengal, the eighth day is especially important as it celebrates Durga slaying Mahishasura and is marked with the sacrifice either of black goats or a substitute sacrifice of pumpkins. The festival culminates with street processions of large painted clay icons of Durga that are later dissolved in the nearby river or the sea. Everywhere the "victorious tenth day," *Vijaya Dashami*, is celebrated as it commemorates Rama's slaying of the demon Ravana.

Diwali *Diwali*, the grand five-day "Festival of Lights" is celebrated in October. For many Hindus, it commemorates Rama's rescue of Sita and heroic return to Ayodhya, although several other myths are invoked as an explanation for the festival in different regions of India. Many twinkling oil lamps are set out on doorsteps and window ledges and floating lamps are placed as offerings in rivers and reservoirs to signify the triumph of good over evil. Fireworks are lit on the night of the new moon, when Lakshmi is worshiped. The third day of *Diwali* marks the end of the harvest season, and *Lakshmi Puja* is performed to thank the goddess for the abundance that she has given. New clothes are worn and gifts are exchanged. *Diwali* is also celebrated by Sikhs and Jains.

Holi *Holi*, a spring festival, is Hinduism's most colorful holiday. Celebrated in either February or March, festivities commence the night before with the lighting of bonfires and the sacrificial breaking of coconuts. The next day a kind of carnival celebration commences as social and gender hierarchies are temporarily inverted and crowds of young and old alike frolic in the streets, mischievously spraying colored water and staining one another with brightly festive powdered pigments.

This festival reenacts the story of the demoness Holika, who devoured a small child every day. On the day that a poor widow's son was to be sacrificed to appease the demoness, a wise holy man intervened, and asked all the children to gather together and fearlessly confront their attacker with insults. Under the assault, the demoness Holika died of her own rage and shame. To commemorate this event, on the eve of the main festival day, people build a giant effigy of Holika and burn it in an enormous bonfire.

Fun and frolic characterize the spring festival of Holi as participants mischievously smear colored powders upon one another or spray each other with colored water.

Performance Traditions

There are a multitude of performance traditions in Hinduism, many of which cross over into the realm of ritual. Even the act of publicly reciting the *Ramayana* in Hinduism is understood as invoking deity and thus transforms the performance site into sacred space. Hindu sacred performance traditions include almost every genre one could imagine: theatre, puppetry, dance, music, storytelling, processions, and street festivals.

Ram Lila The *Ram Lila* (*The Play of Rama*) is one of Hinduism's most well-known and popular performance traditions. During the month of September, North Indian villages and cities alike host *Ram Lila* festivals to coincide with the ten days of the festival of *Dashera*. These festivals, lasting anywhere from ten days to a month, are elaborate costume-dramas based on the *Ramayana*. The most famous and elaborate *Ram Lila* is sponsored by the Maharaja (the hereditary ruler) of Ramnagar, a city located across the Ganges from Varanasi. The Ramnagar *Ram Lila* attracts pilgrims from all over Northern India who come not only to participate in this annual festival but also to have *darshan* of Rama. The roles of Rama, Lakshmana, and Sita (the three principal characters of the *Ramayana*) are played by young upper-caste boys. For the duration of the *Ram Lila*, these boys are worshiped as the embodiments of divinity. Every evening, a priest waves a lamp, illuminating the principal characters, who give *darshan* to the assembled pilgrims and devotees. Just as in a temple, where God is actively present in the icon, here too the very act of performing the *Ramayana* enables the young boys to embody divinity.

Sacred Songs: *Kirtan* and *Bhajan*   The term *bhajan* (Sanskrit, "worship" or "adoration") refers specifically to devotional songs in Hinduism and Sikhism. Such songs are usually composed in accordance with North Indian classical music that utilizes simple melodies and rhythms. The *bhajan* helps the gathered community to contemplate the nature and character of the divine. This is usually achieved through repetition of key phrases and lines, and also through a call-and-response format of singing. Often profound mystical concepts are presented in simple language that everyone may fully enjoy.

Bhajan may be contrasted to *kirtan*, which is neither formal in form or structure nor constrained by setting. *Kirtan* may be performed in lively sing-along processionals that roam the streets. Instruments are not necessary for *kirtan* performance, although they are often used. There are two different types of *kirtan* performances: in one type, the *kirtan* leader and the chorus alternate singing the divine name; and in the other, a hymn is communally recited, usually with an opening invocation and then the body of the composition that describes the pastimes of the deity. For Hindu devotees, *kirtan* is a key spiritual practice, and it continues to be popular today particularly in *Vaishnava* sectarian contexts.

Storytelling   The primary way in which a vast majority of Hindus encounter their religion is through storytelling. This goes beyond the bedtime stories families share with their children, although such tales are also vitally important means of transmission. Even today, as in centuries past, professional storytellers continue to travel particular routes throughout India to visit local festivals, where they sing the epics and other myths in a series of all-night performances.

Modern Hindus enjoy sacred narratives through new and equally vibrant mediums such as movies, television, and even comic books. Throughout the history of Hinduism there have been numerous versions of sacred narratives, the *Ramayana* being perhaps the most obvious example of this tendency. In recent decades, sacred narratives have been invigorated through print, TV, radio, and the Internet, and we continue to see ever-new and imaginative retellings of these ancient stories.

THE HISTORY OF HINDUISM

Hinduism is a vibrant tradition that has exhibited dynamic change and a willingness to embrace theological innovations. At the same time, Hinduism has preserved many of its most ancient elements into the present day, cherishing some traditions that go back more than 3,000 years.

The history of Hinduism can be traced back to the Indus Valley civilization (c. 2600–1700 B.C.E.) and to the Indo-Aryan peoples who compiled the Vedic corpus (c. 1500–900 B.C.E.). But even as we point to these, it is important to remember that Hinduism developed from countless other influences and circumstances.

Indus Valley

As its name suggests, the Indus Valley Civilization developed along the river Indus. It reached its developmental peak between 2300 and 2000 B.C.E., when thriving cities enjoyed the highest standard of living at that time. Extensive archaeological excavations at Indus Valley sites have yielded a vast number of stone seals that were perhaps used to "stamp" products for trade. These are adorned with beautiful depictions of animals and people and with a script that has not yet been deciphered. There are many theories about the language of the Indus Valley people. Most recent scholarship argues that the script represents an early Dravidian language related to those spoken today in South India.[8]

Some scholars believe that the Indus Valley seals are somehow connected with the religious views of Hinduism. The most famous seal has been called the Pashupathi Nath (Sanskrit, "the Lord of the Animals") or the "Proto-Shiva" seal, as it is thought to be an archaic form of the Hindu deity, Shiva. It is dated roughly at 2250–2150 B.C.E. This seal is usually described as depicting a figure of a god seated in a yoga posture, with a buffalo-horned headdress and possibly three faces. The figure is surrounded by various totemic animals, such as an elephant, a tiger, a rhinoceros, a water buffalo, and

TIMELINE
Hinduism

4000 B.C.E. Settlements in Indus Valley.

2600–1700 B.C.E. Indus Valley Civilization (great cities: Mohenjodaro and Harappa c. 2300).

2000–1300 B.C.E.* Migration into Northwest India of Indo-European speakers (Aryans).

1500–1200 B.C.E.* *Rg Veda* II–IX.

1200–900 B.C.E.* Later *Vedas, Brahmanas.*

900–600 B.C.E.* Early *Upanishads.*

400 B.C.E.–400 C.E.* *Mahabharata.*

200 B.C.E.–200 C.E.* *Ramayana.*

c. 0–400 C.E. Tamil literature of the Sangam period.

c. First century C.E.* *Bhagavad Gita.*

100–500 C.E. Expansion of Hinduism to Southeast Asia.

c. 320–540 Gupta Dynasty; rise of Hindu temple culture.

300–500 Earliest *puranas* (such as the *Vishnu Purana*); Hindu law books.

700 Flourishing of *bhakti* in the South.

800–900* Composition of *Bhagavata Purana* (some sections may be much earlier).

999–1226 Mahmud of Ghazi; repeated raids of India.

?–1168 Basavanna; founding of Virasaivism.

1350–1610 Virasaivism as state religion in Mysore.

Fifteenth century Ravidas and north Indian *bhakti* movement.

1526–1757 Moghul rule in India.

1651 The East India Company opens first factory on the Hugli River in Bengal.

1784 Sir William Jones founds the Asiatik Society in Calcutta.

1828 Brahmo Samaj founded by Ram Mohan Roy.

1834–1886 Life of Sri Ramakrishna.

1875 Arya Samaj founded by Swami Dayananda Saraswati.

1893 Swami Vivekananda at the World Parliament of Religions, Chicago.

1925 RSS founded (Rastriya Svayamsevak Sangha).

1947 India gains independence; partition with Pakistan (and Bangladesh).

1948 Assassination of Gandhi.

1964 VHP (Vishva Hindu Parisad).

1992 Destruction of Babri Masjid and widespread riots.

2003 Founding of the Sri Ganesha Hindu Temple of Utah.

Note: Asterisks indicate contested or approximate dates.

The great bath can be seen amid the ruins of the ancient cityscape of Mohenjo-Daro. The towering granary can be viewed in the distance. Mohenjo-Daro, Pakistan, 2600–1800 B.C.E.

two antelopes or deer. But without a decipherment of the script, it is difficult to make sense fully of the images that are depicted on the seals.

Archaeologists working in the Indus Valley have also discovered a number of terracotta figures depicting full-breasted women, which have been identified as representing a mother goddess. Some scholars argue that the veneration of goddesses in the ancient Indus civilization is the source for the widespread worship of goddesses in Hinduism.

Sometime around 1800–1700 B.C.E. there was a sudden decline in the Indus Valley civilization, which became fragmented by about 1500 B.C.E. The cause seems to have been related to climate change and severe annual flooding. The Indus Valley civilization did not die out entirely but rather adapted by abandoning its larger settlements. It is possible that as nomadic Aryans moved in from the regions of present-day Iran and Afghanistan, the Indus Valley people were absorbed into this more militarily advanced society. Hinduism's origin may ultimately lie in a blending of ancient Aryan and Dravidian cultures.

Who Are the Aryans?

The brilliant English linguist Sir William "Oriental" Jones (1746–1794) was appointed in 1783 as a judge for the Supreme Court of Bengal in India. His fascination with languages had inspired him to take up the study of Sanskrit, the language in which most of the ancient literature of India was composed. This study led him in 1786 to a most extraordinary discovery: that Sanskrit, Latin, and Greek—and likely the Persian, Gothic, and Celtic languages as well—all evolved from a common source.

Much like the Romance languages (such as French and Italian), which can be easily traced back to Latin, Jones suggested that a common ancestor linked Europe's classical languages to Sanskrit and Persian. Those languages are referred to as "Indo-European" and probably stem from a lost language we call "Proto Indo-European." Jones' discoveries astounded Europeans, who soon learned that Sanskrit was closest to the original language spoken by the earliest Indo-Europeans. The impact of this revelation, according to the modern scholar Thomas Trautmann, led to a phenomenon described as "Indomania."[9]

What does this landmark linguistic discovery of the eighteenth century have to do with the history of Hinduism? The ancient speakers of Sanskrit who moved into the Indian subcontinent around 1500 B.C.E. referred to themselves as the "Arya" (or Aryan), a Sanskrit word that means "noble, cultivated, and civilized." Scholars in the 1830s adopted the term to designate the family of Indo-European languages and their speakers. But part of the "Indomania" that followed the revelation of these linguistic linkages fueled a quest for "origins," and the term was soon misappropriated by some Europeans in the late nineteenth century to create the mythos of a Teutonic race of "supermen." Initially, the term was coined solely as a linguistic marker—not a racial one. Therefore, when we use the term Aryan in this chapter, we are using it only to designate a group of people who spoke an early form of Sanskrit and moved into the Indian subcontinent around 1500 B.C.E.

The Pashupathi Nath or the "Proto-Shiva" seal.

The Aryans, skilled at handling the horse and chariot, were a nomadic group. Cattle herding and war were most important, and it is possible that the desire for larger herds and wider pastures on which to graze their livestock led to the Aryan expansion. Around the beginning of the second millennium B.C.E., nomadic Aryans entered the Indian subcontinent. They were the minority, but with the technological advantage of the chariot they must have quickly moved into a position of being the dominant elite.

Like other Indo-European cultures, the Aryans revered the horse, placed special importance on sacrifice, and organized their society into a three-part structure. For the Aryans, sacrifice was a means to maintain order in the universe, and they had ritual specialists who conducted and performed these sacrifices. These ritual specialists/priests (*brahmins*) occupied the top rung of the social order because of the ritual power they wielded. The warrior class (*kshatriyas*) was equally important, although they might have been subordinate to the priests. Last were the traders and farmers (*vaishyas*). Since the Aryans did not place a great deal of emphasis on agriculture, one can see why the *vaishyas* would occupy a lower social position. This threefold social structure was also shared with other Aryan tribes that spread into Europe, the Middle East, and Central Asia.

The Aryans have left us a vast body of texts composed in Sanskrit, of which the earliest example is the *Vedas* (1500–900 B.C.E.). Some of these texts are still used for various Hindu rituals. It is to these texts and how they influenced the development of Hinduism that we turn to next.

The Vedic Period

The word *Veda* (Sanskrit, "knowledge") refers to four compendiums of sacred hymns that tradition holds were not composed but were directly perceived by a group of ancient sages called *rishis* (Sanskrit, "seers"). Of these four Vedic hymnals, the oldest and most important is called the *Rig Veda*. The *Vedas* were transmitted orally by the *rishis* and were committed to memory by other priests and sages. Many Hindus regard them as the font of all sacred knowledge and the cornerstone of religious authority. But

VISUAL GUIDE
Hinduism

In Hinduism, folding one's hands and offering salutations by saying "*namaste*" (naam-us-tae) signifies to some a simple way of giving a respectful greeting or a way of showing deference to an elder or superior, but to others it is understood as an expression where the divine within one person acknowledges and bows down to the divine within another.

Om or *Aum* is the most sacred syllable in Hinduism and may be traced back to the *Vedas*. It is the oldest of mantras and is regarded as the sound that both creates and pervades the universe. Composed of the first and last Sanskrit vowel (A & U) and the final consonant (M), it is believed to encompass all sound. It is employed by Hindus, Jains, Buddhists, and Sikhs.

The name *swastika* or *svastika* is derived from the Sanskrit *su* (good) + *asti* (it is), meaning fortunate or auspicious. It is an ancient solar symbol and denotes harmony, balance, and good fortune. It is venerated by Hindus, Buddhists, and Jains and regarded as equally auspicious whether the arms of the symbol spiral out toward the left or the right.

Hindu forehead markings: *bindi, tripundra,* and *namam. Bindi* (drop) is a decorative mark on the forehead signifying auspiciousness. It has evolved into a popular fashion accessory; fancy stickers have often supplanted

more traditional forms of forehead markings. Traditionally, these marks are made with *kumkumam* (a red powder made of saffron or turmeric and lime).   *(continued)*

not all Hindus accept the *Vedas*, or hold them as important. Some see them merely as archaic texts used to sanction priestly domination. Today, only a very small number of Hindus study or understand any of the *Vedas*.

These profound and intriguing texts were painstakingly preserved and passed down in an unbroken oral tradition, with whole *brahmin* lineages being dedicated solely to their conservation. Composed and compiled somewhere between 1500–900 B.C.E., the *Vedas* were not written down until nearly a thousand years after they were compiled.

Vedic Ritual and Gods Ritual was of ultimate importance in Vedic times as rites of sacrifice were held to sustain cosmic order and delight the gods. The four *Vedas* are essentially liturgical texts that record the hymns used in conjunction with such ritual. Much of ritual sacrifice involved the pouring of offerings (such as *ghee*, rice, barley and other grains, milk, and stalks of the soma plant) into a sacrificial fire as Vedic hymns were recited. While the construction of their fire altars became quite elaborate, the nomadic Indo-Aryans had a very "portable" religion, with no fixed buildings or icons, and the sacred texts carried only in the memory of the priests.

In Vedic times, as today, fire was regarded as a god on earth known as *Agni* (cognate with *ignus* in Latin and the English word "ignite"). He was the mouth of the gods and the gateway to the celestial realms, so offerings were magically transported through Agni to whichever god was invoked.

In Vedic mythology it is Indra, God of Thunder and Lightning, and the virile god of fertility itself, who is the most powerful of the Vedic gods. More hymns in the *Vedas* are addressed to Indra than to any other god, but in later Hindu tradition and mythology he is somewhat comical: haughty, proud, and often drunk, he is depicted as repeatedly losing his throne to the *asuras* (titans) and turning to Vishnu or Shiva to intervene to preserve the cosmic order. Many of the Vedic gods continue to play a part in the later Hindu pantheon, but endure only in a subordinate status.

Purusha: The Cosmic Man New deities emerged in the later portions of the *Rig Veda* that were more abstract, pervasive, or cosmic. Of these various "ultimate" deities, one that has enduring influence is the *Purusha* (literally, "Man"), who is praised and described in a famous Vedic hymn known as the *Purusha Sukta*. This later Vedic hymn is significant for the ways in which it asserts the centrality of sacrifice, and it continues to be recited in Hindu rituals even today.

The *Purusha Sukta* describes the sacrifice of a primordial, cosmic man out of whose body the universe is created. As a creation myth, it has parallels in numerous Indo-European traditions. As we have already seen in the section on *varna*, the *Purusha Sukta* not only details the first sacrifice but also delineates the structuring of Aryan society. Thus, it is a creation myth in every way, explaining both the beginnings of the material world—the sun, the moon, breath—as well as the fabric of society.

> When they divided *Purusha*, how many pieces did they prepare? What was his mouth? What are his arms, thighs, and feet called? The priest was his mouth, the warrior was made from his arms; His thighs were the commoner, and the servant was born from his feet. The moon was born of his mind; of his eye, the sun was born; From his mouth, Indra and fire; from his breath wind was born; From his navel there was the atmosphere; from his head, heaven was rolled together; From his feet, the earth; from his ears, the directions.[10]

On the most profound level this passage asserts that the macrocosm is in the microcosm, that the

An additional "dot" is often applied by women to the top of the head where the hair is parted to denote married status. But the mark between the eyes is situated there to signify "the third eye," the eye that looks inward. It is thought to help concentrate the mind and also protect the wearer from negativity and the malicious projections of others. Some forehead markings denote sectarian affiliation, such as the three vertical lines of sacred ash worn by worshipers of Shiva, called the *tripundra*, which signify the destruction of ego, *karma*, and illusion. The vertical "V" of the worshipers of Vishnu is usually made of sacred clay called *naamam* or *tilaka* and is a stylized representation of Vishnu's feet supported by a lotus. The red "drop" in the middle is the descent of grace in the form of Lakshmi, the Goddess of Fortune.

The term *yantra* means "device," but these sacred diagrams may also be referred to by the term *mandala*, or "circle." They vary in form and function. Some are used to map cosmology, embody deities, act as talismans, or for other magical purposes. Many of these geometrical designs are used in meditation to concentrate the mind or aid in cosmological contemplation of the divine order. Most will have a dot or *bindu* in the center that signifies the primordial consciousness of God or Brahman that is the axis of the universe, while at the perimeter there will be four stylized gates that represent the four directions. Shown here is the Sri Yantra, "the auspicious yantra" that is used by Shaktas in Hinduism and some Vajrayana Buddhists.

A *yajna* or fire sacrifice, which is one of the most archaic of Hindu rites, is performed by priests before an image of Durga during the Durga Puja festival in Calcutta, India.

cosmic man is every man, and that the infinitude of the universe can be found within each individual. But on a more pragmatic level it organizes society, asserting that everyone has a specific place—high or low—that is not only predetermined by the divine order but is necessary to the maintenance of that very order.

One thing to note is that the threefold social structure found in most Indo-European societies is amended in the *Vedas* with the addition of a fourth tier—a new servant "caste"—presumably as tribal peoples were integrated into Aryan society. The *Purusha Sukta* refers to this servant class as the *shudra*.

Thus far we have examined the distinctive properties of the pre-Vedic and Vedic antecedents of Hinduism that are most contiguous with later theological developments. For example, Vishnu, a peripheral solar deity in the *Vedas* who assisted Indra in slaying the serpent Vrithra, is later equated with Purusha. Through establishing the equivalence between Purusha and Vishnu, later *Vaishnavas* claimed Vishnu's supremacy.

In later Hinduism, Rudra, an even more marginalized Vedic god, became one of the most important gods of theistic Hinduism. In the *Vedas*, Rudra (Sanskrit, "The Howler") is a marginal, frightening deity. He rides the storms and wields a bow that fires arrows of disease. But he is also thought to live in the high mountains and reveal the secrets of the healing herbs to be found there. These ascetic qualities enable Rudra to be identified with Shiva, while the *Kesins*, Rudra's wild Vedic worshipers, may have been the prototypes of the yogic ascetics, who became the preeminent devotees nearly a millennium later.

Ascetic traditions began to assert significant influence in transforming theology in the later Vedic period as they inspired philosophical innovations that supplanted the Vedic emphasis on sacrifice. Most of the last hymns composed for the *Rig Veda* were compiled in its first and tenth books. And it is in the tenth book that Vedic religion begins to take a decisive turn. Here, we find a shift from an emphasis on myth, cosmology, and sacrifice to a keener interest in philosophy and introspection. For example, the unique account of creation that appears in the *Nasadiya Sukta* (*Rig Veda* 10:129) speaks of "The One" (a nondualistic and all pervasive form of deity), how desire is the compelling agent of creation, and how the *rishis* apprehended within their own hearts the nature of ultimate reality. The text goes on to say that the gods emerged later in the creation, and that even the highest of the gods might not have known the true nature of creation's mystery. It implies that perceiving the nature of existence is more important than servicing the cosmic order through sacrifice.

In the beginning Love arose, which was the primal
germ cell of the mind. The Seers, searching in their
hearts with wisdom, discovered the connection of
Being in Nonbeing. . . .

　　Who really knows? Who can presume to tell it?
Whence was it born? Whence issued this creation?
Even the Gods came after its emergence. Then who
can tell from whence it came to be?

　　That out of which creation has arisen, whether it
held it firm or it did not, He who surveys it in the highest heaven, He surely knows or maybe He does not![11]

Krishna reveals his universal form to Arjuna, as described in the *Bhagavad Gita*. The scene evokes earlier representations of Purusha, whose body pervades the universe.

Late Vedic hymns like the *Nasadiya Sukta* mark a transition toward what would be the philosophical revolution of the
speculative texts known as the *Upanishads*.

The Early *Upanishads* (900–600 B.C.E.)

The *Upanishads* are a group of philosophical texts that seek to
explain the hidden meaning of ritual. They are believed to have
been closely guarded secret teachings. This is implied by the literal rendering of *Upanishad* (Sanskrit, "to sit near"), as though
their insights were being whispered in one's ear. These texts
signal a significant shift away from emphasis on the external
performance of sacrifice that marked the Vedic era. In the *Upanishads*, the significance of sacrifice is reimagined. The primary function of sacrifice is no longer seen as
maintaining order in the universe. Instead, these texts seek to understand the esoteric
meaning of sacrifice. In doing so, the *Upanishads* recast sacrifice as an internal meditative event in which breath becomes the sacrificial fire and the body the altar. Such a
radical rethinking of sacrifice, which was the most fundamental ritual action of the
early *Vedas*, had an enormous impact on the development of Hinduism. It propelled
the development of the contemplative disciplines of yoga and meditation, and influenced the philosophical concepts found later in the *Bhagavad Gita*.

The shift away from the Vedic preoccupation with ritual is difficult to explain. The
Upanishads are also significant for propagating for the first time the mysteries of *karma*,
samsara, transmigration of the soul, and the soul's immortality, which were initially
closely guarded secrets. During the time of the *Upanishads*, contemplative reflection
became more widespread as asceticism was quickly moving from the margins of society
to its center, bringing with it immense philosophical innovation. There was a kind of
exodus of theologians and mystics from urban areas, as many packed up and moved
to the forest to lead simpler lives as hermits. Some took their families with them and
formed hermit colonies. Others simply threw themselves on the mercy of the cosmos
and practiced fierce austerities in the total solitude of the jungle. Still others became

ZOROASTRIANISM

When the Aryan peoples set out southward from their original homeland in the vicinity of the Caspian Sea, one branch migrated into India while another established itself in ancient Iran. The earliest literature of these people was a collection of seventeen hymns called the *Gathas*. These hymns were reputedly authored by Zarathustra, the founder of the Zoroastrian faith. Later included in the *Avesta*, a wider canon of Zoroastrian sacred lore, the *Gathas* represent a profound theological and cosmological shift in the belief system of the Indo-Aryans instigated by the prophet, Zarathustra.

Similar to the religion of the Vedic Aryans, the religion of the Indo-Aryans of Iran and Afghanistan was a nature-oriented polytheistic faith officiated by a priestly class whose principal ritual practice involved tending the sacred fire. Some of its teachings were later transformed by Zarathustra. The many deities were organized into a hierarchy of divinities who served the one god, Ahura Mazda, in his eternal struggle against the forces of darkness. Zarathustra's reform brought a new monotheistic faith that is often regarded as having had a pronounced influence on Judaism, Christianity, and Islam. While it is difficult to map the full extent of Zoroastrian influence, we may note many beliefs shared with the Abrahamic religions: a source of evil that works in opposition to God's will, clearly defined notions of heaven and hell, the existence of angels and demons, foretelling of a coming messiah, resurrection of the body, and final judgment.

Direct linkages of Zoroastrianism to Vedic religion are well established not only on linguistic grounds but also in priestly rites and regalia (such as the *kusti*, the "sacred thread" of Zoroastrian priests), and most clearly in the direct naming of divine beings who appear in both the *Avesta* and the *Vedas*. For example, the Asura, the "old" gods of the *Vedas*, are called Ahura ("Lord") in the *Avesta*. Other Vedic deities found in the *Avesta* include Vayu (the wind-god); Indra (the rain-god), and Varuna (the Vedic sky-god, who protected the social order, enforced the cosmic law, and is sometimes thought to be the basis of Ahura Mazda himself). But Indra, like some other gods mentioned in the *Vedas*, becomes despised in the hymns of the Avesta.

MITHRA

Perhaps the most intriguing shared deity is Mithra. Zoroastrians believed Mithra to be a divine judge, a guardian of crops and cattle and witness to sacred oaths. He was sometimes associated with the sun. In the *Avesta*, Mithra's name means "contract, ally or bond." In Sanskrit the name "Mitra" means "oath, treaty and friendship," and he was the Vedic god of friendship and social obligation.

About a century after Alexander the Great's conquest of Persia, the Parthians rose to power and maintained dominance in the region (B.C.E. 247–226 C.E.). Mithra became their chief deity. During this era of Greek influence Mithra's association with the sun led to his equation with the Greek god Apollo as an all-seeing god of truth. By the first century B.C.E. Mithraism had spread so vigorously throughout the Roman empire that it might well have become the dominant religion of Europe and the Middle East had it not been displaced by Christianity after Constantine. To the Zoroastrians, Mithra remained an (albeit important) servant of the one god, Ahura Mazda.

ZOROASTRIANISM (*continued*)

ZOROASTER OR ZARATHUSTRA

In Greek, the Persian name "Zarathustra" was rendered as "Zoroaster." It is from the Greek name of this prophet that the religion of his followers takes its name. Zarathustra was a religious reformer who lived in Iran perhaps in the sixth century B.C.E. Born into a priestly family, he married and had children. He then spent ten years in prayer and meditation roaming the mountains. When he was 30 years old he was wading in the river Daitya when he saw a wondrous light. An angelic being named "Good Thought" appeared before him and carried his soul to the Court of Ahura Mazda. There, Zarathustra realized that Ahura Mazda ("Lord of Wisdom") was the one eternal, uncreated God, beyond all others.

Upon his return, Zarathustra set out to reveal to a polytheistic society a new monotheistic cosmology. After the conversion of a local king, he made great inroads in converting a population sometimes hesitant to accept his radical new beliefs. Zarathustra is said to have lived to the age of 77, when an assassin stabbed him in the back as he was deep in prayer.

BELIEFS AND PRACTICES

Zarathustra's religious reforms went beyond monotheism. Zoroastrian cosmology is built around an ethical dualism, pitching the universal forces of good and evil against each other in a cosmic struggle. These two forces are the twin offspring of Ahura Mazda. He offers all of creation a choice regarding how to live, but cherishes truth and goodness above all. One of his twins came to embody truth; the other embraced falsehood. All must make a similar choice, deciding where they stand in the divine struggle. In this way, ethics and human destiny are irrevocably linked in the teachings of Zarathustra. This passage is from *Yasna* 30 in the *Gathas*:

> Hear with your ears the best things.
> Reflect with clear purpose, each man for himself, on the two choices for decision, being alert indeed to declare yourselves for Him before the great requital. Truly there are two primal Spirits, twins renowned to be in conflict. In thought and word, in act they are two: the better and the bad. And those who act well have chosen rightly between these two, not so the evildoers. And when these two Spirits first came together they created life and not-life, and how at the end Worst Existence shall be for the wicked, but (the House of) Best Purpose for the just man. (30.2–4)

When death comes, all souls must cross over the "Bridge of the Separator." It is a wide road for the righteous, but for the wicked it narrows to the width of a knife's edge. The wicked invariably fall into the abyss of torment below, while the righteous pass on and achieve heaven (the "House of Purpose").

As part of choosing the righteous life, Zoroastrians pray five times a day (perhaps because of Islamic influences). They may also go to the Fire Temple and have the priest recite special prayers. Temple priests, who maintain strict ritual purity, are clad in white and even cover their mouths with a special cloth so as not to desecrate the purity of the sacred fire with their breath. In these temples the sacred fire, a symbol of divine presence, power, and purity, is kept continuously burning.

(continued)

ZOROASTRIANISM (continued)

The funerary practices of Zoroastrians are especially interesting. The deceased is clad in white holy vestments and a sacred cord and then wrapped in white linen. After friends and relatives pass by the body to pay their respects, it is carried to the top of the "Towers of Silence." These round funerary towers, traditionally placed on the tops of hills, expose corpses to vultures that circle in the sky above. After a few days the bones are gathered and deposited in a well-like structure.

MODERN ZOROASTRIANISM

The *New York Times* reported in 2006 that Zoroastrians numbered less than 190,000, but other estimates count fewer than 100,000 adherents. Approximately three-quarters of them live in India where they are called "Parsis." They are descendants of a mass migration of Zoroastrians to the Indian state of Gujarat in the century following the Islamic conquest of Iran in 651 C.E. This community thrived in India and quickly rose to prominence. Because of their small numbers they are a fairly insular community even though respected in wider society for their philanthropy and trustworthiness in business. They denounce marriages outside the faith and seek no converts. Nevertheless, small communities of Zoroastrians have flourished in many places around the world.

wanderers, going from town to town begging for food and engaging in lively debates with other philosophers as their main pastime and method of spiritual inquiry. All was done in hopes of somehow transcending desire and achieving oneness with God.

The philosophical system that emerged out of the *Upanishads* is called **Vedanta**, which in Sanskrit means "the end of the *Vedas*." Here, "end" does not just mean "conclusion." Rather, the *Upanishads* are explications of the Vedic texts, although many *Upanishads* explicitly reject the ritual action of the *Vedas*. They bring an "end" in that they lead to the utmost fulfillment of all Vedic sacrificial endeavor. The *Upanishads* are the means to the end as they reveal the truth about *samsara* and the path to final liberation. As the *Upanishads* are often abstract, there has never been one single way to interpret them. Predictably, this resulted in a number of perspectives within *Vedanta*, which became its ten major schools. Each school of *Vedanta* has sought to understand the precise nature of the relationships between *Brahman* (God), *atman* (self), and the world.

The impact of *Vedanta* on the development of Hinduism cannot be overestimated. As different Hindu sects emerged, their individual, distinctive understandings of *Vedanta* shaped their philosophical orientations. Of the ten schools of *Vedanta*, the three most important are *Advaita*, *Vishishta Advaita*, and *Dvaita*.

Advaita Vedanta denies the distinction made between spirit and matter, regarding the *atman* as being identical to *Brahman*. This school of thought grew directly out of the *Upanishads* but was further developed in the eighth century C.E. by Shankara, its most famous proponent. Shankara was a young *brahmin* theologian and reformer who strove to win India back from the Buddhists and Jains and reinstate the orthodoxy of the *brahmins*. Shankara posited that the world is illusory and that it causes ignorance, which in turn obscures the true nature of the self (*atman*). According to Shankara, it is ignorance, manifesting as attachment to desire, that keeps one bound to the cycle of birth, death, and rebirth. When one uses discrimination, one can cut through ignorance and recognize the inherent unity of all things, including the oneness of *Brahman* and *atman*. This in turn results in a complete dissolution of one's individual self.

Many of the sects that worship Vishnu differ on the subtler aspects of the relationship between *Brahman* and *atman*. For *Vaishnavas*, *Brahman* was identified with Vishnu. The school of *Vishishta-Advaita*, founded by the twelfth-century C.E. philosopher Ramanuja, declared that all is *Brahman* and that the material world and individual souls are also real. The world is not illusion; rather, it is the body of God. Unlike Shankara, Ramanuja interpreted the ignorance that obscures true knowledge as forgetfulness—in particular, the forgetfulness of Vishnu. In this manner, Ramanuja's *Vedanta* marries philosophy to the devotional, sectarian traditions of Vaishnavism.

The school of *Dvaita Vedanta*, founded by the thirteenth-century theologian Madhva, advocates a complete distinction between *Brahman* and *atman*. It posits that there are five acknowledged aspects of complete separateness or difference: between the soul and *Brahman*, between *Brahman* and matter, between the various souls, between the souls and matter, and between various forms of matter. This philosophical strain, too, is associated with the worship of Vishnu, particularly in his *avatara* as Krishna.

During the "Indomania" of the nineteenth century, the earliest translations of Hindu philosophical works such as these appeared in Europe and America. They had a profound impact in America, particularly among writers and thinkers such as Ralph Waldo Emerson (1803–1882) and Henry David Thoreau (1817–1862), who founded the "Transcendentalist" movement, one of the first wholly American philosophical movements.

The Rise of Theistic Hinduism

Many Hindus draw a distinction between scriptures that are revealed, or *shruti* (literally, "heard," by the ancient *rishi*), and those that are man-made, or *smriti* (Sanskrit, "remembered"), and passed down by way of memory. *Shruti* works are immutable and of divine origin. They include the *Vedas* and *Upanishads*. Texts that are *smriti* are human records that preserve sacred knowledge, such as the two great Sanskrit epics, the *Ramayana* and *Mahabharata*; ancient collections of myths (**puranas**); and treatises on law.

Despite the higher status attributed to *shruti* texts like the *Vedas* and *Upanishads*, *smriti* works such as the epics and myth collections form the basis of both classical and modern Hinduism, and they radically revise Vedic myth and cosmology.

The Epics and *Puranas* The period from the fourth century B.C.E. to the fourth century C.E. saw the composition and transmission of the two great Sanskrit epics, the *Ramayana* and the *Mahabharata*, and was a key formative era in the development of theistic Hinduism. The epics are concerned with political problems, dynastic successions, duty, and obligations, as well as asserting the intervention of the divine in the world.

In addition to the rich storehouse of narrative material in the epics, there exists an equally important collection of mythic stories known as *purana*s (from Sanskrit *purana*, "ancient"). They date from the fourth century C.E. to the modern era. The formulation of the *puranas* is similar to that of the epics in that these texts were initially transmitted orally. *Puranas* was also important because they contain useful historical data such as the genealogies of different regional kings.

The *puranas* reflect the rise of theistic Hinduism, and so are primarily narrations of the deeds of the great deities of Hinduism: Shiva, Vishnu, and Devi. While early *puranas* are concerned with the mythic deeds of various deities, later *puranas* often exalt specific pilgrimage sites. This is a logical development, as many sacred sites develop as the mythical exploits of gods are localized in specific places. The purpose of these later tales is to assert the singular sacredness of a particular place and the site's efficacy in delivering the pilgrim from the coils of mundane existence.

Hindu Expansion in the Age of the Guptas

Most scholars characterize the time of the Gupta empire (c. 320 to 540 C.E.) as a flowering of creativity—of art, innovation, and introspection. The Guptas, who ruled much of Northern India, patronized the arts, sciences, and literature. Their reign was an era of relative peace and prosperity, often described as "the Golden Age of India." It was during this period that the epics took on their definitive forms and the first of the *puranas* was compiled. Radical changes in worship were introduced as temple institutions arose. In particular, the Guptas began to rethink the relationship between the king and God, and the worship of Vishnu received particular royal patronage under their leadership. New roles of royal patronage in the development of religious ideas, institutions, and the arts quickened the spread of the (mostly) devotional orientation of the budding theistic sects. The Guptas, however, equally patronized other sects and religious traditions; indeed, some of the most renowned pieces of Buddhist art were produced under their patronage. This era marks the spread of Hinduism and Buddhism throughout Southeast Asia (extending all the way to Vietnam), where these faiths often intermingled and took on the unique character of the local culture.

The Development of *Bhakti*

The theistic strain of Hinduism began under the Guptas, but it took on new life in the South of India between the sixth and ninth centuries C.E. in the form of the ecstatic movement of *bhakti*. From the South, this movement and ideology spread all over India, changing and adapting to its new regional and linguistic circumstances. Like the radical innovations of the *Upanishads* and the *Bhagavad Gita*, *bhakti* changed the course of Hinduism, giving it an ecstatic, experiential, and lived dimension that expressed itself through poetry, art, architecture, and temple-building. *Bhakti* was instrumental to the development of the various sectarian orientations of Hinduism and the development of Hinduism's vibrant temple cultures. Closely linked to the most important dynasties of the time, *bhakti* was equally important for the challenge it issued to caste and gender hierarchies.

Bhakti receives its first sustained treatment in the *Bhagavad Gita*, where it is re-vealed that *bhakti* is in and of itself an efficacious means out of *samsara*. But more significantly, it is the *Gita* that systematically outlines for the first time how *bhakti* is achieved through dedication, surrender, and devotion to Krishna. Although the *Gita* approaches *bhakti* in abstract terms, it was in the deep south of India, in the hands of wandering poet-saints, that the concept reached its full flower.

By the late fifth century C.E., Jainism and Buddhism were deeply entrenched in South India. *Bhakti* arose as a challenge to these traditions. Over the next four cen-turies, poets roamed the Tamil country, converting royalty and commoners alike to Hinduism. Royal patronage for Jainism and Buddhism waned, and kings sought le-gitimacy through poets' songs that presented the kings as the representatives of the great gods Shiva and Vishnu on earth. The religious networks forged by the itinerant poets transformed into political networks, and as extraordinary temples rose into the sky, soon dominating the South Indian landscape, even stronger alliances were forged between religion and politics.

Although it is difficult to pinpoint exactly *why* ecstatic *bhakti* emerged in South India in the late fifth century C.E., we can explore *how* it occurred. In the Tamil re-gion of the deep south of India (where Dravidian cultural modes were most deeply insulated from northern assimilation), a literary and religious culture developed and flourished independent of the Vedic and Sanskrit traditions. While Sanskrit culture was not entirely absent from South India, Tamil culture maintained its own distinc-tive language and identity. This Tamil culture valued poetry and poets, military valor, and generosity. All of these qualities were embodied in the intimate relationship be-tween the king and the wandering bard. In the Tamil South, poetry was the primary means of propagating one's fame: the bard sang in praise of a king's unmatched valor and generosity, and in return the king rewarded the bard with wealth. The symbiotic relationship between king and bard is essential to understanding how *bhakti* estab-lished itself in South India and why poetry was its preferred means of expression. But the *bhakti* movement was equally indebted to the Sanskrit traditions, and it was so successful because it effortlessly merged Tamil and Sanskrit cultures. Tamil poetry mingled easily with Sanskrit myths. Put another way, Tamil gave *bhakti* its form (poetry) and Sanskrit its content (myth).

The earliest identifiable extant Tamil *bhakti* poem, the *Tirumurukarruppatai* ("A Guide Poem to Lord Muruga"), dates from the period between the second and fourth centuries C.E. Muruga was worshiped in North India as a god of war and in the South as a god of love. He is Shiva's son, the brother of Ganesha. In this poem, the wandering bard's praise is not directed to the mortal king, but to the god, Muruga. The poet wanders from place to place in search of him, recognizing Muruga's presence in the abundance and beauty of the natural world. He also recognizes the god in the faces of fellow devotees who also tread the path. The poem is significant not just because it is the earliest Tamil *bhakti* work but because it anticipates many of the themes and ideas that dominate *bhakti* poetry over the next several centuries. The poem emphasizes two things: first, that god is local, accessible, and immanent, while also impossible to know—like the benevolent kingly sponsors that poets had praised before—and second, that a community of like-mined devotees is essential to gaining the ecstatic experience of *bhakti*.

In Tamil country, the production of *bhakti* poems accelerated in the sixth century, with the emergence of the rival *Shaiva* and *Vaishnava* sects. The two most important Tamil *Shaiva* poets, Appar and Sambandar, seemed to anticipate the philosopher Shankara, who was himself reasserting the authority of the *brahmins* and mounting a challenge to Buddhist philosophy.

Appar, a Jain monk, converted to *Shaivism* and in turn converted the influential Pallava king. He made a number of pilgrimages to various sacred sites, and his poetry helped to establish those sites as large religious institutions. Similarly, Sambandar converted the Pandya king, defeated the Jains in debate, and supported the effort to drive the Jains out of the South (some stories speak of a mass Jain genocide ordered by the converted Pandya king). Although they did not form the strong political alliances that the *Shaivas* did, the *Vaishnava* poets also wandered the Tamil country and established important temples and religious institutions. But unlike their *Shaiva* counterparts, these poets were not much concerned with the Buddhists and Jains, and made little effort in their poems to reviling those rival traditions.

By the twelfth century, both the *Shaiva* and *Vaishnava* poets were canonized as saints and their poems were accorded the highest status. The temples and places mentioned in their poems became the holiest of sites, and their compositions were given an integral role in temple worship. To this day, Tamil *Shaivas* and *Vaishnavas* learn, memorize, recite, and sing the verses of these poets, both in private and public ritual. It would be no exaggeration to state that most Tamil Hindus know more of the Tamil *bhakti* corpus than they know of any of the Sanskrit philosophical texts.

The *bhakti* movement did not confine itself to Tamil country, but moved quickly through the Indian subcontinent. By the twelfth century, it entered what is now the

Indian state of Karnataka, located to the northwest of the Tamil-speaking region. Here, *bhakti* took on a new form. It became a weapon wielded against caste, class, and gender prejudice. It rejected empty ritual and temple-based worship, insisting that the body is itself the temple and that God resides in every individual. This new *bhakti* movement was known as *Virashaiva* ("Heroic *Shaivism*"), and the participants of the movement were devotees of Shiva.

The *Virashaiva* movement was begun by Basavanna, a *brahmin* man born into considerable privilege. He forsook both power and position to advocate inter-caste marriage, a rejection of religious and temple ritual, and a simple but complete love of Shiva. His radical ideas were exemplified in his poetry. Rather than choosing the artificial, elaborate devices of court poetry, Basavanna and other *Virashaivas* composed poems that were simple, direct, and colloquial, composed in a manner as to be accessible to anyone. As in the Tamil *bhakti* poems, the form of the poem was as important as its content. The works of Basavanna and other *Virashaiva* poets continue to be used by contemporary *Virashaivas* in their spiritual practices today.

The *bhakti* movement established itself all over the South of India. Innumerable poets produced innumerable texts, many of which are part of popular religious practice to this day. Sometimes temples were built to the poets themselves, and the sites associated with their lives became sacred places and pilgrimage destinations. In a curious turn, the *bhakti* poets became objects of *bhakti* themselves, lauded for their extraordinary vision and closeness to god.

The ecstatic strain of *bhakti* arrived in North India by the fifteenth century and is almost exclusively devoted to the love of Vishnu in his *avataras* as Krishna or Rama. In the poetry of the North, the poet loves a specific deity with specific attributes. But in another strain of *bhakti* that developed concurrently, God is unknowable yet all pervasive and is often evoked through the sacred name alone. Similar to the *Virashaivas*, this *bhakti* is iconoclastic, sometimes irreverent, and prone to offering social critiques.

Caste and *Bhakti*   Many scholars argue that the *bhakti* movement had such a far-reaching impact because it was egalitarian, revolutionary, and anti-Brahmanical. Bhakti poet-saints of both *Vaisnava* and *Shaiva* leanings represented a variety of caste backgrounds. Furthermore, rather than using Sanskrit, which was the languages of philosophy, the *bhakti* poets used vernacular languages like Tamil, Kannada, Marathi, and an early form of Hindi. The choice of accessible, local languages strengthened the *bhakti* poets' assertion that caste and birth did not determine one's access to God. Rather, it was the quality of one's surrender that mattered. While a text such as the *Bhagavad Gita* espoused similar ideas, that text also simultaneously stressed the importance of one's duty according to caste. In locating one's sole duty as the practice of perfect surrender to god, the *bhakti* poets were revolutionary. Nonetheless, the radical ideas espoused by the poets were often blunted when absorbed into mainstream Hinduism.

Many low-caste *bhakti* poet-saints leveled scathing critiques against the bigotries of caste, gender, and religion. The relationship between caste and *bhakti* is illustrated by the story of Ravidas (fl. fifteenth–sixteenth century C.E.), a poet-saint whose devotion emerged from the social and caste-based prejudice he had experienced throughout his life. Ravidas came from one of the lowest, most "polluted" and denigrated of castes. He was a leatherworker who regularly handled the corpses of animals. Within the caste system a leatherworker was considered an "untouchable," part of a community that today would be referred to as *Dalit* ("oppressed").

In his poetry, Ravidas evokes a community of devotees. Through *bhakti*, social order is reorganized, and people who are traditionally on the lowest rung are reimagined as residing at the very apex. *Bhakti* gives a voice to the voiceless—to women and *Dalits*—because it is believed to express that which is inexpressible. Ultimately, for Ravidas and other *bhakti* poets like him:

> He who becomes pure through Love of the Lord
> exalts himself. . . .
> For he's drunk with the essence of the liquid of life
> and he pours away all the poisons.
> No one equals someone so pure and devoted—
> not priests, nor heroes, nor parasolled kings.
> As the lotus leaf floats above the water, Ravidas says,
> so he flowers above the world of his birth.[12]

Tantra

Bhakti was not the only revolutionary new idea to challenge the strictures of gender, class, and caste. Around the same time (sixth or seventh century C.E.), another compelling ideology—*Tantra*—emerged. *Tantra*, which claimed to be superior to all other theological innovations, promised a fast track to enlightenment through rites that had awesome magical power. By the seventh and eighth centuries *tantric* symbolism began to infuse all manner of sectarian and theological perspectives throughout South Asia—not just Hinduism, but Buddhism and Jainism as well. It was an intricate system of metaphor, symbol, and ritual that was adaptable enough to be grafted onto or appropriated by different sectarian groups. The *tantric* orientation exerted a very strong influence on most *Shaiva* and *Shakta* sects.

Tantric cosmology makes use of overtly erotic symbolism. Sexuality, which is understood to be the creative matrix through which all sentient beings take form, is projected onto the entirety of existence as the governing basis of Being itself. It is in the moment of union—the joining of two polar opposites of male and female—that a crucible of pure creativity is formed. *Tantra* reveres the magic manifested through bringing these two opposites into conjunction.

Tantra presumably arose among ascetics in Kashmir, Nepal, and possibly Bengal and Assam. Like other ascetic renouncers, they asserted that the ritual transgression of social boundaries can help create a set of conditions ideal for experiencing transcendence or even complete and instantaneous enlightenment. Such rituals were designed to break through the narrow confines of what one assumes the self to be. While adherents spoke of a new spiritual technology that could help humanity sidestep lifetimes of evolution and bring about an instantaneous enlightenment, there were also grave warnings that one might be seduced by the magical abilities that arose along the way or the very real dangers of mental breakdown and madness. And certainly the nature of these rites might have a special appeal to hedonists interested only in the pursuit of pleasure. Hence, *tantric* initiation was carefully veiled in secrecy.

Sanskritization

Despite the numerous challenges mounted against orthodox Sanskritic Hinduism, it not only has survived but has also thrived. Even as *bhakti* in its many guises rejected Sanskrit texts, Brahminical authority, and caste, it was nonetheless absorbed into it. *Tantra* also found a place within the Sanskrit tradition. And the numerous local, village gods were given a place at the table in the ever-expanding Hindu tradition. One explanation for such radical transformations, and the reconciliations of such opposite and opposing traditions, can be found in the phenomenon called Sanskritization.

Indian sociologist M. N. Srinivas (1916–1999) coined the term "Sanskritization" to describe the process by which alternate religious ideologies are appropriated and adopted into Hinduism.[13] Simply put, rather than rejecting revolutionary ideas such as *tantra* or *bhakti* as heretical, or characterizing local deities as false, Sanskritization is a process of theological appropriation that asserts that these were just different expressions of the dominant tradition. Through Sanskritization, Brahminical modes of worship that use the Sanskrit language and a Vedic cosmology absorb local forms of myth, ritual, and belief. This process occurs in a number of ways. A local goddess may be seen as a manifestation of the great goddess, Devi; a folk deity may be marshaled as an attendant figure of Vishnu; a fierce local goddess may be domesticated by marrying her off to Shiva. Popular *bhakti* poets are made saints, and temples are built to honor and worship them. Alternately, a revolutionary tradition might make claims to be part of the Sanskrit tradition. For example, the revolutionary poems of the Tamil *bhakti* poets are legitimated by claiming that they are revealed and are equivalent to the *Vedas*.

A similar process is also adopted for legitimizing kingship. Kings that have descended from tribal populations or more marginal communities have employed the Sanskritization process as a means of validating their rule. Their priests often furnish them with a pedigree tracing their lineage back to the solar or lunar dynasties of Vedic kings; grant them proper caste status via a mythology that maps the history of their community; or, in some cases, link their local or tribal deity with one of the main Hindu gods.

Sanskritization may account for the mind-boggling number of deities and sects that come under the umbrella of Hinduism as folk gods, local traditions, and practices are continually absorbed into the religion. Throughout its long history, Hinduism has constantly remade itself, continually adapting to new environments and circumstances. In more recent times, colonialism and then Indian nationalism posed significant challenges as well as opportunities for Hinduism.

Colonial Critique and the Hindu Reformers

When employees of the British East India Company established an imperial presence in India in the late eighteenth and early nineteenth centuries, they initially adapted themselves to Indian customs and practices. They learned regional languages, married into local families, and even embraced local religious beliefs. One particularly colorful example is that of an Irish general in the Bengal Army, Charles Stuart (1758–1828). Stuart was such an avid admirer of Hinduism that his colleagues nicknamed him "Hindoo Stuart." His book, *Vindication of the Hindoos* (1808), was intended to discourage the ever-growing support for British missionaries trying to convert Hindus to Christianity. It was often on matters of Hindu mythology that these missionaries ridiculed Stuart, but he eloquently countered: "Whenever I look around me in the vast region of Hindoo Mythology, I discover piety in the garb of allegory: and I see Morality, at every turn, blended with every tale; and, as far as I can rely on my own judgment, it appears the most complete and ample system of Moral allegory that the world has ever produced."[14]

But not everyone involved with the British East India Company admired Hindu belief and custom. Many felt that the "primitive backwardness" of Hindu belief was enough to warrant colonial intervention. By the middle of the nineteenth century, and certainly after the 1857 Indian Uprising (referred to as the "Mutiny" by British chroniclers, but as the "First War of Independence" by many Indian historians), there was a sharp turn away from the vibrant, multicultural world represented by figures like Hindoo Stuart and Sir William "Oriental" Jones. As the imperial presence of the British East India Company gave way to the colonial control of the British Crown, critiques of Hinduism became an increasingly important means of exerting political power over the subcontinent.

Even as British scholars followed Jones' example in translating Sanskrit texts into English, they were also leveling criticisms at what they perceived as the barbarism of Hinduism. They could see no correlation between the abstract philosophies of the *Upanishads* and the ecstatic dancing, singing, and elaborate ritual worship in the temples. To their minds, the pure rationality of the *Upanishads* had been forgotten and replaced with inexplicable practices. These clearly needed to be reformed, they believed, so that Hinduism could be returned to its original glory.

By the mid-nineteenth century, English-educated Hindus took up the work of reform as a response to colonial critiques of Hinduism. They too began deriding

Hinduism's many gods, erotic symbolism, temple worship, and rituals as crass corruptions of the purity of the authentic Hinduism embodied in the *Vedas* and *Upanishads*. They sought to transform Hinduism from within.

The reformer Raja Ram Mohan Roy (1774–1833) was from a wealthy Bengali *brahmin* community. He translated the *Upanishads* into English as well as his native Bengali and also wrote works on Christianity. He established the Brahmo Samaj (Community of *Brahman* Worshipers) in 1828 as a neo-Hindu religious organization open to all, regardless of religious orientation. He advocated a strict Upanishadic monotheism and was against image worship. Roy is often credited as the first to use the term "Hinduism," in 1816. He was particularly concerned with issues involving the protection of women, such as child marriage, polygamy, dowry, and the practice of *sati*. *Sati* was an upper-caste practice in which a widow immolated herself on her husband's funeral pyre. This ritual suicide was believed to bring great honor to the family and raise the status of the dead widow to a goddess. Roy campaigned for the abolition of *sati* in two major pamphlets published in 1818 and 1820. He argued that there was no scriptural basis in the *Vedas* for this practice. Finally, in 1829, *sati* was made illegal in Bengal. Roy was among the first members of the Indian upper classes to visit Europe, traveling there in 1830 as an ambassador of the Mughal empire to ensure that the *sati* law was not overturned. He died in 1833 and was buried in Bristol.

Another influential reform figure was Dayananda Saraswati (1824–1883). He was born a *brahmin* but became a wandering monk early in life. He studied under a blind sage who influenced him to campaign for a return to the pure and original Vedic religion. Saraswati rejected the epics and *puranas* as eroding the purity of the *Vedas* and spoke out against all aspects of temple tradition, image worship, and pilgrimage. In 1875 he founded the Arya Samaj (the Noble Community) as a "Vedic" religious organization whose social reform platform condemned child marriage and untouchability while promoting the equality of women. He rejected social hierarchies in the form of *jati*, but thought *varna* should be decided based on one's character, which the organization would determine in a public examination. The Arya Samaj distinguished itself from the Ram Mohan Roy's Brahmo Samaj as it cultivated a keen sense of Hindu nationalism and anticipated the more extreme nationalist groups that appeared in the early twentieth century.

Other movements and figures, less influenced by colonial and Christian critiques of Hinduism, did not assume such an apologetic stance. One important figure was the enormously popular Bengali mystic, Ramakrishna (1836–1886). A devotee and temple priest of the Goddess in her fearsome form as Kali, he is said to have had ecstatic experiences since his early childhood. Although some thought he was mad, his fame as a great mystic spread and he began to attract disciples from all over Bengal. Among his many middle-class Bengali disciples was a progressive law student, Narendranath Datta (1863–1902). A member of the Brahmo Samaj, Datta thought of himself as a rational intellectual, but he was curious if anyone had ever

SWAMI VIVEKANANDA
(1863 - 1902)

Temple volunteers unveil a statue of Swami Vivekananda at the Hindu Temple of Greater Chicago, Saturday, July 11, 1998, in Lemont, Illinois. The statue honors Vivekananda as "the first man to bring Hindu religion and the practice of yoga to America."

directly met God "face to face." After hearing of Ramakrishna during a college lecture, Narendranath went to meet him and eventually became a disciple. He took monastic vows during Ramakrishna's last days, and was thereafter known as Swami Vivekananda. He founded the Ramakrishna Math, an order of monks belonging to the lineage of Ramakrishna.

As Swami Vivekananda, this initially skeptical law student had an enormous impact on the manner in which Hinduism was represented in the West, particularly in America. In 1893, Vivekananda visited America to represent Hinduism to the World's Parliament of Religions at the Chicago World's Fair. Quoting from the *Bhagavad Gita* in his speech, he represented Hinduism as a tolerant and universal religion. Like his teacher, Ramakrishna, Vivekananda asserted that all religions are true. His stirring speech ensured his fame and popularity in America, and he stayed on for an additional two years, during which time he founded the "The Vedanta Society of New York." During his visit he established the first Hindu institutions in the West. Today, there are numerous Vedanta Societies; 110 of them are found outside of India.

Gandhi, Hinduism, and Indian Nationalism

Mohandas Karamchand Gandhi (1869–1948), a towering religious, political, and social reformer in India, recast many Hindu ideas in the service of the fight for Indian independence. Born into a middle-class family from the merchant *jati*, Gandhi was an English-educated lawyer and a deeply religious man. As a law student in England he read for the first time the *Bhagavad Gita* (in an English translation), and it had a profound impact on him. He held this text dear for the rest of his life.

Gandhi's political career began in South Africa, where he worked as a lawyer. It was here, in a struggle against apartheid, that he began to develop his political philosophy of nonviolent resistance. He characterized this nonviolent resistance as *satyagraha* (Sanskrit, "grasping the truth") and explained that it derived its very power from its commitment to nonviolence (*ahimsa*).

Gandhi returned to India in 1915 to join the fledgling Independence movement, which sought to free India from British colonial rule. Profoundly influenced by Thoreau's writings on civil disobedience, Gandhi established an ashram (school) to train freedom fighters. The ashram chose as its motto a statement from the *Upanishads*:

satyameva jayate, "the truth alone will prevail." Like his *Upanishadic* forbearers, Gandhi believed that truth could be sought only through perfect self-effacement, which in itself could be achieved by disciplining the body through fasting and celibacy.

Gandhi did not hesitate to criticize certain Hindu beliefs and practices, particularly that of *varnashrama dharma*, the ancient system by which society was ordered. He worked tirelessly to abolish untouchability, although he urged the "untouchables" (*Dalits*) themselves to remain passive in the fight for social equality. For this reason, many *Dalits*, whom he called *harijans* ("children of god"), rejected Gandhi's advocacy and looked within their own fold for a leader.

Gandhi was so influential a figure and his charisma was so great that even in his lifetime he was revered as a saint or *Mahatma* (Sanskrit, "Great Soul"). People flocked to have *darshan* of this slight man, who embodied truth, nonviolence, and self-sufficiency. Although a Hindu all his life, Gandhi also advocated the universality and truth of all religions and sought throughout his life to reconcile Hinduism and Islam. He was assassinated in 1948 by a Hindu fanatic who believed that Gandhi was too lenient with Muslims. He died as he had lived: with quiet strength and dignity and with the name of God on his lips.

Hindu Nationalism and *Hindutva*

While figures like Ram Mohan Roy, Vivekananda, and Gandhi sought to build bridges with the West or with other religions, other figures, such as V. D. Savarkar (1883–1966), insisted on the distinctiveness of Hinduism. Savarkar called this concept **hindutva** (Sanskrit, "Hindu-ness"). The term, coined in a 1923 pamphlet, was for Savarkar a force to unite Hindus in repelling all dangerous foreign influences. As president of the Hindu Mahasabha, a Hindu nationalist political party that embraced Savarkar's notion of *hindutva*, he argued that India was an exclusively "Hindu Nation."

In 1925, the Rashtriya Svayamsevak Sangh (RSS; "The National Volunteer Corps") was founded. Although it has presented itself as a Hindu cultural organization, its members have a long history of staging political actions that have intensified communal tensions, precipitated violence, and propagated ideals of religious intolerance. The RSS was founded by K. B. Hedgewar (1889–1940), who was himself inspired by V. D. Savarkar's concept of *hindutva*. The RSS was meant to be a training ground for the self-empowerment of Hindu youth who were committed to defending a Hindu nation from the perceived threat posed by the Muslim world. On January 30, 1948, Nathuram Godse, a RSS activist and a member of Savarakar's Hindu Mahasabha, assassinated Gandhi because he thought Gandhi was too accommodating of Muslims. Godse was executed on November 15, 1949. Gandhi's two sons and Jawaharlal Nehru (1889–1964), who was the first prime minister of India, felt that Godse was a pawn of RSS leaders and fought against his execution, believing that it would dishonor everything that Gandhi represented.

After Gandhi's assassination, the Hindu Mahasabha was fully implicated in the conspiracy and many of its members were arrested (though Savarkar himself was acquitted). The political backlash led many Mahasabha members to leave the party and ally themselves instead with a new political organization called the Bharatiya Jana Sangh (Indian People's Alliance). Its founder, Syama Prasad Mookerjee (1901–1953), had been a member of both the Mahasabha and the RSS when he organized the Indian People's Alliance in 1951. This was a Hindu nationalist party specifically created to oppose the Indian National Congress, the party of Jawaharlal Nehru and Mahatma Gandhi. In 1981 the Indian People's Alliance became the Bharatiya Janata Party (BJP), and is currently second only to the Congress as one of India's two political heavyweights.

Today, organizations espousing Savarakar's *hindutva* ideology come under an umbrella group called the Sangh Parivar ("the Family of Associations"). The RSS is the cultural wing, the BJP is the political wing, and the Vishwa Hindu Parishad (VHP; World Hindu Organization) is the religious wing. The RSS continues to attract mostly lower-middle-class male youth, who feel empowered by the strong sense of cultural identity that it advocates. While this has helped awaken a deep sense of cultural pride among Hindu youth, it does not change the fact that RSS members have been leading participants in most of the communal violence of recent years.

In 1991 the BJP led a pilgrimage around India gathering bricks to build a temple to Rama in Ayodhya, India. However, this was to be no ordinary temple. The pilgrims claimed that a fifteenth-century C.E. Islamic mosque called the Babri Masjid ("mosque") had been erected over an older Hindu temple that marked the exact birthplace of Rama. Their purpose was to tear down the mosque and build a grand Rama temple in its place. Members of Sangh Parivar rallied around the cause, which culminated in more than 200,000 participants converging on Ayodhya and demolishing the mosque with their bare hands. RSS youth then targeted the local Muslim community, destroying other mosques, ransacking Muslim homes, raping Muslim women, and murdering Muslim men. The backlash of these events echoed throughout India and Bangladesh, resulting in more than a thousand incidents of riots and communal violence perpetrated by both Hindus and Muslims. By the time calm had been restored, more than 4,000 people had been injured and at least 1,100 had lost their lives.

But the BJP has also employed less aggressive strategies to motivate Hindus to fight for a Hindu India. During the BJP's peak years of political power, it attempted to rewrite Indian history by implementing new school textbooks throughout India. These textbooks reflected the BJP's unique political vision, characterizing India as a Hindu nation and Hinduism as a unified, monolithic tradition. Most importantly, and dangerously, this rewriting minimized Muslim contributions to the development of India and described Muslim rulers as foreign invaders. The RSS also has a strong presence in the diaspora communities in Europe and North America. A number of

Hindu immigrants send their children to RSS youth camps to give them a sense of their Hindu identity.

The Future of Hinduism

The pressures of modernity and increasing globalization have caused an inward turn in Hinduism. Encouraged by nationalist groups and political parties in India, some Hindus see Hinduism as monolithic, homogenous, and impermeable, closed off from the perceived corrupting influences of the West and outside religious traditions. Simultaneously, we also discern a movement that seeks to transcend traditional boundaries—as, for example, in the founding of a Ganesha temple described at the beginning of this chapter—as it reaches out to the larger community. While classical Hindu texts give little agency to women, Hindu women today are assuming leadership roles in the Indian community in an unprecedented fashion. Women are acting as priests in villages and diaspora temples and wield influence as spiritual teachers, monastics, and theologians. One of the most important female **gurus** with a transnational presence is Mata Amritanandamayi Devi, known to her followers as Ammachi (b. 1953). Believed by her devotees to be the embodiment of Devi, the divine mother, Ammachi's message of tolerance, caste equality (she herself is from a low-caste background), and ecumenism speaks eloquently to Hinduism's global presence.

CONCLUSION

This chapter explores the rich history of the many religious traditions that make up Hinduism and the varied beliefs and practices of its adherents. We have seen how concepts such as *samsara* and *karma* bind Hindus together despite this diversity. We have also observed that what many people consider to be the central organizing ideologies of Hinduism—the notions of ritual purity and caste—have been repeatedly challenged and rejected throughout its long history. While many might tend to think of Hindu reform as taking place in the nineteenth century as a response to colonialism, it is clear that reform has played an important role throughout the entire development of the various strains of Hinduism. *Bhakti* movements, *tantra*, and the ascetic and renouncer traditions can all be regarded as responses to the crystallization of Brahmanical orthodoxy. This is equally true in the contemporary period. On the one hand, the rise of Hindu nationalism has on occasion led to deplorable violence. On the other hand, figures like Gandhi exemplify a Hinduism synonymous with nonviolence and tolerance. Today, women gurus and women priests break all kinds of traditional taboos, and the vibrancy of the diaspora communities mingle Hinduism peacefully with the religious traditions of Africa, North America, and Southeast Asia.

Hinduism can truly be said to be a global religion. Having long ago left the land of its birth, Hinduism now thrives throughout the world, continuing to adapt, grow, and change in response to new circumstances in which it finds itself.

SEEKING ANSWERS

What Is Ultimate Reality?

Most Hindus believe that *Brahman* pervades and transcends all of creation. Thus, all things are inherently divine. Humans are unable to apprehend this ultimate reality because of attachment, delusion, and identification with the limited ego-self. *Maya*, the illusory or magical divine power, conceals the underlying oneness of things or the intimate eternal relationship on all things with God or Brahman. A deeper understanding of the true nature of the world ultimately culminates in reunion with *Brahman* and further expansion of the nature of consciousness itself.

How Should We Live in This World?

All Hindus believe in the *atman*, the eternal, undying soul, which reincarnates upon death. The nature of one's experience both in this life and in future lifetimes is determined by the result of one's actions. If one has earned plenty of merit, one might for a time even take birth in the realms of gods or celestials. If, on the other hand, one has accrued de-merit, he or she might spend time in a hell realm. But these realms are only temporary, and when the fruits of egregious acts of good or ill are spent, the soul returns to the world again. Some Hindus believe that the last thought in one's mind at the moment of death can significantly influence the state of one's next birth. When Mahatma Gandhi was shot, he had the presence of mind to say Rama's name three times before he died. Human birth is seen as particularly useful for the purpose of quickening the spiritual evolution toward the ultimate attainment of enlightenment (*moksha*) as it is neither too pleasurable nor too painful. Human existence offers the ideal place to see the mystery of action (*karma*) and to transcend it either through using the powers of discrimination to disassociate with the temporal phenomenal self and identify with *Brahman*, the absolute self, or through an act of devotion to surrender the individual ego self to god and relinquish the fruits of action.

What Is Our Ultimate Purpose?

While most Hindus believe in the illusory nature of material existence, they differ on its purpose or reason. Some Hindu sects consider the illusory nature of the world to be a result of divine play. Some don't presume to know God's intention but simply relish the unfolding of life in all its magnitude as God's divine performance. On the other hand, some sects regard illusion as a simple result of ignorance, which is itself born from attachment to the senses and the sense objects. Most agree that the purpose of life is to achieve *moksha* or enlightenment. For some, this is described as a complete union with God or *Brahman* and is usually attained through relinquishing identification with the limited phenomenal self that is attached to sensory objects and thinks itself the agent of action. For

---

SEEKING ANSWERS *(continued)*

---

some Hindus *moksha* is a complete realization of the soul's deep and perpetual loving relationship with God that is perfected through realizing that God works intimately through all of creation and is the true agent of action. Here, *moksha* may mean eternally abiding at "play," in loving service to God. Both of these realizations bring about a cessation of *karma* and a release from *samsara*.

REVIEW QUESTIONS

For Review

1. Describe some of the various types of Hindu worship.
2. Explain the concept of *darshan* in terms of Hindu iconography and temple worship.
3. What is the relationship between the ideas of *karma* and of *moksha*?
4. Describe the various roles that women have played in Hindu tradition and in worship.
5. Describe the history of *bhakti*. What are the earliest sources? How does *bhakti* change as it develops through time and moves from region to region?

For Further Reflection

1. How does theistic Hindu philosophy differ from the philosophy of the *Upanishads*? How is it the same?
2. How has Hinduism changed since the British Colonial period?
3. How would you characterize the impact that many Hindu saints have had on society?
4. How would you explain the difference between theistic Hinduism and what might be called Upanishadic Hinduism? How might both of these differ from Vedic Hinduism? Are there any aspects shared by all three?
5. How is the concept of the *avatara* different or similar to other religious traditions that speak of "God on earth"?

GLOSSARY

arati (aah-ra-tee; Sanskrit) A ceremony involving the waving of a lamp before one's object of worship; it is often conceived as a purificatory rite that removes *drishthi* (the evil eye or negative projections).

atman (aat-mun; Sanskrit) The self or soul; lit. "the one who breathed."

avatara (ah-vah-taah-rah; Sanskrit) A divine incarnation, God taking physical form.

bhakti (bhah-k-tee; Sanskrit) Devotion.

Brahman (braah-mun; Sanskrit) God, ultimate reality, the all-pervasive, the ground of the universe.

brahmin (braah-mun; Sanskrit) A member of the priestly caste.

Dalit (daah-lit; Marathi, "oppressed") The preferred term of self-representation for people who had been traditionally branded as untouchables in the caste system.

GLOSSARY (*continued*)

darshan (dur-shaan; Sanskrit) "An auspicious sight." The act of seeing and being seen by a divine being or saint.

dharma (dhur-mah; Sanskrit) Lit. "that which is upheld": (1) religion, (2) religious prescriptions and ordinances, (3) sacred duty, (4) law, (5) moral virtue, and (6) social or caste obligation.

guru (goo-roo; Sanskrit) A teacher or preceptor. Lit. "one who is heavy."

hindutva (hin-doot-vah; Sanskrit, "Hindu-ness") A modern term that encompasses the ideology of Hindu nationalism.

karma (kur-mah; Sanskrit) Action or cause; the law of causation.

mantra (mun-trah; Sanskrit) A sacred sound, name, or verse that can be used as an object of meditation, ritual adoration, or magical invocation.

moksha (mohk-shah; Sanskrit) Enlightenment; complete liberation from the bonds of *karma* and *samsara*.

nirguna (nir-goo-nah; Sanskrit) "Without qualities." Referring to God as being beyond description.

phala (puh-lah; Sanskrit) Fruit, effect (as in the "fruit" of action).

prasada (pruh-saa-dah; Sanskrit) Consecrated offering, considered to be imbued after worship with the merciful blessing of the deity.

puja (poo-jah; Sanskrit) Worship.

purana (pooh-raa-nah; Sanskrit) "Ancient"; a compendium of myth, usually with a sectarian emphasis.

puranic (pooh-raa-nik; Sanskrit) Pertaining to the *puranas*.

sadhana (saah-dhah-nah; Sanskrit) Spiritual discipline or practice.

saguna (saah-goo-nah; Sanskrit) "With qualities." Referring to God as having specific identifiable traits or characteristics.

samsara The cycle of birth, death, and rebirth.

samskara (sum-skaah-rah; Sanskrit) Rite of passage.

sannyasi (sun-nyaah-see; Sanskrit) Monk-hood; formal renunciation.

Shaiva (shay-vah; Sanskrit) A devotee of Shiva.

Shakta (shah-k-tah; Sanskrit) A devotee of the Great Goddess, Devi.

tapas (tuh-pus; Sanskrit) The purifying heat of austerity.

Vaishnava (vie-sh-na-vah; Sanskrit) A devotee of Vishnu and his *avataras*.

Vedanta (veh-daan-tah; Sanskrit) Lit. "the end of the *Vedas*." A comprehensive term for the philosophy that originated in the *Vedas*.

Vedic (veh-dik; Sanskrit) Pertaining to the *Vedas*.

yoga (yoh-gah; Sanskrit) Lit. "union," from the Sanskrit root *yuj*, "to yoke." Spiritual practices oriented at controlling the mind and senses.

SUGGESTIONS FOR FURTHER READING

Eck, Diana. *Darshan: Seeing the Divine Image in India*. Chambersberg: Anima Press, 1981. An excellent discussion on the significance of *darshan* and traditions of Hindu temple worship.

Flood, Gavin. *An Introduction to Hinduism*. Cambridge: Cambridge University Press, 1996. A concise and in depth study of Hinduism.

Flood, Gavin, ed. *The Blackwell Companion to Hinduism*. Oxford: Blackwell Publishing, 2003. A presentation on select special topics that are key to understanding Hindu belief and practice.

Hawley, John Stratton and Mark Juergensmeyer. *Songs of the Saints of India*. Oxford: Oxford University Press, 2006. A survey of the lives of medieval bhakti saints, with excellent translation of some of their poetry.

Hawley, John Stratton and Vasudha Narayanan. eds. *The Life of Hinduism*. Berkeley: University of California Press, 2006. Special topical articles that explore personal voices and perspectives on Hindu life experience.

Klostermaier, Klaus K. *Hindu Writings: A Short Introduction to the Major Sources*. Oxford: One World Publications, 2000. A keen survey of excerpts from many of the important textual sources that inform Hindu belief.

ONLINE SOURCES

The Internet Sacred Text Archive of Hinduism
www.sacred-texts.com/hin/
The Internet Sacred Text Archive of Hinduism provides an excellent array of the many genres of Hindu sacred texts with multiple public domain translations of key works.

The University of Wyoming Hinduism Website
uwacadweb.uwyo.edu/religionet/er/hinduism/index.htm
The University of Wyoming Hinduism Website offers concise but in-depth discussions on numerous aspects of Hindu tradition, literature, and belief.

Understanding Hinduism
www.hinduism.co.za/index.html
An informal collection of articles and information on key topics offering some range of viewpoints.

The Sri Vaishnava Homepage
www.ramanuja.org
The Sri Vaishnava Homepage is a unique resource for adherents to this important sect of Hinduism, yet is accessible and informative for outsiders.

The Shaivam.org Site
www.shaivam.org/index.html
The Shaivam.org Site is a unique resource in that it explores multiple sectarian views of Shaivism yet is vast in scope and rich in detail.

The Internet Sacred Text Archive on Yoga
www.sacred-texts.com/hin/yoga/index.htm
The Internet Sacred Text Archive offers an extensive array of works on yoga including both original sacred texts in translation as well as modern explorations of the subject.

BUDDHISM

THE FULL MOON HANGS luminous above the western horizon. To the east the light of the morning sun spills across a valley nestled amid low mountains. Those furtive rays glint softly on the red adobe of a Zen temple, making it shimmer like a mirage. Standing at its open doorway Jisen notices that the morning sun has begun to warm the good firm earth beneath her feet.

She used to feel that moving through life was like being caught in the undertow of the world, as if she was being dragged out to sea. But the past years of her Buddhist practice had given her a new sense of buoyancy—an ease with navigating life's challenges. Jisen likes the simple joy of feeling the earth firm beneath her feet. Buddhism has given her a subtle grace of insight, and now her preparation to take on the mantle of a Buddhist priest is about passing that gift ever onward. What she had freely received, she would freely give.

In preparation for leaving home, she had spent the week leading up to her ordination sleeping outdoors under the "Jizo" tree. It grew midway between the monastery and the river and was honored as a living embodiment of the monk Jizo. Like all **bodhisattvas**, Jizo once vowed to postpone achieving personal enlightenment until he had helped to free all other beings from sorrow and despair. Before dawn, Jisen had walked from the tree down to the river. Then, as she stood wearing only

Tonsure ceremony of a Buddhist nun.

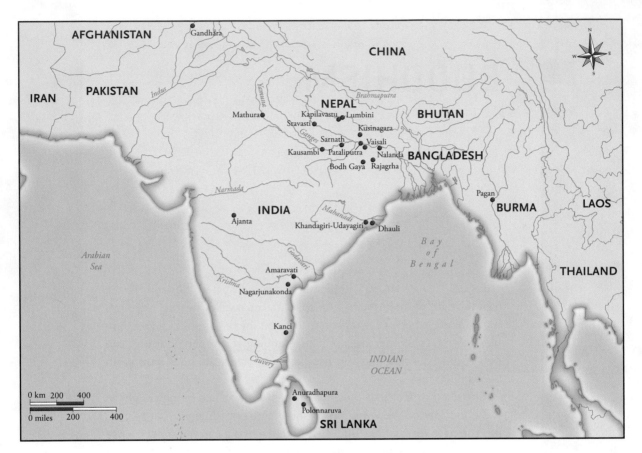

Significant sites of early Buddhism.

her white ceremonial under-robes, a small group of her brother and sister monks had shaved her head, leaving only a single strand at the crown.

Now, as the procession leads her into the temple for ordination and final hair-cutting, she feels the warmth of the monastic community surrounding her and the love of her parents who have come to say good-bye. As the last sonorous notes of the processional music fade into silence, the sharp, wooden "Clack!" of the *zuichin* clappers announce that the ordination has begun. Kneeling before the altar she listens as the Preceptor of the monastery invokes all the Buddhas, *Bodhisattvas*, and Great Teachers of their lineage. Then the Preceptor turns and addresses Jisen:

"The Mind Source is completely calm and the sea of the **Dharma** is fathomless; one who cannot realize it wanders eternally and one who realizes it is immediately at home. To be able to play freely in the field of enlightenment, it is necessary to drop attachments. Vow to drop them, let them go.

"Do not doubt! Cutting one's hair is cutting the root of human attachment, and if one cuts off human attachment even just a little bit, one's True Body is immediately revealed. Changing your clothes you step out of worldly delusion, and can thus attain freedom. Therefore, among all the Buddhas in the Three Worlds, not one attained enlightenment without dropping attachments and penetrating dualistic views. . . . Even though you do not yet know your enlightenment, by dropping attachments, you already are the true child of Buddha. . . .

"Jisen . . . Reflect! Your body-mind is suddenly turning from eternal transmigration and you are being irreversibly and eternally born in the no-birth country of Buddha. Clinging and delusion do not cease, yet your original true nature has been revealed. After entering the priesthood, heaven neither covers nor does the earth sustain. Having nothing with which to cover your round head and your robes embodying enlightenment, you stand out. . . . You will now be able to dedicate this life freely to the welfare and service of all beings."

As the ordination robe is placed in Jisen's outstretched arms, the elder monks and nuns in her monastic community gather round to help dress her in it. The Preceptor then asks: "Now, the last strands of your hair will be cut. Only the Buddha can cut the last strand of hair. Will you allow me to cut it?"

Three times the question is asked and three times Jisen acknowledges that the Preceptor and all beings have the Buddha-nature, by softly answering, "I will." With the final strand of her hair cut, Jisen recites: "Though my form is completely altered I remain faithful to my purpose, parting with human attachment and thus renewing myself. Leaving home, I seek the Enlightened Way; I vow to free all creations." She then intones the four great vows of the *bodhisattva*:

> Vast is the Robe of Liberation. . . .
> A formless field of benefaction. . . .
> I wear the Tathagata teaching. . . .
> Saving all Sentient Beings.

The Preceptor ceremoniously invests Jisen with the begging bowl of a Zen priest, and she is called to atone for any harmful actions done in both this and all previous existences. Having formally committed herself to observing the sixteen Buddhist precepts of her order, Jisen is now an ordained nun. The whole community gathers round her as she stands at the altar. Smiling at one another and bowing, everyone recites together: "Buddha recognizes Buddha and Buddha bows to Buddha." Smiling gently through her grateful tears, Jisen stands at the juncture of a new way of living, with a new resolve to aid all sentient beings. Outside the temple, the sun has risen on a bright new day.[1] ☀

The Buddha, the founder of the Buddhist **dharma** (Sanskrit, "religion, path, teaching"), was a historical figure named Gautama Siddhartha. The word "**Buddha**" means, in Sanskrit, "the Awakened One." Thus, as everyone has the potential for enlightenment, anyone can become a Buddha. However, throughout this chapter we will refer to the historical figure Gautama Siddhartha as "the Buddha," while using "Buddha" or "a Buddha" to invoke the generic notion of an enlightened being. The remainder of the chapter will address the complex array of Buddhist doctrines, sectarian viewpoints, and practices and will outline the social institutions that have preserved and transmitted the Buddha's teaching from his period to the present.

THE TEACHINGS OF BUDDHISM

Many Buddhists believe that there are ultimately as many "Buddhisms" as there are beings in the universe. Everyone "must be a lamp unto themselves"; everyone must find their own way. The beliefs and practices of the religion have grown and developed as Buddhism has moved from region to region across space and time. The one constant, however, is the inspiration drawn from the personal life of the Buddha, the journey of discovery he took, and the questions he asked. Therefore, it is appropriate that we begin our encounter with Buddhism with the story of the life of the Buddha.

Meeting the Buddha

The man who came to be known as the Buddha blended logic, reasoning, meditation, and compassion into an integrated system for alleviating human suffering. His practical approach to confronting life's most vexing problems with clarity and insight has ensured his place as one of the most significant religious figures in human history.

Though little reliable data exist from his historical era, the story of his life has been retold in many cultures, contexts, and time periods. Each version has lent a bit of new color to the picture of one individual's personal quest for understanding.[2] The first part of this chapter begins with an account of the Buddha's life story based primarily on a text called the *Buddhacarita* (Sanskrit, "The Acts of the Buddha"), composed in the second century C.E. in India. Where applicable, other interesting variations on his life story will be noted. While much of the story of the Buddha's life and deeds may have been added later, and it is difficult to separate legend from history, the story nonetheless serves as an inspiration for Buddhists everywhere. So, let us begin to explore Buddhism through the life of the man who first developed Buddhist teaching and practice.

The Life of the Buddha

Siddhartha Gautama, who was to become the Buddha, was born in 563 B.C.E. to King Suddhodana and Queen Maya of the Shakya Dynasty, who ruled from the city of Kapilavastu (in the south of what is modern Nepal). It is said that his mother Maya "immaculately" conceived the child after dreaming that a divine white elephant with six tusks flew down from heaven and entered her womb. Ten months later, in the garden at Lumbini (in present-day Nepal), she suddenly went into labor, clutching the bough of a *sala* tree that bent down to support her. The infant Siddhartha emerged from her side, immediately took seven steps, and proclaimed to the four directions: "I will reach the highest *nirvana*. I shall be the first among beings. This will be my last birth. I will cross the ocean of existence."[3]

Royal astrologers and diviners observed thirty-two auspicious marks on the body of the child that indicated that he was destined to conquer the world. But there was some question as to which world it would be: Would he conquer the outer world as a victorious monarch? Or would he conquer the inner world as a holy sage? However the child's life might unfold, it was clear that Siddhartha was fated to transform the world around him radically.

King Suddhodana began to get a real sense of this only when he took his newborn son to the temple to be blessed by the tutelary deities of the Shakyas. Here, as the king tried to get the baby to bow at the feet of the gods, the sacred icons came alive. Stepping down from their pedestals, the icons all bowed down to the child instead. Seeing this miracle, Suddhodana himself bowed down before his own son and addressed him as *Devatideva* (Sanskrit, "Foremost of the Gods"). Even while witnessing these wonders, King Suddhodana was resolved to ensure that his son would follow in his footsteps and would one day become the King of the World. The king would go to great lengths to insulate his son from those troubling aspects of life that inspired wandering mendicants and philosopher-hermits to abandon the worldly life for a religious calling. But despite the king's best intentions to shield Siddhartha from pain, it seemed the cards were stacked against the well-intentioned king when, just seven days after the baby's birth, his mother died.

Her death had a profound effect on the boy, yet the king still struggled to distract the young prince from the cares of the world. As Siddhartha grew up, he was surrounded by luxurious palaces, sumptuous food, and beautiful women. Not only did he seem to have the perfect life, but he also seemed to be the perfect prince. A brilliant student and accomplished athlete, he won the hand of the lovely princess Gopa by besting the greatest warriors of the kingdom in a contest of martial prowess.[4]

Prince Siddhartha was young, handsome, and gifted with every virtue. He had a beautiful wife and lived surrounded by wealth and opulence, with a vast retinue of devoted servants and eager concubines. Yet something began to stir in him that made him see cracks in the façade of his life, that made him long to burst free of his gilded cage. The simple notion that not everyone enjoyed this same life of ease began to take root in his mind.

One morning the prince accompanied his father to celebrate the annual festival that marked the first sowing of the fields. Seated in the shade of a rose apple tree, Siddhartha saw the oxen straining beneath their yokes and the ploughmen soaked in sweat. He noticed a worm writhing in the heat of the upturned soil, only to be gulped down by a frog. As he watched, the frog was then devoured by a snake, which was in turn eaten by a peacock; the peacock was then killed by a hawk, which was then itself attacked by an eagle. Watching the circle of life and the food chain in action stirred something in the young prince, and his mind withdrew into the first level of meditative trance.

Late in the afternoon, the king and the ladies of the palace came to look for Siddhartha and found him still seated beneath the rose apple tree, deep in meditation.

Though the shadows of all the other trees had shifted, the shade of that rose apple remained unmoved, sheltering the still form of the young prince. The king bowed down before his son a second time.

The third and final turning point in Siddhartha's life came when he insisted on taking his chariot out of the palace for a pleasant ride to the park. His father had the streets cleared of any distressing elements that might encourage his son's philosophical turn of mind. But this day ultimately spelled failure for Suddhodana's plan to shelter his son. Some accounts claim that even the gods were conspiring against the king when they descended to earth to manifest as "the Four Signs."

As Siddhartha rode out of the palace, he encountered the first sign: an old gray-haired man teetering on a cane. He asked his charioteer, "What kind of man is this, is it mere chance that made him this way?" Siddhartha was shocked to learn that everyone—even himself—would eventually become old. He next saw a sick man, and then a corpse, and was again startled to learn that sickness and death are also an intrinsic part of life. In this way Siddhartha learned the *First Noble Truth*, "that suffering is inherent in existence." But then he spied the "fourth sign:" a wandering monk who seemed to be utterly at ease with both himself and the world around him. It struck the prince that there might be some way to make sense of this world and possibly even find a way out of the suffering that all beings seem to endure.

Siddhartha cuts his hair. Mural depicting the Life of Buddha, Jogyesa Temple, Seoul, South Korea.

Setting Forth on the Journey The king, sensing his son's turn of mind, began to have premonitory dreams that the prince's departure was imminent. He took extra precautions to ensure that the prince could not flee the palace. But the night Siddhartha left home, all of the palace guards had by some miracle fallen into a deep sleep. Before leaving the palace, he went one last time to see his wife and newborn son, Rahula, sleeping peacefully on a bed strewn with jasmine blossoms. Although Siddhartha wanted to hold his baby boy one last time, he knew that his wife might wake up and he would then never be able to leave. So, in a moment, he was gone.

When Siddhartha was finally alone in the wilderness, he took off his expensive ornaments and clothes. He drew his sword and cut off his hair. From that moment, Siddhartha would have to "diligently work out his salvation" all on his own.

Siddhartha immediately sought out a teacher. He began to study with a master of philosophy and a yoga master. Both helped to deepen his meditative practice. But ultimately he recognized that these abstract states of expanded consciousness were not the same as true enlightenment. While they did allow him to explore consciousness and transcend his senses, they did not enable him to directly grasp the ultimate nature of reality.[5] Realizing that true enlightenment could not be achieved under their tutelage, he ventured off alone again and began to perform extreme ascetic practices, including yogic breath retention and the kind of fasting usually ascribed to Jain mendicants (Chapter 6).

Meditation, Austerity, and the Quest for Freedom As time passed, five other ascetics began practicing their own severe austerities nearby, hoping that Siddhartha would soon achieve enlightenment and guide them to the next level of being. After a long period of intense fasting that left him all skin and bones, Siddhartha went to bathe in the river. There, he overheard a music teacher plucking a lute and explaining to his student that if the string was too tight, it would break, yet if it was too loose it wouldn't sound. Siddhartha realized that there must be a kind of **Middle Way** for his own bodily instrument as well. The Buddha would later invoke this analogy of tuning the mind like a musical instrument—finding that perfect pitch, so that the mind resonates in harmony with reality. Seeking this profound harmony, Siddhartha began to eat and sleep again, but always in moderation. The five ascetics, disgusted with his lack of discipline, promptly abandoned him. A local woman, however, offered Siddhartha a bowl of porridge to sustain him in his meditation. After eating, he cast the bowl in the river where it floated upstream—a sign that his enlightenment was at hand. He would not eat again for the next forty-nine days.[6]

It had been six years since he left home, and Siddhartha's resolve to obtain complete clarity was unshakable. He wandered to a village in northern India, now known as Bodh Gaya. Under a full moon, he sat down beneath a *bodhi* tree, vowing that though his body might shrivel and his flesh and bones dissolve, he would not move until he achieved complete enlightenment.

Nirvana: "Blowing Out" the Fires of Longing and Despair With this new insight and resolve Siddhartha stood at the brink of enlightenment. But it was here that he faced his greatest challenge. Mara the Tempter, the Personification of Death and Rebirth,[7] appeared before him. Mara summoned a vast legion of demons, monsters, and wild beasts to attack Siddhartha and sent nine storms to shake him from his meditation, but Siddhartha remained unmoved. Their razor-sharp weapons turned to a shower of blossoms, their blazing meteors became a gentle cloud of powdered sandalwood, and those gale-force winds hardly rippled his robe.

The light streaming from Siddhartha's body shielded him from the assault of Mara's dark minions. In desperation Mara summoned his three daughters, *Tanha* (Desire), *Raga* (Lust), and *Arati* (Aversion), to dance enticingly before Siddhartha. But all the energy and vitality of his being were firmly fixed on peering into the very heart of reality, and he remained utterly indifferent.

At last the Tempter wrung his hands, appeared before him, and screamed: "Who do you think you are? How is it that you can challenge my position as Lord of this World? That seat of enlightenment you occupy should be mine. Since the dawn of creation I have been the most generous! I have fulfilled the desires of countless beings.

Buddha's enlightenment, "Calling the Earth to Witness."

Who can attest to your mercy and merit?" Silently, Siddhartha took his right hand and gently touched the earth beneath him. With this "Gesture of Calling the Earth to Witness," the ground shook, the voice of Mother Earth herself gave a resounding affirmation, and Mara wept and dissolved into shadow.

Touching the earth, Siddhartha's enlightenment was at hand. He sank deeper into meditation. In the course of the night he perceived what are called the "Three Marks of Existence." First, he peered deep into the past. He saw all of his former lives in great detail: life, death, rebirth. He grasped the concept that one's existence is constantly in a state of flux, with a shifting sense of "self" arising in response to a given set of conditions. Second, he looked out at the cosmos through a "divine eye." He witnessed the whole cycle of *karma*, where every individual's actions and intentions determined the circumstances of their next rebirth. Third, he tuned his awareness to see reality "as it is," cleared of the mind's distortions.[8] Here he realized the Doctrine of **Interdependent Origination** (Sanskrit *pratitya-samutpada*), which many regard as the pinnacle of Buddhist insight. This Doctrine holds that humans are prisoners in a house built on ignorance, attachment, and aversion. By removing ignorance, the prison crumbles, leaving humanity free under an open sky.

With this final vision, prince Siddhartha had truly become a Buddha, an awakened being. He was permanently freed from all that binds living beings and would not be reborn again. His awareness was now incomprehensibly expansive, without beginning and without end: the state of *nirvana* that he often called "the deathless." It was then that the Buddha opened his eyes and announced to the world:

> Through the round of many births I roamed without reward, without rest,
> seeking the House-builder.
> Painful is birth again and again.
>
> House-builder, you're seen!
> You will not build a house again.
> All your rafters broken, the ridge pole destroyed,
> gone to the Unformed, the mind has come to the end of craving.[9]

He was awake!

The Teaching Buddha and His Journey Home   For seven weeks the Buddha remained in the vicinity of the *bodhi* tree under which he had obtained enlightenment. For the first week he simply sat there, rapt in bliss. For the second week he stood a little ways off, staring, unblinking, at the place where he had sat. The next week he just walked back and forth beside the tree. He passed a few more weeks reflecting on his new understanding and the nature of consciousness. By the seventh week he realized that although he would like to assist all beings in achieving the same clear understanding and enlightenment that he had attained, ultimately individuals would need to perceive it directly. It defied all explanation. It wasn't something that could be spoken of or described.

But Brahma, the Hindu creator god (Chapter 4), in his kindness did not want humanity to miss this rare opportunity to learn the path to freedom from a living Buddha. So he came down from heaven and implored the Buddha to teach and pass on his insight. Brahma assured the Buddha that there were people in the world who could understand his teaching and attain enlightenment.

So the Buddha set out to teach the world. He went first to a deer park at Sarnath (near Varanasi in modern India), where the five disciples who had abandoned him were performing harsh austerities. The disciples could see the light pouring from the Buddha's body, and they realized that he had broken through to some new understanding. The disciples gathered around the Buddha, who gave them his first teaching—a moment that later Buddhist biographers refer to as "the Setting in Motion of the Wheel of the *Dharma*."

From Sarnath, the Buddha began to retrace his steps back home. Along the way he met a variety of unique individuals and extraordinary sages who were immediately struck by the simple directness of his insight. Many never left his side after their chance encounters, and they became the first Buddhist community of monks. As the ranks of this emerging monastic body began to swell, King Suddhodana heard that the Buddha was teaching in Rajagriha in northern India. He immediately sent a minister, accompanied by a thousand attendants, to convey a royal invitation for his son to come for a visit. The 1,001 men arrived, but before the message could be conveyed they heard the Buddha speak. Forgetting their mission, all of them requested to be ordained as monks right on the spot. Similarly, after Suddhodana sent nine more retinues of ministers and none returned, he asked Udayin, the Buddha's childhood friend, to go and convey the invitation. Udayin was also enraptured by the Buddha's teaching and decided to become a monk. But he didn't forget his duty to the king. When autumn came Udayin told the Buddha that the cool season was ideal for travel and that it would be the perfect time to visit his family.

The Shakyas excitedly gathered to receive the Buddha in a grove on the outskirts of Kapilavastu. Yet when the Buddha approached many were too proud to bow to him. The Buddha knew the karmic implications of not showing proper reverence to a Buddha. Fearing for them, he levitated into the sky and manifested a host of miracles before their astonished eyes. King Suddhodana bowed down to his son a third time.

The Buddha devoted considerable time to teaching and ministering to his family and fellow Shakyas. At least another 500 of them, many of whom were family members and friends, were ordained as monks. When they all wished to convert en masse, the Buddha had the low-caste barber Upali ordained first. Upali became the senior member of the **sangha** (Sanskrit, "community"), elder to all the upper-caste Shakyas ordained after him. This strategy worked to weaken caste hierarchy in the region. Later, so many men were becoming monks it seemed impossible for the lay community to be able to support the *sangha* or itself because of the loss of income. Eventually, King Suddhodana helped the Buddha formulate a rule that only one person from each family could be ordained as a monk.

Suddhodana slowly came around to recognize that what his son had achieved went far beyond anything that he could have ever hoped for Siddhartha. The king became a great friend and ally to the ever-expanding Buddhist community as he began to understand the Buddha's teaching. Other close members of the royal family were initially even more dramatically affected by his teaching. Siddhartha's stepmother, Queen Mahaprajapati, achieved the first level of insight upon meeting the Buddha for the first time. She also had a hand in reorganizing the Buddhist monastic institution by persisting in her requests for an ordination system that would allow herself and other women to formally become nuns.

Final Days and Last Words For forty-five years the Buddha wandered, teaching kings, ascetics, erudite *brahmins*, gods, supernatural beings, outcasts, madmen, murderers, and thieves. Some texts claim that he traveled as far west as Afghanistan, as far south as Sri Lanka, and as far east as Burma.[10] He skillfully debated adherents of rival philosophical viewpoints, but often won the hearts and minds of the people by some inexplicable quality they perceived in his demeanor. They took comfort in his ability to face the changes of life calmly, with eyes wide open, and they found healing in the unpretentious honesty of his teaching.

At the age of eighty, three months before his passing, the Buddha announced to his attendant Ananda that the moment of his death was fast approaching. He had been very ill but had used his meditative prowess to transcend the constraints of his time-ravaged body and to sustain him as he presented his final teachings. Eventually the time came as he and Ananda were en route to the rustic little town of Kushinagari in northern India.

In a grove on the outskirts of the village, Ananda made a bed for the ailing Buddha between two *sala* trees. As the Buddha lay down on his right side, celestial music began to echo in the air as the two *sala* trees suddenly burst into bloom and showered bright blossoms upon his body. The normally calm Ananda, who knew the time was at hand, was rattled. He began to lament: "Too soon! The great liberation (*parinirvana*) comes to the Blessed One too soon! Too soon the Eye of the World will be put out!"

Rock-cut reclining statue of the Buddha preparing to enter *nirvana*, in cave 26, a shrine in the Buddhist cave site at Ajanta, carved from a gorge in the Waghore River, Ajanta, Maharashtra State, India. Fifth century C.E.

Wandering monks and laypeople scattered about the area began to gather, frantically seeking a final fragment of the Buddha's wisdom to hold on to as he passed on. Even the very air about him seemed crowded with celestials and gods, who hung in space to catch his final words.

They asked what they would do without him to teach them, and he responded that the precepts would continue to guide them.[11] As he had taught them: "Be a lamp unto yourselves. Be refuges unto yourselves. Let the *Dharma* be your lamp. Let that be your refuge."[12]

The Buddha did not name a successor. He simply said: "All composite things must decay; be diligent in striving for freedom." Closing his eyes, he went deep into meditation, returning to the gate to enlightenment he passed into all those years ago under the *bodhi* tree. He shut the door behind him. The earth shook and he was gone.

> *Gate, Gate, paragate, parasamgate, bodhi svaha!*
> (Gone. Gone. Gone beyond. Gone beyond the beyond. Awake!)[13]

In the Tibetan accounts of the Buddha's life it is said that when the Buddha lay dying a celestial musician named Sunanda descended from heaven to meet him. The Buddha took from him his divine thousand-stringed lute, and then the Buddha began to play the most beautiful and haunting melody on it. As he played, one by one, he cut the strings of the lute. But the music played on. Even after he cut the last string, the music still played on.

The Basics of the Buddha's Teaching

The Buddha made his motives for becoming an ascetic clear to his disciples: observing old age, illness, and death around him, he became aware of life's fragility. He saw clearly that our bodies decay, from age or disease or both, until eventually we die. He understood that hiding this reality—as his father had tried to do—or trying to forget about it only postpones the pain of clinging to transient things. The Buddha spent some forty-five years of his life teaching. This section explores the ten key ideas that are essential to understanding Buddhist thought.

Most of the world's religious teachings begin by addressing the big questions of life, like "Is there an eternal soul?" "Is there life after death?" and "What is the nature and purpose of existence?" But the Buddha was more concerned with beginning right where we stand, right at the heart of the human experience.

In a teaching entitled "The Questions That Tend Not to Edification,"[14] he explained that the reason that he did not emphasize these abstract philosophical issues is that our immediate circumstances are what most require our attention. When we fixate on questions such as these, he taught, it is as if we were like a man wounded by an arrow soaked in poison who before allowing his family to fetch a doctor to help remove it first demands to know: "Who was the man that shot us?" and "Where did he come from?" The Buddha's point is that, just as if you are wounded by a poisoned arrow, you immediately pull it out, the urgency of our present circumstances demands our attention most.

The Buddha taught that much of human suffering is rooted not only in our presumptions of "how things are" but also in our assumptions of "who we are." He demonstrated how we limit our awareness of ourselves by trying to adhere to a fixed self-image that we hold in our minds. In the process, we each become a kind of patchwork imposter formed of mere conceptions. So the Buddhist teaching stresses that "a self *defined* . . . is a self *confined*." The Buddha declared that there are "Three Marks of Existence"—impermanence (*anitya*), suffering (*duhkha*), and no independent self or soul (**anatman**). For the Buddha, understanding these truths is the path to a life of peace. Even as the Buddha acknowledged the problems of human existence, his teaching began by offering a solution.

Some early European scholars[15] posited that Buddhism is not a religion at all, but neither can it be seen as just an abstract speculative philosophy. It is not simply about believing something, or "being a Buddhist," or theorizing about the nature of the world and existence. Rather, Buddhism is rooted in the experiential. It can be regarded as a therapeutic balm for the troubles of life, implemented through a profound "letting go," which includes freeing oneself of all fixed views.

Impermanence (*Anitya*)   The concept of impermanence is at the heart of Buddhist insight. Everything is in a state of flux; nothing remains the same. All things are in the process of becoming something else. In Buddhist cosmology, the universe is made up of shifting patterns of interacting energies that are constantly combining, dissolving, and recombining into a seemingly infinite variety of forms. People imagine that they are separate entities, but they like all other things are formed of threads that are woven into the larger fabric of existence. The Buddha stressed that much of human suffering arises as a result of misreading this shifting pattern of constituent parts for a sense of "self" that is both autonomous and permanent.

Direct Perception   The Buddha left behind a legacy of religious institutions with an emphasis on monastic tradition, yet he is also believed to have asserted at the end of his life that "*You must be a lamp unto yourself.*" While his emphasis on monasticism may appear disempowering to the individual layperson, ultimately his teachings make each individual the primary authority in spiritual matters. Each person must diligently strive to see into the nature of things. No one can tell anyone else what the truth is; one must see it for oneself. He cautioned: "Don't be misled by reports, or tradition, or hearsay. Don't be misled by the authority of religious texts, not by mere logic or inference, not by considering appearances, not by the delight in speculative opinions, not by seeming possibilities, not by the idea 'This is our teacher.' When you know for yourselves that certain things are unwholesome and wrong and bad, then give them up. And when you know for yourselves that certain things are wholesome and good, then accept them and follow them."[16] For the Buddha, even the *dharma* (the Buddhist teaching) was merely a "raft," a means to cross to the other shore (i.e., *nirvana*), but once *nirvana* was achieved the teaching was then to be let go of.[17] In the final analysis, to the Buddha any fixed view was merely a crutch. Though a particular vantage point might for a time enable one to see into the nature of things, it is only a means to an end—a means that should eventually be transcended or discarded.

"Non-Self" (*Anatman*) The Buddha grew up during an age of profound introspection in India, when the emphasis on sacrifice and ritual of the previous era had largely given way to philosophical inquiry and asceticism. By the Buddha's lifetime a number of his contemporaries were espousing descriptions precisely delineating the nature of the soul, or the *atman*, which was often regarded as the indwelling aspect of the divine *Brahman* that creates and pervades all things. Some of the sages steeped in the philosophy of the *Upanishads* (Chapter 4) would assert that the *atman* resided in the heart, was no bigger than the thumb, and that to know it was to be immortal.[18] While this scriptural understanding of the nature of being probably reflected the firsthand insights and experiences of the sages of bygone eras, for the Buddha it was not the same as directly apprehending reality oneself. As profound and revolutionary as these teachings were, the Buddha noticed that this kind of supposition led many to cling to presumptions that obscured their ability to see the truth for themselves.

Presumptions and misapprehension are a poor foundation upon which to build an understanding of reality. So to avoid making false assertions regarding what the nature of being is, the Buddha instead spoke in terms of the self as the *anatman*, the "un-self" or the "non-self." This is a tricky issue in Buddhist doctrine as the Buddha would sometimes speak in terms of a self for some disciples and of a "non-self" for others. Essentially, the early Buddhist position held that there are five "aggregates" or "components" (Sanskrit **skandhas**; "heaps" or "bundles") that together make up our sense of being: form, feeling, perception, mental formations, and consciousness. These *skandhas* give rise to a false sense of identity through apprehending them as an integrated and autonomous whole. Arising when mind and body come in contact with the external world, these aggregates are in a perpetual state of flux, but collectively generate the sense of a constant and changeless self or soul.

Without this conventional "self" or soul, one might ask, "What is it, then, that reincarnates?" For Buddhists, one's intentions and actions leave a kind of karmic residue that is housed in the "bundle" of mental formations (or "conditioned tendencies of thought," the fourth *skandha*). This in turn impresses itself upon consciousness, the fifth *skandha*. Consciousness, then, leaves the body at death and is reborn—reincarnated—in a new form. Because the self is also in a constant state of flux, it is not a changeless permanent or eternal soul as the *Upanishads* described. The five aggregates together are the basis of that which we cling to and consider as "the self"; this clinging, according to Buddhist teaching, is the primary source of human suffering. A movement toward the cessation of suffering comes from letting go of this idea of "me" and "mine," allowing one to flow mindfully in the shifting river of being.

There is considerable disagreement about what is behind the illusory web of "self" woven by the *skandhas*. Some Buddhists speak in absolute terms that there is no "higher self" or consciousness beyond the illusion, that nothing is there to be found. On the other hand, other Buddhists say that the Buddha's teaching clearly implied that ultimately there is "something" there but that he refused to reveal it—not wanting to replace one projection on the nature of reality with another.

Some might argue that this "something-Self" later coheres into the doctrine of the **Tathagatha-garba** (Sanskrit, "Womb-Matrix of the Thus-gone-one"). It asserts that while the constituent aggregates (*skandhas*) cast an illusory sense of self that is false, there is an eternal "Buddha-nature" in all beings. But this "true" self can only be experienced when one has fully awakened.

Interdependent Origination (*Pratitya-samutpada*) Arguably the subtlest of the Buddha's teachings is that of Interdependent Origination (Sanskrit *pratitya-samutpada*). The keystone of all Buddhist thought, in literal translation it means "arising on the ground of a preceding cause," but it is also commonly rendered as "dependent origination," "dependent co-origination," or simply "causality." Shariputra, one of the original disciples of the Buddha, said: "Those who understand Interdependent Origination, understand the teaching of the Buddha, and those who understand the teaching of the Buddha, understand Interdependent Origination."[19] The Buddha himself taught that when one does not rightly understand this law of Interdependent Origination, the world appears as "a ball of tangled thread," "a bird's nest," or "a dense thicket" from which one cannot escape.

Knowledge of Interdependent Origination begins with an understanding that our sense of "self" arises spontaneously in response to a set of conditions. These conditions are born of a vast network of relationships that are inextricably linked to all phenomena. Each juncture of this web of being is in turn linked to other conditions. Thus, all things are the result of antecedent causes and our sense of *independent* existence is merely an illusion. This is analogous to how an ecosystem defines the nature of the plants and animals within it.

A more practical Buddhist approach to understanding Interdependent Origination is illustrated in the Buddha's "Twelve Link Chain of Causation." Here, each link in the chain that binds us to the wheel of death and rebirth leads to the next link in the chain:

1. Ignorance
2. Volitional activity/karmic formations
3. Consciousness
4. Name and form
5. Sensory functions
6. Contact
7. Feeling

8. Craving
9. Grasping
10. Becoming
11. Birth
12. Old age and death[20]

These links should be understood not only as part of a causal process but also in terms of the psychological factors that shape our experience of "reality." Among them, ignorance, craving, and grasping are the three "weakest links" in the chain—they are most readily broken, thereby ending the process of causation and bringing about *nirvana*.

In **Mahayana** Buddhism a new doctrine develops that is intimately linked to that of Interdependent Origination. This is the doctrine of **shunyata** or "emptiness," which is sometimes described as a "profound openness" or "unlimitedness." Going beyond the teaching of *anatman* or the "un self," *shunyata* asserts that all phenomena lack independent existence. As with the teaching on Interdependent Origination it stresses the relational underpinnings of each and every component of existence. It goes as far as to assert that even "emptiness" is empty. Through such subtle, paradoxical reasoning it seeks to jar the mind from clinging to any objects or fixed assumptions by removing the distinction between external objects and the consciousness that views them.

Suffering: *Duhkha* Buddhists universally employ the term *duhkha* (Sanskrit, "the absence of joy and ease") to refer to the kind of human limitation that drove Siddhartha to ascetic practice. He boldly confronted the fact that life is fraught with constant change and that sickness, old age, and death—with all their accompanying feelings of loss and pain—are part of that change. Often translated simply as "suffering," the term *duhkha* also refers to the uneasiness and stress that can be found in aspects of life that we might not initially associate with "suffering." For example, *duhkha* is hidden in the subtle underlying feeling of always wanting something else or longing for more than what we have. The Buddha described as "clinging" any kind of behavior that could produce *duhkha*, and he carefully catalogued its manifestations: wanting something we don't have, hoping to avoid something we fear, trying to get away from what we don't want, or trying to hold onto something we know we'll eventually lose. From a Buddhist point of view, a subtle thread of *duhkha* can be detected even in those aspects of life usually regarded as pleasurable. A lurking sense of dissatisfaction

Pema Chodron is an American-born Buddhist nun whose books, such as *When Things Fall Apart: Heart Advice for Difficult Times*, address skillful ways to cope with everyday suffering and how to keep one's heart open in the face of adversity.

underlies even those aspects of life that we delight in and cherish most because they too will inevitably pass no matter how hard we try to hold on. But contemporary Buddhist teachers often assert that cultivating a willingness to let go in the face of change in turn allows our deepest wounds, disappointments, and regrets to let go of us.

Four Noble Truths The Buddha's process of engaging suffering was systematic. He was called *Bhisakko*, or "the Peerless Physician," and he structured his most fundamental teaching as if it were a medical diagnosis. His Four Noble Truths follow the four steps ancient Indian doctors used to diagnose and treat illness: (1) identifying a symptom, (2) discovering its cause, (3) determining if there is a possible cure to remove that cause, and (4) prescribing a therapy to enable that cure. As a process of treating the "dis-ease" of life, the Four Noble Truths empower all individuals to analyze the root cause of suffering and to provide their own cure. That this particular teaching is so essential to Buddhism is reflected in the fact that some version of these "Truths" are articulated in a variety of different forms and contexts throughout much of the Buddhist canon. The Buddha also linked the Four Noble Truths to the Noble Eightfold Path, discussed later in this chapter. The Four Truths and the Eightfold Path are not intended to be taken as a full description of the Buddha's direct perception of reality but, rather, as a prescription for apprehending it for oneself.

The Buddha did not usually discuss the Four Truths unless he felt a particular listener or group was ready to understand its depth. He usually prefaced its teaching by first reviewing principles of ethical conduct, the implications of *karma*, and the need for mindfulness and concentration. Though they are deceptively simple, the Four Noble Truths are the bedrock upon which the subtlest of Buddhist doctrines are built. Traditionally these truths are spelled out in four Sanskrit words: There is suffering (*duhkha*). It has a cause (*samudaya*). There is a means to bring about its end (*nirodha*). This is by following the path (*marga*) that goes beyond it.

Because most introductions to Buddhist thought begin with a discussion of the Four Noble Truths, a cursory glance at such a doctrine leads many to perceive Buddhism as being overly pessimistic and morose. But this recognition of the problem of human suffering is merely a part of the process of transcending it. And most Buddhists place emphasis on cultivating joy as much as on eliminating sorrow.

THE FOUR NOBLE TRUTHS

1. "*Suffering* is inherent in life."
2. "The *cause of suffering* is desire."
3. "Put an end to desire and you put *an end to suffering*."
4. "The way to do this is to follow *the Eightfold Path*."

The Noble Eightfold Path and the Middle Way You will recall that when Siddhartha overheard the teaching of the lute-player, the strumming of those strings led to his discovery of a "Middle Way." This discovery set Siddhartha on the right course to achieving full enlightenment as the Buddha. To assist in formulating a clear system to guide others between the extremes of life, the Buddha formulated the Noble Eightfold Path. It is the most direct presentation of Buddhist practice. While presumably the earliest and most widely accepted of such formulas, it is but one of a number of methods in which this notion of the Middle Way has been systematized.

The Buddha's teachings have often been referred to as "*prati-pada*" (Sanskrit, "the tracing of [his] footsteps [along the Path])." The structure of his teachings is meant to enable one to effectively follow in his footsteps, to navigate through the world toward the ultimate freedom that is *nirvana*. Examining this eightfold system, you can see that its eight areas of Buddhist endeavor can be further divided into three different spheres that together form a holistic approach to living. The first sphere, *shila* (Sanskrit, "ethical conduct") is reflected in Right Speech, Action, and Livelihood; the second sphere attends to *samadhi* (Sanskrit, "mental cultivation") with Right Effort, Mindfulness, and Concentration; and the third deals with perfecting **prajna** (Sanskrit, "wisdom") through Right View and Resolve. Let us briefly review how these three dimensions of the Buddhist path are implemented.

Ethics and "Skillful Means" For many Buddhist laypersons, the path to *nirvana* begins with ethical conduct. This may be as simple as serving the Buddhist community and supporting its institutions. Some Buddhists formally commit themselves by observing the Five Precepts (*Pancha-shila*), which include: (1) not killing (or causing

THE NOBLE EIGHTFOLD PATH

1. **Right View**: seeing clearly the nature of suffering, the workings of *karma*, and the mystery of Interdependent Origination.
2. **Right Resolve**: cultivating an unshakable commitment to tread the path to enlightenment.
3. **Right Speech**: cultivating the virtue of addressing others with kindness, while abstaining from lying, divisive, or abusive speech and idle chatter.
4. **Right Action**: abstaining from killing, stealing, and sexual misconduct.
5. **Right Livelihood**: choosing a livelihood that harms no one and benefits all.
6. **Right Effort**: striving to prevent unskillful qualities from arising and to abandon those that have arisen; to develop skillful qualities and to fully cultivate those that have arisen.
7. **Right Mindfulness**: awareness of body, feelings, mind, and qualities of the mind.
8. **Right Concentration**: withdrawing from sensuality and unskillful mental qualities and cultivating four stages of concentration leading to equanimity beyond pleasure and pain.

harm),[21] (2) not stealing, (3) not committing inappropriate sexual acts, (4) not lying, and (5) not imbibing intoxicants. On the other hand, the monastic community usually observes a much more complex code of behavior called the *Vinaya* (discussed later in this chapter).

Beyond these more formalized codes of behavior, the Buddha also taught how to cultivate a more practical approach to formulating a personal system of ethics. In this regard, he focused on the distinction between "skillful" and "unskillful" action. The Buddha defined skillful action simply as that which avoids harmful consequences, noting that such action is free of passion, aversion, and delusion. In contrast, unskillful action is imbued with qualities that ultimately harm oneself or others. He emphasized that one can learn to distinguish between the two kinds of actions by paying close attention to one's intentions, the surrounding environment, and the effects of our actions. But he also pointed out that simply understanding the distinction between skillful and unskillful action, and especially the results of such actions, leads in itself to positive consequences in the present scheme of things and favorable rebirths in the future. Buddhist sermons and stories commonly describe the desirable and undesirable rebirths in higher and lower forms of life (including in various heavens and hells) that await those who consistently act in skillful or unskillful ways. As a whole, Buddhist culture particularly emphasizes the importance of friendliness, generosity, and compassion toward all beings and recognizes good conduct as essential to assisting our process toward enlightenment.

For Buddhists, responsible and compassionate action is never simply discerned through an understanding of "right" and "wrong." Ethics for many Buddhists transcends mere adherence to a formalized system of "dos and don'ts," and requires instead the application of creativity and insight to every situation. In later forms of Buddhism the notion of ***upaya*** (Sanskrit, "Skillful Means") was developed into a form of practice that encourages the imaginative application of wisdom to whatever circumstances one is in to assist in easing suffering or cultivating insight.

A story found in the text known as the *Lotus Sutra* is often used to illustrate this point. One day, a man came home to find that his house was on fire. His children were inside playing, so he ran in and frantically pleaded with them to get out fast. But as the children were in a lighthearted and frivolous mood, they thought he was joking and simply laughed. Time was of the essence and the man could see that the children were in no mood to abandon their toys. So he decided to take a different approach. He warmly smiled and announced that he had brought them wondrous gifts: toy oxen and gilt carts that were awaiting them just outside the gates. Hearing this, they all ran laughing outside their burning house, saving their lives. Clearly, the man had broken the fourth Precept by telling a lie. Yet that lie had saved those he loved most from suffering a terrible death.

But *upaya* is more subtle than simply knowing when to break the rules. It has more to do with seeing one's limitations or negative tendencies and finding a way to turn them into assets that can ripen into real understanding. It is a precise—and often sudden—application of wisdom and compassion to undo the constraints of a given circumstance. With Skillful Means, even those aspects of life that are a source of suffering, confusion, and folly can, if properly applied, be a means to enlightenment. Certain Buddhists, like the Mahasiddhas of India and the **Ch'an** and **Zen** monks of Japan, are the subjects of many humorous stories and anecdotes that reveal the skillful ways in which one's own foolishness can suddenly bloom into wisdom.

Karma, Rebirth and the Afterlife   The Noble Eightfold Path is meant to set up the ideal conditions to aid one's spiritual evolution. Yet the Buddha's own personal journey toward achieving enlightenment did not just begin in his life as Siddhartha but was set in motion long before. A collection of stories known as the *Jataka Tales* contains the Buddha's own recounting of many of his previous lives that demonstrated how he cultivated skillfulness in facing life's difficult situations. One such *Jataka* story tells of the time that the Buddha was reincarnated as "Prince Five Weapons" (Sanskrit *Panchayudha*):

At the age of sixteen Prince Five Weapons apprenticed under a famous teacher who lived in Takkasila. After finishing his training, he was given five weapons by his master, and set out to return home. At the outskirts of a dark forest Prince Five Weapons met a man who warned him that the forest he was about to enter was haunted by a horrible ogre named "Sticky Hair," who killed anyone who entered his domain. The young prince, unafraid, boldly walked on. When he reached the heart of the forest, the ogre stepped out of the shadows. He rose up tall as a palm tree, wide-eyed, with a head the size of a building, a beak like a hawk, and massive tusks which jutted out like turnips. His belly was covered with purple spots and his hands and feet were dark blue.

"Where do you think you're going?" the ogre roared. "You'll make a tasty snack for me!"

The Prince replied, "Monster, I came here trusting in myself. Take care in how you choose to approach me. I have a poisoned arrow notched on my bow that will surely put an end to you." The demon was undeterred, so Five Weapons loosed his arrow, which harmlessly stuck to the ogre's shaggy coat. The Prince let more arrows fly, again and again, until fifty had all hit their mark but hung there like fruit on a tree. The ogre just snapped them off and threw them down at the Prince's feet with a grin. So the Prince drew his sword. But when he swung, it just stuck on the ogre's pelt. The Prince next jabbed the ogre with his spear, which became entangled beside his sword. He swung his mighty club, which was just as useless.

When the Prince saw his club dangling there too, he said: "Demon! Perhaps I didn't trust enough in my weapons but I still have my fists. I'll grind you to dust!" He swung with his right. He gave him his left. He kicked first from the left and then from the right. Entangled in the hair of the beast, he fought on, head-butting the demon with all his might. But it was of no use—his head was stuck fast like all the rest of his weapons.

Five times snared and caught in five places, the Prince was held in the demon's grip. But he remained unafraid. Sticky Hair thought to himself: "This man is a lion,

Prince Five Weapons
entangled in the shaggy
mane of the ogre, Sticky
Hair. This story originally
appeared in the *Jataka
Tales*, a collection of
stories the Buddha told
of his previous lives
before he was born as
Prince Siddhartha.

truly noble and unique. Caught in my grasp he doesn't shrink or even bat an eye. I've never seen such a man! Why isn't he afraid?" Thinking this, he simply couldn't bring himself to eat the young prince. Finally he asked, "Young man, why aren't you afraid of death?"

"Why should I fear?" replied the prince. "In one life a man can die only once. Besides, there is a thunderbolt in my belly. Were you to eat me, you could never digest it. It would rip you to shreds and we'd both be dead. So I have nothing to fear."

Then the ogre thought: "He speaks the truth. To eat the smallest morsel of such a man—even the size of a pea—would be too much for me. I'll let him go." Setting Prince Five Weapons free he told him to go home and gladden the hearts of his family.

The Prince said, "Okay. I'll go. But just remember that it was the wickedness of your former lives that compelled you to take birth as a blood-sucking monster, who cruelly hungers to lick the gore and eat the flesh of others. Were you to go on this way, it would lead you only from darkness to more darkness. But now that you've seen me, I trust that you will leave this cruelty behind you. To destroy life only ensures that you will be reborn as an animal or in the realm of the hungry-ghosts or demons. And even if you took birth in the world of men your days would be cut short."

The Prince went on to speak of the mysteries of actions and their consequences, of death and rebirth. He transformed the heart of the beast, filling him with a spirit of selflessness and a commitment to abide by the Five Precepts. In the end, the ogre Sticky Hair became a protector of the forest, and people feared him no longer.[22]

A belief in transmigration, reincarnation, or rebirth is common to all Buddhists. Until enlightenment is reached, one experiences an (almost) endless cycle of death and rebirth known as **samsara.** As Prince Five Weapons explained in his discourse to the ogre, a combination of one's actions and intentions are the primary basis for determining whether or not one will receive a favorable rebirth. But the Buddhist conception of rebirth differs fundamentally from that of Hinduism (Chapter 4) and Jainism (Chapter 6) in one primary aspect: While Hindus and Jains conceive that there is an eternal and changeless soul or self that is each time reborn, Buddhists argue that all things in *samsara* are in a constant state of flux and there can be no independent self or soul. This idea initially seems at odds with the Buddhist belief in rebirth and its assertion that a continuity of karmic repercussions carry over from one life to the next. As such it has been at the root of Buddhist sectarian schisms from the very beginnings of Buddhist history.

The more conventional Buddhist analogy for this mysterious and somewhat ambiguous process is that the causes and conditions construed as a "self" are transferred, as the flame of one torch is passed to another. The flame on the new torch is neither the same nor is it different, but part of a changing continuum of conditionality. In this way, some form of "being" passes on from one incarnation to the next. It is important to remember that the goal in Buddhism is not simply to secure a favorable rebirth but ultimately to end the cycle of death and rebirth entirely. Causality and the doctrine of Interdependent Origination are keys to understanding how this goal is fulfilled.

Nirvana *Nirvana*, the ultimate goal of Buddhist practice, refers to the final liberation from the suffering of cyclic existence (*samsara*). In Sanskrit, *nirvana* means "to blow out or extinguish," but it might best be understood as "cooling down" or "allaying" the pain born from the unquenchable thirst of being. The Buddha often spoke of it in simple terms as relinquishing the compulsive tendency toward "me-making" and "mine-making."[23] This undoing of a limited sense of self has led *nirvana* to sometimes be defined as an "unbinding," in which one's true nature is revealed. While the many sects of Buddhism offer variations in technique on how to attain it, there is a universal understanding among Buddhists that once *nirvana* is achieved, one becomes a Buddha, an awakened one.

Buddhists universally insist that all human beings have the potential to develop the perfection of wisdom that leads to *nirvana*. A number of later Buddhist texts liken this universal hidden potential to an unseen embryo in a pregnant woman (*tathagatagarbha*) and may go so far as to say that all beings in the universe are already Buddhas, while acknowledging that few have cultivated the insight to realize it.

Some contemporary Buddhist teachers describe enlightenment as an evolutionary process that involves tuning awareness (like a radio receiver) to a level of perception in which reality is completely apprehended in one all-encompassing vision. But there are many polemics, or religious disputes, about the nature of this process. There has been much dissension among the various schools of Buddhism as to whether enlightenment is a gradual process or is born of a sudden flash of insight.

God in Buddhism? In addition to the ten points discussed earlier, a brief look at Buddhist teachings about "gods" is in order. Buddhists do acknowledge the presence and power of a variety of gods and other supernatural beings, but they argue that their divine status does not in itself guarantee them access to the liberating vision that the Buddha teaches. Indeed, Buddhists observe that the gods themselves are subject to the winds of change. For the most part, the gods are subject to rebirth and are bound just as much to their celestial roles as humans are on earth. But there are exceptions. While not yet Buddhas, there is a class of gods called "the Non-returners," who, perched on the cusp of complete enlightenment, no longer reincarnate. Buddhist tradition might most precisely be called "transtheistic," rather than nontheistic, since it points to the attainment of insight into *dharma* as more important than the support received from any divine being.

Buddhist Sects and Texts

Over the centuries, a vast number of Buddhist sects have arisen. In this section we will more closely examine the two primary schools of Buddhist thought: *Theravada* (Pali, "the Doctrine of the Elders") and *Mahayana* (Sanskrit, "the Great Vehicle"). We will also examine **Vajrayana** (Sanskrit, "the Thunderbolt Vehicle"), a unique form of Buddhism that grew out of the *Mahayana* school.

In the centuries following the Buddha's death, itinerant monks and nuns increasingly settled into permanent communities, rather than observing the previous practice of only temporarily remaining in one place during the rainy season. Over time, these communities became increasingly insular yet geographically dispersed. Furthermore, without a single unifying authority, variations in practice and doctrine led to a number of distinct sectarian splits within Buddhism. This movement toward fragmentation was attested to even during the Buddha's lifetime, but the Second Buddhist Council (300 B.C.E.) is often regarded as marking the first major schism in Buddhism when the *Mahasamghika* (Sanskrit, "the Great Community") sect broke off from the earlier *Sthaviras* (Sanskrit, "Elders") sect.

After this initial schism, it is traditionally held that some eighteen different sectarian schools or branches arose within a span of two centuries. These eighteen schools today are commonly referred to as "Mainstream Buddhism" or "*Nikaya*" (Sanskrit, "collection") Buddhism. Only *Theravada* Buddhism can still trace its origin back to these eighteen sects of *Nikaya* Buddhism. Although *Mahayana* philosophical texts were also studied by these early schools, it was only much later that some of them evolved into distinctly Mahayanist sects. By the seventh or eighth century C.E., new symbolism and ritual technologies brought about the development of *Vajrayana* Buddhism, which gained a particularly powerful foothold in Tibet. Let us now examine the distinctive features of these three primary Buddhist paths and the sacred texts that inform them.

Theravada Buddhism *Theravada* means "The Doctrine of the Elders" and views itself as representing the original authentic teaching of the Buddha.[24] While it evolved over time to adapt to a variety of social and cultural contexts, it is also a tradition that has continually struggled to establish a rigorous continuity amid these disparate cultural settings. With over 100 million *Theravada* Buddhists around the world today, its institutions have historically had a profound influence in both the social and political spheres in which it predominates. As the main Buddhist tradition in Southeast Asia, it is currently found in Sri Lanka, Thailand, Cambodia, Laos, and Burma.

One of the key defining features of *Theravada* is the central role that the conservative monastic community has in maintaining and interpreting Buddhist teaching. This may be most readily seen in the emphasis placed on the accumulation of merit by the laity through formally extending offerings and esteem to monks. In many countries where *Theravada* is dominant, the monastic body acts as advisors to governments or rulers and provides teaching to the lay community, and its monks also serve as ritual specialists during festivals, at funerals, or in rites that confer supernatural protection. Some monks also specialize in crafting protective amulets, which may be specifically constructed to provide a variety of magical effects and which are widely sought after and collected by talisman connoisseurs. All of these functions are keenly tied to established monastic institutions. *Theravada* Buddhists emphasize three orientations: (1) toward enlightenment, which is mainly pursued through meditation; (2) toward merit-making to improve future rebirths, primarily pursued through service to the *sangha* and society at large; and (3) toward transcending the law of *karma* through magic, ritual, and talismans.

The historical Buddha is clearly the dominant figure of *Theravada* Buddhism. In the sphere of popular worship *Theravada* Buddhists may also venerate certain Hindu gods, nature spirits, saints, or even a few of the *bodhisattvas* of *Mahayana* Buddhism at local shrines, but these are worshiped mostly for "this-worldly" purposes. This "auxiliary pantheon" is not as important as the Buddha himself, who almost invariably occupies center stage, as do his original teachings contained within the early canonical group of Buddhist texts: the *Tripitaka*.

Tripitaka ("The Three Baskets") After the Buddha's death his teaching was transmitted orally, spreading first to the rest of India and then, over the course of the next thousand years, outward to different parts of Asia. Tradition asserts that four centuries passed between the Buddha's death and when a group of 500 monks met at the Aluvihara cave temple in Sri Lanka to write down his teachings for the first time. By that time there were already significant differences in reports of what the Buddha had said, so these monks labored to firmly and finally fix the canon in written form. In order to study the Buddha's teaching, then, one must first understand the basic categories of canonical sources and the distinctive Buddhist traditions that produced them.

Mainstream (*Nikaya*) monasteries referred to their collections of sources as the *Tripitaka* (Sanskrit, "three baskets"), which derives from the fact that in ancient times, manuscripts were written on palm leaves, which were then stored in baskets. Different schools wrote down their *Tripitaka* using different languages and scripts. *Theravada*'s collection of "the three baskets" was recorded in Pali, originally spoken in one region of north India; it is the only complete version of the *Tripitaka* that has survived to the present day.[25] Other mainstream schools used a form of Sanskrit, and scholars have recovered fragments of these other *Tripitaka* collections that were translated and studied outside of India. The different versions of the *Tripitaka* are generally regarded as basic sources for understanding Buddhist history and teachings, and this canon of texts is revered by all schools of Buddhism.

The first of the three "baskets" is the **sutra** (Sanskrit, "a thread [of discourse]"). The opening verses of the *Dhammapada*, one of the texts included in the *sutra* "basket," afford a glimpse into the way verses are structured in Buddhist *sutras* and how they poetically summarize key ideas:

We are what we think.
All that we are arises with our thoughts.
With our thoughts we make the world.
Speak or act with an impure mind
And trouble will follow you
As the wheel follows the ox that draws the cart.

We are what we think.
All that we are arises with our thoughts.
With our thoughts we make the world.
Speak or act with a pure mind
And happiness will follow you
As your shadow, unshakable.

"Look how he abused me and beat me,
How he threw me down and robbed me."
Live with such thoughts and you live in hate.
"Look how he abused me and beat me,
How he threw me down and robbed me."
Abandon such thoughts, and live in love.

In this world
Hate never yet dispelled hate.
Only love dispels hate.
This is the law,
Ancient and inexhaustible.[26]

One cannot assume that everything recorded in the *sutras* is the literal word of the Buddha. Yet the overall content of the *sutras*, even considering the differences between mainstream schools, is remarkably consistent in portraying the Buddha's teaching, suggesting to a significant extent the ideas, practices, and personality of the Buddha himself.

The second of the three "baskets"—the *vinaya* (Sanskrit, "setting down" or regulations)—contains hundreds of monastic rules reportedly prescribed by the Buddha and stories that illustrate how those rules originated. Most Buddhist monks and nuns regularly recite and pledge their allegiance to these rules, which deal with infractions ranging from the very serious (such as killing and stealing) to the less serious (such as lying, not respecting seniors, and hoarding possessions).

The third and last "basket" is known as *abhidharma* (Sanskrit, "higher philosophy"), which distills and elaborates on the teachings contained in the *sutras*. These highly scholastic sources focus on the nature of consciousness, epistemology (or the nature of knowledge), cosmology, and meditation. They seek to reorganize and systemize the teaching in the *sutra*, often manifesting the endless enumeration of lists for which Buddhism is so famous.

Mahayana Buddhism   *Mahayana* Buddhism is comprised of countless sects and subsects spread across China, Korea, Japan, Tibet, Mongolia, Nepal, Bhutan, and Vietnam, with other pockets of adherents in Southeast Asia. The main characteristic that distinguishes *Mahayana* Buddhism from *Theravada* Buddhism is that the primary goal of *Mahayana* Buddhism is not to secure one's own personal enlightenment but, rather, to work to bring all beings to *nirvana*. The centrality of this emphasis may be seen in the fact that most Mahayanists expand the daily threefold prayer of refuge practiced in *Theravada* Buddhism with a "vow of the *bodhisattva*" that formally confirms their commitment to forgo the quest for personal enlightenment in favor of working for the salvation of all beings. (The term *bodhisattva*, originally used to refer to the Buddha before he attained enlightenment, referred to "a being [resolved to achieve] enlightenment." But in the *Mahayana* context *bodhisattva* refers to a highly evolved being who abides at the cusp of enlightenment, forsaking his or her own liberation for the sake of assisting others in attaining the bliss of *nirvana*.)

The *Mahayana* contrasted itself to mainstream schools by referring to them as the *Hinayana* (Sanskrit, "Lesser Vehicle"). A clearly pejorative designation, its use probably stems from *Mahayana* critique that Hinayanists ignore the final dispensation of the Buddha's teaching (the *Mahayana Sutras*) by selfishly pursuing their own *nirvana*, ignoring the spiritual welfare of other beings. To *Mahayana* Buddhists this emphasis on the *bodhisattva* ideal must be seen as a logical extension of the belief in *anatman* and Interdependent Origination, as this doctrinal development seems to ask, "How can one be free if not all are free?"

But this distinction between *Mahayana* and *Hinayana* (or *Theravada*) over the issue of pursuing the liberation of all beings is to a great extent an artificial one. Most *Theravada* Buddhists also include in their practice a daily dedication prayer to offer the merit of their efforts to aid all beings toward *nirvana*. Therefore, it is probably best to look to institutional emphasis and other doctrinal issues when contemplating sectarian distinctions.

Other features of *Mahayana* teachings include an emphasis on meditation instead of textual study, the importance of faith, desire-less action (as in the Hindu *Bhagavad Gita*, Chapter 4), and a vastly expanded pantheon of spiritual friends, such as wise and merciful *bodhisattvas* who work toward the liberation of all beings and other Buddhas who preside over paradisaical worlds where enlightenment comes easier.

No inscriptional or archaeological evidence in India describing an independent sectarian body of "*Mahayana* Buddhism" can be found until after the fifth century C.E. But it seems likely that early *Mahayana* texts were in circulation by the second or first century B.C.E. The fact that the textual history of *Mahayana* is disconnected from inscriptional and other historical evidence has led many early scholars to assert that *Mahayana* arose as a reaction of the laity to monastic Buddhism.[27] Yet much of *Mahayana* literature strives to return Buddhism to older ascetic ideals, and while these texts critique the scholastic preoccupations of the monasteries of the day, the antisocial quality of this emphasis on asceticism makes lay Buddhists an unlikely source for these works. In addition, the mainstream schools of that time were engaged in composing a vast body of storytelling literature that was much more accessible to the lay community than these huge and complex *Mahayana* texts.

Mahayana also developed a pronounced emphasis on devotional practices that held a special appeal to the laity, but again it is difficult to use these later developments to assert a lay origin for the tradition. The intense devotional and ritual orientations of *Mahayana* only begin to develop around the fourth century C.E. Some scholars ultimately ascribe the origin of *Mahayana* to a kind of "Cult of the Book," in which individuals (mostly monks and nuns in mainstream monasteries) realigned their Buddhist orientation to specific texts. The fact that they maintained the vows of a given community would not have led to sectarian schisms and would explain why *Mahayana* doesn't appear as an independent entity until much later.[28]

This emphasis on new sacred texts is even reflected in the *Mahayana* pantheon, which expanded to incorporate a host of powerful and angelic *bodhisattvas*. Perhaps the earliest and one of the most popular was Manjushri (Sanskrit, "Soft Glory"), Patron of Buddhist Scholars and Lord of Wisdom, who is often represented with his flaming sword of discriminating insight in one hand and the *Perfection of Wisdom Sutra* in the other. The *Bodhisattva* of Compassion, Avalokitesvara (Sanskrit, "the Lord Who Looks Down"), is yet another important divine figure (in China this *bodhisattva* is known as a female deity, Kuan Yin).

Mahayana Sources Buddhists in both mainstream and later *Mahayana* schools have revered a wide spectrum of sources that are not included in the traditional *Tripitaka*. These *Mahayana sutras* depict the Buddha's teaching in remote settings to huge crowds of *bodhisattvas*. While differing from the simple and stark discussion that comprises much of the Pali *sutras*, *Mahayana* works often present profound yet enigmatic discourses in the midst of fantastic imagery, which helped to stimulate a flowering of Buddhist art in the first millennium.

One of the earliest of these *Mahayana* works was the *Perfection of Wisdom Sutra*, which was probably initially composed around the first century B.C.E. Increasingly longer versions of it appeared in the centuries that followed. But between 300 and 700 C.E. important new condensed versions arose, such as the *Diamond Sutra*[29] and the *Heart Sutra*, both of which have occupied a central place in a number of *Mahayana* sects. These variants encapsulate the essence of the early *Mahayana* adherents as they set out to define the *Bodhisattva* path by stressing the cultivation of **bodhicitta** (Sanskrit, "awakened thought"; the aspiration for achieving enlightenment to benefit others) and the Six Perfections (giving, morality, patience, vigor, meditation, and wisdom).

Among the most widely venerated Buddhist works in East Asia is the *Lotus Sutra*, composed in Sanskrit in the second century C.E. While exploring the path of the *bodhisattva* it places particular emphasis on skillful means, a concept discussed earlier in this chapter. In this regard the *Lotus Sutra* presents the startling revelation that the Buddha had actually achieved enlightenment untold ages ago, but his life as Siddhartha was just a "skillful" drama to inspire people of the present day to take up the quest for enlightenment. Another important *Mahayana* text, the *Lankavatara Sutra* of the fourth century C.E., provides a detailed study of the nature of consciousness and explores how the mind has both the propensity to generate illusory, dualistic misperceptions as well as the potential to clearly apprehend the unity of existence. In the later part of the second century C.E. another theological innovation appears in the *Land of Bliss Sutras,* which introduced Amitabha Buddha and the devotional practice that leads to attaining rebirth in his Buddha Realm, Sukhavati ("the Land of Bliss"), a kind of heaven where the faithful are reborn in a divine world ideally suited to quickly bring about enlightenment. This text becomes central for Pure-Land Buddhism, an important subsect of *Mahayana* popular throughout East Asia.

Zen The various important subsects of *Mahayana* are too numerous to offer a detailed survey of in the context of this brief introduction. Nevertheless, one would be remiss not to mention Zen (Japanese, "Meditation"; in Sanskrit, the term is *Dhyana*; Chinese, *Ch'an*; Korean, *Seon*; and Vietnamese, *Thièn*). It originated with the South India sage Bodhidharma, who transplanted it in China. The forms of Zen that flourished in Japan have become most widely known in the West. In Zen, doctrine does not merely take the back seat to meditative insight; rather, it is considered an obstacle. This school echoed earlier preoccupations with practice rather than doctrine. It saw doctrine as a crutch or often a distraction from immediate sudden, spontaneous enlightenment called *satori*. Zen sayings included such statements as, "If you meet the Buddha on the road, kill him." This saying is meant to underscore the pretentiousness of even being a "Buddhist" as yet another mask that obscured one's true face. Zen *koans* (Japanese; literally, "public case," but might best be defined as "paradoxical riddles") similarly offered impossible questions to aid the quizzical mind to turn spontaneously upon itself, so it might suddenly see its own true nature. "What is the sound of one hand clapping?" and "Show me your Original Face before your mother and father were born" are some of the most famous Zen *koans*.

These Zen practitioners have always had a unique way of bringing the contemplating mind into everyday artistic expression in creative ways that allow the abstractions of meditative experience to find articulation beyond the constraints of language. This creative aspect of Zen and certainly its deeply ingrained sense of humor helped to popularize this form of Buddhism in American pop culture and subculture, beginning especially with its influence on the Beat poets of the 1950s, such as Jack Kerouac and Gary Snyder.

Vajrayana Vajrayana Buddhism (Sanskrit, the "Diamond" or "Thunderbolt" Vehicle) arose mostly in northwest India between the sixth and seventh centuries C.E. It merged *Mahayana* ideals with a highly esoteric system of symbolism, ritual, and the yogic practice known as *tantra*. *Vajrayana* remains dominant today in Tibet, Nepal, Bhutan, and Mongolia. While the forms of *Vajrayana* in these regions are fairly similar, other early forms of *Vajrayana* arose in China as *Chen-yen* Buddhism and in Japan as *Shingon* Buddhism.

Vajrayana is one of the most distinctive of *Mahayana* schools. It maintains many unique practices, such as the identification of reincarnate **lamas** (Tibetan, "teachers") known as **tulkus** (like the Panchen Lama and Dalai Lama); uses a perplexing array of abstract symbols; and invokes an enormous pantheon of Buddhas, *bodhisattvas*, and folk deities. *Vajrayana* has developed a complex host of contemplative technologies such as the construction of sand *mandalas*, deity yoga, and the recitation of ritual incantations, and it employs visualization as an essential component of all these disciplines.

While Tibetan Buddhism preserved two large canonical collections of *tantras* and traditional *sutras*, it has also maintained a tradition (dating back to the eleventh century C.E.) that allows for the flexibility of its canon through something called *terma* (Tibetan, "hidden treasures"). *Termas* are hidden texts or other relics, usually conceived of having been concealed by the great Indian pundit and *tantric* adept Padmasambhava, who first brought *Vajrayana* Buddhism to Tibet in the eighth century C.E. A class of *tantric* specialists called *terton* (Tibetan, "treasure finders") are said to discover the *termas* as the "time-lock" spells of Padmasambhava come undone and the world is ready to receive the new "revelation" that they portend. As a result, *Vajrayana* Buddhism has been enabled with more adaptability in revising the canon than many other Buddhist schools, a major strength for the tradition in the face of change.

Buddhism died out in India sometime between the twelfth and the fifteenth centuries C.E., while *Theravada* and *Vajrayana* traditions survived just outside India's modern borders in Sri Lanka and Nepal. But in the latter part of the twentieth century, *Vajrayana* monks and nuns fleeing the Chinese invasion of Tibet (c. 1950) reestablished themselves in India. This diaspora has stimulated exponential growth of *Vajrayana* not just in India but in the world at large.

Diversity of Buddhist Beliefs Given Buddhism's long history and its diversity of sects and subsects, neither any single sect nor an authoritative canon of the Buddha's teachings has ever been universally accepted by all Buddhists. As reported by later *Theravada* chronicles, some of the mainstream schools attempted to arrive at a universally accepted canon. Later, the different schools incorporated additional sources— *sutras* emphasizing particular sectarian ideas, stories, legends, rules for monastic life, and so on—with each school pointing out to its followers which sources were most significant and useful.[30] Monks often argued against the validity of certain sources that other schools claimed were authoritative, but no one group was ever able to force a consensus. Though such doctrinal conflicts seem irreconcilable, nevertheless, in recent years there has been more dialogue among Buddhists across sectarian lines.

Women in Buddhism

As in most other religious traditions, it is primarily men who formed the Buddhist institutions which have recorded, transmitted, and interpreted its teachings. In mainstream monasteries nuns did not seem to have much of a place in the preservation and transmission of the *dharma*. But Buddhist women did take on more central roles outside of monasteries, both as lay Buddhists and as wandering ascetics, and their significance is acknowledged in many sources. Powerful political figures such as Empress Wu Zetian of Tang Dynasty China (late seventh century c.e.) or Camadevi (seventh century c.e.), the legendary queen of Haripunjana in northern Thailand, have left an indelible mark in the history of Buddhism as patrons whose support and example helped to spread Buddhist traditions.

But beyond the historical influence of Buddhist women as powerful secular leaders, several important female spiritual leaders have emerged since the very beginnings of Buddhism. Even in the early formation of the *Tripitaka*, one collection called the *Khuddaka Nikaya* (Pali, "Group of Short Texts") canonized a group of early saints in two collections of poems: the *Theragatha* (Pali, "Poems of Male Elders") and the *Therigatha* (Pali, "Poems of Female Elders"). So very early on, the tradition acknowledged and preserved the compositions of its women saints. Other women saints, particularly in *Vajrayana* Buddhism, have stood out as great virtuosos and innovators of the highest esoteric practices.

In 2003 there were approximately 125,000 Buddhist nuns. But historically in many parts of the world lineages of Buddhists nuns either disappeared (such as in the eleventh century in Sri Lanka) or never existed in the first place (such as in Thailand). Only in China, Korea, Taiwan, and Vietnam were nuns traditionally given full ordination and regarded with the same respect as their male counterparts. In other countries only novitiate ordination (that is, a beginning or trial initiation) has been conferred on women, if at all. Even in Tibet, nuns were originally only allowed to observe "Eight Precept" or "Ten Precept" vows offered to lay practitioners, as opposed to the 253 vows of male monks.

Resistance to women taking an active role in Buddhist monastic institutions goes all the way back to the time when Mahaprajapati, the Buddha's stepmother, petitioned for women to be allowed ordination. Though the Buddha eventually relented, he noted that allowing nuns into the order would only hasten the demise of the Buddhist teaching. Even those regions that allowed nuns placed additional constraints on female monastics. Conversely to the situation later found in Tibet, the *Pratimoksha* vows of monks and nuns in the Buddha's time required women to abide by 311 vows while men needed only observe 227.

Where there have been some nunneries attached to *Theravada* monasteries, the nuns have often been relegated to serving the domestic needs (such as cooking and cleaning) of the monks. But some women, like the *maechi* (female renunciants) of Thailand, have preferred solitary ascetic life to the limitations of ordination in the male-dominated monastic institutions.

Katherine Sei is an American Buddhist who lives in California. She is a practitioner of *Vajrayana* Buddhism and has been a student of Lama Lodru Rinpoche for nearly three decades. She is the facilitator of the Sacramento branch of *Kagyu Droden Kunchab*.

As a Buddhist, what is the most important aspect of human existence? What should Buddhists do or focus on in life?

Katherine Sei

The most important aspect of human existence, to me, is that we have an opportunity to evolve as beings. This evolution encompasses uncovering our true nature. This true nature is comprised of a spontaneous, natural compassion and a clear wisdom as to "what is really going on here." I've found through all the years of meditation that we all tend to really limit our minds, and the expression of our true wise and benevolent nature. As I uncover and begin to understand my mind's true nature, and learn to let go of my limiting definitions of self, others, and events in my life, suffering diminishes. Life becomes more joyful, more peaceful, and I feel more interconnected with everyone. Life also becomes very, very interesting as I begin to become aware of all the interconnections of karmic causes and effects, and I can relax into the "play" of events.

Does Buddhism give you a unique outlook on life? How so or why?

I'm not sure if Buddhism gives a unique outlook as much as a useful outlook on life in this culture. The teachings of Lord Buddha are not necessarily unique to Buddhism—I think many aspects of Hinduism, Christianity, Judaism, and Islam provide a framework for becoming a more loving and wise person. What may be unique in terms of Buddha's teachings is that one can examine one's mind and one's life through meditation practices. It's more like a science than a religion, analogous to a physicist learning mathematics to explore the universe. I've found through meditation that life isn't quite as rigid as we often make it out to be. Knowing that, one can learn to let go of many of the emotional habits and knee-jerk reactions. One can find many creative solutions to life's problems, big and small, from "What is death?" or "What does it all mean?" to "How do I deal with my angry boss?" "How do I deal with the stress in my life?" and so on.

What single event in your life would you characterize as your most meaningful religious experience?

It's hard to pick one single event in my life that I consider most meaningful. Three come to mind. First would be when I took refuge with Trungpa Rinpoche in the 1980s. At that time, I discovered that I could treat others and myself with more gentleness. The second event would be when I met Ven. Lama Lodru Rinpoche, my direct teacher for the past twenty-seven years. Lama Lodru has taught me the same meditation practices that Tibetan lamas go through in a formal three-year retreat, but spread out over fifteen years. In doing this, he demonstrated that anyone can learn to meditate and apply it in their day-to-day life. One doesn't have to become a monk or nun to become liberated. The third event was having the nature of my mind pointed out by Mingyur Rinpoche. Mingyur Rinpoche is a Tibetan Lama who had to overcome panic attacks when he was a teenager. He showed me how applicable Buddha's teachings on meditation are to all aspects of life.

Recently, in most of the *Theravada* world, full ordination of nuns has begun to be revived. Women renouncers have been proactive in these regions, adopting ascetic disciplines and formal vows on their own or forming small groups of female practitioners. And there has been an explosion in the number of notable women Buddhist leaders in the West, who have profoundly influenced Buddhist women around the world in finding a voice and getting organized. Because of their efforts, new opportunities for women to receive ordination have begun to open up in many countries as women are transforming the Buddhist institutional landscape.

One such example is that of Ayya Khema and the First Council of Buddhist Nuns that she organized. Born in 1923 to a Jewish family in Berlin, Ayya Khema (d. 1997) was evacuated from Germany along with hundreds of other children in 1938. Her parents eventually escaped to China, where she was reunited with them in Shanghai. Unfortunately the war followed them to China, and when the Japanese invaded the family was placed in a prisoner-of-war camp. Ayya Khema's father died in the camp before the Americans liberated it. After these life-altering experiences, Ayya Khema traveled extensively throughout the world during the next few decades, including time spent studying meditation in the Himalayas. The experiences that grew out of her meditation practice led to her taking ordination as a Buddhist nun in Sri Lanka in 1983. At this time she received her *dharma*-name, "Khema" (Pali, "safety"). She also founded an international training center for Buddhist nuns in 1983 at Dodanduwa, Sri Lanka, called the Parapuduwa Nuns' Island. In Germany she helped organize thirty-seven different meditation groups. But Ayya Khema is most widely remembered for organizing the first international council for nuns in Buddhist history. This conference led to the founding of a worldwide Buddhist women's organization called Shakyadhita. In May 1987 Ayya Khema became the first Buddhist nun to ever address the United Nations.

BUDDHISM AS A WAY OF LIFE

Buddhists engage the Buddha's teachings in the context of a variety of practices: meditative disciplines, daily worship, annual festivals, and rites that mark the transitions of life from birth to death (and beyond). Many Buddhists grow up as active participants in these rituals even before gaining a formal understanding of Buddhist teaching.

This section of the chapter focuses on Buddhist practice, emphasizing those that are most influential today. It observes the disciplines and worship practices of

Buddhist monastics, ascetics, and laypeople, while pointing out how cultural and sectarian context both inform and transform them. Beyond touching on these differences, this section primarily seeks to highlight key elements of religious activity shared by all Buddhists.

Meditation and the Cultivation of Mind

Buddhism may be regarded first and foremost as a mechanism for training the mind. In studying Buddhism within an academic context it is possible to lose sight of the fact that the Buddha's insights grew directly out of meditation. The intellectual sophistication and keen logic employed by many Buddhist scholars can make the tradition seem rooted in a kind of philosophical enterprise. But, in actuality, Buddhism may be regarded as a complex of meditative exercises that seek to transcend the linear nature of everyday mental processes. For many Buddhists, meditation is the true fount of wisdom and the primary means of achieving enlightenment. It is often said that the full implications of Buddhist teaching cannot be rightly understood without devoting oneself to meditative practice. Over the past 2,600 years, Buddhism has generated a huge variety of meditative disciplines as well as textual discussions on the process, nature, and significance of meditation.

Meditation: *Shamatha* and *Vipassana*   Early Buddhism originally approached meditation through two basic types of practice: *shamatha* (Sanskrit, "calm abiding" or "stabilizing meditation") and *vipassana* (Sanskrit: *vipashyana*; "insight"). This division is still maintained today, but both have evolved into various forms among the many Buddhist sects.

Shamatha, a precursor to later forms of meditative development, cultivates the ability to hold an unwavering awareness effortlessly upon a single object of concentration. Sometimes this may be a physical object or even a blank wall, but usually the focal point is the breath. In this case, awareness might be anchored upon the specific sensation of the breath as it first passes into the nostrils, or perhaps the rising and falling of the abdomen, or possibly the whole respiratory process at once.

In comparison, the main object of *vipassana* meditation is consciousness itself. This form of meditation is formally defined as a profound mindfulness that enables the meditator to see through physical, emotional, and mental states to apprehend the nature of phenomena as inherently characterized by the three marks of existence (impermanence, suffering, and no independent self or soul). *Vipassana* meditation too begins with a focus on the breath, which enables the meditator to cultivate a deep concentration and a stable mind. This stability is characterized by an abiding mindfulness and an open, fluid, and expansive awareness. *Vipassana* uses this mindfulness to transcend one's typical response to thoughts, feelings, daydreams, and the other "dramas" that are endlessly enacted in the theatre of the imagination. It enables the meditator to lucidly observe, as if from a distance, the arising and passing away of all mental and physical phenomena—neither obsessing, reacting, nor judging, but simply "allowing" them to be, without actively engaging them. The goal of *vipassana* is to anchor awareness, moment to moment, to the immediate experience and thereby to allow consciousness to expand spontaneously beyond the minutiae of compulsive and restless thought.

> When walking, just walk.
> When sitting, just sit.
> Above all, don't wobble.
> —Yunmen (d. 949 C.E.; Tang Dynasty founder of the Yunmen school of Ch'an Buddhism)[31]

Walking Meditation As part of their standard iconography, Thai Buddhists frequently venerate icons and other images of the Buddha walking. The Buddha taught that there are four postures in which one should practice meditation: sitting, standing, walking, and lying down. Any activity, he asserted, is an opportunity for meditation. Many Buddhist traditions practice a form of walking meditation as a means to take the serenity and insight of the meditation hall out into the world effectively.

For example, the approach of the contemporary Vietnamese monk Thich Nhat Hanh (b. 1926) to walking meditation is centered on relinquishing the impulse to always get "somewhere," instead encouraging the mindful enjoyment of the simplicity of each breath while letting each step lovingly caress the earth. To emphasize the spontaneity and naturalness of walking meditation, Hanh often alludes to the Chinese Zen master Ling Chi (d. 866), who taught that while most people think it is a miracle to walk across burning hot coals, to walk on water, or to walk through the air, the real miracle is simply to be walking upon the earth.

A large contemporary image of the Walking Buddha in Thailand. Thai images often stylistically craft his right arm to represent the graceful swaying trunk of an elephant.

Other Buddhist schools, such as Zen, are more formal in their approach to the practice of walking meditation. In most *Zendo*s (Japanese, "meditation halls"), meditators engage in the formal practice of *Kinhin* (Japanese, "walking meditation"). *Kinhin* is characterized by very slow movements that assist the beginner in dynamically perceiving each subtle shift in posture, breathing, and sensation. After slowly rising, *kinhin* practitioners encircle the left fist with the right hand, holding it in front of the heart, and then take a step. Feeling the pull of gravity and the solidity of the body, they observe the ball of the foot as it rises up off the ground, the air accompanying the forward movement of the foot, and the slow shifting of the weight as the heel is set on the ground again. As the weight shifts forward they notice the points of contact between the sole of the foot and the Earth—a movement from heel, to flat, to toe—and all the sensations that accompany propelling the density of the physical body through space.

Regardless of the manner in which it is practiced, walking meditation is an important mechanism for enabling one to take the clarity of meditation out onto the street and integrate mindfulness more fully into one's daily life.

A contemporary Tibetan *tanka* painting of the *Bodhisattva* of Compassion, Avalokiteshvara (Sanskrit), also known as Chenrezig (Tibetan).

Visualization, Deity Yoga, and Inner *Mandalas* Another important form of meditation entails the practice of visualization. Practices involving the mental contemplation of the body of the Buddha developed early in the history of Buddhism. The visualization of Buddhas and *bodhisattvas* came to occupy a central place in the meditation practices of such *Mahayana* sects as the Pure Land Buddhists, who relish imagining the luminous body of Amitabha in his paradise. But undoubtedly it is in *Vajrayana* Buddhism that a true virtuosity for employing these practices developed. In practices referred to as deity yoga in the West or "actualization" in Tibetan (*lha'i mgnong rtogs*), the deity (such as a Buddha or *bodhisattva*) is coaxed to emerge from the latent potentiality of the meditator's mind. Through a combination of visualization and *mantra* the very substance of the practitioner's mind comes to embody the deity that is invoked.

VISUALIZATION: SHORT FORM OF THE CHENREZIG SADHANA

This text is a visualization of Avalokiteshvara, the *bodhisattva* of compassion. The text is recited accompanied by visualization of its content.

On the crown of the head of myself and all beings,
On a moon, on a lotus, is the syllable HRI.
Chenrezig arises from this.
He radiates clear white light.
He gazes with compassionate eyes and loving smile.
He has four arms: the first two are folded in prayer.
The lower two hold a crystal rosary and white lotus.
He is arrayed in silks and jewels.
He wears an upper robe of antelope skin.
His head ornament is Amitabha,
Buddha of Boundless Light.
His two feet are in the *vajra* posture.
A stainless moon is His backrest.
He is the essence of all those in whom we take refuge.

Make the following prayer, thinking that all beings are making it with you as if in a single voice:

Lord, not veiled by any fault, white in colour,
Whose head a perfect Buddha crowns in light,

> Gazing compassionately on all beings,
> To You, Chenrezig, All-seeing One, I prostrate.

(Repeat as many times as you wish.)

> By having prayed like this one pointedly,
> Light shining from the holy form
> Removes all impure karma and bewilderment.
> The outer realm becomes the realm of bliss.
> The body, speech, and mind of beings within it
> Become the body, speech and mind of Chenrezig.
> All knowledge, sound and all appearances become inseparable from
>   emptiness.

Meditate like this as you recite the *mantra*:

> *"Aum Mani Padme Hum"*

Finally, let the mind remain absorbed in its own essence, without distinction between subject, object, and act.

Then repeat:

> Everyone appears in the form of Chenrezig;
> All sound is the sound of His mantra;
> Everything that arises in the mind is the great expanse of wisdom.

Dedication:

> Through the virtue of this practice may I now quickly
> Achieve the All-seeing One's great state.
> And to this same state may I come to lead
> Every being, not one left behind.[32]

Other visualization techniques employ the contemplation of **mandalas.** *Mandalas* are circular cosmological diagrams that often map out how a Buddhist deity or group of deities manifest both *in* and *as* the universe. These deities embody the function and interaction of archetypal forces within the sphere of being. As with deities they are also venerated externally, sometimes in the form of a *tanka* ("tapestry"), a sand painting, or as a three-dimensional model. But in the formal meditative context *mandalas* are invoked as a realm of cosmological essence that both surrounds the practitioner and also emanates from the core of their being.

Mantra, Liturgic Ritual, and Chanting

The Buddha was himself rather critical of the preoccupation with ritual in his own time and generally discouraged the formalization of such practices among the *sangha*. Nevertheless, ritual does take on an incredible variety of forms in the Buddhist world, where it is of immense importance. Perhaps the most pervasive form of Buddhist ritual practice is chanting, which is one form of ritual that can be found in virtually every sectarian context. Most Buddhist services include liturgical chanting that reflects the philosophical orientation of that particular tradition. The content of the chant and its function can vary greatly. Some chanting consists of entire *sutras*, while others consist of key passages of particular philosophical works. Still other traditions use ritual formulas (*dharani*), or perhaps a simple **mantra** (ritual incantation), as their chant. *Mantras* and *dharanis* don't always have a specific lexical meaning, as they are often considered to be composed of vibrations that are believed to produce a magical effect or to induce a particular kind of meditative state.

But not all *mantras* are used for generating a shift in consciousness or for invoking or venerating a Buddhist deity. Some are used to cultivate compassion or generate merit, while others are believed to have magical or protective properties. For example, a Sanskrit *mantra* from the *Sutra of the Celestial Place Filled with Jewels* directs Buddhists to recite three times each morning: "*Om Khrechara Ghana Hung Hrih Svaha*" (*mantras* such as this have no direct lexical translation). After reciting it one is directed to spit on the soles of one's feet. This practice is said to make all insects crushed beneath one's feet be reborn as gods.

Refuge and the Three Jewels   All Buddhists in all sects across history have engaged in a regular declaration that they take refuge in the Buddha, his teaching, and the Buddhist community. In *Theravada* Buddhism a very early version of this *sharana* (Sanskrit, "refuge prayer") is regularly recited in the Pali language:

> *Buddham sharanam gacchami. Dhammam sharanam gacchami. Sangam sharanam gacchami.*
> "I take refuge in the Buddha. I take refuge in the *Dharma*. I take refuge in the *Sangha*."

"Taking refuge" can be considered the most fundamental ritual practice in Buddhism. The daily observance of formally taking refuge in these "three jewels"—the Buddha, the *dharma*, and the *sangha*—is regarded by many as being the closest thing to a Buddhist "creed" and is regarded as the definitive act that makes someone a "Buddhist." But beyond a rudimentary affirmation of faith, and a commitment to follow in the Buddha's footsteps, "going for refuge" is first and foremost a simple acknowledgment that one cannot (and need not) tread the path alone. It speaks both to one's dedication to and reliance upon the Buddha, his teaching, and those in the wider community who have also taken up the path. It ultimately marks a radical reorientation in one's approach to life in terms of intention, and resolve, as well as one's primary goal. *Vajrayana* Buddhists take refuge in a fourth jewel—the guru or teacher—before the other three, and *Mahayana* Buddhists usually append to the daily refuge prayer a "*bodhisattva* vow," meant to generate **bodhicitta** (Sanskrit, "the aspiration for enlightenment") or a commitment to seeking enlightenment first and foremost for the benefit of others. These refuge prayers are recited in a variety of forms and languages throughout the Buddhist world.

Ordination and "Being a Buddhist"

As noted earlier, most Buddhists consider a simple heartfelt recitation of the refuge prayer sufficient to make one a "Buddhist." A striking example of this occurred in 1950 at Pune, India, when thousands of *dalits*, members of the lowest caste of Hinduism, recited the refuge prayers and converted to Buddhism en masse under the leadership of the *dalit* activist Dr. B. R. Ambedkar (1891–1956). While this mass conversion was as much a political act as it was a religious one, the majority of Buddhist laity participate in more formal rites that are conducted in the presence of the *sangha* and a revered senior monk, lama, or spiritual teacher. During these rites, individuals seeking to be ordained or converted also take vows to abide by the Five Precepts.

In contrast to lay conversion, monastic ordination also confers legal status and authority on the newly ordained individual and demands the presence of a quorum of qualified monks. In most Buddhist countries ten monks are required to form this ordination quorum, while in remote areas only five are needed. Typically there are two different levels of monastic ordination. The first is that of the novice, which can be conferred as early as the age of 7 or 8 in *Theravada* or 19 among East Asia Buddhists. The novice agrees to abide by ten precepts and essentially functions as a student under the direct guidance of his preceptor. The second, higher ordination of a full-fledged monk requires them to be at least 20 years of age. In both cases (but to varying degrees) the recipient of the ordination makes a commitment to embody, maintain, and transmit the Buddhist *dharma*.

At the beginning of this chapter we had a glimpse into the form and structure of an ordination ceremony where the nun Jisen became a novice. The authority conferred in this kind of ceremony is primarily transmitted through the formal acknowledgment that the initiate is part of a lineage that can be directly traced back to the Buddha. Sometimes a scroll or document tracing this spiritual genealogy is presented to the newly ordained. We can imagine how moving it must be to see one's name at the bottom of a list headed by the actual Buddha and indicating that one has been formally admitted into the Buddha's own "family."

Sacred Places and Objects of Worship

In his own lifetime people clearly treated the Buddha as they would a great king, with formal rituals signaling profound honor and respect. Those coming to receive teachings or advice often arranged their upper garment in a certain way, bowed low when approaching, and then sat quietly to the side until addressed; on some occasions a person would walk around the Buddha three times as an outward expression of veneration for the spiritual gravity he embodied. But what followed after his passing?

The Buddha expressed two ways his followers might remember him: by worshiping Buddhist *stupas* (Sanskrit, "dome"), reliquary mounds originally constructed in ancient Indian culture to hold bones and other remains of cremated kings and saints, and by visiting sites linked to events in his life. Pilgrimage and the veneration of reliquary mounds and shrines (dedicated to Buddha, *bodhisattvas*, and other saints) became a universal expression of Buddhist worship. But it is important to keep in mind that the Buddha also taught that the teaching itself would serve as his "*dharma*-body" after his physical body passed away. As a result, the veneration of Buddhist texts also quickly became an important focus of devotional practice.

Because the Buddha did not want people to fixate on his individual personality or physical form, the convention of venerating icons and images of the Buddha was a much later development. It seemed to emerge first in the northwestern region of the Indian subcontinent at the time of the Kushana empire (probably beginning during the reign of Kanishka, r. 127–151 C.E.). Earlier Buddhist artifacts and arts never depicted the Buddha directly, and instead had a tendency to symbolize him more as an absence than a presence. In this regard, the Buddha was often indicated by an empty chair, a pair of footprints, or the *bodhi* tree he sat under when he obtained enlightenment.

The Great Stupa of Sanchi. Early Andhra Dynasty, first century B.C.E., Great Stupa, Sanchi, Madhya Pradesh, India.

Cherry blossom trees in front of a five-storied pagoda, Goju-No-To Pagoda, Miyajima, Itsukushima, Hiroshima Prefecture, Chugoku Region, Japan. A Japanese adaptation of the Indian *stupa*, where the central shaft with its stylized umbrellas extends down through all five stories to a reliquary casket below. It was built in 1407 C.E.

Early Buddhists also worshiped other aniconic images (that is, symbols that represented the Buddha in the particular roles he played during his life without depicting his bodily form). To this day, for example, all *bodhi* trees continue to be objects of reverence, as it was beneath the shade of a *bodhi* tree that the Buddha first achieved enlightenment. Another commonly venerated symbol is the wheel. In ancient India the wheel had represented the temporal law and order preserved by great kings. But Buddhists used the wheel to represent the *dharma* that the Buddha revealed through his teaching. Many early stone carvings show Buddhists standing with folded hands around a wheel mounted on a pole (most notably at the site of the Buddha's first sermon at Sarnath), as the symbol implies the Buddha's teaching in general and his first sermon in particular.

The symbolic resonance of the wheel takes on intriguing new forms of worship as Buddhism evolves. For example, part of the *tantric* dispensation of *Vajrayana* Buddhism encouraged the development of new technologies and mechanisms for insight and the production of merit that cleverly augment the efforts of the practitioner. One such technology is the prayer wheel, which is a commonly used ritual device in *Vajrayana* Buddhism. The prayer wheel is a device filled with printed scrolls, which, when rotated, is believed to emit thousands of prayers and *mantra* recitations at once. It is similar in premise to the printed prayer flags that automatically unfurl scores of sacred invocations as they flutter in the breeze, a familiar sight to trekkers in the Himalayas and visitors to Nepal and Tibet.

For about the last 1,800 years, Buddhists have also used sculpted images to remember more vividly the form of the Buddha, as well as other Buddhas and *bodhisattvas*. While icons of the Buddha tend to be quite consistent in their portrayal, subtle iconographic cues—such as hand gestures (in Sanskrit, *mudras*), posture, or objects held by the deity—can make special reference to particular events in the life of the Buddha or saint, address the specific function of that manifestation of deity, and reveal the sectarian orientation of its worshipers. As in Hinduism, it helps to remember that with *Mahayana* and *tantric* images multiple arms indicate how the deity acts or functions in the world, while multiple faces each reveal how the deity manifests or presides over specific spheres of spiritual influence.

Festivals

As Buddhism straddles so many cultural contexts, there are numerous Buddhist festivals. For the sake of simplicity, we will here examine primarily those Buddhist festival days that are more transregional in character, while still taking into account important local variations.

Most Buddhist festival days are determined by the lunar calendar and fall on different dates each year. The importance placed on the lunar calendar keeps Buddhists in touch with the natural cycles and rhythms of life. In this regard the moon's cycle stands as a poignant reminder of the cyclical nature of *samsara*, and in early times the *sangha* would gather on all full and new moon days for *uposatta* (Pali, "observance day"), a special observance of reaffirmation to follow the *dharma* path.

Wesak As one might expect, much of the Buddhist festival calendar is built around celebrating key moments in the life of the Buddha. By far the most important of such holidays is *Wesak*. This Singhalese name for the festival is derived from *Vishakha*, the Sanskrit name of the month in which it falls (late May–early June). It was on the full moon day of *Vishakha* that the Buddha was not only born, but attained enlightenment and died (achieving the ultimate state of **parinirvana**, "supreme release"). This is celebrated as the high holy day of the Buddhist calendar year.

On *Wesak*, *Theravada* Buddhists decorate local shrines and light lamps to symbolize the Buddha's enlightenment and the spreading of his awakened insight throughout the community and the world. People send out greeting cards that depict the key events in the life of the Buddha. Some lay Buddhists observe eight precept vows and stay up all night in meditation as the Buddha had done on the night of his enlightenment.

In Tibet this festival is called *Saga Dawa*. It occurs around the same time and also celebrates the Buddha's birth (his enlightenment and death, however, are celebrated six days later). Tibetan Buddhists also light lamps and strictly observe the Buddhist precepts. As in most Buddhist countries devotion is expressed through circumambulating shrines and *stupas*, but Tibetans also frequently show reverence and acquire merit through repeated prostrations—lying face down in supplication before the sacred site or object. Worshipers also observe *Saga Dawa* by gathering together, with each person taking turns to ritually bathe an image of the infant Buddha by pouring a spoonful of water over the icon. This bathing practice is performed in Japan as well during a festival known as *Hana Matsuri* (Japanese, "The Flower Festival"). There, the Buddha's birthday is celebrated on April 8, in order to coincide with the blooming of the cherry blossoms.

Father and child bathe a statue of Buddha as a baby in a Taipei temple during the April 2001 celebration of the Buddha's birth in Taiwan.

Asala In *Theravada* Buddhism, *Asala* is the holiday that traditionally marked the beginning of the three-month rainy season. During this time monks would traditionally cease to wander and would remain instead in the monastery for a period of extended retreat, meditation, and introspection. In Burma and Thailand some of the laity take temporary ordinations and live as monks for this three-month period of extended practice. *Asala* also commemorates the "First Turning of the Wheel of the *Dharma*," when the Buddha gave his first teaching, so many sermons are given to the laity at this time. In Tibet, where this festival is called *Chokor*, grand processions parade the scriptures and other sacred objects through the streets to echo the time when the Buddha first spread the *dharma*.

Other Festivals The conclusion of the three-month retreat season coincides with festival observances that also mark the time when the Buddha returned to earth after he had ascended to the *Tushita* heaven to preach to his mother. This usually occurs in October and is called the *Kathina* ceremony by Theravadins, when the laity offer new robes to the monks and make special requests for spiritual guidance and intervention. The Tibetan form of this holiday is called *Lhabap* and is characterized by feasting and visits to temples as Buddha's benevolence is dynamically present at this time and the monks and Buddhist institutions are especially spiritually charged after the season of retreat.

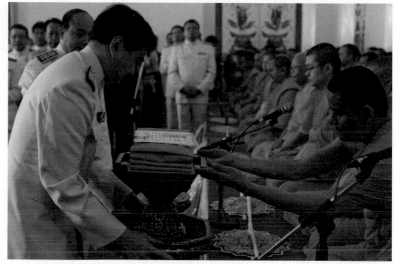

Prime Minister Abhisit offers Kathina robes to monks at a 2010 Kathina ceremony in Bangkok, Thailand.

There are many other important culturally specific Buddhist festivals that lack corollaries in other regions. To mention just one interesting example among these, we may note the "Festival of the Hungry Ghosts" (*Ullambana*) in China and its Japanese corollary "the Feast of the Dead" (*O-bon*). Here, ghostly ancestors are placated with food offerings and monks are called on to recite *sutras* in order to transfer ritually the karmic fruits of meritorious deed to aid the departed in securing a favorable rebirth.

Funerary Rites

The role played by Buddhist monks in the funerary rites of South and Southeast Asian Buddhists is first and foremost to comfort the living and to "transfer" merit to the deceased. The bereaved also accumulate "transferable" merit (potentially aiding the departed in securing a more favorable rebirth) by feeding monks on the one-week, three-month, and one-year anniversaries of their loved one's death.

Tibetan funerary practices are particularly interesting. One set of traditions that is still widely observed today dictates that after death the body be covered with a white cloth and monks ritually recite the scripture known as *Bar-do Thos-grol* into the ear of the deceased for a period of three to five days as it guides the departed through the early stages of the afterlife. Sometimes translated as *The Tibetan Book of the Dead* (or, more accurately, *Liberation in the Intermediate State Through Hearing*), the *Bar-do Thos-grol* maps out the *bardos* (Tibetan, "between two"), the three intermediary states the dead traverse between death and rebirth. The first state, known as the *clear light state*, is experienced at the moment of death as the sensory experience dissolves. If one is able to realize that this clear light is reality, liberation is immediately achieved; otherwise one passes on to the second *bardo*. In this second state, as the personality dissolves, another vision appears in the form of a *mandala* of forty-two peaceful deities and another one of fifty-eight wrathful deities, all appearing sequentially. This provides another opportunity to awaken by recognizing this as a vision of ultimate reality.

Finally, if the departed still has not spiritually awakened, he or she must pass on to the third *bardo*, where the momentum of past *karmas* propels consciousness to take birth in one of the six realms (that of the gods, demigods, humans, animals, hungry ghosts, or demons).

The realms of the *bardos* are thought to be traversed between the seventh and forty-ninth days after death. But what of the body that is left behind? After lying in state for a period of mourning, the body is stripped, put in the fetal posture, and wrapped in a wool blanket in preparation for burial. Burial in Tibet can take a variety of different forms depending on the status of the individual. Ordinary people receive a "sky burial." Beggars, the destitute, and widows receive a water burial. Thieves, murderers, and those who die of leprosy or smallpox are buried in the earth. Nobles and high-ranking monks are cremated. Finally, *stupa* internment is reserved for high lamas, like the Tashi Lama or Dalai Lama.

In the case of sky burial, an undertaker hauls the corpse on his back to a remote mountain outcropping. A fire is kindled and a pinch of roasted barley flour is thrown in to send up smoke signals that invite awaiting vultures to gather. The "meat" of the corpse is then stripped from the bone by the *rogyapa* ("body-breakers"). The *rogyapa*

Diffusion of Buddhism across Asia.

Routes of Trade and Religious Dissemination in Asia
- ——— Silk Road
- –·–·–▶ Spread of Buddhism into Korea and Japan
- ––––▶ Spread of Mahayana Buddhism
- ——▶ Spread of Theravada Buddhism
- ·······▶ Spread of Tibetan Buddhism

sets the flesh aside and goes to work on grinding the bones to dust. The powdered bone is mixed with flour and fed first to the congregated carrion birds before the meat is served. The idea is that even in death one can compassionately give their body to sustain the lives of other creatures.

The Wider Implications of Buddhist Ritual and Practice

This survey of Buddhist practices makes it clear that for ordinary followers, as for the Buddha, seeking *nirvana* has always involved the intermingling of the human and the sacred. The Buddha, other Buddhas, and *bodhisattvas* are honored through worship of their human forms (relics, objects, images, and the places where they lived and taught) through bowing down, making offerings, and the recitation of sacred texts and *mantras*. Yet all this engagement with the everyday physical domain serves as a "vehicle" to apprehend ultimate reality.

THE HISTORY OF BUDDHISM

The final part of this chapter revisits the social institutions, sectarian communities, and philosophical developments discussed earlier, and situates them within their wider historical contexts. This history explores the expansion of Buddhism in India, follows its subsequent spread to other regions of Asia, and notes its movement onto the global stage. This section maps change and innovation in Buddhism, paying particular attention to points of contention and interaction both within and across sectarian and cultural lines.

The Period of the Buddhist Councils

According to traditional Buddhist accounts, immediately after the death of the Buddha a council was convened at the town of Rajagriha in northeast India. It was the first of a series of such councils, which would define Buddhism by addressing key doctrinal shifts as they arose at particular times and places in its history. This First Council gathered because the direct disciples of the Buddha reportedly wished to ensure that everyone accurately remembered each word of his teaching. Buddhists had begun to recite and commit to memory *sutras* and stories during the Buddha's own lifetime, and the preservation of these sources must have become increasingly important after his death, as precise memories of him and his teachings began to fade. So the early *sangha* gathered, recited the *sutras*, and compared variants that had been compiled during the forty-five years the Buddha taught. The monk Upali recited the disciplinary rules (*vinaya*), and the Buddha's attendant Ananda—who is said to have achieved enlightenment on the evening before the council—recited the *sutras* (doctrine). They thereby formalized an oral canon and established an authority for the community that had lost its teacher.

The Buddha had made it clear that he did not wish for any individual or institution to have authority over the *sangha* after he was gone. As a result, in the years that followed, monks and nuns settled in various monastic institutions, with each locale

VISUAL GUIDE
Buddhism

The Buddha achieved enlightenment while seated beneath a bodhi tree. This was already considered a sacred tree long before the Buddha lived, but during his lifetime it came to directly symbolize his enlightenment. It is often regarded as a kind of cosmic axis, the divine hub in the wheel of time, seated at which one may perceive eternity and achieve omniscience. Monks gather at Bodh Gaya, the site of the Buddha's enlightenment in India, to venerate a descendant of the original bodhi tree under which he sat.

Before the Buddha was ever depicted, beginning around the first century C.E., Buddhists venerated the footprints of the Buddha to indicate that he had gone into *nirvana*. While Buddha statues that actually depict his form are common, the convention of worshiping his footprints continues today and reminds the worshiper simultaneously of the immediacy of Buddha and also of universal law of impermanence. The footprints of the Buddha mark as much a presence as an absence. These are inscribed with the sacred marks that Siddhartha is said to have been born with and that foretold his impending enlightenment.

Buddhists of all sects demonstrate their reverence for the Buddha by formal practices of bowing or prostrations. Often the full body of the worshiper lays face down on the ground in supplication. Similar practices of bowing in reverence are found in Hinduism and Jainism as well. In the Tibetan Nongdro (*sngon'gro*) or preliminary practices of *Vajrayana*, many Buddhists will perform 100,000 prostrations *(continued*

forming their own consensus on matters of discipline and doctrine. Even amid diverse monastic settlements, the doctrine of these early schools remained largely consistent, although in matters of discipline (*vinaya*) this was not always the case.

Approximately 100 years after the Buddha's passing, a "Second Buddhist Council" was purportedly held in Vaishali, in northern India, which seemed to pave the way for the first great schisms among the Buddhist community that would eventually splinter Buddhism into countless sects. This council was convened to debate the issue that the monks of Vaishali had begun to accept money. The conflict over this point had escalated when monks visiting the region refused to accept money and were then persecuted by the local *sangha*. With some 700 monks in attendance, a total of ten different monastic infractions were debated and unanimously condemned. But even though traditional accounts present this council as functioning to reinstate solidarity in the community, sectarian schisms were clearly beginning to divide the *sangha* at this time.

The same sources that describe these early councils also note that certain Buddhist elders emerged who were revered as important leaders of the Buddhist community during the several generations after the Buddha's death. Beginning even with some of the Buddha's own disciples, a shift in emphasis characterized how each of these teachers approached the *dharma* in his own unique way. There were also many solitary practitioners who chose an ascetic lifestyle, cultivating their own unique method of practice. Without a central authority beyond a loosely defined canon (which was itself open to varying interpretations and dispute), the tradition was bound to evolve dramatically in the face of both internal and external factors.

External factors included the fact that those settled in monasteries interacted with and were more dependent upon the support of the laity. In some cases they began to take on many of the characteristics of the other religious specialists of that era, employing and adapting Buddhist teaching to allow them to serve a ritual function similar to that of *brahmin* priests. Part of Buddhism's burgeoning appeal to the wider lay community in this era must have been linked to the fact that the Buddhists seemed to embody a little of both of the main religious specialists of the time: the scholastic and ritual savvy of the *brahmin* priest and the world-transcending discipline and mystic power of the wandering ascetic. This deepening interaction with the laity clearly impacted the development of Buddhism from the outset.

Ashoka and the Third Buddhist Council

The renowned emperor of the Mauryan Dynasty, Ashoka (r. 268–232 B.C.E.), continues to this day to embody the ideal of Buddhist kingship. He united the subcontinent of South Asia on a scale unseen either before or after his time. It was not until the British colonized India in the eighteenth and nineteenth centuries that a larger portion of the subcontinent would be unified under a single ruler.

The Mauryans rose to power in the years after Alexander the Great (355–323 B.C.E.) had conquered northwest India and when the Indo-Greek rule he had established in nearby regions began to wane. It was then that Ashoka's (Jain) grandfather, Chadragupta Maurya (r. 321–297 B.C.E.), began to take advantage of the vulnerability of neighboring small states throughout the region of the Indus River. With the same aggressively expansionist tactics of Alexander, he effectively consolidated Mauryan rule throughout Northern India. His grandson Ashoka skillfully renewed this policy of conquest through brute force. But while he was among the most remarkable warriors of ancient India, Ashoka later profoundly regretted the violence involved in his conquests. Legend had it that he underwent a conversion experience immediately following his triumph over the Kalingas in 260 B.C.E. It is said that after the battle he looked down from the top of Dhauli Hill (near modern Bhubaneswar in eastern

as an act of purification. Some Buddhist pilgrims will show reverence by measuring the journey to a sacred site by bowing in prostration every step of the way. Special padding to the hands and body will afford the devotee some protection during this arduous practice.

As in Hinduism and Jainism, the lotus in Buddhism is a symbol of both purity and enlightenment. The lotus has its roots in the mud of the world but rises up as its pure blossom expands ever outward in the light of the sun.

While *mandalas* are used in Hinduism, where they also function as cosmological diagrams used for meditation, some Buddhists utilize them in unique ways. In *Vajrayana* Buddhism monks may spend two weeks or more painstakingly constructing sand *mandalas*, like the Avalokiteshvara Mandala or "The Circle of Bodhisattva of Compassion" (shown here). The sacred image will then be swept toward the center and destroyed in only a few moments, as the ephemeral art also contemplates impermanence. The sand of these sacred constructions is then ceremonially carried to a lake or mountain and poured out so that this vision of harmony and mercy spills out and brings blessings to the valley below and the world beyond.

TIMELINE
Buddhism

563 B.C.E. Siddhartha Gautama (563–483 B.C.E.), the man known as "the Buddha," is born in Kapilavastu (in modern Nepal) and lives for eighty years.

486 B.C.E. The First Buddhist Council.

386 B.C.E. The Second Buddhist Council.

272–231 B.C.E. Reign of Ashoka.

c. 250 B.C.E. The Third Buddhist Council.

247 B.C.E. Ashoka's son Mahinda brings Buddhism to Sri Lanka.

100–0 B.C.E. The *Lotus Sutra* is written.

c. 25 B.C.E. The first written version of the *Pali Canon* is made in Sri Lanka.

0–100 C.E. Though historically unlikely, tradition holds that Kanishka I was inaugurated at Fourth Buddhist Council.

0–200 The initial spread of *Mahayana* Buddhism.

100–200 Ashvagosha authors the authoritative biography of the Buddha, the *Buddhacharita* (*The Deeds of the Buddha*).

In South India, Nagarjuna develops Madhyamaka philosophy and expounds the Mahayana emphasis on the idea of *shunyata*.

148 An Shin-kao brings Buddhism from Parthia along the Silk Road to the Han capital at Loyang and begins translating texts.

401 Kumarajiva (344–413) arrives in Chinese capital of Chang'an and the emperor empowers him to oversee the first Buddhist translation bureau in China.

527 Rulers of the Silla Kingdom in Korea adopt Buddhism.

593 Prince Shotoku (r. 593–622) comes to power and promotes Buddhism in Japan.

597 Bodhidharma, the first Patriarch of Chan (Zen) Buddhism, arrives in China from Kanchipuram, India.

629 Xuan Zang (596–664), the Chinese monk, begins his sixteen-year journey to India to collect Buddhist texts.

775 Samye, the first monastery in Tibet is built, after the Buddhist magician Padmasambhava is invited from India by Trisong Detsen.

800–900 Borobudur stupa is built in Java.

868 The oldest existing book in print, a copy of the *Diamond Sutra*, is printed in China.

(continued)

India) and surveyed the blood-drenched fields below. It was at this moment that he experienced a deep change of heart and was overcome with both compassion and remorse. He abandoned his compulsive expansionist policies and began to channel his efforts into a kind of social reform grounded in Buddhist ethics.

Ashoka had been influenced by Buddhist ideals even before his conquest of Kalinga, but this event was clearly the pivotal moment of his reign. The many edicts he ordered disseminated throughout his empire, often carved on rock pillars, proclaimed his desire to promote moral purification and self-awareness, to end unnecessary violence done to animals, and to honor and respect all religious viewpoints. Ashoka offered only a subtle critique of Hindu traditions as his edicts extended his support and praise to both Brahminical and Buddhist religious teachings, but he stressed the importance of cultivating inner virtues over outer worship and condemned animal sacrifices for religious purposes. Buddhists were gathering *sutras* and stories of the Buddha long before Ashoka's time, but did not begin writing them down until several centuries after the emperor's reign. Therefore Ashoka's edicts, which are still preserved today, are the earliest verifiable evidence for the widespread influence of Buddhist ideas, though the exact nature of his allegiance to the Buddha's teaching is ambiguous.

Later Buddhists revere Ashoka as the first great royal sponsor of the Buddha's teaching and as the ideal model for all later Buddhist kings. Legends celebrate Ashoka's efforts to excavate the remains and personal artifacts of the Buddha from eight *stupas*, originally constructed after his death, and then to redistribute them among 84,000 newly built *stupas* (each with an accompanying monastery) all over the empire. One of the most beautifully preserved of these structures is the *stupa* he built at Sanchi, with its elegant and distinctive gates that open out to each of the four directions. But beyond helping to propagate the Buddha *dharma* through distributing new sites of reliquary worship throughout his domain, Ashoka's building projects clearly functioned ritually to assert his sovereignty and engender a sense of unity to a culturally diverse empire.

Ashoka himself reportedly convened the Third Buddhist Council in his capital at Pataliputra around 250 B.C.E. Those present attempted to define the acceptable sources of the Buddhist teaching. Various (heretical) sectarian viewpoints were discussed and later collected in a Pali Abhidharma text called the *Kathavatthu* (Pali, *Points of Controversy*). One such sect, called the *Sarvastivada* (Sanskrit, "Those Who Hold to the Doctrine That All Exists"), were expelled from the capital following the council. But interestingly, the *Sarvastivada* was among the most important groups in Buddhist history as its doctrines contributed much to the rise of the *Mahayana*. In contrast, this council ultimately concluded that the *Vibhajyavada* sect (Sanskrit/Pali, "the Distinctionists") represented the authentic and orthodox viewpoint of the Buddha. The *Vibhajyavadas* were an offshoot of the *Sthaviras* (Sanskrit, "Elders"), and they eventually gave rise to *Theravada* Buddhism. They are the only one of the eighteen *Nikaya* or mainstream Buddhist sects that still exists today.

Aside from the major Buddhist texts, some early secondary sources allude to another council that was also convened at Pataliputra before Ashoka's reign (either 137 or 116 years after the Buddha's death). These sources indicate that shortly after the Second Council, when the Buddhist *sangha* was still unified, King Mahapadma of Nandin gathered the community to address whether the Buddhist canon should be regarded as the final authority and whether or not the early monks who recorded them were fallible. Those who held the majority vote were thereafter named the *Mahasanghika* (Sanskrit, "Greater Community"), and they agreed that one need not cling solely to the texts but, rather, that the transmission of the Buddha's teaching can come in many ways. The minority (who considered themselves more conservative on these points) called themselves the *Sthaviras*. In the years following, subdivisions within both groups quickly arose that seemed to herald the events of Ashoka's Third Buddhist Council.

TIMELINE *(continued)*
Buddhism

1197 Nalanda University is sacked by Turkic Muslim invaders.

1881 The Pali Text Society is founded by Thomas W. Rhys David in London.

1893 The first American formally converts to Buddhism on American soil following speeches given by two Buddhist leaders at the World Parliament of Religion in Chicago.

1899 The Buddhist Churches of America is founded in San Francisco by Japanese immigrants of the Jodo Shinshu sect.

1900 Over 40,000 Buddhist and Daoist texts are rediscovered in a cave at Dun Huang.

1956 Ambedkar (1891–1956) converts to Buddhism along with 400,000 *dalits* ("untouchable" caste in India).

1959 The 14th Dalai Lama flees to India from Tibet.

1989 The 14th Dalai Lama is awarded the Nobel Peace Prize.

1994 The entire Pali canon becomes freely available online for the first time.

2006 A plan is formalized to rebuild Nalanda, to again become a great Buddhist University at the original site in Bihar, India.

The Brahmi script is an ancestor of all modern Indian scripts, from the sixth pillar edict of Emperor Ashoka, 238 B.C.E.

ACTIONS TAKEN DURING EACH OF THE BUDDHIST COUNCILS

First Council: preserved the teaching and created a canon (soon after the Buddha's death)

Second Council: preserved vows and banned handling money or selling religious services

King Mahapadma's Council: asserted that the *dharma* teaching is not bound by canon and can be modified (only mentioned in some secondary sources)

Third Council: defined what the "authentic" view of the Buddha is and acknowledged the *Vibhajyavada* sect as representing that view (under Ashoka's reign)

The Period of Expansion

During the centuries of relative political disunity that arose after Ashoka, Buddhist teaching and practice expanded and spread considerably. Some monasteries began writing down their *Tripitaka* collections for the first time in the first century B.C.E., while new storytelling traditions began to make the teaching more accessible to the layperson.[33] These legends depicted the lives of saints, many of whom were the Buddha's contemporaries, and had a tendency to glorify the ways of solitary sages, living and practicing in the wilderness like lonely heroes set apart from the familiar institutional settings of the monastery.

The great ascetic Kashyapa is one such figure. Renowned as the foremost leader of the Buddhist community following the Buddha's death, Kashyapa is often credited with organizing the First Buddhist Council. Tales began to be told about how he never died, but lives on in a profound state of trance, buried inside the remote peak of Cockfeet Mountain (Sanskrit *Kukkutapada Giri*) in northern India. There he waits, guarding the robe of the Buddha that he will present to the future Buddha, known as Maitreya (Sanskrit, "the Loving One"), when he at last appears. Just as the *Jataka Tales* speak of when the Buddha met the past Buddha Dipankara, in a previous incarnation, all Buddhists await the coming of Buddha Maitreya, who will someday descend from Tushita heaven to reestablish the Buddha-*dharma* on Earth.

Another popular tale emerged of a monk named Upagupta who lived during the time of the emperor Ashoka. He is said to have accompanied

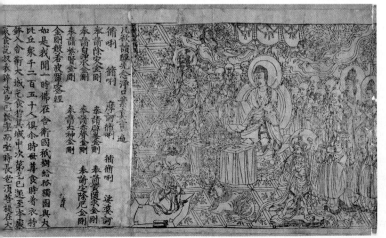

Frontispiece of the Diamond Sutra of Dun Huang, 868 C.E. This manuscript, currently on display in the British Museum (London), is the oldest known printed book in the world; it appeared 587 years before the Gutenberg Bible.

Gilded bronze Sitting Maitreya statuette. Like Rodin's *Thinker*, he is seated on his throne in deep contemplation with his hand touching his chin. Three Kingdoms period, seventh century. National Museum, Seoul, Korea, The Maitreya of Korea and Japan.

"The Laughing Buddha." He is a form of Maitreya that is popularly found in China, where his fatness symbolizes prosperity and joy. Here, his belly is rubbed for good luck. He is also associated with a portly saint named Hotei who always carried a bag of treats for children. People try their luck by touching a Maitreya relief during the New Year temple fair at the Huayan (Avatamsaka in Sanskrit) Temple on the Laoshan Mountain in Qingdao, east China's Shandong Province. Over 30,000 people come to the annual temple fair to pray for good luck.

Ashoka on pilgrimage and is sometimes credited with inspiring his Buddhist missionary campaign. Upagupta supposedly spent the early part of his life managing his family's perfume business. Yet everything changed when he met a solitary wandering teacher who instructed him in meditation practice.[34] He soon became a wandering beggar himself and quickly obtained enlightenment. But it wasn't long before Mara the Tempter showed up. Stumbling across the saint lost in deep meditation, Mara thought to perplex him by placing a wreath of flowers on his head. When Upagupta returned from his meditative trance and found himself mysteriously crowned in flowers, he again withdrew his awareness into a deep *samadhi* state and sought to determine who had done the deed. Realizing it was Mara, Upagupta thought it would be amusing to return the favor, so he garlanded the demon in turn—but, instead of flowers, he used a shriveled corpse that clung around Mara's neck. Mara tried with all his might and magic to pull it off, but it would not let go. In the end he had no choice except to return to Upagupta, admit what he had done, and humbly petition the saint to remove it. Upagupta agreed, but on the condition that Mara first manifest himself in the form of the Buddha, complete with all the auspicious marks upon his sacred body. Mara did so. This sent Upagupta into a great ecstasy upon seeing the magnificence of the Buddha, and he fell down before him in worship.

It is said that having been tamed (or even "converted"), Mara eventually became the teacher not only of fellow ascetics but also of ordinary people and the preceptors of mainstream monasteries. The subtext of this story suggests that wandering ascetics of this period also taught laypeople and that there was a rise in devotional practice (directed toward the sacred image of the Buddha) that coincided with these new hagiographies. Upagupta continues to have a significant cult following today, particularly amongst the laity of Burma.

Bodhisattvas Alongside these emerging hagiographies, we begin to find several *Mahayana* ideas move in from the margins to the forefront of Buddhist thought. One such idea acknowledges that the world is filled with *bodhisattvas*, spiritual heroes who will become Buddhas, but only after they have fulfilled their vow to first help usher all sentient beings across the gateway of liberation. Back in the period of the early Buddhist councils, the term *bodhisattva* had been used almost exclusively to refer to the Buddha before he attained *nirvana* and thus became a Buddha. But in the period of expansion, Buddhists began to depict a vast multitude of *bodhisattvas*. Many of these figures had already attained insight and power nearly equivalent to that of a Buddha and would intervene in the lives of both ordinary people and aspiring saints by employing a liberal mixture of pithy wisdom, psychic faculties, and skillful magic. They often no longer even needed human bodies, dwelling instead in heavenly realms and appearing to those who prayed to them.

"Manjushri, *Bodhisattva* of Wisdom" appearing with the flaming sword of discrimination and a copy of the *Prajnaparamita Sutra* in the blooming lotus of enlightenment. Kopan monastery, Kathmandu, Nepal.

The Story of Bhusuku and How He Met the *Bodhisattva* Manjushri Bhusuku (also known as Shantideva) authored the *Bodhicaryavatara* (*A Guide to the Bodhisattva's Way of Life*), which was to become one of the most famous works in *Mahayana* Buddhism, around 700 C.E. His systematization on the process of becoming a *bodhisattva* was key to the development of *Mahayana*. Bhusuku also advocated and helped spread the Madhyamaka or "Middle Way" philosophy of Nagarjuna (c. 150–250 C.E.), another essential aspect in the development and spread of *Mahayana*.

Nagarjuna had expounded the doctrine of emptiness (Sanskrit *shunyata*) as a powerful tool to free the mind of its constant tendency to imagine that all things are fixed, instead of fluid. *Shunyata* stresses that even the underlying building blocks of reality, or *skandhas*, are themselves empty and have no independent existence. Here, even "emptiness" is "empty;" so the mind has no firm object on which to stand and so must radically adapt and evolve how it engages reality.

There is a charming popular story told about Bhusuku's life. As a monk at the University of Nalanda, he was a very lazy and poor student. Because he neglected his studies and spent all his time eating, sleeping, and just wandering about, the other monks named him "Bhusuku" ("Lazy Bum"). Eventually he was ordered to recite the *sutras* publicly or be expelled. With the day of the test fast approaching, the abbot noticed that Bhusuku, though trying earnestly, was making little progress. So he taught Bhusuku the *mantra* of Manjushri, the *Bodhisattva* of Wisdom, and told him to pray for Manjushri's help by staying up all night. Bhusuku tied a rope so he would sit upright all night and began to recite the *mantra* "*A-Ra-Ba-Tsa-Na*" without cease.

As the night wore on and the still silence of the wee hours were about to yield to dawn's first light, Manjushri appeared before the bleary-eyed Bhusuku, saying, "Oh Bhusuku! How are you?"

Absentmindedly the student monk complained: "In the morning it will be my exam, so I have been praying to Manjushri for help."

Manjushri said: "Don't you recognize me?"

Bhusuku squinted. "No, sir. I do not."

"I am Manjushri!"

Bhusuku started. "Oh Manjushri! Please help! Grant me the power of the most excellent wisdom!"

Manjushri said: "In the morning prepare your *sutras.* I'll give you the knowledge you seek."

All the other monks gathered that morning to laugh at Bhusuku, but he sat at the head of the congregation looking particularly radiant. Bhusuku asked the king and the professors who were in attendance: "Shall I recite the *sutras* as they traditionally have been recited, or should I explain them in my own way?" They all laughed and the king said, "You have inaugurated a way of eating and sleeping and wandering about like we have never seen before, why not expound the *dharma* in a way we are yet to hear!"

Bhusuku began to speak. His teaching was beautifully eloquent and profound. As he talked he floated up into the air, while everyone dropped to their knees and called out: "You are not a *bhusuku!* You are a master!!" They began calling him Shantideva ("Peaceful Deity") because his own unique wisdom could quiet the pride of both scholars and kings.[35]

The Development of *Mahayana* in Monasteries

Between the fourth and sixth centuries C.E., *Mahayana* practices and ideas became more formally integrated into monastic institutions, ensuring their preservation and propagation up to the present day. This coincided with the rule of a north Indian dynasty known as the Guptas, who culturally and politically reunited parts of Ashoka's great empire. By 1000 C.E., numerous versions and translations of *Mahayana sutras* were widely available, and their once secretive traditions became well established and revered throughout Asia. During this period of integration the short *Mahayana sutras* composed in verse, which were probably the earliest to appear, began to be revised into significantly longer prose versions, often four to twenty times the length of the original.

Many mainstream monasteries in India adopted *Mahayana* ideas and practices during the early part of this period. In the fourth and fifth centuries C.E., records of donations to settled monasteries indicate that some monastic heads were openly supporting "Greater Vehicle" teachings and praising their members as *Mahayana* adepts. In addition, East Asian monks from the fifth century onward regularly traveled back to India to study and bring home copies of *Mahayana* sources. The accounts of these East Asian pilgrim monks confirm that *Mahayana* ideas and sources increasingly influenced the daily practice and reflection of Indian Buddhists.

By the seventh century, a significant number of monasteries were allying themselves with the *Mahayana*, the greatest concentration of which were found in northwest India where king Kanishka (121–157 C.E.) had ruled half a millennium earlier.

Vajrayana or *Tantric* Buddhism: The "Diamond Vehicle"   By the seventh century, influential Buddhist teachers in northeast India were promoting yet another distinct "vehicle" known as the *Vajrayana* (Sanskrit, "Thunderbolt Vehicle"). If the image of an ocean liner (in contrast to a simple raft) is used as a metaphor for *Mahayana*, this new thunderbolt "vehicle" might be described as a supersonic jet. It was conceived as a method of such intense power and speed that it could catapult an ordinary human adept to the stage of an advanced *bodhisattva*—a level of awareness that would normally take many eons to attain—in a single lifetime. This tradition is also sometimes referred to as the "Diamond Vehicle," emphasizing both the crystal-like clarity of the wisdom it teaches and its ability to cut through all misperceptions of reality.

Compared to the Buddha's words in *Mahayana sutras*, the methods of *Vajrayana* are intended for even more advanced adepts. These esoteric techniques are described not in *sutras* but in sources called *tantras* (Sanskrit, "weavings"), a special class of sacred text that discusses the mysterious modes of ritual and practice that characterize these traditions. One scholar defined *tantra* as "a technique for magically storming the gates of Buddhahood."[36] These sources are full of mysterious language and often shocking symbols that can only be understood after receiving secret initiation and instruction from a qualified teacher. Many claimed that the Buddha took on a special radiant form as *Vajradhara* (Sanskrit, "Thunderbolt-bearer") to teach this method to special disciples. Some thought that this transmission even took place psychically while the Buddha imparted other, less esoteric teachings to a wider audience, appearing simultaneously in both his thunderbolt and his ordinary human form.

Vajrayana Buddhist sources became influential in northeast India during the seventh through eleventh centuries, especially in the region of Bengal. *Vajrayana* tradition looks to a group of eighty-four *Mahasiddhas*—a wild order of mystic saints, magicians, and yogic adepts—as those who first formulated and spread this tradition. (Bhusuku, the student monk who was suddenly enlightened, is counted among them.) A number of Buddhist universities were founded in this period, from where *Vajrayana* was transmitted to nearby Tibet and Nepal, and subsequently to Mongolia and Bhutan, as well as certain parts of East and Southeast Asia.

Withering Roots in South and Central Asia Scholars often point to the year of 1197 C.E. as the beginning of the end of Buddhism in India. It marked the date of one of the more virulent incursions by Muslim Turks into India. These raids were particularly damaging to Buddhist institutions, which no longer garnered the royal support and protection given in preceding eras. It was the destruction of the Buddhist universities of Nalanda and Vikramasila (circa 1200) that most historians assert struck the final blow.

Inaugurated in 427 C.E., Nalanda (in northeastern India) has often been regarded as the first great learning institution in human history. At its height it had 2,000 professors and 10,000 students and offered a well-rounded curriculum that extended far beyond Buddhist *dharma*. But it was not just the loss of these institutions that spelled doom for the Buddha-*dharma* in India; Buddhism was clearly waning long before Nalanda was sacked. By the tenth century Indian Buddhist monasteries had fallen into a state of decline from which they never recovered. It is unsure what factors brought this about. Was it the political fragmentation that came after the sixth-century fall of the Guptas? This period of smaller warring kingdoms clearly weakened the mechanisms of support and patronage that Buddhist monasteries and other institutions had relied upon since Ashoka's time. Was it the growing hostility of the Brahminical establishment that began making concerted efforts to reinforce its supremacy? Perhaps it began when the *bhakti* movement in the south became openly hostile to Buddhism and Jainism, or when renowned Brahminical theologians actively combated the growth of Buddhism in the public domain. Whatever the cause, by the eighth and ninth centuries, Hinduism had won back the lion's share of both royal and lay support. When the Tibetan monk Dharmasvamin wrote of his travels in the mid-thirteenth century, he despaired that almost no one in India would openly profess to being a Buddhist. Nevertheless, small pockets of Buddhism did endure in India, particularly in South India, until the seventeenth century.

Buddhism Beyond India

Even as the light of Buddhism dimmed and sputtered out in India, it was thriving beyond that country's borders and spreading in all directions. Many of Buddhism's sectarian transformations arose as adaptations to new cultural contexts. Keeping in mind that Buddhism died in the country of its birth, we can see how its journey and adaptation in other lands becomes all the more poignant. In the limited context of this brief introduction to Buddhism it is impossible to do justice to the subtle complexities of these processes. But the following discussion paints with a broad brush a rough sketch of the initial transformative journey Buddhism has taken outside of India.

The Southern Transmission Sri Lankan legend has it that King Devanampiyatissa (250–210 B.C.E.) was converted to Buddhism by Ashoka's own son, Mahinda. The newly converted king had a huge monastery complex called Mahavihara (Pali, "Great Monastery") built in his capital at Anuradhapura. Ashoka's daughter, Sanghamitta, also came to the island to plant a sapling from the Buddha's own *bodhi* tree and to establish the first order of Sri Lankan nuns.

Monastic institutions were strong in Sri Lanka from Buddhism's earliest period, and monasteries competed with each other for royal patronage. Although there were times when disputes over patronage led to irreconcilable schisms among the *sangha*, Sri Lanka has been for more than a millennium renowned as a bastion of exemplary *Theravada* Buddhism. One interesting development came around the beginning of the fourth century when King Mahasena (r. 275–301 C.E.), coming under the influence of a South Indian monk, aligned himself with the *Mahayana*. Much to the shock and horror of its monastic body, he decided that the Mahavihara monastery should become a *Mahayana* institution as well. The monks there simply packed up and left. King Mahasena had the Mahavihara pulled down and the Jetavana Vihara monastery built in its place to accommodate his Mahayanists. The next king had the Mahavihara rebuilt and invited back the monks who had left. But for centuries these and other monasteries were at odds. These sectarian tensions remained until the reign of King Parakkama Bahu I in the twelfth century C.E. who, favoring the lineage of the Mahavihara, "purified" the *sangha* by abolishing all other sects.

Burma became another important center to diffuse *Theravada* throughout Southeast Asia. It also claims to have had a visit from Ashoka's emissaries in the third century B.C.E. Historically, however, much of early Buddhism in mainland Southeast Asia was transmitted among the Mon people, who occupied southern Burma along with parts of both Thailand and Laos. Ultimately, the pivotal moment for Burmese Buddhism occurs in 1057 C.E. when Anawr, the Bamar king of Pagan, invaded the Mon kingdom of the south to establish the first Burmese empire (1057–1287) by uniting Upper and Lower Myanmar. As the spoils of his conquest he carried off Buddhist relics, Pali texts, and a retinue of monks to whom he granted control of the *sangha*. Thus, *Theravada* suddenly became the new state religion of this new empire. Much of these developments are said to have arisen because of the influence of a Burmese monk named Chapata, who took his ordination at the Mahavihara in Sri Lanka, following the Buddhist reformations of King Parakkama Bahu I (r. 1153–1186). This reform impacted the spread of *Theravada* Buddhism throughout Southeast Asia, and echoed the theological transitions of Thailand, Laos, and Cambodia, where between the twelfth and fifteenth centuries an earlier mingling of various Buddhist sects, Hinduism, and indigenous traditions gave way to state-sponsored *Theravada*.

It is important to note that *Mahayana* too did have a significant place in the history of these regions. In Cambodia, kings frequently identified themselves as *bodhisattvas*, and the worship of Lokeshwara (Avalokiteshvara) was of prime importance during the latter part of the Angkor period (twelfth–fifteenth centuries C.E.). *Mahayana* also reigned supreme in Indonesia

Lokeshwara peers out in all directions from the temple towers at the Angkor Wat temple complex in Cambodia. These colossal faces were identified both as Shiva and as Avalokiteshvara by their worshipers.

and on the Malay Peninsula, where even *tantric* forms proliferated. By the seventh century, sites like Srivijaya in Sumatra were important centers of Buddhist training and attracted monks from as far away as China. The renowned Indian monk Atisha (982–1054) came to study in Srivijaya under the great master Dharmakirti before journeying to Tibet in 1042, where he founded the Kadampa sect of *Vajrayana*, from which the Gelugpa school of the Dalai Lamas eventually arose.

The Sailendra Dynasty, on the isle of Java, patronized a blending of *Mahayana* Hindu and Hindu Shaivism that was popular throughout these regions and built at Borobudur (around 800 C.E.) one of the most beautiful *stupas* ever constructed. True to its *tantric* orientation, it took the form of a gigantic multi-tiered *mandala* wrought in stone and comprised of seventy smaller *stupas*, each enclosing an image of one of the Five Meditating Buddhas. Winding one's way upward and inward toward the central apex of the *stupa*, thousands of bas relief sculptures transport the viewer across vast eons through the depiction of key episodes in the past lives of the Buddha, enabling the pilgrim to share in the Buddha's journey through *samsara* to *nirvana*. This hybrid Tantrism continued to develop during the twelfth and thirteenth centuries but was deposed by a fifteenth-century Muslim rebellion. Islam, which entered Sumatra in the ninth century, came to dominate most of the region by the sixteenth century.

Borobadur Stupa, Java, Indonesia, c. 800 C.E. One of the many hidden Buddhas stands revealed. Usually, worshipers would have to peer in through the diamond-shaped holes on the *stupas* to see these hidden sacred forms.

The Northern Transmission Buddhist communities were also founded in Central Asia shortly around Ashoka's time. Besides sending Buddhist missionaries to Afghanistan, it is said that Ashoka sent his son, Kustana, to the region northwest of Tibet, where he founded the kingdom of Khotan in 240 B.C.E. Later, the Central Asian ruler Kanishka I (r. 110–139 C.E.?), after inheriting the portions of Bactria and northwest India conquered by his Kushan predecessors, is said to have embraced and vigorously supported Buddhist tradition in the second century C.E. Some of the earliest Buddhist images date from the period of his reign. These were clearly influenced by the Hellenistic Greek artistic styles left over from Alexandrian times and by artisans from the Roman empire, who commonly traveled along the trade routes crossing Asia from the Middle East. Indeed, the oldest existent image of the Buddha shows up on a coin of Kanishka, where the influence of Indo-Greek culture is still evident as the Buddha's name appears in Greek characters. Kanishka is also sometimes credited with convening a Fourth Buddhist Council.

Buddhism Comes to East Asia We may assume that the first importation of Buddhism to China came in the first century C.E. along the arduous overland trade routes extending through Central Asia to both Persia and India. Most likely it was initially brought by monks and missionaries of Central Asia, who accompanied merchants along the Silk Road to China. When Buddhism arrived in the refined world of the late Han Dynasty (206 B.C.E.–220 C.E.), it was not construed as a civilizing force as it was often regarded when welcomed in other lands. Nonetheless, it was received as a rare and precious import.

One of the major ways in which Buddhism entered and was adapted in China was through the process of translation. What this meant is that in China, Buddhist culture was not so much adopted as adapted. It required some transformation to conform to the deeply embedded Chinese cultural landscape. This process began in 148 C.E. when An Shin-kao came from Parthia along the Silk Road to the Han capital at Loyang. He was the first of a series of missionary-translators welcomed in China. Like him, Lokaksema of the Kushans also came from Central Asia and first translated *Mahayana* works into Chinese in the later half of the second century C.E., but there were many others. Translation into Chinese was a tricky process. It usually began with reciting the text from memory in Sanskrit, followed by the writing of a rough draft in Chinese. The work was then polished into a format in keeping with the Chinese literary conventions of the day. Not unexpectedly, this often produced a fair amount of deviation from the original source. Early on, rough Taoist equivalents stood in for Buddhist philosophical terms and only later were new Chinese words coined to better convey abstract Buddhist concepts.

The earliest known image of the Buddha appears on the reverse of a coin minted by the Kushan King, Kanishka. Previously, the Buddha was never depicted in physical form but was depicted more as an absence than a presence, symbolized with images such as footprints or an empty chair.

After the Han Dynasty fell around 311, the court fled to the south and many Buddhist monks went with them, taking the *dharma* into new territory. It quickly became a kind of intellectual discipline that appealed to the ruling classes. Confucianism had lost some of its credibility in the wake of these upheavals and Buddhism was primed to take its place. It resonated nicely with the contemplative and mystic introversion of Daoism (Chapter 8) but was more systematized and spoke directly to the sorrows and sympathies of the man on the street. By this time, Indian transmissions of Buddhism had also reached Southern China by sea. Amid the chaos of the North, Buddhist intellectualism had given way to an emphasis on practice. Here in the North, "barbarian" kings patronized Buddhist ascetics and magicians who had roots in Central Asian traditions.

New approaches to translation came into practice in the fourth century as Buddhists began to question how Daoist terminology distorted their understanding of Buddhist doctrine. Indian monks were then imported to the translation center at Ch'ang-an (modern Xi'an) to work alongside Chinese scribes. Among them was the illustrious Kumarajiva (344–413), who assisted in a massive retranslation project that also introduced a host of "new" *Mahayana* texts. Their appearance would propel Chinese Buddhism into its own unique flowering of creative insight.

Among the *Mahayana* sects of today, many took on their (historically recognized) definitive form in China. In this regard, the old *Mahayana* conventions of devotion or alliance to a particular text can be clearly seen as informing the primary character of these schools. Thus, we can understand why the efforts of Kumarajiva were so essential in mapping this history. Traditionally, China counts ten separate Buddhist schools that emerged on its soil. Most of them are built around a principal *sutra*, each proffering some interesting developments in their relationship to Indian textual traditions. Two of the ten schools were primarily not oriented around Indian textual traditions, but on practice. The main emphasis of the *Chen-yen* ("True Word") *School* (a.k.a., *Mi-tsung*; Japanese, *Shingon*) was *tantric* initiation and the esoteric use of *mantras*, *mandalas*, and *mudras*. It was later supplanted by Tibetan *Vajrayana*, but it managed to be transplanted to Japan by Kukai (774–835) before it died out in China. The *Ch'an*, or "Meditation" School, is called *Son* in Korea, but is best known by its Japanese name, *Zen*.

Without doing full justice to the rich forms of Buddhism that develop as these many schools pass to Korea and then Japan, let us briefly note the early history of their transmission to other parts of East Asia. Buddhism arrived in Korea around the fourth century C.E. and closely emulating the Chinese systems, originally developed Five Doctrinal Schools. Four of them were derivatives of the Chinese (text-based) prototypes, while the fifth was purely a Korean syncretism called *Popsong*. When *Son* (*Ch'an/Zen*) was later introduced, its iconoclastic nature put it at odds with the doctrine-based schools that preceded it, yet it has always remained particularly strong in the region. In Japan, Buddhism was first introduced in 552 C.E. when the Korean King of Paechke presented Emperor Kinmei of Japan (r. 531–571) with a gift of *sutras* and an icon of the Buddha. By the Nara period (710–784) six schools of Buddhism were imported directly to Japan from China. In the Heian period (794–1185) *Tantric* Buddhism (*Shingon*) and the Lotus *Sutra* sect (*Tiendai*) were added, and by the Kamakura period (1185–1333) "Pure Land," Zen, and *Nichiren* (an indigenous fusion of the last three) came to essentially define the sectarian complexity of Buddhism in Japan. Among these, Zen would later have the most enduring and greatest impact on Japanese culture and have a uniquely broad influence in inspiring the arts.

Although Buddhism took root in Tibet later than in China, its transmission came directly from India between the seventh and the eleventh centuries C.E. Since its arrival in Tibet around 650 C.E., the region has remained a stronghold of *Vajrayana* or *Tantric* Buddhism, although it initially met with a great deal of resistance. The shamans and court "wizards" of the indigenous Tibetan *Bön* religion held sway among the nobility. But legend has it that when King Songtsen Gampo (c. 617–649) arranged marital alliances with the daughters of the King of Nepal and the Emperor of China, he found that his new wives were both Buddhists (and later legend even held them to be incarnations of *bodhisattvas* of mercy—the "Green Tara" and the "White Tara"). Their arrival began to soften the Tibetan attitudes to Buddhism, and the king built the first Buddhist temple and made arrangements for the translation of *sutras* into Tibetan. As monks and teachers poured into Tibet, Buddhism flourished.

During the reign of Trisong Detsen (c. 742–798), Tibet's first Buddhist king, the Buddhist scholar Shantarakshita (d. 800?) was invited to come from Nalanda and preside over the building of Tibet's first monastery. But local priests said his arrival was marked by ill omens sent by local demonic forces. Before fleeing the country, Shantarakshita told the king that he needed a powerful *tantric* adept to subdue these dark forces and advised him to send for the Indian pundit and adept Padmasambhava (see p. 172). When Padmasambhava arrived he not only managed to subdue and convert the local gods and demons, but endeared himself to the Tibetan people. Shantarak-shita was invited back, and the king and these two sages consecrated the Samye monastery in 775 C.E. as well as ordained members of the Tibetan aristocracy.

In the early ninth century, Buddhism was again under siege in Tibet and forced underground during the reign of King Lang Darma (r. 838–842 C.E.). When the king was assassinated and his dynasty collapsed, Buddhism was blamed for instilling weakness in the military. After serving as dean at Nalanda the scholar monk Atisa arrived in Tibet in 1042 C.E. A disciple of the Indian *tantric* master Naropa, he provided Tibet with an effective synthesis of the *Theravada*, *Mahayana*, and *tantric* forms of Buddhism that had previously undermined the cohesion of the *sangha*. Atisa instituted the practice of formal initiation into *tantric* lineages, which still characterizes Tibetan *Vajrayana* today.

During the thirteenth century, Tibetan Shakya masters entered into a "patron-priest" relationship with the Khans (descendants of Genghis Khan) who ruled a Mongolian empire that extended from China to Eastern Europe. This inaugurated a tradition in Tibet, whereby monastic leaders took on the role of the social and political guardians of the Tibetan people. In 1578 C.E. the head of the Gelugpa monastery, Sonam Gyatsho (1543–1588), converted Altan Khan, the ruler of the Mongols. The Great Khan bestowed upon Sonam Gyatsho the title *Dalai Lama* (Mongolian, "Ocean [of Wisdom] Teacher"). Since Sonam Gyatsho was already identified as a *tulku* or "reincarnate lama" as the third incarnation of the sage Tsongkhapa, tradition calls him the "third" Dalai Lama. However, it was the fifth Dalai Lama (1617–1682) who took full advantage of Mongol patronage. Backed by Mongol troops he took over all of Tibet and sent other sects with conflicting political aspirations fleeing to other Himalayan locales across the Himalayas. By the seventeenth century, with the Dalai Lama as the primary ruler of Tibet, great efforts were made to identify and reinstate him in this role each time he died and took rebirth. Many Dalai Lamas, however, fell victim to political assassination.

Vajrayana spread through Mongolia, Bhutan, southwestern China, northern India, and even parts of Russia. Among the Newar people of Nepal, *Vajrayana* Buddhists have lived in a fairly symbiotic relationship with the state-sponsored Hinduism that defines the majority in the country of the Buddha's birth.

Through all of these many transplantations into many regions and countries, Buddhism adapted to the culture it moved in, was imbued with local color, and integrated indigenous beliefs. These patterns of transformation have also extended to Buddhism's encounter with Europe and America in the modern and postmodern contexts.

The Beginnings of the Western Transmission

Over the past two centuries, Buddhist traditions came increasingly into contact with Western observers, who reported and interpreted Buddhist teachings and practices to Western audiences. Among them were many of the first Western converts to the Buddhist faith who both anticipated and helped inspire the growing popularity of Buddhism in Europe and America today.

Much of this story begins in the early nineteenth century, when T. W. Rhys-Davids (1843–1922), a British colonial administrator and later professor of Pali at the University of London, first "discovered" Buddhist teaching while stationed in Sri Lanka. He founded the Pali Text Society in 1881 to translate these Buddhist works systematically into English. His translations sparked a whirlwind of interest among an English-speaking audience. The impact of modernization that accompanied the Industrial Revolution, and an unshakable veneration of the power of reason, drew readers of these translated works to the Buddha's teaching. Many saw the Buddha as a radically independent, "self-made" man who relied only on his own introspection and insight. Fixating on the "logic" of Buddhism, many Western readers[37] considered sections that held the slightest trace of magic or mystical thinking as later misrepresentations of the Buddha's purely rational impulse. Consequently, early Western readers of Buddhist texts preferred to characterize Buddhism primarily as a "philosophy" that radically contrasted with the anti-rational dogmas of Western religion. One might argue that this oversimplification of Buddhist tradition is still widespread among many Western Buddhists.

In recent years, Western adherents have increasingly been moving away from the simplistic and subjective interpretations of previous decades, valuing instead a deeper commitment to particular lineages and a more well-rounded understanding of the subtle complexities of specific systems of Buddhist practice.

Chinese and Japanese immigrants had a lot to with the first establishment of Buddhist institutions on American soil around 1900. But the first formal Buddhist conversion or lay ordination was conducted in 1893 when Charles T. Strauss formally converted, following a series of lectures he heard at the World Parliament of Religions in Chicago. But it was the American subcultures of the 1950s and 1960s, particularly the Beats and Hippies, who helped catalyze a deep and abiding interest in Buddhism for Americans. Some might argue that this culminated in 1974, when Chogyam

As a young Vietnamese monk, Thich Nhat Hahn appears alongside Dr. Martin Luther King Jr. at a Chicago news conference as King suggests a halt in bombing of Vietnam, May 31, 1966. King also said there is not a direct parallel between Buddhists who put themselves to death by fire and Americans who die in the civil rights cause.

In 1963 the Vietnamese Buddhist monk Thich Quang Duc, while seated in meditation, burned himself to death in Saigon's Market Square to protest the government's religious policies.

Trungpa (1940–1987)—the first Western-educated Tibetan *tulku*—founded Naropa University in Boulder, Colorado. Yet clearly the noble character of Buddhist leaders as political dissidents and peace activists also inspired these new generations of American Buddhists. Martin Luther King's nonviolent approach to civil rights activism was informed by Buddhist practice. King's admiration for the Vietnamese Buddhist monk and peace activist Thich Nhat Hanh, whose caring and commitment to community service helped to heal the emotional wounds of many American veterans of the Vietnam War, led King to nominate Hanh for a Nobel Peace Prize in 1967. The ever-growing popularity of the 14th Dalai Lama, Tenzin Gyatso (b. 1935), who was awarded the Nobel Peace Prize in 1989, also exemplifies the identification of Buddhism with peaceful political dissidence in America.

Buddhists in the World Today

Today, "*dharma*-talks" are delivered as podcasts. Apps that help Buddhists time their meditations or look up specific *sutras* are available for the iPhone. In Japan, you can purchase pocket-size plastic replicas of some of the most revered Buddhist icons out of vending machines. Chinese animated hagiographies of saints and *bodhisattvas* can be easily downloaded, and, in America, the warmly irreverent creators of *South Park* offer free online versions of old Zen lectures by Alan Watts accompanied by Trey Parker and Matt Stone's own "cartoon commentaries."[38] In the world of American comic books, an increasing number of superheroes are turning Buddhist (such as "Xorn" of the X-men; there are also frequent references to the Buddhist training Batman has received in Tibet). Yet even as far back as the 1930s and 1940s there were similar mystic American heroes trained in Buddhist practice, such as The Shadow and The Green Lama, who appeared in pulp magazines, radio serials, and comic books.

A modern Cambodian monk at work on his computer.

Today, no scribes are needed to copy *sutras* as the vast majority of the Buddhist canon is available for free online, along with virtual zendos, *mandalas*, and temples to visit without stepping outside one's door. Today new technology and media are continually challenging Buddhists to adapt, expand, and explore new environments. But Buddhism has encountered a multitude of cultures in its spread throughout Asia (and beyond) over the past 2,500 years and has always found skillful ways of applying new technologies. Indeed, the earliest printed text in the world was a copy of the *Diamond Sutra* dated 868 C.E. and made on an early Chinese printing press. Just so, we are now witness to the instantaneous worldwide distribution of those same sources via the Internet. Buddhists continue to develop innovative ways to integrate modern realities into an ancient Buddhist worldview, as they convey traditional teachings through contemporary mediums that preserve the sacred *sutras*, stories, and songs that are the Buddhist tradition.

CONCLUSION

We began this chapter by reflecting on the Buddha's own life because for most Buddhists his quest for freedom helps map the evolutionary journey of us all. His was an expedition from the oscillations of time and circumstance, from the sorrow inherent in clinging to impermanence to a timeless joy that springs from simply letting go and acknowledging the interconnectivity of all things. The Buddha's teaching intended to dislodge the mind from holding to the illusion of fixity, to embrace change, and to empower each individual to see for himself or herself the nature of reality.

Through its history we have seen that Buddhism has always had a unique ability to adapt to any cultural context. Much of its versatility was fostered in the earliest teaching of the Buddha when he insisted that wherever Buddhism is transplanted, local custom, convention, and religious observance should always be maintained. This allowed Buddhism to be incredibly adaptable and to syncretize easily with regional beliefs and theologies, as its predisposition was not to displace but to augment. But Buddhism also needed to adapt to internal factors as new insights and understanding of the *dharma* arose. Some of the fundamental concepts of Buddhism inspired insights, challenged earlier assumptions, and interrogated the established conventions of Buddhist ethos. This generated powerful schisms among the *sangha* and created a diversification of ways of practice. Many Buddhists see this diversification as a natural development of the Buddhist *dharma* as it manifests in countless forms to adapt to as many different aptitudes and inclinations as there are sentient beings. In other words, many Buddhists believe that there are ultimately as many "Buddhisms" as there are beings in the universe. Everyone must find their own way. Everyone "must be a lamp unto themselves."

In the modern context, Buddhism has inspired social dissidence and been employed to liberate the individual from social constraints, as in 1956 when B. R. Ambhedkar led 400,000 Hindu *dalits* to convert en masse to Buddhism to free themselves from the caste-based shackles of untouchability. But, as with other religions, Buddhist institutions have also at times functioned as mechanisms of social control and supported state-sponsored violence, as may be seen in the fact that there have often been "fighting monks" in Tibetan and East Asian monastic traditions that developed various martial arts traditions, often to enforce both sectarian and political agendas.[39] Nevertheless, many modern Buddhist leaders have come to exemplify the power of nonviolent modes of resistance and reform, such as the Burmese Buddhist dissident Aung San Suu Kyi (b. 1945), whose commitment to peaceful resistance resulted in her receiving the Rafto Prize in 1990, the Sakharov Prize for Freedom in Thought in 1990, and the Nobel Peace Prize in 1991, among other awards and accolades.

A new development in the modern context—and one that has emphasized the teaching of Interdependent Origination—views ecology as a primary model for embracing the interrelational underpinnings of reality. This trend, which sees the individual and the environment in perpetual relationship, embraces a global vision as a key adaptive evolution of the *dharma* that is both timely and essential to where we stand today.

SEEKING ANSWERS

What Is Ultimate Reality?

For most Buddhist sects, ultimate reality is the luminous and expansive nature of consciousness itself. Ultimate reality is primarily apprehended by understanding the nature of the mind, which mediates our experience of existence. A famous Zen *koan* illustrates this concept succinctly. Two monks are standing at the foot of a flagpole, staring upward contemplating the flag as it flutters in the breeze. One monk turned to his companion and said, "The flag is moving." The other quietly observed, "The wind is moving." Old Hui Neng, the Sixth Patriarch, happened to be passing by and said: *"Not the wind, not the flag, mind is moving."* To many Buddhists material reality is simply a product and projection of the mind.

Many *Mahayana* and *Vajrayana* Buddhists would assert that being born into this world, with all its suffering and strife, places us in the ideal situation to achieve enlightenment. It is the very fragility of life that evokes the compassion and empathy essential to achieving enlightenment.

How Should We Live in This World?

Buddhism's five precepts are ethical guidelines that seek to minimize the suffering one inflicts on others as well as oneself. The first three are concerned with ethical prescriptions that limit the harm we cause others: not killing, not stealing, and not committing inappropriate sexual acts. The last two seek to limit the suffering that one inflicts on oneself: not lying and not imbibing intoxicants. The other fundamental guide to life is Buddhism's Eightfold Path. By advocating neither extreme asceticism nor worldly hedonism, the Noble Eightfold path charts a Middle Way. It suggests an integrated way of living that embraces a balanced cultivation of both the outer and inner life and is meant to optimize fully the expansion of consciousness and evolutionary development.

What Is Our Ultimate Purpose?

For Buddhists, one's ultimate purpose is to break free of *samsara* and achieve *nirvana*. For many *Mahayana* Buddhists, the vow of the *bodhisattva* embellishes this primary goal. Thus, many Buddhists strive not only for their own enlightenment, but for the enlightenment of all sentient beings. For most Buddhists meditation is the fundamental means through which one can apprehend the true nature of reality. That direct apprehension, combined with an understanding of *karma*, *shunya*, Interdependent Origination, and the relationship between *samsara* and *nirvana*, create the ideal conditions to bring about enlightenment. But some Buddhists find their life utterly transformed simply by emphasizing the cultivation of *bodhicitta* (compassion).

REVIEW QUESTIONS

For Review

1. List some of the very distinctive ways in which Buddhism differs from other religions.
2. How does the Buddhist concept of "enlightenment" differ from that of Hinduism, Jainism, Sikhism, and Taoism?
3. How would the Buddha have regarded practices of Buddhist worship?
4. Discuss the various kinds of narrative traditions found in Buddhism and how they impart Buddhist teaching.
5. Describe some of the varieties of Buddhist meditation and the various sectarian contexts in which they are employed.
6. What are some of the more "devotional" forms of Buddhism, and how are they distinguished?

For Further Reflection

1. Give a specific example of what Buddhists might describe as "Skillful Means." Take note of both action and circumstance.
2. What is the primary reason for the theological shift to *Mahayana* Buddhism, and how specifically is that reflected in Mahayanist practice?
3. Explain how Interdependent Origination is "interdependent."
4. Describe the philosophical continuities that carry over from Jainism and the *Upanishads* into Buddhism.
5. How did the three main branches of Buddhism develop? What are the special properties of each, and how do they assert their own superiority over the other systems?
6. Explain the problems with the theory that *Mahayana* arose to serve the needs of the laity.

GLOSSARY

anatman (un-aat-mun; Sanskrit) No independent self or soul.

bodhicitta (bow-dhi-chit-ta; Sanskrit, "the awakening mind or heart") In *Mahayana* it is the wise intention to enlighten all beings.

bodhisattva (bow-dhi-sut-tva; Sanskrit, "an awakened being") One on the verge of awakening. In *Mahayana* it refers to an adept who has made the vow of the *bodhisattva* to remain in *samsara* until all beings are free.

Buddha (bood-dha; Sanskrit, "the Awakened One") A fully enlightened being.

Cha'an or *Zen* (chah-aahn/Zehn) Respectively, the Chinese and Japanese names for the "meditation" school of Buddhism that values meditative experience far and above doctrine.

dharma (dhur-mah; Sanskrit, "that which upholds") In the Buddhist context it refers to Buddhist teaching, or Buddhism as a religious tradition.

Interdependent Origination (Sanskrit: *pratitya-samutpada*, "arising on the ground of a preceding cause") The realization that our sense of "self" arises spontaneously in response to a set of conditions. These conditions are born of a vast network of relationships that are inextricably linked to all phenomena. All things are the result of antecedent causes, and our sense of independent existence is merely an illusion.

karma (kur-mah; Sanskrit) Action or cause; the law of causation.

lama (laah-mah; Tibetan) A teacher. But usually a degree or title reserved for one who has completed a three-year retreat.

(continued)

GLOSSARY (continued)

Mahayana (muh-haah-yaah-na; Sanskrit, "greater vehicle") Characterized by emphasizing the *bodhisattva* path and developing between 100 B.C.E.–100 C.E.

mandala (muhn-daah-la; Sanskrit "circle") Typically circular cosmological diagram used for *tantric* meditation.

mantra (mun-trah; Sanskrit) Sacred sounds or syllables used as a focus for meditation, as an invocation of a deity, or as a protective spell.

Middle Way Buddha's teaching on avoiding extremes, that is systematized by the eightfold path.

nirvana (nihr-vaah-nah; Sanskrit, "blowing out") The ultimate goal of Buddhist practice and refers to the final liberation from the suffering of cyclic existence (*samsara*; endless cycles of death and rebirth). Lit. "to blow out or extinguish," but it might best be understood as "cooling down" or "allaying" the pain born from the unquenchable thirst of being.

parinirvana (pah-ree nihr-vaah-nah; Sanskrit, "supreme release") Refers to the death of a fully enlightened being.

prajna (prudg-naah; Sanskrit) Wisdom.

samadhi (sah-maahd-hee; Sanskrit, "hold together") A profound state of meditative trance.

samsara (sum-saah-ra; Sanskrit, "continuous flow") This term refers to the endless cycle of life, death, and rebirth or reincarnation.

sangha (suhn-ghaah; Sanskrit/Pali) "Assemblage or community [of Buddhists]."

shunyata (shoon-yah-taah; Sanskrit "emptiness") This asserts that all phenomenon, even the momentary components of experiential reality, are devoid of ontological, independent, intrinsic existence. As with the teaching on Interdependent Origination it stresses the relational underpinnings of each and every component of existence.

skandha (skuhn-dhaah; Sanskrit, "heaps" or "bundles") Five aggregates (form, feeling, perception, mental formations, and consciousness) that give rise to a false sense of identity through apprehending them as an integrated and autonomous whole.

stupa (stooh-puh; Sanskrit, "heap") Reliquary mounds in which the remains or personal objects of Buddhist masters are buried and venerated.

sutra (sooh-trah; Sanskrit, "a thread") Verses of text or scripture.

Tathagatha (tuh-tha-gaah-tah; Sanskrit, "the Thus-gone [One]") The Buddha.

Tathagatha-garba (tuh-tha-gaah-tah   gaar-bhah; Sanskrit) The Womb Matrix of the Buddhas; i.e., the inner Buddha or the potentiality for awakening found in all beings.

Theravada (thair-ah-vaah-duh; Pali, "the Way of the Elders") Established in 240 B.C.E. at the Mahavihara in Sri Lanka, the earliest existent school of Buddhism that is predominant in Southeast Asia.

tulku (tool-kooh; Tibetan) A reincarnate lama or Tibetan teacher who often provides indications to his disciples before his death as to where he will next be reborn. Ritualized modes of testing the child are employed to ensure that he or she is the reincarnation of the lama, usually involving identifying the personal items of the lama from a group of similar objects.

upaya (ooh-paah-ya; Sanskrit, "expedient means") "Skillful Means" was developed into a form of Buddhist practice that encourages imaginatively applying wisdom to whatever circumstances one is in to assist in easing suffering or cultivating insight.

Vajrayana (vaah-jiraah-yaah-nah; Sanskrit) The diamond or thunderbolt (*vajra*) vehicle. A kind of Esoteric Buddhism based on *tantric* teachings that mostly date back to the seventh century C.E. Considered a more dangerous but quicker means of achieving enlightenment.

SUGGESTIONS FOR FURTHER READING

Buswekk, Robert E. Jr., ed. *Encyclopedia of Buddhism.* New York: Macmillan Reference USA, 2004. A highly detailed illustrated reference tool.

Byrom, Thomas. *The Dhammapada: The Sayings of the Buddha.* New York: Vintage Books, 1976. A very accessible and readable version of a key early Buddhist text.

de Bary, William Theodore, ed. *The Buddhist Tradition in India, China and Japan.* New York: Vintage Books, 1972. A concise but systematic treatment on the evolution of Buddhist ideas and the formation of different sects.

Faure, Bernard. *Buddhism.* New York: Konecky & Konecky, 1977. A richly illustrated and descriptive introduction to Buddhism.

Lopez, Donald. *Buddhist Scriptures.* London: Penguin Books, 2004. A well-chosen survey of Buddhist scripture.

Skilton, Andrew. *A Concise History of Buddhism.* Birmingham: Windhorse Pub, 1994. An excellent and accessible history of Buddhism.

Snelling, John. *The Buddhist Handbook: The Complete Guide to Buddhist Schools, Teaching, Practice and History.* Rochester: Inner Traditions, 1998. A guide to Buddhism that includes a detailed directory of contemporary institutions.

Strong, John S. *The Buddha: A Short Biography.* Oxford: Oneworld Publications, 2001. An exhaustive study of the story of Buddha's Life that examines variations in textual retellings.

Suzuki, Shunryu. *Zen Mind, Beginner's Mind.* New York: Weatherhill, 1997. An excellent introduction to meditation practice.

Williams, Paul. *Mahayana Buddhism: The Doctrinal Foundations.* 2nd ed. New York: Routledge, 2008. A history of *Mahayana* that places emphasis on the veneration of certain Buddhist texts.

ONLINE RESOURCES

The Wikipedia Buddhism Portal
en.wikipedia.org/wiki/Portal:Buddhism
The collection of articles in the Wikipedia Buddhism series are generally quite reliable and extensive in scope.

***A Manual for Buddhism and Deep Ecology* by Daniel H. Henning**
buddhanet.net/pdf_file/deep_ecology.pdf
Explores environmental issues and a relationship to nature from a Buddhist perspective.

Access to Insight: Readings in *Theravada* Buddhism
accesstoinsight.org/canon
Includes very helpful summaries and substantial translated portions of the Pali Tipitaka.

The Berzin Archives
berzinarchives.com/web/en/index.html
An excellent collection of translations, teaching, and scholarship on the *Vajrayana* tradition.

JAINISM

IN A SMALL VILLAGE in the southern Indian state of Karnataka, a middle-aged man stands silently in the main room of the home of Mr. and Mrs. Chandra, lifelong residents of the village and followers of the Jain religious tradition. Mr. Chandra carefully places small amounts of food in the cupped hands of his visitor. Other family members look on reverently, respectful and admiring both of the man who is receiving the food and of all that he represents—even though they have not met him before this day. These morsels of food—thirty-two altogether—and the small amount of water to follow are the only things he will ingest on this or any other day. His sole possessions consist of a gourd for drinking water and a broom for sweeping the path before him as he walks, lest he accidentally destroy a living being even as small as an ant. As a monk of the **Digambara** (literally, "sky-clad") sect of Jainism, this visitor does not even possess clothing. He stands naked before the Chandra family and, during his annual eight-month period of wandering about the land, goes naked before the elements.

Along with illustrating the austerities of the Jain monastic life, this ritual of giving, known as *dana*, indicates certain distinctions between ascetics (which includes both monks and nuns) and laypeople. The Chandras and the other laypeople who have gathered to participate in this *dana* represent the great majority of Jains in the world today. As

Jains worship in a temple at Ranakpur, India. Splendid marble temples such as this are a common feature of the Jain tradition.

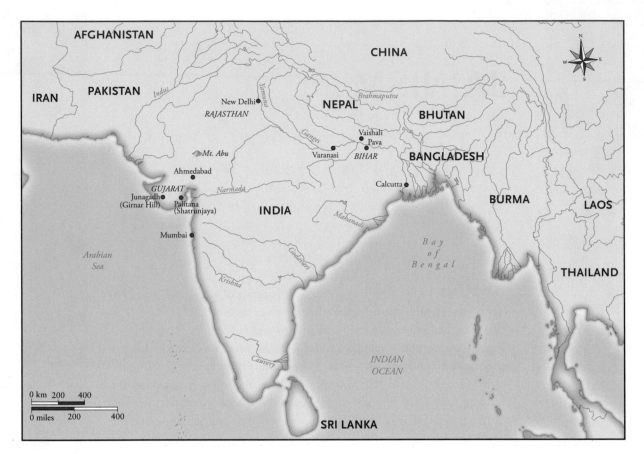

Significant sites in the development of Jainism.

members of the laity, their religious duties differ from those of the ascetics, who exemplify Jainism's highest ideals of nonviolence and self-denial. The layperson depends on the ascetic for spiritual nourishment. But this in no way diminishes the sanctity or relevance of the lay religious life. The reverence shown by the roomful of admirers is as true to Jainism as is the monk's extraordinary self-discipline as he follows the ascetic path. Through such acts as *dana*, the lay participants can positively affect their **karma**, the moral law of cause and effect that determines prospects for a good rebirth. At the same time, the ascetic depends on laypeople like the Chandras for physical nourishment and support.

Viewing the scene from a more distant perspective, we can note other features of Jainism. For one thing, Mr. and Mrs. Chandra painstakingly prepared the food and carefully strained the water in preparation of the ritual, in order to avoid harming any living organism such as a tiny plant or insect in the water. They had invited the monk to partake of the food, for it would not befit one so venerated as a Digambara monk actually to have to beg for his food. The monk's accepting of the offerings was not a foregone conclusion. Had he for any reason found the circumstances objectionable and refused, the Chandras' reputation would have been damaged. In other words, the ritual of *dana* is played out within an interwoven network of religious and social ideas and forces. The fact that the monk stands naked with cupped hands is proof that he is a member of the Digambara sect, the more prevalent sect in southern India. In any number of households across India on this very morning, we could find similar scenes, but with some variations. Members of Jainism's **Shvetambara** sect, for example, don white robes and hold alms bowls for receiving their food. Or the ascetic could be a nun, in which case she would be clothed, even if of the Digambara sect.

Stepping back even further as we view this ritual of *dana*, we can observe a number of correlations with other South Asian religions. A nonviolent ethical stance, the ascetic path, *karma*, rebirth, and *dana* are also prominent aspects of Hinduism and Buddhism. Compared to those two religions, Jainism is a very small one with just over 5 million adherents, the great majority of whom live in India. Because it rejects the authority of the *Vedas* (Chapter 4), Jainism (along with Buddhism) is considered to be distinctive relative to the Hindu traditions. Through the centuries, Jainism has earned a special reputation for having exemplified the ideal of nonviolence. ☼

This chapter sheds light on the main elements of Jainism, with regard to both the ascetics and the laity—and the interplay between the two groups. We have already identified some central Jain teachings: nonviolence, the need for an ascetic lifestyle, and the ultimate need to attain perfect knowledge. In the following section we explore in more detail these central elements and how they relate to the Jain understanding of the nature of the universe, the human condition, and the quest for spiritual deliverance. But first we will look to the distant past, to the foundational figures whom all Jains revere as the *jinas* ("conquerors"), those the Jains believe have shown the way to spiritual deliverance.

THE TEACHINGS OF JAINISM

Most of the world's religions look to a glorious founding figure, who is typically regarded both as an exemplar of the religious life and as the revealer of the religion's most significant teachings; the Buddha, Confucius, Jesus, and Muhammad are examples of such founding figures. Jainism looks not to just one but to a series of founding figures, the *tirthankaras*, "makers of the ford (or river crossing)." Each is considered to be a *jina*, "conqueror"—whence comes the name Jainism. Through having conquered the realm of *samsara*, the "cycle" of moving from one birth to another (also a concept prominent in Hinduism and Buddhism), the *tirthankara* has, metaphorically, successfully crossed the river from the worldly realm to the beyond—the realm of the liberated.

The most recent of the *tirthankaras*, Mahavira, is especially significant. We begin this section by considering his captivating and highly influential life story.

Mahavira, the Twenty-fourth and Last *Tirthankara* of This World Cycle

Nataputta Vardhamana, popularly known as Mahavira ("great hero"), was probably born near Vaishali (located in the northern Indian state of Bihar). He lived, according to the Shvetambara sect, from 599 to 527 B.C.E., although the Digambaras date his death at 510 (and scholars tend to date it later still, to sometime in the second half of the fifth century B.C.E.). The earliest biography of Mahavira is from the ninth century C.E. (the Sanskrit work *Vardhamanacarita*, by the poet Asaga), and so it is not possible to determine with historical certainty the details of his life. One thing, though, is agreed on by all: Mahavira was a contemporary or near-contemporary of Gautama the Buddha, who lived in the same area of northern India and preached his last sermon at Vaishali. There is no record of the two having met, but their legendary biographies are strikingly similar.

Vardhamana is said to have been born into the ruling class (the *kshatriyas*), the second son of a *rajah* or local ruler who was also a pious Jain. Vardhamana grew up amidst the luxuries of the palace, eventually marrying a princess named Yashoda (although the Digambara sect denies that he married), with whom he had a daughter. Eventually, however, he yearned for more than his princely life could offer, and so at age 30 he asked for permission to leave and become a monk. He joined a group of Jain ascetics who were followers of Parshva, the last *tirthankara* to have lived prior to Mahavira.

Vardhamana soon set off from the other ascetics and wandered about for over twelve years, naked and exposed. Fasting, going for long periods without sleep, withstanding the verbal and physical abuse of human opponents, and enduring the bites of insects rather than doing them harm, Vardhamana exemplified the ideals of nonviolence and asceticism, thereby earning his epithet "great hero," Mahavira.

In the thirteenth year of his ascetic wanderings, Mahavira is believed by Jains to have attained the state of **kevala**, or omniscience, the complete and perfect knowledge that leads at the time of death to liberation from the realm of *samsara*. The tradition recounts that Mahavira attained this enlightenment after spending two and a half days fasting in the heat of the sun, squatting near a tree but out of its shade. With these acts of extreme asceticism, his steadfastly nonviolent approach to life, and his supreme spiritual achievement of attaining *kevala*, Mahavira exemplifies Jainism's central ideals.

Now perfectly enlightened, Mahavira set about preaching the tenets of Jainism. His followers included eleven *ganadharas*, or disciples, who had been Hindu *brahmins* before hearing Mahavira's message. All of them eventually attained *kevala*, ending with Jambu, who is regarded as the last human being ever to attain *kevala* in this world cycle.

Mahavira preached for some thirty years until, at the age of 72, he died in the town of Pava (like Vaishali, located in the northern Indian state of Bihar). Now liberated from his body, Mahavira's perfected soul is said to have ascended to the top of the universe in a state of eternal bliss.

It is helpful at this point to recall the similarities between the Buddhist accounts of Gautama's path to enlightenment (Chapter 5) and Mahavira's path to *kevala*. Both men practiced severe austerities. But whereas Mahavira continued on the path of strict asceticism to the very end of his life, Gautama, at the time of his enlightenment, rejected strict asceticism and instead embraced the Middle Way, which calls for moderation in the treatment of one's body. The distinction is highlighted during the climactic moments of each story, for while Gautama is said to have sat underneath the *bo* (or *bodhi*) tree when he experienced enlightenment, Mahavira is said to have squatted in the scorching heat of the sun, near a tree but apparently intentionally avoiding its shade.

Sculpture of Mahavira in the cave temples of Ellora, India.

Whatever the historical accuracy of these accounts, clearly the two traditions diverged over the question of the degree of ascetic rigor. Indeed, Buddhists typically held Jains in contempt for their extraordinary rigor, which for Jains has always been the hallmark of their religion and a mark of honor. And so, even though Buddhism and Jainism have a considerable amount in common doctrinally and even in terms of practice, the two traditions seem not to have engaged much with each other. Apparently it was this way from the beginning, for while Mahavira and Gautama the Buddha seem to have been at least near-contemporaries, none of the texts claim that they ever met.

An Eternal Succession of *Tirthankaras*

Jainism, like Hinduism and Buddhism, is categorized by scholars as being an "eternal" religion in the sense that it subscribes to an ongoing succession of world cycles, without beginning or end. Jains believe that twenty-four *tirthankaras*, or *jinas* (Sanskrit, "conquerors"), have appeared in this current world cycle. Mahavira is the latest in an infinite line of previous *tirthankaras*, but he is not expected to be the last.

All twenty-four *tirthankaras* of this world cycle are known by name and by their specific symbols, Mahavira by the lion, for example, and Parshva—of whom there are more sculptures in India than of any other *tirthankara*—by the serpent. Along with Parshva and Mahavira, however, the only additional *jinas* who play a prominent role in the scriptures and in the tradition generally are the first, Rishabha (symbolized by the bull), and the twenty-second, Nemi (symbolized by the conch shell). Rishabha, who is clearly legendary and not historical, is believed to have been the father of Bharata, whom Jains regard as the first world emperor of this world cycle. Nemi, in addition to being the predecessor to Parshva, is traditionally thought to be a relative of Krishna, whom many Hindus revere as an *avatar* (human incarnation) of the god Vishnu. The nineteenth *tirthankara*, Malli (symbolized by the jar), is also especially notable, for,

Sandstone sculpture of Parshva, the *tirthankara* most commonly depicted in Jain art.

according to the Shvetambara sect, Malli was a woman. The Digambaras, who in general are more conservative, deny this.

Jainism and Hinduism

Throughout the centuries, Jainism has coexisted with Hinduism. The list of interesting and relevant points of contact between the two religious traditions is almost endless. Here we shall make note of just a few, in order to shed some light on the cultural interplay.

Jains commonly worship deities of the Hindu pantheon, and they tend to think of them in similar ways. There are, however, certain rather glaring exceptions. For example, Hindus would probably be surprised to learn from one popular Jain text that Rama and Krishna were both pious Jains. Also, the various Jain renditions of the *Mahabharata*, the great epic poem that, in its more standard form, is regarded with devotion by almost every Hindu, transform Krishna into a devious trickster. On the other hand, the *Bhagavad Gita*, which forms a very small portion of the *Mahabharata* and is typically regarded as Hinduism's most popular text, has been very favorably received by Jains. As for Hinduism's part in this cultural interplay, devotees of the god Vishnu have at times adopted the *tirthankara* Rishabha as being an *avatar* of their god. These few examples suffice at least to indicate the extensive interaction between Jain and Hindu religious and other cultural aspects.

Cultural interaction and similarities notwithstanding, Jainism is very much its own tradition. Among its more distinctive features is the very special status assigned to the *tirthankaras*. Jains believe them to be human—not gods or *avatars* of gods—but nevertheless to deserve the highest degree of veneration.

Jain reverence for twenty-four *tirthankaras*, as opposed to focusing on just one founding figure, is instructive with regard to some basic elements of the religion. Why, one might wonder, would more than one *jina* be needed? Human nature, Jainism would answer, is depraved to the point of needing repeated assistance from these spiritual masters. In a related manner, Mahavira is the last *jina* of the present world cycle because human nature has become continually *more* depraved. In the present state of affairs, *kevala* is no longer a possibility in this world, having been attained for the last time by Jambu, the disciple of Mahavira.

So, the next logical question is, what hope do human beings have if they are confined to this realm of *samsara?* What needs to happen before a *tirthankara* once again appears to show humanity how to cross the river from this shore to the beyond, the eternal realm of complete freedom and perfect bliss? Answers to such questions call for an analysis of Jain teachings.

We will now turn to a brief survey of Jain scriptures, the main source of Jain teachings. All Jains agree that, originally, there were fifty-eight books of scripture based on the preaching of Mahavira, who in turn based his views on the earlier *tirthankaras*. These books are divided into three categories: *Purva*, *Anga*, and *Angabahya*. But much is believed to have been lost. The Digambaras believe that only excerpts from one of the books of *Purva* survive; these excerpts, together with later commentaries written about them, constitute Digambara scripture. The Shvetambara sect, on the other hand, officially rejects the Digambara texts and follows instead eleven books of *Anga* and thirty-four books of *Angabahya*.

Ahimsa and Asceticism: Jainism's Ideals

We have observed how, in the ritual of *dana* ("giving") and in the ascetic practices of Mahavira, the principle of nonviolence functions as a basic ethical norm in Jainism. This principle, commonly known by its Sanskrit name **ahimsa**, is prevalent throughout the traditional religions of India. Hindus and Buddhists, for instance, all tend to favor vegetarianism due to its relative nonviolence. Jainism emphasizes the place of *ahimsa*, the "pure, unchangeable, eternal law" in this well-known passage from the *Acarangasutra*, the first book of the *Angas*:

> All breathing, existing, living, sentient creatures should not be slain,
> nor treated with violence, nor abused, nor tormented, nor driven away.
> This is the pure, unchangeable, eternal law which the clever ones, who
> understand the world, have proclaimed.[1]

All aspects of life are set in the context of avoiding injury toward "sentient creatures," an extensive category that includes not only human beings and animals but also plant life. Jain ascetics expand the category nearly to its logical extreme, striving even to avoid harming the atomic particles believed to pervade the natural elements.

The most distinctive characteristic of Jain doctrine, then, is *ahimsa*, the avoidance of doing injury to any life form. Or, put differently, Jains strive toward constant friendship with all fellow living creatures. As this striving becomes more intense, an ascetic lifestyle emerges naturally. Denying the body anything beyond what is necessary to sustain life lessens the risk of injuring other forms of life. Restricting one's diet to vegetables, for example, avoids doing violence to animals. On a more subtle level, straining one's water before drinking it (as we saw in this chapter's opening account of the Chandra household) and, indeed, drinking only as much water as is absolutely necessary, further decreases violence, in this case to the small organisms that live undetected in drinking water.

Interrelated aspects of *ahimsa* are helpfully set forth by two other Jain concepts: *anekantavada* ("nonabsolutism") and *aparigraha* ("nonpossessiveness"). As stated in this introductory section of *Jain Way of Life*, a publication of the Federation of Jain Associations of North America, these three concepts—AAA—set forth the foundations of Jain teachings:

> Jainism is a religion and a way of life. For thousands of years, Jains have
> been practicing vegetarianism, yoga, meditation, and environmentalism.

Jains have three core practices: Non-Violence, Non-Absolutism, and Non-Possessiveness (Ahimsa, Anekantvad, and Aparigraha—AAA).

Non-Violence is compassion and forgiveness in thoughts, words, and deeds toward all living beings. For this reason, Jains are vegetarians.
Non-Absolutism is respecting views of others. Jains encourage dialog and harmony with other faiths.
Non-Possessiveness is the balancing of needs and desires, while staying detached from our possessions.[2]

Another basic doctrine of Jainism is the need to diminish *karma* through limiting one's actions. In order to understand *karma* and Jain beliefs regarding spiritual fulfillment, it is best first to consider Jain cosmology, or its theory of the universe.

Theory of the Universe

According to tradition, Mahavira taught extensively and in detail about the nature of the universe, its makeup and its functioning. He did so not merely as an intellectual exercise, but because, as he saw it, understanding the universe had sweeping implications for the spiritual quest. Thus, to understand Jain doctrine, one must understand Jain cosmology. We begin with considering the Jain concept of time, which incorporates the notion of eternally recurring cosmic or world cycles. Then, we examine the makeup of the universe and all that exists within it.

Cosmic Cycles of Generation and Degeneration   In keeping with the general Indian notion of *samsara*, Jainism conceives of time as cyclical and envisions the cycles as upward and downward turnings of a wheel. During the upward turning of the wheel (which proceeds through six spokes, or ages), the world is in a state of ascendancy, with all aspects of existence, notably including the moral propensity of human beings, in the process of improvement. The three upper spokes are considered to be a golden age of goodness and prosperity. Once passing the top of the wheel and entering into its downward turning, however, things begin gradually to decline, until the end of the age of the sixth spoke, at which point the universe reaches utter moral deprivation. Then the wheel once again begins its turn upward. And so it continues, eternally.

The traditional length of each of the six ages is 21,000 years. Currently, the world is said to be in the age of the fifth spoke of the downward turning, called *Kali Yuga*, to be followed by the sixth, final period of degeneration. In this sixth age, the theory goes, people are more prone to immorality, and physically become smaller. The consequences for the spiritual quest are pronounced, for human beings can no longer hope to attain *kevala* in this world until the wheel has once again begun its upward turning. Mahavira is the last of the *tirthankaras* of the turning of the wheel in which we now live, and his eleven *ganadharas*, ending with Jambu, are the last people to achieve liberation during this cycle. The wheel will need to advance considerably into its upward motion before anyone else can hope again to attain *kevala* in this world.

Notably, Rishabha, the first *tirthankara* of this downward turning of the world cycle, is believed to have appeared during the third spoke. Before that, the world was so healthy morally and spiritually that human beings did not need a *jina* to show them the way to liberation. Rishabha and the other early *tirthankaras* are understood to have been of greater physical stature than their successors.

The concept of *Kali Yuga* and the continuing downward turning of the wheel gives rise to a fundamental and serious question. If indeed *kevala* is no longer a possibility, what purpose is there in continuing to pursue the religious life? Thinking again of the *dana* ritual, why should laypeople like the Chandras go to the effort of giving so conscientiously to monks? And why would anyone opt to undergo the physical hardships of the ascetic life? Part of the answer depends on the nature of *karma*, which we will address next. Another part of the answer is provided through consideration of the composition of the universe, which Jains call the ***loka*** and regard as containing within it three distinct lands inhabited by human beings.

The *Loka*   The *loka* is understood to be vast almost beyond description. Over the centuries, Jains have speculated as to just how vast the *loka* is, deriving a unit of measure known as the "rope," which is strikingly similar to the "light year" of modern astrophysics. According to one account, the *loka* is fourteen ropes from top to bottom. This means, according to traditional Jain calculations, that it would take a god, flying at the speed of 10 million miles per second, seven years to traverse its full span. These attempts at specifying the size of the universe are probably to be taken figuratively rather than literally. Still, a tendency toward something like scientific understanding is in keeping with the Jain belief that perfect and complete knowledge is attainable and indeed has been attained—namely, by Mahavira, his disciples, and the countless numbers of those who have achieved enlightenment before them.

The *loka*, then, is a vast and yet a finite space, within which all beings dwell. Beyond the *loka* there is nothing but strong winds. The *loka*, together with everything in it, has always existed and will continue to exist eternally. Jainism thus does not believe in a creator god.

Jains sometimes depict the *loka* as a diagram in the shape of a giant man, the *purusha*. Across the midsection runs a relatively small band known as the Middle Realm, which contains a series of oceans and continents, three of which together form the region inhabited by human beings. This region is further divided into various lands, one of which is India and another of which, Mahavideha, is not affected by the corruptness of this world cycle, and thus continues to be the home of *tirthankaras* and of human beings who still can attain *kevala*. This notion is crucial when considering the quest for spiritual liberation that takes place in this corrupt world. As we shall discuss in more detail shortly, living a good life that is true to Jain ideals leads to a good rebirth, perhaps even in a land like Mahavideha, where *tirthankaras* currently reside and where *kevala* is a possibility.

Below the Middle Realm is a series of progressively darker hells, whose denizens suffer agonizing torments. At the very bottom of the *loka*, below the lowest hell, there are only clouds. Above the Middle Realm is a series of progressively brighter heavens, inhabited by deities who enjoy pleasures not unlike those of earthly rulers. For both the denizens of hell and the deities, their stays in those realms are only temporary, as they will eventually be reborn in another realm. In other words, just as is in Hinduism and Buddhism, the realm of *samsara* extends well beyond the human domain. Because only humans can ever attain *kevala*, however, the Jains believe that even being reborn as a deity in one of the brightest heavens is ultimately not as fortunate as it might seem. The best rebirth is as a human being, so that the quest for spiritual fulfillment can be continued.

At the top of the *loka*, in the crown of the head of *purusha*, is a roof that is described as having the shape of an umbrella. Called the "slightly curved place," this is the eternal home of the souls that have been liberated from the realm of *samsara*.

Categories of Existence: *Jiva* and *Ajiva*   Jain scriptures spell out the categories of existing things in meticulous detail (in keeping with the belief in the omniscience of Mahavira and others who have attained *kevala*). The categories of existence can be said to begin with a simple distinction: that between the living, which is termed **jiva**, and the nonliving, **ajiva**. The nonliving is further divided into four: motion, rest, atoms, and space. These four basic entities plus the *jiva* are the five building blocks of all that exists in the universe. The entities interact, but forever maintain their individual existence. This view contrasts with the main form of Hindu cosmology, which envisions an ultimate union of all being. Furthermore, Jainism holds that the universe has an infinite number of atoms, forever distinct from one another, along with an infinite number of *jivas*, or souls.

Each *jiva* ("soul") is eternal, completely without form, and yet capable of interacting with the atoms of the body it inhabits in such a way that it can control the body's mechanisms. While avoiding the notion that the *jiva* is in any way dependent upon the body, Jainism does posit a complex integration of soul with body. Thus, while bodies do act, it is the soul that wills actions and therefore is held responsible for their moral quality.

All *jivas* are essentially equal, regardless of the bodies they inhabit. For example, the *jiva* of an insect is considered to be of identical quality as that of a large animal or a human being. This belief has significant implications with regard to the doctrine of *ahimsa*, since it encourages equal treatment of all living beings.

The great variety of bodies inhabited by the *jivas* produces many different life forms. Jainism's detailed classification of these life forms is among its most fascinating features, and one that shows remarkable similarities to the modern field of zoology. A simple twofold approach distinguishes life forms that are stationary, such as plants, from those that are moving. Another approach categorizes life forms based on the number of senses they have. In the words of one text:

> Up to the vegetable-bodied ones, selves have one sense [i.e., touch].
> Worms, ants, bumblebees, and men each have one more than the one preceding.[3]

Human beings are thus categorized with life forms having five senses: deities, denizens of hell, and most animals aside from insects. Flying insects ("bumblebees" and the like) are thought to lack the sense of hearing, while most that crawl on legs also lack sight. Along with such insects as worms, shellfish are thought to have only the senses of touch and taste. Plants and "microbes" (a large category of the most basic life forms) are devoid of all sensations but touch.

More elaborate systems of classification abound in Jain scriptures. This fascination with the intricacies of life forms supports the religion's general concern for their welfare, and for maintaining the attitude and practices that secure this welfare as best as possible. To some extent, the attitude and practices of the religious life are expected of nonhuman life forms as well. Lions, for example, are said to be able to learn to fast. Even plants and the simplest microbes are believed to have some basic religious capacity that they can apply for spiritual advancement. Ultimately, however, all *jivas* must be reborn as human beings before they have any chance of attaining *kevala* and release from the realm of *samsara*.

Liberation and Salvation

Many religions typically emphasize teachings concerning salvation or liberation, and Jainism is no exception. As our account will make clear, salvation depends on understanding the challenges of *samsara* and how to overcome them.

To begin, salvation in no way depends on the power of a deity. Just as Jainism has no creator god, neither does it have one to assist with the all-important quest for liberation. Some would thus label Jainism an atheistic religion, but this is not quite accurate. We have seen that in the Jain cosmology, deities inhabit the various heavens. Many of their names would be recognizable to the student of Hinduism, for the pantheons are similar. Thus, Jainism might best be labeled transtheistic[4] in the sense that there are gods (in fact, a great variety of gods), but ultimately the religion moves beyond them when it comes to the truly crucial issues of salvation. To understand why this is, let us first examine Jainism's concept of *karma*.

Karma and the Human Condition Notwithstanding the intricate categories of existence, so far as the human condition is concerned, Jainism is best understood in terms of two categories: soul (*jiva*) and matter (*ajiva*). As noted earlier, the *jiva* is essentially pure and formless. And yet, for reasons that defy explanation, souls have become entwined with impure matter, causing them to be weighed down and bound to *samsara*. Human beings are born into this state. The religious life strives to clean away the dirt that tarnishes the *jiva*, returning it to its original state of pristine purity and releasing it from *samsara*, so it can ascend upward to the "umbrella" ceiling of the *loka*, the realm of liberated souls.

For Jains, the term *karma* refers to the process in which matter dirties the soul. In both Hinduism and Buddhism, *karma* is commonly understood as being the moral law of cause and effect. This general definition applies for Jainism as well, but here the term's more literal meaning of "activity" is stressed. Because all actions encumber the *jiva* with matter, whenever the soul wills an action, it risks tarnishing itself. Immoral actions, those that violate the principle of *ahimsa* or other Jain ethical teachings, are especially damaging because they dirty the *jiva* with heavier impurities. Highly virtuous actions, on the other hand, bring about only small quantities of light matter that neither cling to the soul nor weigh it down.

Along with this emphasis on the material aspects of *karma*, Jainism also emphasizes the intentions behind one's actions. That is, the immorality that tarnishes the soul with heavy matter lies mainly in the evil intention, not in the consequence of the action. Similarly, an action that might appear to have evil consequence could be considered moral if good was intended. For example, the accidental killing of microbes, provided proper means were taken to avoid it, would generally not be immoral and thus would not lead to the dirtying of the *jiva*.

Kevala: Omniscience That Leads to Liberation   *Kevala* is best translated as "omniscience"; one who has attained this state is a *kevalin*. Whereas Buddhist enlightenment (*bodhi*) incorporates the sort of knowledge that is vital for spiritual perfection (Chapter 5), Jain *kevala* is knowledge of everything: the nature of one's inner self, of one's past lives, and of the external world and all things, including fellow living beings (and their past lives, and future lives) that inhabit it. Little wonder that Jainism so boldly sets forth cosmological explanations, based as they are on the omniscience of Mahavira and the other *tirthankaras*.

The most significant feature of *kevala* is that it frees the *jiva* completely from the tarnishing effects of *karma* so that it may be liberated. The final experience of liberation or release is known as *moksha* (as it is in Hindu traditions). *Moksha* and *kevala* are distinguishable in that one who has attained *kevala* normally goes on living in the physical body, confined to the realm of *samsara*, while one who achieves *moksha* is liberated from the body. Mahavira, like the *jinas* before him, passed many years as an enlightened one (sometimes referred to in Jainism, as in Buddhism, as *arhat*) before experiencing *moksha* at the time of his death, which finally freed him completely from any impurities that would bind him to the material world.

One might ask at this point whether omniscience leads to the purity of the soul or whether purification of soul brings about omniscience. A Jain might respond by asserting that the two work together harmoniously. This notion of religious impulses working in harmony is embodied in the Jain concept of the Three Jewels of the religion:

right faith (*darshana*), right knowledge (*jnana*), and right practice (*caritra*). All three are integral to the religious quest. Right faith, which for Jainism involves a proper outlook or mindset, the correct way of "seeing" (which is the root meaning of *darshana*), nurtures right knowledge and practice. Likewise for the other Jewels; they function together like three legs of a stool.

The Quest for a Heavenly Rebirth We have noted that Jambu, the last of Mahavira's eleven disciples to attain *kevala*, is believed to be the last person of this world cycle ever to achieve liberation. But this does not imply that for Jains living since Jambu's time it is meaningless to seek liberation. Every living being remains destined for rebirth, and the nature of rebirth depends on *karmic* status. A good rebirth, into the delights of one of the heavens or back into the human realm, therefore requires living a good life.

In contrast to Hindu and Buddhist beliefs, Jainism understands rebirth as occurring immediately after death. This has various implications that set Jainism apart from Buddhism and Hinduism, especially in regard to the need to perform rituals on behalf of the dead. For Jains, such rituals are deemed superfluous—which is not to say that Jains forgo mourning rituals or that they fail to honor their deceased loved ones. But the most crucial thing, the destiny of the deceased's soul, is determined as soon as the person dies. In fact, the soul is believed immediately to begin animating another life form.

Having examined the primary teachings of Jainism, we now turn our attention to the various ways these teachings have been manifested in Jain society and rituals.

JAINISM AS A WAY OF LIFE

In the opening section of this chapter, we glimpsed a moment in the religious life of Jainism, the ritual of giving known as *dana*. While illustrating concern for the central Jain principles of *ahimsa* and the ascetic path, the ritual also indicates some of the diversity of the religion. For example, we noted features of the Digambara version of *dana* that are not found among Shvetambaras, and the basic distinction between the ascetics and the Jain laity was evident. In this section, we examine in greater detail these varieties of Jainism and consider other significant practices and characteristics of the Jain religious life.

Digambaras and Shvetambaras

Before highlighting those things that distinguish the Digambaras from the Shvetambaras, it is important to acknowledge the many things they share in common, including a general heritage of teachings and similar forms of practice. Still, the differences are interesting and instructive, helping to illustrate Jainism's rich diversity.

Digambara (or "sky-clad") monks, as their name infers (and as we have witnessed in the *dana* ceremony), go about naked; Digambara nuns do not, donning simple white garments like their counterparts in other Jain sects. From the Digambara perspective, wearing clothes puts monks back into the ordinary category of the laity.

VOICES: An Interview with Girish Shah

Girish Shah was born in the Indian state of Gujarat, which is home to many Jains and to important pilgrimage destinations. He attended college in Mumbai and then left India to attend graduate school in the United States, where he now lives. A founding member and director of the Jain Center of Northern California and the Federation of Jain Associations in North America, Mr. Shah is dedicated to educating people about his religion.

Girish Shah

What do you consider to be the most important reason for living a proper Jain religious life?

The goal is to become free of *karma*. To make your soul and its properties of infinite knowledge, infinite vision, infinite strength, and infinite capacity to character "clean," you have to get rid of all the *karmas* that are polluting it. For one to live a religious life it is important to achieve that. . . . But for me, the more important part of living the proper religious life is that it is the way you will support each other, it is the way you will serve each other. You are helping each other grow, and you are reciprocating, giving back. We need to have empathy toward everyone. Forgiveness is not for those who have done nothing to you; forgiveness is for someone who has hurt you.

Do you consider Jainism to be an atheistic religion?

I think the question is what you mean by "atheistic religion." If you mean by atheistic religion god the creator and god the controller and god the sustainer; that there is an entity that created the world, that controls the world, that sustains the world, and that judges everybody, then no. We do not believe in god in that sense, but we do believe in the quality of the soul, which is godliness. Infinite compassion—that is the characteristic of soul. The knowledge, the vision, and working with and relating to everybody, comes from infinite compassion. And that has the power, that has the godlike characteristics. It doesn't control anything. Even our enlightened or *tirthankaras* cannot make me achieve *moksha*. They can show me the path, but cannot say, such as the gods will say, "I bless you." There is no blessing. There is no divine grace that anyone can give. Forgiveness has to be done by you, by your own action. The burden is on you completely, but you can achieve it. Jainism is the religion that says: "I am god" (if we call the *tirthankara* "god," which is the common word that we use). No other religion tells you that you can become god. But Jainism says everyone can become god.

How important to you are vegetarianism and other forms of *ahimsa*?

Very important. The idea is to minimize the amount of *himsa* that you are doing, and so you give up some of these things—at least for the important religious days, if not all the time. Some people will take vows to give up this or that for their entire lifetime. Increasingly I am becoming vegan, knowing that there is so much *himsa* in dairy. I have not become fully vegan, but hopefully some day I'll get there. Traditionally, milk was okay, because of the way cows were treated before. Now things have changed, and so we have to evolve and look at it. It's just sensitivity to it. Here is another example. I ask myself: "Why am I wasting natural resources?" I have a nice home. I have never felt the need to go beyond. This is my first house and my last house. I have no attachment to the house. People say, "Girish, you should be living in a beautiful big home," and I say, "What beautiful big home? Why do I need one?" It's all internalizing. I don't have the need. I have a four-bedroom house; it's big enough. That's plenty of space, 1,800 square feet. Why do I need a 7,000 square foot house, why do I need a 10,000 square foot house? Just because I can afford it doesn't mean that I should have it. . . . This is all part of *ahimsa*. It's all part of *ahimsa* because then you are not wasting your resources. Charity is a form of *ahimsa* because you are now using money that you made for the benefit of others, for their growth, their progress, their betterment of life. People need to have betterment of life beyond their basic needs in order for them to spiritually think. If you don't have enough even to eat and to think, you're not going to have spirituality.

You immigrated to the United States from India. What do you consider to be the most notable differences between being a Jain in India and being a Jain in the United States?

For Jains in India, things are taken for granted, whereas being a Jain here, you have to put up with a lot of issues. Every time I go shopping, it takes a half hour reading the ingredients to see how many animal products are in it. There is no green mark on food packaging here like we have in India, where you can look at it and say, green—it is vegetarian. Also, I can't walk to places here. In India, you walk to places. You don't have to use the car. To go shopping, to go to the temple, you walk. Here in California you have to drive, particularly when you drive here in summer, your car windshield is filled with all those butterflies that you're killing on the way. And so my wife refuses to travel at night. You're going to get up in the morning and go. You're not going to kill all those butterflies, just to get there at night.

Nuns are not esteemed quite as highly as monks, and in general, Digambara doctrine is more severe than the other sects when it comes to spiritual deliverance of men versus women. In short, women (including nuns, even though they perform the same ascetic practices as monks) are deemed incapable of attaining *kevala;* they must await rebirth in a male body in order to reach the potential of final deliverance.

Another identifying feature of the Digambara sect involves the ascetics' avoidance of alms bowls as means of collecting food, using instead only their cupped hands. The reasoning is based in the principle of *ahimsa:* washing of bowls presumably would bring about greater harm to living beings. The same reasoning supports the "sky-clad" practice of monks, for the washing of dirty clothes causes harm. Finally, as previously noted, the Digambaras have their own official collection of scriptures.

A sizable majority of Jains are Shvetambaras. Since about the thirteenth century c.e., they have followed their set of forty-five sacred texts as authoritative. Unlike

A Jain monk wearing the *muhpatti* in order to prevent unnecessary harm to airborne insects.

the Digambaras, they use alms bowls when begging for food; they accept the possibility of a woman attaining *kevala;* and, of course, they wear clothing (monks and nuns alike), consisting of upper and lower white garments.

Within Shvetambara Jainism, two distinctive sects, the Sthanakvasi and the Terapanthi, have features that distinguish them somewhat from their parent. Most significantly, they both reject the worship of images, which is a common religious practice among the majority of Shvetambaras. The Sthanakvasis are also distinguishable by the ascetics' practice of constantly wearing the *muhpatti* ("mouth-shield"), a cloth that protects insects from accidentally being inhaled as the monks and nuns traverse the land.

The Ascetic Life

Through their biographies and teachings, the *tirthankaras*, "makers of the river crossing," show the way to liberation to all Jains. However, since neither the *tirthankaras* nor any Jain deities can bestow salvation, all individuals must make their own spiritual progress and eventually attain their own deliverance. Moreover, as noted, Jains believe that the ascetic life offers the spiritual path that best replicates the lives and follows the teachings of the *jinas*. Still, no one expects the average Jain to enter upon this arduous path. Simply having entered into the human realm does not imply that one is ready for the ascetic life. A Jain takes this life on gradually, after having become an accomplished layperson who fulfills all religious duties successfully and with a pure disposition. When the circumstances are right, whether in this lifetime or in a future lifetime, the decision to renounce the lay life and become an ascetic is made.

It almost goes without saying that the decision of renunciation is not to be made lightly. The initiation ritual, *diksha*, marks the point at which the individual becomes completely committed to the ascetic life. Through the centuries, minimum age requirements have been imposed—young adulthood for the Digambara sect, younger for the Shvetambaras (historically, as young as age 6, although today only the Terapanthi sect permits the initiation of young children). The ceremony includes a symbolic removal of hair (via the traditional method of being pulled out tuft by tuft) and presentation to the initiate of the whisk and other implements of the ascetic life, such as the alms bowl for Shvetambaras. *Diksha* is overseen by a teacher, who typically continues to provide guidance to the new ascetic. The ritual marks the symbolic rupturing of the participant's past and future lifestyles, usually involving total separation from one's family, although Shvetambara nuns are on occasion allowed to interact with family members.

Ascetics depend on the almsgiving of the Jain laity, and sometimes of Hindus, in order to eat. Usually wandering in groups, they spend eight months of the year traversing the land, and then four months, during the rainy season, with lay communities. By remaining settled during this wet period, the ascetics do not jeopardize the well-being of life forms, which tend to be on the roads in greater numbers due to the rains. So, once again, the principle of *ahimsa* underlies Jain practice.

The Five Great Vows All ascetics commit to five "Great Vows" that serve as the doctrinal groundwork of both their inner purity of intention and their outer purity of action:

1. Avoid inflicting violence (*ahimsa*) on other life forms.
2. Abstain from lying.
3. Do not take what has not been given.
4. Renounce sexual activity.
5. Renounce possessions.

Jain texts expand on these vows in great detail, elaborating on the subtleties of their content and means of satisfactorily fulfilling them. As you might expect, most attention is devoted to the first vow, as *ahimsa* is understood to be the foundation of the entire ethical outlook of Jainism. Each of the other four vows is interrelated to *ahimsa*. For example, the third vow (not to take what is not given) is interpreted to mean, in its most profound sense, not to take a life. The fifth vow is understood also to imply avoidance of violence, for to renounce possessions is to deflect the passion that arises through attachments to them. Passion is thought to be a primary cause of violence.

Ascetic Practices The basic impulse toward asceticism, so pervasive throughout the history of Jainism, is grounded in two objectives: the avoidance of further dirtying of the *jiva* with *karmic* matter and the eventual burning off of the matter that has already tainted it. Specific practices are prescribed in Jain texts, notably the Six Obligatory Duties, which for the Shvetambara sect are enumerated as follows (the Digambara list differs only slightly):

1. Equanimity, achieved through meditation
2. Praise of the *tirthankaras*
3. Veneration of teachers
4. Repentance
5. Laying down the body (standing or sitting motionless for varying periods of time)
6. Abandonment (renunciation of specific foods or activities for a certain period of time)

The Six Obligatory Duties are to be performed by all ascetics, and ideally by laypeople as well. Specifics of each duty are developed in the texts. The duty of repentance, for example, involves acknowledging wrongdoings before one's teacher twice daily and ends with the recitation of a passage well known to Jains: "I ask pardon from all living creatures. May all creatures pardon me. May I have friendship for all creatures and enmity towards none."[5]

Perhaps the most startling Jain ascetic practice in the view of outsiders is *salle-khana*, the intentional fasting of oneself to death. Although this practice was quite common in earlier times and is believed to have been the form of dying adopted by Mahavira and other great ascetics of the past, today it is rare. Insistent that *sallekhana* is in no way suicidal, Jains argue that, since the act of eating generally involves the risk of harming other life forms, fasting even to the point of ending one's own life is a highly effective means of warding off *karma*. In general, an individual's mindset at the moment of death is considered to be a significant factor for the prospects of rebirth, and so *sallekhana*, lacking the passion and violence that regularly accompanies suicide and instead fostering a tranquil and meditative state, is thought to provide an ideal means of death.

The Religious Life of the Jain Laity

Although Jainism is best known for its asceticism, a balanced understanding of the religion demands a careful look at the role of the laity. For one thing, lay adherents constitute the great majority of Jains. Also, even as the laity looks to the monks and nuns as exemplars of Jain ideals, the ascetics themselves depend on the lay community for their livelihood and support. These two components, in other words, function hand in hand. The worship activities of the Jain laity are rich and diverse and have for centuries been a vital part of the religious life of India.

Jain worship occurs on two separate levels. At the more mundane level, the objects of worship are various gods who, as we have noted, tend to be the same as those worshiped by Hindus. While having nothing to do with the ultimate religious pursuit of liberation, the gods are believed to respond to material needs, such as providing weather favorable for agriculture and cures for health maladies.

On a more sublime level, Jains worship the *tirthankaras*—even though they, like the gods, are unable actively to assist a worshiper in achieving salvation. Nevertheless, worship of the *tirthankaras* nurtures a properly devout religious attitude; its net effect is to burn off the dirtying *karma* that weighs down the soul. It is this second level of worship that warrants our consideration here.

Religious Places   In its most visible form, Jain worship concentrates on images of the *tirthankaras*, although the Sthanakvasis and Terapanthis shun this. Most of this worship takes place in temples, some of which rank among India's most impressive architectural achievements. For example, the Dharna Vihara at Ranakpur in the state of Rajasthan, which is dedicated to the *tirthankara* Rishabha, is remarkable for its unique four-directional design, four-faced image of the *tirthankara*, and 1,400 carved columns. Along with such spectacular temples as the Dharna Vihara, many temples coexist with shops and offices on city streets, indistinguishable from the neighboring buildings.

The Dilwali Temple on Mount Abu in the state of Rajasthan is famous for its exquisite, delicate carvings and architectural design.

Jain sacred places also include various sites in the countryside, such as Mount Shatrunjaya in Gujarat in western India, one of five sacred mountains for Shvetambara Jains. Hundreds of shrines are located at Mount Shatrunjaya, and one textual tradition predicts that nineteen future *tirthankaras* will spend time preaching there.

Pilgrimages to places like Mount Shatrunjaya constitute an important aspect of lay worship. In fact, every Jain strives to make at least one pilgrimage in his or her lifetime. Typically undertaken at considerable expense, the pilgrimage offers each lay individual an opportunity to experience through the interruption from normal life and the rigors of journeying to the site an ascetic lifestyle for a temporary period. This experience allows for the concentration of effort in gaining *karmic* merit. Traditionally, pilgrimages were made on foot, and this is still the mode of transportation for ascetics. Today, laypeople often travel by train or other modern means. Sometimes the expenses for entire groups of pilgrims are paid for by one person, who is thought to gain much *karmic* merit through the act of benevolence.

Shatrunjaya, a hill near the town of Palitana, India, and for centuries an important Jain pilgrimage site, features 863 temples of various sizes and styles.

Rituals and Observances In addition to the relatively rigorous periods of pilgrimage, the religious life of the Jain laity overlaps with that of the ascetics in some everyday aspects. All Jains are careful with regard to their eating habits. They are diligently vegetarian, and go well beyond abstaining from meat by avoiding such things as eggs, vegetables, and fruits with a large number of seeds, in order not to destroy life forms unnecessarily. Fasting, a very common practice among ascetics, also is quite common among the laity, especially among women, who generally are less involved than men in business and other professional concerns and therefore have more time and energy for fasting.

These similarities notwithstanding, it is easy to observe that in almost every way, the ascetics' religious life demands significantly more by way of exertion and endurance of physical hardships than does the religious life of most laypeople, who strive mainly to behave morally in order to ebb the flow of harmful *karma* and thus to foster a good rebirth. As we observed at the outset of this chapter, the ritual of *dana* (the giving of food to monks and nuns) provides one opportunity to be a good Jain layperson and to enhance one's *karmic* status. A somewhat similar practice involves bidding for the right to sponsor rituals, with any extra money being donated to charitable causes and the winning bidder gaining in social esteem. Whenever a new image of a *tirthankara* is erected or installed in a temple, for example, rituals are performed to celebrate each of the "five auspicious events" of a *tirthankara's* life: conception, birth, renunciation, attainment of *kevala*, and *moksha*. The person who sponsors the building

VISUAL GUIDE
Jainism

Jain emblem. Incorporating a variety of symbols, the Jain emblem's outline represents the *loka*, or universe. The swastika, an ancient and common symbol in Hinduism, Buddhism, and other religious traditions, is very prominent in Jainism; its four arms represent the four realms of life (heavens, human realm, animal realm, hells). The hand represents *ahimsa*.

Tirthankara. Sculptures of *tirthankaras*, like this one of Rishabha, whom Jains revere as the first of the current world cycle, are objects of Jain worship.

Whisk. Shown here with a book of Jain scripture, the whisk is used by ascetics to clear away, and thus to protect, insect life. It symbolizes *ahimsa*.

of such an image and funds the rituals is said to acquire very positive *karmic* merit, so that the person likely will be born into a world blessed with a living *tirthankara*.[6]

A formalized system of religious observance features the Twelve Vows for the layperson. The first of the Vows, for instance, makes clear that it is the intentionality, rather than specific action, that most matters with regard to *ahimsa*. Proper intentionality is involved, for example, in choosing the right profession, one that would not likely result in violence toward sentient life forms. As a result, Jains through the centuries have tended to engage in trade and other forms of business. Obviously harmful occupations such as hunting and fishing are strictly prohibited; farming is acceptable because it can be done without *intentionally* harming life forms. Trade and business, however, are generally considered optimal because they can be done without causing any harm at all.

THE HISTORY OF JAINISM

In the previous section, we have focused attention on Jain teachings, the differentiation of Jain sects, and some of the specific practices of the Jain religious life. Next, we turn to a consideration of the general place of Jainism in the context of Indian religions and to some notable features of the Jain tradition in its more recent history.

The Indian Historical Context

Earlier in this chapter we learned about the traditional understandings of Jainism's historical foundations. Here, our attention shifts to the scholarly understanding of Jainism's historical foundations, so we can observe some features of Indian religious culture that helps situate the stories of the *tirthankaras* within a broader context.

Jains themselves do not regard Mahavira as having founded their religion. Historians, too, tend to agree with the traditional view that Mahavira himself followed an already established form of Jainism—possibly that of Parshva, the twenty-third *tirthankara* of this world cycle. Scholars situate Parshva's lifetime in the eighth century B.C.E.

As noted previously, there are more sculptures in India of this *tirthankara* than of any other, Mahavira included, indicating his great popularity as an object of Jain devotion.

In the eighth century B.C.E., the probable period of Parshva, Indian civilization was beginning an important transition. The Vedic period, named for the Sanskrit texts that form the scriptural foundation of Hinduism, was ending, as was the domination of the priestly leadership of the *brahmin* caste (Chapter 4). Now began a period of religious diversity that included philosophical speculation on the *Upanishads* (themselves, technically, the last section of the Vedic corpus) and religious movements that eventually gave rise to Buddhism and the devotional forms of Hinduism that continue today. Parshva, and Mahavira after him, fit into a general category of religious movements that emphasized asceticism as a means of spiritual development.

Perhaps because of Jainism's belief in a never-ending succession of world cycles, Jains have not kept a detailed historical record of their own tradition. As we have seen, the dates for the lifespan of Mahavira are a matter of dispute, and so, too, is the place of his birth. The texts that contain the accounts were written hundreds of years after the fact. Much of the story of Jainism through its early centuries similarly does not lend itself to precise historical reckoning. With the religious changes of the period around 1000 C.E., the historical record begins to become clearer.

The Legacy of the *Tirthankaras*: Jainism through the Centuries

In the ninth century C.E., about the time that the influence of Buddhists was severely diminishing in India, the country's religious landscape was undergoing a rather sudden shift with the influx of Islam. Muslim rule was established in 1192 in the form of the Delhi Sultanate, which was succeeded in 1526 by the Moghul empire. During the early centuries of Muslim rule, relations between Muslims and Jains were not always friendly. There are accounts of large-scale destruction of sacred Jain sites, for example, the pillaging by Muslims in 1313 of Mount Shatrunjaya, a major Jain pilgrimage site in the western state of Gujarat. But during the period of Moghul rule, and especially

TIMELINE
Jainism

800–700 B.C.E.* Probable period of Parshva, the twenty-third *tirthankara*.

500–401 B.C.E.* Probable period of Mahavira (Shvetambara traditional dates 599–527 B.C.E.*).

(From antiquity through the medieval period, there is scant evidence for historical events, though there is much evidence for general involvement by Jains in the cultural life of India, through the building of temples and monuments, founding of schools and sects, and interaction with other religions.)

1313 C.E. Pillaging of Mount Shatrunjaya by Turkish invaders.

Fifteenth century Period of Lonka, precursor of Sthanakvasi and Terapanthi sects.

1526 Founding of the Moghul empire.

1556–1605 Akbar the Great (who maintained good relations with Jain leaders).

Seventeenth century Period of the founding of the Sthanakvasi sect.

1726–1803 Acarya Bhikshu, founder of the Terapanthi sect.

1867–1901 Shrimad Rājacandra, teacher and mystic, friend of Mahatma Gandhi.

1893 Lecture on Jainism delivered by Vircand Gandhi at the World Parliament of Religions at Chicago.

1900–2000 Period of geographical expansion of sizable Jain communities outside of India.

Note: Asterisks indicate contested or approximate dates.

at its apex during the reign of Akbar the Great (1556–1605), remarkably close relations developed. Akbar himself was the close friend of a Jain leader, and he issued several decrees promoting the protection of animals, motivated apparently by learning about the Jain emphasis on *ahimsa*.

During the eighteenth and nineteenth centuries, Jainism became somewhat more diverse, through the establishment of the Sthanakvasi and Terapanthi sects. In the twentieth century, immigration led to the establishment of Jain communities in various places around the globe.

Jainism in Today's World

The total number of Jains today is about 5 million, with all but about 100,000 living in India. Still, in India Jainism is dwarfed numerically by the Hindu population, which now numbers near 1 billion. In light of these numbers, the influence that Jainism has on Indian culture is quite remarkable. To some extent, this influence can be measured in financial terms. For centuries, Jains have been very successful in business, perhaps due to their religiously motivated focus on trade as opposed to agriculture. Also, the Jain community is highly respected for its charitable giving. In keeping with their profound emphasis on *ahimsa*, Jains commonly take in and care for animals that are maltreated or are targeted for slaughter. Although they generally do not actively seek converts to their religion, Jains tend to be outspoken advocates of universal vegetarianism, and so have exercised wide influence in this regard.

Among the recent remarkable Jain figures, Shrīmad Rājacandra (1867–1901) is especially known outside India due to his connection to Mohandas (Mahatma) Gandhi. Both from the state of Gujarat, they met in 1891, and according to Gandhi's autobiography, Rājacandra made a strong impression and had a very positive impact on his spiritual development. Gandhi, of course, is perhaps the most famous advocate of *ahimsa* the world has ever known, even though he never overtly adopted Jainism as his religion.

Jain ascetics and impressive religious monuments, such as this nun on pilgrimage at Sravanabelgola, are common sights in India. Through its diaspora population of some 100,000 people, Jainism also has a significant presence outside of India.

Jain influence has also reached well beyond India through the Indian diaspora population. More than 45,000 Jains currently live in North America, 25,000–30,000 in Great Britain, 20,000 in Africa, and 5,000 in Asia outside of India.[7] Their centuries-old focus on business has made life in the modern world a relatively natural thing for the Jain laity. For ascetics, of course, life outside their traditional homeland is especially challenging; and indeed, it is quite rare, as only the Sthanakvasi and Terapanthi sects even allow for monks and nuns to journey in the world at large. The Terapanthis are responsible, too, for having founded the first Jain university, recently established at Ladnum in the state of Rajasthan.

CONCLUSION

In this chapter, we have learned about the teachings, way of life, and historical development of Jains and their religion. One of the world's oldest traditions, Jainism today remains relatively small, with just over 5 million adherents, and also relatively confined to its place of origin, with the great majority of Jains living in India. This tendency for the tradition to maintain itself demographically and geographically is natural for Jains, who do not actively seek converts to Jainism and, even when living outside of India, tend to maintain strong ties to the motherland.

Like every religion in the world today, however, Jainism has become diverse, as indicated by the differences between the sects. Some aspects of the religion are more adaptable to modernization, pluralism, and other contemporary forces, and some are less adaptable. In this regard, Jainism as a whole can perhaps best be summed up as a tradition that is both eternally constant and constantly evolving. At one extreme, a group of monks and nuns wandering the countryside, sweeping ahead of their bare feet with their whisks, hardly fit into the picture of the modern world. Paradoxically, these same ascetics carry on a tradition of cosmology that appears remarkably modern relative to most traditionally religious points of view. Moreover, the social consciousness of Jains—expressed in their advocacy of vegetarianism and other forms of nonviolence—is in step with many who are concerned over the state of the world, the environment, and humanity's plight.

SEEKING ANSWERS

What Is Ultimate Reality?

Like Hinduism and Buddhism, Jainism maintains belief in *samsara*, the wheel of life. Time is conceived of as being cyclical, such that this world is but one in an eternal sequence of worlds that have come to be. The Jain perspective on space features the *loka*, a vast expanse that includes three realms inhabited by human beings. Jainism does not emphasize the importance of deities, even to the point of appearing atheistic; it can be considered a transtheistic religion. Souls (*jivas*) and matter (*ajiva*) are believed to exist eternally. Ultimate reality for Jainism might best be identified as *kevala*, the supreme state in which the eternal soul is perfectly pure.

How Should We Live in This World?

Jainism bases its ethical teachings on the principle of *ahimsa* (nonviolence) and on the accompanying value of asceticism. Both are exemplified by Mahavira and the other *tirthankaras*, and Jain monks and nuns continue to act as exemplars. Jainism understands human

(continued)

SEEKING ANSWERS (continued)

beings—like every other sentient being—to be made up of a soul (*jiva*) combined with bodily matter (*ajiva*). This matter is believed to contaminate the soul, and thus to weigh it down and to prevent it from attaining spiritual perfection. Jains explain this through their doctrine of *karma*, understanding the term in its literal sense as "actions."

What Is Our Ultimate Purpose?

Jains believe that eventually every soul will become perfectly pure, allowing it to rise to the top of the *loka* in the transcendent state of *kevala*, the Jain equivalent of Buddhist *nirvana* or Hindu *moksha*. But the current state of the world is too degenerate for anyone to attain *kevala*. But the impossibility of achieving this ultimate state in this life does not mean that the spiritual quest is futile. Jains believe that the rebirth of an individual's soul, which is understood to occur immediately after death, is determined by the adequacy of one's spiritual and moral life in this world. Death, then, does not "end it," and mortality for Jains involves the prospect of a good rebirth.

REVIEW QUESTIONS

For Review

1. What is the role of Mahavira as one of Jainism's *tirthankaras*?
2. How do Jain practices of asceticism promote the cause of *ahimsa*?
3. What is the *loka*?
4. Identify and briefly describe the various Jain sects.
5. Differentiate the main religious duties of the Jain laity from those of the ascetics, and explain what religious advantages a monk or nun might have over members of the laity.

For Further Reflection

1. Compare the biographies of Nataputta Vardhamana (Mahavira) and Siddhartha Gautama (the Buddha), focusing especially on the episodes of attaining enlightenment.
2. What is the relationship between Jain cosmology and the Jain perspective on spiritual liberation? Consider especially the classification of reality into *ajiva* and *jiva* and how this relates to the quest for spiritual liberation.
3. What is *kevala*? How does it compare to Buddhist *nirvana*? To Hindu *moksha*?

GLOSSARY

ahimsa (ah-him'suh; Sanskrit, "nonviolence," "not desiring to harm") Both the avoidance of violence toward other life forms and an active sense of compassion toward them; a basic principle of Jainism, Hinduism, and Buddhism.

ajiva (uh-jee'vuh; Sanskrit, "nonsoul") Nonliving components of the Jain universe: space, time, motion, rest, and all forms of matter.

dana (dah'nuh; Sanskrit, Pali, "giving") Ritual of giving.

Digambara (dig-ahm'buh-ruh; Sanskrit, "those whose garment is the sky") The second largest Jain sect, whose monks go about naked so as to help abolish any ties to society; generally more conservative than the Shvetambara sect.

jina (ji'nuh; Sanskrit, "conqueror") Jain title for one who has "conquered" *samsara;* synonymous with *tirthankara.*

jiva (jee'vuh; Sanskrit, "soul") The finite and eternal soul; also the category of living, as opposed to nonliving, entities of the universe.

karma (Sanskrit, "activity") The moral law of cause and effect of actions; determines the nature of one's reincarnation; for Jainism, all activity (*karma*) is believed to involve various forms of matter that weigh down the soul (*jiva*) and thus hinder the quest for liberation.

kevala (kay'vuh-luh; Sanskrit) Shortened form of *kevalajnana,* literally, "isolated knowledge" (isolated from the effects of *karma*); the perfect and complete knowledge that is Jain enlightenment; marks the point at which one is free from the damaging effects of *karma* and is liberated from *samsara.*

loka (loh'kah; Sanskrit, "world") The Jain universe, often depicted as having the shape of a giant man.

Shvetambara (shvayt-ahm'buh-ruh; Sanskrit, "those whose garment is white") The largest Jain sect, whose monks and nuns wear white robes; generally more liberal than the Digambara sect.

tirthankaras (teert-hahn'kuhr-uhs; Sanskrit, "makers of the river crossing") The Jain spiritual heroes, such as Parshva and Mahavira, who have shown the way to salvation; synonymous with *jinas.*

SUGGESTIONS FOR FURTHER READING

Dundas, Paul. *The Jains.* 2nd ed. London: Routledge, 2002. A thorough and scholarly study that has become a standard reference work for students and academics alike.

Jain, Shri Satish Kumar, and Kamal Chand Sogani, eds. *Perspectives in Jaina Philosophy and Culture.* New Delhi: Ahimsa International, 1985. Helpful insights from within the Jain tradition.

Jaini, Padmanabh S. *The Jaini Path of Purification.* 2nd ed. Columbia, MO: South Asia Books, 2001. The first comprehensive work in English that offers a sympathetic study of the religion, this modern-day classic has been revised and updated.

Lopez, Donald S. Jr., ed. *Religions of India in Practice.* Princeton, NJ: Princeton University Press, 1995. Offering some translations for the first time, this anthology presents a wide range of texts well beyond the usual collections of sacred writings.

Radhakrishnan, Sarvepalli, and Charles A. Moore, eds. *A Sourcebook in Indian Philosophy.* Princeton, NJ: Princeton University Press, 1957. A standard anthology of sacred texts in English translations.

ONLINE RESOURCES

The Wabash Center

wabashcenter.wabash.edu/resources/result_browse.aspx?topic=575&pid=361

The Wabash Center, a trusted resource for all aspects of the academic study of religion, offers links to a wide variety of dependable Internet resources on Jainism.

The Jaina

jaina.org

The Jaina (Federation of Jain Associations in North America) website is especially useful for studies of Jainism in North America.

SIKHISM

MANJIT KAUR, a 16-year-old girl, and Sandeep Singh, a 14-year-old boy, stand in the **gurdwara**, the place of Sikh worship, in their small village in northwestern India. Here in the region known as the Punjab, Sikhism's ancestral homeland, Manjit and Sandeep are members of the majority religion, and *gurdwaras* are common sights in the farming villages that dot the land. Most of the village has gathered together to witness the proceedings, and Sandeep and Manjit have spent the morning preparing for this momentous event—their initiation into the Sikh **Khalsa**, or community of "Pure Ones." They have both bathed and washed their long hair carefully and have dressed especially for the occasion. Most notably, they both don the five articles of faith, known as the Five Ks: uncut hair, a comb, a steel wristlet, a short sword, and a pair of shorts.

Manjit and Sandeep join a group of five older villagers who also don the Five Ks and who for this ceremony play the part of the *Panj Piare*, or "Beloved Five." They are established members of the Khalsa and will oversee the initiation. The grouping of five recalls the founding of the Khalsa centuries ago, when Guru Gobind Singh (1675–1708 C.E.), the tenth in a line of Gurus going back to Guru Nanak (1469–1539 C.E.), chose five original initiates who had distinguished themselves for their loyalty to the Guru and for their commitment to Sikh ideals. On this day

The five Sikh men who participate in the Amrit *sanchar* represent the original "Beloved Five" in commemoration of the founding of the Khalsa.

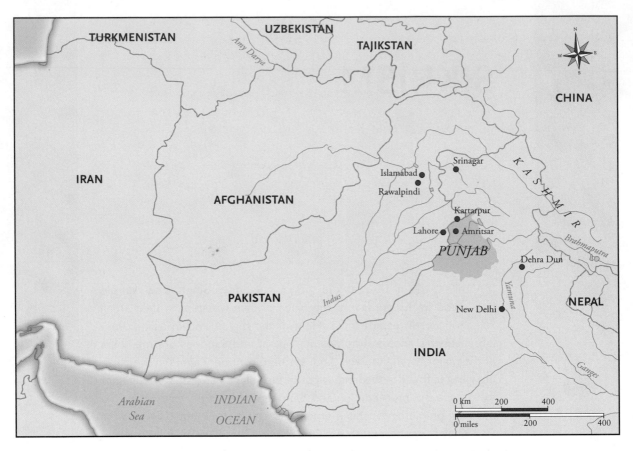

Significant sites in the history of Sikhism.

of *Amrit sanchar*, the Khalsa initiation ceremony, the stirring memory of these founding figures and the ideals they embody is palpably felt. But the most vital presence of all is a large book, lying opened on a special platform. It is Sri Guru Granth Sahib, or the **Adi Granth**, the sacred scripture of Sikhism, and the Sikhs' **Guru**, or spiritual teacher, from the time of Guru Gobind Singh forward.

Sandeep and Manjit stand before the *Panj Piare*, one of whom explains the basic principles of Sikhism. They agree to accept these principles by nodding, the ritual action that makes the initiation official. The new members of the Khalsa are then served **amrit** ("immortalizing fluid"), a special drink made from water and sugar crystals, which has been mixed by the *Panj Piare* in an iron bowl and stirred with a two-edged sword. Meanwhile, hymns from the Adi Granth are sung by the congregation. The *amrit* is drunk and sprinkled on the eyes and head of the initiates, who recite the **Mul Mantra**, the summary of Sikh doctrine that comprises the opening lines of the Adi Granth. The *Panj Piare* then instruct Manjit and Sandeep about the ethical requirements of the Khalsa. These include prohibitions against the cutting of one's hair, the eating of meat that has been improperly slaughtered, extramarital sexual relations, and the use of tobacco. The initiates are also told that all Sikhs are brothers and sisters and there should not be any distinctions made on the basis of caste.

Manjit and Sandeep are among a minority of Sikhs, approximately 15 percent, who undergo the traditional ceremony of initiation into the Khalsa. Some 70 percent of the approximately 23 million Sikhs in the world,[1] however, are popularly considered to be members of the Khalsa, insofar as they observe the Five Ks, or at least the one that is generally deemed most important: not cutting one's hair.[2] And regardless of percentages or degrees of membership, the traditional ways of the Khalsa greatly influence the practices and customs of the entire **Panth**, or Sikh community. We can thus glimpse in this ceremony, with its powerful ties to tradition and its rich symbolism, key aspects that are at the heart of Sikhism. ☀

In this chapter we shall study these and other key aspects, attending in turn to the founding of Sikhism and its primary doctrines, its most prevalent rituals and worship practices, and its historical development. By virtue of its size alone, Sikhism is among the major religions of the world. Theologically, Sikhism's intermixing of concepts that are common to some Hindu traditions on one hand and to Islam on the other make it a very interesting subject for the comparative study of religion. And with about 2 million Sikhs living outside of India, and Sikh communities being found today in most of the large cities of the West, Sikhism clearly is a global tradition that has a significant impact on the world.

THE TEACHINGS OF SIKHISM

The term *Sikh* is derived from ancient Indian terms that mean "disciple." Sikhs are thus disciples, specifically of the ten Gurus, beginning with Guru Nanak and ending with Guru Gobind Singh, founder of the Khalsa. Thereafter, Sikhs have been disciples of Sri Guru Granth Sahib, the traditional name for their most important sacred text, the Adi Granth. A sound understanding of Sikhism therefore must begin with a consideration of the origins of this line of Gurus.

By the time Guru Nanak had come on the scene, the important role of the guru had long been established within Hindu traditions of northern India. A **guru** is a spiritual teacher. *Guru* is actually used in three slightly different ways in Sikhism. Along with being the title of Guru Nanak and his successors, and of the sacred text (Sri Guru Granth Sahib), it is used as a name for God. (In fact, *Vahiguru*, "Praise to the Guru," is the most common name for God used by Sikhs today.) In each case the guru functions as the revealer of Truth, or God's will. As Sikhs believe that God lovingly reveals the divine will to humans, God, too, thus functions as Guru.

We now consider the career of the guru of northern India whose extraordinary life experiences and bold spiritual leadership were to have such a profound impact that a new religion would arise.

The Life of Guru Nanak

Nanak was born in 1469 C.E. in a small village near Lahore (in present-day Pakistan) to Hindu parents of the ruling class (the *kshatriyas*). His parents arranged for him to marry early, when he was still in his teens, as was customary at the time. Soon Nanak was the father of two sons.

The legendary accounts of Nanak's early life emphasize his dissatisfaction with typical forms of employment and his general rejection of traditional forms of Hindu worship. It seems that he sought out the company of a variety of holy men, both Hindu and Muslim. (Islam had for several centuries since been a prevalent religious tradition in northwestern India.) His spiritual searching led him to a religious outlook that asserted the oneness of God and the need to move closer to God. This could best be accomplished, Nanak believed, through meditation and singing hymns in praise of God. Eventually Nanak began composing his own hymns. With his friend Mardana, a Muslim musician, accompanying him on the *rebab* (a stringed instrument), Nanak sang his hymns at communal worship gatherings. These hymns are included in the Adi Granth and are sung in Sikh services today.

According to tradition Nanak was a spiritual leader even at this early stage of his life. He would rise before dawn and bathe in the river, meditate, and then lead others in singing hymns of praise. The crucial experience leading to the origin of the Sikh tradition, though, occurred when Nanak was about 30 years old.

Receiving God's Revelation One morning Nanak did not return from bathing in the river. He was presumed drowned, and yet his body was not found. Three days later Nanak returned to the village, but remained silent for a day. When he finally spoke, he proclaimed: "There is neither Hindu nor Muslim so whose path shall I follow? I shall follow God's path. God is neither Hindu nor Muslim and the path which I follow is God's."[3]

Sikhs pay homage to Guru Nanak, the founder of Sikhism, in a crowded room in Lahore, Pakistan.

When he explained what had happened, Nanak said that he had been escorted to the court of God, who gave him a cup of *amrit* (the same drink that is used in the Khalsa initiation ceremony) and said to him:

> This is the cup of the adoration of God's name. Drink it. I am with you. I bless you and raise you up. Whoever remembers you will enjoy my favor. Go, rejoice in my name and teach others to do so. I have bestowed the gift of my name upon you. Let this be your calling.[4]

The Journeys of Guru Nanak Deeply moved by this revelation, Guru Nanak spent the next stage of his life, from age 30 to about age 50, on a series of travels. The traditional account depicts four long journeys to various places: eastward to Assan; southward to Sri Lanka; northward to the Himalayas; and westward, reaching as far as Mecca and Baghdad. He visited holy sites and encountered a wide variety of religious people. He also proclaimed and practiced his own teachings, sometimes to hostile audiences.

Several incidents during Guru Nanak's travels illuminate the new message he proclaimed. On one occasion, while visiting a famous Hindu shrine, he found himself among *brahmins* throwing water toward the rising sun as an offering to their dead ancestors. Nanak turned and threw water the other way, explaining, "If you can send water to your dead ancestors in heaven, surely I can send it to my fields in the Punjab."[5] On another occasion, Nanak was awakened from sleep by an angry Muslim, who chastised him for sleeping with his feet pointing toward the Ka'ba in Mecca, the most sacred site in Islam. (Showing the soles of one's feet is considered by many Muslims to be a grave insult.) Nanak responded: "Then turn my feet in some other direction where God does not exist."[6]

Such stories as these illustrate a general theme of Nanak's religious outlook. He consistently rejected traditional rituals and "proper" religious protocol, whether Hindu or Muslim.

Founding the Sikh Community Drawing from his revelation experience and years of journeying, Nanak continued proclaiming his own understanding of the truth. In doing so he attracted a large following. At about the age of 50, Nanak built a new township called Kartarpur ("abode of the creator") in what is now Pakistan. Here he and his followers formed the first Sikh community and established the lifestyle that has characterized Sikhism to this day.

Guru Nanak erected a special building, a *dharamsala* ("abode of faith"), for worship. In so doing, he provided the prototype of the *gurdwara*, which today is the central structure of any particular Sikh community. (The term *dharamsala* gradually was replaced in the eighteenth century with *gurdwara* to designate the Sikh place of worship.) He also built a hostel to accommodate the many visitors to Kartarpur. Nanak, though in most respects a regular member of the community, sat on a special seat when addressing the congregation. Followers recognized the nature of the Guru as merely human and yet also as very spiritually advanced. Today the Adi Granth, Sikhism's sacred text, occupies the role once held by the Gurus. The Adi Granth sits on a special seat within the *gurdwara*.

On September 22, 1539, after leading the Kartarpur community for about twenty years, Guru Nanak died. According to tradition the Guru, aware of his approaching death, settled a dispute regarding the proper disposal of his body. In keeping with their respective traditions, his Hindu followers intended to cremate him; the Muslims, to bury him. Nanak instructed them that when he died, the Hindus should lay flowers at his right side, and the Muslims at his left. Those whose flowers were still fresh in the morning were to do as they wished with his body. The Guru covered himself with a sheet in preparation for death. When the sheet was removed, the body was gone, and the flowers on both sides were still fresh. Even with his death, Guru Nanak encouraged that the differences between Hindus and Muslims be transcended and that peace should prevail.

Guru Nanak's example powerfully informs the beliefs and practices of Sikhs up to the present day. We will next turn our attention briefly to Sikh scripture, the collection of texts that contains the doctrinal position as set forth by Guru Nanak and his successor Gurus.

Sikh Scripture

We have previously identified the Adi Granth, commonly known as Sri Guru Granth Sahib, as Sikhism's most important sacred text. This is without question true for all Sikhs today. There are, however, other texts that most Sikhs would classify as scripture, of which the most important are the Dasam Granth and the *rahit-nama*, both of which we consider here. In addition, works by two disciples of the Gurus are granted sufficient status to be recited in the *gurdwara:* Bhai Gurda (disciple of Guru Arjan and Guru Hargobind) and Nand Lal (disciple of Guru Gobind Singh). A collection of stories about the life of Guru Nanak, called the *janam-sakhi*, also deserves mention.

A Sikh reads from Sri Guru Granth Sahib.

The Adi Granth Compiled by Guru Arjan in 1603–1604, the Adi Granth contains the works of his four predecessors, along with his own hymns and various works by poets, such as Kabir (c. 1440–1518). Through the centuries, the Adi Granth has occupied a central place in Sikhism. Whereas the Gurus once sat on a special seat amid Sikh disciples, the Adi Granth now occupies the same type of seat in the middle of any place of worship. And whereas the Gurus were once the authorities on religious matters, now Sikhs consult the Adi Granth.

The name "Adi Granth" ("the Original Volume" or "the First Book") is standard among scholars. Sikhs commonly express their reverence for the scripture by referring to it as Sri Guru Granth Sahib (*sahib* is a title of respect). Every copy is identical in both script and page number; there are 1,430 pages in every copy. It was composed using the Gurmukhi script and a variety of languages that were used in northern India at the time, most prevalently Punjabi. It also contains some words in Arabic, Persian, Prakrit, and Sanskrit. All of these factors render the Adi Granth somewhat difficult to read as well as difficult to translate. Today, however, English and French translations are available. Many Sikh families have at least a condensed version of the Adi Granth, containing all of the works used in daily prayers, including Guru Nanak's *Japji*, which is the only portion of the entire Adi Granth that is chanted, rather than sung.

For Sikhs, the Adi Granth rings with brilliance when it is set to music and proclaimed in its original language. In the words of one commentator: "The poetic excellence, the spiritual content, and the haunting, lilting melodies of the hymns of the Adi Granth are Sikhism's greatest attraction to this day."[7]

The Dasam Granth The composition of the Dasam Granth ("Volume of the Tenth Master") has been traditionally attributed to Guru Gobind Singh, although many Sikhs today regard only some parts to have been authored by the Guru. The first compilation of works into the Dasam Granth is thought to have taken place in 1734 (twenty-six years after the death of Guru Gobind Singh), although in the ensuing decades variant versions appeared. In 1902, the version that is used today was officially authorized.

During the eighteenth century, the Dasam Granth was considered to be Guru alongside the Adi Granth. Today however, only one group of Sikhs, the Nihangs, bestow equal honor on the Dasam Granth. Nevertheless, the sections of the text that all Sikhs attribute to Guru Gobind Singh can safely be categorized as Sikh scripture. These sections include the well-known *Jap Sahib* and the *Ten Savayyas;* both are recited daily in morning prayers.

The Rahit In the chapter's opening, we observed that the *Amrit sanchar*, the Khalsa initiation ceremony, is undertaken only by a minority of Sikhs, even though the Khalsa continues to exemplify the ideals of Sikhism. These ideals are spelled out in written form in *rahit-nama*, a collection of texts compiled over the centuries and collectively referred to as the **Rahit**. Traditionally, the contents of the Rahit are believed to stem from the teachings of Guru Gobind Singh himself. In both this section on Sikh doctrinal teachings and the following section on Sikh religious life, we shall draw frequently from the contents of the Rahit.

On God, the Human Condition, and Spiritual Liberation

More than anything else, Sikhism is a religious path to spiritual liberation through devotional praise of God, most especially by way of meditation on the divine Name. This meditation is often done through prayerful recitation of sacred words. In this section, we take up in more detail three main aspects of Sikh teachings that will shed light on this religious path: the nature of God and the "divine Name"; the nature of the human condition and its need, through the aid of the Guru, to move from darkness to enlightenment; and the nature of liberation, which is release from *samsara*, the cycle of rebirth.

Sikhism teaches that the ultimate purpose of life is to attain spiritual liberation, which is similar to Hindu *moksha* (and sometimes Sikhs use this same term), "release" from *samsara*, the cycle of death and rebirth (a concept also adopted from Hinduism). This release is believed to bring about an experience of union with God, a state of eternal bliss.

God: Formless One, Creator, True Guru Guru Nanak's understanding of the nature of God is the center from which all Sikh teachings emerge. It is fitting that the Adi Granth begins with a concise summary of Sikh theology. This summary is known as the *Mul Mantra*, the passage recited by initiates to the Khalsa (as we noted in the beginning of the chapter) and by most Sikhs daily as part of their morning prayers.

> There is one Supreme Being, the Eternal Reality, the Creator, without fear and
>   devoid of enmity, immortal, never incarnated, self-existent, known by grace
>   through the Guru.
> The Eternal One, from the beginning, through all time, present now, the
>   Everlasting Reality.[8]

Much of this description should sound familiar to those who know about the monotheistic traditions of the West (Judaism, Christianity, and Islam). God is one, eternal, self-existent, and "Creator." The Punjabi term that the Gurus used for God is *Akal Purakh*, "The One Beyond Time." Guru Nanak sometimes used the name *Nirankar*, "Without Form." For Sikhs, then, God is without form and beyond all attributes that humans use to describe reality. God is without gender and is referred to as "he" in Sikhism only begrudgingly and when grammatically necessary due to the limitations of language; there is no neuter pronoun in Punjabi. Sikhs actively strive to avoid assigning such human attributes to God.

For reasons beyond the grasp of human comprehension, God decided to create the world and all that is in it, including human beings. Akal Purakh (we'll use this traditional name, although modern Sikhs commonly refer to God as *Vahiguru*, "Praise to the Guru"), in addition to being the Creator, is also the Preserver and the Destroyer. Sikhism here draws from the important Hindu triad of gods and their respective functions: Brahma (Creator), Vishnu (Preserver), and Shiva (Destroyer). All Sikhs, though, insist that their God is one. These three functions are thus different aspects of the one God.

In God's primary state, to which Guru Nanak referred when he used the name *Nirankar* ("Without Form"), God is distinct from his creation in much the same way that an artist remains distinct from her or his artwork. And yet God dwells within creation—within nature and within human beings. God is thus said to be immanent, or indwelling (as opposed to transcendent, or beyond creation). In this state of immanence, Akal Purakh is personal and approachable through loving devotion. Because of God's immanence in creation, it is possible for humans to make contact with God and come to know God. To extend our analogy, one can know something of an artist by seeing the artist's works. So too can one come to know Akal Purakh through experiencing God's creation. Indeed, part of the ongoing purpose of creation is that God, through loving grace, might reveal the divine self to human beings. It is in this capacity that God is referred to as Guru, for in this manner God delivers humans from darkness to enlightenment.

The Human Condition: Self-Centered and Bound to *Samsara* Human beings are especially near to Akal Purakh. Though Sikhism advocates kindness to living things, it also holds that other creatures are here to provide for us. (Unlike most Hindus and all Jains, therefore, Sikhs are not opposed to eating meat—although vegetarianism is the preference of many.) More importantly, Akal Purakh is believed to dwell within all human beings and is actively concerned about their spiritual welfare. Humans, however, tend to neglect the need to center their lives on God.

Rather than being God-centered, humans are inclined to be self-centered. The primary shortcoming of the human condition is expressed in the Sikh term ***haumai***, which is difficult to translate accurately into English. Various possibilities include "self-reliance," "pride," and "egoism." *Haumai* is humans' insistence to make do on our own rather than to acknowledge dependence on Akal Purakh. When life is dominated by *haumai*, its five accompanying vices—lust, anger, greed, attachment, and pride—tend to run rampant. *Haumai* and its vices increase the distance between the person and God.

This distance from Akal Purakh is compounded through ignorance. The world and its charms are mistakenly believed to be the true object of attention. Rather than seeking the Creator, humans in their ignorance seek God's creation. In this manner, creation itself can be a pitfall because it presents the vices with countless attractions. Lust and greed for the world, anger and pride regarding the world, and attachment to the world: these are the evil workings of *haumai*. As long as ignorance, *haumai*, and the other vices persist, humans are destined to remain in *samsara*, the ongoing cycle of death and rebirth.

Spiritual Liberation through Union with God Sikhs believe that because of the problem of *haumai*, individuals tend to be selfishly attached to the charms of this world. But creation itself is good, and in fact provides for human beings the necessary means for overcoming *haumai*. God's immanence in creation is perceivable in ***hukam***, the divine order. Through *hukam* Akal Purakh asserts the divine will on the world and communicates truth to the human heart. Under these circumstances the quest for spiritual liberation is a constant struggle between the self-centeredness to which humans are naturally inclined and the call to live in accordance with the will of God.

Akal Purakh plays an essential role in determining the outcome of this struggle, for it is through God's grace that humans acquire the potential for perceiving God. In the words of the *Mul Mantra* cited earlier, Akal Purakh is "known by grace through the Guru"—the Guru being either one of the historical Gurus or Sri Guru Granth Sahib. (Since the *Mul Mantra* was composed by Guru Nanak, we can assume that the original meaning was the historical Guru.) Through humbling oneself, thus denying the normally dominating powers of *haumai*, a person is opened to the power of God's grace. Having received God's grace, the task is to respond in loving devotion through meditation on the nature of God. The term most often used in the Adi Granth to denote the nature of God is *nam*, the "divine Name." Meditation on the *nam* or recitation of the *nam* is prescribed repeatedly as the path to spiritual liberation. A chapter of the *Japji* sets forth these points:

> The Eternal One whose Name is Truth speaks to us in infinite love. Insistently we beg for the gifts which are by grace bestowed. What can we offer in return for all this goodness? What gift will gain entrance to the hallowed Court? What words can we utter to attract this love? At the ambrosial hour of fragrant dawn meditate on the grandeur of the one true Name. Past actions determine the nature of our birth, but grace alone reveals the door to liberation. See the Divine Spirit, Nanak, dwelling immanent in all. Know the Divine Spirit as the One, the eternal, the changeless Truth.[9]

The significance of the *nam* for Guru Nanak, and thus for the entire Sikh tradition, can hardly be overstated. In the words of one modern commentator, "Anything that may be affirmed concerning Akal Purakh constitutes an aspect of the divine Name, and a sufficient understanding of the divine Name provides the essential means to deliverance."[10]

Spiritual liberation, or "deliverance," amounts to moving beyond all human shortcomings to a state of complete union with God. This state of salvation is eternal, infinitely blissful, and forever beyond *samsara*, the cycle of death and rebirth. It should be noted that Sikhism's doctrine of spiritual deliverance is not dependent in any way on one's caste status or gender. Also, the focus is on inward meditation and piety, rather than on outward forms of worship, such as festivals or pilgrimages—although Sikhism is not entirely without such forms of worship, as we shall consider shortly. But before we move on from this section on Sikh teachings, we next consider elements introduced with the foundation in 1699 of the Khalsa, the community of "Pure Ones," and take up the crucial question of the relationship of the Khalsa to the Panth or Sikh community at large.

Teachings of Guru Gobind Singh and the Khalsa

The teachings that Guru Gobind Singh proclaimed to the *Panj Piare*, the "Beloved Five" who became the first initiates into the Khalsa, are believed by Sikhs to comprise the Rahit, the regulatory code that spells out correct belief and behavior for members of the Khalsa.

The Rahit contains vital teachings pertaining to the religious life. As we observed in the opening of the chapter, Manjit and Sandeep, as part of their initiation into the Khalsa, were taught certain norms of behavior, all of which are contained in the Rahit. Among the teachings are four cardinal prohibitions (*kurahit*): cutting one's hair, eating meat that has been improperly slaughtered (specifically, slaughtered according to Muslim regulations), engaging in extramarital sex, and using tobacco. Along with these and other prohibitions, the Rahit also sets forth requirements, including the requirement to don the Five Ks, so named because all five of the items begin in Punjabi with the letter "k." The Five Ks are:

- *Kes*, uncut hair, symbolizing Sikh belief that one should not interfere with natural, God-given form
- *Kangha*, a small comb worn in the hair, a reminder of cleanliness
- *Karā*, a steel wristlet, affirming constant connectedness with God
- *Kirpan*, a sword, a sign of devotion to truth and to the defense of just causes
- *Kachh*, a pair of shorts tied with a drawstring, symbolizing chastity

Gurbaj Singh Multani (right) wears a ceremonial dagger, known as a *kirpan*, after a news conference on Parliament Hill in Ottawa March 2, 2006. Multiculturalism and religious freedom trumped safety concerns in a Canadian Supreme Court decision that will allow orthodox Sikh students to carry traditional daggers to school.

To some extent, both the meaning and the practical implications of the Five Ks have varied somewhat through the centuries. At the time of the founding of the Khalsa, for example, the wearing of a sword would have suggested true preparedness to fight. Today, the *kirpan* is usually only five to eight inches long and often is concealed underneath clothing in order not to appear threatening.

Study of Sikh doctrine, especially as set forth in the Rahit, has led us naturally to a consideration of some aspects of Sikh worship and lifestyle. In the next section, we take up specific forms of the religious life.

SIKHISM AS A WAY OF LIFE

One aspect of Guru Nanak's teachings was the rejection of the outward forms of religion that he found troubling in the Islam and Hinduism of his day. Focused as he was on seeking the indwelling God through meditation on the divine Name, Guru Nanak regarded the external forms of religion as useless.

Guru Nanak's rejection of outward forms of religion, however, has not resulted in complete avoidance by Sikhs of religious observances. For one thing, Sikhs through the centuries have continued to celebrate annual festivals that are generally features of northern Indian culture. We noted previously that Guru Gobind Singh founded the Khalsa on the day of an important annual festival, Baisakhi Day, the first day of the Indian year (according to the Western calendar, this day occurs in March or April). For Sikhs, Baisakhi Day has the special significance of commemorating the founding of the Khalsa. Another important festival celebrated by Sikhs as well as by Hindus and Jains is Divali, the Festival of Lights (which takes place in October or early November). Other religious observations were instituted by the Sikh Gurus, most notably by Guru Gobind Singh, and are unique to Sikhism.

VOICES: An Interview with Onkar Singh

Onkar Singh is a Sikh who was born and raised in the Punjab; earned a Ph.D. (Entomology) from the University of California, Berkeley; and served in India, Nigeria, Sudan, Liberia, and Indonesia before immigrating to the United States and becoming a U.S. citizen. He has devoted his retirement years to educating his fellow citizens about Sikhism.

What is the significance of the Name of God, and does the fact that your name, "Onkar," is one of the Sikh names of God have special significance?

God's name is used to remember Him, to meditate on Him, to pray to Him, and to seek His blessings. People are named after different names of God (*Bhagwan, Govind, Hari, Indra, Kartar, Eshwar, Ram,* etc.) or gods and prophets (*Krishan, Shiva, Jesus, Moses, Mohamed,* etc.). I was named Onkar, after the most common name of God in the Sikh Holy Scriptures, following the tradition of choosing a name starting with the first letter of the hymn when Sri Guru Granth Sahib is opened at random.

Onkar Singh

What is the primary purpose of prayer?

The primary purpose of Sikh prayer is to thank God (*Vahiguru*) for all His blessings thus far and to seek His blessings for the success of the task about to be started. Sikhs also ask for His continued blessings so that they submit to His Will and continue to remember Him at all times. The prayer ends with a request for their optimism and for the welfare and prosperity of the entire humanity.

How does wearing the turban relate to your religious beliefs?

In South Asia and Southwest Asia, the turban is a symbol of dignity, honor, respect, and responsibility. Guru Hargobind, the sixth Sikh Guru, asked his followers to wear turbans, carry arms, and ride horses, in opposition to a ban imposed on non-Muslims by the rulers. Further, in 1699, Guru Gobind Singh, the tenth Sikh Guru, prescribed the five articles of faith including uncut hair (and the turban) mandatory for the Khalsa. I wear a turban as per the dictates and practice of my Sikh faith.

To what extent are the Golden Temple and the Sikh homeland of Punjab in general of special meaning for you, living in the United States?

The Golden Temple, Amritsar, is the most visited Sikh shrine. More people, of different faiths, castes, etc., visit the Golden Temple than the Taj Mahal. Guru Arjan Dev, the fifth Sikh Guru, built this temple. He invited a famous Sufi saint, Mian Mir, to lay its foundation stone. Further, he compiled, edited, and installed the first edition of the Sikh Holy Book in this temple in 1604. The Golden Temple Complex houses the SGPC (Shromani Gurdwara Parbandhak Committee) and includes the Akal Takht and some historic *Gurdwaras.* Besides the Golden Temple, the Sikh homeland of Punjab has three *Takhats* and numerous historic *Gurdwaras.* Sikh Americans, irrespective of the country of their birth, look upon

Punjab as the Land of their Gurus, who preached Unity of God, practiced equality of humanity, and worked lovingly to unite the populace.

What is the most important thing that non-Sikhs in the United States need to understand about your religion?

Non-Sikhs in the United States should understand that almost all who wear turbans in America are followers of Sikhism, which is not a branch of another religion (e.g. Hinduism or Islam), and has its own founder (Guru Nanak) and Holy Book (Sri Guru Granth Sahib), and worship places (*Gurdwaras*), where all are welcome.

In this section we focus on the ideals of the religious life, paying attention to the actual degree of participation among Sikhs today.

Daily Devotional Practices

Guru Nanak emphasized the importance of *nam simaran*, "remembrance of the Name." This can be done simply by repeating one of the names used to refer to God. Recall that Guru Nanak composed many hymns; *kirtan*, the singing of hymns, is another form of *nam simaran*. A third form involves meditation practices designed to contemplate the divine Name and ultimately to bring one into perfect harmony with God. On one hand, these methods are straightforward and easy to practice on one's own. On the other hand, to make significant progress normally takes years of diligence.

Daily prayers are another form of devotional practice that can (and should) be done by every Sikh. The Khalsa Rahit, which spells out the ideal regimen for much of the religious life, gives the following instructions:

> A Sikh should rise early (3 a.m. to 6 a.m.) and having bathed he should observe *nam japan* by meditating on God. Each day a Sikh should read or recite the order known as the "Daily Rule" (*nit-nem*). The Daily Rule comprises the following portions of scripture: Early morning (3 a.m.–6 a.m.): *Japji, Jap,* and the *Ten Savayyas.* . . . In the evening at sunset: *Sodar Rahiras.* . . . At night before retiring: *Sohila.* At the conclusion of the selections set down for early morning and evening (*Sodar Rahiras*) the prayer known as *Ardas* must be recited.[11]

To follow such a regimen requires much diligence and much time: altogether, these prayers cover about twenty pages in English translation. While some Sikhs, especially those more advanced in age, commonly do this on a regular basis, the majority do not.

Sikh Worship in the *Gurdwara*

Gurdwara literally means "doorway of the Guru" (a variant translation is "by means of the Guru's [grace]"). Any building that contains a copy of the Adi Granth is, technically speaking, a *gurdwara*, a Sikh house of worship. There is at least one *gurdwara*

Volunteers prepare food for the *langar* meal at the Golden Temple in Amritsar. Many thousands of people share meals together here daily, at no cost to the visitor.

in virtually every village in the Punjab. Most *gurdwaras* have a characteristic Sikh style, with minarets and chalk-white paint. Aside from the presence of the Adi Granth, which usually sits atop cushions and under a canopy, there are no specific requirements regarding the interior.

The *gurdwara* serves mainly as a place for Sikh men, women, and children to congregate for worship. This they do frequently, on no particular day of the week. Worship usually takes place in the evening, though the early morning is also a popular time. Worship in the *gurdwara* is preceded by bathing and consists of singing the Gurus' hymns, reading from the Adi Granth, or telling a story about one of the Gurus. No formal requirements govern the exact nature of worship. It generally ends, though, with a sharing of a special pudding made of wheat flour, sugar, and ghee (clarified butter), known as *karah prasad*. This act is symbolic of the unity of the Panth.

The sharing of food is an important feature of Sikhism. Each *gurdwara* typically has within it a community kitchen, called the *langar*, where Sikhs gather at various times to share in the preparation and consumption of a meal. The food served in the *langar* is strictly vegetarian; even eggs are not allowed. Again, this sharing of food symbolizes the equality of all. It also provides food for the needy.

Life Cycle Rituals

In the chapter's opening description of the *amrit sanchar*, the Khalsa initiation ceremony, we witnessed an example of a Sikh ritual that marks a certain point in the individual's life and does so through detailed actions and rich symbolism that are steeped in tradition. Having already considered the Khalsa initiation ceremony in some detail (and bearing in mind that only about 15 percent of Sikhs undergo initiation), we now turn to considering other important rituals of the life cycle.

Birth and Naming On the birth of a child, Khalsa Sikhs can choose to undertake a ritual that resembles an aspect of the initiation ceremony. A sweet drink is made by stirring water and sweets with a *kirpan* (the short sword, one of the Five Ks), while reciting from the *Japji*. A few drops are given to the baby, and the rest is drunk by the mother.

A short time after giving birth, the parents and child proceed to the *gurdwara*, where hymns are sung and the Adi Granth is opened randomly. The child's first name is chosen based on the first letter that appears on the left-hand page of the Adi Granth, the letter with which the name is to begin. If the child is a girl, she is also given the name Kaur; if male, he is given the name Singh. The names Singh or Kaur normally correspond to an English last name. No distinction is made between girls' and boys' first names. The "last name" of Kaur or Singh serves to make this distinction.

Tying a Turban When a boy reaches the age of 10 or 11, Sikh families often undertake a ceremonial tying of his first turban. This symbolizes the great respect that Sikhs hold for the turban. Even though wearing the turban is not technically required, it is regarded as a natural corollary of *kes*, not cutting one's hair (one of the Five Ks). Indeed, because one's hair is typically kept inside the turban, it is really the turban, not the hair, that is the most visible sign that one is a Sikh.

Traditionally, the turban is tied in a specific way that is both easy to do (once one has learned how) and effective, keeping the turban securely on the head. The style and color of the turban may sometimes indicate regional, political, or religious affiliation. The turban is generally considered to be highly practical, providing protection both from the summer sun and from the cold of winter. Women rarely wear turbans; instead, they traditionally wear a scarf or veil that can be used to cover the head.

Marriage Proper Sikh marriage, according to the traditions established by the Khalsa, is arranged by the parents of a child of marriageable age through the assistance of a relative, who seeks out a suitable spouse and sets up meetings with the families. The parents thus can become acquainted with their child's potential bride or groom. The same type of meeting takes place with the other set of parents. Once both families have agreed on a match, the marriage ceremony is planned. According to the Rahit, a Sikh woman is only to be married to a Sikh, but no account whatsoever of caste status is to be taken into consideration. In actual practice, however, there are many exceptions. Caste status commonly dictates the choice of marriage partners, and Sikhs (men more commonly than women) sometimes marry outside the tradition. As we have remarked previously, common practice by no means always complies with Khalsa ideals.

The ceremony takes place at the *gurdwara*, with Sri Guru Granth Sahib the central focal point, just as it is in everyday worship. First seated before the Adi Granth during the singing of hymns, the couple then stands and receives instruction in the teachings of the Gurus on marriage, nodding their assent to the Adi Granth, and afterward walking around it. This focus on the scripture exemplifies the central role that the Adi Granth is to play in the life of the married couple.

The ceremony concludes, like other worship services in the *gurdwara*, with the distribution of *karah prasad*, the special pudding made of wheat flour, sugar, and ghee.

Death Traditional Sikh mourning rituals center around the process of cremation. The body is washed and dressed in clean clothing and adorned with the Five Ks. A hymn is recited, and the body is carried to the cremation grounds, which women do not enter. The funeral pyre is lit by a son or other male relative or friend, while the other mourners sing funeral hymns. The *Kirtan Sohila*, the prayer that is recited daily when retiring for the evening, is then sung.

Once the fire has burned out, the ashes are recovered and are either buried there at the cremation site or immersed in running water. Then the entire Adi Granth is read, within a period of ten days if possible. (The Rahit specifies that a full reading takes forty-eight hours, if done without interruption.)

Worship, Work, and Charity

Like every global religion, Sikhism is continually in contact with people of other traditions. In this chapter, we have seen how Guru Nanak inspired followers who were both Muslims and Hindus. While the common notion that Sikhism somehow resulted from the mixing of Islam and Hinduism is not an accurate one, clearly Guru Nanak and Sikhs after him helped to bridge differences among these two major religions of India. Sikhism has generally maintained peaceful relations with other religions and with other peoples, both in their homeland and abroad. Indeed, Sikhs have a well-deserved reputation for reaching out and helping to improve their communities. From its beginnings, Sikhism has been on the side of religious freedom and justice for oppressed people. Justice is carried out partly through the regular donation of one-tenth of one's income to charitable causes.

Three guiding principles of Sikh life are worship, work, and charity, as embodied in the popular Punjabi proverb, *nam japo, kirat karo, vand chhako*: "Repeat the divine Name, work, and give a share [of your earnings to the less fortunate]."[12] An outsider need only pay a visit to a Sikh *gurdwara* and witness the worship and afterward partake of the carefully prepared food in the *langar* to experience these guiding principles in action.

Women and Sikhism

Sikhism, like every religion, has both its ideals and its practical realities. Such is the case with the place of women over the centuries. The ideals are set forth straightforwardly, for instance in these words by Guru Nanak:

> From women born, shaped in the womb, to women betrothed and wed,
> We are bound to women by ties of affection; on women man's future depends.
> If a woman dies he seeks another, source of society's order and strength.
> Why then should one speak evil of women, they who give birth to kings?
> Women also are born from women, as are all who have life and breath.[13]

Sikhism has always maintained this ideal of gender equality with regard to the crucial issue of spiritual liberation. But this does not ensure equality in society, even in religious society. Sikhism, through the centuries and up to the present day, has tended to be quite patriarchal, with positions of institutional power occupied by men. (Notably, the ten Gurus were all men.) The wedding ceremony that we have considered suggests a certain patriarchal tendency with its prescribed vows. The groom promises to be "protector" of the bride and her honor; the bride promises to accept her husband as "master of all love and respect."

As is the case with all of the world's major religions, the degree of gender equality in Sikhism varies from circumstance to circumstance. Generally speaking, modern times have brought changes. As we will learn at the end of this chapter, the rapid growth of the Sikh diaspora in places where gender equality is held up as an ideal suggests that such changes will bring new opportunities for women to occupy roles of power in Sikh religion and society. With regard to the issue of gender equality, too, the Panth will need to continue to make adjustments as it orientates its way as a global religion.

As we conclude this section on Sikh religious life, we can look back and note some features of Sikhism that give rise to further questions. It is one thing for Sikhs in their traditional homeland of the Punjab to practice worship and rituals in the manner here described, but what about Sikhs who live abroad? For that matter, to what extent has modernity affected the traditional religious life of Sikhism? And in these times of increased screening at airports, what of a Khalsa Sikh who wishes to don the *kirpan* (the sword or knife, one of the Five Ks) when traveling about? To answer these questions, we need to take a closer look at the development of Sikhism since the time of Guru Nanak's death and its evolution as a global religion in the modern world.

THE HISTORY OF SIKHISM

Guru Nanak has remained the most prominent and revered of the ten Gurus of the Sikhs. Yet his nine successors contributed significantly to the development of the religion. Young Sikhs like Manjit and Sandeep learn about all of them as a natural part of their upbringing, celebrating their heroic life stories.

VISUAL GUIDE
Sikhism

Ik Onkar. Literally meaning "one God," *Ik Onkar* is the primary Sikh symbol of monotheism. The *Mul Mantra*, recited daily by most Sikhs, begins with these words.

Five Ks. Objects symbolizing membership in the Khalsa: *kes*, uncut hair; *kangha*, a small comb worn in the hair; *karā*, a steel wristlet; *kirpan*, a sword; *kachh*, a pair of shorts tied with a drawstring.

Golden Temple. Located in Amritsar in the Punjab, the Darbar Sahib ("Court of the Lord") or Golden Temple, was built by Guru Arjan in about 1600 C.E., providing Sikhs to this day with a geographical center.

Composed (from the center outward) of a double-edged sword, the circular *Chakar*, and two *kirtans*, the *khanda* symbolizes the balanced unity of Sikh spiritual and worldly life.

Guru Nanak's Successors

All ten Gurus are considered to have been revealers of truth and to have been linked to one another through sharing the same divine essence. This made them spiritually more adept than ordinary people. They were not, however, thought to be divine incarnations of God. The Gurus thus are not to be worshiped by Sikhs, though they are greatly revered. Guru Nanak constantly stressed his human limitations, humbly referring to himself as God's slave. All the Gurus were highly prestigious persons. They were revered for their spiritual gifts and acquired much worldly prestige as well. The Moghul (therefore, Muslim) emperors who ruled northern India knew the Gurus

TIMELINE
Sikhism

1469 C.E. Birth of Guru Nanak, founder of Sikhism.

1520s Establishment by Guru Nanak of the township of Kartarpur, the first Sikh community.

1539 Death of Guru Nanak.

1606 Death (execution?) of Guru Arjan, under Moghul emperor Jahangir.

1675 Execution of Guru Tegh Bahadur, under Moghul emperor Aurangzeb.

1699 Founding of the Khalsa by Guru Gobind Singh.

1708 Death of Guru Gobind Singh and establishment of the Adi Granth as Guru.

1799 Establishment of independent Sikh kingdom by Ranjit Singh.

1849 Annexation of Sikh kingdom by the British.

1947 Partition of Punjab with the establishment of India's independence.

1984 Indian army attacks and occupies Sikh holy sites, including the Darbar Sahib.

1999 The Panth celebrates the third centennial of the establishment of the Khalsa.

personally and tended to respect them, in some cases developing strong friendships with them.

Nanak's successors are responsible for a wide variety of impressive accomplishments that gradually transformed the Sikh community. Arjan, the Fifth Guru (from 1581 to 1606), deserves special mention. For one thing, he compiled the scripture that would come to be known as the Adi Granth ("the Original Volume," distinguishing it from the later Dasam Granth), thus giving the Sikhs their most important sacred scripture. He included, by traditional count, 2,312 of his own compositions, beautifully melodic hymns that are considered to be among Sikhism's most impressive musical accomplishments. Arjan also constructed at the city of Amritsar the Hari Mandar ("Temple of God"), now called Darbar Sahib ("Court of the Lord") or the Golden Temple. This provided the Sikhs with a geographical center.

The Darbar Sahib remains one of the world's most impressive and important religious buildings. Along with being architecturally magnificent, it is rich in symbolic meaning, beginning with the building process itself. At Arjan's invitation, Mian Mir, a Muslim *Sufi* saint, laid the foundation stone. Even as the Sikh community was gaining independence from its Muslim and Hindu neighbors, Sikhism served as a bridge between religions. In contrast to Hindu temples, which typically have only one door, Arjan designed the Darbar Sahib with four doors. Traditionally this is interpreted as representing Sikhism's openness to all people—to adherents of all four of northwestern India's major religious traditions of the time (Hinduism, Islam, Buddhism, and Sikhism); to people of all four classes of the prevalent Hindu caste system; and to people of the north, south, east, and west. In light of this it is ironic that, in recent times, the Darbar Sahib has become associated with controversy and discord, having been the site of the bloody military action in 1984 known as Operation Blue Star, which we shall consider in more detail below.

Guru Gobind Singh and the Khalsa

The tenth Guru, Gobind Singh (1666–1708), is revered as the greatest Guru after Nanak. His strength of character and spiritual adeptness made him a successful and memorable leader. By the time he became Guru at the age of 9, he had already begun training in the art of warfare and hunting, along with the ways of religion. A modern history of the Sikhs makes note of the enduring impression made by the Guru's appearance:

THE TEN GURUS

The guruship of each begins with the death of his predecessor.

1. Guru Nanak (1469–1539)
2. Guru Angad (1504–1552)
3. Guru Amar Das (1479–1574)
4. Guru Ram Das (1534–1581)
5. Guru Arjan (1563–1606)

6. Guru Hargobind (1595–1644)
7. Guru Hari Rai (1630–1661)
8. Guru Hari Krishan (1656–1664)
9. Guru Tegh Bahadur (1621–1675)
10. Guru Gobind Singh (1666–1708)

Every description of Guru Gobind Singh's person delineates him as a very handsome, sharp-featured, tall and wiry man, immaculately and richly dressed as a prince. Decked with a crest upon his lofty, cone-shaped turban with a plume suspended behind from the top, he was ever armed with various weapons, including a bow and a quiver of arrows, a sword, a discus, a shield and a spear. His choice steed was of bluish-grey color and on his left hand always perched a white hawk when he sat on the throne or went out hunting.[14]

Whereas Guru Nanak is traditionally depicted as being contemplative and the master of things spiritual, Guru Gobind Singh is depicted as a worldly prince, ever ready for battle.

Guru Gobind Singh contributed significantly to the growth of Sikh militarism and engaged in many armed conflicts during a period when revolts against the Mo-ghuls, which had been occurring periodically for about a century, were common. Due to his success in consolidating and strengthening the Panth, the Sikhs had a realistic possibility of establishing independent rule. Most notably, Guru Gobind Singh brought about two innovations that forever changed the structure of Sikhism. As we have already noted, he instituted the Khalsa, which would redefine the Panth, and he installed the Adi Granth, the sacred scripture, as Guru, which radically altered the nature of leadership.

Founding the Khalsa In the year 1699, in the midst of a period of great unrest and violent confrontations between Sikhs and Moghuls, the

A woman prays at the Golden Temple in Amritsar, India.

Sikh devotees celebrate the 345th birth anniversary of Guru Gobind Singh on January 11, 2011, in the northern Indian city of Jammu.

Sikhs had gathered to celebrate the annual festival of Baisakhi Day, the first day of the Indian year. Perceiving a desperate need for loyalty and cohesion among the Sikhs, Guru Gobind Singh addressed the multitude. Raising his sword, he challenged any Sikh who was willing to die for him to come forward. An uncomfortable silence followed. Then one man stepped out of the crowd, expressing his willingness even to give his life if that's what his Guru demanded. The man followed Guru Gobind Singh into his tent. The stunned crowd heard the thud of a falling sword, and the Guru emerged alone, with bloodstained sword in hand. And yet, from the silenced crowd stepped another man, and the process was repeated. Three more men followed in turn. The crowd waited anxiously. Eventually Guru Gobind Singh emerged with all five men, alive and well.

These men forever afterward have been known as the *Panj Piare*, the "Beloved Five." As we noted in the opening description of the initiation ceremony, they were the original members of the Khalsa, the community of "Pure Ones," an order of men and women within Sikhism based on the principle of loyalty exhibited by these five men. After initiating them, Guru Gobind Singh is said to have had the *Panj Piare* initiate him into the Khalsa, and soon thousands more joined. All the men were given the additional name Singh, which means "lion," and all the women were named Kaur, which means "princess." To this day, these names indicate a family's affiliation with the Khalsa (although they no longer imply that one has undergone initiation).

By the time of his death in 1708, Guru Gobind Singh had managed to befriend the Moghul rulership and to ease tensions between the peoples, although his own death came at the hands of a Moghul assassin. Before dying, he is said to have declared that he was to be succeeded, not by another individual, but by the Adi Granth and by the Panth, to both of which he assigned the title "Guru."

Sikhs and Nationalism

Over the centuries, the Punjab has tended to be a volatile region, marked by political and military strife. In the century following the death of Guru Gobind Singh in 1708, the Sikhs struggled through a period of especially violent confrontations with the Moghul empire, eventually managing to establish independent rule. Under the leadership of Ranjit Singh (1780–1839), who ascended to the throne in 1792, the Sikh community thrived as a sovereign kingdom in the Punjab. In 1849, the kingdom was annexed by the British, who had established control over India and had commenced the period known as the British Raj.

When India gained independence from the British in 1947, the Punjab was divided, with India gaining control of the east and Pakistan gaining control of the west. Most Sikhs living in the western region migrated eastward, favoring the Hindu-dominated India over the Muslim-dominated Pakistan. These Sikhs left behind their traditional homeland and many significant sites, including Nanak's birthplace.

In recent times, a new nationalist movement for independence, commonly called "Khalistan," has involved the Sikhs in conflict, both within and outside the Sikh community. The most violent tragedy of all took place in 1984 when, in an attempt to control the more radical aspects of the independence movement, the Indian government launched "Operation Blue Star," which culminated in the occupation of Sikh holy sites, most notably the Darbar Sahib (or Golden Temple), by Indian forces and the death of as many as 10,000 Sikhs. (Estimates of the death count vary widely, with various sources citing from 500 to 10,000.) This led to the assassination of Indian Prime Minister Indira Gandhi by two of her Sikh bodyguards on October 31, 1984. Today, the Khalistan movement is not nearly so prevalent as it was in the 1980s. That in 2004 a Sikh, Manmohan Singh, for the first time became India's prime minister perhaps signals a new degree of assimilation of Sikhism within Indian society.

Sikh Identity

This chapter has assumed all along a rather malleable definition of who is a Sikh. On one end of the spectrum, we have considered the rigorous regimen of observance as spelled out in the Rahit, which calls for the recitation of some twenty pages of prayer every morning before six o'clock. At the other end of the spectrum, there are those who cut their hair, and yet one cannot go so far as to deny that they are Sikhs.

This malleable definition is quite in keeping with the Sikh perspective. Every religious tradition sets forth ideals that are not necessarily put into practice by all of its followers. Sikhism openly acknowledges this. It is also important to recognize that "Sikh" can refer broadly to an ethnic group, without necessarily implying adherence to the religion of Sikhism. For centuries, Sikhs maintained a society in the Punjab that was quite distinctive, and the vast majority of today's Sikhs are themselves descendants of Punjabi Sikhs. There is thus both a societal and a hereditary aspect of being Sikh, neither of which necessarily involves the explicitly religious aspects of belief or conduct.

Sikhs in the Diaspora

Sikhism clearly has become a global religion. When it comes to issues involving Sikh identity, however, we observe an enduring influence of the Khalsa and of other more traditional aspects of Sikhism as it has been practiced for centuries in its homeland. At the beginning of this chapter, we noted that there are approximately 23 million Sikhs in the world,[15] of which approximately 70 percent follow at least the basic requirement of the Khalsa and do not cut their hair. Only about 15 percent of Sikhs have undergone the traditional ceremony of initiation into the Khalsa.

With approximately 2 million Sikhs now living in the diaspora[16] (that is, outside of the Punjab and of India), issues of these Sikhs have gained prominence. Many of the traditional practices taken for granted in the Punjab simply are not feasible—or, in some cases, even legal—in other lands. Consider, for example, the funeral ritual described earlier. According to the Rahit, and in keeping with longstanding tradition, the body of the deceased is to be born to the pyre on a bier, not in a coffin, and the fire is to be lit by a close relative or friend. In countries like the United States, such a practice is not permitted; as a result, adjustments are made. The ceremonial departure for the cremation site is replaced by placing the coffin into a hearse, which then proceeds to a crematorium. (Or the ceremony is held at a funeral home that is equipped with a crematorium.) The lighting of the pyre is replaced by the chosen person pushing the button that conveys the coffin into the cremation furnace.

Another challenging situation for Sikhs in the diaspora involves the wearing of uncut hair and, for men, the turban. As we have noted, wearing of the turban, which is almost universal among male Sikhs in their traditional homeland, is an important symbol of Sikh identity. But in many places in the diaspora, wearing a turban is not so easily done. In the United States, for example, there are laws requiring that helmets be worn when driving a motorcycle.

In some cases, governments attempt to accommodate Sikhs. In the United Kingdom, for example, motorcycle helmet laws have been modified. But in many situations, such traditional practices as wearing the turban have led at least to inconvenience, and sometimes even to tragedy. In the aftermath of the attacks on the World Trade Center and Pentagon of September 11, 2001, Sikhs have been mistaken (presumably due to the wearing of the turban) for Muslims and have become targets of hate crimes, including murder.

Uncut hair (one of the Five Ks) and the wearing of the turban by men is a crucial mark of Sikh identity. For Sikhs living in the diaspora, this issue of identity needs to be weighed against practical concerns, sometimes even involving one's safety. Whereas most Sikhs in the Punjab continue to follow the injunction not to cut their hair, most living in Western countries do not. The Panth, as a global religious community, must contend with this complex mix of issues and concerns.

A Sikh man greets Hillary Clinton, at the time Senator of New York, at the United States National Day of Prayer Ceremony in 2007.

CONCLUSION

In this chapter, we have learned about the teachings, the way of life, and the historical development of Sikhs and their religion. Founded by Guru Nanak (1469–1539), Sikhism is relatively young compared to other major world religions. It nevertheless is firmly rooted in tradition that is historically rich, theologically and ritually sophisticated, and adorned with impressive musical and architectural achievements. Especially because of the central role of the Khalsa, with its Five Ks and other standards for Sikh behavior and identity, the Panth tends to be a community with well-defined ideals. All of these factors contribute to the considerable holding power of Sikh tradition, even as the modern world invites—and sometimes forces—adaptations.

Sikhism today is a global religion, as vital in places like Toronto, Canada, and the central valley of California as it is in its ancestral homeland of the Punjab. As it continues to draw upon the richness of its eventful historical tradition, Sikhism shows every sign of continuing also to adapt to modernity in the various places across the globe that it has come to call home.

SEEKING ANSWERS

What Is Ultimate Reality?

Sikhism is strictly monotheistic, emphasizing the oneness of God, while also teaching that God dwells within creation. For reasons that cannot be understood by human beings, God created the world. Knowing the divine nature can be considered as analogous to knowing the nature of an artist through contemplation of her artwork. Sikhism holds that the world is good, that God is immanent in the world, and that the world is permeated with divine order, called *hukam*. If this divine order can be recognized, it stands to reason that human beings can come to know God.

How Should We Live in This World?

Sikhs believe that God dwells within everyone. Humans tend, however, to be self-centered, rather than God-centered, a concept known as *haumai*, the self-reliance or pride that poses the primary obstacle to spiritual fulfillment. Sikhs further believe that the world is permeated with *hukam*, or divine order. To live in accord with *hukam* naturally requires proper ethical conduct. The Khalsa, though technically made up of only a minority of Sikhs, continues to be the authoritative source for ideals on the right way to live.

What Is Our Ultimate Purpose?

Immanent in creation, God is knowable to human beings. The flaws of *haumai* can be overcome through attention to the presence of the divine, most effectively through meditation on *nam*, the Name of God. As the term suggests, liberation, which for Sikhism is complete union with God, is the complete overcoming of the human condition. Sikhism teaches that the ultimate purpose of life is to attain spiritual liberation, and thereby release from *samsara*, the cycle of death and rebirth. In general, the Sikh perspective on *samsara* is very similar to that of Hinduism. In addition, Sikhs cremate their dead, which marks another similarity to Hinduism.

REVIEW QUESTIONS

For Review

1. What is the meaning of the term "guru"?
2. Compare the contributions of Guru Nanak and Guru Gobind Singh for the development of Sikhism.
3. Identify at least three of the names for God in Sikhism. Why do you think there is more than one name? What is the relationship of the names to each other?
4. What is the Khalsa? What is its ongoing relevance for Sikhism?
5. How do the "Five Ks" of Sikhism serve to strengthen Sikh identity?

For Further Reflection

1. What aspects of the Sikh God would Jews, Christians, or Muslims find familiar?
2. Describe the Sikh state of spiritual perfection. How does this compare to other religions— for example, to Hindu *moksha* or Buddhist *nirvana*?
3. Compare Sikh worship in the *gurdwara* with the forms of worship in religions with which you are familiar, either through studies or through personal experience. What are the notable similarities and differences? What do these comparative points regarding worship suggest about the nature of the religions, in general?

GLOSSARY

Adi Granth (ah'dee gruhnth; Punjabi, "first book") Sikhism's most important sacred text and, since the death of Guru Gobind Singh in 1708, Sikhism's primary earthly authority; traditionally known as Sri Guru Granth Sahib.

amrit (ahm-reet; Punjabi, "immortalizing fluid") A special drink made from water and sugar crystals, used in the Khalsa initiation ceremony.

gurdwara (goor'dwah-ruh; Punjabi, "doorway of the Guru" or "by means of the Guru's [grace]") A special building for Sikh worship that houses a copy of the Adi Granth; the central structure of any Sikh community.

Guru (goo'roo; Sanskrit, "venerable person") A spiritual teacher and revealer of truth, common to Hinduism, Sikhism, and some forms of Buddhism. When the word *Guru* is capitalized, it refers to the ten historical leaders of Sikhism, to the sacred text (Sri Guru Granth Sahib, or Adi Granth), and to God (often as True Guru).

haumai (how'may; Punjabi, "self-reliance," "pride," or "egoism") The human inclination toward being self-centered rather than God-centered, which increases the distance between the individual and God.

hukam (huh'kahm; Punjabi, "order") The divine order of the universe.

Khalsa (khal'sah; Punjabi, "pure ones") An order within Sikhism to which the majority of Sikhs belong, founded by Guru Gobind Singh in 1699.

Mul Mantra The summary of Sikh doctrine that comprises the opening lines of the *Japjī*, Guru Nanak's composition that in turn comprised the opening section of the Adi Granth. (See p. 244 for an English translation of the full text.)

Panth (puhnth; Punjabi, Hindi, "path") The Sikh community. In lower case, *panth* ("path") is a term applied to any number of Indian (primarily Hindu) religious traditions.

Rahit (rah-hit'; Punjabi) The *rahit-nāmā*, a collection of scripture that specifies ideals of belief and conduct for members of the Khalsa and, by extension, for Sikhism generally; the current authoritative version, the *Sikh Rahit Maryādā*, was approved in 1950.

SUGGESTIONS FOR FURTHER READING

Cole, W. Owen, and Piara Singh Sambhi. *The Sikhs: Their Religious Beliefs and Practices*. 2nd rev. ed. Brighton, United Kingdom: Sussex Academic Press, 1995. A highly readable and informative account, organized in such a way as to make easily accessible the main figures and ideas.

Mann, Gurinder Singh. *Sikhism*. Upper Saddle River, NJ: Prentice Hall Inc., 2004. A clear and up-to-date overview, with focus on modern times.

McLeod, Hew. *Sikhism*. London: Penguin Books, 1997. A detailed yet accessible overview of the religion, with a helpful appendix of primary source material.

McLeod, W. H., ed. and trans. *Textual Sources for the Study of Sikhism*. Totowa, NJ: Barnes & Noble Books, 1984. A helpful collection of source material that goes well beyond the Adi Granth and presents texts in such a way as to clarify the identity of authors.

Singh, Khushwant. *A History of the Sikhs*. 2 vols. Princeton, NJ: Princeton University Press, 1963–1966. A detailed and authoritative resource.

ONLINE RESOURCES

Wabash Center
wabashcenter.wabash.edu/resources/result_browse.aspx?topic=585&pid=361
The Wabash Center, a trusted resource for all aspects of the academic study of religion, offers links to a wide variety of dependable Internet resources on Sikhism.

SikhNet
sikhnet.com
SikhNet offers an extensive "insiders' view" on Sikhism, with information on many aspects of the religion.

CHINESE RELIGIONS: CONFUCIANISM and DAOISM

TODAY IS *QINGMING*, a "pure and bright" day (the literal meaning of this Chinese compound word) that arrives once a year, 105 days after the winter solstice. It is a day for all Chinese families to remember their dead relatives and ancestors in a very public way. Spring is definitely in the air. The days have been getting longer and warmer. The rice seedlings, standing in neat rows in ankle-deep water in the paddy fields, wave gracefully in the gentle breeze. Their luxuriant greenness is most pleasing to the eyes of Chen Liang,[1] a peasant from Southern China in his early fifties. He and his two sons have been working hard in the past couple of months to plow and flood the paddy fields, seed the nursery plots, and then transplant the young seedlings one at a time into their current location. It is a tedious and back-breaking job that the Chen family has been doing for generations.

But today there will be no work in the fields. *Qingming* marks the renewal of spring. It also celebrates the rekindling of the kitchen fire. Two days earlier the old fire was put out, so only cold food had been served. Chen Liang and his wife get up today at the crack of dawn to light a new fire in the kitchen. Leftovers from the previous days' cold meals are wrapped in rice pancakes and fried, making "spring rolls" that many Chinese restaurants the world over serve regularly on their appetizer menu. They prepare for an important family gathering at the ancestral graves of the Chen clan. During this annual event, family members gather at and sweep the graves of their relatives and ancestors to renew their kinship ties with both the

Woman making offerings in front of her ancestor's tomb

Important Confucian
and Daoist sites in China.

dead and the living. Platefuls of fruits, freshly steamed chickens, a whole roasted pig, bottles of wine, bundles of incense sticks and bright-red candles, strings of firecrackers, as well as piles of make-believe paper money and paper clothing for the dead—are all ready to be carried to the lineage burial ground just outside the village.

At the gravesite, where several generations of the Chen clan are buried, Chen Liang meets up with his three brothers, his five cousins, and their families. The children, numbering more than twenty, are all dressed in brightly colored clothing, giggling and playing. They help remove overgrown weeds, clean the tombstones, and arrange food in front of the graves. Then, by generation and birth order, all members of the Chen clan take part in the annual ritual. They bow before their ancestors, address them in silent prayers, offer them wine and food, send them clothing and stacks of under-world money by burning paper imitations of those goods, and set off firecrackers to scare off wandering ghosts unrelated to the family.

Afterward a picture is taken of the entire gathering in front of the graves. The families divide up the fruits and the meats to be consumed later back at their respective homes. The men linger to talk about the weather and the crops, the women catch up on family news, and the children play. ☀

Gatherings similar to that of the Chen extended family are replicated millions of times throughout China in observance of *qingming*. It is through this activity of paying homage to the ancestors and reaffirming kinship relations that the Chinese act out one of their most basic religious assumptions. At the core of this ritual is the Confucian notion of filial piety (honoring parents, elders, and ancestors) and of the centrality of the family in Confucian teaching. Equally on display is the Daoist (Taoist) attentiveness to changes in season and in nature, as well as the practice of warding off unwelcome ghosts through exorcistic exercises and thunderous explosives. From this single family ritual we see that Confucianism and Daoism can coexist quite harmoniously among the Chinese, with no sense of incompatibility or mutual exclusivity. Indeed, except for extreme partisans in each tradition, most Chinese often embrace both religions with no sense of tension or conflict. How is that possible?

In this chapter you are invited to step into the religious world of the Chinese and to see how these two native Chinese religions both rival and complement each other. (Even though Buddhism is the third main religious tradition in China, we will only give passing notice to it in light of its alien origin and its totally different worldviews; see Chapter 5 for a complete treatment of Buddhism.) By focusing on the history, beliefs, and practices of Confucianism and Daoism, we can appreciate the true religious nature of the two traditions as well, even though in content and expression they may differ from most other world religions.

This chapter, unlike most others in this book, does not begin with a discussion of teachings and beliefs. Because it is difficult to make sense of the teachings and practices of Confucianism and Daoism without some understanding of the larger context in which the two traditions developed, this chapter begins instead with a discussion of the historical background that gave rise to both traditions, followed by an examination of the teachings and practices of each.

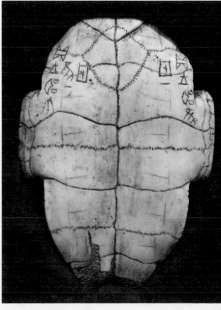

A Chinese oracle bone made of tortoise shell.

THE HISTORY OF CONFUCIANISM AND DAOISM

It should be observed from the outset that before Confucianism and Daoism, an ancient religion already existed in China. This ancient Chinese religion took shape no later than 1500 B.C.E., fully a thousand years prior to the rise of the two traditions. In fact, both Confucianism and Daoism may be regarded as two divergent extensions or outgrowths of this ancient Chinese religion. In order to understand the religious nature and practice of Confucianism and Daoism, therefore, this ancient Chinese religion needs to be examined first.

Ancient Chinese Religion

The earliest time in Chinese history for which we have both written records and archaeological evidences is the Shang Dynasty, whose traditional dates are 1751–1122 B.C.E. Representative of these records and evidences are the "oracle bone inscriptions," carved messages on smoothed-out oxen shoulder

VISUAL GUIDE
Daoism and Confucianism

This is an iconic image of Confucius as a learned scholar and an exemplar of human moral accomplishment. Traditionally the Chinese did not see religion as a separate realm of activity, hence the pursuit of scholarship and the enactment of moral behavior within the family and community were very much part of their religious experience.

Though not strictly Confucian, this yin-yang symbol surrounded by the eight trigrams does reflect the Chinese belief in the complementarity of opposites and the harmonious unity of the cosmos. More than any other visual symbol, it represents Chinese religiousness.

Family cohesion and respect for elders are central Confucian values. A daughter and her husband pay a visit to her parents on Chinese New Year's Day to renew her kinship tie with her natal family.

Statue of Laozi carved out of a huge rock in Fujian province, China. This legendary founder of Daoism symbolizes wisdom and irreverence for conventional thinking. He is understood as the yin to Confucius' yang, and the image of passive acceptance of what nature has ordained to Confucius' active attempt at improving society.

(continued)

blade bones or tortoise shells that include questions put to (and supposed answers from) deceased members of the Shang royalty. The questions covered a wide spectrum of issues, from actions to be undertaken by the ruler (such as the decision to go to war) to intimate, personal matters of the imperial family (such as the gender of royal offspring about to be born). After the questions were put forth, heat was applied to a predrilled hole in the bone or shell, causing cracks to appear. Patterns formed by these cracks were read by the shaman-diviner, and occasionally the Shang ruler himself, and were interpreted as answers to the original questions posed.

The Ancient Chinese Concept of Ancestor Worship and the Divine

The oracle bone divinatory practice of the Shang royal house reveals a central concern with ancestor worship. The ancestors were not just dead, buried, and forgotten. Instead, they continued to play an active role in the lives of their living descendants. They were consulted often on matters both major and minor. From the very beginning, then, Chinese religious practice focused on kinship ties and practical living. It was not exclusively located in a separate "sacred" realm.[2] The ancestors' presence in the life of their descendants has remained a central and characteristic aspect of Chinese civilization, not just for the Shang Dynasty or for the imperial family but for all subsequent ages and for every family in China. It is in this sense that the depiction of *qingming* at the opening of this chapter is so demonstrative of Chinese religious behavior.

In the Shang period, the spirits of the ancestors were sometimes asked to carry messages to a higher deity for decision and response. This higher, more authoritative deity was ***Shangdi***, the Lord on High, who was the most powerful god in the Shang spiritual world and who also happened to be the ancient ancestor of the Shang imperial house. This Lord on High was the controlling power in the cosmos.

Along with the spirits of the ancestors, *Shangdi* monitored the behavior of the royal descendants, dispensing rewards and meting out punishments as appropriate. It was precisely for this reason that the Shang rulers needed to maintain close contact and good relationship with *Shangdi* and the other ancestral spirits, for the spirits were their source of kingly power. This power was termed ***de***, commonly translated as "virtue," but more accurately as "potency." It was through the timely and correct performance of sacrificial rites to the ancestors and to *Shangdi* that each Shang ruler could claim this power, which may be more appropriately understood as the charismatic influence he possessed. With *de* the Shang king ruled with authority and legitimacy.

But sometime near the end of the second millennium B.C.E., a former minister of the court staged a rebellion that overthrew the Shang Dynasty and founded the next regime, the Zhou Dynasty (1122–256 B.C.E.). This power shift was rationalized primarily in religious terms. The defeat of the Shang, as the victorious Zhou founders explained it, was in fact sanctioned by *Shangdi*, who turned out to have a different name and was in fact a different kind of deity. *Shangdi* was now known as ***Tian***, literally, "the sky," but more properly "the force above." (Regrettably most books and articles written in English on Chinese religion and philosophy translate *Tian* as "Heaven," which is both inaccurate and misleading. In this chapter we will continue to use the term *Tian* rather than any English equivalent in order to avoid any mistaken notion of *Tian* being a paradise-like location.)

Tian was believed to be the source of all things in the universe, the ultimate divine entity that provided order throughout the cosmos. More significantly, *Tian* was also a "will" that would support only the morally deserving as king. This made *Tian* radically different from *Shangdi*, who was understood to be partial to the Shang kings, its quasi-biological descendants, and subject to their sacrificial "bribery." *Tian* was not swayed by claimed blood-ties or sacrificial offerings; instead, it insisted on the demonstration of moral uprightness as the only condition for its award of political authority and legitimacy, which was labeled ***ming***, or ***Tianming***. This was the "mandate" or "charge" given by *Tian* to the person and the imperial line who was to rule on *Tian*'s behalf. Moreover, this *ming* could be revoked and withdrawn and could be transferred to another person or family, any time its provisional holder was found wanting in morality. This event was known as "*geming*," the revocation of the "*ming*." To this

TIMELINE
Daoism and Confucianism

	Daoism	Confucianism
Spring and Autumn (c. 722–481 B.C.E.)		Confucius (551–479 B.C.E.)
Warring States (c. 480–221 B.C.E.)	*Neiye* [Inner Cultivation] (fourth century B.C.E.) Zhuangzi (365–290 B.C.E.) *Laozi* (earliest extant ed. c. 300 B.C.E.)	Mencius (371–289 B.C.E.) Xunzi (c. 310–211 B.C.E.)
Early Han Dynasty (206 B.C.E.–9 C.E.)	Worship of Xiwangmu (Queen Mother of the West)	Confucianism declared orthodox (136 C.E.); *Five Classics* designated
Later Han Dynasty (25–220 C.E.)	Laozi deified as Taishang Laojun. Tianshi [Celestial Master] Movement founded by Zhang Daoling (142 C.E.) *Laozi bianhua jing* (Classic of Laozi's Transformations) (170s*)	Confucian classical commentaries and Scholasticism
Period of Disunion (221–589)	Shangqing [Highest Clarity] Movement (fourth century) Lingbao [Numinous Treasure] Movement (fourth century)	
Tang Dynasty (618–907)	First attempt at compiling canon. State patronage of Daoism	First stirring of Neo-Confucianism
Song Dynasty (907–1279)	Quanzhen [Complete Perfection] Movement founded by Wang Zhe (1113–1170)	Neo-Confucianism: Zhu Xi (1130–1200)
Yuan Dynasty (1279–1368)		*Four Books* designated as civil service examination curriculum (1313)
Ming Dynasty (1368-1644)	*Daozang* compiled (1445)	
Qing Dynasty (1644–1911)		Civil service examination abolished (1905)
Early twentieth century	Chinese intellectuals criticized Daoism as superstition	Chinese intellectuals rejected Confucianism as feudal and reactionary
Communist China (1949–present)	Cultural Revolution (1966–1976) devastated Daoism Daoism gradually recovering since 1980s	Cultural Revolution (1966–1976) devastated Confucianism Confucianism gradually recovering since 1980s

Note: Asterisks indicate contested or approximate dates.

day, *geming* in Chinese means "revolution—the withdrawal of the current regime's mandate to rule."

According to the religious mindset of the Zhou, *Tian*'s workings in nature and in the human world is its **dao**, its "way" or "path." It is the *dao* of *Tian* that provides order and regularity in nature and in human society. By following and obeying this *dao*, both the natural as well as the human worlds would reach their optimal fulfillment. This implementation of the *dao* of *Tian* is the duty and obligation of the human ruler. Thus what had happened to the Shang regime actually validated this belief in *Tian*'s mandate. Shang's last ruler, who was, according to the Zhou founders, a corrupt and immoral individual, was no longer fit to exercise *Tianming*, hence his violent removal from power.

As the chosen deputy of *Tian* in the human world, the Zhou king (and all subsequent imperial rulers in China) called himself *Tianzi* ("Son of *Tian*"), the person who had been entrusted with the power to rule *Tianxia* ("domain under *Tian*," i.e., the entire known world). The king was therefore not just a political leader exercising power over both territory and people; he was also a religious figure who served as intermediary between *Tian* and humanity, as well as the natural world. To fulfill his roles as both king and priest, the Zhou ruler had to observe a set of behavioral practices collectively referred to as **li** ("rituals" or "rites"). It was the correct and sincere performance of *li* that would convince *Tian* of the ruler's moral worth, ensure *Tian*'s continuous favor, and guarantee the ruler's power through his *de*, his "potency." *Li* covered every aspect of kingly behavior—from matters of state, to relation with ancestors, to conduct on important familial occasions such as marriage and funerals, and even involving military campaigns. It would in time govern all the ritual conduct of the king's ministers as well, as their proper behavior also contributed to the stability and legitimacy of the regime.

Ancient Chinese Texts Such prescribed rites for the king and his ministers would later be codified into a text known as the *Record of Rites* (*Liji*). However, the beliefs in the source of kingly power and the underlying assumptions of imperial moral obligations are fully addressed in two other texts, the *Book of Odes* (*Shijing*)[3] and the *Book of History* (*Shujing*).[4] The former is an anthology of poems and ballads expressing the sentiments of both nobles and commoners, while the latter consists primarily of recorded activities and pronouncements of kings and aristocrats. Another work, the *Book of Changes* (*Yijing*), contains early Chinese views of cosmology and the supernatural. Collectively these texts, which existed in some form after the founding of the Zhou regime, provide most of the information on the ancient Chinese religion from which Confucianism and Daoism would evolve. The Confucians, in particular, would revere these texts as classics and as sacred texts. The four just mentioned, along with the *Spring and Autumn Annals* (*Chunqiu*), purportedly compiled by Confucius himself, would constitute the Confucian **Five Classics**. The Daoists, while recognizing the authority of these texts, especially the *Book of Changes*, would create their own corpus of scriptural works, as we shall see in later sections.

History of Confucianism

In this chapter, the term Confucianism is used with reservation. The Chinese refer to this tradition as the "Teaching of the **Ru** (scholars and ritualists)." Even though Confucius has been rightfully credited with giving this tradition prominence and profound religious meaning, he is by no means its founder, nor is he worshiped as a supernatural savior figure like Jesus Christ in Christianity or the Buddha in Mahayana Buddhism. Therefore, "Confucianism" is quite a misleading term, suggesting a parallel to Christianity and Buddhism that is simply not there. In fact, the name "Confucius" is equally problematic, as it is actually a Latinized way of representing the Chinese reference to "Kong Fu Zi," the honorific way of addressing "Master Kong." Master Kong's full name is Kong Qiu, whose dates are conventionally given as 551–479 B.C.E.

Confucius, the Man and His Time At the time of Confucius' birth, the entire political system and moral framework put in place by the early Zhou kings, as described in the previous section, was in disarray. Powerful feudal lords jockeyed for position to become the next *Tianzi*, the Son of *Tian*, and to replace the current Zhou king. The more capable and ambitious among them actively sought the service of talented men outside the hereditary aristocratic circles, thereby creating upward social mobility for some among the commoners. Conversely, powerful lords could become commoners overnight as a result of their defeat by their rivals, creating a downward social spiral as well.

Statue of Confucius at the entrance to the Confucian Academy in Beijing, China.

These critical social developments gave rise to the increasing prominence of a class of experts and specialists known as **shi** (men of service). Drawn from lower aristocratic or commoner backgrounds, they entered the employ of feudal lords and imperial rulers. The *shi* performed two major categories of duties: military and civil. The military men of service, the knights, were referred to as *wushi*, while their civilian counterparts, the scholars, were known as *rushi*, or simply **ru**. *Ru* were scribes and record keepers, masters of rituals and ceremonies, as well as diviners and religious professionals. To perform their duties well, *ru* had to acquire expertise in history, poetry, religious rites, divination, dance, and music.

Confucius was just such a *ru* who was born into a family of former aristocrats in the feudal domain of Lu (located in present-day Shandong province in North China). His father died when he was still an infant, so he had to do menial work as a young man to support himself, his sickly older brother, and his widowed mother. What enabled Confucius to lift himself up from poverty and anonymity was his desire for and success in scholarship. He apparently had an extraordinarily inquisitive mind and a voracious appetite for study, especially of the ancient texts of history, rituals, and poetry. By the age of 30 he was well known for his expertise as a *ru*. His service in government was limited to a number of minor posts, but his greatest accomplishment was in his vocation as a teacher. Confucius offered fresh insight into the human condition, creatively reinterpreting the belief system he inherited from the early Zhou. In addition, he communicated a forceful message of the need for improvement of individuals and society through moral cultivation and benevolent government. Aided by an intense and charismatic personality, Confucius became a popular private teacher with a huge following.

After age 50, as he realized that the feudal lord of his native Lu did not value his service, Confucius left with a number of trusted disciples in tow and headed for other feudal domains. His hope was that other lords would embrace his ideas and would implement his political blueprint for restoring order to the world. For the next thirteen years he traveled all across Northern China, going from one feudal domain to another in search of opportunities to carry out his reform proposals. He was met with disappointment everywhere, at times suffering much indignity, deprivation, and even physical danger. In the twilight years of his life, he returned to his home state of Lu with his political ambition unfulfilled and devoted the remainder of his life to teaching, writing, and editing the ancient texts. Confucius died in his early 70s.

Confucius is believed to have put the major classical works into their final form. He supposedly edited the *Book of Odes* and the *Book of History*, wrote important commentaries on the *Book of Changes*, and contributed to the *Record of Rites* as well as the no-longer-extant *Book of Music*. He also supposedly authored a book on the history of the late Zhou period from the vantage point of his native state of Lu, which is entitled *Chunqiu* (*Spring and Autumn Annals*). The work covers the years 722–481 B.C.E., a period which since has been known as the Spring and Autumn period in Chinese history.

Toward the end of his long life, Confucius gave a telling summary and assessment of his intellectual development as recorded in the *Analects*, a work compiled by his followers that contains his celebrated sayings:

> At fifteen I set my mind on learning
> At thirty I had become established [as a *ru*]
> At forty I was free from doubts
> At fifty I knew the decree of *Tian* (*Tianming*)
> At sixty my ears became attuned [to what I heard from *Tian*]
> At seventy I could follow my heart's desires without transgressing what was right
>   —Analects 2:4

As we shall see, this intellectual and spiritual autobiography of Confucius illustrates the pattern of his development from a scholar to a religious figure. His biography shows that he was a fully human figure with no claim to supernatural origin or power and was the consummate representative of the *ru* tradition and an exemplary teacher. Eventually, however, Confucius would be honored as a sage and a semi-divine figure deserving of worship.

Later Defenders of the Faith The Chinese world after Confucius took a turn for the worse. Warfare among the feudal states became even more frequent and brutal. The centuries between Confucius' death in 479 and 221 B.C.E. are known as the Warring States period in Chinese history. Confucius's original vision of moral cultivation and benevolent government seemed impractical and quixotic. Internally, the Confucian tradition was rocked by self-doubt and resignation, as his *ru* followers became mere functionaries for the feudal lords, enjoying little influence or self esteem. Externally, rival traditions such as Daoism and other more pragmatic schools competed for attention and attacked many of the Confucian ideas.

Into this picture came Mencius (a similarly Latinized rendition of "Master Meng") (371–289 B.C.E.?), born a full century after Confucius' death. A second-generation disciple of the grandson of Confucius, Master Meng was very much aware of what ailed the Confucian tradition. Claiming to be the rightful successor to Confucius, Mencius reaffirmed moral cultivation as a religious calling. He provided the moral elite with a strong sense of mission that bordered on a martyr's commitment to a religious cause. Mencius also made one lasting contribution to the Confucian belief system with his insistence on the basic goodness of human beings, thus upholding Confucianism's optimistic view of human perfectibility.

A younger contemporary of Mencius was Xun Qing (298–238 B.C.E.?), or Master Xun (Xunzi), who actually exerted far greater influence on the Confucian movement through the second century C.E. than Mencius did. Xun Qing's rationalism and pragmatic approach to rituals and learning had given a decisively secular and worldly bent to the Confucian tradition, resulting in a noticeable neglect of its religious nature. His view on human nature as evil also contradicted the Mencian version. Nevertheless, Xun Qing shared with Mencius an abiding faith in the transformative influence of moral cultivation and the perfectibility of humanity through self-effort. Eventually, however, Xun Qing was rejected by later Confucians as heterodox, and the text bearing his name was never recognized as a Confucian scripture.

Confucianism as Orthodoxy When China was unified by the Qin (Ch'in) state in 221 B.C.E., the Confucian tradition was initially a target of state persecution. Its call for benevolent government and individual moral autonomy was rejected by the First Emperor of Qin as impractical and subversive. But the Qin Dynasty soon fell, replaced by the Han (205 B.C.E.–220 C.E.), a much more hospitable regime for Confucian teaching. By the middle of the second century B.C.E., the Confucian tradition finally surpassed all its competitors by becoming the state-designated orthodoxy, in recognition of its usefulness in fostering effective governance and enhancing social cohesiveness. Yet its orthodox status also necessitated fundamental changes in its orientation. From a teaching that called for high-minded personal moral cultivation and benevolent government, Confucianism in the Han Dynasty became a scholastic tradition and a tool for state control and patriarchal authoritarianism. In fulfilling that role, Confucius was showered with grandiose titles by subsequent generations of Chinese rulers who scrambled to outdo one another in their adoration of him, culminating in the breathtakingly exuberant title of "Ultimate Sage of Greatest Accomplishment, King of Manifest Culture" given to him by an emperor in 1308. "Temples" dedicated to Confucius were built in all the administrative and political centers throughout the empire. Nevertheless, these temples served more as memorials, such as those dedicated to Thomas Jefferson or Abraham Lincoln, than as places of worship, and Confucius himself remained by and large an exemplary human figure worthy of veneration, rather than a god promising salvation and demanding pious submission.

Confucian Patriarchy and the Role of Women One of the most prominent features of Confucianism during the Han Dynasty and beyond—in addition to its emphasis on the obedience of the young to the old and the subject to the ruler—is the submissiveness of the female to the male. Cleverly manipulating the traditional *yin-yang* belief into an argument for the priority of *yang* over *yin*, hence the male over the female, Han Confucians and their successors in later dynasties insisted on women to submit to their fathers when young, their husbands when married, and their sons when old and widowed. This aspect of Confucianism in imperial China became a major cause of criticism of the tradition in the modern period as egalitarian values came to be embraced by the Chinese.

The Apricot Platform (Xingtan) is traditionally identified to be the location where Confucius lectured to his students.

The Neo-Confucian Tradition Though Confucianism served nominally as China's orthodoxy from the second century B.C.E. to the beginning of the twentieth century C.E., a span of over 2,000 years, it coexisted with Daoism and Buddhism during that entire period, and at times was even overshadowed by them. Since the twelfth century C.E., however, through a revitalization movement known in the West as Neo-Confucianism, it regained the initiative over its Daoist and Buddhist rivals and became the predominant religious tradition in China until the modern era. Indeed, as advocated by its most eloquent representative, the scholar Zhu Xi (1130–1200), its new scriptural corpus, the **Four Books**, comprised of the *Analects*, the *Mencius*, the *Great Learning*, and the *Doctrine of the Mean* (the latter two texts were supposedly written by two of Confucius' immediate disciples), would constitute the main curriculum upon which the civil service examination of late imperial China would be based. Between 1313 and 1905, all aspiring scholars and government officials in China had to study and were examined on their mastery of this set of canonical works, which provided the basis of their worldview and their outlook on life.

A new slogan for ethical and social achievement was advanced by the Neo-Confucians. "Inner sagely moral perfection and outer political ability and administrative skills" (**neisheng waiwang**) became their ultimate religious mission. Personal moral perfection and universal transformation of the human community formed one continuum in their religious quest.

Confucianism in the Modern World Confucianism entered a period of sharp decline in the modern age. This process began after the Opium War of 1839–1842, in which China was handily defeated by Great Britain. Other foreign powers quickly followed suit to demand enormous concessions from a weakened and disgraced China. For China's patriotic young generation of intellectual elite, this humiliating development exposed the shortcomings of their Confucian heritage. Confucianism was blamed for China's political, social, and economic backwardness. As a result, the New Culture Movement that began in the second decade of the twentieth century made Confucianism their main target of assault. "Down with Confucius and sons!" was now the popular call for rebellion against the tradition. The logic was that unless the roots of the Confucian tradition were eradicated completely, China would not survive the onslaught of modernity. Indeed, the birth of the Chinese Communist movement was in part attributable to this rebellious mode of thinking. From the perspective of the radical revolutionaries, Confucianism was a reactionary ideology of the ruling elite in China's feudal past that should be cast into the dustbin of history.

But the obituary for Confucianism appears to have been written prematurely. Despite repeated and sometimes violent attempts to rid China of the harmful influence of Confucianism, the "anti-Confucius" campaign of the Cultural Revolution period (1966–1976) on Mainland China being the most glaring example, the tradition has survived. As the opening vignette demonstrates, Confucianism as a religious tradition is still very much alive in contemporary China. The central importance of the family, the persistence of ancestral remembrance, and the value placed on education and self-improvement are evidence of the resilience of the Confucian ethos among many Chinese, and even East Asians in general. Some argue that the economic and industrial progress of the "Four Dragons" of Taiwan, South Korea, Hong Kong, and Singapore since the 1980s, and a similar development underway in China as well, might have been brought about by the Confucian heritage in these East Asian countries.

At the same time, an emergent group of "New Confucians," both inside and outside China, has been active as advocates for the revival of the Confucian teaching on philosophic and religious grounds. This group finds a new relevance for the Confucian tradition in the postmodern world on the ground that it expresses values of universal significance. These new defenders of the Confucian faith seek to rearticulate Confucianism for our time in the same way Confucians of the past had re-articulated it for theirs.

Equally notable is the new popularity enjoyed by Confucianism in China within the last decade, in part endorsed by the Chinese government. Academies devoted to the study of the Confucian tradition have been established, instruction on and the memorization of the *Analects* for school-age children are widely promoted, and even TV programs dedicated to the explanation of the relevance of Confucian teaching to contemporary Chinese society are eagerly viewed by a growing audience. The Chinese government also provides partial funding for the establishment of "Confucius Institutes" in European and North American universities to encourage interest in Chinese and Confucian studies.

History of Daoism

As we pointed out at the beginning of this chapter, the ancient Chinese religion that gave rise to Confucianism also served as the fountainhead for Daoism. Daoists, when they finally assumed an identity that distinguished them from the Confucians, partook of the same cosmological assumptions that formed the basis of Confucian teaching. They shared with the Confucians such central ideas as *Tian*, *Dao*, and *De*, even though their understanding and usage of these concepts were quite different. Consequently, the Daoist views of the ultimate meaning in life and the ideal mode of human conduct were also very different from that of the Confucians.

Laozi (Lao-tzu) and Zhuangzi (Chuang-tzu) Indisputably, the best known and earliest identifiable Daoists were Laozi (Master Lao) and Zhuangzi (Master Zhuang). The former, more of a composite figure than an actual person, was the reputed author of the ***Laozi***,[5] alternatively known as the ***Daodejing*** (*Tao-te Ching*) (*The Scripture of the Way and Its Potent Manifestation*). The latter was an obscure individual active in the late fourth-century B.C.E. who was credited with authorship of the second most influential Daoist text, the ***Zhuangzi***. Both texts are more representative of certain modes of thinking than of individual thinkers, as they are actually anthologies containing different strands of thought rather than coherent and logical teachings of single authors. One thing, however, is clear: they are consciously non-Confucian in that they express a decidedly alternative understanding of the *dao* and of ideal human action. In addition, both the *Laozi* and the *Zhuangzi* also contain descriptions of perfected human beings who possess amazing powers of magic and immortality. Both texts suggest that, through intense inner psychic journeying and mystical conditioning of the human body, individuals can acquire impressive powers of transformation and invulnerability to the decaying agents in nature.

The Deification of Laozi A crucial development that contributed to the rise of Daoism as an organized religion was the divinization of Laozi, the purported author of the *Daodejing*. Sometime between the second century B.C.E. and the second century C.E., Laozi came to be seen as a human incarnation of the *Dao*. Remarkably, the belief arose that the *Dao* could now intervene in human affairs and directly and personally impart teaching to the faithful through its human form. As the *Dao* incarnate, Laozi was the object of worship, thereby making the *Dao*, for the first time, a human-like being that demanded and

Laozi riding on the back of a water buffalo as he retires into the realm of the immortals.

received religious devotion. In a text entitled *Laozi bianhua jing* (*Scripture of the Trans-formations of Laozi*), compiled around the middle of the second century C.E., the vari-ous incarnations of Laozi over time, particularly as a messianic figure dedicated to the salvation of the world, were recounted. One of the titles Laozi assumed in these incar-nations was *Taishang Laojun*, the Venerable Lord of the Most High.

Even more significantly, Laozi as *Taishang Laojun* could give instructions to se-lected individuals on the esoteric secrets of the *Dao* as part of his scheme to save the world. This deified and messianic Laozi thus turned the Daoist teaching into a divine revelation on salvation, which has since become a major tenet of organized Daoism. Once Laozi was venerated as the *Dao* incarnate, as well as a dispenser of redemptive instructions, Daoism became a salvational faith. A whole pantheon of deities, both in nature and within the human body, came to be worshiped as physical manifestations of the *Dao* and as agents of deliverance.

Daoism as Organized Religion Beginning in the middle of the second century C.E., Daoism became an organized and large-scale movement among the common people. In the year 142 C.E., a man by the name of Zhang Ling (or Zhang Daoling) allegedly had a fateful encounter with the deified Laozi, who indicated to him that the world was in great trouble and he was the one who would be taught the right knowledge and proper practice to save it. He was to adopt the title of **Tianshi** (Celestial Master), and the teaching he was to transmit would be called *Zhengyi* (Orthodox Unity).

Zhang Ling later transferred the *Tianshi* title to his descendants down through the ages until the present day (in Taiwan). The movement would be known variously as "Celestial Master," "Orthodox Unity," or "Five Bushels of Rice," the last derived from the amount of contributions members were expected to make to the organization at their initiation. During the second half of the second century C.E., the movement acted as a theocratic shadow government, providing material aid and physical healing services to its membership, in addition to offering a vague hope of messianic salvation. A contemporary and parallel movement, alternatively known as "Great Peace" (*Tai-ping*) and "Yellow Turbans" (more accurately, Yellow Kerchiefs) (*Huangjin*), took the messianic message more seriously and rebelled against the Han court in an attempt to usher in a new age. This movement was ruthlessly suppressed, even though the dream of *taiping* would live on.

Later Daoist Historical Development The Celestial Masters made an arrangement with the government in 215 C.E. whereby it abandoned its theocratic base in south-western China and migrated closer to the political center in the north. But soon the Han Dynasty fell, and the subsequent short-lived regimes failed to maintain their power in the face of devastating invasions by nomadic non-Chinese groups such as the Huns, forcing the political and cultural elite to flee south toward the Yangzi River basin. The Celestial Masters followed, and became popular there as well, setting up its headquarters on the Dragon and Tiger Mountain in Jiangxi province in southeast

China. During the ensuing Period of Disunion, three centuries when China was politically divided between north and south, Daoism entered a most creative period.

First, both the *Laozi* and the *Zhuangzi* were given new philosophical interpretations that downplayed, if not totally eliminated, the religious elements on meditative transformations and magical physical transmutations in the two texts. Then someone who was much more closely related to the Celestial Masters, a certain Ge Hong (283–343 C.E.), who styled himself the "Master Who Embraces Simplicity" (*Baopuzi*), vigorously asserted the possibility of attaining physical perfection in the form of immortality through various techniques involving alchemy.

But the most significant development in Daoism was in the area of textual revelations and ritual reforms. Responding both to the competition offered by a rapidly expanding Buddhism and to the need to distinguish itself from the "uncouth" and "coarse" practices of popular religion, Daoist leaders from aristocratic families created new texts and devised new rituals that they claimed were revealed to them through ecstatic encounters with an ever-growing number of Daoist deities.

In the south, the Shangqing (Highest Clarity) and the Lingbao (Numinous Treasure) set of texts and rituals began to emerge almost simultaneously in the fourth century C.E. While the former emphasized individual experiences of spiritual fulfillment through meditation and mental visualization, the latter focused on ritual precision and use of talismans for the purpose of universal salvation, though there was considerable overlapping between the two as well. In the north, similarly intense and creative activities also took place under the claim of new revelations from *Taishang Laojun*, the deified Laozi. A Tuoba (a people outside of the Great Wall) ruler, Emperor Taiwu of the Northern Wei Dynasty, was touted as the "Perfect Lord of Great Peace" (*Taiping zhenjun*) and declared that the ideal world had arrived.

Common among the various Daoist groups of this period was the belief in and anticipation of an impending cataclysmic disaster that would radically transform the existing world. There was an anxious yet exciting expectation of the imminent arrival of a savior-like figure who would protect the devout followers from harm and ensure them a safe journey to the world to come—a perfect world populated by the faithful alone. This eschatological (vision of the end of time) and apocalyptic (revelation of a secret divine design) feature of the Daoist movement resembles many millennial traditions in other cultures.

Because of the proliferation of revelatory texts and the diverse array of rituals, the Period of Disunion also witnessed the first attempts made to classify and standardize them. The Lingbao master Lu Xiujing (406–477 C.E.) was the first to propose the notion of the "three caverns" (*sandong*) to categorize the growing corpus of texts. This tripartite principle of organization was a conscious imitation of the *Tripitaka* (Three Baskets), the canonical corpus of Buddhist texts. Subsequent centuries and regimes would see the organization of the texts become more elaborate with the addition of "four supplements" (*sifu*). This form of classification would constitute the framework of the entire Daoist canon, known as the ***Daozang***, the most complete and monumental version of which was printed in 1445 C.E. in 480 sections, 1,120 titles, and over 5,300 volumes.

During China's medieval period, lasting from the seventh to the fourteenth centuries, organized Daoism enjoyed imperial patronage and became very much a part of the cultural life of the elite. Along with a very popular Buddhism and the nominal state ideology of Confucianism, it was one of the "three religions" (*sanjiao*) of the realm. Its emphasis on nature and a free spirit informed much of the art and literature of the time. The breathtaking monochrome landscape paintings and cursive calligraphic art of the elite scholars reflected central Daoist values.

Several new orders also gained prominence during this time, the most influential among them being the *Quanzhen* Sect (Complete Perfection). Founded by Wang Zhe (1113–1170 C.E.), this school of Daoism embraced elements from both Confucianism and Buddhism. From Confucianism it took moral values, and from Buddhism it adopted monasticism and clerical celibacy. In addition to the *Daodejing*, the Confucian *Classic of Filial Piety* and the Buddhist *Heart Sutra* were given the highest prominence by this tradition. The *Quanzhen* Sect was the most popular religious organization in Mongol Yuan China (1279–1368 C.E.), even overshadowing Buddhism. It is one of the only two Daoist groups that still exist today, the other being the Celestial Masters.

During the late imperial period in Chinese history (fourteenth to nineteenth centuries), Daoism was put on the defensive by the triumphant Neo-Confucians. Its clergy was tightly controlled by the state through the highly regulated issuance of ordination

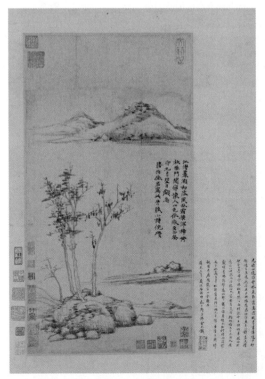

This painting, *Wind among the Trees on the Riverbank* by Ni Zan (1306–1374), is best known for the quietude and balance in nature it expresses. China, Yuan Dynasty (1271–1368), dated 1363.

certificates. Though individual emperors might have supported Daoism, as evidenced by the printing of the complete *Daozang* in 1445, as a religious tradition it was overshadowed by Confucianism. While the Confucian elite grudgingly acknowledged the "philosophic" brilliance of the *Laozi* and *Zhuangzi*, they regarded organized Daoist groups as nothing more than a degenerated form of pristine, original Daoism. Organized Daoism was marginalized as superstition, unworthy of elite attention. This contempt for Daoism continued beyond the imperial period, was intensified in the early twentieth century, and was adopted as official policy under the Communist regime since 1949.

Daoism Today Because of elite hostility and government neglect, if not active persecution, Daoism as a religious tradition has fared generally very poorly in the modern period. While the intellectuals still recognized the philosophic ideas in the *Laozi* and the *Zhuangzi* as properly Daoist, they totally ignored the meditative exercises and amazing magical powers of the Daoist seekers of perfection discussed in the two texts, along with the entire corpus of the *Daozang*, the Daoist canon. Daoism was lumped with shamanic popular religion and viewed with disdain. The New

Culture movement of the 1910s and 1920s regarded both Daoism and Confucianism as unwelcome remnants of China's feudal past. The Cultural Revolution (1966–1976) that did so much damage to Confucianism also proved devastating to Daoism. Many historic Daoist shrines and sites were destroyed or sacrilegiously defaced, while all performances of Daoist rituals and liturgies were banned. For all intents and purposes Daoism as an organized religion ceased to exist in mainland China. Yet the tradition survived, if only barely, outside China among Chinese communities in Taiwan, Hong Kong, and Southeast Asia. Since the late 1970s, however, a Daoist revival of sorts has begun. Daoist ceremonies are once again openly observed in China, and a new generation of Daoist priests has been trained to carry on the tradition and to rebuild the shrines. Academic study of Daoism, primarily by Japanese and French scholars at the beginning, and now joined by Americans and Chinese themselves, has created new understanding of the tradition both from the point of view of doctrines and

This painting of the poet Li Bo (Li Bai, 701–762) shows him as a Daoist immortal.

practices. Some of the scholars have actually become ordained Daoist priests of either the Celestial Master or the Complete Perfection tradition to arrive at more accurate and authoritative interpretations of Daoism. In recent decades, *qigong* exercises (meditation and respiration techniques designed to enhance the body's vital energy), martial arts, and food therapy are popular both in China and abroad. Though not strictly associated with organized Daoism, such phenomena are nevertheless in part based on and inspired by Daoist views on nature and the human body. Respective Daoist practices in breath circulation, gymnastics, and dietetics, discussed in more detail later in this chapter, attest to the continued relevance of Daoism in the modern world.

THE TEACHINGS OF CONFUCIANISM AND DAOISM

In the preceding pages, we have conducted a rather lengthy examination of the history of Confucianism and Daoism. It is now time to turn to another dimension of the two—their beliefs and teachings. To put their beliefs in proper context, the content of the ancient religion that preceded them needs to be examined more closely.

Ancient Chinese Religious Views

The *Book of Changes* represents the earliest expression of the Chinese religious mindset. It conveys a worldview that has been described as "organic,"[6] meaning that every single component of the cosmos belongs to an organic whole and that all the component parts interact with one another in a continuous self-generating process. Unlike the foundational texts of most religions, the *Book of Changes* does not include a creation myth. This absence of a creation myth may be attributed to the dominance of the spirit of ancestor worship in China since antiquity. When most of the spirits who populate the supernatural world are former human beings who share the same qualities as the living, the sense of mystery and "otherness" of a creator being may be difficult to envision. Instead, from an original state of "undifferentiated chaos" (*hundun*)[7], two polar yet complementary energies known as *qi* ("breath," "energy," or "force") emerged. One is called *yang* (literally the south-facing, sunny side of a mountain), and the other *yin* (the north-facing, shady side of a mountain). Representing all binary entities and concepts (such as day and night, male and female, hot and cold), *yang* and *yin* interact and alternate ceaselessly to form a continuum or spectrum, generating the myriad elements of the creation.

In this kind of a worldview, nothing exists outside the cosmos; therefore, everything is subject to its operating principles. Even the aforementioned *Tian*, along with its complementary counterpart *Di* (earth), is part of the cosmos, not external to it. This absence of a "wholly other" creator in the early Chinese cosmological myth has very significant implications. That is, the classical Chinese view uses the metaphor of procreation or giving birth, not creation or fashioning something out of nothing, for the creation of the universe. A biological link exists between the procreator and progeny, for they share the same genetic attributes and are therefore no different qualitatively from each other. In the Chinese view, the lack of any notion of a wholly transcendent ultimate cause makes it difficult to produce the idea of an almighty god preceding and existing outside of creation. Correspondingly, the notion of an active evil dedicated to undermining the plans of a supposedly benevolent creator is similarly absent in the Chinese cosmological view. In other words, no frighteningly personified devil competes with a benign god to win the hearts and minds of humans. In this world without sin (at least sin as understood by the Abrahamic faiths of Judaism, Christianity, and Islam), humanity is released from an acute sense of guilt. Instead, harmony and balance are good and preferable. Disharmony and imbalance are not.

The cosmic tango of *yang* and *yin*, spontaneous and unceasing, is manifested in the ***wuxing*** ("five elemental phases"), the five paradigmatic states of metal, wood, fire, water, and soil. These five states or elements correlate with many categories in nature. In the human body, they correspond to the Five Viscera (heart, liver, spleen, lungs, and kidneys). In the sky they are represented by the Five Planets (Venus, Jupiter, Mercury, Mars, and Saturn), and then there are the Five Colors (red, blue, yellow, white, and black) and the Five Flavors (sour, sweet, bitter, spicy, and salty). These five states are at the same time mutually nurturing and mutually destructive. Water sustains wood, wood feeds fire, fire reduces everything back to ashes (soil), soil produces ores (metal), and ores melt into liquid (water). Conversely, water douses fire, fire melts metal, metal chops down wood, wood draws nutrients from soil, and soil blocks water. Ultimately, like the swinging of the pendulum, what drives this dynamic process is the principle of alternation: when one extreme is reached, it reverts to the other. Such is the way the cosmos operates.

Notice that the two halves of the circle are not perfectly divided right down the middle. Instead, they are interlocked and mutually penetrating. Each half also contains the seed of the other. Thus the entire cosmos is involved in a ceaseless flow of alternation and change.

Human Body and Soul As fundamental energies of the cosmos that constantly interact with each other, *yin* and *yang* make solid matter when they coalesce and remain immaterial when diffused. Thus their interplay can manifest in coarse and materialistic things, as well as in subtle and spiritual entities. It is in this context that the constitution of human beings can be understood.

All humans have a physical body, seen as the corporal manifestation of the interplay between *yin* and *yang*. But all humans also have an immaterial aspect, subdivided into *hun* and *po*. *Hun* reflects the *yang* component, being light, pure, and upward-rising. *Po*, on the other hand, indicates *yin*, being heavy, turgid, and downward-sinking. *Hun* and *po*, introduced into the physical body when the fetus is gestating, together make up the spiritual aspect of the individual. For lack of a better term, they constitute the soul matter of the individual. As long as they stay with the human body, with only short and temporary absences during the dream state or when in a coma, the individual remains alive. At death, however, *hun* departs from the body permanently, rising skyward, and *po* settles down on earth alongside the interred and decomposing body. Both *hun* and *po* eventually dissipate and become reconfigured in different proportions to form future beings.

The Spiritual World of Gods and Ghosts After death, as long as the energy remains to keep the current identity of *hun* and *po* intact, the spirit of the deceased lingers. Though only a pale shadow of its former self, the spirit of one who dies at a ripe old age and is properly cared for by the descendants may become **shen**, a benevolent power that protects and brings benefit to the living. On the other hand, the spirit of one who dies tragically or prematurely, and one who is not given a suitable burial or sacrifice, will become **gui**, a vengeful and malevolent ghost who visits disasters on people. *Shen* is a generic term for all kindly deities and gods whose power and efficacy are sought to fulfill people's wishes for health, wealth, progeny, and status. Conversely, *gui* refers to all spiteful ghouls, demons, and ogres who wreak havoc in people's lives. Motivated both by longing and fear, the Chinese from the ancient times to the present strive to cultivate good relations with both *shen* and *gui*. This, of course, is in addition to their primary obligation in the worship of their ancestors. The line of demarcation between the spirits and humans thus cannot be sharply drawn. Humans can indeed possess or exhibit qualities that in other cultures or beliefs may be considered spiritual, or even divine.

The Teachings of Confucius

Confucius inherited the entire package of ancient Chinese religious views discussed in the preceding pages. This is made clear in the single most important work that contains his main teaching, the *Lunyu*. Literally meaning "comments and sayings"

The yin-yang symbol best represents the Chinese religious mentality. It portrays a bipolar and complementary view of the cosmos that assumes mutual dependency and interpenetration of opposites rather than mutual exclusivity and incompatibility. This worldview recognizes differences, but also harmony among the differences.

but customarily translated as the *Analects*, this text is believed to have been compiled by Confucius' leading disciples after his death. It serves as a record of statements he had made, exchanges with students he had conducted, and even remarks some of the students had offered. As such it is an authoritative source for the examination of Confucius' teaching. Despite the possibility of later interpolations and the apparent lack of organization, the extant twenty "Books" of the *Analects*, taken as a whole, reflect a coherent picture of Confucius' major concerns and aspirations. A careful analysis of the content of the *Analects* shows that while accepting many of the preexisting cosmological notions and religious beliefs of ancient China, Confucius and his immediate followers offered many new insights and creative interpretations regarding them. In the end, these "comments and sayings" contributed to the formation of a distinct tradition with unique views on humanity and its relationship with the divine. The following are some of the most notable topics addressed in the *Analects*.

The Primacy of *Tian*   As you recall from the previous section on the life and times of Confucius, he lived during the last decades of the Zhou regime, a period of unmistakable dynastic decline. The supposedly perfect order established by the Zhou founders was tearing at the seams, and society was in turmoil. The notion of the possible revocation and transfer of *tianming* could not be too far from the minds of the weak Zhou ruler, the ambitious feudal lords serving under him, and the "men of service" who were seeking new opportunities for social and political advancement. Confucius was no exception. What he has conveyed in the *Analects* is a reinvigorated and fresh understanding of *Tian*, *Tianming*, and their relationship to humans, especially the moral elite.

The *Tian* of early Zhou was an august and aloof divine power whose interaction with human beings was largely confined to the ruler who alone could worship it. By contrast, the *Tian* of Confucius was a far more intimate religious and ethical entity. It had a conscious will that no longer reached out to the Zhou rulers and the various feudal lords (as it had done in the past), but to moral and noble men of diverse backgrounds so that they might revive a moral order on the verge of total collapse. Confucius saw himself among this moral vanguard and encouraged his followers to join him in the task of redeeming this world. Confucius thus understood *Tian* as a cosmic moral will that intervened in human affairs in order to maintain and protect an ideal human order. *Tian* accomplished this by endowing certain worthy individuals with a historic mission to restore this order, which had been established at the beginning of each of the known dynastic regimes of Xia (a legendary period not yet confirmed by archaeology), Shang, and Zhou.

Tian's message to the moral elite is not verbal or revelatory. Unlike the Biblical God or the Qur'anic Allah, *Tian* silently manifests itself in the course of the seasons and in the records of human events to allow perceptive individuals to detect the full content of its command. Once the individual moral person firmly understands that imperative, a special relationship with *Tian* becomes possible. That person feels that *Tian* "knows" him and that he in turn has direct access to *Tian*.[8] He becomes an obedient mouthpiece through which *Tian*'s message will be spread, resulting hopefully in a general uplifting of society. Various passages in the *Analects* attest to this Confucian faith in the primacy and imperative of *Tian*. The following are particularly illustrative.

TIAN IN THE ANALECTS

A border official from the town of Yi requested an audience with the Master. . . . After emerging from the audience, he remarked [to the Master's disciples], "The world has long been without the ideal Way. *Tian* intends to use your Master like a wooden clapper for a bell [to awaken the world]"
—Analects *3:24*

When Huan Tui, the Minister of War of the principality of Song, tried to kill Confucius (who was visiting), Confucius exclaimed, "It is *Tian* who has endowed me with virtue. What harm can Huan Tui do to me?"
—Analects *7:23*

When under siege in the principality of Kuang, the Master declared, "With King Wen (founder of Zhou Dynasty) dead, does not civilization rest now on me? If *Tian* intends to have civilization destroyed, those who come after me will have nothing. But if *Tian* does not intend to have civilization destroyed, then what can the men of Kuang do to me?"
—Analects *9:5*

The Prime Minister asked Zigong, "Your Master is a sage, is he not? So how come he is skilled in so many menial tasks?" Zigong answered, "Surely *Tian* has ordained that he be a sage. But it has also given him many talents."
—Analects *9:6*

The Master lamented, "Alas, there is no one who understands me." Zigong said, "How is it that no one understands you?" The Master continued, "I do not complain against *Tian*, nor do I blame my fellow men. I study what is mundane to reach what is transcendent. If there is anyone who understands me, it is *Tian!*"
—Analects *14:35*

The Master sighed, "If I could only give up speech!" Zigong (a disciple) said, "If the Master did not speak, how would we disciples receive any guidance?" The Master replied, "What does *Tian* ever say? Yet the four seasons are in motion and the myriad things are alive. What does *Tian* ever say!"
—Analects *17:19*

What these passages show collectively is the centrality of *Tian* in Confucius' thinking. *Tian* is clearly the highest religious authority as well as ultimate reality in the *Analects*. The *Analects* suggests a conscious *Tian* who "intends" human beings to have civilization in the form of a perfect order. To that end it reaches out to a few noble individuals. It does so not by direct revelation but through the quiet natural course of nature as well as through human events, and it charges those individuals with the mission to sustain and protect this civilization. This is *Tian*'s mandate or imperative (*ming*). Such is the way Confucius reconceived the notion of *Tianming* as an individual mission and a personal commitment to the monumental task of saving and preserving civilization. *Tianming*, to Confucius, is no longer an endowment of dynastic power and legitimacy for the political power-holders but a call to moral perfection and close relation with the divine ultimate for the spiritual elite.

Some scholars of Confucian studies have noted the "prophetic voice" in Confucius and his followers. William Theodore de Bary of Columbia University is a forceful advocate of this aspect of the Confucian tradition. His observation is worth quoting:

> "Prophetic" I use here to indicate an extraordinary access to and revelation of truth not vouchsafed to everyone, which . . . gives new meaning, significance, and urgency to certain cultural values or scriptural texts. Confucian tradition does not customarily speak of such a revelation as "supernatural," but it has an unpredictable, wondrous quality manifesting the divine creativity of Heaven [*Tian*].[9]

To be sure, unlike Moses or Muhammad, Confucius did not see himself as the messenger of a personal God; nevertheless, he criticized the authorities of his time and condemned their departure from the normative ideal by appealing to *Tian*. He invoked his own power as someone who, because of his endowment with *Tian*'s command, had that right to do so. In effect Confucius changed the very nature of *Tianming*. It became the self-ascribed duty of the moral individual to serve as mouthpiece to a *Tian* that did not speak itself, to be inspired and motivated by the sense of mission, indeed of commission, by *Tian*. The men of virtue, the *Analects* insists, must be "strong and resolute, for their burden of responsibility is heavy and the journey is long. Taking upon themselves the burden of humaneness, is that not heavy? Stopping only at death, is that not long?" (*Analects* 8:7). This is truly a revolutionary and radical claim, not unlike that of the prophets of ancient Israel. Just as YHWH turned away from the corrupt rulers in favor of the prophets outside the existing power structure for his direct communication with the people of Israel (Chapter 10), *Tian* in the *Analects* spurned the power-holders of a decadent age and instead entrusted the awesome responsibility of protecting the ideals of the human order to a nonruler like Confucius.

The Content of *Tian*'s Imperative—the *Dao* Just what is this message that *Tian* seeks to convey through the spiritual elite? It is the *Dao*, the Way, or the ideal human order that the sage kings of the past established in accordance with *Tian*'s command but that is now in decline. In other words, it is an achievable and universal order that had existed in the past and can be recaptured in the present. In the *Analects*, the precarious state in which this ideal human order found itself is lamented throughout the text. Confucius often complains in the *Analects* that the "*Dao* is not in practice" (*Analects* 5:7), or the "*Dao* does not prevail in the world" (*Analects* 16:2). What he means by the *Dao* is the total normative socio-political-ethical order with the prescriptions for proper ritual behavior publicly as well as the moral rectitude privately. However, when men in power were incapable or unwilling to uphold this order, as was the case during Confucius's time, men of virtue and uprightness must take it upon themselves to protect and preserve this ideal or civilization would be doomed. It is for this reason that Confucius regards the search for and embodiment of the *Dao* to be the ultimate, paramount task in life. He proclaims: "If I can hear the *Dao* in the morning, I will die contented that evening!" (*Analects* 4:8).

As *Dao* represents the entire normative human order, Confucius focuses on certain key aspects for detailed discussion: *ren* and *li*.

Ren Perhaps the single most important article of faith held by Confucius is **ren** (benevolence, humaneness, virtue)—the kernel of humanity that exists in all human beings. It is the entity implanted in humans by *Tian* that separates them from the animals. It is the germ of moral consciousness that enables human beings to become fully actualized noble beings. It is the root and the foundation of the perfect human order, and at the same time it also represents the highest state that human beings can accomplish. Etymologically, it points to the interrelatedness among humans, for in writing it is a combination of the character for person (人) and the character for the number two (二), signaling that it is in a "state of person-to-person" that *ren* (仁) can be enacted. Throughout the *Analects* the importance of *ren* in Confucius's teaching is evident. Many of his leading disciples ask him about it, and he gives various answers to drive home the idea that *ren* is all-rounded and multifaceted. Indeed, *ren* is so fundamental a concept that Confucius allows the giving of one's life in order to preserve it (*Analects* 15:9), implying that a life without *ren* is meaningless.

People who can preserve and develop their *ren* can be entrusted to carry out the imperative of *Tian*. "When the root is firmly established, the *Dao* will grow. Filial piety and brotherly deference, are they not the basis of *ren*?" (*Analects* 1:2). It is the cultivation and nurturing of this root of moral propensity that constitutes the actualization of the *Dao*. Note that Confucius here is not asserting the perfection of all human beings. Rather, he is advocating their perfectibility through self-effort. This inner moral disposition needs to be expanded and developed before it can sustain the *Dao*. What is remarkable about this view is the belief that this moral potentiality is not a monopoly of those in power, or those of noble birth, but is in fact possessed by all humans. This accessibility makes it possible for someone like Confucius to teach others how to achieve *ren* and how to become men of virtue themselves.

Moral authority, in other words, is no longer merely the province of kings and feudal lords. It belongs, rather, to all who aspire to be good. Furthermore, this goodness is exemplified by filial piety (**xiao**) and brotherly deference, as well as by a sense of dutifulness (**zhong**) and reciprocity (**shu**). Filial piety honors one's indebtedness to the family elders and to the parents, while brotherly deference acknowledges the natural hierarchy in birth order among siblings. Thus, it is within the family that humans first acquire their moral education. The family is precisely the domain where authority and obligation are exercised and performed through natural sentiments and close blood ties. It is the first school of ethics in which traits or virtue are taught and nurtured. Outside the family, one should interact with other people according to the principle of exerting one's utmost effort in fulfilling one's diverse roles in society. This effort arises from one's sense of dutifulness, and "not doing unto others what one does not want done unto oneself" (*Analects* 15:24), which is the height of reciprocity. One of Confucius' principal disciples, Master Zeng, concludes that "the *Dao* of the Master is nothing more than dutifulness and reciprocity," for the two form the "single thread" that runs through the entirety of the Master's teaching (*Analects* 4:15). *Ren* is thus the entire human moral repertoire, which, when developed and enacted, will produce harmony in the human world and in the relationship that humans maintain with *Tian*.

Li   Ren alone, however, is not enough to enable one to preserve the *Dao*. This inner potentiality for goodness and benevolence has to be manifested by an external performance of prescribed behavior within the family, the community, the entire human society, and the spiritual world beyond. This is referred to as ***li*** (rites, rituals, normative behavior) in the *Analects*, a word that in ancient China meant only the sacrificial and behavioral rituals of the kings and the nobles. The ideograph for *li* shows a sacred ritual vessel, indicating that the etymological origin of the word has something to do with sacrifice to the gods or the ancestors (禮). In Confucius' understanding of the term, *li* encompasses the entirety of proper human conduct vis-à-vis other human beings, dead ancestors, and the spirits. In a thought-provoking work published some thirty years ago, the scholar Herbert Fingarette proposed that *li* be regarded as "holy rite" or "sacred ceremony."[10] In Fingarette's analysis, human beings live in an interlocking world of roles. Those roles function smoothly and harmoniously only when the people involved behave in a sincere, dignified, and effortless way. This requires a learned pattern of behavior that, when combined with the moral propensity present in each individual, will produce a "magical power" in human relationships as well as in relations with the spirits. Once a ritual gesture is initiated in the proper ceremonial context and performed with grace and sincerity, the magical result of goodwill, trust, and harmony will follow. This is the irresistible and invisible power of ritual itself.

The *Analects* is most optimistic about the efficacy of *li*: "If a ruler's comportment is correct, he will be obeyed even if he does not give any order" (*Analects* 13:6). "What did Shun [the sage-ruler] do? He merely made himself reverent and took his proper ritual position facing south, that is all" (*Analects* 15:5). Such magical potency, however, is not limited to the kings and lords. In a famous response to his favorite student's question about *ren*, Confucius states: "Restraining oneself and returning to *li*, this is *ren*" (*Analects* 12:1). The humanity of *all* human beings is expressed by their performance of rituals and observance of proper etiquette. Only through ritualized interaction with others and with the spirits can one realize one's full potential as a human being. The mastery and performance of *li*, then, is in fact a "process of humanization."[11]

Li transforms an ordinary human being into an exemplary model of perfect virtue. *Li* is brought to life by the authentic, model human who infuses it with the spirit of *ren*. *Li* is the externalization of *ren*. Conversely, *ren* is the inner source of *li*. This is why Confucius asks rhetorically: "A man who is not *ren*, what has he to do with *li?*" (*Analects* 3:3). Prescriptions for *li* have to be learned and mastered through a rigorous process of self-cultivation. It is often accompanied by such refined cultural pursuits as poetry and music. In fact, Confucius instructs his followers to "find inspiration in poetry, take one's stand in *li*, and achieve perfection through music" (*Analects* 8:8).

Junzi Confucius uses the term **junzi** (the noble man, the man of virtue, the superior man) for the noble *ru* on whose shoulders rests the burden of reviving and preserving the *Dao*. This is Confucius at his most creative and revolutionary in the usage of terminology. Originally used to refer to the scions of feudal rulers, *junzi* in Confucius' refashioning comes to mean men of moral rectitude. From someone highborn, *junzi* becomes someone high-minded. From those of noble birth, *junzi* now means those of noble worth. They are the prophet-like individuals discussed earlier who, though holding no political office or having no privileged positions, nevertheless heed *Tian's* call. They undertake the most arduous task of implementing *Tian's Dao* in the human world. The *Analects* puts the issue most plainly: "Without knowing the imperative of *Tian*, one cannot be a *junzi*" (20:3).

The *junzi* has three traits: "They are *ren*, thus they do not have anxieties. They are wise, thus they are not perplexed. They are courageous, thus they do not have fear" (*Analects* 14:28). Their self-cultivation and constant vigilance have earned them a power (*de*) similar to that possessed by the ancient sage rulers. It is a charismatic, non-coercive, potent influence that both inspires and persuades, and coaxes and shames, people into doing what is right. In the *Analects* Confucius confidently declares: "The *de* of the *junzi* is like wind, while that of the common people is like grass. When the wind blows over the grass, the grass cannot help but bend in the direction of the wind" (12:19). The epitome of the *junzi* is the sage (**shengren** or simply **sheng** 聖), the rarest of human beings who are perfect in their moral standing and kingly in their worldly accomplishments. The traditional Chinese character for sage contains three components: ear, mouth, and ruler (耳, 口, 王).

The sage is someone who hears or listens to the Way of *Tian*, discloses and manifests it through the mouth, and acts in the capacity of the ancient ruler whose job it is to link up the three realms of Heaven, Earth, and Humankind. Through auditory reception and oral transmission of the wisdom of *Tian*, the sage serves as the intermediary between it and humanity. Thus the sage is decidedly a religious figure, a saintly person who is at once a messenger of *Tian* to the human world and an exemplar of human perfection in the eyes of *Tian*.

The Religious Vision of the *Analects*   Taken as a whole, the vision of the *Analects* offers an amazingly clear picture of Confucius' ultimate concern. The religious aspect of this Confucian vision is unmistakable. It has been justly pointed out that, unlike many other religious figures, Confucius envisaged no escape from the world and human society, nor did he insist on ascetic self-denial as a precondition for spiritual progress. In a similar vein, Confucius did not consider concern with the afterlife or with the spirits of primary importance. The following exchange between him and his student Zilu on that subject is famous: "Zilu asked about serving ghosts and spirits. The Master said, 'When we are not yet able to serve fellow humans, why worry about serving the ghosts and spirits?' 'What about death?' [Zilu persisted]. 'When we do not yet know enough about life, why worry about death?' [the Master replied]" (*Analects* 11:12).

Then in what sense is the Confucian teaching religious? Here the definition of religion discussed in Chapter 1 becomes relevant. Confucius has an abiding faith in the transcendent ultimate *Tian*. He feels an intimate relationship with it. He has a keen awareness of its command (*ming*) given to the moral and spiritual elites (*junzi*) to create the ideal human order (*Dao*). He firmly believes in the *Tian*-endowed human capacity for perfection and genuine humanity (*ren*) through self-cultivation, and enthusiastically participates in sacrificial rituals and familial and social rites (*li*). These are all components of his religious outlook. To be sure, this religiosity does not express itself in faith in a personal God and the need for salvation through divine grace. Rather, it distinguishes itself as a form of "this-worldly transcendentalism." It treats the "secular as sacred," and it imparts deeply religious meaning to participation in the mundane. Thus, it expresses a different mode of religiousness. For this reason, it has been paradoxically labeled a "humanistic religion" and a "religious humanism."[12] The distinction between the human and the divine, clearly drawn in the Abrahamic traditions, is not found here. For Confucius, the ultimate goal for humans is to heed the instruction of *Tian* by transforming themselves from potential goodness to actual goodness. This process of transformation toward the absolute is the religious nature of the Confucian teaching, and it is right there in the *Analects*.

The *Mencius*   Next to the *Analects*, the *Mencius* is significant as a Confucian scriptural text. Seeing himself as the direct successor to Confucius, Mencius is immodest in his aspiration. Unlike Confucius, who does not regard himself as a sage—a title he reserves only for the few legendary rulers in ancient China—Mencius not only boldly declares his predecessor's sagehood but also insists on his own as well. Indeed, he considers every human being a potential sage, as he deems that each possesses all the innate qualities to become one. It is based on that assumption that he asserts the intrinsic goodness in human nature, which he compares to the natural tendency of water to flow downward (*Mencius* 6A, 2:2). This is Mencius' fundamental article of faith.

Identifying four "sprouts of morality" in all humans—the inborn sentiments of commiseration (not bearing to witness the suffering of others), shame, deference and yielding, and sense of right and wrong—Mencius proclaims them to be the roots of benevolence (*ren*), righteousness (*yi*), propriety (*li*), and wisdom (*zhi*), respectively. With this belief as his religious premise, he constructs a logical progression from moral cultivation to the ultimate attainment of divine spirituality. He states, "That which is sought after is called 'good.' To have it in oneself is called 'true.' To possess it fully is called 'beautiful,' while making it shine forth with brilliance is called 'great.' To be great and be able to transform others is called 'sage.' To be sage and be beyond understanding by others is called 'spiritually divine.'" (*Mencius* 7B, 25). Through our moral progress, Mencius suggests, we can become not only good, true, beautiful, and great, but also sagely and ultimately divine. With utter conviction, then, he maintains, "Probing one's heart/mind to the utmost, one will know one's nature. Knowing one's nature, one will know *Tian*. To preserve one's heart/mind and nurture one's nature is to put one in the service of *Tian*" (*Mencius* 7A, 1:1). Once one has embodied the moral imperatives of *Tian*, Mencius reasons, one will find all other concerns secondary. In one of his most celebrated statements, Mencius declares: "I like fish, and I also like bear's paw. If I cannot have both, I will give up fish and keep the bear's paw. Life is what I desire, but so is righteousness. If I cannot have both, I will give up life but cling to righteousness" (*Mencius* 6A, 10:1). With morality as his ultimate concern, Mencius is willing to sacrifice his own life in order to preserve it. This is certainly reminiscent of Confucius' commitment to benevolence (*ren*), for the preservation of which he too is willing to suffer death. This is demonstrative of the spirit of the martyr and a deeply held religious sentiment.

The *Great Learning* and the *Doctrine of the Mean*   The remaining two texts of the Four Books, completing the Confucian religious corpus, are the *Great Learning* and the *Doctrine of the Mean*, supposedly compiled by two of Confucius' prominent students. Both are chapters from the *Book of Rituals* that have been excerpted as independent texts because of their religious significance. The former refers to learning about what is of primary importance. It prescribes a practical step-by-step roadmap for self-cultivation, starting with individual inquiries and ending with the transformation of humanity as a whole. Listing eight steps in personal cultivation, the *Great Learning* outlines a sequence of individual and social effort made to manifest "illustrious virtue," "love the people," and reach the "ultimate good," which is nothing short of the *Tian*-ordained perfect world order. Thus learning involves far more than the acquisition of knowledge, but is actually an ethical-religious program of personal and communal transformation.

The *Doctrine of the Mean* begins with a bold declaration: "What *Tian* has ordained is called human nature. Following this nature is called the *Dao*. Cultivating the *Dao* is called teaching" (*Doctrine of the Mean* 1:1). These three statements articulate the fundamental Confucian articles of faith, representing what Confucianism regards as self-evidently true. The text asserts that humans are born with a benign nature imparted by *Tian*, the ultimate religious authority. This nature provides them with the inner strength to reach their fullest potential as perfect beings. Furthermore, when extended beyond the individual, this human nature can bring about an ideal socio-political-ethical order, the actualization of which is the purpose of education. The text further maintains that the real possibility for achieving perfect goodness exists because of the special relationship between human beings and *Tian*. But human endeavor and devotion to the task are essential to the accomplishment of the goal. Nothing is going to happen spontaneously, and the ultimate prize will not be handed to humans without their unwavering and sustained effort. There is therefore a logical progression from self-generating moral effort to the perfection of the faithful and the world around them: "The *junzi* [noble person] cannot avoid not cultivating his person. Thinking of cultivating his person, he cannot neglect serving his parents. Thinking of serving his parents, he may not avoid knowing other humans. Thinking of knowing other humans, he cannot ignore knowledge of *Tian*" (*Doctrine of the Mean* 20:7). It is clear that human beings must fully engage themselves with others in order to actualize their genuine humanity and divine potential.

There are five cardinal human relations for such interaction—three within the family and two outside of the family : that between father and son, husband and wife, elder and younger brothers, ruler and subject, and friends. The attainment of the ultimate religious goal is not the result of a hermitic and lonely search for the divine, but the end product of a comprehensive engagement in the familial and social context. It is the entire human community that provides the setting for the religious quest. The *Doctrine of the Mean* offers a climactic conclusion to the process of self-cultivation:

> Only the most authentic and genuine person can fully develop his nature. Able to fully develop his nature, he can then thoroughly understand the nature of other people. Able to fully understand the nature of other people, he can develop the nature of things. Able to fully develop the nature of things, he can assist in the transforming and nourishing process of *Tian* and *Di*. When he assists in the transforming and nourishing process of *Tian* and *Di*, he forms a trinity with them!
> —Doctrine of the Mean *22:1*

This euphoric assurance of the final outcome of human moral cultivation is breathtaking in its grandeur. Not only does the person who realizes his own nature to the full become a paradigm of genuine humanity, he actually becomes a "co-equal" with *Tian* and *Di* through his participation in their nurture and sustenance of the myriad things. Forming a trinity with the ultimate numinous entity in the cosmos is without a doubt the highest accomplishment for any religious seeker in the Confucian mode.

In the preceding paragraphs, we have analyzed the content and the religiosity of the Four Books. These four texts neatly annotate the Neo-Confucian goal of "*neisheng waiwang*"—inner moral cultivation and external skillful management of society and state. This is believed to reflect the original vision of Confucius, namely, to pursue a personal relationship with the ultimate reality through moral improvement, culminating in an ordering of society and state in accordance with the Way ordained by *Tian*.

This religious mission is best expressed by a famous Neo-Confucian scholar by the name of Zhang Zai (1020–1077):

> To establish the mind of *Tian* and *Di*
> To inculcate an understanding of [*Tian's*] command (*ming*) for the multitudes
> To revive and perpetuate the teachings of the sages of the past
> To provide peace and stability for all future generations

This is indeed the religious aspiration of Confucianism in a nutshell!

Confucianism and Women

Like the proverbial elephant in the room, the issue of Confucianism and sexism needs to be addressed. Despite its lofty religious teaching, Confucianism is not without its shortcomings. As we have already pointed out in the "History" section of this chapter, Confucianism has been portrayed as a sexist, patriarchal ideology responsible for the oppression of women in China by its critics since the beginning of the twentieth century. The insidious Chinese practices of footbinding, concubinage, disallowance of women-initiated divorce, prohibition against remarriage, and encouragement of widow suicide have all been blamed on Confucianism.

To a certain extent, this blame is justified. To begin with, Confucius himself had shown little regard for specifically female concerns. Instead, on one isolated occasion in the *Analects*, he compared women to the "petty people" who would be contemptuous of you when you were on familiar terms with them and who would whine when you stayed aloof (17:25). In the Han Dynasty, the Confucian elders clearly deemed women inferior to men, just as *yin* was regarded as inferior to *yang*. Subsequently, as the official, orthodox teaching of the Chinese state and society for over 2,000 years, Confucianism cannot escape its responsibility of being the underpinning of the oppressive Chinese political and social structure.

However, as the discussion of the Confucian teaching in this section has shown, this reductionist view of Confucianism as no more than a rationalization of hierarchical exploitation and rigid gender oppression overlooks the very intellectual and religious dynamism of Confucianism as a teaching of human improvement and self-cultivation. Confucianism as a state orthodoxy whose central purpose is social control and political manipulation is indeed incompatible with modern values. However, Confucianism as an ethical and religious teaching aiming at human transformation and even sanctification can easily be made gender neutral to serve as a worthy partner in the feminist endeavor to create an egalitarian and harmonious world. "Confucian feminism" may not be an oxymoronic label at all.[13]

Teachings and Beliefs of Daoism

We have pointed out earlier that Daoism evolved out of the same ancient Chinese religious mindset as Confucianism did. But instead of regarding *Tian* as the Absolute Ultimate, as the Confucians do, Daoists from the beginning hold *Dao* to be supreme.

It should be recalled that the term *Dao* is also central to the Confucian tradition. However, the Daoists articulate a very different understanding of the *Dao*. It is this alternative apprehension of the *Dao* that serves as the point of departure for their entirely different mode of religious experience from that of the Confucians. Let us begin with the basic Daoist texts.

The *Laozi* The eighty-one-chapter *Laozi*, also known as the *Daodejing* (*The Scripture of the Way and Its Potent Manifestation*), is undoubtedly the most translated and most popular Chinese text in the West. Virtually all the different movements and lineages within Daoism regard this work as the founding scripture of the tradition. Yet its authorship and date of composition remain uncertain. Much ink has been spilled to determine the broad outlines of the biography of its reputed author Laozi, the "Old Master," yet there is not even consensus among scholars that an individual by that name actually existed at all—or, if he had, what years he lived. There are indications that Laozi may be a composite figure, a group of "old masters" who represents the ideal Daoist sage.

In contrast to the Confucian *Dao* being the ideal ethical-social-political order ordained by *Tian* for human beings, the *Dao* of the *Laozi* antedates *Tian* and acts as the basis of the natural order. Here *Dao* is the primordial entity that exists in an undifferentiated state prior to the coming into being of the myriad things, including *Tian* and *Di*, which now stand for nothing more than nature itself. The lofty primacy of the Confucian *Tian* is supplanted by the nebulous *Dao* of the *Laozi*, as indicated by the following celebrated passage:

> There was something undifferentiated and yet complete, which existed before
>   *Tian* and *Di*
> Soundless and formless, it depends on nothing and does not change
> It operates everywhere and does not stop
> It may be regarded as the "Mother of the world"
> I do not know its name; I call it *Dao*
>   —Laozi, *Chap. 25*

In one broad stroke, the entire Confucian cosmological scheme is turned upside down. It is *Dao*, not *Tian*, that gives birth, like a mother, to the myriad things. It is *Dao*, not *Tian*, that serves as the primal source of the cosmos. Echoing the cosmogonic view of the *Book of Changes*, the *Laozi* gives an even terser summary of the generating process of the cosmos:

> The *Dao* gives birth to the One [Being, Existence]
> The One brings forth the Two [*Yin* and *Yang*]
> The Two give rise to the Three [*Tian, Di*, and Humans]
> The Three engender the Ten Thousand Things [world of multiplicity and diversity]
>   —Laozi, *Chap. 42*

Again, the primacy of the *Dao* as the procreator of the entire universe and everything that is in it is unequivocally asserted here. As the ground of all beings, this *Dao* is compared to a "mysterious female," "water," "infant," and "uncarved block," all alluding to the beginning of life and form. However, unlike the Confucian *Dao*, which requires superior human beings (the *junzi* [men of virtue] and the *shengren* [sages]) to exert their utmost effort to actualize its ideal design, the *Dao* of the *Laozi* can only maintain its pristine form when humans leave it alone. Thus the ideal course of action for the insightful and wise human beings is to observe **wuwei** (actions without intention) and **ziran** (natural spontaneity) in their attempt to return to the *Dao*. These two ideal approaches to life are indicative of *Laozi*'s belief in the innate perfection and completeness of the *Dao*. *Wuwei* calls for a minimalist and noninterventionist attitude in human action, while *ziran* rejects any artificiality and contrived undertaking as detrimental to human well-being. Ultimately, the *Dao* in the *Laozi* is indescribable, for it defies verbalization and precise definition. "The *Dao* that can be [verbally] expressed is not the constant *Dao*," insists the *Laozi* in its first verse. This ineffability of the *Dao* qualifies it as the numinous entity in Rudolf Otto's idea of the holy (Chapter 1).

Yet the transcendent *Dao* is, at the same time, manifested in the myriad things through its presence in them as *de*—the very "potent manifestation" of each thing. In contrast to the *de* of the Confucians, which is the charismatic power of the moral elite, the *de* of the *Laozi* points to the concrete expression of the *Dao* in all things. *De* is the "thingness" of a thing—that which makes a thing what it is. The combination of *Dao* and *de*, then, helps to bridge the gap between the transcendent and the immanent for the author(s) of the *Laozi*. The *Dao* is the transcendent ground of being, yet through its expression in the *de* of the myriad concrete things, it is also fully immanent.

The *Zhuangzi* The extant version of the *Zhuangzi* consists of thirty-three chapters divided into three sections—"Inner," "Outer," and "Miscellaneous." The first seven Inner chapters are generally believed to be the authentic writings of Zhuang Zhou, the putative author. Yet as in the case of Laozi, we have only a vague biographical account of Zhuang Zhou, and little of substance is known about him. Also, like the text *Laozi*, the book of *Zhuangzi* is an anthology of disparate ideas compiled by multiple hands. Its date of circulation is also traceable back to the late Warring States period of the late fourth and early third centuries B.C.E.

The *Zhuangzi* is overall a different kind of text from the *Laozi*. Whereas the *Laozi* is terse and aphoristic in language, the *Zhuangzi* is effusive and vividly narrative. The *Laozi* idealizes the feminine and regards the *Dao* as mother, but the *Zhuangzi* does not. The *Laozi* gives much emphasis on politics and the techniques of rulership; the *Zhuangzi* is overtly adverse to politics. The *Zhuangzi* tells stories with a witty, playful, irreverent tone that is totally absent in the *Laozi*. In terms of basic worldview and cosmological assumptions, however, the *Zhuangzi* shares much in common with the *Laozi*, hence their grouping together by later historians and bibliographers as representatives of the "School of the *Dao*."

In the *Zhuangzi*, the *Dao* is not only the ineffable transcendent entity that gives rise to all things but also the immanent core that exists in all things, from the loftiest perfected beings to the lowliest broken tiles and excrement. It is therefore omnipresent, making all things ultimately equal. As such the *Dao* transcends all polarities, dichotomies, and dualities, which the human mind is inclined to create. Hence the use of the human cognitive and rational approach to apprehend the *Dao* is futile and unproductive, as it can only be realized intuitively through the abandonment of the intellect. The mind must be able to be free from all conventional distinctions and established views, hence the advocacy of "carefree wandering" (*xiaoyao yu*) in the *Zhuangzi*. In this connection the discussion of "fasting the mind/heart" (**xinzhai**) and "sitting and forgetting" (**zuowang**) becomes pertinent, as both practices dispense with rationality and deliberative cognition in order to arrive at the perfect understanding of the *Dao*.

Mystical and Magical Elements in the *Laozi* and the *Zhuangzi* Having identified the metaphysical nature of the *Dao* as discussed by these two texts, we will next explore the impact the two have had on the later development of Daoism as a religion. The following passages from both texts are highly intriguing.

EXCERPTS FROM THE *LAOZI*

In letting our *hun* (pure, light soul matter) and *po* (turgid, heavy soul matter) embrace the One, can we keep them inseparable?
In concentrating on the *qi* (breath, vital force) and making it soft and supple, can we be like the infant? . . .
In opening and shutting our natural gates, can we be like the female?
—Laozi, *Chap. 10*

He who does not lose his proper place lasts long
He who dies but does not perish has longevity.
—Laozi, *Chap. 33*

I have heard that people who are good at preserving their lives will not encounter wild bulls or tigers when traveling on land, and will not need to protect themselves with armor when in the army. Wild bulls will find nowhere to thrust their horns, tigers will have no place to sink their claws, and weapons will find no point to insert their cutting blades. And why is that? Because in them there is no room for death.
—Laozi, *Chap. 50*

He who is richly endowed with *de* is comparable to a newborn baby: poisonous insects will not sting him, ferocious beasts will not seize him in their claws, and birds of prey will not snatch him with their talons.
—Laozi, *Chap. 55*

EXCERPTS FROM THE *ZHUANGZI*

Far away on Mt. Guye there dwells a divine person (*shenren*) whose skin is like ice and snow, and who is gentle and shy like a young girl. He does not eat the five grains; but [only] inhales the wind and drinks the dew. He ascends the clouds, mounts flying dragons, and wanders beyond the four seas. His spirit is focused, thus he saves creatures from sickness and plagues, and guarantees bountiful harvests.

—Zhuangzi, *Chap. 1*

Ziqi of Southwall sat leaning on his armrest, facing skyward and exhaled slowly—vacant and unfocused, as if bereft of his soul. [His student] Yancheng Ziyu, who stood in attendance in front of him, said, "What is this? Can the body really be made to be like withered wood? Can the heart/mind be made to be like dead ashes? The one leaning on the armrest now is not the one who leaned on it before!"

—Zhuangzi, *Chap. 2*

The ultimate person (*zhiren*) is spirit-like. Though the great marshes are set ablaze, they will not make him hot. Though the rivers and streams freeze up, they cannot chill him. Though violent thunder splits the mountains and howling gales churn the ocean, they will not frighten him. A man like this rides the clouds and mist, mounts the sun and moon, and goes beyond the four seas. Death and life have no effect on him, how much less will profit and loss?

—Zhuangzi, *Chap. 2*

The perfected individuals (*zhenren*) of old . . . could go up to high places without getting frightened, enter water without getting wet, and go into fire without feeling hot. Only those whose knowledge ascends the height of the Dao can be like this. . . . The perfected breathe with their heels, while the ordinary men breathe with their throat.

—Zhuangzi, *Chap. 6*

After three days, he could put all in the world beyond him. . . . After seven days, he could put things beyond him. . . . And after nine days, he could put life beyond him. Once he was able to put life beyond him, he could see with the clarity of morning light. Seeing with the clarity of morning light, he could discern the One. Able to discern the One, he could forget past and present. With no past and present, he could enter the realm where there is no life or death.

—Zhuangzi, *Chap. 6*

> Blowing and breathing, exhaling the old and inhaling the new, [imitating the postures of] bear strides and bird stretches—these are all undertaken for the purpose of longevity. They are pursued with fondness by people who practice gymnastic calisthenics (*daoyin*) and body nourishments (*yangxing*) in hope of [attaining the longevity] of Patriarch Peng.
> —Zhuangzi, *Chap. 15*

> The perfected individual walks under water without hindrance, treads on fire without being burnt, and moves about high places without fear.
> —Zhuangzi, *Chap. 19*

As shall be discussed later, many of the terms and concepts used in these two texts are repeated in later Daoist scriptures. The ideals of the infant and the newborn baby, the virginal and mysterious female, the divine person, the ultimate person, and the perfected person inspire the later religious Daoist yearning for, experience of, and union with the *Dao*. These exemplars of the *Dao* display amazing magical power and physical invulnerability. The two texts also make reference to numerous physical-spiritual exercises to attain that power. Taken literally, the two texts provide an inventory of the physical techniques and the magical attributes of the practitioners of the *Dao* at the time they were compiled. The practices of meditation, respiratory control, avoidance of grains and other dietetic regimens, imitation of animal movements, and calisthenics are mentioned. The effectiveness of these practices in producing clear vision, a sense of union with all things, the ability to soar into the sky and travel far and fast, a resistance to physical harm, and ultimate immortality is also asserted.

What these two texts suggest, at the very least, is that the numinous *Dao* (the holy), is accessible by potent (that is, healthy) individuals and that holiness and robust health are closely related. As described by the *Laozi* and *Zhuangzi*, the early practitioners of the *Dao* were people who, through their use of various bodily techniques, acquired powers that enabled them to experience the divine. These techniques and powers would very much become the concern of later Daoists. The later Daoist traditions that appeared since the middle of the second century C.E. were thus far from being degenerate and distorted expressions of the "philosophical" teachings of the *Laozi* and the *Zhuangzi*. Rather, they may be seen as a continuation and further expansion of a particular strand of thought in these highly eclectic and heterogeneous texts. In short, the *Laozi* and the *Zhuangzi* can be perceived as "proto-Daoist" by virtue of their distinctive view of the *Dao* and their reference to various practices and powers that anticipate those of the later organized Daoist groups.

Other Contributing Beliefs in the Daoist Tradition Though the *Laozi* and the *Zhuangzi* are the best known scriptural sources of Daoism, other texts and ideas are equally important in the formulation of the full Daoist belief system. One such text is long-overlooked brief treatise entitled *Neiye* [*Inner Cultivation*], which first appeared in the mid-fourth century B.C.E. It articulates an understanding of the human body that has a profound effect on later Daoist beliefs and practices. The text identifies three intrinsic entities within the human body—*jing* [vital essence], *qi* [life energy], and *shen* [spiritual consciousness]—and teaches a way to harness them through meditation and ritual purification for the purpose of building up one's potency. By instructing people how to exercise rigorous and conscious control over their thought, emotion, and action, the text dovetails well with the physical-spiritual practices discussed in the *Laozi* and *Zhuangzi*.

Immortality and Alchemy One major Daoist preoccupation is with the notion of **xian** (immortal or transcendent), long a folk fascination since the late fourth century B.C.E. but articulated most eloquently in the *Baopuzi* [*Master Who Embraces Simplicity*], a text authored by Ge Hong (283–343 C.E.). Central to this belief in *xian* is the conviction that physical transformation, invulnerability to disease, longevity, and ultimately immortality, can be acquired through proper diet, physical exercise, and drugs. People with the right recipe, formula, or prescription (**fangshi**) would teach these esoteric techniques and provide ready-made elixirs to those who had the financial resources and the necessary devotion to secure their services. The First Emperor of the Qin Dynasty and Emperor Wu of the Han (respectively the champions of Legalism and Confucianism as their state orthodoxy) were known for their trust in the *fangshi* and the huge expenses they were willing to incur in dispatching missions to, respectively, the Eastern Ocean and to Mt. Kunlun in the West in search of the elixirs of immortality.

Inherent in the belief in immortality are the ancient Chinese assumptions about the human body and the measures that can be taken to keep it healthy and even immortal. The Chinese believed that the human body is the microcosm that reflects the macrocosm of the cosmos. In other words, there is a direct correspondence and parallel between the human body and nature. All the myriad things in the universe are produced by the interaction of the vital energies (*qi*) of *yin* and *yang*. They also manifest the qualities of the five elemental phases (*wuxing*), follow the principle of alternation and constant return, while maintaining balance and harmony with one another. There are three central nodal points in the body called **dantian** (locations for the production of pills of immortality)—in the head, the chest, and the abdomen—connected by meridian circuits through which the *qi* (energy) flows. And, since the body is the cosmos writ small, just as there are gods and deities inhabiting the physical world outside, there are also numerous spiritual beings residing in various organs of the human body.

Based on this whole series of assumptions, the techniques of **yangsheng** (nourishing life) are developed. First mentioned in the *Zhuangzi*, *yangsheng* has the goal of refining the body so that it can overcome its earthly limitations and be in perfect harmony with the *Dao*, making it last as long as the universe. It

A Taoist immortal flying through the clouds, 1750. Portrayed is the sage mother of Dongling, who studied the Way and could cure illnesses. One day, amidst a throng wishing to thank her, she ascended to the clouds.

involves an entire spectrum of exercises, including deep meditation, controlled breathing, therapeutic gymnastics, dietary regimens, even sexual techniques. Recent excavations of Han Dynasty tombs dating back to the second century B.C.E. have retrieved numerous medical manuals that shed much light on *yangsheng* practices. They include:

1. Interior visualization (*neiguan*) through meditation to make contact with the various spirits inside the body
2. Guided breaths through the entire circuitry linking the three Fields for the refinement of the immortal pill in the form of fetal respiration (breathing like a fetus—that is, not through the lungs, *taixi*)
3. Yoga-like movements of the body and limbs to regulate the circulation of *qi* with a gymnastic routine known as *daoyin*
4. Avoidance of eating grains (*pigu*) to deny the harmful spirits within the body of their sustenance
5. "Techniques of the bed-chamber" (yoga-like sexual practices, *fangzhong shu*) which are designed, not so much to enhance pleasure of the flesh, but to increase the production of seminal fluids to be channeled up through the spine to replenish the brain (*huanjing bu'nao*)
6. Various forms of massage
7. Acupuncture

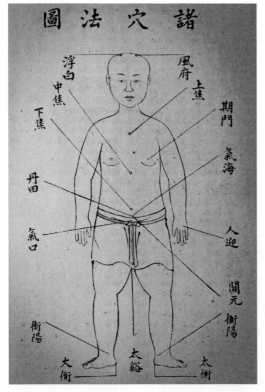

A Daoist view of the major nodal points in the human body through which the *qi* (energy) flows.

All these measures of nourishing life have been practiced by religious Daoists since the second century C.E. and are grouped under the general heading of **neidan** (internal alchemy).

While these *yangsheng* techniques aim at the regeneration and reinforcement of the human body by making use of what the body originally possesses, the *fangshi* also focus on the compounding and refining of elixirs with substances (herbal and mineral) from nature. The aforementioned missions dispatched by the rulers of Qin and Han to the Eastern Ocean and the western mountain of Kunlun were intended precisely to secure such medicine of immortality in the form of pills (*dan*). References to "refining gold" (*lianjin*) and transmuting cinnabar (mercury sulphate) in some Han Dynasty texts indicate a growing practice of alchemy for the purpose of attaining longevity and immortality. This pursuit of alchemical manufacturing of *dan* with minerals and plants would eventually lead to the **waidan** (external alchemy) tradition in Daoism.

All the internal and external alchemical techniques discussed here are intended to produce a new body that grows within the old so that, in time, the old self will be replaced by the new in the same way cicadas and snakes regenerate themselves.

Daoist Deities As the Daoist tradition matured, the most exalted god on the Daoist equivalent of Mt. Olympus became the *Yuanshi tianzun* (Celestial Venerable of Primordial Beginning), who is head of a trinity of Three Purities (*sanqing*). Below the *sanqing* are innumerable deities of both genders who fill up various ranks in a mind-boggling celestial bureaucracy that loosely corresponds to its human counterpart.

The lowliest among the spiritual bureaucrats is the local Earth god (*tudi gong*), while the head of the celestial government is the Jade Emperor (*Yuhuang*). Many of them have divine origins, of course, but many also are former humans whose merits warrant their promotion to godly status. Some of the deities have national appeal, such as Lord Zhenwu [Perfect Martiality] of Mt. Wudang, while others are more local in influence, including the Stove god (*zaojun*) in each household.

Daoist immortals staff a very elaborate ranking system. Here is one such deity officially installed into the divine bureaucracy.

Daoism and Women

Because of the feminine emphasis of the *Laozi*, it is generally assumed that Daoism, unlike Confucianism, treats women fairly and kindly. Yet the situation is more complicated than it might appear at first thought. The positions and roles of women in organized Daoism have to be examined in the larger context of Chinese society, which until recent times has indeed been patriarchal and sexist. It is therefore not surprising that women only play limited roles even in Daoism.

And yet it is also undeniable that because of women's believed greater sensitivity to the spirits and their keener communication ability with the divine and invisible world, they do have access to roles and positions denied to most women in Chinese society at large. Women's special power to intercede with the deities often makes some of them more outstanding and influential practitioners of Daoism than men.

The Celestial Masters identified five classes of women suited to be Daoist practitioners: young unmarried women, women unable to marry because of their inauspicious horoscope, women forced into marriage, rejected (divorced) wives, and widows. All these were vulnerable individuals to whom the Celestial Masters offered an escape and a way to assert their worth. In the Tang Dynasty (618–907 C.E.), women from aristocratic families became Daoist nuns in substantial numbers, either between marriages or as widows. There were also imperial princesses ordained as Daoist priestesses.

Equally noteworthy are a number of major Daoist goddesses who play key roles in the religion, chief among them are Xiwangmu (Queen Mother of the West), best

Xiwangmu (Queen Mother of the West) is one of the most prominent female Daoist deities. She rewards her devout followers with immortality by feasting them with magical peaches.

known for her granting the power of immortality to the faithful, and Mazu, the virginal protectress of fishermen and merchants who is still very popular in southeast China and Taiwan today. Some women were actually founders of Daoist sects, most notably Wei Huacun (252–334 C.E.) of the Shangqing [Highest Clarity] tradition and Zu Shu (most active during 889–904 C.E.) who initiated the Qingwei [Pure Subtlety] tradition. Sun Bu'er (1119–1182 C.E.) was a famous female disciple of the founder of the Quanzhen [Complete Perfection] sect who became a senior leader in the movement with the power to teach and ordain other female practitioners.

No comparable number of women can be identified as prominent Confucians. It is thus accurate to conclude that women generally fare better in Daoism than in Confucianism.

CONFUCIANISM AND DAOISM AS A WAY OF LIFE

The two Chinese religions discussed in this chapter are not just a collection of precepts and beliefs. More importantly, they are lived and practiced traditions. It is in the living and practicing of the two traditions that their true meaning and value can be gauged.

Confucian Rituals

From the very beginning, the Confucian tradition has put great emphasis on ritual as a crucial expression of humanity. As "moral behavior," ritual teaches people to conduct themselves with dignity and decorum, making them authentically human. As "holy rites," ritual enables them to communicate effectively with the spiritual powers and interact harmoniously with one another. It is in the latter, more overtly religious, sense that Confucian ritual will be addressed in this section.

In addition to the mundane rituals of familial and social interaction with other human beings in accordance with the prescribed rules outlined in the classic texts, the most important aspect of religious ritual in Confucianism in the premodern period was the sacrifice (*jisi*), or the making of offerings to the spirits, including ancestors, in the form of animals, other food and drink, even jade and silk. These sacrificial rituals were performed at different levels—the state, the community, and the family. The grandest of the rituals were, of course, conducted at the state level. And chief among

The Temple of Tian (Tiantan), where the Chinese emperor prayed to *Tian* on behalf of his subjects and in his capacity as "Son of Tian," is now a popular park in Beijing.

the state rituals were those connected with sacrifices to *Tian* and *Di*—and to Confucius once his teaching was exalted to orthodoxy.

Sacrifice to *Tian* and *Di* *Tian*, it should be recalled, was the source of legitimate political power since the Zhou Dynasty. As son of *Tian* (*Tianzi*), the Chinese ruler carried out *Tian*'s mandate (*Tianming*) to exercise his imperial prerogatives over the entire realm under *Tian* (*Tianxia*). The worship of *Tian* thus became the ruler's exclusive privilege and obligation. Later, with Confucianism imbued with *yin-yang* cosmological ideas in the Han Dynasty, *Tian*, the *yang* element, was paired up with *Di* (earth), the *yin* element, and worship of *Di* was added, though with much less pomp and ostentation.

In late imperial China, the worship of *Tian* and *Di* took place annually. On the day of the summer solstice, the emperor made sacrifice to *Tian* at the Temple of *Tian* (*tiantan*) located in the southern suburb of Beijing. Correspondingly, on the day of the winter solstice, worship of *Di* was conducted at the Temple of Di (*ditan*) located at the northern suburb of the capital. The rituals involved nine steps, including the purification of the participants, the performance of dance and music, the reading of prayer documents, and the offering of sacrifices.

A far more elaborate rite known as "*feng* and *shan*" has only been performed a total of six times in all of Chinese history.[14] *Feng*, literally meaning "to seal," was the rite of worshiping *Tian* atop Mt. Tai, the "Sacred Eastern Peak" located near Confucius' native town of Qufu in modern Shandong province. *Shan*, literally meaning "to yield"

The Hall of Praying for an Abundant Harvest (Qi'nian dian), Temple of Tian (Tiantan), Beijing. The whole complex was built in 1420 under the emperor Yongle and restored in 1530 and 1751. Here the emperor celebrated the sacrifice to Tian for a good harvest. The decorated ramp between the two stairways was reserved for the emperor's palanquin.

VOICES: An Interview with Jason Ch'ui-hsiao Tseng

Jason Ch'ui-hsiao Tseng is a Taiwanese man in his fifties with a master's degree from an American university. He engages in educational exchange for Chinese students wishing to study in the United States.

Do you consider yourself a Confucian or a Daoist?

I do not consider myself exclusively one or the other. Both have influenced me deeply and I regard their teachings as equally valid and complementary.

How is that possible, as their teachings often conflict with each other?

They are not in conflict, they merely represent the polar opposite of the other. They complete each other. For most Chinese, there is no necessity to choose one or the other. We think of them as the two sides of a coin—without both there is no coin. The two together constitute our native Chinese religious outlook. As a matter of fact, we also consider Buddhist teaching a third way of guiding our religious life. These teachings are generally not jealous of one another. They do not demand total exclusive devotion. They provide meaning to different aspects of our lives. There is religious pluralism for most Chinese.

How is that so?

We do not believe that one teaching alone corners the market. As a respectful son and an upright citizen, I embrace Confucian values. They teach me to put family and society ahead of myself and to value education as the most important undertaking to improve myself. In my views on how my body works, how my health can be maintained, how different ingredients should be used to achieve balance in my food, and how I can relate to the spirits in the invisible world, I follow the Daoist teaching. And Buddhism gives me hope for a good afterlife. Together they make me a complete person.

Jason Ch'ui-hsiao Tseng

or "to clear away," was the ritual of sacrificing to *Di* at the lesser peak of Liangfu at the foot of Mt. Tai. The ultimate purpose of the *feng* rite was to seal a new covenant between the ruler and the numinous Absolute that gave him his legitimacy to rule. Similarly, the *shan* performance was meant to establish a bond with the Earth. Because of the huge expenses and elaborate arrangements involved, *feng* and *shan* were conducted consecutively on the same trip.

Before being carried up steep mountain paths to reach the top of Mt. Tai, the emperor and his retinue of high officials had to go through a rigid purification ritual lasting three days, during which time they secluded themselves in special chambers where they took ritual baths, ate pure food, abstained from sex, and conducted serious self-reflection. Once he reached the flat platform at the top of Mt. Tai after an arduous and exhausting uphill climb, the emperor would kneel facing south and would announce his receipt of the mandate. The tablet with his seal would then be enclosed with stone slats that in turn would be bound with cables of gold and cemented with a paste of gold and quicksilver. The coffer formed by the sealing paste and packed earth was painted the five colors—red, blue, yellow, white, and black, symbolizing the four cardinal directions and the center, thus the entire known world. The emperor then bowed, and the assembled officials shouted, "May His Majesty live ten thousand years!" with a sound that echoed throughout the peaks. A few days later, the emperor would perform the *shan* rite to Di on the northern slope of Mt. Liangfu. In this fashion the ruler ritually enacted the sacrosanct relationship he had with *Tian* and *Di*.

Confucius serves as an object of veneration and commemoration. He is the "Utmost Sage and Late Teacher," as the tablet in front of his statue declares.

Sacrifice to Confucius The state cult of Confucius began in the Han Dynasty with the designation of Confucianism as orthodoxy. The descendants of Confucius were first given a hereditary fief, and later, the Master himself was given increasingly laudatory titles and ducal honors. Finally temples commemorating Confucius were ordered to be built in every county and major city throughout the empire. In time, wooden tablets commemorating some of his prominent students, as well as those of successive generations of Confucian worthies such as Mencius and Zhu Xi, were installed in these temples. Though the frequency and elaborateness of the sacrificial rites conducted at these temples varied with time and locale, the traditional birthday of Confucius (the twenty-seventh day of the ninth month) was generally observed. These rites involved dance and music accompanied by drums and bells, proclamations and didactic lectures given by local dignitaries and government officials, as well as offerings of incense and animals. It should be noted that Confucius' divinity was never claimed at these ceremonies, nor was his intervention sought in solving human problems. Rather, they were expressions of veneration and respect for a human culture hero who had helped to define Chinese civilization.

The most magnificent Temple of Confucius, as can be expected, is located in his native county of Qufu, not far from Mt. Tai. Built and maintained at state expense, the Qufu Confucian Temple has a main building with a palatial design supported by dragon decorated pillars, all meant to accord the Master the highest honor comparable to that of a ruler. Stone steles are engraved with the calligraphy or essays of various emperors in Chinese history, all lauding the moral and cultural accomplishments of the

Confucius' tombstone boldly declares that he is the "Ultimate Sage of Greatest Accomplishment, King of Manifest Culture."

sage. This Confucian Temple in Qufu was a pilgrimage site for generations of scholars and aspiring literati and is still popular among tourists today.

Family Rituals Ancestor worship in China started long before the rise of Confucianism, going back to the very dawn of recorded Chinese history—the Shang period. But Confucianism lent further theoretical support to the practice with its discussion of *xiao* (filial piety). The Confucian teaching maintains that one's filial obligation to parents and ancestors is the core of one's humanity. Thus while the state monopolized the worship of *Tian/Di*, and the educated elites controlled the sacrifice to Confucius, all people could participate in the family ritual of honoring parents and ancestors. Sacrifice to ancestors, in particular, is important because it gives the descendants a sense of belonging and continuity, and thereby a religious appreciation of the chain of life that links them to their forebears.

In the *Family Rituals* (*Jiali*), compiled by the Neo-Confucian scholar Zhu Xi, detailed step-by-step liturgies are provided for ceremonies associated with ancestor worship. Chapters describe daily "looking in" on the ancestors; more elaborate semi-monthly "visits," "reports" on major family events such as births, weddings, and deaths; and formal "offerings" on festival days and seasonal sacrifices. What follows is a summarized version of Zhu Xi's instructions for the rites of making seasonal offerings to the ancestors.[15]

In the preparatory phase, the date for the sacrifice is selected by divination performed in front of the ancestral shrine in the preceding month. Then, three days before the event, the designated leading man and woman will each lead family members of their respective gender to perform purification rituals in their designated quarters, men in the outer and women in the inner. The men also make the main hall sparkling clean and arrange the place settings for each generation properly. The women will set the incense burner and incense box, as well as prepare wine racks and containers, along with meat plates for the ancestors.

On the day of the event, when the sun is fully up, the wooden tablets containing the names of the different generations of ancestors, separated by gender, are moved to their proper places in the main hall. Then the spirits of the ancestors are greeted, and food is offered to them three times. The ancestors are entreated to eat the food and are given privacy to do so with everyone from the presiding man on down exiting the main hall and the door is closed. After a suitable interval, the master of ceremony coughs three times to announce his intention to reenter, then he opens the door and everyone else comes back in. Tea is offered to the ancestors to supposedly cleanse their mouths. Then the presiding man receives the sacrificed food from the master of ceremony. With reverence the presiding man bows and prostrates himself to taste the food and drink the wine. Then the entire group takes leave of the ancestral spirits, returns their tablets back to their original locations, and clears away the offering tables. The presiding man supervises the division of the sacrificial food to be consumed by all the family members later that day. This brings an end to the ritual of the ancestral sacrifice. The intended effect of this ritual is apparent—to create familial cohesiveness and to recognize the unseverable bond between the living and the deceased family members. You may notice that the opening scene of *qingming* observance at the beginning of this chapter has similar rituals.

Daoist Practices

As can be deduced from our discussion of Daoist beliefs, Daoism is essentially lived, not merely believed. Whether it is the amazing feats of the immortals and perfected beings in the *Laozi* and the *Zhaungzi*, or whether it is the physical-spiritual regimens and alchemical techniques of the later Daoists, there is always an understanding and expectation that the beliefs need to be put into practice to be truly meaningful. Returning to the *Dao*, warding off physical deterioration, and attaining actual immortality involve a whole spectrum of undertakings and practices.

Daoist Communal Festivals and Liturgies To ordinary believers, those who have no hope of going through the rigor and the expenses of pursuing immortality, the Daoist religion as practiced by the Celestial Master Sect offers the promise of health, long life, even collective salvation. Membership in these organized movements during the tumultuous centuries after the collapse of the Han Dynasty meant a special sense of belonging to a select group destined to survive those trying times. Noteworthy in their beliefs was the idea of chosenness—that they constituted a special group of people who, because of their embrace of an apocalyptic ideology, were favored by the gods. Referred to as *zhongmin* (seed people), they confirmed their "elect" status through their participation in collective rituals called ***zhai*** (fasts). Lasting several days each, these fasts involved abstinence from food, public performance of penance for past moral transgressions, submission of written memorials to request pardon from the deities, and communal prayers for the salvation of the faithful.

The Fast of Mud and Soot (*tu-tan zhai*) in China's medieval period

A group of Daoist priests perform a ritual service for a member of the community.

reflected the general tenor of *zhai* rituals. With hair disheveled and face smeared with soot, believers prostrated themselves like condemned criminals before a raised altar to ask for forgiveness from the gods. Moved by their emotions, many fell to the ground and rolled about amidst loud wailings. Such public acts of penance were performed to earn pardon and spiritual merit. Another liturgical ritual was the Fast of the Yellow Register (*Huanglu zhai*) during which the participants performed penitence for their ancestors going back seven or nine generations. The names of deceased ancestors, entered in registers, were read by the officiating priests and were then considered to have gained postmortem immortality. In this way the filial obligation of the faithful was ritually expressed.

Another communal ceremony, the **jiao** (offering), is popular even down to the present day. It is a public liturgy performed usually by the Daoist priests on behalf of the entire community to petition the gods to bestow good fortune, health, and prosperity on all. Sometimes labeled as a rite of cosmic renewal, the *jiao* brings together the community to participate collectively in a religious ritual that is loud, colorful, and dramatic. Depending on the needs of the community, a *jiao* is conducted at periodic intervals (ranging from once a year for the affluent communities to once every 60 years for the poor communities) or to give special thanks to the deities for having successfully protected the entire community by, for example, warding off an epidemic.

A *jiao* ceremony usually lasts several days. The dates are chosen for their astrological auspiciousness. Daoist priests are contracted to perform the ritual with efficacy and precision. Prior to the official dates of the ceremony, "memorials" are submitted by the priests to the celestial bureaucracy of the gods to give notice of the scheduled *jiao*. Then the location where the liturgy takes place, usually both the inside and the outside of the largest local temple or shrine, is marked off by hoisted lanterns to signal the enclosure of the sacred space. Afterward the local deities are invited to take their honored seats within the enclosure by having their statues or wooden tablets carried there by community elders. The procession of the deities through the community is accompanied by lion or dragon dances, made even more boisterous with lots of firecrackers. Then the ritual proper begins in earnest.

Reenacting the beginning of the cosmos in a ritual called *fendeng* (spreading the light), the chief Daoist priest, in full vestment, blows on a buffalo horn and rings his "thunder" bell, to the accompaniment of an entire music ensemble, and repeats the forty-second chapter of the *Laozi* by announcing that "the *Dao* gives birth to the One [Being, Existence]; the One brings forth the Two [*Yin* and *Yang*]; the Two give rise to the Three [*Tian*, *Di*, and Humans]; and the Three engender the Ten Thousand Things [world of multiplicity and diversity]." Entering a meditation-induced trance, he transforms his body into the body of the *Dao*. He takes prescribed steps that are dancelike, spins on himself, and sanctifies the ritual enclosure by requesting the dispatch of heavenly troops to guard the place. At the same time, to placate the wandering ghosts in the neighborhood and to warn them against intrusion into the sacred ground, he provides a feast for them while lecturing them on the reasons for their suffering.

At some point during the ceremony, the names of every member of the community will be posted on a roster and read aloud by the priests to signal their financial and spiritual support of this elaborate and expensive event, as well as to ensure that they will receive their share of the benediction of the gods. There is great interest among the community members to check the posted name list to make sure that the names are written accurately and that they have not been inadvertently left out.

The climax of the ceremony occurs when the highest of the Daoist deities, the Three Purities and the Jade Emperor, are invited to take part in the ceremony. Piercing prepared talismans with his sword, the chief Daoist priest burns them with great dramatic effect to appeal to the august deities. Once the gods are properly seated, a blanket pardon of every immoral act committed by every member of the community between the last *jiao* and the present one is announced. In grateful response, the community performs a public charitable act of "releasing life"—setting cages of captured birds free and returning to a stream bucketfuls of live fish. On the last night of the ceremony, a grand feast for all ghosts trapped in hell is hosted by the community. Once again, the Daoist priests exhort the ghosts to behave themselves and to refrain from wreaking havoc in the lives of the living. Balance is restored among the worlds of humans, gods, and ghosts. The rite concludes with the sending off of the celestial gods and the local deities and the distribution of food and buns to the spectators and the performance of operas for the entertainment of all.[16]

CONCLUSION

In this chapter we have invited you to explore the religious world of the Chinese through a study of their two native religious traditions—Confucianism and Daoism. We have highlighted the religious nature of both traditions. In the case of Confucianism, we have established that it is not just a teaching of ethics and good government but is in fact informed by a deep religious faith in a numinous Absolute—*Tian*. This faith, moreover, mandates dedicated human effort to transform the individual and the world. At the same time, we have also identified the ritual dimensions of this tradition, from the ornate and solemn state observations of the past to the simple familial ceremonies that are still practiced today.

As for Daoism, we have clarified that it is not confined to the metaphysical discussions of the *Laozi* and the *Zhuangzi*, but that it is richly informed by an elaborate belief in the cosmological importance of the human body, a salvational message of communal redemption, and an abiding yearning for physical transformation and perfection. We have also documented the colorful ritual performance of Daoism in the community.

Both Confucianism and Daoism (along with a Chinese form of Buddhism) have contributed to the shaping of the Chinese religious mindset. Both have experienced ups and downs in their respective history, at times being the dominant ideology of the realm, and at times being eclipsed by other traditions in influence. Nevertheless, both have maintained their central importance to the Chinese people, at no time risking irrelevance or extinction. Despite suffering a brutal critique and rejection in the twentieth century by the modern Chinese intellectual elite in the name of rationalism and egalitarianism, both have remained resilient. In fact, there are signs of their revival and rejuvenation at the dawn of the twenty-first century. Confucian values continue to inform Chinese familial ethics and social and political behavior, while Daoist concerns for the well-being of the human body and harmonious relationship with the spiritual world shape contemporary Chinese attitudes toward health, medicine, cuisine, and the environment.

Most importantly, we have attempted to justify the inclusion of both Confucianism and Daoism in the study of world religions. Confucianism treats the fulfillment of the human potential as an ultimate concern. The tenacity with which Confucianism exhorts people to strive for human perfection in our mundane lives as a form of divine calling—thereby making the secular sacred—demonstrates an interesting type of religiosity. Its assertion of human co-equality with the divine offers an intriguing contrast with other religious traditions as well. Daoism is similarly a significant world religion. Its perception of the divine Absolute as a life-generating, feminine entity; its call for a harmonious coexistence between humans and nature; its emphasis on healthy improvement of the human body as a religious mission; and its promotion of communal cohesiveness through ritual participation make it all the more relevant in a postindustrial world.

SEEKING ANSWERS

What Is Ultimate Reality?

Confucianism and Daoism share the same cosmological myth they inherit from ancient China. The natural world is not in a fallen state. There is no almighty creator, nor is there a demonic counterpart. There is no definite beginning of the world, and there is no predicted end. Instead, the world unfolds cyclically and operates like a pendulum, arcing between two extremes and alternating between two polar but complementing opposites. Human beings are not caught in a tug of war between good and evil, and the side they choose does not result in a permanent fate in paradise or hell. Emphasis is placed on balance, coexistence, and harmony. For the Confucians, ultimate reality is *Tian* (Neo-Confucians

(continued)

SEEKING ANSWERS (continued)

sometimes use the term *Taiji*, Supreme Ultimate). *Tian* is the procreator of the cosmos and all the myriad things in it. Moreover, *Tian* has a special relationship with humans and communicates with chosen individuals its grand design for humanity. This communication does not occur through dramatic and ecstatic encounters such as that between god and the prophets in Abrahamic traditions. Instead, *Tian*'s message is discerned by perceptive and insightful human representatives through their keen observation of nature and diligent study of human affairs as recorded in history and enacted in the present. It is in this sense that Confucianism is not a revelatory religion in the conventional sense. In contrast, Daoism, in its organized form, is a revelatory religion. Its ultimate reality is the *Dao*, the "mother of the universe." Originally formless and undifferentiated, it later takes on human and divine forms, giving instructions and revealing texts to the faithful. Daoism can also be salvational in its message, complete with prescription for repentance and thanksgiving.

How Should We Live in This World?

Both Confucianism and Daoism inherit the ancient Chinese religious view regarding the human condition: human beings are, like everything else in the cosmos, the product of the interaction between *yin* and *yang*. They have a corporeal aspect (the body) and an incorporeal aspect (the "soul"), consisting of *hun* and *po*. There is no notion of any alienation from or disobedience of an almighty god, thus a total absence of sin. However, this does not mean that human beings are already perfect and need no improvement from their current state. There is still a yawning gap between human beings as they are and human beings as they should or can become. For the Confucians, the right way to live is to live ethically, in accordance with the moral dictates of *Tian*. Humans alone have the responsibility to model and exemplify *Tian*'s moral imperative, thereby making themselves co-partners in creating harmony and prosperity throughout the cosmos. In concentric circles extending outward from the individual, moral behavior will transform the family, the community, and the world at large. "Do not do unto others what you do not want done to you" is the minimal moral guide for correct living in Confucianism. For the Daoists, the right way to live is to live healthily. To be sure, ethical behavior is part of desirable living, but Daoists also emphasize the human body as a microcosm reflecting perfectly the macrocosm of the cosmos. Thus, taking care of one's body through both internal and external "alchemical" means is a way of living life properly in accord with the Dao. Similarly focusing on the intimate connection between the individual, the community, and the cosmos, Daoists prescribe diet, exercise, and preservation of health and energy as a way of approaching the holy.

(continued)

SEEKING ANSWERS *(continued)*

What Is Our Ultimate Purpose?

Confucians and Daoists differ in their answer to this question. For the Confucians, humans are potentially perfect and inclined toward the good. Yet this potentiality and inclination need to be rigorously nurtured and developed through scholastic learning, moral introspection, and ethical behavior. Learning to be authentically human, to enact the "way" of *Tian*, is the way to improve the human condition and to perfect it. The highest achievement of human endeavor is to become the co-equal of the divine ultimate—*Tian*.

Daoists regard humans on the same level as all the myriad things—they are all concrete expressions of the *Dao*, the numinous Absolute. Through their ignorance or negligence, however, humans dissipate their primordial endowment of the vital energy, the *qi*, resulting in their vulnerability to disease and death. Consequently, the Daoist prescription for improving the human condition is to engage in exercises and rituals designed to replenish the body and the spirit, making it once again as immortal as the *Dao*. Confucians and Daoists also diverge in their beliefs about what happens after we leave this life. Confucius himself famously brushed aside a student's inquiry on death. He just did not consider it an issue worthy of exploration. His priority was to pay exclusive attention to life and how to improve it. This "prejudice" has affected all subsequent Confucians, none of whom showed any strong interest in addressing death or its religious meaning. Even the Confucian practice of ancestor worship and respecting the dead can be explained as a way of bypassing the issue, as dead ancestors are treated very much as living members of the lineage and the family. Daoists, on the other hand, confront the topic of mortality by emphasizing the possibility and the desirability of immortality. Even with the appearance of death as inevitable, Daoists explain it as a stage of transformation to a higher plane of existence, a way of attaining true immortality. Thus the deeper meaning of death is equally ignored by Daoists.

REVIEW QUESTIONS

For Review

1. Why should the term "Confucianism" be used with caution? In what way may it be a misnomer?

2. How do Confucianism and Daoism define such terms as *Tian, Dao,* and *de* differently?

3. Why is Daoism more than the teachings of the *Laozi* and the *Zhuangzi*?

4. Why is Confucianism a religious tradition despite its lack of concern for the afterlife?

For Further Reflection

1. In what ways do Confucianism and Daoism complement each other, and in what ways do they oppose each other?

2. Compare and contrast the Confucian notion of *Tian* with the Christian concept of God.

3. Compare and contrast the Daoist notion of *Dao* with the Hindu concept of Brahman.

4. Having examined Confucianism and Daoism, have you arrived at any conclusion regarding Chinese religiosity? How does it differ from that of other religious traditions?

GLOSSARY

dantian (dahn'-teen'ən) "Fields for the refinement of the immortal pill"; major nodal points in the human body where the "pill" of immortality can be refined through alchemical means.

dao (dow) A fundamental concept in Chinese religion, literally meaning the "path" or the "way." In Confucianism, it specifically refers to the entire ideal human order ordained by the numinous Absolute, *Tian.* In Daoism, it is the primary source of the cosmos, the very ground of all beings.

Daodejing (dow'-duh-jing) Basic Daoist scripture, lit. "The Scripture of the Way and Its Potent Manifestation"; also known as the Book of *Laozi,* the name of its purported author.

Daozang (dow' zahng) Literally "Treasury of the Dao," this is the Daoist Canon that contains the entire corpus of Daoist texts. The most complete version, still in use today, was first published in 1445.

de (duh) Another fundamental concept in Chinese religions, meaning "virtue" or "potency." In Confucianism, it is the charismatic power of the ruler or the man of virtue, while in Daoism it means the concrete manifestation of the *dao.*

fangshi (fahng-shər) "Magicians" who allegedly possessed the recipe for immortality.

Five Classics The five canonical works of Confucianism designated in the Han Dynasty. They are *Book of Odes, Book of History, Book of Changes, Record of Rites,* and *Spring and Autumn Annals.*

Four Books The four texts identified by the Neo-Confucian Zhu Xi as fundamental in understanding the Confucian teaching. Between 1313 and 1905, they made up the curriculum for the civil service examination. They are *Analects, Mencius, Great Learning,* and *Doctrine of the Mean.*

gui (gwei) Ghosts and demons, malevolent spirits.

jiao (jee'au) Daoist communal sacrificial offerings to signal cosmic renewal and collective cohesion.

junzi (ju'un zee) The personality ideal in Confucianism; the noble person.

li (lee) Etiquette and proper manners; rituals and holy rites.

ming (see *Tianming*)

neidan (nay'-dahn) Daoist "Internal" alchemy designed to attain immortality through meditation, breath control, gymnastics, diet, and massage.

(continued)

GLOSSARY (*continued*)

neisheng waiwang (nay'-sheng' wī'-wahng) Neo-Confucian ideal of "inner sagely moral perfection and outer political skills."

qi (chee) Breath, force, power, material energy.

ren (rən) Human-heartedness, benevolence; the unique moral inclination of humans.

Ru (rōō) Scribes and ritual performers of the Zhou period; later used exclusively to refer to Confucians.

Shangdi (shahng'-dee) The August Lord on High of the Shang period.

shen (shən) Gods and deities; benevolent spirits.

shengren (shəng rən) (or **sheng**) The Confucian sage, the epitome of humanity.

shi (shər) Men of service; lower-ranking civil and military officials in the Zhou period.

Tian (tee'ən) The transcendent, numinous entity in ancient Chinese religion; the conscious Will that regulates the cosmos and intervenes in human affairs; conventionally translated as "Heaven."

Tianming The mandate or command of *Tian* that confers political legitimacy to the ruler; also understood by Confucians as the calling to morally improve oneself and to transform the world.

Tianshi (tee'ən shər) "Celestial Master"; reference to a Daoist salvational figure as well as an organized movement.

waidan (wī dahn) Daoist "external" alchemy involving refining of "pills" with herbs and minerals for ingestion so that immortality can be attained.

wuwei (wōō way) Daoist notion of action without intention; actionless action.

wuxing (wōō shing) The five elemental phases of metal, wood, water, fire, and soil that mutually support and overcome one another.

xian (shee'ən) Daoist immortals and perfected individuals.

xiao (shee'au) Filial piety; respect and care for parents and ancestors.

xinzhai (shin jī) "Fasting of the Mind" in the *Zhuangzi*.

yang (young) Lit. the south-facing side of a mountain, representing the energy that is bright, warm, dry, and masculine.

yangsheng (young shəng) Daoist techniques of nourishing life and attaining immortality.

yin Lit. the north-facing side of a mountain, representing the energy that is dark, cold, wet, and feminine.

zhai (jī) Daoist "fasts" designed to seek redemption of transgressions by the gods.

Zhuangzi (juahng-zee) A fourth century B.C.E. Daoist figure as well as the title of the book attributed to him.

ziran (zee'-rahn) Daoist notion of natural spontaneity.

zuowang (zoh'-wahng) "Sitting and Forgetting" in the *Zhuangzi*.

SUGGESTIONS FOR FURTHER READING

de Bary, Wm. Theodore. *The Trouble with Confucianism.* Cambridge, MA: Harvard University Press, 1991. A thought-provoking discussion of the "prophetic voice" in Confucianism.

Fingarette, Herbert. *Confucius: The Secular as Sacred.* New York: Harper Torchbooks, 1972. A creative interpretation of the Confucian notion of *li* as holy rites.

Gardner, Daniel K., trans. *The Four Books: The Basic Teachings of the Later Confucian Tradition*. Indianapolis: Hackett Publishing, 2007. A handy translation of important excerpts from the scriptural corpus of Confucianism.

Kirkland, Russell. *Taoism: The Enduring Tradition*. London: Routledge, 2004. An impassioned monograph by a specialist to correct many of the misconceptions regarding Daoism and its history.

Kohn, Livia, ed. *Daoism Handbook*. Leiden: Brill, 2000. A magisterial and encyclopedic collection of essays on various aspects of Daoism, ranging from history to schools to texts.

Schipper, Kristofer. *The Taoist Body*. Berkeley: University of California Press, 1993. An authoritative discourse by an ordained Daoist priest on the rituals and practices of Daoism as they relate to the texts and teachings.

Taylor, Rodney L. *The Religious Dimensions of Confucianism*. Albany: State University of New York Press, 1986. A convenient collection of mostly previously published essays by the author to argue for the religiousness of Confucianism.

Yao, Xinzhong. *An Introduction to Confucianism*. Cambridge: Cambridge University Press, 2000. An authoritative basic text on the entire Confucian tradition.

ONLINE RESOURCES

Research Centre for Confucian Studies
cuhk.edu.hk/rih/confucian/index.htm
This useful website for Confucian studies is maintained by the Research Center for Confucian Studies, Chinese University of Hong Kong. It contains a rich resource guide for Confucian studies.

The Daoist Foundation
daoistfoundation.org
The Daoist Foundation was created by two American academics who, having studied and practiced Daoism for many years, "are committed to fostering the flourishing of authentic and tradition-based Daoist practice, community, and culture with attentiveness to the needs and concerns of Western students."

Center for Daoist Studies
daoistcenter.org
This useful website is the education and research branch of the Daoist Foundation.

SHINTO

THIS IS THE LAST day of the three-day Sanja Festival in Asakusa, a historic precinct in Tokyo. The climax of the festival is the wild parading of **mikoshi**, portable shrines carrying the "essence" of the patron deities of the various neighborhoods and merchant groups.[1] As one of the most popular annual festivals in Tokyo, the Sanja Festival attracts upward of half a million spectators and participants during the three-day festivities.

At 5 a.m. on the third Sunday in May, Satoshi Tanaka, a young grocery clerk in his twenties, is waiting expectantly outside the Asakusa Shrine. Along with hundreds of other young men (and some brave women), he has signed up months in advance to form teams of shrine carriers sponsored by local merchants and civic groups. Though ordinarily preferring to sleep late, Satoshi finds himself in a state of excited anticipation and alertness this morning. Dressed in colorful shirts and shorts with matching headbands, he waits with others to receive their purification by the Shinto priests so that he will be considered spiritually clean and ready for the sacred task ahead. Even though he does not see himself as a seriously religious person, Satoshi feels perfectly comfortable in being a shrine carrier at this Shinto festival. It is his way of interacting with his community, and with the deities he believes are present.

The job of these carriers is to carry the *mikoshi* through the streets of Asakusa so that all in attendance can share a moment of intimacy with the deities temporarily housed in these portable shrines. These ornately

Throngs of portable shrine carriers with their respective *mikoshi* outside of the Asakusa Shrine in Tokyo.

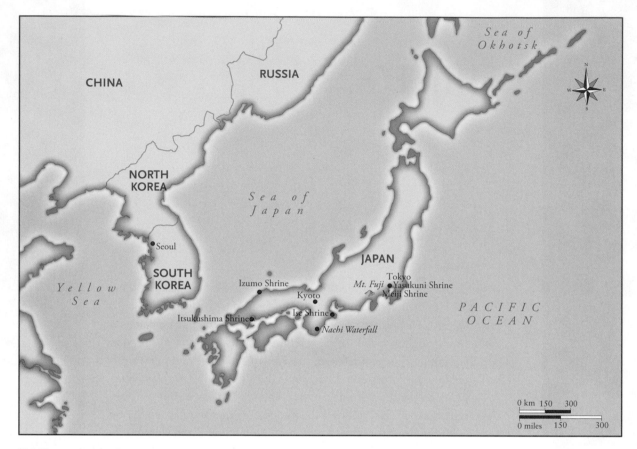

Significant sites in the history of Shinto.

decorated *mikoshi* rest on poles that are carried on the shoulders of the carriers. Shouting and grunting in unison, to the accompaniment of much drumming, cymbal clanging, and loud cheers from the crowd, the carriers attempt to move the portable shrines along. But since no one among them is in total control of the direction of the *mikoshi*, all the carriers move back and forth or sideways more or less blindly. The movement of the portable shrines can thus be wild and unpredictable, subject to the unconscious collective will of the entire group of carriers (or, supposedly, that of the deity inside). This cumbersome and potentially dangerous parade lumbers down narrow streets and broad boulevards amidst large crowds.

Quite frequently one shrine will cross paths with another, resulting in great commotion and competition for attention from the throngs of spectators. Sweating profusely and hoarse from too much shouting and chanting, individual shrine carriers drop out and are quickly replaced without disrupting the progress of the shrines. Thirsty and hungry, the temporarily retired carriers sit or lay on the ground in total exhaustion. Meanwhile, the spectators watch; take pictures; applaud; cheer; visit the main shrine; purchase the sundry food, drink, and souvenirs offered by enterprising street vendors; and make a day of it. ☀

The preceding scene is typical of a ***matsuri***, a Shinto festival in contemporary Japan that helps to create religious awareness and social solidarity within the entire community. The *matsuri* is both a religious and a social occasion. Though the oldest surviving religion in Japan, Shinto has, by and large, coexisted with Buddhism and Confucianism, which were introduced into the country from China by way of Korea in the sixth century C.E. While there has been rivalry and competition among the three religions over the centuries, there has also been accommodation and acceptance. There is an observation about Japanese religious behavior that says that the Japanese are born and wed in Shinto, die Buddhist, and live in accordance with Confucian ethical principles. In other words, most Japanese do not see the three religions as mutually exclusive or incompatible. Rather, they regard them as mutually reinforcing and relevant in separate aspects and stages of their lives. In this chapter, we will invite you into the life of Shinto believers as they practice their religion in the context of recognizing, and sometimes actually embracing, the other faiths. We will do so by discussing its beliefs, ritual practices, and history.

THE TEACHINGS OF SHINTO

The term **Shinto** is an elegant reference to the longest existing religion in Japan. "*Shin*" is the Japanized pronunciation of the Chinese word "*shen*," which refers to gods and deities (Chapter 8). "*Tō*," alternatively "*dō*," is the Japanese way of pronouncing the Chinese word "*dao*," which suggests the "way." Hence Shinto literally means "the way of the gods." As a matter of fact, the term Shinto did not come into existence until the Japanese used it to distinguish their preexisting religion from Buddhism, which, when first introduced into the country in the middle of the sixth century C.E., was known as "*Butsudō*," "the way of the Buddha." In more colloquial form Shinto is known as *kami-no-michi*, "the way of the ***kami***," as the core of Shinto is the belief in the existence and power of *kami*, a broad term that suggests a whole range of meanings.

The Meaning of *Kami*

The complexity of the word *kami* is best illustrated by the great eighteenth-century Japanese scholar Motoori Norinaga (1730–1801). As an articulate advocate for the revival of Shinto in a Japan dominated by Confucian orthodoxy and Buddhist piety, Motoori points out the diverse meaning of the term *kami*:

> I do not yet understand the meaning of the term *kami*. Speaking in general, however, it may be said that *kami* signifies, in the first place, the deities of heaven and earth that appear in the ancient records and also the spirits of the shrines where they are worshiped. It is hardly necessary to say that it includes human beings. It also includes such objects as birds, beasts, trees, plants, seas, mountains, and so forth. In ancient usage, whatsoever was outside the ordinary, possessed superior power, or was awe-inspiring, was called *kami*.[2]

Put simply, then, *kami* refers to anything that is out of the ordinary, awe-inspiring, mysterious, powerful, marvelous, and beyond human control or comprehension. The awe and marvel accorded the *kami* seem to date back to the earliest times in Japanese history. A closer examination of the Shinto beliefs and practices will bear this out.

Belief is the least precise aspect of Shinto, as this religion has no identifiable founder, nor does it have a sacred book similar to the Bible. Our discussion of Shinto beliefs cannot then rely on a professed creed or doctrine. Rather, it is based on a set of highly revered texts, dating back to the eighth and ninth centuries C.E. The **Kojiki** (*Record of Ancient Matters*, completed in 712 C.E.) and the **Nihon shoki** (alternatively known as **Nihongi**, *Chronicles of [the Land Where] the Sun Originates*, compiled in 720 C.E.) are the two authoritative texts for the study of ancient Shinto mythologies and beliefs. The following narrative is primarily based on the former.

Creation Myth in the *Kojiki*

The *Kojiki* begins with several generations of invisible divinities at the beginning of time, all of whom have titles that end with the word *kami*, until the primordial pair, **Izanagi** and his wife **Izanami**, appears. The couple is credited with bringing the world out of its original chaos. Standing on the Heavenly Floating Bridge, they lower a jeweled spear to stir the ocean below. When they lift up the spear, the brine dripping down from its tip forms an island. In like manner, "the grand eight islands" of the Japanese archipelago are created. The divine couple then descends to take up residence there, and through their sexual union they produce the various nature deities.

Izanami is burned to death while giving birth to her last child, the fire god. Izanagi follows his wife to Yomi, the underworld of the dead where, upon seeing her putrefied and decomposing body, he is horrified and beats a hasty retreat. After his return to the world of the living, Izanagi washes himself in a stream. From his eyes are born the solar goddess **Amaterasu**-no-Ōmikami (The Great August Kami who Shines in the Sky)[3] and the lunar god Tsukiyomi. From Izanagi's nose comes the violent and ill-tempered storm god Susa-no-o.[4]

When the *Kojiki* continues, the focus shifts to the relationship between Amaterasu and her brother Susa-no-o. Petulant and mischievous, Susa-no-o gives much grief to his sister. He ravages her heavenly domain, destroys her rice fields, and desecrates her house. Annoyed and frightened, Amaterasu retreats into a cave, thereby plunging the world into darkness. The other deities try to lure her back out with all sorts of tricks, but to no avail, until a goddess by the name of Uzume performs a lewd dance that causes so much raucous laughter among the gods that the curious Amaterasu is finally enticed to emerge from her hiding. (This is an ingenious Shinto attempt at explaining solar eclipse.) Susa-no-o is forced to apologize to his sister and is banished to Izumo, a region facing the Japan Sea (also known as the East Sea) on the other side of the main island from Ise, the future home of Amaterasu's grand shrine. In Izumo Susa-no-o settles down and locates a sword, which he presents to Amaterasu as a token of his apology and goodwill. The sword will later become one of the "three imperial regalia" Amaterasu bestows on her descendants who occupy the Japanese throne.

The final cycle of the narrative in the *Kojiki* deals with the successors of Susa-no-o and the descendants of Amaterasu. Ninigi, grandson of Amaterasu, is instructed by her to rule all of Japan. But his mission is thwarted by Susa-no-o's successors in Izumo, who refuse to yield to the Amaterasu line until she promises to honor her young brother by building him a grand shrine. After Izumo's accommodation with the Sun Goddess group, the descendants of all the other deities also fall in line, and Ninigi's own grandson, the Emperor Jimmu, is the first human ruler to claim imperial authority over all of Japan. He is provided with the three imperial regalia of the sword, the mirror, and the curved jewel as symbols of his power, which he is believed to have exercised in the Yamato region near present-day Nara. According to tradition, this momentous event took place in 660 B.C.E., and the imperial line has continued uninterrupted to the present time.

From the *Kojiki* story just outlined, major themes of Shinto belief can be identified: the divine creation of Japan, a concern with fertility and purification, the importance of the feminine, an absence of ethical teachings, a corresponding lack of absolute good or radical evil, and a profound intertwining of divinity with imperial power.

Japan as a Divine Creation The core belief of Shinto centers on the *kami* and Japan's unique relationship with them. Representative of the Shinto notion of the sacred or the holy, *kami* are mysterious and tremendous powers in nature and in the human world, powers that have been the object of worship in Japan since prehistoric times. Most *kami* are believed to be the source of blessing and protection, hence worship of them is understood either as thanksgiving or as pleading for more divine gifts. But some *kami* are ill-tempered and even ill-intentioned, so worship of them is a necessary and prudent act of preventing disaster.

Kami are most evident in nature. Illustrious objects in the sky such as the sun and the moon, majestic mountains such as Fuji, serene waterfalls such as the Nachi, and strange-shaped rocks are all regarded as *kami*.

Furthermore, the *Kojiki* story of creation reflects a fundamental Japanese sentiment that their island nation was created by the *kami* as a paradise on earth. Nature, then, with its awesome power and captivating beauty, is the very expression of divine presence. Human beings, who themselves are also descendants of divinity, have the duty to respond in celebration and adoration to the gifts and blessings of the *kami*. The *kami* among humans—the ancestors of clans and communities, the heroes and powerful individuals, the emperors and some of their high officials, all exemplify godly qualities. They therefore equally deserve veneration and worship.

In the prehistoric or quasi-historic periods prior to the fifth or sixth century C.E., when Japan had no centralized imperial rule or institutionalized

The Meoto-iwa (Husband and Wife rocks) in Mie Prefecture is an iconic landmark in Japan that symbolizes the union between Izanagi and Izanami.

governmental structure, only clans and communities existed. With the ascendancy of the Yamato clan that claimed descent from the Sun Goddess Amaterasu, the chiefs and heads of the various clans and communities surrendered their power to the Yamato ruler in return for recognition and position in the divine/political power structure. The result was the entire country of Japan forming a network of *kami* with strong local identities that were loosely linked to the worship of the emperor as a deity.

Fertility and Purification   Early Shinto is centrally concerned with fertility. In the *Kojiki* cosmogonic (explanation of how the cosmos came about) myth, the main function of the primeval pair of *kami* is to "fertilize" the land and to procreate the other gods. Much emphasis is placed on the sexual union between Izanagi and Izanami in the population of the world, especially Japan, with plants, animals, and people. This procreative power of the original divine couple continues even after the death of the wife when Izanagi, on his own, manages to bring forth more deities through ritual washing. At the same time, this mythic story highlights the Shinto fear of contamination and defilement, as well as its emphasis on purification. Despite the love that he has for his wife, Izanagi is so horrified and repulsed by Izanami's decomposing form after her death that he abandons her in the netherworld and hurries back to the world of the living. Death, disease, and blood are thus seen as polluting; persons connected to those things are considered spiritually impure and must be ritually purified before they can approach the *kami*. The arrangement of the typical Shinto shrine and the main ritual responsibility of the Shinto priests illustrate well this vital aspect of Shinto belief, as we shall see later in this chapter.

The Feminine in Shinto   It is highly noteworthy that in the Shinto myth, the sun, the most illustrious object in the sky, is portrayed as female, this despite the later patriarchal (male-dominated) nature of Japanese society. It is equally significant that the Sun Goddess Amaterasu is also the ancestress of the Japanese royal family and that at least up through the tenth century c.e., it was not uncommon for the imperial ruler to be a woman. Also prominent in early Shinto is the role of the shamanic figure, often a female. The ecstatic dance of the goddess Uzume to lure Amaterasu out of hiding, thereby saving the world from perpetual darkness caused by solar eclipse, is indicative of the power of the female shamanic dancer. In addition, both the *Kojiki* and the *Nihongi* mention the mother of Emperor Jimmu, the first human ruler of Japan, whose name is Tama-yori-hime. This name suggests her role as a female shaman, as it literally means "a princess (*hime*) in whom dwells (*yori*) the spirit (*tama*) of the *kami*." Equally noteworthy is the account of Emperor Sujin in the *Nihongi*, whose rule is assisted by two female diviners, one being his own aunt, and the other a charismatic commoner named Ōtataneko, the favorite woman shaman of the deity of the Yamato region. It is the latter who is credited with the peace and prosperity of Sujin's reign, as she is known for her capacity to commune with the *kami* and be possessed by them.

The high prestige of female shamans in ancient Japan is further attested by the story of Empress Jingō, also recorded in the *Nihongi*. Jingō is a capable shamanic diviner for her husband, Emperor Chūai, who, after his death, personally leads an armada to invade Korea because of the oracle of assured victory she receives from the gods. It is the extension of Japanese political control over Korea that paves the way for the powerful reign of her son, Emperor Ōjin. Scholars today speculate that Empress Jingō's legendary account is modeled after the story of Himiko in Chinese historical records dating back to the fourth century C.E. They describe a female shamanic ruler of a region called Yamatai (suspected to be a variation of Yamato) in the country of Wa (Japan) whose bewitching control over the people is the source of her power. One possible interpretation of the term Himiko is "*miko* of the Sun (*hi*)." At the same time, *miko* to this day refers to unmarried women attendants at Shinto shrines who possess shamanic power to communicate with the *kami* through dance and other ritual performances. Himiko's central role as medium for the Sun Goddess can thus be imagined. Jingō's possible association with Himiko only highlights the critical importance of female diviners in ancient Shinto.

Ethics, Good, and Evil Conspicuously absent in early Shinto belief is any reference to ethics. While much emphasis is placed on fertility and purity, the *Kojiki* cosmogonic story does not address the issue of morality at all. Though causing the death of his mother Izanami, the fire god is not depicted as a villain. Though abandoning his wife in the eternally dark and terrifying underworld, Izanagi is not blamed for being a heartless spouse. Though causing much distress to his sister Amaterasu with his destructive and willful behavior, Susa-no-o is not portrayed as an evil culprit. Likewise, the explicitly lewd behavior of the *kami* in drawing Amaterasu out of her hiding is not seen as immoral. In other words, the early Shinto account of creation and the relationship between the gods gives no instruction on proper ethical conduct. There is no supreme god giving moral instructions and laws. Nor is there any hint of a cosmic struggle between good and evil. Whether in the primeval divine realm of the gods, in the natural world, or within the human community that comes into being afterward, there is no existence in Shinto beliefs of a radical evil entity that is bent on subverting the will and the handiwork of a benevolent creator god. Divine and human actions are judged only as fertile or unproductive, pure or impure, desirable or undesirable. Wayward behavior can be remedied and impurities can be removed. What are most offensive to the gods are not sin and guilt, but pollution and defilement.

The notable absence of ethical concerns in early Shinto myth by no means signals that the Japanese are not governed by moral principles in their behavior. What it does mean is that the Japanese adopted their ethics from other sources, primarily from Buddhism and Confucianism. The introduction of these two alien traditions in the history of Shinto will be discussed later.

State Shinto One controversial issue in Shinto that must be addressed is the religion's tie to the imperial state and to the worship of the emperor. As early Shinto texts make clear, the divine origin of the imperial family and of the reigning emperor had been asserted right from the beginning. As descendant of the Sun Goddess, Amaterasu, the Japanese ruler (both male and, not infrequently, female—at least up to the tenth century C.E.) traditionally wielded both political and religious power. As a matter of fact, government affairs, and government in general, were originally referred to as *mat-surigoto*, "matters relating to festivals." Meanwhile, the principle of **saisei-itchi**, "the unity of the religious and the political," theoretically guided government operations. Sentiments showing strong advocacy of Japan's special position and the emperors' sacred nature based on Shinto beliefs were expressed by nationalists and royalists since the fourteenth century. In a work entitled *Jinnō shōtōki* [*Direct Succession of Gods and Sovereigns*], published in 1339 by Kitabatake Chikafusa (1293–1354), the superiority of Japan and the divine status of the emperors were forcefully asserted: "Great Japan is the divine land (*shinkoku*). The heavenly progenitor founded it, and the Sun goddess bequeathed it to her descendants to rule eternally. Only in our country is this true; there are no similar examples in other countries."[5] But it was during the eighteenth and nineteenth centuries C.E., when an intense Shinto revivalist movement took hold in Japan, that such sentiments came to be even more extravagantly expressed. Known as National Learning (*Kokugaku*), this movement aimed at preserving the very essence of Japanese culture by ridding the country of all foreign elements, including Confucian and Buddhist influences. These concepts were advanced in the *National Learning Writings* of Motoori Norinaga (1730–1801) and Hirata Atsutane (1776–1843).

> Our country's Imperial Line, which casts its light over this world, represents the descendants of the Sky-Shining Goddess (Amaterasu). And in accordance with that Goddess' mandate of reigning "forever and ever, coeval with Heaven and Earth," the Imperial Line is destined to rule the nation for eons until the end of time and as long as the universe exists. That is the very basis of our Way. That our history has not deviated from the instructions of the divine mandate bears testimony to the infallibility of our ancient tradition. It can also be seen why foreign countries cannot match ours and what is meant by the special dispensation of our country.
> —*Motoori Norinaga*

> [A]s a special mark of favor from the heavenly gods, they gave birth to our country, and thus there is so immense a difference between Japan and all the other countries of the world as to defy comparison. Ours is a splendid and blessed country, the Land of the Gods beyond any doubt, and we, down to the most humble man and woman, are the descendants of the gods. . . . Japanese differ completely from and are superior to the peoples of China, India . . . and all other countries of the world, and for us to have called our country the Land of the Gods was not mere vanity. . . . This is a matter of universal belief and is quite beyond dispute.[6]
> —*Hirata Atsutane*

These chauvinistic sentiments, buttressed by a revived nationalistic Shinto, became a prime motivating force that eventually brought down the last feudal military government and ushered in an imperial Restoration in 1868. With the help of Shinto nationalism and deep respect for the imperial line, the fifteen-year-old Meiji emperor emerged from the shadow of centuries of domination of the royal family by military commanders to reclaim his divine right to rule. A "State Shinto" was implemented to promote the worship of the emperor as a living *kami*, at once sacred and inviolable, and to propagate a form of ethnocentric nationalism. It was this State Shinto that was responsible for the cult of emperor worship and the rise of ultra-nationalism in Japan in the twentieth century, a subject to which we will return in the Historical Development section of this chapter.

VOICES: An Interview with Watanabe Minoru

Mr. Watanabe Minoru is a Shinto priest in his fifties at a shrine in the Nerima district of Tokyo.

Why did you want to become a Shinto priest?

My family has been in charge of a shrine at my native city of Shizuoka for generations. Both my grandfather and father were chief priests there. So, ever since my childhood, I have been expected to carry on this family profession also.

Did you have to go to a special school in order to be a Shinto priest?

After high school, I attended the Kokugakuin University in Tokyo to learn all about being a Shinto priest. The university is pretty much like all other universities, except that it is one of the two main training centers for Shinto priests, the other being Kōgakkan in Mie prefecture, near Ise. In addition to Shinto culture and practices, the university offers numerous other disciplines, including economics and law. I led a typical college student's life. I was even president of the judo club during my senior year.

What does it mean to be a Shinto priest?

To me, being a Shinto priest is more than knowing all the Shinto teachings and ritual performances. Most importantly, it is to serve as "cement" for the community by bringing all the neighbors together through year-round shrine activities. The shrine should be a place where people can come and interact with the *kami* and one another on all sorts of occasions and for all kinds of needs whenever they want to. It is a fundamental aspect of Shinto to have a sense that *kami* is so close to us that we can communicate with it whenever we need guidance and protection. Respect of the *kami* and closeness to it either as an individual or as a community form the very basis of our Japanese cultural identity. As a Shinto priest I consider it my solemn duty to preserve this identity and to invite people to appreciate and respect this identity.

SHINTO AS A WAY OF LIFE

Far more important to Shinto than beliefs are ceremonies and ritual practices. Some scholars even argue that Shinto beliefs are "more acted out than thought out".[7] It is often the case that many Japanese perform some of the Shinto rituals and daily habits without full knowledge or consciousness of their doctrinal and theoretical underpinnings. It is certainly the rituals, both public and private, that enable Shinto practitioners to directly experience the presence of the divine *kami* and to recognize their bond with the *kami* as well as with one another. The young shrine carrier Satoshi Tanaka, whom we met at the beginning of this chapter, is representative of this Shinto mindset. Though he does not consider himself a deeply religious man, he finds fun and meaning in his participation in the Sanja Festival. Let us examine how the Shinto beliefs discussed in the previous section of this chapter are lived and acted out in the daily lives as well as the ceremonial occasions of the believers.

Fertility Rites

A major emphasis of Shinto is fertility. In villages throughout Japan, one can still find phallic symbols and representations of the female sex organ on display and worshiped. The Shinto ritual calendar to this day gives prominence to ceremonies revolving around fertility and productivity. In early spring, the *kinensai* (festival for praying for good harvest) is celebrated when the fertility-dispensing *kami* are believed to be physically present in their shrines. Processions of worshipers greet these deities, carry them into the fields on portable palanquins, and dance to celebrate their divine powers while rice seedlings are being planted or transplanted. In the fall, the *niiname matsuri* (harvest festival), the largest event of the ritual year, is observed, when the *kami* are honored and thanked for the bounteous crops with joyous and boisterous celebrations.

The harvest festival is also closely linked with the Shinto belief in divine kingship. The Japanese emperor, the *tennō* ("august heavenly ruler"), had until 1945 both religious and political responsibilities, as he was regarded as a direct descendant of the Sun Goddess Amaterasu and thereby entrusted to rule over the land. One such religious responsibility was the guarantee of fertility of the soil and bountiful harvest. This is consummated ritually each fall at the *niiname* festival, presided over by the emperor as high priest. The most spectacular expression of this magical power of the Japanese ruler is the *daijosai* ("the great food festival"), which is performed by a new emperor the year after his ascension to the throne. In an elaborate and ancient ritual, rice and wine from specially cultivated fields are presented by the new ruler to the deities in the middle of the night, a gesture that consecrates the emperor's religious power and political legitimacy. This rite, still performed as the climax of a royal accession in modern Japan, marks the very distinctive religious foundation of the Japanese imperial institution.

Women in Shinto

As we have seen, Shinto mythology includes many powerful female figures and forces. It should also be noted that though small in number and usually more junior in rank, Shinto priestesses constitute an integral part of the Shinto clergy and can be found in many of the larger shrines all over Japan. They participate fully in all the Shinto rites performed by their male counterparts, though serving as chief ritualist remains rare. Yet it is also true that the most supreme religious figure at the Grand Shrine of Ise, the home of the Sun Goddess Amaterasu, is the *saishu*, the female priestess who is usually a relative of the imperial family, and is ranked above even the chief priest there!

The role of the *miko* (unmarried female shrine attendants) cannot be overlooked. Practically all Shinto shrines have *miko* performing a variety of important, though subordinate, functions. Because of the persistent belief in the shamanic power of these young women to communicate with the *kami*, they are entrusted to perform the sacred dance of *kagura* (music of the *kami*) at festivals and other ritual occasions as an indispensable complement to the prayers and purifying acts of the priests. In addition, they serve as secretaries in shrine offices, sell amulets and other trinkets at shrine gift shops, and generally interact with the public by providing a feminine touch on behalf of the shrine.

Rites of Purification, Presentation, Petition, and Participation

The Shinto ritual event generally involves a four-step sequence of purification, presentation, petition, and participation. The first three steps are performed by priests, while the last one involves the "congregation" in attendance. The rationale for the sequence is first to make the participants (both clergy and laity) physically and spiritually clean for their encounter with the *kami*. The second step is to present food offerings to the *kami* in an attempt to show respect and good will and to pave the way for the next act. This is to formally plead with the *kami*, through beautiful and correct words intoned with reverence and awe by the chief priest, for the concrete benefits being sought. Finally, the last sequence of the ritual is to have the entire worshiping audience fully participate in the ceremony through the watching of performances, sharing of ritual drinks, and the gift of shrine souvenirs.

The Japanese word for the purification ritual performed by the Shinto priest is **harae**, the purpose of which is to please and soothe the *kami*. The ceremony is deemed necessary to prepare the faithful for their encounter with the deity or to remove the defilement that results from any contact with pollutants. All sorts of occasions call for the performance of *harae*, which may take place at the shrine, or the priest may go to the place where it is needed. It is common to call in the Shinto priest to perform the *harae* before moving in to a new home, occupying a new office building, opening a new highway, or even driving a new car. The priest, dressed in sacramental vestments, waves an *onusa* (the wand of stripped paper or an evergreen branch) over the person(s) or the object(s) to be purified, first on the left, then the right, and finally back to the left. Ritual bathing is another form of purification. In a practice known as **misogi**,

Entry of the bridal procession at a Shinto wedding, walking through the shrine gate, led by *mikos*. Yasaka Shrine, Maruyama Park, Kyoto, Japan.

Shinto believers purify themselves by standing under a waterfall or immersing themselves in ocean water. As is well-known, the Japanese are a meticulously clean people who enjoy long and frequent baths during which they scrupulously clean and scrub themselves. This national trait certainly has Shinto roots.

Salt also plays an important role in the *harae*. Its snowlike appearance symbolizes purity, and its potency as a purifying agent is widely accepted in Japan. The Shinto priest often sprinkles salt over the place, the people, or the object to be purified. Sumo wrestlers, whose characteristic Japanese spectator sport has strong Shinto connections, are purified with salt before each match. This belief in salt as spiritual purifier also makes its way into many aspects of Japanese life. After attending a funeral service, people sprinkle salt in the doorway before reentering their home so as not to carry the defilement of death inside. Shop owners also put small mounds of salt on either side of their store front to ward off evil spirits. The Shinto concern with purification is evident in these examples.

The presentation component involves the offering of rice, fish, fruit, rice wine, water, and salt to the *kami*. It should be pointed out that there is absolutely no blood sacrifice in the offerings, as blood is considered repulsive and polluting in Shinto. (For the same reason, menstruating priestesses cannot participate in the *harae* ritual, thus making them less available and qualified to officiate at Shinto rites.) The petition takes the form of the priest reverently reciting the **norito** (prayers or "words spoken to the *kami*"), which is usually written in advance in very elegant and flowery language and read aloud with a rhythmical cadence, ending with a vowel that slides down an octave in pitch and the volume tapering off slowly. The worshipers' participation in the ritual event includes receiving purification by the priest; watching the dance of the *miko*; listening to the performance of the musicians; and, when over, taking small sips of rice wine called *omiki*, as well as bringing home leafy sprigs of the native Japanese *sakaki* tree to complete their encounter with the divine. All of these activities are designed to create bonding between the worshipers and their *kami* as well as among themselves.

The Shrine The Shinto shrine is generally the location where Shinto rituals are carried out. It is referred to as the **jinja**, the "dwelling place of the *kami*." It is here that the *kami* can be approached and worshiped. In early Shinto and in some remote, isolated sacred locations today, the *jinja* can be a tree, a waterfall, or an extraordinarily shaped rock, which local people believe to be a source of spiritual power. These *kami* dwellings are filled with awe-inspiring mystery and great natural beauty. They are often marked with nothing more than a pile of rocks, or sometimes an ornamental rope to suggest the approach to sacred space. Most *jinja*, however, are enclosed areas with a few simple structures. Entry into them requires a purified body and, ideally, a purified mind, as godliness in Shinto is synonymous with cleanliness. Thus the shrine is a holy space, of which the visitor is immediately reminded by two guardian stone lions, one on each side of the entry approach. (In the case of the shrines of the grain goddess Inari, the stone lions are replaced by foxes, which are believed to be her preferred

There is an ancient belief that every part of the island of Itsukushima is so sacred that even the hills and surrounding waters are gods. Inspired by this most unusual belief, a deeply religious twelfth century military commander named Taira no Kiyomori had this shrine complex constructed as an integral part of the natural environment. When the tide is high, the main sanctuary and other structures appear to be floating. The shaded sanctuary's stage is used for events such as dreamlike *takigi* Noh performances illuminated at night by burning wood. The shrine was added to the list of World Heritage Sites in 1996. The island is within the district of Miyajima-cho, Hatsukaichi City, Hiroshima Prefecture.

messengers.) The entry path then passes under the distinctive Shinto crossbar gateway, known as the **torii**, whose literal meaning is "bird dwelling," probably reflecting the earliest function of it as a roost for sacred birds.

In its most characteristic form, the *torii* of today is painted red and consists of two upright posts joined by one or two crossbeams, with the upper crossbeam gently curved in the middle toward the ground. This use of red paint and the curved line in the upper crossbeam indicates both Chinese and Buddhist influence and would not have been found in the early days of Shinto. The *torii* is not meant merely to be a decorative gateway. It is a magical protective device that guards the shrine against all impurities and contaminants. Sometimes visitors have to pass under multiple *torii*, and on occasion an extended series of them are set so close together that they form a veritable tunnel.

Once inside the shrine grounds, all visitors perform a simple purification ritual by approaching a basin or trough of purified water called **tem-izuya** (usually a natural stone basin filled with clear water from the mouth of a sculpted dragon) and, using a bamboo dipper, taking a ladleful of water to rinse their mouth and hands. They are now ready for communion with the *kami*. The *jinja* generally has two buildings—the *haiden* and the *honden*. The former, the "worship sanctuary," is the more public of the two. As its name implies, the *haiden* is where the faithful can approach and worship the *kami*. One very noticeable feature of the *haiden* is the **shimenawa**, a huge rope

The Fushimi Inari-taisha Shrine in Kyoto Japan is dedicated to the god of rice and sake. Here, a tunnel of *torii* arches guarded by pair of foxes.

made of rice straw that marks the boundaries of the building that has been purified or an area in which the kami might be present. Strips of paper called *shide* are hung from the rope.

Worshipers stand in front of the building, clap their hands twice, and ring a suspended bell to attract the attention of the deity. Then they bow their heads and, with hands clasped and sometimes eyes closed, silently utter their prayer of requests or thanksgiving. Occasionally they also deposit offerings into a money chest. The *haiden* is also the place where the priests conduct their ordinary ceremonies on specific occasions on behalf of the community or the state, but sometimes also purely private matters for individuals or small groups.

In the courtyard facing the *haiden*, visitors display their interaction with the *kami* through two specific objects: the **ema**, wooden tablets on which are written their pleadings with the *kami* for success in marriage, childbirth, investment, and entrance examinations; and the **omikuji**, paper fortunes wrapped around tree branches as a form of divination to gauge the future outcome of an undertaking.

Beyond the *haiden* and more hidden from public view is the *honden* ("main sanctuary"), the place where the *kami* resides. It is generally raised higher than any other structure on the premise and has steep access stairs in front and at the sides. Only priests can enter this building, for it is regarded as the shelter of the **shintai**, the "body of the deity" that is the very physical embodiment of the *kami*. This *shintai* is the kernel of sacredness, the symbolic representation of the *kami* honored at the shrine. In and of itself the *shintai* has little intrinsic value. It may be a stone, a scroll, a mirror, a sword, or a small statue. Yet it is regarded with such awe and reverence that even the priests are prohibited from gazing upon it or handling it except on special occasions. As the soul of Shinto holiness and cleanliness, the *shintai* is both inviolably sacred and pure.

The Grand Shrine at Ise, the main sanctuary of the Sun Goddess Amaterasu and official shrine of the imperial family, deserves special mention in connection with this Shinto concern for purity and cleanliness. Though originally built more than thirteen centuries ago, it is completely torn down and rebuilt every twenty years for the purpose

Top: The *shimenawa* marks off a sacred space at a Shinto shrine.

Bottom: These prayer plaques express the hopes, aspirations, and requests for blessing of the shrine visitors.

The inner shrine of Amaterasu at Ise.

The empty lot, adjacent to the existing shrine, is where an identical new shrine will be erected in 2013. The temporary plaque announces that this is the location for the future Inner shrine.

of regular purification and renewal. According to tradition, this practice was inaugurated in 690 C.E. by Emperor Jitō. The design, however, is meticulously copied each time. The shrine we see today is supposedly an exact replica of the original one, and the next rebuilding will take place in 2013.

The carpenters for the Ise shrine come from families that have been hereditarily entrusted to undertake the task. Only natural cypress wood is used for the main structures, and only hand tools are allowed to work on the wood. There are no metal braces or nails used in construction, and the different parts of the shrine are held together by complex and intricate wooden joints. The cypress wood is carefully selected years in advance of the rebuilding and is paraded through different communities throughout Japan to drum up support for and interest in the shrine rebuilding project. Thus the Ise Shrine is simultaneously the oldest and the newest, as well as the purest, shrine in Japan.

Religious Observances throughout the Year

Because of the diversity in Japanese religion, the yearly round of customary ritual observances (*nenjū gyōji*) is correspondingly diverse in religious orientation. Excluding the various local festivals that pay tribute to particular Shinto *kami* and Buddhist feasts that honor the Buddha and specific *bodhisattvas*, the following are the most popularly observed annual ritual occasions.

New Year (*Oshōgatsu*) People prepare for the New Year each January 1 by cleaning their houses thoroughly in an attempt to get rid of both physical and spiritual dirt. On New Year's Eve near midnight, they visit one of the major Shinto shrines such as the Meiji Shrine in Tokyo or a prominent Buddhist temple such as the Honganji in Kyoto to welcome in the New Year. Beginning on New Year's Day, they visit friends and relatives to offer their greetings and renew their relationship.

The Turn of the Seasons (*Setsubun*)   This festival is observed on February 3, the last day of the winter season. A special purification ritual is performed by the entire family, which involves the throwing of roasted beans from the house into the yard, yelling *Oni wa soto!* (Demons get out!) and, from the yard into the house, calling out *Fuku wa uchi!* (Fortunes come in!). Shinto shrines in the community do the same, though on a much larger scale.

Doll Festival (*Hina Matsuri*)   March 3 is devoted to the celebration of girls and daughters in the household. A notable feature of the observance of this special day is the prominent display of tiers of dolls with elaborate costumes that represent the styles of the court ladies of the ancient imperial period. These dolls are expensively made and are seen as reflection of the family's financial standing.

Boys' Day (*Tango no Sekku*)   This the counterpart of the Doll Festival is celebrated on May 5. Dedicated to celebrate the healthy growth of boys, this day refers to the annual festival (*sekku*) held on the day of the horse (*go*) at the beginning (*tan*) of May. It also involves the display of figurines of armored fighters and the flying of carp-shaped paper or fabric streamers on a tall pole.

Star Festival (*Tanabata*)   This festival was introduced from China to commemorate the romantic story of two stars, Vega and Altair, personified respectively as a young weaver maiden and her lover the cowherd, who are allowed this one-time-a-year rendezvous in the heavens. Observed on July 7, it is a festival for young lovers and for unmarried girls who want to improve their chances of marriage by honing their skills in weaving, sewing, and embroidery, or any arts and crafts requiring manual dexterity.

Ghost Festival (*Obon*)   Unlike the other festivals listed here, the Ghost Festival's date each year is not determined by the solar calendar. Instead, it falls on the fourteenth day of the seventh month in the lunar calendar. This is the Japanese version of the *Yülanpen*, a Chinese Buddhist festival. *Bon* is the Japanese pronunciation of the Chinese word *pen* (bowl of offerings), and *o* is the honorific. This is the festival to welcome the ancestral spirits to return home with food and offerings. Families clean the graves of their ancestors and wash the headstones. On the previous evening, people build a small fire outside the gate of their homes to greet the returning spirits. Sometimes Buddhist monks are invited to the house to recite *sutras* to soothe the souls of the deceased and comfort the living. Over the next two days, people participate in communal folk dances called *bon odori* to please the spirits and to enhance communal solidarity.

Harvest Festival (*Niiname-sai*) This giving of thanks by the community for rice harvest occurs on November 23. In modern Japan, it is renamed "Labor Thanksgiving Day" (*Kinro kansha no hi*) and designated a national holiday. Celebrating the harvest with the people, the Japanese emperor traditionally would taste the newly ripened rice and would offer it to the *kami* on behalf of his subjects. The festival also links all local shrines to the imperial court, as the emperor is believed to be the representative of the people to thank the *kami* for providing fertility and bountifulness.

THE HISTORY OF SHINTO

The long history of the Shinto tradition can be divided roughly into three periods: ancient, medieval, and modern. The ancient period lasted from prehistoric times to the unification of the country by the Yamato leaders sometime prior to the sixth century C.E. We have already discussed the major tenets of this ancient Shinto as revealed in the classical works of the *Kojiki* and the *Nihongi*, compiled in the eighth century C.E.

Medieval Shinto

By the time the *Kojiki* and *Nihongi* had been compiled, Shinto had actually begun its second (medieval) stage of development. This stage was marked by the new religious and political challenge from the continental culture of China through Korea. In the year 538 C.E., Confucianism and Buddhism were formally introduced into Japan by the Yamato leaders who had consolidated their power over all other rival clans. This was an accomplishment confirmed by the mythological accounts that describe the submission of the various *kami* (who were believed to be the founding ancestors of these clans) to Amaterasu, the ancestress of the Yamato rulers.

Confucianism and Buddhism gave a great jolt to the established Shinto faith, addressing issues it had ignored or had no interest in. Confucianism (Chapter 8) provided an ethical framework for state, society, and family, while Buddhism (Chapter 5) gave special attention to the issues of suffering and death. The clearest evidence of the influence of the two alien traditions can be seen in the "Seventeen Articles Constitution" promulgated in 604 C.E. by Prince Shōtoku, regent to his aunt the Empress Suiko. More a vision statement than a constitution in the modern sense, the document clearly acknowledges the strengths of Confucianism and Buddhism

TIMELINE
Shinto

10,000–300 B.C.E.* Jōmon period.

300 B.C.E.–300 C.E.* Yayoi period.

300–500 C.E.* Kofun period.

538 Introduction of Buddhism and Confucianism to Japan.

593 Prince Shōtoku becomes regent.

712 *Kojiki* (Record of Ancient Matters) completed.

720 *Nihon-shoki* or *Nihongi* (Chronicles of Japan) completed.

794 Heian (present-day Kyoto) becomes the permanent capital.

1185 Beginning of samurai rule in Japan.

1339 Kitabatake Chikafusa publishes the *Jinnō shōtōki*.

From 1750s* Rise of *Kokugaku* (National Learning, Neo-Shinto).

From 1780s* Birth of founders of New Religions.

1868 Meiji Restoration begins, creation of State Shinto.

1937 Beginning of Pacific War, fought in the name of Emperor Showa.

1945 Japan surrenders to Allies, Shinto separated from state.

Note: Asterisks indicate contested or approximate dates.

VISUAL GUIDE
Shinto

This image contains three major aspects of Japanese religiosity—the sun, the Shinto *torii*, and cherry blossoms. The sun is the chief deity responsible for the rise of the Japanese state, the *torii* (lit. "bird perch," hence the bird atop the arch) marks off the sacred space of the Shinto shrine ground, and cherry blossoms convey the Japanese sense of fragile beauty and transience.

Mt. Fuji is probably the most recognized mountain in the world, with its perfect cone shape and white top for a good part of the year. It is also believed by the Japanese to be a *kami*—a deity with awesome power. Framed by blooming cherry blossoms in early spring, it offers a breath-taking sight.

The *shimenawa* in front of a Shinto shrine. A giant rope made of rice stalk, the *shimenawa* marks off the sacred space within the shrine complex. Worshipers believe that beyond the line resides the spirit of the *kami*.

The Nachi Waterfall in Kumano, Japan. Like Mt. Fuji, the Nachi Fall is an iconic Shinto symbol long revered in Japan. Also considered a *kami*, it is a popular site for Shinto pilgrims who appreciate not only its magic power but also its scenic beauty.

A Shinto priest at the Itsukushima Shrine in Miyajima, Japan. The priest acts as bridge between the worshipers and the *kami* housed at the shrine. He makes presentation to the deity on behalf of the community, purifies the shrine visitors with prescribed rituals, and presides over community events.

in giving guidance to harmonious living and purpose in life. Article One declares the primacy of Confucian harmony as the operating principle of both state and society, while Article Two professes hearty adherence to the Buddhist Three Treasures: the Buddha, his teachings (the *Dharma*), and the community of monks he created, the *Sangha*.

In the face of strong challenge from such potent rivals, the reaction of Shinto practitioners was accommodation and adaptation. With no clear inherent ethical orientation (as noted earlier), Shinto adopted Confucian moral principles with little resistance. With respect to Buddhism, the Shinto reaction was more complicated. The Buddha was initially vehemently rejected as a foreign *kami* with no relevance to Japan. In time, however, when Buddhism was fully embraced by the Japanese court during the Nara period (710–784 C.E.), Shinto *kami* became guardians and protectors of the newly arrived Buddha and his various manifestations. Some time later, Buddhas and *bodhisattvas* in turn became saviors of the *kami!* It was common for Buddhist scriptures to be recited before the altar of *kami*, and conversely Buddhist monks were in charge of Shinto shrines. At the end, though, the accommodation between Shinto and Buddhism became nearly a total merger, when Shinto *kami* were worshiped as Buddha or *bodhisattva*, and the alien Buddhist deities were likewise regarded as Japanese *kami*. Using the Tōdaiji temple in Nara as example, the Vairocana Buddha housed there is known as Dainichi, the "Great Sun," a conscious effort to equate and identify with Amaterasu the Sun Goddess. By the Heian period (794–1191), a perfect amalgamation of Shinto and Buddhism was complete.

One interesting form of this Shinto-Buddhist merger at the folk level was the emergence of a lay Buddhist and occult Shinto group known as Shūgendō ("The Way of Cultivating Magical Power"). Practitioners of this faith usually underwent austere training in the mountains to acquire mysterious powers of healing, divination, and exorcism. Commonly referred to as *yamabushi* ("those who sleep in the mountains"), they were ascetics with no formal affiliation with either established Shinto or Buddhism, but were revered as shamanic healers and exorcists, as well as guides for pilgrims making their way to remote sacred sites.

The convergence of Shinto and Buddhism (and Confucianism for that matter) in Japan has been credited with the formulation of the *samurai* ("sword-wielding warriors") code of conduct in premodern Japan. Known alternatively as *Bushidō* ("Way of the warrior"), this *samurai* ethics emphasizes purity of the heart and soul, contempt for pain and death, and undying loyalty to the feudal lord. It aims to combine the best elements of Shinto, Buddhism, and Confucianism within Japan's cultural heritage.

The Modern Period

The modern period of Shinto history began with its attempt at recovering its pristine past and its claim of superiority over the non-native traditions. Stirrings of this sentiment can be detected after the abortive Mongol invasions of Japan in 1274 and 1281. The near disasters aroused in the Japanese a strong sense of national consciousness, resulting in their reevaluation of their native beliefs and those coming from abroad. The aforementioned nationalistic sentiment of Kitabatake Chikafusa, whose writing insisted that Japan was superior to all other countries because of its single line of emperors descended from the gods, reflected this trend in the political realm.

With the rise of the *Kokugaku* (National Learning) movement in the eighteenth century, a call was made for the return of Japan to the pristine beliefs and practices of ancient times before the introduction of "inferior" alien traditions such as Buddhism and Confucianism had contaminated Japanese culture. Meanwhile, with reinvigorated effort, the priests of the Grand Shrine at Ise actively promoted pilgrimage to the shrine by groups from all over Japan. This helped to create a sense of national unity, binding all Japanese together under one common Shinto faith.

State Shinto All these developments paved the way for the establishment of State Shinto after the Restoration of the Meiji Emperor in 1868. In 1870, the Meiji government proclaimed that "the Way of the *Kami*" would be the guiding principle of the nation. Reversing the previous Tokugawa military regime's practice of requiring all households to register in Buddhist temples, the new government mandated every household to enroll in the shrine of the local *kami*. The government also actively encouraged Shinto funeral rites in a deliberate effort to deprive Buddhism of its monopoly in conducting funeral services. Indeed, Buddhism was forcefully separated from Shinto, and Buddhist monks who had been affiliated with Shinto shrines were ordered to return to secular life.

But it was the Meiji government's promotion of the emperor cult that constituted the core of State Shinto. The emperor was venerated as a "living *kami*"—a god in flesh and blood. During the Meiji reign, a special shrine was built in Tokyo (formerly known as Edo), the seat of power of the just-toppled Tokugawa shogunate, which had become the new capital. The shrine, named Yasukuni Jinja ("Shrine for the Pacification of the Nation"), was dedicated to those who had sacrificed their lives for the royalist cause at the time of the toppling of the last feudal regime and the restoration of imperial authority in 1868. All of them had been elevated to *kami* status, as would others who were subsequently enshrined there after each of Japan's foreign wars in the twentieth century, including the Russo-Japanese War of 1904–1905 and the Second World War. Because of its close association with State Shinto and the emperor cult, both of which have been blamed for Japan's imperialistic expansion in Asia (the colonization of Taiwan and Korea in 1895 and 1910, respectively; the occupation of Manchuria in the 1930s; and the outright invasion of China and Southeast Asia during the Pacific Wars of 1937–1945), the Yasukuni Shrine has become a controversial symbol. That it also houses the remains of some of the most notorious government leaders and commanders at the end of World War II makes matters even more sensitive. Japan's neighbors (China and Korea in particular), who were victims of Japan's ultra-nationalistic aggression in the first half of the twentieth century, invariably file official complaints whenever prominent Japanese political figures (such as the prime minister) pay formal visits to the Yasukuni Shrine.

State Shinto has also been blamed for the fanatical nationalism among many Japanese, particularly among the rank and file of the military, during World War II. Japanese soldiers ravaged much of Asia in the name of their imperial ruler, Emperor Hirohito (r. 1926–1989). They considered their foreign aggression a divine mission, to be carried out without remorse or hesitation. Even when Japanese defeat appeared inevitable by the early 1940s, the military commanders sent suicide pilots to plunge their planes into Allied battle ships in a desperate attempt to reverse the fortune of the war. Calling the pilots *kamikaze* ("divine wind"), they tried to evoke memory of the Japanese defeat of the invading Mongol troops in 1274 and 1281 thanks to the alleged assistance of the divine storm (*kaze*) sent by the *kami* to protect the nation. State Shinto's hold on Japan during those war years was unmistakable.

But the best illustration of the emperor cult in State Shinto was the building of the Meiji Shrine that began in 1915 and was completed in 1920. Constructed to enshrine the *kami* spirits of the Meiji Emperor and his wife, the shrine was a tremendous undertaking funded by the government. Located in the heart of Tokyo, the Meiji Shrine covers close to 200 acres of prime real estate, surrounded by elaborate gardens and wooded areas. It remains to this day a popular site for New Year's celebrations and other festivals.

Sect Shinto The Modern period of Shinto also saw the rise of Sect Shinto and other new religions. A combination of Shinto, Confucianism, Buddhism, Shūgendō, and folk beliefs, Sect Shinto arose at the end of the Tokugawa period and became popular throughout the Meiji period. Thirteen such sects have gained official recognition. Grouped with other eclectic religious organizations that arose in the 1920s and 1930s under the general category of "New Religions," they include such influential sects as Tenrikyō ("Teaching of Heavenly Principles"), Konkōkyō ("Teaching of Golden Light"), and Kurozumikyō ("Teaching of the founder, Kurozumi Munetada" [1780–1850]).

Although different in doctrine and practice, these religious groups share a number of common features. Their founders were charismatic individuals steeped in the shamanic tradition of Shinto, the esoteric teachings of Buddhism, and a whole host of other folk beliefs. A noticeable number of them were women. Mostly of farming origin, they appealed to the anxiety and unease experienced by the lower classes during a time of rapid social change and political upheaval, as was the case in much of modern Japanese history. Explaining that calamity and disaster emanate from disturbances in people's spiritual state, they offered their shamanic powers to bring peace, harmony, health, and prosperity to their followers. The emphasis on worldly benefits was often accompanied by the promise of the impending arrival of a new age and a new world. To impress the faithful and the larger society around them, they have built imposing headquarters and even whole cities of great beauty. Their teachings generally stress clean living, hard work, moral conduct, familial cohesion, and social solidarity. The sectarian nature of these groups has made their believers more fervent than members of the established traditions of Shinto and Buddhism.

Shinto In Japan Today

Japan's defeat at the end of World War II in 1945 fundamentally changed the religious landscape of the country. The State Shinto that sponsored the cult of the emperor and government support of the shrines was, in theory at least, abolished. The divinity of the Japanese emperor was officially disavowed. Yet the imperial family continues to enjoy great affection by the majority of the Japanese people. Public reference to members of the emperor's family, even children, has to be couched in honorific language, and great throngs of people visit the grounds of the Imperial Palace on New Year's Day to greet the imperial family. The emperor opens each session of the parliament as the constitutional monarch and officially receives each new prime minister upon his assumption of office (a female prime minister is yet to be elected in Japan). Members of the imperial household, particularly the Crown Prince, visit the Grand Shrine at Ise periodically to signal their claimed lineage tie to the Sun Goddess Amaterasu.

Meanwhile, Sect Shinto in the form of the many new religions discussed previously has flourished. With their charismatic leaders and their emphasis on this-worldly benefits, the various Shinto-inspired groups attract large followings by serving the practical needs of the faithful. Local, regional, and even national shrines are maintained largely with nonofficial sources of funding, providing quiet locations of escape from the hustle and bustle of urban living and scenic sanctuaries where people can commune with the numinous forces in nature. Shinto values continue to give the Japanese people their sense of identity and aesthetics, as well as solace and comfort after disasters. In the aftermath of the 9.0 earthquake and its subsequent nuclear leak and devastating tsunami that wreaked so much havoc in northeastern Japan in March 2011, Shinto beliefs about life renewal and rejuvenation, as well as its emphasis on purification and decontamination, have provided the Japanese people with the purpose and resolve to carry out a massive program of reconstruction and revival of the stricken areas. Shinto remains at the core of Japanese culture. As the opening vignette illustrates, it is the ritual and social functions of Shinto that continue to provide solidarity for the Japanese people and justify the relevance of this religion for the Japanese nation.

CONCLUSION

We have established in this chapter that Shinto is the longest surviving and most distinctive religious tradition in Japan. It pervades much of Japanese life and informs much of Japanese behavior. It also provides a sense of identity and unity to the Japanese people. Shinto belief in the ubiquitous presence of the *kami*, both in nature and in human society, makes the Japanese view nature and community with awe and respect. Though lacking an ethical code and detailed understanding of the afterlife, Shinto is complemented by Confucianism and Buddhism to allow the Japanese the full experience of a religious life.

SEEKING ANSWERS

What Is Ultimate Reality?

According to Shinto, the world is a sanctified place divinely created and ordained by the *kami*. The *kami* reveal themselves in living and nonliving things, in both nature and in the human world. They are responsible for the fertility of the world, and they prefer purity and cleanliness. Humans, some of whom are *kami* themselves, must pay constant attention to their relationship with the *kami*, for that is the only way that life can be fulfilled. Because the world is the creation of the *kami*, humanity is obligated to maintain the world's sanctity by acting as its guardian and caretaker. Shinto believers are extremely sentimental about nature and are easily moved by its beauty. Much of Japanese literary compositions express this Shinto affirmation of the divine and sanctified nature of the world.

How Should We Live in This World?

Original Shinto gives little emphasis on morality or ethical living. There is no revealed moral code. Instead, it teaches right living primarily as fertile and pure living. The human condition is defined more in terms of purity and defilement. Death, blood, improper food, or improper behaviors are sources of contamination that make humans unfit to interact with the *kami*. However, these are temporary conditions. Constant attention to maintaining cleanliness and purity will ensure favor from the deities. As a result, rituals of purification

(continued)

and sanctification are meticulously performed by Shinto believers to seek good interaction with the *kami*.

What Is Our Ultimate Purpose?

Unlike many other religions, Shinto does not perceive the human condition as a fallen state or intrinsically flawed by sin. Humans are therefore not evil by nature; thus, there is no need for improvement or transcendence. Conversely, Shinto has no belief in an almighty benevolent God who has made humans in an initial state of perfection. Humans are therefore not good by nature either. Instead, humans are very much a part of nature, striving to live in harmony with it through interaction with its various spiritual manifestations, the *kami*.

REVIEW QUESTIONS

For Review

1. What is the Shinto version of creation?
2. Why is the concept of *kami* so central to Shinto beliefs?
3. How does Shinto view death?

For Further Reflection

1. If Shinto does not address ethics in its original outlook, what is the source of morality for the Japanese?

2. Discuss the role played by women in Shinto.
3. What role does Shinto play in bolstering the nationalistic sentiments of the Japanese people?
4. While there are rivalry and competition among the three major religions in Japan, there has been a conspicuous absence of religious wars based on doctrinal or theological differences. Please explain.

GLOSSARY

Amaterasu (ah-mah'-te-rah'-soo) "Deity that shines in the sky," the Sun Goddess in Shinto. Enshrined at Ise, Amaterasu is the *kami* of the imperial family. As the Sun Goddess, she is the most august of all deities. Her descendants are considered the only rightful rulers of Japan.

ema (ə-mah') Wooden tablets expressing pleadings to *kami* for success in life.

harae (hah-rah'-ə) Shinto purification.

Izanagi (ee-zanah'-gee) The male *kami* who is the procreator of the Japanese islands.

Izanami (ee-za-nah'-mee) The female *kami* who is the procreator of the Japanese islands.

jinja (jin'-ja) Shinto shrine.

kami (kah-mee) Shinto deity and spirit with awe-inspiring power.

Kojiki (koh'-jee-kee) *Record of Ancient Matters*, compiled in the eighth century C.E.

matsuri (mah-tsu'ree) Shinto religious festival.

miko (mee'-koh) Unmarried female Shinto shrine attendants.

(*continued*)

GLOSSARY (*continued*)

mikoshi (mee-koh'-shee) Portable shrine temporarily housing a Shinto deity.

misogi (mee-soh'-gee) Shinto ritual of purification with water.

Nihon shoki (nee-hohn shoh-kee) *Chronicles of [the Land Where] the Sun Originates.*

norito (noh-ree'-toh) Invocational prayer offered by Shinto priests to the *kami.*

omikuji (oh'-mee-koo-jee) Paper fortunes wrapped around tree branches at shrines.

saisei-itchi (sai-sei ik'-kee) Unity of the religious and the political realms.

shimenawa (shee-mə' nah-wa) Huge rope hung in front of the worship sanctuary of a shrine.

shintai (shin-tai) The "body" of a *kami* housed in a shrine or temporarily in a *mikoshi.*

Shinto (shin-toh) The Way of the Gods. Traditional Japanese religion that acknowledges the power of the *kami.*

temizuya (te mee' zoo-ya) Purification fountain at a shrine.

torii (toh- ree' ee) Cross-bar gateway leading up to the Shinto shrine.

SUGGESTIONS FOR FURTHER READING

Ashkenazi, Michael. *Matsuri: Festivals of a Japanese Town.* Honolulu: University of Hawaii Press, 1993. An anthropological and sociological description of Shinto in practice at Yuzawa, a town in Japan's northern region.

Bellah, Robert N. *Tokugawa Religion: The Cultural Roots of Modern Japan.* New York: The Free Press, 1985. A classic sociological study of the religious roots of modern Japan, with an in-depth look at possible parallels to the Protestant ethic.

De Bary, Wm. Theodore, et al., eds., *Sources of Japanese Tradition*, Vols. I & II, 2nd ed. New York: Columbia University Press, 2001, 2005. Though not exclusively focused on religious writings, this two-volume anthology is a gold mine of information for the study of Japanese religion.

Earhart, H. Byron. *Religion in the Japanese Experience: Sources and Interpretations*, 2nd ed. Belmont, CA: Wadsworth Publishing Co., 1997. An informative collection of source materials on Japanese religion, arranged topically and with insightful comments.

Ellwood, Robert, and Pilgrim, Richard. *Japanese Religion: A Cultural Perspective.* Englewood Cliffs, NJ: Prentice Hall, 1985. A concise volume for the cultural study of Japanese religion.

Kasahara, Kazuo, ed. *A History of Japanese Religion.* Tokyo: Kosei Publishing Co., 2002. An English translation of a two-volume work in Japanese that contains chapters written by scholars on different stages in the historical development of Japanese religion.

Kitagawa, Joseph M. *Religion in Japanese History.* New York: Columbia University Press, 1990. A detailed historical narrative of the development of Japanese religions.

Nelson, John K. *A Year in the Life of a Shinto Shrine.* Seattle: University of Washington Press, 1996. An ethnographical description of the ritual cycle at the Suwa Shrine in Nagasaki.

Ono, Sokyo. *Shinto: The Kami Way.* Tokyo: Charles E. Tuttle, 1962. This remains a very convenient single volume on Shinto.

ONLINE SOURCES

Encyclopedia of Shinto

eos.kokugakuin.ac.jp

This useful, English-language resource is maintained by the Kokugakuin University in Japan. In addition to the *Encyclopedia of Shinto*, it includes various images and video clips of Shinto objects and rituals.

Tsubaki Grand Shrine of America

tsubakishrine.com

The Tsubaki Grand Shrine, located near Seattle, is the North American branch of one of the most ancient Shinto shrines in Japan. This English-language website provides information about Shinto as well as a schedule of observances at the Tsubaki shrine.

JUDAISM

IT IS A SATURDAY morning, and Seth is waiting to read from the Torah—the most ancient of Jewish Scriptures. Seth has spent the past ten months preparing for this moment, and he is about to become a *Bar Mitzvah* (Hebrew, "son of the commandment"). In late antiquity, a young Jewish male became a Bar Mitzvah simply by turning 13 years old, but by the later Middle Ages a formal rite of passage had developed that signaled a young man's entry into religious manhood. By demonstrating that he can read directly from and comment on the Torah, Seth is proclaiming, before an entire congregation of worshipers, his intention to enter the Jewish community as a literate adult.

Moving a silver pointer shaped like an outstretched hand and index finger across the Torah scroll, Seth reads the passage assigned for that particular Sabbath morning. The sacred text before him is especially difficult to decipher because, as in ancient times, it is written in the consonantal script (that is, without vowels of Hebrew); however, Seth has reviewed this passage many times and has practically memorized it. After the service, Seth will be joined by friends and family who will celebrate his accomplishments with a party, gifts, and lavish praise. This coming-of-age ritual has been enacted countless times over the centuries in Jewish communities throughout the world, but it is only recently—since the 1920s—that the privilege of participating in this ritual has been

The *Bar Mitzvah* stands behind a lectern, facing an open Torah scroll, preparing to read his scriptural passage in Hebrew.

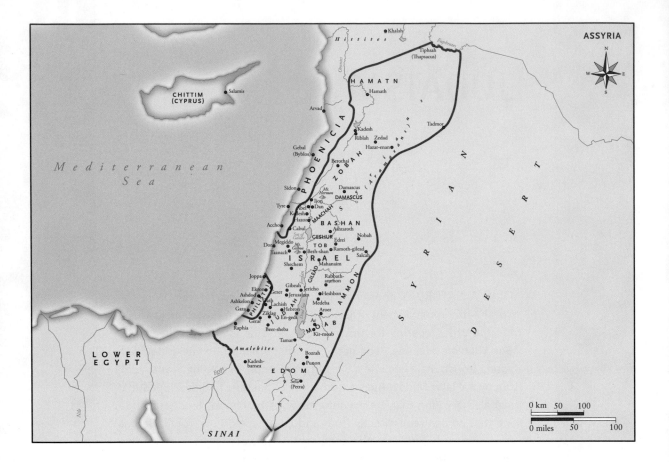

Ancient Israel.

extended to young women (in which case the young woman in question becomes a **Bat Mitzvah**—a "daughter of the commandment"). Nevertheless, it has become quite common today for 12- and 13-year-old Jewish girls to perform the same ritual acts their male counterparts do and to receive the same recognition.

Of all of the life-cycle events in Judaism, the Bar and Bat Mitzvah rite is the one ritual occasion where we see the most fundamental of Jewish beliefs on display. For at the core of the Judaic belief system is the assumption that a very special historical and spiritual relationship—referred to, traditionally, as a *covenant*—exists between the one God of heaven and earth and the people of Israel. By demonstrating both a degree of religious literacy and a willingness to freely embrace a life of sacred duties and obligations, adolescent Jewish boys and girls renew that covenant in a public and deliberate way.

The Bar or Bat Mitzvah ritual is not, however, a prerequisite for membership in the Jewish community. Historically, the one and only precondition of Jewish identity has been biological: that is, whether or not one has been born to a Jewish mother. While Judaism has always accepted converts, the majority of the world's Jews have been persons whose ancestors are also Jewish. Nevertheless, this rite of passage has achieved its present popularity precisely because it symbolizes a commitment to a communal religious life and to Judaism as the collective faith-experience of the Jewish people. ☼

Judaism is one of the world's oldest extant religions. In order to best understand the teachings and practices of the Jewish religion, we must first understand the historical context out of which they emerged and to which they responded Therefore, in this chapter we will begin by retracing the history of the Jewish people. We will then be better able to appreciate how Jewish teachings reflect the many challenges faced by Jews over the millennia and to see how Jewish practices often reflect, commemorate, mourn, or celebrate historical events.

THE HISTORY OF JUDAISM

The earliest reference we have to the Jews—known variously as "Hebrews," "Israelites," and "the people of Judah" (depending on the era and the context)—dates from the late thirteenth century B.C.E. On a commemorative stone, inscribed at the request of the reigning Egyptian ruler, Pharaoh Merneptah (c. 1210 B.C.E.), the following inscription appears: "Israel is laid Waste, its seed is no more." No other reference to "Israel" or the "Israelites" appears in Egypt or anywhere else for centuries. Most of what we know about ancient Israel, as well as the beliefs and religious practices of the ancient Israelites, is derived from Jewish Scriptures, referred to in Hebrew (the ancient language of the Jews) as **Tanakh**, and commonly called the **Hebrew Bible** in English. (Christians refer to these books as the "Old Testament" because, in the formation of their own sacred writings, early Christianity decided to incorporate Judaism's Bible into its own scriptures and needed to differentiate specifically Christian books from more ancient Jewish writings. Jews, however, do not generally employ this term.)

TIMELINE
Judaism

c. 1210 B.C.E.* Pharaoh Merneptah's victory over "Israel."

c. 1000 B.C.E.* King David unites kingdom.

922 B.C.E. Division of Kingdom of David and Solomon.

722 B.C.E. Israel conquered by Assyrians.

587 B.C.E. Destruction of First Temple; Babylonian Exile.

539 B.C.E. Cyrus of Persia conquers Babylon.

333–323 B.C.E. Alexander the Great conquers Egypt, Palestine, and Persia

167–140 B.C.E. Maccabean revolt against Seleucid rule.

140 B.C.E. Establishment of the Hasmonean dynasty.

63 B.C.E. Pompey invades Syria-Palestine; Judea becomes Roman province.

66–70 C.E. First Jewish War with Rome.

70 Destruction of the Jerusalem Temple.

132–135 Second Jewish War with Rome.

135 The defeat of the would-be Messiah Bar Kochba.

c. 200 Rabbi Judah the Nasi compiles the *Mishnah*.

c. 500 Completion of the Babylonian Talmud.

882–941 Saadia ben Joseph serves as Gaon of Sura, Babylonia.

1135–1204 Moses ben Maimon (Maimonides) flees Spain for Egypt.

1492 Jews expelled from Spain.

1570–1572 Rabbi Isaac Luria establishes a community of mystics in Safed, Palestine.

1666 Shabbetai Zevi declares himself the Messiah.

1700–1760 Israel ben Eliezer establishes the Hasidic movement.

1792 France confers citizenship on the Jews.

1845 Reform Movement of Germany defines the movement's goals and beliefs.

1894–1899 The trial and re-trial of Capt. Alfred Dreyfus.

1917 The Balfour Declaration.

1939–1945 The Second World War and *Shoah*.

1948 State of Israel established.

1951 The Israeli Parliament declares the 27th of Nisan as *Yom HaShoah* (Holocaust Remembrance Day).

1967 Six-Day War between Israel, Egypt, Syria, and Jordan.

Note: Asterisks indicate contested or approximate dates.

VISUAL GUIDE
Judaism

The Torah scroll is placed on a table where the reader will use a *Yad* (a pointer) to read each word aloud.

The Palm Branch, the Willow, and the Myrtle make up the Lulav; the Lemon (or Etrog) and the Lulav are held together during Sukkot prayers.

The Passover plate is prepared for the *Seder*, with an egg, a shank bone, parsley, chives, and bitter herbs.

The Star of David is a medieval symbol of Jewish identity placed in the center of the flag of Israel.

Dispersion, Assimilation, and Collective Identity

The composite portrait of ancient Israelite society and its faith that one finds in the books of the Hebrew Bible is one of seemingly endless conflicts and successive divine revelations. For the authors of the Hebrew Bible the central conflict was over one issue: Would Israelites remain loyal to their one God (referred to, in Hebrew, by the consonants **YHWH**), or would they worship the deities of Egypt, Assyria, and Babylonia and the gods of the Canaanite peoples among whom they lived? This was a politically relevant question as well as a spiritual one, as the people of ancient Israel struggled to maintain their political and cultural independence for several centuries. Eventually, however, the tides of imperial Near Eastern politics swept over them, and after a series of devastating military defeats—first at the hands of the Assyrians in 721 B.C.E. and later at the hands of the Babylonians in 586 B.C.E.—the once independent Israelite kingdoms of Israel and Judah were destroyed. Thousands of the Israelites were driven into exile or simply absorbed into the Assyrian and Babylonian empires.

Yet despite this history of conquest and dispersion, the people of Israel retained their national identity and their collective memory, and while living in exile they began to assemble a continuous history of their people and of their relationship with their God. Once completed, that history became a library of sacred books. With the earliest copies of these books in hand, exiles from the kingdom of Judah began returning to their homeland after 538 B.C.E., believing that YHWH had at last forgiven them. Over the next few centuries, Jewish communities could be found not only in the historical land of Israel (which Greek and Roman geographers later named "Palestine") but also in Mesopotamia and throughout the Mediterranean. These communities were referred to as the Jewish **Diaspora**, and in the many centuries that followed, the number of Jews living outside of their historic homeland ultimately far exceeded those living within its borders.

For more than two millennia, therefore, dispersion, acculturation, and resistance to total assimilation have formed the larger pattern of Jewish life and must serve as the backdrop to any discussion of Judaism as a historical religion.

The Biblical Period

It has become customary to segment the history of Judaism into several discrete "epochs," each marked by certain key events that help to shape the direction of Jewish religious behavior and thought. The earliest of these epochs is the Biblical period, which can be dated roughly from the eighteenth century B.C.E. to the sixth century B.C.E. The key events of this era are the rise of the Patriarchs (Abraham, Isaac, and Jacob); the **Exodus** from Egypt; the formation of the monarchy; and the rise and fall of the two kingdoms, Israel and Judah, that followed. Viewed historically, the Patriarchal period remains shrouded in myth and legend, with the towering figures of Abraham and Jacob as the principal bearers of the **Covenant** that YHWH establishes with the people we later call "Israelites." As we will see later in this chapter, both the concept of the Covenant and the events of the Exodus exert a profound influence on Jewish beliefs and practices.

The Exodus from Egypt remains a problematic event for which little credible evidence exists today. Nevertheless, in the minds of biblical writers—and in the consciousness of Jews for centuries thereafter—it remains one of the crucial turning points in the history of Judaism. For whether or not it occurred exactly as described in the Hebrew Bible, the escape of Israelite slaves from Egypt marked a significant reversal of fortune for the tribes that called themselves "Israel," and it served as proof of God's power and willingness to intervene in history on their behalf.

More than that, however, the Exodus also marked a decisive moment in Israel's history of divine revelation and law-giving, for it was on a mountain peak in the Sinai peninsula (variously identified as Mt. Horeb or Mt. Sinai) that divine instruction (Hebrew, *torah;* this meaning is distinct from the five books of the bible also known as the *Torah*) was provided to their leader **Moses**, who then imparted these teachings in written form to the assembled Israelite masses. From this era on, "Israel" could no longer regard itself as a simple tribal society, cherishing memories of remote patriarchal leaders. The moment Israel encountered YHWH at Sinai it became a "confessional" community, bound together by a common faith in a Creator-God and committed to His service. As for the land the Israelites were poised to invade, that was understood to be a gift from YHWH, as well as the fulfillment of promises made to their ancestor Abraham. But it was theirs only as long as they remained faithful to the God who had brought them into their "Promised Land" and true to the Covenant He had established with them.

Kingdoms of Israel and Judah As a nation-in-the-making, Israel only began to emerge as a distinctive political entity in the tenth century B.C.E., with the establishment of the dynasty of King David (c. 1000–961 B.C.E.). For a time, David managed to unite a warring tribal society under his leadership, finally passing on the throne to his son Solomon (c. 961–922 B.C.E.), whose even more exalted reign—at least in the eyes of biblical writers—brought a united monarchy to its height of power and fame.

The most important achievement of Solomon's reign, however, was not the extent of his legendary wealth and power, but rather the construction of the First Temple—a permanent sanctuary, designed to replace the portable tent (or "Tabernacle") of Moses' time, wherein prayers and animal sacrifices were offered to YHWH. By building this Temple in the capital city of Jerusalem, Solomon ensured not only that the political and religious life of Israel would be geographically concentrated within one "holy" city but also that the Davidic monarchy would forever be associated with the most sacred site in Judaism.

Following Solomon's death, the northern tribes seceded to form a kingdom of their own, subsequently identified as the kingdom of Israel. The southern tribe of Judah remained loyal to the house of David and his descendants, and it bore the name of the kingdom of Judah. Both of these kingdoms were relatively short-lived, and each in turn was overrun by the armies of more powerful empires: the northern kingdom was destroyed by the Assyrians in 722 B.C.E., and the southern kingdom by the Babylonians in 587 B.C.E. Of the two invasions, it was the second that resonated most powerfully with Jews for centuries thereafter, if only because it was the occasion for the destruction of Solomon's Temple. In time, the loss of the First Temple and of the kingdom of Judah became the archetype of all later tragedies of displacement that the Jews were to endure and would be commemorated in both prayer and practice.

The Second Temple Period

The second great epoch in the history of Judaism, known as the Second Temple period, began with the gradual return of a relatively small band of Judean exiles from Babylonia, following the Persian conquest of the Babylonian empire in 539 B.C.E. The rebuilding of the First Temple (c. 516 B.C.E.), which the Babylonians had earlier destroyed during their siege of Jerusalem in 587 B.C.E., signaled the renewal of a centralized ritual life for Jews in what was formerly the kingdom of Judah, and now was merely a province within the Persian empire. However, the movement of Jews between Babylonia and "Yehud" (as the Persians called Judah) not only provided for the repopulation of Jerusalem and its restoration as a center of religious life but also provided for the passage of ideas and literature from Mesopotamia to the land of Israel.

Even at the beginning of the Second Temple era, a "canon" or collection of sacred Jewish writings was slowly taking shape. Thus, the formation of Jewish Scriptures can be dated most reliably from this period, and the persons most likely responsible for the gathering and editing of these books were scribes and priests. Using the historical and theological perspectives of earlier prophets like First Isaiah (late eighth century B.C.E.) and Jeremiah (late seventh–early sixth century B.C.E.) as their guides, these priestly redactors selected works that embodied a recurrent pattern of teachings about divine promise, judgment, and hoped-for restoration, binding together this diverse collection of sacred works with an archetypal vision of Israel's past and anticipated future.

Though politically turbulent, the Second Temple period saw both the growth of the Jewish Diaspora and an increase in the Jewish population of Palestine, as one empire succeeded another in turn (Persian, Ptolemaic, Seleucid, Roman). In the absence of a Jewish nation-state, religious leadership within the Jewish community fell to the priesthood and to an intellectual class connected to the priesthood. These two groups are said to have formed a leadership "council," known as the "Men of the Great Assembly." Tradition assigns to this body the decision to "close" the canon of divinely revealed (or inspired) Scripture. Scholars differ today on the probable period in which religious authorities—whether in Jerusalem or Babylonia—considered the period of prophecy (and therefore the process of revelation) to have ended.[1] However, it is commonly assumed that by the third century B.C.E. the writing and editing of the first five books of the Hebrew Bible, known in Hebrew as the *Torah* (Hebrew, "the Teaching"), had already reached a sufficient state of finality to allow Greek-speaking Jews to translate it from Hebrew into Greek. In time, additional portions of the Hebrew Bible were translated from available texts; these books are collectively referred to as the Septuagint. This translation played a significant role in introducing Judaism to the larger Greek-speaking world, and it was this version of Jewish Scriptures, rather than the Hebrew original, with which most early Christians were familiar.

Division and Revolt One important development within the Second Temple period was the increasing tension within the Jewish community between those who favored social and intellectual assimilation into Greek (and, later, Roman) culture and those who resisted such assimilation in favor of preserving "traditional" values and religious practices. This struggle became openly violent during the Maccabean revolt of 166–164 B.C.E., as the leaders of the revolt found themselves fighting against not only Syrian-Greek armies but also their more assimilated countrymen who sided with the Syrian king, Antiochus IV (c. 215–164 B.C.E.) Although this conflict finally resulted in the reestablishment of an autonomous Jewish state (c. 140–63 B.C.E.), one of the results of this internal struggle was the gradual appearance of religious "parties" whose influence on Jewish belief and practice grew during the period of Roman domination and occupation of Palestine.

The first-century Jewish historian Josephus (37–c. 100 C.E.) identified the most important of these parties as the Pharisees, who appear to have commanded the attention and the loyalty of the Jewish masses. Central to the Pharisees' form of Judaism was their belief in the "Oral Torah"—that is, the body of teachings imparted by God to Moses on Sinai (but never written down) and subsequently transmitted orally to later generations. For the Pharisees, these interpretive readings of Scripture were an integral part of "Scripture" itself, and therefore just as binding. Thus, the Pharisees taught that *torah*—in the most inclusive sense of the totality of divine revelation to the Jews—incorporated a belief in both the immortality of the soul and the resurrection of the dead. In the eyes of the common people, the Pharisees' knowledge of the biblical text and their familiarity with biblical law made them more reliable guides than the often corrupt and politically compromised priesthood, and it is from the followers of the Pharisees that we derive our sense of what the dominant form of Judaism may have been by the end of the first century C.E.

A second group that Josephus identified were the Sadducees (named for the legendary figure of Zadok, who served Solomon as high priest), whose influence upon the Judaism of the time was much weaker. Drawing their constituents largely from priestly families, the Sadducees regarded the written Torah as exclusively sacred and authoritative, and therefore rejected the very notion that an "Oral Torah" existed. Unlike the Pharisees, the Sadducees tended toward literalism in their understanding of Scripture and therefore could find no warrant for believing in either immortality or resurrection. In politics, they tended to be sympathetic to—or at least accommodating of—Roman authority, and therefore less likely than the Pharisees to favor revolutionary leaders.

The third, and most reclusive, community Josephus refers to is that of the Essenes, a general term designating groups of devout Jews who had withdrawn from society in protest against the moral and spiritual corruption of their contemporaries. These traditionalists viewed the Temple priesthood with disgust and held the radical view of history that the "End-Time" of divine judgment and global catastrophe was at hand. Such beliefs, which religious scholars refer to as **eschatological**, had become increasingly widespread during the late Second Temple era, particularly when coupled with a belief in a **Messiah**. While such beliefs were well-known throughout the Jewish world, Essenes held to their faith in the imminence of the world's end with particular fervor, and they looked forward to a Messianic Age, when the Temple would at last be purified and the Romans defeated by armies of angels. We will learn later in this chapter about the profound influence Messianic concepts have had in shaping Jewish beliefs and practices.

Many historians today associate the Essenes with a community of sectarian Jews who withdrew from Judean society and built a settlement near the northwestern shore of the Dead Sea, at a place called Khirbet Qumran, sometime during the second century B.C.E.[2] The religious literature written and preserved by this group was hidden away in caves near their settlement, and it was not until 1947–1956 that these ancient scrolls were discovered. Collectively, they are referred to as the **Dead Sea Scrolls**, and almost half of these are fragments of books from the Hebrew Bible. These copies of biblical texts are the oldest copies of the Jewish Scriptures known to exist today.

Last, and most transitory in their influence on Judaism, were those revolutionaries Josephus termed the Zealots. Like the Pharisees and the Essenes, the Zealots were eager to see the Romans driven from the land of Israel and looked forward to a restoration of Israel's sovereignty and of its monarchy. However, believing that God would fight on their side, the Zealots sought to expel the Roman army through direct action, and Zealot agitation and rebellion were underlying causes of the First Jewish War against Rome (66–70 C.E.). Even after this war ended in the defeat of Jewish forces and in the destruction of the Second Temple, a group of Zealots continued to hold out against the Romans until 73 C.E., when their mountain fortress of Masada wasbesieged and overrun by the Roman army. Rather than surrender, the remnant of the Zealot fighters, along with their women and children, committed suicide (according to Josephus) rather than be taken alive by their enemy.

The Formative Age

The fall of Jerusalem and of Masada, and the destruction of the Second Temple, signaled the end of the Second Temple era and the beginning of

Masada was the last stronghold Zealots held before taking their lives, rather than yield to the Roman army (73 C.E.).

the third epoch of Judaism's history, known variously as the Rabbinic Age or the Formative Age (c. late first century C.E.–sixth century C.E.). As long as the Temple stood, it served as both a treasured symbol of Israel's biblical past and the operational center of Jewish ritual life throughout the world. Once it lay in ruins, however, the Jewish people needed a new institutional center—a replacement sanctuary, until such time as the Temple could be rebuilt. The **synagogue**, whose remote origins can be traced back to the beginning of the Babylonian exile, provided just such a substitute, but unlike the Temple it was never a place of animal sacrifice, nor was it under the control of a priesthood. In all likelihood, the synagogue began simply as a place of assembly at which Judean exiles could meet and study together. With the Temple gone, however, Jews had no other place to turn to for religious leadership or for communal prayer by the second and third centuries C.E.

Unlike the Temple, which could only stand in one place (namely, Jerusalem), a synagogue could be built anywhere. Synagogues had already begun to appear even while the Temple was still standing. Moreover, almost anyone could build a synagogue or serve as a communal leader. Priests had no role to play in the ritual or social life of a synagogue, which made it a more democratic institution from the start.

The Tuoro Synagogue, built in Newport, Rhode Island, in 1759 is the oldest synagogue in the United States.

The Rabbis In time, the synagogue acquired a clerical leadership all its own, which brings us to the second major historical change that defines the Formative Age: the emergence of a class of religious intellectuals known as Rabbis (Hebrew, "my master"). The word was a term of honor conferred on someone whose piety and learning caused him to stand out among his contemporaries and whose teachings (or legal rulings) were sufficiently memorable that subsequent generations viewed him with respect and even reverence.

One such figure, who had come from Babylonia to study in Jerusalem, was Hillel (fl. 30 B.C.E.–4 B.C.E.), whose compassionate nature was as remarkable as his scholarship. According to legend, it was Hillel who, when asked (mockingly) by a pagan to teach him *torah* while he stood on one foot, replied: "What is hateful to you, do not do to your neighbor; the rest is commentary"—a version of the so-called Golden Rule. Like Hillel, many of the early Rabbis saw themselves as more than just legal scholars whose expertise in biblical law allowed them to advise common folk on matters of correct observance. They also saw themselves as sages or wisdom teachers whose insights into human nature complemented their knowledge of divinely revealed law.

The Compilation of the Talmud The signature accomplishment of the rabbinic scholar-class during the Formative Age is the writing and compilation of the **Talmud**, a composite work that, in time, was seen as a second Torah, or at the very least, as an indispensable addendum to the Jewish Scriptures. On one level, the Talmud is a collection of expansive, often highly imaginative interpretations of biblical law. The format of the Talmud is dialogical (that is, a series of question-and-answer exchanges). Nearly every page consists of some portion of a rabbinic debate over the alternative ways in which a particular biblical statute can be understood or implemented. The practical objective of all these debates was the creation of an authoritative form of ritual behavior—referred to in Hebrew as *halacha*—that would enable the observant Jew to sanctify daily life and fulfill the commandments imparted to Moses on Sinai. God gave *torah* to Israel, the Rabbis believed, and now it was their responsibility to clarify its terms and relate them to daily life. In the Practices section of this chapter, we will see how *halacha* informs the ways many Jews today live their faith.

The Babylonian version of the Talmud, compiled at the beginning of the sixth century C.E., consists of sixty-three separate volumes covering a wide range of legal issues. The historical process by which these volumes came into being, however, can be studied in two stages: the earlier stage, known as the *Mishnah* (Hebrew, "repetition"), is written in Hebrew and consists of economical formulations of *halacha*, often accompanied by an attribution to a particular rabbinic scholar; the later stage, referred to as the *Gemara* (Hebrew, "completion"), is written in Aramaic (a Semitic language, very close to Hebrew), and the rabbinic debates recorded there often take up where the Mishnah leaves off.

This process of recording and summarizing rabbinic debates continued, in both Palestine and Babylonia, during a period of roughly four centuries. As the body of rabbinic commentary evolved toward the next stage of completion—first in Jerusalem in the fifth century C.E. and later in Babylonia at the beginning of the sixth century C.E.—the Mishnah was combined with the far more expansive text of the Gemara. Together these two scholarly works make up the Talmud. Judaism's greatest challenge during this period, however, was not simply that of preserving the teachings of its religious elite, but was, more importantly, that of protecting itself from a rival, "sister" religion—namely, Christianity—whose political might increased throughout the Roman empire in the course of the fourth and fifth centuries, at the same time that Judaism's declined.

The Conflict between Judaism and Christianity

Christianity, as you will learn in Chapter 11, began life as a splinter movement within Judaism, following the death by crucifixion of its central figure, Jesus of Nazareth, in 30 C.E. Over the next two generations the early Christian community gradually pulled away from mainstream Judaism and redefined both the nature and role of Jesus in Christian thought, largely under the influence of an ex-Pharisee known as Paul of Tarsus. Those early followers of Jesus, who may have thought of him as a prophet, or even as a Messiah-figure, were soon displaced by those who saw Jesus as the "Son of God," and who eventually came to believe in him as the incarnate human form of YHWH. As the letters of Paul (mostly written between 50 and 64 C.E.) clearly testify, most contemporary Jews viewed these teachings as heresy and quickly banished Jewish followers of Jesus from the synagogue. By the turn of the second century the split between Judaism and Christianity was irreversible, and out of the matrix of Judaism a new (and largely antagonistic) faith had been born.

The philosophical conflict between Judaism and Christianity sprang from a number of incompatible views on the nature of God, the covenant, and salvation from sin. For rabbinic Judaism, the deity was a transcendent being. Any material representation of God—either in the form of an image or a living human being—was barely acceptable, and even then only as metaphor. For Christianity, on the other hand, the embodiment of the divine in Jesus as the "Christ" soon became a central doctrine of the early Church. As for God's covenant with Israel, Paul argued that the Christian community had—at least at that moment in time—displaced the Jews as true heirs of the biblical promises made to the Patriarchs and the prophets; the Jews, he insisted, had alienated God by their rejection of Jesus and had (if only temporarily) forfeited their intimate relation to the deity. That the Christian and Jewish communities would, before long, rejoin each other in an expanded covenanted relationship with God was Paul's fervent wish and expectation.

As the bearer of a new covenant, made possible through the vicarious sacrifice of Jesus—who took all of humanity's sins on his shoulders—the Church was uniquely empowered to enable those in a state of sin to achieve forgiveness and true righteousness. Paul contrasted this method of obtaining release from sin with the process of repentance in Judaism, insisting that—contrary to Jewish beliefs—no amount of good works (or performance of *mitzvot*) could ever accomplish the goal of obtaining divine mercy. Only heavenly "grace," imparted to each sinner who believed in Jesus' redemptive power, could free one from the burden of guilt and sin. Taken together, these beliefs constituted a significant departure from Judaism's understanding of God's being and of the meaning of *torah*. With the Roman Emperor Constantine's conversion to Christianity early in the fourth century, Judaism found itself facing not only a determined religious antagonist in the Christian Church but also an even more powerful political antagonist, as a succession of Christian emperors sought to stifle Judaism throughout the Roman empire by imposing punitive legislation on the Jews and by condoning acts of violence against synagogues. In the eyes of the late fourth-century Christian theologian St. John Chrysostom (c. 347–407 C.E.), the Jews were the devil's spawn, their synagogues the dwelling-places of all evils, and any civil relations between Christians and Jews, he argued, represented a betrayal of God.[3] Against such a background of institutionalized hatred, the Jews of Christian Europe struggled for the next millennium to maintain not just their faith, but their very lives.

The Age of Philosophy and Mysticism

The fourth great epoch in the history of Judaism, extending from the Early Middle Ages (sixth–seventh centuries C.E.) to the Early Modern period (sixteenth–seventeenth centuries C.E.), can be thought of as the Age of Philosophy and Mysticism. During this period the Jewish Diaspora stretched from China and India in the East to England in the West. Historians frequently employ the following terms to identify these historical/cultural groupings: Ashkenazim, representing those Jews living in Europe; Sephardim, or Jews living in Spain, Portugal, and parts of North Africa; and Mizrachim, or Jews living in various parts of the Middle East. Each of these communities underwent periods of prosperity and decline, but throughout most of this period some of the most creative developments in Judaism took place: first in Babylonia (present-day Iraq) and later in Spain.

As the Palestinian Jewish community dwindled in numbers and prestige in the course of the sixth and seventh centuries, the center of Jewish intellectual life shifted to Babylonia and to the principal rabbinic academies of Sura and Pumpeditha. And it was Sura, in the early tenth century, that gave rise to one of the major figures in Jewish philosophy: Rabbi Saadiah ben Joseph (889–942). Two challenges faced Saadiah during his career; the first, from within the Jewish community; the second, from an entirely new religion.

The Karaites The challenge from within the Jewish community came from a group of anti-rabbinic Jews, known as Karaites, who (like the Sadducees of the first century) rejected the very notion of an "Oral Torah," and therefore rejected both the Talmud and whatever claims to religious authority the Rabbis had asserted since the beginning of the Common Era. For Karaite scholars the only sacred texts in Judaism were those books that made up the Hebrew Bible, and no work of commentary could possibly claim equal, or near-equal, status.

Such views clearly threatened the existence of the rabbinical class, as well as the structure of interpretive and juridical power the Rabbis had constructed over the centuries. As a representative of the rabbinical tradition, Saadiah rose to its defense. The interpretation of Scripture, he argued, rested not only on a profound knowledge of the language of Scripture but also on "reliable tradition," since no generation of scholars could claim a monopoly upon insight or knowledge. In addition, unlike the Karaites, Saadiah did not encourage his contemporaries to believe that the Messiah would arrive momentarily or to assume that the End of Days was at hand. His comparatively realistic view that the Messiah would arrive when the time was right—whenever that might be—made the rest of his views on the Torah seem that much more reliable to his readers.

The Encounter with Islam   Saadiah's second great challenge came from outside Judaism altogether, in the form of a competing faith—namely, that of Islam (Chapter 12). The founder of Islam, Muhammad (570?–632 C.E.), claimed to have received a new work of Scripture—the Qur'an—in the form of oral communications from the Angel Gabriel, and which he saw as a more reliable revelation than that given to either the Christians or the Jews. Viewing himself as one in a long line of prophets that included both Moses and Jesus, Muhammad clearly expected the Jews of Arabia to accept his claim to be the last (or "seal") of the prophets and to embrace his revelation as the definitive message of God (or "Allah" as the one Creator-God is referred to in Arabic) to humanity.

When it became apparent that the Jews of Mecca would accept neither him nor his new *torah*, Muhammad turned his full attention to his pagan audience, whom he found more receptive to a new monotheistic faith. Muhammad's success in propagating his religious message was matched by his military success in defeating many of his more powerful enemies (which included some of the prominent Jewish tribes of Arabia), and after his death the faith of Islam spread rapidly throughout many of the lands in which Jews had settled centuries before. While Muhammad's attitude toward the Jews, as expressed in the Qur'an, remained understandably ambivalent, from the eighth century on Jews were accorded a degree of tolerance within Muslim societies that they rarely encountered in Christian lands.

Like many Jewish scholars of his generation, Saadiah had learned a great deal from reading Muslim philosophical literature of the ninth and tenth centuries. The remarkable similarities between Judaism and Islam allowed him to apply many of the insights that had been used in the defense of the Muslim faith to a Jewish context, while at the same time remaining true to his biblical and rabbinic heritage. Foremost among Saadiah's concerns, therefore, was the need to present Judaism to an educated Jewish audience already familiar with the teachings of both Islam and Greek philosophy, and to do so in a way that did not contradict Jewish Scriptures.

The result of this investigation, which Saadiah published as *The Book of Beliefs and Opinions* (933), is the earliest example of scholasticism in Jewish thought—that is, a systematic attempt to reconcile faith and reason by relating mainstream religious beliefs to contemporary philosophical arguments. By engaging Greek and Islamic philosophy in dialogue, Saadiah sought to prove the unique character of God's revelation to Israel, as well as the rational character of many (though not all) biblical commandments, and thereby strengthen Jewish belief in the uniquely trustworthy nature of Judaism's Scriptures.

Maimonides   The tradition of philosophical inquiry produced at least one more intellectual giant during this period: Moses ben Maimon, better known as **Maimonides** (1135–1204). In Maimonides, Judaism found one of its supreme philosophers; much of Orthodox Jewish theology derives directly from his writings. Maimonides, the son of a respected rabbinic scholar, was well-prepared by his background and early education for this role. When his family was forced to flee their native city of Cordoba, Spain, to escape the tyrannical rule of a militant Muslim regime, they found refuge in Egypt under the more tolerant rule of the celebrated Muslim ruler Salah-Al-Din (c. 1138–1193). Maimonides was better known to his Muslim hosts as a physician than as a philosopher, though it is the latter role that concerns us here.

Maimonides' passion for logic and intellectual clarity is evident in all of his writings. In his *Mishneh Torah*, for example, he listed every single one of the 613 biblical commandments, revealing (even to the casual reader) that many of these *mitzvot* could no longer be fulfilled in the absence of the Temple in Jerusalem. Similarly, in his *Commentary to the Mishnah*, Maimonides clearly describes what he believed to be the thirteen essential "articles" of Jewish belief, thereby creating a dogmatic framework for any subsequent discussion of Judaism as a faith-system.

The enduring popularity of this compact statement of faith guaranteed that it would survive its time and place. It has continued to serve many generations of devout Jews as a useful reference point in any discussion of what today is called "Torah-true" (or "Orthodox") Judaism.

Ironically, Maimonides' most celebrated work, *The Guide for the Perplexed*, evoked considerable controversy when it finally became public, though Maimonides had not intended it originally for widespread publication. In this philosophical treatise, which he worked on toward the very end of his life, Maimonides attempted to grapple with some of the more problematic philosophical issues of his day: the existence and attributes of God, the nature of creation and prophecy, the problem of evil, divine providence, and the purpose of human existence. Throughout the *Guide*, Maimonides makes it clear that he distrusts any comparison between humanity and the eternal creator. At best, he argued, we can speak of God mostly in negative terms. For example, instead of saying that God is a being who lives forever, Maimonides advises that it is preferable to say that He has no temporal limits. This particular approach to theology (and inevitably, to biblical interpretation) emphasizes God's "otherness" and tends to remove God from the material world and beyond the limitations of the human mind.

Like many of his Jewish contemporaries, Maimonides looked forward with some eagerness to the advent of the Messianic Age, though he was shrewd enough not to assign a date to that hoped-for event. Interestingly, however, Maimonides' view of both the Messiah and the era of his arrival is largely naturalistic, and it contrasts sharply with the more supernaturalist traditions that both preceded and followed him:

> "The 'days of the Messiah' refers to a time in which sovereignty will revert to Israel and the Jewish people will revert to the land of Israel. Their king will be a very great one, with his royal palace in Zion. . . . All nations will make peace with him, and all countries will serve him out of respect for his great righteousness and the wonders which will occur

through him. . . . However, except for the fact that sovereignty will revert
to Israel, nothing will be essentially different from what it is now."
—*Helek Sanhedrin, Ch. 10*[4]

This demythologized version of messianic Judaism was Maimonides' principal
legacy to future generations of acculturated Jews. But one important segment of the
Jewish community, those drawn to mystical thinking, rejected Maimonidean scholasticism and its celebration of reason and sought to restore to Judaism some of its rich
mythological past.

The Kabbalah Collectively, the many diverse traditions that make up the world of
Jewish mysticism are sometimes referred to as **Kabbalah** (lit. "received" tradition),
but when historians use that term they are thinking primarily of a school of mystics
whose beginnings can be traced to twelfth-century France and thirteenth-century
Spain. Common to all these writers was an acknowledgment that the hidden "essence"
of YHWH— as Maimonides taught—cannot be fully grasped, and certainly never
directly perceived or represented.

In a late thirteenth-century work many regard as the "bible" of Kabbalah—
the **Zohar**—this entire structure of divine qualities and emanations is laid out in
the form of a biblical *midrash*, that is, an extended interpretation of select passages
from the Book of Genesis. Central to this form of mystical thought is the idea that

THE ESSENTIAL ARTICLES OF JEWISH BELIEF

1. God the Creator exists.
2. God is uniquely "one."
3. God is incorporeal (and therefore all scriptural images of a divine "body" are mere figures of speech).
4. God is eternal.
5. God alone is worthy of worship and obedience.
6. The teachings of the biblical prophets are true.
7. Moses is the chief of all prophets.
8. The Torah comes directly from God (through Moses).
9. Both the Written and the Oral Torah represent the authentic word of God, and nothing can be added or taken away from either.
10. God is omniscient.
11. God rewards the good and punishes the wicked.
12. The Messiah will undoubtedly come (though no exact date can be known for his coming).
13. The resurrection of the dead will occur in the World-to-Come.

however imperfect the human race may be, we are still capable of interacting with, understanding, and even influencing God. This theology of immanence—or, more precisely, of divine-human interaction—is quite obviously at odds with Maimonides' view of a profoundly transcendent Creator. Consequently, the kabbalists felt free to evoke the Creator in explicitly anthropomorphic language (i.e., portraying God in very human terms).

By the sixteenth century, the kabbalistic system had matured to the point that a powerful and highly imaginative cosmology emerged, mainly through the teachings of one man: Rabbi **Isaac Luria** (1534–1572). The *Ari* (or "holy lion"), as he was known to his disciples, left no writings at the end of his short life, but his followers disseminated his thought throughout much of the Jewish world, and of all the many variants of Kabbalah, the "Lurianic" system is at once the most influential and the most complex, as we will see later in this chapter. Luria taught that the individual believer could liberate the divine "spark" within by careful observance of the divine commandments and acts of self-discipline and meditation. In addition, in sharp contrast to mainstream Jewish belief, Luria envisioned each soul undergoing a series of reincarnations, as the soul constantly strives to return to its Source.

The potential danger—as well as the enormous appeal—of Lurianic Kabbalah became quite apparent a century after the Ari's death in the sensationalistic career of a messianic pretender, Shabbetai Tzevi (1626–1676). A Turkish Jew of obviously unstable temperament, Shabbetai became convinced early in life of his extraordinary spiritual powers after studying Lurianic texts. At the encouragement of one of his most fervent disciples (a self-styled prophet named Nathan of Gaza, whom he had met on a visit to Palestine), Shabbetai declared himself the "King Messiah." In 1666, he presented himself before the Sultan of Turkey, asserting his messianic credentials and his "royal" right to the historic land of Israel. The Turkish response to this mystical drama was, first, to imprison Shabbetai for a year, and then to offer him a minor position at court following his conversion to Islam. Shabbetai's acceptance of this offer not only exposed him as an apostate, but it also sent shockwaves throughout the Jewish world, particularly among those who had firmly believed that Shabbetai was indeed the messianic deliverer he claimed to be.

The Rise of Hasidism Shabbetai Tzevi was neither the last nor even the most important religious figure to base his teachings on Lurianic thought, however. Within two generations of Shabbetai's death yet another mystical teacher arose, this time in Poland. The **Baal Shem Tov** (c. 1700–1760) also taught the necessity of releasing the sparks of holiness within and thereby hastening the approach of the Messiah. His given name was Israel ben Eliezer, but his disciples commonly referred to him as the "Master of the Good Name" (Hebrew, *Baal Shem Tov*), a title that conveyed to contemporaries the belief that he possessed secret "names" of God that he could use in incantations. Orphaned as an infant, the Baal Shem Tov was given a rudimentary education, and at no time during his career as a spiritual guide was he regarded as a great scholar. Instead, his fame derived from his faith healings and exorcisms. In time, the Baal Shem Tov gave up the life of an itinerant healer and began to attract a growing number of disciples who were drawn by his reputation for wisdom and spirituality.

At the heart of the Baal Shem Tov's teachings was a profoundly immanental vision of God's omnipresence. For the Baal Shem Tov and his followers—who were soon called **Hasidim** (Hebrew, "pious ones")—God could be found everywhere, and everyone was at least potentially capable of spiritual communion with the Creator. To worship God properly, the Baal Shem Tov taught, one need not be a master scholar, nor engage in acts of self-mortification, nor even engage in constant prayer. The most ordinary of everyday acts, he insisted, if performed with an awareness of God's nearness and in a spirit of joy and love, become acts of spiritual devotion and serve to make everyday life sacred. No one was too humble or too depraved to turn (or return) to God, who required only a burning desire to perform His will. Only when believers are capable of this level of religious enthusiasm will their prayers begin the process of world-healing.

At the communal level, the key to success within this system of mystical devotion lies with its leadership, and the Baal Shem Tov urged his disciples to choose a spiritual guide, or *tsaddik* (meaning "righteous one"), to provide a living example for themselves and the rest of the community of what it is like to live a life of intense religious commitment and intimacy with God. After the Baal Shem Tov's death, the Hasidic movement he helped to create spread rapidly throughout Russia and much of Eastern Europe. In each major geographical center of Hasidic activity, *tsaddikim* appeared to carry on the teachings of the Baal Shem Tov. Each of these leaders formed a "court," or spiritual circle of followers; in time Hasidic dynasties appeared, as one generation followed another and as the loyalty to the father was transferred to the son. Many of these dynasties, formed in the nineteenth century, still exist today, with the result that virtually all Hasidic communities are centered around the personality and religious leadership of one man—often referred to in Yiddish as the *Rebbe*—whose authority in all things is largely unchallenged.

Opposition to the Hasidic movement arose soon after the Baal Shem Tov's death, and for the next two generations established rabbinic authorities in Russia and Poland sought to stifle popular interest in Hasidic teachings, even encouraging secular authorities to arrest prominent Hasidic leaders. Their principal fear was that Hasidism would lead to a revival of a messianic cult like that which formed around Shabbetai Tzevi. Yet despite the determined opposition of the rabbinic establishment, Hasidism flourished, and by the mid-nineteenth century official opposition to Hasidism waned as Europe's rabbinic leadership realized that it faced a far more formidable opponent in the Jewish reform movements that

A young Israeli Hasid with curled sideburns, commonly worn by men in his community.

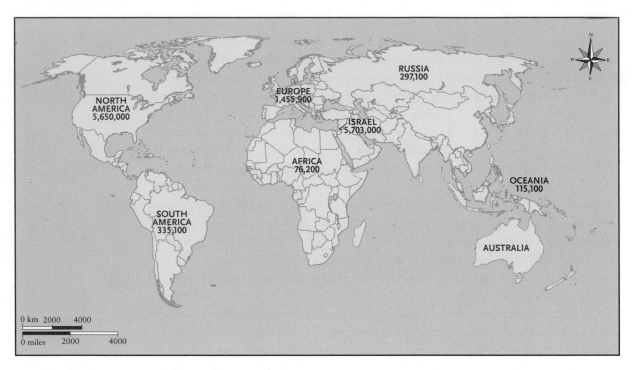

RUSSIA
297,100

EUROPE
1,455,900

NORTH
AMERICA
5,650,000

ISRAEL
5,703,000

AFRICA
76,200

OCEANIA
115,100

SOUTH
AMERICA
335,100

AUSTRALIA

0 km 2000 4000

0 miles 2000 4000

Total number of Jews presently living throughout the world.

suddenly emerged in response to Enlightenment values during the late eighteenth and early nineteenth century.

The Modern Era

The modern era in Judaism can be studied on at least two levels—the political and the philosophical—for until the Jews of Western Europe had achieved a certain degree of political emancipation, they were unable to fully acculturate within European society or benefit from the intellectual revolutions of the seventeenth and eighteenth centuries. For centuries, Jewish life in the West was characterized by both physical and cultural containment, the most visible symbol of which was the Jewish Quarter of many cities (or Ghetto, as it was known after the sixteenth century), where Jews were forced to reside. By law, Jews were also restricted to certain trades and professions, especially money-lending, but by the late eighteenth century many of these restrictions began to be removed. As more prosperous and highly educated Jews were permitted to intermingle (and increasingly, intermarry) with their Christian contemporaries, Judaism itself began to change.

Moses Mendelssohn No better example of this pivotal transformation in Jewish life can be found than Moses Mendelssohn (1729–1786), the son of a Torah scribe and the principal representative for his time of the Age of Enlightenment (referred to in Hebrew as the *Haskalah*). Since Jews were not yet permitted to attend universities, Mendelssohn was largely self-taught in modern philosophy and several European languages. Before long, his philosophical writings began to attract the attention of non-Jews within his native Germany and beyond. His impact on the Jewish community was just as profound, and through his translation of the Hebrew Bible into modern German and his various other publications Mendelssohn became one of the most effective advocates for educational reform and the modernization of Jewish intellectual life.

What Mendelssohn is best remembered for today, however, is his eloquent defense of religious freedom, coupled with a defense of the Jewish faith, in a volume entitled *Jerusalem* (1783). In this polemical masterwork, Mendelssohn entered a plea on behalf of religious tolerance and in defense of the integrity of Judaism. He argued that all higher religions share certain common beliefs (such as the existence of a benevolent Creator-God, or the immortality of the soul) and that since Judaism also held such beliefs it was as much an expression of the "common religion of humanity" as Christianity or Islam.

What was distinctive to Judaism, Mendelssohn proposed, was not so much its belief system as its sacred legislation—its *Torah,* understood here strictly as divinely revealed law—and its emphasis on doing God's will rather than professing correct ideas about God or the afterlife. The essence of Judaism, Mendelssohn insisted, was orthopraxy (correct conduct), and not orthodoxy (correct beliefs), though Mendelssohn himself led a traditionally observant life. This interpretation of Judaism, it should be noted, was not acceptable to more conservative religious authorities, but it did appeal to more secularized Jewish readers who were prepared, in the next generation, to carry the logic of Mendelssohn's argument even further and to attempt to transform the belief structure of Judaism in more radical ways.

Reform Movements in Europe and the United States

The European Enlightenment, and the revolutionary political changes it inspired, impacted Judaism in various ways, but its most direct influence can be seen in the early stages of the Reform Movement in the first decades of the nineteenth century. Beginning in Germany, where admirers of Moses Mendelssohn called for the political "emancipation" of European Jews and their gradual assimilation to Western society, and soon spreading to France, England, and ultimately the United States, the idea of "reforming" Judaism drew support from both lay community leaders and from a younger generation of rabbis who had been permitted to receive a university education. From the outset, the Reform Movement sought to accomplish two goals: first, the modernization of Jewish thought and ritual practice, and second, the acculturation of Jews to the secular culture of nineteenth-century Europe and America. As in any "reformation," however, a split soon developed between those who were determined to achieve these objectives by radical means and those who were not.

At first, reformers seemed content with largely ceremonial innovations, insisting, for example, that rabbinic sermons be delivered in the vernacular language of the nation in which they were living in (rather than in Yiddish, the Germanic language of European Jews) or that men and women be permitted to sit together in synagogue during religious services (as opposed to separate seating, which had been the norm for hundreds of years). By the 1840s, however, the demands of the more aggressive reformers became increasingly anti-traditionalist and theologically innovative, as reformist rabbis increasingly embraced the idea of Judaism as an evolving religious culture. All of these changes were opposed vigorously by more traditionalist rabbis, who, from this time forward, came to be described as "Orthodox" religious authorities.

Reform Judaism This more radical type of reformist thinking flourished in the United States after the Civil War. By the late 1880s Rabbi Kaufmann Kohler (1843–1926) had drafted a set of principles and objectives—known today as "The Pittsburgh Platform of 1885"—that defined the "essence" of Judaism for Kohler and many of his reformist contemporaries. The most important features of this "platform" can be found in its most negative statements, namely, that the Reform movement rejected the biblical idea of a direct, finite, and exclusive revelation from God—the traditional understanding of the concept of *torah*. The reformists opted instead for the concept of an evolving (and therefore universal) revelation, an idea that was easily gleaned from the writings of Moses Mendelssohn. This way, Kohler and his colleagues were able to renounce the dietary code and all other forms of "Mosaic legislation" deemed unacceptable to the Reform rabbinate (such as circumcision and rigorous Sabbath observance) on the grounds that they were "not adapted to the views and habits of modern civilization." And in language designed specifically to suppress any sympathy for Jewish aspirations to return to the historic land of Israel, the Pittsburgh Platform declared boldly that the Jews were no longer a nation and therefore no longer desired to return to, or to restore, a nation-state in Palestine.

Conservative Judaism However acceptable these innovations may have seemed to those American Jews who identified with the Reform Movement, they were clearly unacceptable to the overwhelming majority of European Jews who began to immigrate to the United States in rapidly increasing numbers during the last two decades of the nineteenth century and the first decade of the twentieth century. As the Jewish population of America increased exponentially, the religious diversity of that community increased as well. By the middle of the twentieth century, the American Jewish community found itself largely divided into three movements: Reform, Orthodox, and Conservative. Of these three, the Conservative Movement had emerged, by the 1950s, as the Reform Movement's principal rival, and its appeal can be explained, historically, as a "counter-reformation" both within and outside of the Reform Movement itself.

Thus, for those Jews who were initially drawn to reformist ideals but who found the more extreme changes advocated by the early Reform Movement distasteful, Conservative Judaism offered a more moderate departure from traditional (or what is now called "Orthodox") beliefs and practices. Like their Reform counterparts, Conservative rabbis acknowledged the evolutionary character of Judaism and embraced the need for substantive change; unlike the leading reformists, however, they were not willing to abandon either principles of faith or religious behaviors that had defined Judaism for many centuries. The result was the formation of a "third way" of responding to the challenges facing Judaism in the modern era, in which a high level of adaptation to secular culture was combined with a selective relaxation of *halacha* (with respect, for example, to travel on the Sabbath) and institutional innovations frowned on by the Orthodox community (like the ordination of women as rabbis).

However, in its formative stages, the most obvious difference between Conservative Judaism and its Reform and Orthodox counterparts was the public support of both its rabbis and laity for **Zionism**. Throughout its more than 100-year existence, the Conservative Movement has been a fervent advocate for both the formation of a Jewish nation-state in what is now Israel and for the emigration of American Jews to this state.

Reconstructionist Judaism One of the most important offshoots of Conservative Judaism first emerged in America in the 1930s. Known today as Reconstructionism, this new school of thought centered on the teachings of Rabbi Mordecai Kaplan (1881–1983). By the 1960s, however, the Reconstructionists had formally separated themselves from Conservative Judaism, first by writing their own prayer-book and later by establishing their own rabbinical seminary. Though few in numbers, Reconstructionists have had a far-reaching effect on the thought and religious practices of non-Orthodox Judaism in the United States.

Philosophically, Reconstructionism occupies a position somewhere between Conservatism and Reform. Unlike their Reform counterparts, Reconstructionists held firm to the concept of Jewish nationhood; in fact, for Mordecai Kaplan, the idea that Jews constituted a separate and distinctive *civilization* was central to his belief system. What followed from that assumption was a desire to retain as many traditional "folkways"— which was Kaplan's way of referring to such ritual practices as the dietary code and circumcision—as modern Jews found meaningful. As a consequence, the Reconstructionist Movement tended to place greater emphasis upon the historical continuity of religious customs than did Reform Judaism.

At the same time, Reconstructionism developed a much more naturalistic conception of God than either Conservativism or Reform were willing to support. For Kaplan and his followers, God could no longer be thought of as a noun—that is, as a metaphysical "entity," separate from humanity—but rather as the expression of whatever moral and spiritual potential human beings possess in their search for holiness and righteousness. Kaplan's virtual abandonment of the traditional concept of divine transcendence signaled a dramatic break with the Orthodox faith in which he was raised.

For most Jews, Reconstructionist theology seemed to be a contradiction in terms: Lacking a true Judaic concept of God, it could be nothing more than a disguised form of secular humanism, and as such an heretical rejection of *torah*. Kaplan's defenders, however, insisted that, as an "evolving religious civilization," Judaism's understanding of God and of the covenant would have to change as well, and in the process absorb contemporary scientific views of the cosmos and of the human mind.

The *Shoah* and the State of Israel

During the twentieth century two of the most extraordinary events in Jewish history occurred: one traumatic, the other transformative. Both events have had a profound effect on the beliefs and practices of contemporary Judaism. The first event, referred to in Hebrew as the *Shoah*—or, more commonly, as the **Holocaust**—can be seen as the single greatest tragedy of modern Jewish life: the most successful attempt in history by anti-Semites to rid the world of both the religion Judaism and the Jewish people.

The *Shoah* The word *Shoah* itself requires some explanation, if only because it has a different connotation than the more familiar word "Holocaust." In Hebrew the word *shoah* literally means "whirlwind," and as a metaphor it captures—as well as any image can—the insane rage of anti-Semitic hatred that was loosed on Europe's Jews during World War II. Many Jews prefer this term, unfamiliar as it may be to English-speaking audiences, precisely because it avoids the connotation of a divinely commanded sacrifice, which is exactly what the biblical term "holocaust" (or "burnt-offering") brings to mind.

For centuries, as we have learned, Jews had been the targets of both Christian and Muslim hostility—and, on occasion, the objects of intense persecution—but until Adolf Hitler and Nazi Germany embarked on the "Final Solution," no ruler or regime ever entertained the idea of total extermination. In Hitler's autobiography, *Mein Kampf* (1925), he described the Jews as a disease organism within the body of European society, a kind of bacillus that he and his followers proposed to destroy forever. The genocidal policies that his government pursued represented a logical outcome of an essentially racist conception of the Jews and their faith. To carry out this genocidal campaign, Hit-

The entrance gate at Auschwitz.

ler mobilized not only the resources of Germany but also the support of willing collaborators throughout Europe. There is little doubt that had German armies defeated the United States, Britain, and the Soviet Union during World War II, the annihilation of the world's Jewish population would have been one of Hitler's proudest accomplishments. Even in defeat, however, the Nazis destroyed roughly one-third of the world's Jewish population, and the legacy of torture and mass murder they left behind has deeply scarred the Jewish consciousness.

Contemporary Jewish philosophers have responded in remarkably diverse ways to the tragedy of the *Shoah*. For one theologian in particular, Ignaz Maybaum (1897–1976), the slaughter of innocents can be seen as a kind of *churban* (Hebrew, "divinely-willed sacrifice"), through which the Jews perform an act of vicarious atonement for the sins of the world.[5] For theologian Richard Rubenstein (b. 1924), on the other hand, such logic is morally insane. Rubenstein insists that the random killing of 6 million Jews (not to mention the untold suffering and murder of many more millions of non-Jews) challenges, at the most fundamental level, Judaism's belief in a just and benevolent Creator who values every single human life. In his book *After Auschwitz*, Rubenstein insisted that Judaism's historic God-concept is "dead" and that no religious philosophy that is still committed to biblical ideas of divine justice and retribution can withstand scrutiny in an age of genocide and mass destruction.[6] For philosopher and rabbi Eliezer Berkovits (1908–1992),[7] however, the mystery of God's presence in history is deepened by the *Shoah*, not refuted by it, and ours, he observes, is not the first generation to reflect either on God's "hiddenness" or on the terrible consequences of human freedom. For human beings to be capable of choice, he argues, God must "restrain" Himself and allow His human agents to exercise their moral will, even if the consequences of divine restraint are catastrophic.

None of these theologians, however, nor most other Jewish thinkers who have reflected on the religious implications of global genocide, are willing to see the *Shoah* as an instance of merited (and therefore inevitable) divine punishment. Their refusal to accept that now-archaic model of God's judgment and response to human sin marks a definitive break with traditional Jewish thought. If much of the world's Jewish population can no longer declare—in the words of the traditional liturgy—"because of our sins were we exiled from the land," then what model of covenant relations can now be invoked to make both human suffering and world redemption meaningful?

For theologian Abraham Joshua Heschel (1907–1972), the only defensible Jewish theology after the *Shoah* is one that posits God's need for, and yearning after, humankind. The covenant relationship, as Heschel understands it, is a reciprocal one in which human moral intelligence and divine "pathos" join in the act of worship and of love. God's longing for us does not, Heschel insists, annul the reality of evil or the terrible freedom with which human beings have been invested. It does, however, establish what Heschel calls an "analogy of being," that is, a hint of divine likeness in every soul, and thereby the capacity to mend a broken world. If all we knew of God, Heschel argues, was a theory of omnipotence or omniscience, then the *Shoah* might very well sweep away that merely conceptual reality. But the truth is, he continues, that we know God at a much deeper level of moral consciousness, and that form of the divine presence abides even in the midst of the most appalling evils.[8]

Statehood for Israel The second pivotal event of modern Jewish history is the establishment of the state of Israel in 1948, what one philosopher has called the "the Jewish return into history."[9] The Zionist philosophy on which the state of Israel rests is really several philosophical/religious arguments in one; we will explore the religious arguments in the Teachings section of this chapter. In its earliest form, "Zionism" is simply a feeling of attachment to an ancestral homeland in which a vast majority of Jews, past and present, have never lived. Even though a comparatively small population of Jews continued to live in Palestine for centuries after the Exodus, most Jews were content to sing "next year in Jerusalem" at the Passover *Seder* without ever really contemplating a return to the land of biblical Israel.

A decisive shift in such thinking occurred, however, in the course of the nineteenth century. The earliest sign that the idea of Zion had become profoundly politicized came in 1862 with the publication of Moses Hess' *Rome and Jerusalem*. Hess (1812–1875), a radical journalist (and friend of Karl Marx), abandoned his socialist dreams in midlife for a renewed appreciation of Judaism and argued passionately for the creation of a Jewish homeland. For Hess, anti-Semitism was an ineradicable presence in Western society, and therefore Jews could never hope to assimilate successfully to a society in which they were bound to be hated. The only solution, he concluded, was to revive their long-dormant sense of nationhood and to reestablish a Jewish state in Palestine.[10] As a largely secular Western European Jew, Hess presumed that the creation of this new state would be the result of renewed Jewish political and cultural activism, and not divine intervention; yet despite the fervor with which he argued the case for a new Zion, Hess' work went largely ignored for a generation.

In the last two decades of the nineteenth century, however, interest in Hess' ideas renewed, even among those who had never read him. What motivated this revival of "political" Zionism, as it came to be called, was the rapid growth of anti-Semitism in various parts of Europe and the oppressive cruelty of the Czarist regime in Russia during this period. For one writer in particular, the Austro-Hungarian Theodor Herzl (1860–1904), the condition of Eastern European Jews had become so precarious that something had to be done—apart from continuing mass emigration to the United States—to deal with the poverty and desperation of the Jewish masses. Herzl's solution was the establishment of an internationally recognized Jewish state, either in Palestine or Argentina. He laid out his ideas in an extended tract entitled *The Jewish State* (1896)[11] and later in a utopian novel entitled *The Old-New Land* (1902).[12] Herzl, who died in 1904, never lived to see any of his ideas come to fruition. The Zionist movement he helped to found continued to solicit support for his ideas, and in 1917 British Zionists found a sympathetic advocate in the foreign minister of Great Britain, Lord Arthur Balfour (1848–1930).

Balfour's private letter—now known as the Balfour Declaration—to the most prominent Jew in England, Lord Walter Rothschild (1868–1937), is the earliest sign that any major power was willing, for whatever reasons, to validate Zionist claims to a political stakehold in Palestine. In carefully guarded

This painting of Herzl is one of many that appear on Israeli currency.

diplomatic language Balfour declared his government's willingness to establish a "national home for the Jewish people," provided that "nothing shall be done which may prejudice the civil and religious rights of existing non-Jewish communities in Palestine."[13] Within a decade of this proclamation, however, both Great Britain and the rapidly growing Jewish community in Palestine discovered just how intense Palestinian Arab opposition to increased Jewish immigration really was. By the late 1930s, as Great Britain sought to limit sharply the number of Jews who could legally enter Palestine, the stage was set for a succession of wars between Arabs and Jews—wars that have continued to the present day.

As a secular ideology, Zionism (in all its variations) rests on a few basic assumptions. The first assumption holds that anti-Semitism may abate from time to time, but it will never disappear, and as long as Jews are hated anywhere in the world, their lives are in peril. The second assumption is that the only guarantee of physical survival in a hostile world is national sovereignty—because only a nation-state can effectively defend its citizens. Third, the guest-host relationship Jews have lived under, whether in Christian or in Muslim lands, has always been inherently unstable, and on occasion threatening to Jewish survival. If Jews are to have any hope of a secure future, they will have to regain their collective autonomy, which can be accomplished only through political means. And if one adds to all of this the specifically religious belief (as we will learn later) that the rebirth of the state of Israel represents the beginning stage of messianic redemption of the world, we have a totality of ideas that have been employed to rationalize the transformation of the world Jewish community back into a politico-religious entity. Viewed from this perspective, Jewish history has come full circle in our time, as Jews search for ways to reconnect their religious lives with their enduring sense of peoplehood.

The Future of Judaism in the Contemporary World

During the last three decades of the twentieth century, and at the dawn of the new millennium, Judaism faced a number of formidable challenges. The sheer loss of human life following the *Shoah* meant more than just a sharp reduction in the Jewish world population. For some Jews, the possibility of collective annihilation carried with it the secondary possibility of the "end" of Judaism itself, or at the very least the dwindling away of what was once a global community. For others, however, the threat of cultural extinction inspired a reexamination of their most basic philosophical assumptions and institutional behaviors. Two of the most far-reaching challenges came from two largely unrelated movements: feminism and radical humanism.

The Feminist Challenge Traditionally, the status of women in Judaism has been that of a respected but subordinate member of the religious community, and for many centuries Jewish women lived in a male-dominant culture. The Orthodox **Siddur** instructs Jewish males to thank God that they were not born a woman, while rabbinic tradition released women from all time-bound religious obligations (such as fixed prayer-times), based on the assumption that a woman's chief responsibility was the raising of children and maintenance of the home. Though women were never prevented from attending synagogue, their very presence necessitated a physical barrier to separate them from male worshipers, who, it was feared, would otherwise be distracted by their presence. Moreover, the privilege of advanced religious study was reserved exclusively for men, who were thought to be better equipped by nature for the mental rigors of scholarly debate.

The Western feminist movements of the 1970s totally rejected such views on the grounds that they embodied a "patriarchal" view of woman's place in society, and as the influence of feminist thought made its presence felt throughout the Jewish community—particularly in the United States—the exclusion of women from positions of religious authority soon came to an end. The American Reform movement took the lead by conferring the title of Rabbi on Sally Priesand (b. 1946) in 1972, and shortly thereafter both the Conservative and Reconstructionist movements in the United States admitted women to their rabbinic seminaries. However, even more transformative changes were underway, affecting the very language and root concepts of traditional Judaism.

At the same time that women were being admitted to the rabbinate in greater numbers, a new approach to both religious language and the interpretation of biblical literature was beginning to manifest itself within the non-Orthodox spectrum of the Jewish community. Feminist scholars in particular focused on the gendered vocabulary that surrounded the biblical idea of God, as well as echoes of a distinctly masculine image of the Deity in traditional prayers, where God is consistently referred to as "Father," "Lord," and "King." Reform liturgists began to experiment with gender-neutral words like "Eternal One" and "Source of Life" as alternatives to the obviously patriarchal terminology of the traditional *Siddur*. In addition, the elimination or revision of prayers that implied the spiritual superiority of the male, or that excluded women from the prayer community by omission, became part of the same revisionist project. Not all of these innovations have proven universally acceptable, but collectively they represent a serious effort to bring the religious discourse of Judaism into the contemporary world.

The Challenge of Humanist Judaism Probably the most far-reaching critique of traditional Jewish concepts and religious practices at the end of the twentieth century came from a very different quarter: the rejection of Judaism's central God-concept by secular Jews who found any form of theism philosophically untenable. For some, the renunciation of Judaism's God was a logical response to the insane violence of the *Shoah* and the absurd wastefulness and cruelty of a world that seemed perpetually at war. No truly just or beneficent God, they argued, could possibly tolerate such slaughter. Therefore, the only reasonable and morally compelling response was to assume that no such deity ever existed—except perhaps in the human imagination.[14]

Of course, anyone who has studied the development of atheism in the modern era has encountered arguments like these. What was new can be found in the insistence of humanist advocates like the American rabbi Sherwin Wine (1928–2007) that one can remain a Jew, culturally and sociologically, while at the same time rejecting any belief in a supernatural Creator.[15] Taking their cue from Mordecai Kaplan and Reconstructionism, humanistic Jews insist that since Jews are a people first, and only secondarily a religious community, their disbelief in a God should not exclude them from the company of their fellow Jews or prevent them from embracing Jewish ethics and folkways.

At present, the appeal of this approach to Jewish life and values appears to be small. Institutionally, very few communities throughout the world have identified themselves with this form of radical humanism or have made the effort to revise their religious calendars and liturgies accordingly. Still, no survey of contemporary Judaism would be complete without some recognition of this radical alternative to mainstream Jewish faith.

THE TEACHINGS OF JUDAISM

As we have learned, Judaism has undergone many changes in its long history. For the purposes of our study, however, we will start by looking at those concepts and values the majority of Jews living today would regard as "normative" or "enduring." Having done that, we will consider the diversity of belief that increasingly characterizes Judaism in the present age, beginning with Judaism's concept of God.

God

The Jewish religion is most commonly referred to as a type of **ethical monotheism**, as it assumes the existence of a Creator God whose benevolence and goodness are reflected in His love of humanity and who has imparted to the Jews ethical principles by which they (and the rest of the human race) are expected to live.

As Jewish philosophy developed over the centuries, an understanding of God's nature deepened, and additional qualities—such as **omniscience** and **omnipotence**—were added to the composite portrait of the deity. Most important for Judaism, however, is the concept of divine "oneness," which can be understood to mean that there is only one divine Being in the universe; this one Being is truly incomparable, and no human being (or anything we can possibly imagine) can be compared to this Being. Judaism's idea of divine **transcendence** presupposes that a fundamental difference in reality exists between God and the world He has brought into existence, and therefore precludes the possibility of God's embodiment or "incarnation" in a particular human personality.

Yet for all its emphasis on God's "otherness," Judaism is not lacking a sense of God's nearness, or immanence. The very fact that Jews pray to God—and do so with the expectation that their prayers will be heard and that those prayers may move the deity to respond—suggests that there are limits to the distance between the divine reality and the world of human consciousness. In Jewish mysticism, as we will learn later in this chapter, that sense of metaphysical separation is largely overcome through visionary and contemplative experiences. Moreover, the ancient liturgical tradition of addressing God through the use of masculine nouns and pronouns (still preserved in many prayer books today) surely suggests that, at the level of common speech, Jews have long thought of God in human terms. As we have learned, contemporary feminist critics of traditional Judaism have repeatedly challenged this practice, arguing that the attribution of gender—that is, employing masculine metaphors (or capitalizing the masculine pronoun) to speak of God—subverts God's transcendent character. Humanist critics have also challenged this practice, arguing that any anthropomorphic imaging of the divine is a false representation of an unknowable reality. Such contending views constitute part of an ongoing conversation within modern Judaism over the nature of the one God Jews have long proclaimed.

One of the great constants in Jewish theology, however, has been its assumption that the Creator-God was also the shaping force or will behind our universe and our human world. Judaism has never conceived of the God of Israel as a deity who abandoned the universe once it was brought into being. On the contrary, Jews have always assumed that God's infinite capacity to create implied a willingness to judge that creation, as well as a determination to see His creative purposes fulfilled in time. Judaism assumes, therefore, that God is moved to respond by every human act of goodness and contrition.

The Problem of Evil How such a God can tolerate the continued existence of evil in a world that He has created is a question that has troubled Jewish philosophers for many centuries. Like their counterparts in other monotheistic faiths, they have sought various solutions to this possibly insoluble enigma. The oldest Judaic response to this question—a question that philosophers today often refer to as the "problem of evil"—takes the familiar biblical form of an accusation: the people of Israel have sinned against God by violating His Covenant, and therefore God has no alternative but to punish those who have rejected Him and His laws.

However, the Nazi genocide against the Jews during World War II has prompted many Jewish theologians to reexamine this traditionalist argument and to reject the cause-and-effect pattern of thinking it presupposes. For some, the spectacle of mass murder or, even worse, the possibility of global annihilation, makes the biblical idea of a just, compassionate, and omnipotent Creator-God insupportable; indeed, according to this argument, such a God-concept is no longer acceptable to a post-Holocaust Judaism.[16] Still others, unwilling to embrace the agnosticism (or atheism) this argument inevitably leads to, insist on reviving the biblical idea of a divine "eclipse": the belief that God periodically conceals Himself from human understanding, thereby creating a seeming void in which evil, for a time, may prevail.[17]

Nevertheless, according to this counterargument, even during this period of divine "absence," God remains present in many human hearts, and in time God will "return" to our world in the form of humanity's moral striving and severe self-judgment. This alternative view of God's role in the world holds that reconciliation with God, and a renewal of those divine values that reside within all enlightened human cultures, is still possible, and that one should never doubt God's continuing love for, and anguish over, the human race.

Torah

In addition to a commitment to monotheism, Judaism also claims to be a "revealed" religion, in that its most basic teachings are believed to be the result of divine revelation. Most of the books that make up the Hebrew Bible—the most ancient work of Jewish scripture—advance this claim. Furthermore, when Jews employ the Hebrew word *torah* (Hebrew, "teaching") in its most inclusive sense, they are referring to the totality of God's revelation to the people of Israel. The very fact that Judaism possesses a sacred scripture presupposes a belief in divine-human communication, as well as a belief in the trustworthiness of those individuals—whether prophets or sages—who served as instruments of divine speech and understanding.

The word **Torah**, however, has secondary and even tertiary meanings, and all of them are crucial to an understanding of Jewish faith. Thus, when reference is made to the scrolls of the Torah (which Seth read from at the beginning of this chapter), what is meant are the parchment copies of the first five books of the Hebrew Bible (known in English as Genesis, Exodus, Leviticus, Numbers, and Deuteronomy). Such scrolls can be found in any synagogue in the world. Jews view this portion of Judaism's ancient scriptures with particular reverence, and not only because these books offer a quasi-historical portrait of the creation of the world and the beginnings of the Jewish people. Even more important, these scrolls contain virtually all the sacred legislation contained within the Hebrew Bible. And given the centrality of the idea of sacred law in traditional Judaism, it is hardly surprising, then, that the word Torah has often been translated as "The Law."

An even more expansive use of the word Torah can be found, as we have seen in the previous section on the Formative Age, in the practice of referring to a comprehensive collection of commentaries on biblical law as the "Oral Torah." This multivolume anthology of interpretive and folkloristic writings, more commonly called the Talmud, represents the final extension in Jewish history of the idea of revelation. The teachers—known as rabbis—whose comments are preserved in these volumes claimed to be passing on the oral instructions of the biblical Moses, to whom God originally imparted His laws at Mt. Sinai. Though not every community of Jews has accepted this claim as historically or theologically valid, the vast majority of the world's Jews have accorded to the Talmud a degree of sanctity and intellectual authority almost equal to that of the biblical Torah, thereby making the Talmud a virtual second scripture in Judaism. Much of the education of rabbis today consists of studying the Talmud, as well as a vast body of interpretive literature (commentaries upon a commentary) that has grown up around the Talmud.

Mitzvot At the core of the Torah tradition (whether understood as written or oral) lies the concept of the *mitzvot* (Hebrew, "commandments"), and it would not be unreasonable to describe Judaism as religion of "divine commandments." By the Rabbinic (or "Formative") Age, the number of such commandments that can be found in the first five books of the Hebrew Bible was fixed at 613, and each of these *mitzvot* was viewed an essential link in a chain of religious laws that could not be broken. Over many centuries, rabbinic commentators (including, as we have seen, Maimonides) have attempted to categorize these commandments into positive and negative precepts or into absolutely obligatory and relatively obligatory commandments, but the simple fact today is that at least half of these laws are no longer applicable, either to contemporary society or to a Judaism without a Temple in Jerusalem, and therefore without a priesthood and a system of animal sacrifice.

However, at the heart of this vast network of sacred law lie the Ten Commandments, which can be found in two slightly different forms in the books of Exodus and Deuteronomy. For all Jews, in every age and in every land, these ten pronouncements have served not only as the bedrock of their faith but also as the basis of their social and philosophical ideals.

It is entirely appropriate, then, that when the Ten Commandments are read aloud in synagogue (at *Shavuot* and on the two Sabbaths when the normal Torah reading includes this portion), the entire congregation stands in honor of these divinely revealed commandments.

However, just like the term "Torah," the word *mitzvot* (singular, *mitzvah*) has taken on another, more informal meaning—that of "good deeds." In ordinary conversation, Jews routinely refer to any act of generosity or good will as a *mitzvah*. In fact, a glance at a traditional prayer book will reveal exactly which good deeds the rabbis expected every adult to feel especially bound by in everyday life. The list includes honoring one's parents, visiting the sick, outfitting a bride, and peacefully resolving quarrels between neighbors. But the greatest *mitzvah*, the rabbis go on to explain, is the study of Torah, since it contains all the moral wisdom God has imparted to the Jewish people.

Nevertheless, there are practical limits to how far anyone can go in the performance of a good deed or the fulfillment of a divine commandment. Those limits are formally acknowledged in rabbinic law under the principle of *pikuach nefesh*, or "the preservation of life." Thus, the rabbis taught that whenever carrying out a *mitzvah* entails imminent risk to one's life or health, one is released from that obligation until the threat to life has passed. The only exceptions to this rule—and these exceptions became the basis for the concept of martyrdom in Judaism—are those situations in which a Jew is commanded to worship another god, to commit adultery, or to murder an innocent human being. In all other cases, the traditionalist view is that laws may be bent, but not permanently broken, to accommodate exigent circumstances.

Covenant and Election

Throughout its long history, Judaism has thought of God's relationship with the Jewish people as an intimate contractual relationship (rather like a marriage) freely granted by God and freely entered into by the biblical Israelites and all their remote descendants.

THE TEN COMMANDMENTS

1. Acknowledge one God only.
2. Worship no other.
3. Never swear falsely in His name.
4. Observe the Sabbath rest.
5. Honor one's parents.
6. Never commit murder.
7. Never commit adultery.
8. Never commit theft.
9. Never give false testimony.
10. Never desire anything that belongs to another.

In Hebrew this type of relationship is referred to as a *b'rit*, commonly translated into English as a Covenant.

In the Hebrew Bible Israel's covenant with God is often portrayed as a kind of treaty, with reciprocal obligations and expectations. On God's side, an unconditional promise is given to the patriarch Abraham that his "seed," or descendants, would be numerous and that they would inhabit the land God had given Abraham as a legacy. The people of Israel, however, are expected to live up to all of God's demands and to obey His *mitzvot*. The penalty for disobeying God is a temporary dissolution of the covenant connection, coupled with such punishments as famine, defeat in war, and ultimately exile from the very land first promised to Abraham and his heirs. Clearly, this later understanding of the covenant idea is both conditional and even punitive in nature, and for many centuries it provided a theological rationale for the worldwide dispersion of Jews and their subsequent statelessness. Since the establishment of the state of Israel in 1948, contemporary Jewish theology tends to deemphasize that theme and to stress, instead, the bond of enduring love, trust, and forgiveness that exists between Israel and God.

Much more problematic than the covenant idea, however, is the accompanying belief in Israel's **election**, or, as this idea is more commonly expressed, a belief that the Jewish people have been "chosen" by God to receive His laws and to live in His presence. No concept in Judaism has evoked more hostility and misunderstanding; yet despite the controversy, it would be difficult to imagine a historically credible form of Judaism that completely lacked this concept. On one level, all that the idea of election in Judaism affirms—and all that the Hebrew Bible attests to—is God's decision to reveal Himself to the people of Israel in a way that is qualitatively different from the way He has related to any other people on earth.

On yet another level of understanding, however, the covenant demands that Israel actively serve God's purposes in history: first by becoming a "holy nation," completely obedient to His will, and second by representing God to the peoples of the world who have no knowledge of His existence. This latter understanding of the doctrine of election is precisely what the biblical prophet Isaiah had in mind when he spoke, on God's behalf, of Israel becoming a "light to the nations." Of course, some biblical writers approached this theme with nationalist feelings in mind, but after long centuries of living in a stateless Diaspora, Jews have come to see their "chosenness" simply as an obligation to serve both God and humanity, rather than as an assertion of moral or religious superiority.

Historically, Jews have thought of the Covenant in ancestral terms, since most Jews are persons born to Jewish parents. Nevertheless, conversion to Judaism has long been open to any non-Jew who wishes to assume the responsibilities (and the hazards) that are a part of membership in the covenant community. Those who enter Judaism by choice are required by tradition to prove their sincerity and to undertake a term of study to prepare for full participation in Jewish religious life. The final stage of conversion customarily entails circumcision for men who are not already circumcised, and for both men and women immersion in a ritual pool (known as a **mikveh** in Hebrew). From that moment on the convert is known as a "son" or "daughter" of Abraham, and no Jew by birth is permitted to treat such a convert as anything but a spiritual equal. Paradoxical as it may sound, therefore, it is possible for anyone to choose to become part of the "chosen people." Nevertheless, since Jewish religious identity is traditionally traced through the mother's line (matrilineal descent), the conversion of a prospective bride is absolutely critical to determining the Jewishness of her offspring, and though the Reform Movement in the United States has attempted to trace Jewish identity through the male line as well (patrilineal descent), the standard practice in most Jewish communities worldwide remains, at present, matrilineal.

Israel

Since 1948, the word "Israel" has been used to identify the Middle Eastern nation-state that bears that name. But for many centuries, beginning with the Hebrew Bible, "Israel" connoted both a political and a spiritual community, a double frame of reference that is still preserved within the synagogue liturgy. In the latter sense, therefore, Israel is that covenant community to whom God imparted Torah and to whom He is bound by promise and affection. Like the idea of election, however, the notion of peoplehood implicit in the concept of Israel has seemed to some either confusing or simply archaic, and its use today can still generate controversy.

Biblical writers, of course, had no difficulty reconciling ethnic identity and religious affiliation: God's covenant, they believed, was established with the *b'nei yisrael*—literally, "the children of Israel" (that is, the lineal descendants of the patriarch Jacob)—and that contractual bond was thought to be unique and therefore without precedent in history. As a consequence, Jews continued to think of themselves over the centuries as members of a single extended family and as a faith community held together by a common set of beliefs.

However, during the modern era Jews found themselves faced with a political dilemma that soon took on religious implications: they could receive citizenship within the now largely secular nation-states of Europe, but only at the expense of their collective historical identity, namely, that of a national religious community-in-exile, or Diaspora. For many Jews, eager to assimilate into modern society and determined to secure civil rights that had been denied them for centuries, the demand that Judaism redefine itself as a religious creed, and nothing more, seemed a small price to pay for political emancipation.

On the other hand, Orthodox Jews, generally suspicious of secular values and distrustful of the process of acculturation, viewed this new understanding of Jewish identity with alarm. In addition, by the end of the nineteenth century, a very different group of secular dissident Jewish intellectuals—early advocates of Zionism, for example, like Theodor Herzl—also rebelled, though for completely different reasons, against the notion that Jews had no claim to nationhood and were just another religious denomination among thousands in the world.

Today, many of those who practice Judaism are comfortable with their double identity as members of both a religious and an ethnic community, while at the same time recognizing the inevitable tension between these two perspectives. For those Jews who have chosen to make *aliyah* (Hebrew, "to ascend")—that is, to immigrate to Israel and become citizens of a Jewish state—this tension almost disappears, though secular/nationalist and religious values continue to clash with one another in contemporary Israeli society. For those Jews who remain in the Diaspora—a majority of the world's Jewish population—the need to establish a balance between national and religious self-identification remains a challenge.

The Messiah and the Messianic Age

One idea that emerged from the matrix of ancient Judaism that has had a profound impact upon the Western world is the idea of a Messiah. From its very beginnings in the Hebrew Bible, however, this concept has meant different things to different audiences. At its root, the term *mashiach* (Hebrew, "anointed one"; translated into English as "messiah") means any person who was ceremonially anointed with oil in preparation for becoming a priest or a king, and when most biblical writers used this term literally, that was all they had in mind.

However, later prophets like the Second Isaiah (c. late sixth century B.C.E.) began to extend the use of this term metaphorically by applying it to either non-Israelite kings or to an unnamed future "prince" who would redeem his people from subjugation to foreign nations. As the beginning of the Common Era approached, the idea of a messiah continued to evolve. In works that lie outside of the Hebrew Bible, such as the First Book of Enoch and the Fourth Book of Ezra, the term *mashiach* took on explicitly supernatural meanings, signifying a heavenly redeemer-figure sent by God to rescue Israel and the world from evil. This more imaginative use of the messiah concept was linked in such books with end-of-the-world visions, complete with predictions of a new world order emerging from a final era of chaos and destruction. Such writers saw the Messiah as an instrument of divine power through whom God would accomplish both the final judgment and the ultimate renewal of life on earth. The Essenes, the ascetic visionaries of the Second Temple period, embraced this more nearly supernatural view of the messianic tradition with particular intensity.

When Christianity identified Jesus of Nazareth with this redemptive/supernatural messiah tradition, it prompted the rabbis of the Talmud to reevaluate the very notion of a "Messiah." What followed in their writings on this subject was a remarkably diverse collection of views, with some religious authorities identifying the biblical king Hezekiah (late eighth century B.C.E.) as a "messiah" who had already distinguished himself in the past as a ruler wholly obedient to God's will, while others deferred the appearance of an equally human Messiah (albeit one from the line of David) to the indefinite future. Yet despite this uncertainty over the Messiah's precise identity, a lively debate ensued, within and beyond rabbinic literature, on which tasks such a Messiah might be expected to accomplish, and whether his mission would be accomplished within the span of human history or only at the "end" of time. Not surprisingly, centuries of longing for the fulfillment of these messianic visions have produced a succession of "false" Messiahs in Judaism; what is more remarkable is the persistence of that faith into the modern era and its active advocacy among traditionalist communities within contemporary Judaism.

The Afterlife

Of all the basic beliefs of Judaism, a belief in an afterlife (Hebrew, *Olam Ha-Bah*—in rabbinic literature, the "world to come"), along with accompanying beliefs in the resurrection of the dead and the immortality of the soul, are among the most elusive. Historically viewed, these beliefs are largely postbiblical in their origin, or at least are not fully articulated until the period of the Talmud. For most biblical writers, the death of the body entailed the passage of the soul into an underworld (Hebrew, *Sheol*; "pit" or "abyss"), where it would remain forever. Still, various biblical texts contain hints of a countertradition; for example, the second Book of Kings depicts the prophet Elijah as ascending directly into heaven on a fiery chariot (2 Kings 2:1–12). But such miraculous transitions from life to a mysterious afterlife are exceptional, and it is only in a very late biblical work, the Book of Daniel, that we come upon an explicit reference to the dead rising again to life.

By the rabbinic era, however, mainstream Judaism had already embraced the idea of a postmortem existence in the "world-to-come," though the rabbis who espoused this belief were notoriously vague as to just what this belief entailed. Thus, questions surrounding the afterlife—such as whether the departed enter the world-to-come automatically upon death or only after some ultimate judgment has been passed upon that soul by God or whether a general resurrection of mankind will precede or follow the appearance of the Messiah—were left unanswered.

By the modern era, many reform-minded Jews, bent on reevaluating (and even rejecting) traditional Judaic beliefs, concluded that any belief in an existence beyond this world was either an archaic folk-belief or an insupportable, unscientific hypothesis. Yet despite such opposition, the classic phraseology of the afterlife, along with references to the resurrection of the dead, persists within most contemporary prayerbooks. In Orthodox communities, Jews continue to insist that these beliefs are an integral part of the Judaism they uphold.

Jewish Mysticism

The origins of mystical thinking in Judaism can be found in the Hebrew Bible, where at least one prophet, the sixth-century figure of Ezekiel, recorded visionary trances in which YHWH appeared to him as a figure of infinite mystery, seated upon a throne:

> Above the expanse . . . was the semblance of a throne, in appearance like sapphire; and on top, upon this semblance of a throne, there was the semblance of a human form. From what appeared as his loins up, I saw a gleam as of amber—what looked like fire encased in a frame; and from what appeared as his loins down, I saw what looked like fire. There was a radiance all about him. Like the appearance of the bow which shines in the clouds on a day of rain, such was the appearance of the surrounding radiance. That was the appearance of the semblance of the Presence of the Lord. When I beheld it, I flung myself down on my face.
> —*Ezekiel 1:26–28*

Visionary passages like these, which can be found throughout the Book of Ezekiel and in other prophetic texts as well (see Isaiah 6:1–7), testify to a tradition of ecstatic meditation in biblical Judaism in which a prophetic writer experiences the presence of God in a manner that is at once direct and mysterious. For centuries, Ezekiel's vision of the heavenly throne (which is also a chariot) served as an inspiration to mystics who sought a comparable glimpse of God and of the heavenly beings who, according to biblical tradition, surround His throne.

Another popular biblical text that served as inspiration for Jewish mystics was the opening chapter of the Book of Genesis, in which the creation of the world and of mankind is described. What distinguished the Kabbalah school of mystical writers from other visionary writers was a fascination with the mysterious process of world-creation and a deep curiosity over the role of the Creator in this process. This type of mystical inquiry is often accompanied by some form of esoteric biblical interpretation, and it often incorporates some of the boldest kinds of cosmological speculation Jewish writers have ever indulged in.

Key to the writings of the Kabbalah is one underlying cosmic metaphor, the image of the *Sephirot*. The *Sephirot* are ten in number, and they can be visualized as connected "spheres" of divine power, or as stages in a process of divine self-revelation.

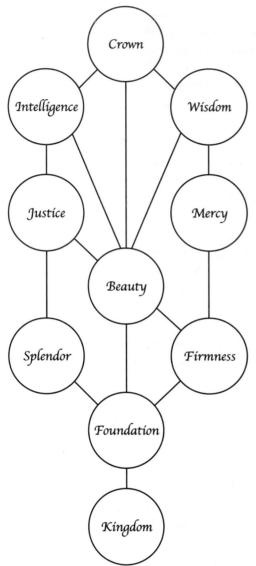

The traditional arrangement of the *sephirot* is designed to evoke either the tree of life or the human body.

As such they come to represent at least one of two things: the primary attributes of God and the dynamic emanations of His creative force.

However, the goal of mystical meditation in kabbalistic writings goes well beyond a desire to describe God or His relation to our world in quasi-mythological terms. The kabbalists were united in their desire to reconnect heaven and earth through a process of contemplative prayer and restorative moral actions. Thus, every blessing that a Jew utters in praise of God, or every *mitzvah* that is performed in strict accordance with tradition, they taught, can now be invested with an almost magical power to "heal" the world (Hebrew, *tikkun olam*) and is directly related to the soul's longing to reunite with its Creator. The end-goal of this longing, kabbalists believe, is *devekut*, or a "clinging" to God that represents the highest state in mystical Judaism of the covenant relationship.

The Lurianic system of kabbalah, as we have seen, has had a particularly powerful appeal. In the "beginning" before creation, Rabbi Luria taught, God (whom kabbalists refer to as the *Ein Sof,* or "Infinite One") withdrew into Himself, thereby creating an empty space within which a material universe could take shape. Having performed this voluntary act of self-contraction (Hebrew, *tzimtzum*), the Creator then allowed rays of light to penetrate the void, resulting in a concentration of this creative force into ten spheres (the *Sephirot*). However, the ten "vessels" God had prepared to hold this *Sephirotic* light mysteriously shattered, leaving the material universe in disarray. According to Luria, this cosmic event was the true origin of evil and disorder in the world, and this partly inexplicable catastrophe resulted in the scattering of divine "sparks" throughout the cosmos, and particularly within the human soul. Within each of us, therefore, is an intermingling of good and evil; even the worst human beings, he believed, retain some small portion of divine goodness. With the coming of the Messiah, all of these sparks would be reunited with God. Until that eschatological event transforms the world forever, each person has the potential to liberate that divine "spark" for himself or herself through a process of repentance and return to God (Hebrew, *teshuvah*).

Ideas and images derived from Kabbalah continue to exert some influence on contemporary Jewish thought, and particularly for those associated with the Jewish "Renewal" movement.[18] Admirers of Rabbi Abraham Joshua Heschel—and, more recently, followers of Rabbi Zalman Schachter-Shalomi (b. 1924)—who are determined to bring about a reinvigoration of Jewish spirituality, insist that concepts like *teshuvah* and *tikkun olam* cannot be confined to the synagogue or to a life of conventional religious observance. For some, *teshuvah* entails a sincere and disciplined internalizing of our longing for God in the form of true piety, affecting every aspect of our behavior. For others, however, *tikkun olam* means, quite literally, actions that benefit humankind and promote peace in the world.

JUDAISM AS A WAY OF LIFE

As Judaism has historically placed great emphasis on the sanctification of time, any consideration of Judaism as a "way of life" should begin with the ways in which Jews mark the passage of time. Like many ancient peoples, Jews in antiquity employed a modified lunar calendar, which allowed them to celebrate each month's appearance of a new moon while at the same time periodically adjusting the lunar year to the solar year. They dated this calendar from what they presumed to be the moment of the world's creation, with the result that the year 2012 in our secular calendar overlaps with the Jewish year 5772. And within this sacred calendar, certain seasons were designated as "Sabbaths," or occasions for religious celebration during which the Jewish community reaffirms its covenant relationship with God.

The Major Festivals

At the core of this system of seasonal religious observances are five major festivals, all linked to each other and to the cycle of nature—**Rosh Hashanah**, **Yom Kippur**, **Sukkot**, **Pesach**, and **Shavuot**—plus a host of relatively minor festivals interspersed throughout the year. Each major festival is biblical in origin, and on each of these occasions Jews are commanded to cease working and devote themselves to prayer. That said, each major *chag* (Hebrew, "sacred occasion") is as individual as the season it celebrates and the ritual function it performs.

Rosh Hashanah Commonly referred to as the Jewish New Year, Rosh Hashanah is traditionally celebrated for two days at the beginning of the month of Tishri (September-October), and it is regarded as both a solemn and a joyous occasion. Though there is some evidence that, in biblical times, the agricultural year began in the early spring, by the rabbinic era, the start of the religious year had already shifted to the early fall. This shift placed a greater emphasis on the internal rhythms of the human heart and a need for self-reflection, as opposed to a celebration of the seasonal harvests.

As a consequence, the year begins with a period of self-reflection, signaled by the blowing of a ram's horn (Hebrew, **shofar**) during the synagogue service. The sound of this instrument, which can be heard 100 times during the service, is designed to awaken the conscience of the worshiper to the need for repentance and reconciliation with God. For that reason Rosh Hashanah is referred to in the liturgy as *Yom Hazikaron*, or the Day of Remembrance. At the same time, the mood created during the two days of Rosh Hashanah is a generally happy and expectant one, and it is customary to eat a dish of apples and honey as an expression of hope that the coming year will be one of sweet fruitfulness and fulfillment. It is also customary on this occasion

Covered in a large *tallit*, this Yemenite Jew blows the *shofar* on Rosh Hashanah.

for Jews to greet each other, at the conclusion of religious services, with the words *l'shanah tovah tikatevu*—"may you be inscribed for a good year"—alluding to the ancient belief that, during the ten-day period between Rosh Hashanah and Yom Kippur, God writes the names of those who will live and die in three separate books: the Book of Life (for the truly righteous), the Book of Death (for the irredeemably wicked), and the Book of Intermediate Souls (for those who have not yet repented their sins). The hope, of course, is that one will be inscribed in the Book of Life.

Yom Kippur Also known as the Day of Atonement, Yom Kippur is unquestionably the most solemn day in Judaism's sacred calendar, and its most important fast day. The purpose of both the dusk-to-dusk fast and the penitential prayers that are recited on Yom Kippur was made clear by the rabbis centuries ago: "For transgressions against God, the Day of Atonement atones; but for transgressions of one human being against another, the Day of Atonement does not atone until they have made peace with one another" (tractate Yoma 8:9). For repentance (Hebrew, *teshuvah*) to be effective, therefore, some restorative action must accompany the process of prayer and self-examination. As a result, the liturgy for Yom Kippur asks forgiveness for a rather lengthy list of all the sins that people are likely to commit against one another, as well as all the acts of defiance that people are likely to display toward God. These confessional prayers, which are recited throughout the day, are collective expressions of guilt and remorse ("Our father, our King, *we* have sinned before You"). But while it is the norm in Judaism to pray as a part of a community, each worshiper is nevertheless expected to internalize the act of repentance and strive for reconciliation with neighbors and with God.

On Yom Kippur a number of restrictions, in addition to fasting, are commonly imposed on those who observe this holy day. Thus, in Orthodox communities it is customary for married couples to abstain from intimacy, for men to wear white garments (symbolic of purification) to synagogue, and to neither shave nor bathe (as if one were in mourning). In addition, no work of any kind may be performed on Yom Kippur, from the evening in which the holy day begins until the following evening when it ends. However, all fasting on Yom Kippur ceases the moment one's health is imperiled, and the rabbis were quite insistent that any seriously ill person first consult with a physician before undertaking a twenty-four-hour fast. Children under 13 and women who are actively nursing infants are generally exempt from the rigors of this day.

Sukkot Five days after the conclusion of Yom Kippur Jews undertake a week-long fall harvest celebration known as Sukkot (Hebrew, "booths"). As with any harvest festival, Sukkot displays symbols of the season, the most important being the palm frond

VOICES: An Interview with Rabbi Brad Bloom

Rabbi Bloom, of Temple Beth Yam, Hilton Head, South Carolina, is a graduate of the Hebrew Union College (a Reform Rabbinic Seminary). He holds a Master's degree in social work, and for almost thirty years he has served congregations in Illinois and California.

How do the High Holy Days evoke feelings of wonder and awe, for you and your congregation?

Rosh Hashanah and Yom Kippur lie at the very core of Jewish religious consciousness. These "Days of Awe," as they are called, challenge us to assess our relationship to God and to each other. We are obliged to ask hard questions and recognize our human frailties, and hopefully discover whatever inner strength we possess to change for the better. The awe and wonder we experience during this period of repentance come from two sources: from our encounters with God and from our communal experience and collective memory, woven together to create a moment of special sanctity.

Of course, our prayers and special rituals are an essential part of that experience. Listening to the *Kol Nidre* chant, for example, we are moved as much by the beauty of the traditional melody as by the thought of unfulfilled vows to God. And similar feelings arise on Rosh Hashanah when the *shofar* is sounded, echoing throughout the sanctuary. These are all sensory responses, but they evoke powerful emotions and even more powerful moments of introspection.

And how does a sense of God's presence enter into these rituals?

For some, God occupies the center stage in this drama; for others, he is thought of as working behind the scenes, eliciting deep feelings of empathy and belonging through our interaction as a congregation. And for still others, God is not present at all; instead, they experience the assembled presence of *K'lal Yisrael*— the world-wide community of Jews joined in solidarity. Taken together, all of these experiences represent the continuum of awe and wonder that are central to the High Holy Days.

Rabbi Brad Bloom

(Hebrew, *lulav*), the citron (Hebrew, *etrog*), and leaves of the willow tree (Hebrew, *aravah*) and the myrtle (Hebrew, *hadassah*). It is customary to adorn the *sukkah*—or temporary hut, from which Sukkot derives its name—with each of these plants while leaving the roof of this structure partly open to the sky. During the seven days of this holiday Jews are encouraged (weather permitting) to eat and sleep in the *sukkah*, so as to reenact, symbolically, the biblical Exodus (i.e., the passage of ancient Israelites through the desert after escaping from slavery in Egypt). Sukkot thus becomes one of three festivals (the other two being Pesach and Shavuot) that recall the Exodus narrative.

It is traditional religious practice to attend synagogue during the first two days and the last two days of the festival, offering thanksgiving prayers attuned to the fall

A decorated *Sukkah*, ready for a midday meal.

season. To that end, each worshiper is required to carry a *lulav* and an *etrog* to morning services, and in the course of this ceremony both the *lulav* and the *etrog* are waved in six directions, signifying God's presence throughout the universe. In addition, the biblical book of Ecclesiastes is read on the Sabbath of Sukkot, highlighting some of the major themes of this festival, namely, the passing of the seasons and the providence of God. At the conclusion of Sukkot an eighth day of prayer and celebration, known as Shemini Atzeret (or "the Eighth Day of Assembly"), is added to the seven days of Sukkot as a culminating moment in the process of expressing one's gratitude to God for the bounty of the world.

Traditionally, Jews living outside Israel divide up Shemini Atzeret into two days, with the second day referred to as *Simchat Torah* (Hebrew, "Joy of the Torah"); on that day, the annual reading of the first five books of the Hebrew Bible comes to an end, and the cycle of weekly readings begins again. In Israel, and in many Reform congregations, Shemini Atzeret and Simchat Torah are telescoped into a single day of observance, characterized by a festive atmosphere in which both children and adults join in celebrating the "gift" of Torah while singing and dancing with their congregation's Torah scroll in their arms.

Pesach   More commonly known as "Passover" in English-speaking countries, Pesach is the second of three pilgrimage festivals, the first being Sukkot and the third being Shavuot. In ancient times, as long as a Temple stood in Jerusalem, Jews made a pilgrimage to it to offer prayers and animal sacrifices to God. With the Roman destruction of the Second Temple in 70 C.E., Jews were left with nothing but a memory of this rite, and the practice of celebrating the Exodus from Egypt then shifted exclusively to the synagogue and to the home. However, long before the tragic end of the First Jewish War with Rome and the loss of both the Temple and its priesthood, Jews were accustomed to gathering in their homes on the first two nights of this week-long festival to recount the Exodus story and to celebrate this event through a ceremonial meal known as a **Seder**—a practice that may well have begun in biblical times.

Like Sukkot, Pesach is celebrated for either seven or eight days during the month of Nisan (March-April), depending, once again, on whether one lives in Israel or in the Diaspora, or whether one follows the Orthodox custom of celebrating Pesach for eight days or the Reform custom of limiting observance to a week. In either case, the first two and the last two days are subject to the same restrictions that govern any *chag*—no work and limited travel. In addition, however, Pesach imposes one more strictly dietary requirement: no foods containing yeast may be consumed during this period (reflecting the fact that Jewish slaves, escaping from Egypt, had no time to allow their bread to rise). In Orthodox and most Conservative households it is the custom, therefore, to rid the home of all breads and foods that contain leavening agents and to prepare for this occasion by either boiling one's dishes and silverware or using a separate set of dinnerware and utensils that are reserved for use on Pesach alone. As we will learn later in this chapter, the dietary rules and regulations collectively known as *kashrut* are fundamentally important to Jewish practice. The number of foods sold in supermarkets bearing a "Kosher for Passover" label testifies to the seriousness with which this practice is observed by many Jews today.

Observance of Pesach begins in the evening in the home, where the *Seder* is celebrated by a gathering of family and friends, followed the next morning by a festival service in the synagogue. The *Seder* consists of two rituals in one: a festive meal, featuring biblical and seasonal foods that reflect the Exodus story, and a liturgy, found in an ancient text called the *Haggadah* (Hebrew, "telling"). The *Haggadah* contains both the story of Israel's escape from Egypt and a collection of hymns and songs and rabbinic commentaries in praise of God, who made that deliverance possible. One of the principal goals of this highly ritualized meal is to leave each participant in the *Seder* with a sense of engagement in the biblical story. Ideally, each person should identify with the enslaved generation that witnessed not only the liberation from bondage but also the giving of the Torah at Mt. Sinai.

Because the Pesach *Seder* is essentially a family event, children play a very prominent role in this rite by being given questions to ask, songs to sing, and stories to listen to. Most temptingly of all, during the initial ceremony that precedes the meal, the prayer leader takes a piece of *matzah* (a type of unleavened flatbread that, according to biblical writers, the escaping Israelites baked in haste while fleeing Egypt) and breaks it in half, hiding one half of this piece—known as the *Afikoman*—so that children can find it by the end of the meal and exchange it for a gift.

In addition to *matzah*, several other foods are either displayed or consumed during the *Seder* meal, including bitter herbs (a reminder of the bitterness of slavery); a mixture of wine, chopped nuts, and apples (symbolically representing the mortar used by Israelite slaves to build cities and pyramids); a roasted lamb shank bone (recalling the sacrifice of lambs by the Israelites before their departure from Egypt); and a roasted egg, a green vegetable (usually parsley), and an additional herb or vegetable. These items all reflect the ancient agricultural context of this celebration—namely, the early spring harvest and the lamb-shearing season that often accompanied that harvest. Finally, participants consume four small symbolic cups of wine during the *Seder* meal, each serving as a reminder of the many blessings God bestowed upon ancient Israel and continues to bestow upon the Jewish people. A fifth cup is set aside for the prophet Elijah, whose symbolic presence at the *Seder* represents the hope that a Messiah will some day appear and bring peace and justice into the world.

What Pesach brings together, at last, is a combined celebration of nature's bounty, historical memories, and redemptive visions of the future, all of which turn upon the ancient miracle of God's intervention on behalf of an enslaved Israel.

Shavuot Seven weeks separate Pesach from the last of the three pilgrimage festivals, Shavuot (Hebrew, "weeks"). (This holiday is often referred to by Christians as "Pentecost.") Between the second day of Passover and the first day of Shavuot, it was the practice in biblical Israel to bring a sheaf of new grain to the Temple, and an obvious connection exists between this festival and the later spring harvest. However, during the rabbinic era Shavuot became associated with the giving of the Torah on Mt. Sinai, and from that moment on Shavuot became a part of the ongoing liturgical reenactment of the Exodus that we have traced through Sukkot and Pesach. Given this new historical association, we can understand why the rabbis decided that the high point of the synagogue liturgy for Shavuot would be the public reading of the Ten Commandments.

Traditionally, Shavuot is celebrated for two days (the sixth and seventh of the month of Sivan [May-June]), though the festivities associated with Shavuot are considerably less elaborate than those connected to Pesach or Sukkot. It is common practice on Shavuot to decorate the synagogue with flowers and to serve meatless meals with honey as a key ingredient—the idea being that the reading of the Torah should be sweet upon the lips, though neither of these practices is obligatory. More common is the public reading of the Book of Ruth, which tells the story of a young Moabite widow who is welcomed into Israelite society and who, centuries later, became the prototype of the ideal convert to Judaism. Finally, there is a custom of staying up the entire first night of the *chag* for the purpose of studying some portion of the Torah. This practice was established for the first time by a community of mystics living in sixteenth-century Safed (northern Israel) who believed that the celebration of the Torah on Shavuot should be preceded by a process of mental and spiritual preparation. Shavuot, therefore, does more than merely commemorate the revelation at Sinai: for Jews it is as much a reenactment as it is a remembrance of that central event in biblical history.

The Minor Festivals

In contrast to the major festivals we have just reviewed, a number of relatively "minor" festivals serve to fill out the Jewish religious year. Yet despite their historically subordinate status, they are no less beloved by Jews and are sometimes observed with equal attention. The distinction between them is mainly ceremonial: the observance of many (though not all) of these festivals does not entail restrictions on labor, diet, or any other activities. In addition, these festivals were never really integrated into the agricultural cycle that is so clearly embedded within the calendar of major holidays, though some indirectly reflect the season in which they appear.

Hanukkah Of all of Judaism's minor holidays, Hanukkah is probably the best-known throughout the Western world, if only because of its proximity to Christmas. It is also one of the most historically aware since it is linked directly to a historical event. Hanukkah commemorates the Maccabean rebellion that began in 167 B.C.E. against the tyrannical rule of the Syrian monarch, Antiochus IV, who sought to suppress the practice of Judaism within Palestine and who "defiled" the Temple in Jerusalem by rededicating it to the Greek gods. For the next two years an armed insurrection, led first by a rural priest named Mattathias and after his death by his eldest son Judah the Maccabee, wrested control of the Temple from Antiochus' army.

The key event that Hanukkah celebrates, however, is the recovery and cleansing of the Jerusalem Temple and the miracle of the lights that Jewish tradition records. According to this legendary account, once the Temple was in Jewish hands it became necessary to rededicate the sanctuary—yet only one flask of the oil necessary to keep lamps lit could be found. Miraculously, however, this one flask continued to burn for eight days, thus attesting to the renewal of God's presence within the Temple and to His continuing commitment to Jewish survival. In commemoration of that miracle, and as an acknowledgment of God's deliverance of His people from a brutal tyrant, Jews light a candle each night for eight nights until a ceremonial candelabrum (known in Hebrew as either a *menorah* or a *hanukkiah*) is completely lit. This candle-lighting ceremony is accompanied by the chanting of prayers, the singing of songs, and, in more recent times, the giving of gifts. In addition, a traditional game of chance is played with a four-sided top known as a *dreidel*, on whose sides are inscribed four Hebrew letters, which stand for the words meaning "a great miracle occurred there." In contemporary Israel, however, *dreidels* bear a slightly altered message: "a great miracle occurred here," referring to the establishment of the Jewish state in 1948.

On the final night of Hanukkah all the candles are lit while children play with the dreidel, a game with toy coins.

Purim Another history-oriented festival, and one that exhibits an even more secular character than Hanukkah, is Purim, which occurs on the fourteenth day of the month Adar (February–March). Purim is a carnival-like holiday whose origins can be found within the biblical Book of Esther. Like Hanukkah, Purim celebrates a victory, this time over an antagonist named Haman, who appears in the Book of Esther as a would-be destroyer of the Jewish people. However, unlike Hanukkah, the underlying festival narrative appears to have little or no historical basis. Still, Purim tells an interesting story of adaptation and survival against all odds, and it is a story that has gripped the Jewish imagination for centuries.

For Orthodox Jews, Purim begins with a fast on the thirteenth of the month of Adar. This fast reflects Queen Esther's request to the Jews of Shushan (the capital of Persia) that they fast for three days before she was to visit the Persian king Ahashueros and identify Haman as the courtier who planned to murder her people. Once the fast is over, however, the festive aspects of Purim begin. These include a reading of the *megillah* (the book or scroll) of Esther. While this scroll is being read, congregants interrupt the narration with shouting and foot stamping every time Haman's name is read aloud. In addition, the rabbis, many centuries ago, sanctioned the practice of drinking to excess on Purim, thereby contributing to an atmosphere of barely controlled anarchy. This near-riotous behavior is coupled with the practice of dressing children in costumes that suggest the principal characters in the Esther story, so it is easy to see why this holiday is sometimes referred to as the Jewish Mardi Gras.

However, Purim also has its more sedate customs: the sending of gifts to friends, or to the poor, and the eating of triangular-shaped fruit-filled cookies known as *hamantaschen*, variously thought to represent Haman's ears, or hat, or pockets. Finally, while there is no prohibition against working on Purim, many Orthodox communities will devote the entire fourteenth of Adar to celebrating this festival.

Tu B'Shevat   The fifteenth day of the month of Shevat (January-February) is identified in rabbinic literature as the "New Year's Day of Trees," and it is often referred to today as the Jewish version of Arbor Day. Typically, trees are planted on this day (especially in modern Israel), and monies are set aside for the poor. In some communities Jews hold a special *Seder* on Tu B'Shevat consisting of recitations from the Bible and the Talmud, combined with the eating of certain fruits and nuts (chiefly figs, dates, carobs, almonds, and pomegranates) that are native to the land of Israel.

Tisha B'Av   The ninth day of the month of Av (Hebrew, *Tisha B'Av*) is, after Yom Kippur, the most solemn day in the Jewish calendar because it commemorates the destruction of both the First Temple by the Babylonians in 587 B.C.E. and the Second Temple by the Romans in 70 B.C.E. Each of these events was a tragic turning point in Jewish history, leading to the loss of national sovereignty and the subsequent exile of the Jewish masses from their homeland. On Tisha B'Av (commonly celebrated in July or August) Jews fast from sunset to sunset as they remember not only these tragedies but other terrible losses that they have suffered during their long history. Like Yom Kippur, Tisha B'Av is a day of collective contrition and virtual mourning, as Jews gather in synagogues to read from the Book of Lamentations and sing hymns that reflect on the double loss of Jerusalem and Jewish nationhood.

In Orthodox and many Conservative communities, congregants forgo the custom of wearing prayer shawls and phylacteries during the morning service, and they sit on low stools in a darkened sanctuary, as if mourning for a close relative. Even though the liturgy for Tisha B'Av plumbs the very depths of Jewish sorrow and despair, it gives way, a week later, to the "Sabbath of Comfort," on which one reads from the fortieth chapter of the Book of Isaiah. Here, the prophet extends both consolation to his fellow exiles and assurance that God has not, and never will, forget them.

Yom HaShoah   Holocaust Memorial Day, or *Yom HaShoah* in Hebrew, is the most recent addition to the sacred calendar in Judaism. In 1951 the Israeli Parliament selected this date (the twenty-seventh day of Nisan [March-April]) as a remembrance day for the millions of Jews who were victims of Nazi genocide during World War II. This date was chosen because it coincides with the beginning of the Warsaw Ghetto Uprising of 1943, and today the overwhelming majority of Jewish communities throughout the world observe this day of collective mourning and reflection. Yom HaShoah, however, is not a fast day, and unlike Tisha B'Av there are no prohibitions on work or other activities. Nevertheless, it has become customary in recent years for Jews to gather on the evening of the twenty-seventh of Nisan and to recite memorial prayers for the roughly one-third of the Jewish world population that lost their lives during the war. Moreover, the practice of lighting commemorative candles in the home has also taken hold and is done in imitation of the mourning rites for a close relative.

The Sabbath

Though it is neither a major nor a minor festival, strictly speaking, the weekly Sabbath (Hebrew, *Shabbat*) forms the core of the sacred calendar in Judaism. Like the major festivals, it is a day of prayer and rest, with its own liturgical tradition and pattern of observance, but unlike any other sacred occasion in Judaism its observance is explicitly mandated in the Ten Commandments. The Torah, in fact, provides two different rationales for Shabbat: in the Book of Exodus (20:8–11) it is identified as the day on which God rested from His creative labors; in the Book of Deuteronomy (5:12–15), however, it is associated with the Exodus from Egypt and liberation from slavery. Each of these explanations, of course, provides a distinctive interpretation of the meaning of Shabbat; the former is supernatural, while the latter is historical. For both interpretations, however, the commanding lesson of the Sabbath remains the same: God's actions, whether at the beginning of human time or at a turning point in the history of Israel, serve as a model for human behavior; the Creator/Liberator has separated sacred time from ordinary time, and so must we.

Shabbat begins at dusk on Friday and concludes at sundown on Saturday (according to tradition, when three stars appear in the sky). This 24-hour period is ushered in by the lighting of two candles in the home, reminiscent of the first act of creation. Customarily it is the woman of the house who lights these candles, though men are not forbidden to do so. Once the Sabbath formally begins observance shifts to the synagogue, where the *Erev Shabbat* (Sabbath evening) service is conducted. The liturgy for Sabbath evening identifies the Sabbath itself as a "bride," and the feelings aroused by the "joy of the Sabbath" are similar to the emotions evoked by a wedding. With the return of the family from prayer the Sabbath meal begins with a prayer of sanctification recited over wine and a blessing said over two loaves of bread. Sabbath bread is called *challah*, and it is usually baked in a shape that suggests a woman's braided hair (yet another allusion to the Sabbath "bride").

A Jewish mother and daughter light the Sabbath candles.

Sabbath morning observance shifts, once again, to the synagogue, where, in addition to the Shabbat liturgy, a weekly portion of the Torah is read, accompanied by a portion from the prophetic books. That service concluded, the remainder of the day is spent in quiet study or in rest until the evening, when the last two worship services of the day are celebrated, and a separation ceremony, known as *Havdalah*, is celebrated with a cup of wine, a braided candle, and a spice box—all reminiscent

A table set for Shabbat: Challah, candlesticks, and wine.

of the sweetness and calm of the Sabbath that has just departed. The rabbis of the Talmud once observed that it was not just Israel that had kept the Sabbath, but the Sabbath that had kept Israel; as the most direct link to the ancient past, Shabbat serves as one of Judaism's primary symbols of historical and spiritual continuity.

Life-Cycle Events

Virtually all religious cultures attempt to locate the sacred within the context of everyday life, and Judaism is no exception. From birth to death, and from day to day, Jews have found myriad ways of testifying to God's presence in their lives and in the life of their community. At each stage in the cycle of living and dying, Judaism offers a distinctive ceremony that marks the passage from one stage to another. The ultimate object of these rites of passage is the sanctification of human life and the desire to deepen the covenant relationship between Israel and God.

Birth The ritual process of entering the Jewish community begins, for male babies, on the eighth day of life with the rite of circumcision. Jews are not the only people today who circumcise male infants (nor were they in antiquity), but in Judaism circumcision is much more than a medical procedure. It is, in fact, a very basic *mitzvah*, a divine commandment imparted to the biblical patriarch Abraham and incumbent upon all of his male descendants from that time forward.

Historically, circumcision has been one of the distinctive physical marks of Jewish identity, and its importance for the overwhelming majority of Jews can be gauged by the fact that the circumcision ritual takes precedence over the Sabbath or any other holy day in the sacred calendar; indeed, the only thing that would delay the performance of this *mitzvah* would be concern for the health of the child. During this ceremony, after the *mohel* (a ritual-circumciser, who is usually a medically trained professional) has removed a portion of the infant's foreskin, the newborn receives his Hebrew name, which traditionally consists of the child's own name and that of the father (for example, Isaac son of Abraham). From this moment on, this is the name by which the child will be known in the Jewish community, particularly on ritual occasions. In many Conservative and Reform communities it has become the custom to add the mother's name to the father's, thereby assigning equal weight to the matrilineal source of the child's identity.

Baby girls enter the Jewish community under slightly different circumstances. There has never been any form of female circumcision in Judaism, nor any fixed naming ritual for the infant female. However, one very popular custom today among Jews worldwide is the practice of bringing the newborn to the synagogue on the first (or, in some communities, the fourth) Sabbath after birth. On that occasion, either the child's father or both parents are called up to the Torah and recite the customary blessings. Then the baby girl is given a Hebrew name, and like her male counterpart it is the name that she will use on all ritual occasions for the rest of her life. This ceremony is sometimes referred to, in Hebrew, as a *brit hayim*, or "covenant of life."

Bar/Bat Mitzvah and Confirmation As you learned from Seth's story at the beginning of this chapter, Jewish males traditionally enter the stage of religious maturity at the age of 13, whether or not they have engaged in the *Bar Mitzvah* ceremony. There is no reference to such a ritual in the Hebrew Bible, nor do the rabbis of the Talmud make mention of any specific rite of passage that marks a young man's assumption of responsibility for fulfilling the *mitzvot* incumbent on an observant Jew. Nevertheless, by the later Middle Ages, something like the *Bar Mitzvah* ceremony we practice today had already begun to evolve, consisting of some demonstration of Hebrew literacy and an ability to read a weekly portion of the Torah. And of all the commonly practiced rituals of contemporary Judaism, the *Bar Mitzvah* is the one ritual that is likely to be familiar to non-Jews.

Regarded as the culminating point of years of study, the young man who becomes a *Bar Mitzvah* is taught to see himself as a scholar-in-training whose entry into adult Jewish life is just the beginning of a lifelong program of study. Though the celebration that follows is often joyous, there is a serious underlying purpose: the preparation of a young person to assume what the rabbis have called the "yoke of Torah." Thus, in addition to reading a portion from both the Torah and the prophetic literature, a *Bar Mitzvah* is expected to deliver a *d'rash*, or brief scholarly explanation of the portion he has just read, thereby demonstrating a mature comprehension of Jewish Scriptures.

The practice of requiring young women (between the ages of 12 and 13) to furnish similar proof of both literacy and religious commitment is of much more recent origin. The first *Bat Mitzvah* to be performed in the United States was conducted in 1922 for Judith Kaplan, daughter of Rabbi Mordecai Kaplan, the founder of the Reconstructionist Movement. What began as a somewhat radical gesture, designed to raise the question of gender equality in modern Judaism, soon evolved into an alternative form of the *Bar Mitzvah* ritual, and today the *Bat Mitzvah* ceremony is as common as the *Bar Mitzvah* in non-Orthodox communities.

Another innovative practice, known as a Confirmation, is almost as commonplace today in non-Orthodox communities as the *Bar* and *Bat Mitzvah*, and it too involves a process of study and ritual performance by both young men and young women. The Confirmation ceremony can be traced back to the early decades of the Reform Movement in nineteenth-century Germany, where some Reform-minded rabbis attempted to find an alternative rite of passage for adolescents rather than the traditional *Bar Mitzvah*. Their solution was to borrow a practice from the Christian church and to require 16-year-old males (and later females) to make a profession of faith during the

Shavuot service, thus connecting their religious coming-of-age with the traditional celebration of the giving of the Torah at Mt. Sinai. Curiously, however, this intended departure from normative Jewish practice was finally reintegrated into the traditional life-cycle after World War II, as many Reform and several Conservative congregations added the Confirmation ceremony to the now-lengthened process of Jewish education. Thus, instead of supplanting the *Bar Mitzvah*, the Confirmation ceremony simply became a secondary stage of the passage to adulthood.

Marriage and Divorce   In Judaism, marriage is a contractual relationship between a man and a woman, rooted in mutual love and respect, and presumed to be both monogamous and enduring—a relationship on which divine blessings can be invoked. However, like all contracts, the marriage contract can be dissolved.

Over time Jews have devised formal procedures for regulating and solemnizing the processes of marriage and divorce. Many centuries ago, the marriage ceremony consisted of two separate rites: the betrothal and the actual nuptials. According to this ancient custom, the future bride and groom became engaged to one another through the exchange of a ring. The couple then returned to the homes of their respective parents for a year, at which time the bride and groom gathered, along with their families, under a marriage canopy (known as the *chuppah*). A rabbi would recite seven blessings, praising God and sanctifying the union, and only at the conclusion of this ceremony would the marriage be consummated. Today, these two ceremonies have been combined, and are accompanied by other, largely symbolic rituals: first, having the bride and groom drink from the same wine cup, and second, having the groom present the bride with her marriage contract (Hebrew, *ketuvah*). Finally, at the conclusion of the ceremony the groom crushes a wine glass with his shoe—traditionally understood to symbolize the destruction of the two Temples— whereupon the attending guests shout *Mazel Tov* (Hebrew, "good luck").

The bride and groom will stand under this canopy during the wedding ceremony.

From a traditional point of view, the presentation of the *ketuvah* by the groom is the core of the marriage rite in Judaism because it states publicly and clearly the groom's intention to provide for his bride's comfort and well-being while he lives and her financial security after he dies, or after they divorce. The *ketuvah*, in short, is a "prenuptial agreement," and its principal purpose is to provide for the future bride so that, in the event of divorce or the groom's death, she will not be left destitute. Traditionally, the groom alone vows to set aside monies in escrow as "marriage insurance," but many modern Jewish couples have opted for a very different kind of *ketuvah*, vowing mutual commitment and support, symbolized by an exchange of rings.

Jewish divorce proceedings are no less formal (albeit much sadder) than the marriage ceremony. After marital counseling has been tried and failed, the couple comes before a rabbinic court (Hebrew, *bet din*) that consists of three rabbis who hear the case. The divorce document (Hebrew, *get*) is then drawn up, releasing both parties from any future obligation to one another. At that moment, the husband (or his representative) must hand the *get* to his soon-to-be ex-wife. He is then declared free of their union and eligible to marry again—that very day, if he chooses. The wife, however, must wait three months to marry again, on the presumption that she may be pregnant and therefore carrying the child of her former spouse. Moreover, if her husband refuses to grant her a divorce—or cannot do so because he is missing—traditional Jewish law leaves her few options for dissolving the marriage. She may find herself bound by religious law to a husband who has abandoned her, or who may have died in some distant land without witnesses to his death. In rabbinic parlance, such a woman is an *agunah* (Hebrew, "chained woman"), and Orthodox communities continue to struggle with this legal dilemma today.

Death and Mourning It is the custom in Judaism to treat the deceased with as much dignity as the living, and every effort is made to ensure that the ceremonies associated with the burial of the dead and mourning are invested with sanctity and respect. Whenever possible, a Jewish burial will take place within twenty-four hours of death (unless the Sabbath or a festival intervenes, delaying burial for a day or two). The body is prepared for burial by being bathed and wrapped in a shroud, then traditionally placed in a simple pine box, thus discouraging ostentation. It is customary during the burial service for mourners to express their sorrow by a symbolic tearing of their clothes—often wearing a strip of torn black cloth, pinned to a garment—while reciting prayers of praise for God and comfort for the soul of the deceased in the afterlife. During this ceremony mourners are consoled by family and friends and gently discouraged from showing excessive grief.

Once burial occurs, those mourners who were closest to the deceased—parents, siblings, children, or spouse—enter into a weeklong period of intensive mourning known as *shivah* (Hebrew, "seven"), interrupted only by the Sabbath. During this period, mourners do not work, remain at home, and receive well-wishers who join with the mourning family in "sitting *shivah*." Since mourners are not expected, during this week, to attend synagogue, it is customary for friends to form a prayer quorum (Hebrew, *minyan*) in the home so that morning and evening prayers may be recited.

Once *shivah* is over, however, mourners are expected to return to the world and everyday obligations, with the understanding that for the remainder of that month mourners will abstain from entertainments of all kinds and remain in a somber state of mind. Once this thirty-day period of diminished mourning is completed, restrictions on the mourner's participation in celebratory events are lifted, though most Orthodox Jews continue a modified mourning protocol until the first anniversary of a parent's death has passed. The erecting of a tombstone does not normally occur until eleven months have passed; thereafter, close relatives are expected to visit the grave at least once a year—usually on the anniversary of the death of that family member—as well as to recite prayers in memory of the dead during memorial services held during all the major festivals. Finally, it is customary to light candles in the home at the time of the yearly anniversary of a loved one's death, and, whenever possible, to place small stones on the gravestone as a sign of one's remembrance of the deceased.

Other Sacred Practices

As a way of life—and not just a creed—Judaism seeks to shape every facet of one's behavior: from the food one eats (or doesn't eat) to the way husbands and wives relate to one another. To someone outside these traditions these religious practices might seem intrusive, but to those living within those traditions they provide a sense of meaning and order, endowing all of life's activities with an aura of holiness.

The Dietary Code   Since antiquity, Jews have observed a restricted diet. While the details of that diet have changed somewhat over the centuries, the underlying assumptions behind these practices have not. In the Torah, the people of Israel are told, repeatedly, that God wishes them to be in a state of "holiness," and when that principle is applied to diet it becomes a multiform discipline of selective food consumption and careful food preparation.

The essentials of the Jewish dietary code—known in Hebrew as *kashrut*—are as follows:

1. The only animals that may be eaten are those that have been properly slaughtered; no animal that has been killed by another or that has died a natural death may be consumed.
2. The only quadrupeds that may be eaten are those with split hooves who also chew the cud (like cows or goats), and once properly slaughtered their blood must be drained away.
3. No fish may be eaten that does not have both fins and scales.
4. No insects may be consumed at all.
5. No meat dish may be eaten at the same time as a milk dish.

The practical consequences for anyone who observes this diet are obvious: no one who is serious about *kashrut* will walk into a restaurant and order a cheeseburger, nor will that person dine at a stranger's home without first inquiring whether the food about to be served is really "kosher" (meaning in conformity to rabbinic standards of food selection and preparation) and whether the plates and cooking utensils are also completely free of contamination from forbidden foods. In fact, within all Orthodox and many Conservative Jewish homes it is customary to find not only kosher foodstuffs on the table, but also duplicate sets of ovens, refrigerators, and dinnerware to make it easier to separate meat dishes from milk dishes. Kosher restaurants carry this process one step further by only ordering meat prepared by kosher butchers and by obtaining rabbinical certification that all food preparation procedures have been followed scrupulously. The phrase "kosher-style" food is therefore a deceptive misnomer; foods and cooking processes are either kosher or non-kosher, but never both.

It is interesting to note, however, that all fruits and vegetables are kosher, and that certain foodstuffs—like Jell-O or margarine—are "neutral" with respect to meat-milk distinctions. Such "neutral" foods are known by the Yiddish term *pareve*, and they may be eaten at either a meat-based or a milk-based meal. Over the centuries, attempts have been made to rationalize this system of food taboos and culinary practices by suggesting an underlying concern with food safety and dietary well-being, but whatever side benefits may be derived from not consuming infected meats, such benefits are largely peripheral to the primary intent of the dietary code, namely, that of separating the observant Jew from a nonobservant food-consuming culture, thereby making the commonplace act of eating a religiously self-conscious event.

Family Purity All Orthodox, and some Conservative and Reform, women, in addition to maintaining a kosher home, are also equally attentive to the practice of ritual "purity," and as a consequence attend a *mikveh* (Hebrew, "pool") at the conclusion of their menstrual period. In fact, in a truly orthodox Jewish home, husband and wife abstain from sexual intimacy not only during the entire period of menstruation, but for seven days thereafter, and only then will the wife attend the *mikveh*. The purpose of this rite of purification, however, is not to remove biological impurities from a woman's body; that can be accomplished simply by bathing. Immersion in a *mikveh* is rather a symbolic act of spiritual preparation—somewhat similar to the practice of baptism in Christianity, which clearly derives from antecedent Jewish practices—and while the *mikveh* is used primarily by women preparing to resume sexual relations with their husbands, it is also used for conversion ceremonies and by orthodox males on the afternoon before Yom Kippur.

The rabbinical laws governing this entire process are referred to as *taharat hamish-pachah* (Hebrew, "purity of the family"), and the remote origin of these practices can be found in the Hebrew Bible, where men are warned against having intimate relations with a menstruating woman. Nowhere, however, in either the Hebrew Bible or in rabbinic literature does Judaism suggest that women's bodies are "unclean" in a hygienic or biological sense. As with the dietary code, so with the laws of family purity: the ceremonial discipline of traditional Judaism requires a heightened degree of self-awareness about the routines of everyday life, a repertoire of symbolic acts associated with the condition of holiness, and an added concern for maintaining a certain distance from the normative behavior of non-Jewish societies. Among Reform and Reconstructionist Jews, however, such practices are rarely observed, and today rigorous application of the purity laws is only a distinguishing mark of family life within the Orthodox Jewish home.

Prayer

From its earliest beginnings, Judaism developed a distinctive culture of prayer. In the Hebrew Bible one can find numerous examples of the principal types of prayer that make up the traditional Judaic liturgy: prayers of praise, confession, petition, and thanksgiving. In the Book of Psalms, for example, the legendary King David (to whom much of that book is attributed) petitions God in the following prayer-like poem:

> Hear my cry, O God,
> Heed my prayer.
> From the end of the earth I call to You;
> When my heart is faint,
> You lead me to a rock that is high above me.
> For you have been my refuge,
> A tower of strength against the enemy.
> O that I might dwell in Your tent forever,
> Take refuge under Your protecting wings.
> —*Psalm 61:2–5*

In poems like this, biblical writers repeatedly addressed God in a language that is at once intimate and awestruck, praising His providential care of those who trust in Him, while requesting His continued protection against evil and misfortune. But no matter what the character of any particular prayer, all prayers in Judaism are addressed directly to God and all assume His compassion and just concern.

With the destruction of the Second Temple in 70 C.E., the principal site of Jewish prayer shifted to the synagogue, where prayer alone, disconnected from animal sacrifices, became the norm. From that point on, the practice of offering prayer—now no longer primarily the privilege of Temple priests—became more democratic. Each community constructed its own house of worship, and before long a recognized liturgy emerged that consisted, in part, of selections from the Hebrew Bible, and prayers for various occasions composed by rabbinic authors. By the Middle Ages these prayers were collected in a single volume, known in Hebrew as the *Siddur*, that became the primary source of the synagogue liturgy for weekdays, Sabbath, and festivals.

The daily routine of prayer appears to have been established during the late biblical period, where we find the exiled Daniel, living in Persia, praying three times a day while turning toward Jerusalem (Daniel 6:11). The architectural arrangement of early synagogues echoed this practice by orienting the entire building in the direction of Jerusalem, though in later centuries Jews were content with placing the Ark—a large, upright cupboard designed to hold several scrolls of the Torah—on the eastern wall. As the rabbinic protocol of prayer developed during the early Middle Ages, the rules governing thrice-daily prayer became increasingly elaborate and formalized, with an additional early afternoon service added on the Sabbath.

The most common setting for prayer in Judaism is communal, and while individual (and even spontaneous) prayer is always valid, the full complement of prayers in any prayer service can only be said once a quorum of worshipers has assembled, either in the home or, more commonly, in a synagogue. That quorum is referred to in Hebrew as a *minyan*, and in Orthodox communities it consists of at least ten males 13 years of age or older; in Conservative and Reform synagogues, a minyan consists simply of ten adults of either gender.

Holding a prayer book, and wearing a *tallit*, *tefillin*, and a *kipah*, a young man prepares to recite morning prayers.

During the morning service (Hebrew, *shacharit*), men traditionally wear a prayer shawl (Hebrew, **tallit**) and phylacteries or prayer-amulets (Hebrew, **tefillin**) throughout, and then remove them at the conclusion of prayers. On the Sabbath it is customary, even in many Reform synagogues, to wear the *tallit* during prayer services, with *tefillin* worn only during weekday prayers. In most synagogues today, a head covering (known variously as a *kipah* or a *yarmulke*) is worn during prayer, chiefly by males, and as a sign of respect. Prayer services are conducted in the late afternoon (Hebrew, *minchah*) and early evening (Hebrew, *maariv*) as well, and like the morning service they consist of certain fixed prayers that represent a succinct summation of the Jewish faith.

One of the most powerful, and the most revered, of all the prayers that are recited during the morning and evening services is the *Shema*, which consists of biblical verses that first declare the unity of God and then declare Israel's commitment to His service:

> Hear O Israel, the Lord is our God, the Lord is one!
> Blessed is God's glorious kingdom forever and ever!
> And you shall love the Lord, your God with all your heart, with all your soul, and with all your might. Set these words, which I command you this day, upon your heart. Teach them faithfully to your children; speak of them in your home and on the way, when you lie down and when you rise up. Bind them as a sign upon your hand, and let them be symbols before your eyes; inscribe them on the doorposts of your house and upon your gates.
> —*Deuteronomy 6:4–9*

This passage is one of the first prayers taught to children at the earliest age of religious instruction, and it is, traditionally, the last prayer one utters before death. It is one of a repertoire of "statutory" prayers that are recited every day in the week, on major festivals, and on the Sabbath.

In Orthodox and many Conservative congregations, it is customary to read aloud a portion from the Torah every week, on Monday and Thursday mornings, and especially on the Sabbath (morning and late afternoon). In addition, an extra passage from the prophetic books is read on both the Sabbath and the major festivals. On each occasion the portion selected from the prophetic books either echoes the themes of the Torah portion or reflects the themes of the festival itself. All these readings are normally recited or chanted in Hebrew, with translations in the local language freely available to the congregation. For centuries, most Jewish males possessed enough Hebrew literacy to follow readings from the Torah, or the liturgy itself, with little difficulty; however, with the dawn of the modern era, Hebrew-reading skills began to decline rapidly, and the question of vernacular language use became a much-debated topic within reformist circles. Today, all Jewish communities employ quite a bit of Hebrew in both the recitation of prayers and in readings from the Torah, though the ratio of Hebrew to the vernacular will vary considerably, with Orthodox synagogues conducting services almost entirely in Hebrew, and Conservative, Reform, and Reconstructionist communities employing a variable mixture of Hebrew and the congregation's native language.

CONCLUSION

Judaism has not merely survived over a period of three millennia (in itself a remarkable achievement); it has also evolved, responding and adapting to changing circumstances as it developed from a geographically and philosophically circumscribed religious culture into a global faith. As the oldest of the Abrahamic religions, it carries within itself the longest memory of formative events and personalities, and with it an abiding sense of the divine purposefulness of human history. Judaism exists, therefore, at a point of intersection between history and theology, as the life experiences of a people intertwine with their experience of the sacred.

At the summit of Jewish faith lies a singular Creator-God—at once familiar and mysterious, judgmental and forgiving—whose very existence guarantees the order and meaning of the universe, and those who inhabit it, while at the heart of Jewish faith lies a covenanted relationship between that God and those who are committed to serving and obeying His will. And even those who doubt the very existence of that God, but who persist in identifying themselves with Jewish history and values, continue to believe in a moral covenant that makes all human communities possible.

SEEKING ANSWERS

What Is Ultimate Reality?

The one God of Jewish faith is understood to be not only the source of all created things but also the highest and most complete form of reality the human mind can imagine. Jewish mystics often refer to this transcendent reality as the *Ein Sof* or Infinite One. Traditionalists believe that God revealed Himself to the people of Israel at Mt. Sinai and that Jewish Scriptures provide a reliable account of that revelation. The biblical view of Creation is, initially, positive: when God views the world He has brought into being He declares it "very good" (Genesis 1:31). However, later mystics, like Rabbi Luria, traced the evil in the world back to a mysterious cosmic error that subverted the design for the created world that God had originally intended. Nevertheless, the presence of divine "sparks" in each of us inspires us to believe that goodness and not evil will prevail.

How Should We Live in This World?

The divine commandments that make up the core of the Torah are designed to enable human beings to achieve true righteousness, that is, to bring the human moral will into conformity with God's will, and thereby ensure that justice and peace will prevail in the world. All ideas of right and wrong—like the Ten Commandments—must, therefore, be referred back to God's revelation of His will at Sinai and the Torah's laws that govern human conduct. Both biblical writers and their rabbinic commentators believed that human beings are created in the "image of God" and, at the same time, are torn between good and bad impulses. In the mystical tradition this conflict can be resolved through study, prayer, and meditation, all of which draw us closer to God.

What Is Our Ultimate Purpose?

Judaism has never believed that human beings are hopelessly evil, nor does it support the view that humanity can never make moral progress. The High Holy Days are dedicated to the belief that both individuals and whole societies are capable of changing their behavior and that, through active repentance, they are even capable of drawing closer to each other and to God.

Jews have long believed that the soul is immortal and survives death. The fate of the soul in the "world to come" and God's judgment of that soul remain a subject of speculation and wonder, even today; some, however, regard these beliefs as obsolete and no longer a part of contemporary Jewish faith.

REVIEW QUESTIONS

For Review

1. What are *mitzvot*, and where can they be found?
2. What does the word *Torah* literally mean, and how many other meanings can be derived from it?
3. What are Maimonides' thirteen Principles of Faith?
4. Who was Mordecai Kaplan, and to which movement in modern Judaism is he connected?
5. What does the term *Shoah* mean, and how is it different from the word "Holocaust"?

For Further Reflection

1. What are the implications for Judaism of the dual concepts of election and covenant? Do Jews see themselves as the only people with whom the Creator-God has communicated? Is it ever possible for a non-Jew to enter into a covenant relationship with Israel's God?
2. How did Judaism recover from the loss of the Jerusalem Temple in 70 C.E.? Why do you think that some Jews living today are

hoping to rebuild the Temple and resume the practice of animal sacrifice? Why are the majority of the world's Jews content with the synagogue and its prayer routines?

3. How does Maimonides' approach to both God and Torah differ from that of the mystics? Do the kabbalists really believe that it is possible for human beings to seek union with God or to find the presence of God within oneself?
4. Among the varied responses to the *Shoah* that modern Jewish philosophers have proposed, which response seems the most compelling to you? If you were a Holocaust survivor, what would your view of life and of faith be now? Would you still find it possible to believe in a just and loving God?
5. What does the word Zionism refer to, and what role did Theodor Herzl play in promoting Zionist ideas?
6. What are the Ten Commandments, and where can they be found?
7. What is the Talmud, and how many volumes (or tractates) does the Babylonian Talmud contain?

GLOSSARY

Baal Shem Tov (1698–1760) A charismatic faith-healer, mystic, and teacher (whose given name was Israel ben Eliezer) who is generally regarded as the founder of the Hasidic movement.

Bar/Bat Mitzvah A rite of passage for adolescents in Judaism, the *Bar Mitzvah* (for males age 13) and the *Bat Mitzvah* (for females age 12–13) signal their coming-of-age and the beginning of adult religious responsibility.

Covenant A biblical concept that describes the relationship between God and the Jews in contractual terms, often thought of as an eternal bond

between the Creator and the descendants of the ancient Israelites.

Dead Sea Scrolls Religious literature hidden in caves near the shores of the Dead Sea (c. second–first centuries B.C.E.).

Diaspora A Greek word in origin, it refers to those Jewish communities that live outside of the historical land of Israel.

election The belief that the biblical God "chose" the people of Israel to be His "kingdom of priests" and a "holy nation." This biblical concept is logically connected to the idea of the Covenant, and

GLOSSARY (continued)

it entails the belief that the Jews' relationship with God obliges them to conform to His laws and fulfill His purposes in the world.

eschatological Any belief in an "End-Time" of divine judgment and world destruction.

ethical monotheism A core concept of Judaism: it is the belief that the world was created and is governed by only one transcendent Being, whose ethical attributes provide an ideal model for human behavior.

Exodus The escape (or departure) of Israelite slaves from Egypt as described in the Hebrew Bible (c. 1250 B.C.E.).

halacha An authoritative formulation of traditional Jewish law.

Hasidism A popular movement within eighteenth-century Eastern European Judaism, Hasidism stressed the need for spiritual restoration and deepened individual piety. In the course of the nineteenth and twentieth centuries the Hasidic movement spawned a number of distinctive communities that have physically separated themselves from the rest of the Jewish and non-Jewish worlds, and who are often recognized by their attire and their devotion to a dynasty of hereditary spiritual leaders.

Holocaust The genocidal destruction of approximately 6 million European Jews by the government of Nazi Germany during World War II. This mass slaughter is referred to in Hebrew as the *Shoah*.

Kabbalah One of the dominant forms of Jewish mysticism, kabbalistic texts begin to appear in Europe during the twelfth and thirteenth centuries. Mystics belonging to this tradition focus on the emanative powers of God—referred to in Hebrew as *Sephirot*—and on their role within the Godhead as well as within the human personality.

Luria, Isaac A sixteenth-century mystic who settled in Safed (Israel) and gathered around him a community of disciples. Lurianic mysticism seeks to explain the mystery surrounding both the creation of the world and its redemption from sin.

Maimonides A twelfth-century philosopher and rabbinic scholar whose codification of Jewish beliefs and religious practices set the standard for both in subsequent centuries.

Messiah A possibly supernatural figure who will judge and transform the world.

mikveh A ritual bath in which married Jewish women immerse themselves each month, after the end of their menstrual cycle and before resuming sexual relation with their husbands.

mitzvot Literally translated, the Hebrew word *mitzvot* means "commandments," and it refers to the 613 commandments that the biblical God imparted to the Israelites in the Torah (i.e., the first five books of the Hebrew Bible).

Moses The legendary leader and prophet who leads the Israelite slaves out of Egypt, Moses serves as a mediator between the people of Israel and God in the Torah and is later viewed as Israel's greatest prophet. It is to Moses that God imparts the Ten Commandments and the teachings that later became the Torah.

omnipotence The divine attribute of total and eternal power.

omniscience The divine attribute of total and eternal knowledge.

Pesach An early spring harvest festival that celebrates the liberation of the Israelites from Egypt, Pesach (better known as "Passover" in English) is celebrated for seven days in Israel and eight days in the Diaspora. The first two nights are celebrated within a family setting.

Rosh Hashanah The Jewish New Year, it is celebrated for two days in the fall (on the first day of the month of Tishrai) and accompanied by the blowing of a ram's horn (a *shofar*, in Hebrew). It signals the beginning of the "ten days of repentance" that culminates with Yom Kippur.

(continued)

GLOSSARY (continued)

Seder A ritualized meal, observed on the first two nights of Pesach, that recalls the Exodus from Egypt.

Shavuot A later spring harvest festival that is celebrated for two days and is associated with the giving of the Torah at Mt. Sinai. Along with Pesach and Sukkot it was one of the "pilgrimage" festivals in ancient times.

Siddur The prayer book that is used on weekdays and on the Sabbath.

Sukkot A fall harvest festival that is associated with the huts (in Hebrew, *sukkot*) in which the ancient Israelites sought shelter during the Exodus. It is celebrated for seven days in Israel (eight days in the Diaspora). During that time Jews take their meals, and if possible sleep, in huts that are partly open to the sky.

synagogue Jewish houses of worship. The focal point of every synagogue is the Ark, a large cabinet where scrolls of the Torah are stored.

tallit A prayer-shawl that is worn during morning prayers (traditionally by men). The fringes of this shawl represent, symbolically, the 613 *mitzvot* found in the Torah.

Talmud A multi-volume work of commentary on the laws of the Torah and on the teachings of the entire Hebrew Bible, composed in two stages: the Mishnah (edited in approximately 200 C.E.) and the Gemara (edited, in its Babylonian version, around 500 C.E.). Traditionally, Jews refer to the Talmud as the "Oral Torah" and regard it as an extension of sacred scripture.

Tanakh An acronym standing for the entire Hebrew Bible: **T**orah (the first five books of the Hebrew Bible); **N**eviim (or "Prophets," which includes works of both prophecy and history); and **Kh**etuvim (or "Writings," a miscellaneous gathering of works in poetry and prose). Taken together, the twenty-four books that make of this collection constitute the core "scriptures" of Judaism.

tefillin Taken from the word for "prayer," the term *tefillin* refers to two small boxes to which leather straps are attached. Traditionally, Jewish males from the age of 13 wear *tefillin* during weekday morning prayers. Inside each of these boxes a miniature parchment containing biblical verses can be found; one box is placed on the forehead and the other is placed on the left arm, signifying that the individual's mind and will are devoted to God.

Torah Literally, the word *torah* means "teaching," and in its most restrictive sense it refers to the first five books of the Hebrew Bible. Less restrictively, it signifies the totality of God's revelations to the Jewish people, which includes not only the remaining books of the Hebrew Bible but also the writings contained in the Talmud.

transcendence The divine attribute of being above and beyond anything human beings can know or imagine.

YHWH These four consonants constitute the most sacred of names associated with the biblical God. The exact pronunciation of this name, according to ancient Jewish tradition, was known only to the High Priest, but after the destruction of the Second Temple the precise vocalization of these letters was lost—only to be recovered in the days of the Messiah.

Yom Kippur Referred to as the "Day of Atonement," it is the most solemn of all of the fast-days in the Jewish religious calendar.

Zionism A modern political philosophy that asserts a belief in Jewish national identity and in the necessity of resuming national life within the historic Land of Israel.

Zohar A kabbalistic *midrash* based on the biblical Book of Genesis (c. 1280 C.E.).

SUGGESTIONS FOR FURTHER READING

Akenson, Donald Herman. *Surpassing Wonder: The Invention of the Bible and the Talmuds*. Chicago: The University of Chicago, 2001. An ambitious, and sometimes argumentative, history of the evolution of biblical and rabbinic literature.

Ariel, David. *What Do Jews Believe?* New York: Schocken Books, 1995. An accessible and nuanced account of traditional and nontraditional Jewish beliefs.

Bauer, Yehuda. *A History of the Holocaust*. New York: Franklin Watts, 2001. A well-researched and readable account of the Holocaust, written by the "Dean" of contemporary *Shoah* historians.

Eisenberg, Ronald. *The JPS Guide to Jewish Traditions*. Philadelphia: The Jewish Publication Society, 2004. A well-researched and comprehensive guide to traditional and nontraditional Jewish religious practices.

Neusner, Jacob, and Avery-Peck, Alan J., eds. *The Blackwell Companion to Judaism*. Oxford: Blackwell Publishing Ltd., 2003. A collection of diverse articles on the history of Judaism, written by some of the leading scholars in Jewish studies.

Robinson, George. *Essential Judaism: A Complete Guide to the Beliefs, Customs and Rituals*. New York: Pocket Books, 2000. A well-written and comprehensive description of Jewish beliefs and practices.

Sarna, Jonathan D. *American Judaism: A History*. New Haven, CT: Yale University Press, 2004. The best account to-date of the historical development of the Jewish community in the United States.

Strassfeld, Michael. *The Jewish Holidays*. New York: HarperCollins, 1985. A nicely illustrated presentation of major and minor Jewish festivals with detailed accounts of religious observances from around the world.

ONLINE SOURCES

My Jewish Learning
myjewishlearning.com
A well-researched site for historical subjects and religious practices.

The Jewish Virtual Library
jewishvirtuallibrary.org
A good site for contemporary subjects like Israel and the Holocaust.

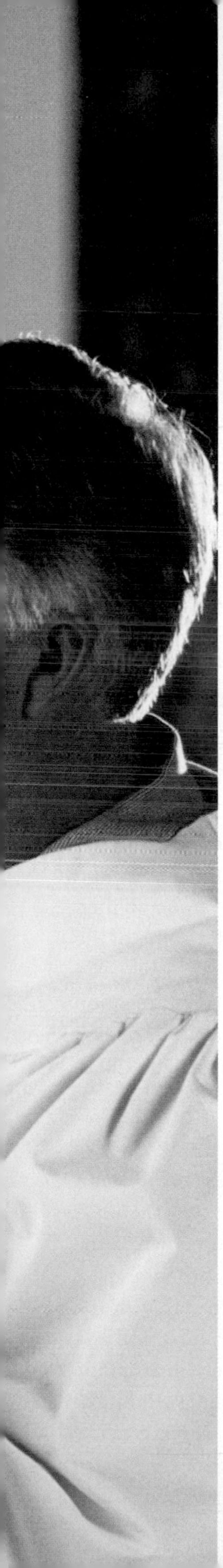

CHRISTIANITY

IT IS EARLY on a bright Sunday morning as the congregation of an Epis-copal church in Boston prepares to welcome a new member. Today there will be a **baptism**. In a ceremony that reaches back 2,000 years, Annie, a college freshman, will join the worldwide community of Christians.

Although infant baptism is common among Christians, Annie's par-ents agreed before she was born to let her decide for herself when, and if, she would be baptized. As a child, Annie attended church regularly and enjoyed activities designed to acquaint children with the Bible and Christian teachings. In her teens, however, she lost interest in religion and attended church only on holidays such as Easter and Christmas. But time and a growing awareness of the great issues in life have led An-nie to reconsider the meaning her family's faith has for her. After much reflection, she has come to believe that the way to God can be found in the life and teachings of Jesus Christ. And so it is that now, standing before the crowded church, Annie can answer joyfully and with convic-tion the questions put to her by the priest:

"Do you turn to Jesus Christ and accept him as your Savior?"

"I do."

"Do you put your whole trust in his grace and love?"

"I do."

"Do you promise to follow and obey him as your Lord?"

"I do."

A young woman is baptized.

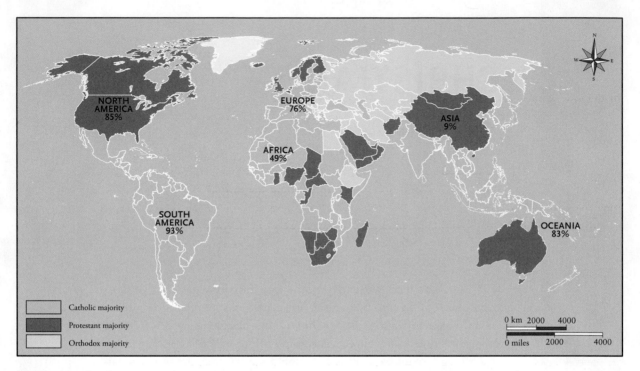

Distribution of major branches of Christianity throughout the world.

Satisfied by her responses, the priest prepares Annie for her baptism. Although most Episcopalians are baptized by a sprinkling or pouring of water on the head, Annie has chosen the ancient rite of full immersion. Standing beside her in a small tub filled with warm water, the priest gently lowers her until her head is covered and then raises her up again. As he does so, he says, "Annie, I baptize you in the name of the Father, and of the Son, and of the Holy Spirit. Amen."

Now that Annie has made her baptismal vows, the members of the congregation reaffirm their own. Then, promising to support Annie in her new life as a Christian, they welcome her into a spiritual communion that includes more than 2 billion Christians worldwide. ☼

There are three great traditions within Christianity. Historically, the **Roman Catholic Church** has been the dominant **church** in the West. In the East, most Christians have belonged to the **Orthodox Church** (also known as the Eastern Orthodox Church). **Protestant Christianity**, which consists of thousands of "denominations," grew out of the Roman Catholic tradition in the sixteenth century. Although these churches have been shaped in different ways by complex historical and cultural forces, they are united by shared beliefs that lie at the heart of Christianity. Christians acknowledge a personal and transcendent God, the creator and sustainer of the universe. The Christian doctrine of the **Trinity** describes God as one in essence, but consisting in three "persons": Father, Son, and Holy Spirit. Christians believe that communion with God, in this life and in eternity, is the ultimate purpose of human existence. But there is an obstacle to be overcome: sin. The violation of God's will in thought or action, **sin** is common to all humanity. Worse, sin separates the individual from God. What is needed is the forgiveness that God gives to all who believe that the sacrificial death of Jesus Christ, the Son of God, atoned for all sin. For Christians, the sacrifice of Christ is the supreme expression of divine love. Similarly, they see in his resurrection and ascension into heaven a sign that not even death can separate from God those who respond to God's love with faith. Although they remain imperfect, Christians believe that the destructive power of sin is no longer the primary force in their lives, for they have been baptized into a new "life in Christ."

We will begin our investigation of Christianity with a survey of its teachings. We will then explore the practices by which Christians give outward expression to their beliefs. Finally, we will trace the history of Christianity from the earliest days after the death of Jesus to the present moment.

THE TEACHINGS OF CHRISTIANITY

By the first century (as we learned in Chapter 10), Palestinian Jews had endured centuries of oppression under foreign conquerors and had struggled to preserve their unique religion and culture. The conquest of Palestine by Alexander the Great in 332 B.C.E. was especially threatening, as some of Alexander's successors had attempted to force Greek polytheism on the Jews, who believed only in the one God described in their scriptures. The situation became far more dangerous with the arrival of the Romans (63 B.C.E.), whose brutality fueled a bitter resentment that ultimately led to a Jewish rebellion. Tragically, the revolt ended with the destruction of the Jerusalem Temple, the center of Jewish religious life, in 70 C.E.

The Jewish people responded to these pressures in different ways. Pharisees defended Jewish tradition through strict observance of the Torah. Sadducees cooperated with the Romans in the hope of preserving social stability. Zealots advocated anti-Roman violence. Essenes withdrew to the desert lands outside Jerusalem to wait for divine deliverance.

Most Jews, in fact, looked for deliverance. Believing that God would soon bring an end to unrighteousness, they awaited the coming of a **Messiah** who would inaugurate a new era of justice and peace. Originally, *Messiah* ("anointed one") was a title given to Israel's kings, who were anointed with oil as a sign of God's favor. Later, it came to mean the deliverer God would send to save the Jewish people from oppression. Some looked for a supernatural Messiah. Others watched for a descendant of David, ancient Israel's greatest king. Most believed the Messiah would rule as king and judge the wicked and the righteous.

The first Christians were Palestinian Jews who believed that Jesus of Nazareth was the Messiah—in Greek, the *Christos,* or "Christ." They proclaimed him as a deliverer not from earthly oppression but from the power of sin. In Jesus, these long-oppressed people saw the beginning of a new era of righteousness and peace evident in his teachings, miracles, death, and resurrection.

The Life of Jesus

Our most important sources for the life and teachings of Jesus are the **gospels** of Matthew, Mark, Luke, and John. Written in the decades following the death of Jesus (70–100 C.E.), the gospels are not biographies of Jesus but early Christian proclamations of the "good news" about him ("gospel," from Middle English *godspel*, translates the Greek *evangelion*, "good news"). As such, they focus on Jesus' ministry, suffering, and death and say little about other aspects of his life. Each of the gospels presents its own understanding of the good news about Jesus, but their essential agreement on most points allows us to discern the general outlines of Jesus' career and teachings.

It is likely that Jesus was born between 4 and 1 B.C.E. in the Judean city of Bethlehem and spent his youth in the Galilean village of Nazareth. At about the age of 30, he made his way south to the Judean wilderness, where he was baptized by John the Baptist in the River Jordan. A prophetic figure who warned of God's imminent judgment, John called on sinners to repent and be baptized in water as a sign of spiritual cleansing.

After his baptism, Jesus began a ministry that lasted no more than three years. The gospels say that as he traveled throughout Galilee he performed healings and miracles that testified to God's presence within him. The gospel accounts also describe Jesus as a charismatic teacher who spoke with authority on the scriptures and urged repentance and baptism in anticipation of the coming **kingdom of God**, a new era of peace and holiness. He was accompanied by a group of twelve disciples led by three Galilean fishermen (Peter, James, and John); people from towns, villages, and the countryside; and women like Mary of Magdala, Joanna, and Susanna, who supported his ministry with their own resources. Indeed, women figure prominently in the gospel accounts of Jesus' ministry. Rejecting the social norms of his time, he befriended women and spoke and ate with them both in public and in private. When even the twelve disciples abandoned Jesus in his final days, it was only his faithful women followers who remained with him.

As enthusiasm for his teachings and miracles grew, Jesus' popularity aroused resentment and opposition among members of the religious establishment. Jesus himself appears to have understood that dark days lay ahead. As he prepared to leave Galilee for Jerusalem, he warned his disciples that rejection, suffering, and death awaited him there.

Jesus arrived in the holy city just before Passover. The gospels describe a triumphal entry in which crowds greeted him as the Messiah. Entering the Temple, he caused a great stir by driving out those who did business there, accusing them of making the sacred place a "den of robbers." For several days Jesus taught in the Temple, but then events took an ominous turn. Within hours after celebrating a "Last Supper" with his disciples, Jesus was brought before a council of Jewish leaders, accused of blasphemy,

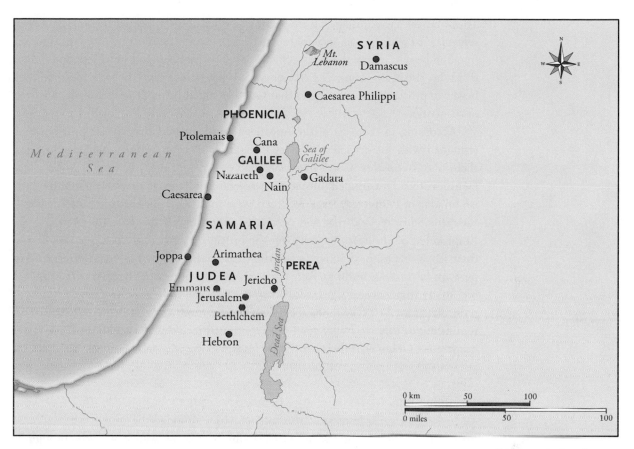

SYRIA

Mt. Lebanon

● Damascus

● Caesarea Philippi

PHOENICIA

Ptolemais ●

Cana ●

Mediterranean Sea

GALILEE

Sea of Galilee

Nazareth ●

Nain ●

● Gadara

Caesarea ●

SAMARIA

Joppa ●

Arimathea ●

Jordan

PEREA

JUDEA   Jericho ●

Emmaus ●

Jerusalem ●

Bethlehem ●

Dead Sea

Hebron ●

0 km	50	100
0 miles	50	100

Palestine during the time of Jesus.

and handed over to Pontius Pilate, the Roman governor. Fearing that he was a threat to public order, Pilate ordered his execution. Jesus was crucified on a Friday, just hours before Passover began and less than a week after he had entered Jerusalem.

The gospels add theological reflections and commentary to this historical outline. Matthew and Luke assert that Jesus' mother, Mary, was a virgin who conceived miraculously in fulfillment of prophecy (Isaiah 7:14). All four of the gospels say that the Spirit of God, or the Holy Spirit, descended upon Jesus at the time of his baptism. According to Matthew, Mark, and Luke, a voice from heaven then declared: "This is my Son, the Beloved, with whom I am well pleased" (Matthew 3:17). In this way, the gospels link Jesus to King David, who is described in Psalms 2:1–7 as God's "anointed" and "son." The gospels also identify Jesus as the "servant" of God who would suffer for the sake of humanity, as foretold by one of Israel's prophets (Isaiah 42:1–4; 53:10–12). In making these connections, the gospels reveal their understanding of the kind of Messiah Jesus was to be: a Son of God who, filled with the Spirit of God, would suffer for the sins of others. Finally, all four gospels report that some of the women who had followed Jesus found his tomb empty at dawn on the Sunday following his crucifixion.

They and the other disciples were overjoyed when Jesus appeared to them and they remembered what he had once told them: "The Son of Man must undergo great suffering, and be rejected by the elders, chief priests, and scribes, and be killed, and on the third day rise again" (Luke 9:22). Convinced that he was indeed God's Messiah, they began to proclaim the good news that God had acted through Jesus for the salvation of the world.

According to the Acts of the Apostles (found in the Christian scriptures), Jesus remained with his disciples for forty days after his resurrection. Then, having sent them out as **apostles** (Greek *apostolos*, "one who is sent out") to preach to Jews and Gentiles alike, he ascended into heaven. Several days later, as they celebrated the Jewish holiday of **Pentecost**, Jesus' followers were suddenly "filled with the Holy Spirit," the same Spirit of God that had descended upon Jesus at his baptism (Acts 2:2–4). Empowered by the Spirit to carry out the mission Jesus had given them, they found themselves able to speak in languages they had not known before, to prophesy, and to perform miraculous healings. According to Acts, the number of believers grew rapidly, for "many wonders and signs were being done by the apostles" (Acts 2:43). Acts also reports that the first Christians spent "much time together in the temple" (Acts 2:46), reminding us that they were Jews who continued to live and worship as Jews. It did not occur to them that their belief that Jesus was the Messiah had given them a new religious identity outside of Judaism.

The Teachings of Jesus

The gospels describe Jesus as a great teacher who astounded the crowds who gathered to hear him, "for he taught them as one having authority" (Matthew 7:29). Though he engaged in debate with learned Pharisees and Sadducees, Jesus also took great interest in ordinary people. He often taught them in **parables**, stories that employed vivid images from everyday life to illustrate spiritual truths.

The central theme in Jesus' teaching was the kingdom of God (in Matthew, the kingdom of heaven). For Jesus, the kingdom of God was not an ordinary realm but the state of affairs that exists when human beings recognize God's sovereignty over the world and respond in love and obedience to God's will. To put it another way, the kingdom of God means the world as it ought to be, a world in which God's love and righteous rule are fully realized. In the gospels, Jesus sometimes speaks of the kingdom as a future event to be heralded by dramatic signs such as a darkening sun and stars falling from heaven. In the midst of these cataclysmic events, the present age would pass away and the kingdom would be revealed in all its glory. But Jesus also spoke of the kingdom as already present within himself and his followers. Asked when it would come, he replied, "The kingdom of God *is* among you" (Luke 17:21). Though still small, Jesus expected the kingdom to grow into something great and wondrous. In one of his parables, he compared it to a tiny mustard seed that "grows up and becomes the greatest of all shrubs, and puts forth large branches, so that the birds of the air can make nests in its shade" (Mark 4:30). Whether speaking of the kingdom of God as present or future, Jesus emphasized its all-surpassing importance. Nothing can compare to the kingdom, he said, and so it is worth any price: "The kingdom of heaven is like treasure hidden in a field, which someone found and hid; then in his joy he goes and sells all that he has and buys that field" (Matthew 13:44).

Jesus taught that the kingdom of God is open to all who repent. By repentance, he meant something more than a mere expression of regret for some wrong one has done. The Greek *metanoia* ("a change of mind") found in the gospels suggests a turning away from anything that might prevent one from doing God's will. Like other Jews, Jesus found God's will expressed in the Torah and its commandments. In his famous Sermon on the Mount (Matthew 5–7), however, he gave the commandments his own interpretation, emphasizing that what God requires is obedience in thought as well as in deed. Thus, true obedience to the commandment against murder goes beyond not killing; it means never harboring anger toward anyone in one's heart. Similarly, the commandment against adultery prohibits not only the act itself but any thought of it (Matthew 5:21–28). For Jesus, it was this absolute obedience to the will of God that constituted the true righteousness of the kingdom of God.

Jesus also taught that true obedience to God's commandments was an expression of love. When pressed by a Pharisee to identify the greatest of the commandments, he cited two (Deuteronomy 6:5 and Leviticus 19:18), explaining that they embody the essence of scripture: "'You shall love the Lord your God with all your heart, and with all your soul, and with all your mind.' This is the greatest and first commandment. And a second is like it: 'You shall love your neighbor as yourself.' On these two commandments hang all the law and the prophets" (Matthew 22:37–40).

The nature of love lies at the heart of Jesus' teachings. Jesus taught that genuine love knows no limits and is offered freely to everyone: "Love your enemies and pray for those who persecute you, so that you may be children of your Father in heaven" (Matthew 5:44–45). Understood in this way, love leaves no room for the condemnation of others: "Do not judge, so that you may not be judged" (Matthew 7:1). Instead, love requires forgiveness: "For if you forgive others their trespasses, your heavenly Father will also forgive you" (Matthew 6:14). These principles are richly illustrated in Jesus' parables. The parable of the Good Samaritan (Luke 10:25–37), for example, demonstrates that even enemies deserve love and compassion. In the parable of the Prodigal Son (Luke 15:11–32), a father greets a dissolute and disrespectful son who has returned home—not with any thought of reproach, but with love and forgiveness gladly given.

These principles of repentance, obedience, and love were exemplified by the life and death of Jesus. The gospels also depict Jesus as living in the expectation of his crucifixion. In Mark, he tells his disciples that his death will be "a ransom for many" (Mark 10:45). Jesus spoke of God as Father, sometimes using the Aramaic *abba* ("papa") to suggest a relationship of special intimacy as well as obedience. He urged his followers to draw close to God as well. They were God's children, he told them. As such, they should approach God in prayer with the words "Our Father"

(Matthew 6:9) and with confidence that, like a loving parent, he would provide for their needs (Luke 12:22–31).

As we shall learn later in this section, these fundamental teachings of Jesus lie at the heart of what Christians believe about sin, divine love, and salvation. But we first turn our attention to Paul of Tarsus, the first great interpreter of the life and teachings of Jesus, to see how Christian beliefs began to take shape in the years immediately following Jesus' crucifixion.

Paul and the Mission to the Gentiles

The most famous of the Jewish Christians who took the gospel and its teachings to Gentile lands was **Paul of Tarsus.** A Pharisee devoted to Judaism, Paul had been a persecutor of Christians, but after a dramatic experience of the risen Christ (Acts 9:1–19) he dedicated himself to preaching Christianity in Asia Minor (modern Turkey), Greece, and Macedonia. In his letters to young churches in Corinth, Thessalonica, Rome, and other cities, we can see Paul breaking with traditional Jewish thought in emphasizing God's love for Gentiles and disputing the necessity of observing the commandments in the Torah. Since Paul was the first to describe the role of Jesus in the salvation of humanity from sin, some have described him as the second founder—and even the *true* founder—of Christianity. It was due in part to his influence that Christianity was transformed in the middle of the first century from a Jewish sect into a largely Gentile movement.

At the heart of Paul's teaching was his belief that in Jesus Christ God had acted to bring salvation from sin to the world. Paul saw sin as a condition affecting all humanity: "All have sinned and fall short of the glory of God" (Romans 3:23). Controlling human beings and separating them from God, sin corrupts and ultimately destroys human life (Romans 6:23). For Paul, the good news of the gospel was that God's promise of salvation from sin, anticipated in the Jewish scriptures, had been fulfilled in Jesus' death on the cross. Though sinless and undeserving of death, Jesus had offered himself as a sacrifice in atonement for all sin. Although Paul's language of "sin," "sacrifice," and "atonement" may sound strange today, it is really quite similar to what we might mean when we say we have done some "wrong" to someone and that we must do something to "make up for it." In Paul's time, Jews and Gentiles alike understood that sacrifice was the means of "making up for" an offense against God, or the gods.

Paul was always emphatic in maintaining that the salvation made possible by Christ's sacrifice is a gift, the ultimate expression of God's love, or **grace**. Salvation, he said, cannot be earned by good works. Instead, salvation rests on faith in God; specifically, that in the death and resurrection of Christ God had saved humanity from the consequences of sin.

But faith does more than bring salvation; it unites the believer with Christ in a "newness of life" (Romans 6:4) so real that Paul could say, "It is no longer I who live, but it is Christ who lives in me" (Galatians 2:20). Like the apostles who had been filled with the Holy Spirit at Pentecost, Paul believed that the Spirit lives in believers and brings them into union with God. To the Christians at Rome he wrote: "You are in the Spirit, since the Spirit of God dwells in you" (Romans 8:9). As a divine presence within, the Spirit encourages the growth of spiritual virtues, the greatest of which is love (1 Corinthians 12:27–14:1). Paul also believed that the Spirit makes all Christians one in the Church, which he often called the "body of Christ" (1 Corinthians 12:12–27).

Like other early Christians, Paul looked forward to a time when Christ would return in glory to bring an end to evil, sin, and suffering (1 Corinthians 15:20–28). But he also believed that the transformation of the world, signaled by the resurrection of Christ, had already begun. Signs of change were especially evident in the lives of believers, who had been renewed, even re-created, through the action of God's grace: "So if anyone is in Christ, there is a new creation; everything old has passed away; see, everything has become new!" (2 Corinthians 5:17).

God, Creation, and Original Humanity

Christian thought about God, the world, and humanity begins with the first verse in the Bible: "In the beginning God created the heavens and the earth" (Genesis 1:1). Here, and in the story of creation that follows, the Bible makes a clear distinction between created things and their Creator. Because God is not to be confused with the world, Christians describe God as transcendent—that is, as existing outside space, time, and the other limiting factors that give the world its order and finitude. While the idea of transcendence suggests an exalted Deity whose place is in the heavens, this does not mean that God exists apart from creation. The Bible also speaks of God as immanent, or present in the world. God is deeply and continually involved in creation, sustaining and caring for all things with a loving benevolence that touches even the least of creatures. Sensing on one occasion that his followers were anxious about their security, Jesus urged them to reflect on God's attentiveness to the needs of lesser beings: "Look at the birds of the air; they neither sow nor reap nor gather into barns, and yet your heavenly Father feeds them. Are you not of more value than they?" (Matthew 6:26).

Christians believe that, much as a work of art reveals something of the thought and character of the artist, creation tells us something about the divine nature. Paul made this point in his letter to the Romans: "Ever since the creation of the world his eternal power and divine nature, invisible though they are, have been understood and seen through the things he has made" (Romans 1:20). The great medieval theologian Thomas Aquinas claimed in his *Summa Theologica* that the very existence of God could be proved by logical arguments based solely on the observation of creation. The fact that creation exists at all, he said, points to the existence of a Creator in whom all its virtues are perfectly realized and who is their source. Christians believe that the goodness, beauty, power, and design evident in the world are all expressions of God's nature. But it is God's goodness, and the consequent goodness of the world itself, that are emphasized in the biblical story of the world's beginnings. At the completion of each stage of creation, it says, "God saw that it was good" (Genesis 1:10, 18, 21, 25, 31). Finally,

Christianity teaches that the entire order of existing things, and especially human beings, is the deliberate and purposeful expression of a divine love that a grateful creation returns to God in praise. "Let heaven and earth praise him, the seas and everything that moves in them" (Psalms 69:34).

Christians believe that, despite its original perfection, the world as we know it today falls far short of God's intentions, plagued as it is by pain, disappointment, injustice, and death. These evils cannot be attributed to God, however, for they are completely opposed to God's perfection. Instead, Christianity points to creation itself—and, more specifically, to humanity.

The story of creation relates that "God created humankind in his image" (Genesis 1:27). For centuries, Christian thinkers have sought to understand all that is entailed by this assertion. Some have found the image of God in the human capacity for rational thought. Others have said that it can be seen in the "dominion" God gave to human beings over all the earth (Genesis 1:26), which resembles God's rule over the entire universe. All Christian thought, however, acknowledges that human beings have a unique ability to relate to God, and to love God, just as God relates to and loves them.

This idea is found in the biblical narrative that describes how God placed Adam and Eve, the first human beings, in a garden-like paradise called Eden. Whether we understand Adam and Eve as literal human beings or as symbols of original humanity—the Hebrew word *adam* means "humankind"—the point of the story remains the same. For as long as human beings related to God in loving obedience, they lived in joyous harmony with their Creator, but their eventual decision to disobey God brought an end to that harmony and, consequently, to the harmony of creation as a whole (Genesis 2:4–3:24). It was through sin that evil in all its forms became a reality in the world. Worst of all, sin separated humanity from God. In the Christian view, the salvation of creation from sin's destructive effects begins with the salvation of human beings. It is only through salvation from sin that they are restored to that original relationship with God in which they find their true place, purpose, and fulfillment. In the words of Augustine, the great fifth-century saint, "You have made us for yourself, and our hearts are restless until they find rest in you."[1]

Andrei Rublev's icon of the Holy Trinity (1411) is considered a masterpiece of Orthodox religious art. It depicts (from left to right) God the Father, God the Son, and God the Holy Spirit. On one level, the three figures are the "angels" through whom God appeared to Abraham in the Old Testament. On a higher level, they represent the Trinity in a way that uses color, light, and imagery to give the viewer a glimpse into its unfathomable mystery.

God as Trinity

Like Judaism, Christianity is a monotheistic faith. But Christianity differs from its parent religion in defining the one God in terms of three aspects of divinity. For Christians, there is a single divine nature that expresses itself eternally in the "persons" of Father, Son, and Holy Spirit.

The doctrine of the Trinity was not put into precise language until 381 at the Council of Constantinople, one of the meetings at which early Christian leaders assembled to establish doctrine. The Council produced the **Nicene Creed,** a statement of the doctrine that many Christians continue to recite in public worship:

(1) We believe in one God, the Father, the Almighty,
  maker of heaven and earth, of all that is seen and unseen.

(2) We believe in one Lord, Jesus Christ, the only Son of God,
  eternally begotten of the Father,
  God from God, Light from Light, true God from true God,
  begotten, not made, one in Being with the Father.
  Through him all things were made.
  For us and for our salvation he came down from heaven:
  by the power of the Holy Spirit
  he was born of the Virgin Mary, and became man.
  For our sake he was crucified under Pontius Pilate;
  he suffered, died, and was buried
  On the third day he rose again in fulfillment of the scriptures;
  he ascended into heaven and is seated at the right hand of the Father.
  He will come again in glory to judge the living and the dead,
  and his kingdom will have no end.

(3) We believe in the Holy Spirit, the Lord, the giver of life,
  who proceeds from the Father *and from the Son.*
  He has spoken through the prophets
  We believe in one holy catholic ["universal"] and apostolic Church.
  We acknowledge one baptism for the forgiveness of sins.
  We look for the resurrection of the dead,
  and the life of the world to come. Amen.

As you can see, the Creed is divided into three parts corresponding to the three "persons" of the Trinity. It tells us about the relationships among the three persons as well as the functions of each.

The opening statement is about God the Father, the omnipotent ("almighty") Creator of all reality, spiritual as well as material, visible as well as invisible. There is one God, upon whom all things depend for their existence.

The second part of the Creed focuses on God the Son, who is "one in Being with the Father"—that is, of the same divine substance or essence as the Father. For the sake of humanity, the Son became fully human as well as fully divine. This is why Jesus, as God incarnate, can say in the Gospel of John: "I and the Father are one" (John 10:30). As a revelation of divinity on earth, the Son enabled those who recognized him as such to come to a greater understanding of God: "If you know me, you will know my Father also" (John 14:7). Beyond revealing the Father, the Son has three other roles.

Adam and Eve Banished from Paradise. In this fresco, the Renaissance painter Tommaso Masaccio (1401–1428) captured both the shame of Adam and Eve and the fear they felt as they were expelled from the Garden of Eden and separated from God.

First, recalling the Gospel of John (1:3), the Creed states that "through him all things were made." Second, the suffering and death of the Son have made salvation possible. Third, the Son, as the risen Christ, will one day return to judge the world.

The final part of the Creed affirms that the Holy Spirit "proceeds" from the Father (the Western Church adds the Latin *filioque*, "and from the Son"), implying his sameness in substance or essence with the Father and Son. Just as the Father represents God's power in the creation of the world, and just as the Son both reveals the Father and redeems a sinful humanity, the Holy Spirit represents God's continuing presence in the world. Since the beginning, when God breathed the "breath of life" into Adam (Hebrew *ruach* means both "breath" and "spirit"), the Spirit has given life to all of creation. Christians believe that since the descent of the Holy Spirit at Pentecost, it has animated, empowered, and guided the Church. Finally, it is the Spirit within that helps believers as they reach out to God in prayer (Romans 8:26) and nurtures virtues such as love, patience, kindness, gentleness, and self-control (Galatians 5:22–23).

Sin and Human Nature

Christianity has always emphasized the sinfulness of human nature. This may seem a harsh way of thinking about humanity. After all, there are good reasons to believe in the essential *goodness* of human nature. Of course, Christians do acknowledge the human capacity to do good things. But they are equally aware of the human capacity for evil and the fact that people are often destructive in their thought and behavior. Christianity teaches that sin is universal: everyone sins. It also insists that the tendency to sin is far more serious than an acquired habit one might overcome through greater self-control or moral effort. The inability of human beings to rise above sin—to be as loving, humble, generous, and righteous as they should be—suggests that something has gone wrong deep within human nature. In the Christian view, since human beings cannot overcome sin on their own, they stand in need of salvation from its power over them—a power that cuts them off from God, the source of all good things.

Grace and Salvation

For Christianity, sin is the fundamental problem of human existence. But it is a problem solved by the good news of God's grace, the love God gives freely to human beings despite their sin. In the Christian view, it is only through reliance on divine grace that salvation from sin becomes possible.

Christianity explains *how* salvation is made possible by using the language of sacrifice, a practice that was central to the Judaism of Jesus' time. In the sacrificial ritual, the sins of the people were symbolically placed on animals, which were then sacrificed as innocent victims for the transgressions of others. For Christians, Jesus' death on the cross was both the end and the fulfillment of this sacrificial practice. It is with his crucifixion that the significance of the Christian teaching that Jesus Christ was both human and divine becomes clear. Christians believe that Jesus' divinity allowed him to do for human beings what they could not do for themselves. As the sinless "lamb of God" (John 1:29), he alone could make the perfect atonement for sin that would allow sinners to be restored to their original relationship with God. As a human being, on the other hand, he could truly suffer the consequences of sin on behalf of humanity. In doing so, Christians say, Jesus fulfilled the words of the Old Testament prophet Isaiah, who spoke of the "suffering servant" of God: "But he was wounded for our transgressions, crushed for our iniquities; upon him was the punishment that made us whole, and by his bruises we are healed" (Isaiah 53:5). Christians see in Christ's suffering for the sake of humanity the supreme proof of God's grace:

> God is love. God's love was revealed among us in this way: God sent
> his only Son into the world so that we might live through him. In this
> is love, not that we loved God but that he loved us and sent his Son to
> be the atoning sacrifice for our sins.
> —1 John 4:8

But grace requires a human response in the form of faith. For Christians, faith is more than intellectual acceptance of the fact that God has made salvation possible through Jesus Christ. Faith involves a wholehearted opening of oneself to God so that God's love replaces sinfulness as the prevailing power in one's life. Christians admit that they are no closer to perfection than anyone else, yet they are confident that faith allows them to "walk in a newness of life" (Romans 6:4) on a path that leads toward rather than away from God.

The Church

Christians do not live the Christian life in isolation. Instead, their faith and baptism unite them with all other believers. In its most basic sense, the Church is simply the sum of all believers. But most Christians believe that the Church is far more than this. The Greek word from which our word "church" derives (*kuriakon*, "that which belongs to the Lord") suggests an intimate connection between Christ and the Church that is well attested in the New Testament. There, Paul describes the Church as the "body of Christ," a body whose diverse members are unified by the Holy Spirit: "For just as the body is one and has many members, and all the members of the body, though many, are one body, so it is with Christ. For in the one Spirit we were all baptized into one body—Jews or Greeks, slaves or free—and we were all made to drink of one Spirit" (1 Corinthians 12:13).

VOICES: An Interview with Mia Sasaki

Mia Sasaki

Mia Sasaki is a university student and "born-again" Christian. She attends a Protestant church identified with the evangelical movement.

Can you describe your "born-again" experience and what it means to you?

It's difficult to tell the story of how I was rescued and how my life was saved in just a few words, but I'll try. I'm a person who has tried in many ways to make my life worth something—to find a meaningful identity. I tried and failed. Still, I found myself wanting to be wanted, wanting to be loved. I was looking for fulfillment, but every promise of fulfillment seemed to wither. I remember hitting rock bottom—feeling empty and thinking I had nowhere to turn. That's when I found God. Or maybe God found me. I'm not sure which is true. I'm not sure I care. What matters is that God became my best friend. Jesus showed me that I was worth saving and worth loving.

God's love doesn't depend on what I do. His grace is freely given and shapes how I live and what I live for now. It's like being born again. The world teaches us that our value and identity are based on how well we perform. Jesus came to free us from this destructive idea. No matter what, I know that on my own I can't be all that I want to be for others and that I can't achieve enough to really matter. I always fall short. Jesus came to say that I have value and identity just because I am loved by the Creator of everything. Sometimes it can be difficult to understand and accept the fact that God loves me with no strings attached, but knowing that he does makes me want to love God with everything I am.

What role does your relationship with Christ play in your everyday life?

Actually, I believe that the most important thing is to live intimately with God as Trinity. People often tend to focus on Jesus, God the Son. I suppose they relate best to him because in him God became human and showed us how to thrive in life.

Many people talk about Jesus as a good man. I agree with them, though I would say that he was the **best** possible man, a perfect human being. But Jesus was more than human. He was and is God, and he was very clear in describing himself in this way in the Bible. It seems to me that there are only two possibilities. One is that Jesus was a liar, or crazy. The other is that he was who he said he was. I find his life and message so compelling, his death and resurrection so amazing, and my own experience so undeniable that I can't believe anything other than that he was God.

In Jesus, we can see the extent of God's love for us. I think that the gospel is an incredible love story. In a way, it reminds me of the story of a prince who was so head-over-heels for a slave girl that he was willing to become a peasant to be near her. Although she did not love him, his love for her was so great that he died in order to release her from slavery.

So, Jesus is my liberator. He's my friend and my lover. He's the one who shows me how to live in freedom. He's my everything.

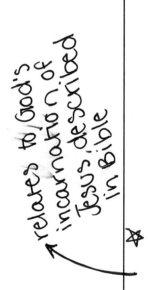

relates to God's incarnation of Jesus, described in Bible

How do you understand the Bible and its place in your life?

The Bible is God's love letter. I think it tells a riveting story of how God has interacted with people in history. The Bible reminds me of Jesus' amazing life and love. It gives me encouragement for each day. I believe that God revealed to the Bible's human authors what should be written and that this is why the Bible is so relevant today. To me, the marvelous story told in the Bible is completely true, though it is not necessarily completely factual as far as some unimportant details are concerned. The most important thing is that the story tells us about the heart of a God who loves the world he (or she) has created and longs for the restoration of wholeness in his relationship with all people.

Scripture

When the first Christians spoke of scripture, they meant the Jewish scriptures. In Greek, these texts were called the *biblia*, or "books"—hence, our English "Bible." It was not long, however, before certain Christian writings had assumed an importance equal to that of the Jewish scriptures. By the end of the fourth century, there was general agreement that twenty-seven of these texts had greater authority than all others. These came to be known collectively as the New Testament. Since then, the Christian Bible has consisted of the Old Testament (the Jewish Scriptures) and the New Testament. In Christian interpretation, the Old Testament, which tells of God's covenant with the Jewish people, anticipates and is fulfilled by the New Testament, which reveals that the Messiah has come and established a new and universal covenant between God and the Church. Roman Catholic and Orthodox versions of the Bible also include several Deuterocanonical ("secondary canon") texts, which they place in the Old Testament. Protestants call these texts the Apocrypha ("hidden texts") and sometimes place them between the Old and New Testaments in their versions of the Bible.

The first four books in the New Testament are the gospels. Although tradition attributes the gospels to specific individuals, some of them disciples of Jesus, none identifies its author by name. For this reason, scholars generally consider them anonymous. Each of the gospels portrays Jesus in its way. In the Gospel of Mark, Jesus is a Messiah who resolutely submits to suffering on behalf of humanity. In the Gospel of Matthew, Jesus is a figure reminiscent of Moses who reveals the true meaning of the Torah. The Gospel of Luke focuses on Jesus' compassion for sinners, women, the poor, and the sick. Finally, the Gospel of John emphasizes the divinity of Jesus. In describing him as God's "Word" (Greek *logos*, "word," but also "divine reason") "made flesh," John presents Jesus as a revelation of God in human form.

The gospels are followed by the Acts of the Apostles, which describes the founding of the Church in Jerusalem and tells the story of Paul's missionary journeys. All but one of the texts that follow Acts are letters, many of them written by Paul. These texts describe the organization of the first Christian churches, tell us about early Christian beliefs and practices, and offer insights into the complex relationship between early Christianity and Judaism. The New Testament concludes with Revelation. Written at the end of the first century, when Christians were beginning to suffer persecution, Revelation is an apocalyptic text that employs vivid imagery in describing the coming of the kingdom of God after a climactic battle between good and evil.

Christians have always seen scripture as the revealed word of God. They turn to the Bible for instruction in doctrine, ethics, and higher truths, confident that this collection of divinely inspired texts has an authority that sets it above all others. But what, exactly, does "divinely inspired" mean? More important, does the Bible make the claim of divine inspiration about itself?

As it turns out, one passage in the New Testament speaks of *all* scripture as "God-breathed" (2 Timothy 3:16). Here, the Greek *theopneustos* ("God-breathed") comes very close to "divinely inspired." Another passage describes the prophets of the Old Testament as men who "spoke from God as they were carried along by the Holy Spirit" (2 Peter 1:21). Two Old Testament passages say that God himself wrote the Ten Commandments (Exodus 24:12 and Deuteronomy 5:22). There are also several Old and New Testament texts that describe Old Testament figures as taking dictation from God when writing small portions of scripture (e.g., Ezekiel 11:5, Matthew 22:43). Beyond this, the Bible says little about divine inspiration.

Until the Reformation of the sixteenth century, divine inspiration was not an issue of great importance. The two great traditions within Christianity, Roman Catholicism and Orthodoxy, agreed that the biblical texts were *somehow* inspired by God, who chose their authors and worked *with* and *through* them, and that seems to have been enough. But the Protestant reformers advanced the doctrine that scripture is the only authority on which Christians can completely rely. This meant that that authority of scripture had to be raised to a level at which it was beyond question. In order to do this, Protestant thinkers formulated a variety of theories in order to explain just how divine inspiration "works." Some of these theories claim that God inspired the biblical writers even to the point of determining every word they chose to use. Other theories say that God has ensured the truth of the message in the biblical texts but without influencing the means by which the biblical authors chose to communicate it.

Today, there is a broad range of opinion on divine inspiration and the Bible. Some Christians credit the authors of the biblical texts for their spiritual insights and leave little or no room for divine influence. Others downplay the human contribution to scripture, some to the point of attributing every word and idea to God.

The issue of divine inspiration is closely tied to the issue of biblical accuracy. As you might imagine, the more one emphasizes God's involvement in writing the biblical texts, the more necessary it becomes to insist on their inerrancy. After all, since God cannot lie or contradict himself, a Bible whose ultimate author is God cannot possibly contain even a single error. Of course, there do seem to be errors and contradictions in the Bible. In such cases, Christians who support absolute inerrancy use biblical, historical, and linguistic arguments to show that they are only apparent, not real. Those who endorse a limited inerrancy say that the Bible is inerrant in matters essential to faith and doctrine but may contain insignificant errors relating to geography and history. For the most part, conservative Protestants favor absolute inerrancy. Liberal Protestants, Roman Catholics, and Orthodox Christians tend to support limited inerrancy.

Tradition

Tradition has great authority in the lives of most people. We look to the accumulated wisdom of the past in forms such as laws and constitutions, scientific discoveries, masterpieces of art and literature, and folklore for guidance in organizing society and understanding the world and our place in it. In a similar way, Christians have always looked to their past for guidance in matters of belief and practice. For them, tradition is the "handing on" (Latin *traditio*) and continuing interpretation of the gospel message through the centuries. The idea of tradition is found in the Bible. In one of his letters to the Christians of Corinth, Paul wrote: "I handed on to you as of first importance what I in turn had received" (1 Corinthians 15:3). While different groups define the content of tradition in different ways, in the broadest sense it includes creeds, forms of worship, doctrines, the decisions of church councils, papal decrees, the works of major theologians, and even the illustration of the gospel in art, music, and literature.

All Christians place great value on tradition. For Roman Catholics and Orthodox, its authority is on the same level as scripture. In fact, some point out that since the earliest Christians were "handing on" the faith even before the first New Testament texts were written, scripture can be seen as a *part* of tradition. Protestants set tradition below scripture but still acknowledge its importance. Most Protestants believe that tradition can be helpful in understanding scripture and accept the ancient creeds, the basic outlines of liturgical worship, and a great many other "traditional" features of belief and practice.

"Last Things"

We have seen that Jesus proclaimed the coming of the kingdom of God—God's loving and righteous rule in the world. Jesus taught that the kingdom was already present in him and in his followers but that its full realization lay in the future. In doing so, he made a distinction between the *now* and the *not yet* that is evident throughout the New Testament.

The Letter to the Hebrews, for example, describes Christians as "those who have once been enlightened, and have tasted the heavenly gift, and have shared in the Holy Spirit, and have tasted the goodness of the word of God and the powers of the age to come" (Hebrews 6:4). Similarly, Paul's letters speak of world-transforming events that had already occurred, such as the resurrection of Christ and the descent of the Holy Spirit upon his followers, but they also look forward to events that would take place at the end of the age. Greek-speaking Christians called these events *ta eschata*, "the last things." They include eschatological events such as the Second Coming of Christ, the resurrection of the dead, the last judgment, and the glorious consummation of the kingdom of God.

Most early Christians assumed that the end of their age was not far off. As time passed, however, many came to believe that the consummation of the kingdom would occur within a spiritual context rather than in an earthly kingdom. There is a biblical basis for this view in the Gospel of John, whose "realized eschatology" holds that events such as judgment and resurrection into eternal life have already been realized in the interior lives of believers. Both points of view are still very much alive today, and so it is fair to say that Christians hold a very wide range of opinions with respect to the time and nature of the fulfillment of God's purposes in the world.

The Afterlife

Like the adherents of many other religions, Christians believe that human existence extends beyond this life. In the afterlife, the consequences of the choices people make now in relation to God and God's grace will be fully realized. Traditionally, Christians have illustrated these consequences with images of heaven and hell. Some Christians also believe in purgatory, an intermediate state between earthly life and heaven.

Christian beliefs about the afterlife have been influenced by the cultures in which Christianity has developed as well as by scripture. As a result, they are extremely varied and complex.

Heaven Perhaps it is best to begin with what most Christians believe about heaven. In essence, heaven is the perfect and eternal union with God, the fulfillment of the true purpose and deepest desire of human beings. Whether understood as an actual place or a state of being, as physical or spiritual, as earthly or celestial, "heaven" always means the ineffable bliss of everlasting existence in the loving presence of God.

Although the New Testament texts make frequent reference to heaven, they do not describe it in detail. The only exception is the book of Revelation, which devotes two chapters to its own unique vision. For the most part, the New Testament authors provide only glimpses of heaven, to which they refer in a variety of ways: as the city of God, the heavenly Jerusalem, life everlasting, the holy place, and the great reward. In the gospels, Jesus speaks of heaven as "paradise" (Luke 23:43) and as a place he will prepare for his followers (John 14:2–3). Paul's letters describe heaven both as the present dwelling-place of God and Jesus Christ and as the future home of believers. According to Paul, Christians can be certain of heaven because their experience of the Holy Spirit in this life gives them a taste of a future reality in which mortality will be "swallowed up by life" (2 Corinthians 5:12).

For some Christians, heaven is not a place but a spiritual state of being. This view evinces the influence of ancient Greek thought, which held that the true self is an immortal soul that can exist apart from the body and beyond space and time. For other Christians, heaven is the abode of God in the starry firmament above the earth. With roots in both the Old and New Testaments, this conception of heaven as a physical place is associated with the belief that those in heaven will possess physical bodies made perfect and immortal following the resurrection of the dead that will occur when Christ returns to judge the world (1 Corinthians 15; Philippians 3:20). Finally, some Christians understand heaven as an earthly phenomenon. The basis for this view is the vision of "a new heaven and a new earth" in the New Testament book of Revelation (21–22). According to Revelation, the day will come when a "heavenly Jerusalem" will become present on earth. Here, evils such as death and disease will no longer exist and God himself will live among his people.

Purgatory One of the most striking differences between Christian views of the afterlife concerns **purgatory**. In Roman Catholic thought, purgatory is an intermediate place or state between earthly life and heaven in which the souls of the dead suffer temporal punishment due for sin. Just as a friend might forgive you for some wrong you have done but still expect you to suffer a bit in demonstrating your sorrow, Roman Catholic doctrine holds that sinners must make reparation or satisfaction for sins already forgiven by God. Traditionally imagined as a cleansing fire, purgatory offers the opportunity to complete the work of reparation left undone in earthly life. The scriptural basis for belief in purgatory is found in the apocryphal book of 2 Maccabees (12:39–45), which describes Jewish belief in the efficacy of prayer offered for the dead so that "they might be released from their sin."

Although Orthodox Christianity does not accept the Roman Catholic doctrine of purgatory, most Orthodox Christians believe that after death souls enter a "condition of waiting" in which they can benefit from prayers said on their behalf. Protestant Christians reject belief in purgatory because they find no basis for it in scripture (since most Protestant Bibles do not include 2 Maccabees)

Hell Hell is not so much God's punishment for sin as the self-imposed consequence of rejecting God through the exercise of free will. Some Christians understand hell as an actual place, others think of it as a state of being, and still others do not believe in hell at all. In describing why hell must exist, one Orthodox writer has said: "God will not force us to love Him, for love is no longer love if it is not free; how then can God reconcile to Himself those who refuse all reconciliation?"[2]

The word translated as "hell" in English versions of the New Testament is Gehenna, the name of a valley bordering Jerusalem where many Jews in the time of Jesus expected that the worst of sinners would one day suffer torment. Thus, Gehenna works well as a means of illustrating the pain of separation from God. While hell clearly refers to a state of existence, there is little basis in the New Testament for understanding it as an actual place. It was not until the early Middle Ages that hell was transformed in the popular imagination into a subterranean pit of fiery horrors.[3] Although hell has long been understood as a necessary expression of divine justice, many Christian thinkers have found this idea to be inconsistent with God's love. Some have taught that God will ultimately save all people from the consequences of sin.

Christianity and Other Religions

Coexisting with other religions, Christianity has always needed to define itself in relation to them. This is particularly true of Judaism, within which it originated. The bitterness felt by Jewish Christians after their expulsion from synagogues late in the first century can be seen in a variety of New Testament passages critical of Jewish piety and religious groups (for example, in Matthew 23 and John 5–8). It must also have influenced the composition of the gospel accounts of the crucifixion of Jesus, which place most of the blame on Jewish authorities rather than on the Romans, who actually carried out the execution. The anti-Jewish feeling evident in passages like these reflects a hostility that existed on both sides as first-century Christianity began to move away from Judaism. Tragically, its presence in scripture continued to influence Christian attitudes toward Jews and Judaism long after the split occurred. The same can be said of New Testament descriptions of the Church, rather than the Jewish people, as the true people of God (for example, Matthew 21:43).

Scriptural passages have been used for centuries to justify hostility and violence against Jews, denounced as Christ-killers and enemies of humanity. In the seventh century, French and Spanish Jews were subjected to forced baptism. In the late Middle Ages, Jews were expelled from England, Spain, France, and Portugal. Anti-Jewish feeling assumed its most virulent form with the rise of fascism in Germany, Italy, and other parts of Europe during the first half of the twentieth century. It was not until after the Holocaust, the genocidal murder of 6 million Jews carried out by Nazi Germany during World War II, that church leaders began working for an end to hostility toward Jews and Judaism. At its inaugural meeting in 1948, the World Council of Churches declared that anti-Semitism is incompatible with the Christian faith and "a sin against God and man." Today, many Christian groups are engaged in efforts to heal the wounds of the past and to encourage a Jewish-Christian dialogue that will foster mutual appreciation and respect.

Historically, the Christian attitude to other religions has been based on the teaching that there is no salvation apart from faith in Jesus Christ. This view is based on passages in the New Testament that speak of Jesus as the only way in which God has been fully revealed to humanity. But the cultural pluralism of today's global society has raised interest in and appreciation for other ways of understanding spiritual realities. In fact, some Christians find a scriptural basis for the possibility of salvation in other religions. They point to Paul's letter to the Romans, which says that those who follow the dictates of their consciences will be judged as righteous on the last day (Romans 2:14–16). Similarly, the letter of James defines "pure" religion not in specifically Christian terms but as caring for the needy and keeping oneself "unstained by the world" (James 1:27). Of course, the meaning of statements like these depends on how one chooses to interpret them, but they have encouraged many Christians to value the spiritual insights of other religious traditions and to enter into cooperative relationships with them. The spirit of this new attitude, expressed in formal statements by many Christian groups, is represented in the *Declaration on Non-Christian Religions* issued by the Roman Catholic bishops who assembled for the Second Vatican Council (1962–1965):

> Prudently and lovingly, through dialogue and collaboration with the followers of other religions and in witness of the Christian faith and life, we should acknowledge, preserve and promote the spiritual and moral goods found among these men, as well as the values in their society and culture.[4]

CHRISTIANITY AS A WAY OF LIFE

There is much more to Christianity than the beliefs Christians hold inwardly. Like the followers of other religions, Christians express their beliefs outwardly in a variety of ways. Some are public, such as formal worship in church, participation in rituals, and the observance of holy days. Others are more private and personal, such as prayer and meditation. Together, these practices constitute much of what Christians do in living the Christian life.

Worship

Because the first Christians were Jews, they patterned their worship on the familiar synagogue service, which consisted of readings from scripture, prayer, and a sermon. To this, they added the celebration of the eucharist, a commemoration of the Last Supper Jesus shared with his disciples. The result was a liturgy (Greek *leitourgia*, "a work of the people") consisting of two parts: the liturgy of the word, including readings from scripture, prayer, and a sermon, and the liturgy of the eucharist. The Western custom of referring to the liturgy as the Mass can be traced back to *missa*, one of the Latin words used to dismiss the congregation: *Ite, missa est* ("Go, the dismissal is made").

Today's Roman Catholic and Orthodox churches are highly liturgical. In worship, members of these traditions feel themselves caught up in ritual rhythms of praise and adoration that reach back through more than two millennia. In contrast, most Protestant groups have adopted much simpler forms of worship that emphasize readings from scripture and preaching over ritual.

Christians have always made Sunday, the day of Christ's resurrection, a day set apart for communal worship. Typically, worship in Protestant churches begins with a hymn followed by an invocation, or opening prayer. After readings from the Old and New Testaments, congregants might sing another hymn in preparation for the sermon. Informal announcements of interest to the congregation often follow, along with a collection taken up for support of the church and its charitable causes. A recitation of the Lord's Prayer (p. 425) follows the collection. The service concludes with a final prayer and a closing hymn. In Roman Catholic churches, worship begins with a formal procession of the clergy toward the altar (a table used in celebrating the eucharist) accompanied by the singing of an opening hymn. Next, in a penitential rite, those present confess their sins and ask God's forgiveness. The liturgy of the word that follows consists primarily of readings from scripture, a short sermon, or homily, and a recitation of the Nicene Creed. At this point, the liturgy of the eucharist begins with the presentation of bread and wine, which are set on the altar. After the priest blesses these elements, there is a special eucharistic prayer followed by a singing of the *Sanctus*, a short hymn taken from the Old Testament (Isaiah 6:3). The congregation then recites an affirmation of faith and the Lord's Prayer. In a final preparatory act, members of the congregation wish each other "the peace of the Lord." It is at this point that the bread and wine are consecrated, making Christ present upon the altar. The members of the congregation then share in the rite of communion, in which each person receives a bit of the consecrated elements of bread and wine. Many Roman Catholic Christians say that it is in this solemn moment that they are most acutely aware of God's loving presence. The liturgy concludes with a final prayer, a benediction (blessing), and the formal dismissal of the congregation. The liturgy celebrated in Orthodox churches follows this same pattern, though additional processions, prayers, and blessings make it more elaborate.

Sacraments

Like worship, the special rituals known as **sacraments** are central to Christian life. Understood as visible symbols of God's grace, the sacraments infuse believers with spiritual nourishment and impart a sacred character to transitional moments in their lives. The Greek word for sacrament, *musterion* ("mystery"—the term preferred by Orthodox Christians), helps to explain the significance these rituals have for Christians. Making use of ordinary elements such as bread, wine, water, and oil, they bring the individual into an experience of something extraordinary—the mystery of God's love. Roman Catholic and Orthodox Christians celebrate seven sacraments. Protestants acknowledge only two: baptism and the eucharist.

The first sacrament celebrated in the life of a Christian is baptism, a cleansing of sin that marks the beginning of a new spiritual life in which one is united with Christ and sanctified by the Holy Spirit. Baptism can take the form of complete immersion in water or a sprinkling of water on one's head. However it is performed, the priest or minister always follows the instruction of Christ to baptize "in the name of the Father and of the Son and of the Holy Spirit" (Matthew 28:19). Roman Catholics, Orthodox Christians, and many Protestants prefer infant baptism. Some Protestant denominations baptize only those who are old enough to determine for themselves whether they wish to make a commitment to the Christian faith, as we saw in Annie's story at the beginning of this chapter.

After baptism, a Christian is entitled to participate in the eucharist, also known as Holy Communion and the Lord's Supper. As we have seen, the eucharist

This baptistry basin was built in the sixth century as part of the Basilica of St. Vitalis in what is now Sbeitla, Tunisia. Candidates for baptism were led down the steps and then baptized by full immersion in water.

commemorates Christ's Last Supper with his disciples before his crucifixion. On that occasion, he identified the bread and wine they shared with his body and blood:

> While they were eating, he took a loaf of bread, and after blessing it he broke it and gave it to them, and said, "Take; this is my body." Then he took a cup, and after giving thanks he gave it to them, and all of them drank from it. He said to them, "This is my blood of the covenant, which is poured out for many."
> —*Mark 14:22–24*

Historically, most Christians have taken these words to mean that Christ is truly present in the eucharist. Only with the Reformation of the sixteenth century did some Protestant groups adopt the view that the bread and wine are mere symbols of Christ's presence. While those who believe in the "real presence" have sought to explain it in various ways, most acknowledge that it is ultimately a mystery. In a sense, it is similar to the gestures we use to communicate inward feeling in everyday life. For example, most of us believe that the love we feel for someone else can be conveyed by a hug or kiss, but we would find it difficult to explain in precise terms how our love is present in the gesture. We can understand the eucharist as a kind of sacred gesture in which God offers grace to human beings. Although they have different ways of explaining how this happens, Christians agree that their participation in the ritual meal of bread and wine brings them into closer union with God and each other.

A third sacrament is confirmation. In the Roman Catholic Church, confirmation is administered to adolescents who have completed formal instruction in the faith. *Because* they understand its teachings, they are recognized as fully responsible members of the Church. In the Orthodox tradition, confirmation usually occurs when an infant is baptized *in order that*, nourished by grace, he or she might grow into a mature understanding of the faith and share in the work of the Church.

The four sacraments that remain are essentially the same in Catholicism and Orthodoxy. Holy matrimony gives a sacred character to marriage. For men who feel called to become priests, the sacrament of holy orders confers a grace that enables them to be effective leaders in the Church. Penance, also known as confession and reconciliation, involves confessing sin to a priest in order to receive his assurances of God's forgiveness and his prescription for the performance of an act of penance or reparation for the sin committed. The final sacrament, anointing of the sick, is meant to strengthen those who are in immediate danger of death.

In addition to the sacraments, Christians make use of a variety of other rituals. Many make the sign of the cross by touching the fingers of the right hand to the

In this celebration of the eucharist, a Roman Catholic priest prays over a wafer of bread and chalices of wine, which are believed to become the body and blood of Christ.

The design and decor of this small Protestant church are simple. The attention of the congregation is directed toward the pulpit, from which the pastor delivers a sermon based on the scriptures.

forehead, chest, and shoulders. In some churches, vessels of holy water blessed by a priest are available near the entrance so that, by dipping their fingers into them before making the sign of the cross, worshipers can perform a simple act of cleansing reminiscent of baptism. Priests sometimes sprinkle holy water over the altar and congregation at the beginning of the Mass and worshipers genuflect by bending the right knee before taking their seats or passing before the altar. In the Roman Catholic and Orthodox churches, incense is used as a symbol of prayer rising to God.

Church Interiors: Sacred Space

The interior design of a church reflects its theology and liturgical style. Most Protestant churches are quite plain and have rows of seats facing a pulpit in the front as their main features. It is from the pulpit, a raised lectern, that the pastor or minister delivers the weekly sermon. Since Protestants emphasize scripture over sacraments, the pulpit generally has a more prominent position than the altar. Protestant churches make sparing use of decorative effects. There may be candles on the altar and a cross displayed on the wall, but little more. The intent behind this simplicity is to create an environment without distractions in which worshipers can meet God in prayer and in the reading and exposition of scripture.

Roman Catholic churches are more elaborate. Because Catholicism emphasizes the sacraments, and the eucharist in particular, it is the altar rather than the pulpit that stands out from the worshiper's perspective. Religious paintings and statues of saints are commonly found, as are crucifixes, or images of Christ

Like all Roman Catholic churches, this church in St. Maarten in the Netherlands Antilles gives the most prominent place to the altar, where the eucharist is celebrated. The priest's homily, or sermon, is delivered from a pulpit set to the side. Images of the saints that Catholics venerate can be seen along the walls.

on the cross. To the side of some churches is a stand supporting rows of votive candles set in colored glass. When music is added to these physical features of the church, the senses are filled with sights and sounds meant to lift the mind and heart to God.

This approach to creating a sacred space is even more pronounced in Orthodox churches, whose design and decoration give worshipers a sense of entering into the heavenly presence of God. The main body of the Orthodox church is separated from the sanctuary in the front by a screen, called an iconostasis ("icon stand"), covered with painted images of Christ and the saints. Icons fill the rest of the church as well, reminding worshipers that they belong to a spiritual communion that includes the whole company of heaven. Even the magnificent domes atop Orthodox churches display iconic murals of Christ and the saints. But the main focus of attention is the sanctuary, which can be glimpsed through several doors that provide access to the priest and his assistants. It is in this sacred space that the mystery of the eucharist is celebrated, with chanting and incense that reveal in the material world the realities of the spiritual realm.

The Interior of a Greek Orthodox church. Note the iconostasis, or "icon screen" at the far end of the aisle. In Orthodox churches, the altar is always located behind the iconostasis. Worshipers sit under a dome, partially visible here, on which images of Christ and the saints are painted.

Prayer

As in other religions, prayer is an essential part of Christian life. For Christians, Jesus provides the ultimate example of prayer's importance. The gospels describe him as praying frequently, often for hours and with great fervency. On one occasion, he taught his disciples to pray in this way:

> Our Father in heaven,
> hallowed be your name.
> Your kingdom come.
> Your will be done,
> on earth as it is in heaven.
> Give us this day our daily bread.
> And forgive us our debts,
> as we also have forgiven our debtors.
> And do not bring us to the time of trial,
> but deliver us from the evil one.
> — *Matthew 6:9–13*

This prayer, known as the **Lord's Prayer**, is just one of many forms of prayer in Christianity. The New Testament describes the apostles as following the Jewish custom of praying at certain times of the day. From this developed the Christian practice of reciting formal prayers at prescribed times. These prayers were gradually combined with hymns and readings from scripture to create public services held throughout the day and night at "canonical hours." Known collectively as the Divine Office, they became an essential part of monastic life. Formal, recited prayers were also integrated into the liturgy. Of course, from the beginning Christians also prayed privately, informally, and silently. Today, it is customary for Christians to offer a prayer of thanksgiving before meals, on rising in the morning, and before going to bed at night. When the troubles and concerns of daily life arise, they ask God for guidance, forgiveness, and peace. In the face of sickness and death, they find in prayer the assurance of God's loving presence.

Most Christian traditions include specialized forms of prayer practiced by those who wish to deepen their spiritual lives. For example, the interior walls of Roman Catholic churches display fourteen images of the passion, or "suffering," of Christ during the final hours of his life. Catholics visit these Stations of the Cross in order, reciting prayers and meditating on each incident as a means of coming to a deeper understanding of Christ's suffering. Another form of Catholic devotion is praying the **rosary**. This involves recitation of a series of prayers counted on a string of beads while meditating on important moments in the lives of Jesus and his mother, Mary.

For instruction in prayer, Orthodox Christians turn to the *Philokalia*, a collection of ascetic and mystical texts written between the fourth and the fifteenth centuries. Containing the words of Orthodoxy's greatest sages, the *Philokalia* is considered a treasury of wisdom concerning the practice of contemplative prayer. While meditation centers on the intellect, contemplative prayer is a "prayer of the heart" in which it is not only the mind but one's whole being that reaches out to God. Its most common form is the Jesus Prayer: "Lord Jesus Christ, Son of God, have mercy on me." Ideally, the Jesus Prayer is recited continually, whether one is driving to work, standing in line, or attending to any other matter. In time, it embeds itself in one's being and its repetition becomes as natural and effortless as breathing. According to one Orthodox saint, "even when [the practitioner] is immersed in sleep, the perfumes of prayer will breathe in his heart spontaneously."[5] In recent years, the Jesus Prayer and other forms of Orthodox contemplation have become increasingly popular among Catholics and Protestants, who share with Orthodox Christians a yearning for communion with God not only at certain times, but throughout the course of each day.

The Liturgical Year

Just as the life of every Christian is punctuated by the sacraments, each year in the life of the Church is defined by the celebration of holy days and the observance of religious seasons that make up the liturgical year. Built around the two great feasts of **Christmas** and **Easter**, the cycle of the liturgical year draws believers into the experience of Christ, allowing them to relive in a vicarious way the events in his life through which God brought salvation to the world.

The first great season of the liturgical year is Advent, a time of preparation and looking forward to the "coming" (Latin *adventus*) of God into the world. Advent culminates in Christmas, a celebration of the birth of Christ on December 25, when expectation turns into rejoicing. The Christmas season ends on January 6 with a celebration of **Epiphany** (from the Greek *epiphaneia*, "manifestation"), which recalls the manifestation of God's presence in the infant Jesus to "wise men from the East" who came to give him gifts (Matthew 2:1–12). In many parts

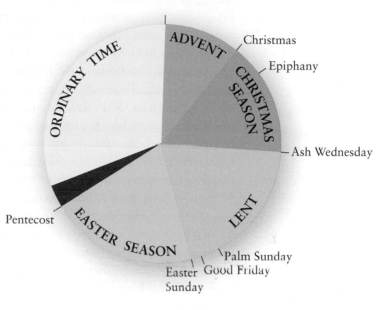

The liturgical year is an annual cycle of holy days and seasons that re-create events and times during the life of Jesus.

of the world, it is Epiphany rather than Christmas that is the central holiday of the Christmas season.

After Epiphany, the liturgical year moves forward to Easter, a springtime celebration of Christ's resurrection. The Easter season begins on Ash Wednesday, when ashes symbolizing human mortality are placed on the foreheads of believers. Ash Wednesday is followed by the forty-day period of Lent, when many Christians practice self-denial as a way of participating vicariously in the suffering of Christ. Awareness of Christ's suffering is heightened during Holy Week, the last week of Lent, when most days have special significance. Palm Sunday recalls Christ's triumphal entry into Jerusalem, when enthusiastic crowds placed palm branches on the road before him. Maundy Thursday marks Jesus' institution of the eucharist at the Last Supper. Good Friday commemorates the crucifixion of Jesus. Holy Week concludes with Easter, the most important of Christian holidays because it is in Christ's resurrection that Christians see his triumph over death and the promise of eternal life. Easter is a truly joyous holiday, filled with signs and symbols of new life. In Orthodox countries, Easter mornings resound with the cry, "Christ is risen!" and the response, "He is risen indeed!" Rejoicing continues through the following weeks as Christians celebrate the Ascension of Christ into heaven and the coming of the Holy Spirit at Pentecost.

After Pentecost the liturgical year moves into six months of "ordinary time." There are no great celebrations during this period but there are saints' days and other occasions that have significance for particular groups. For example, at the end of October Protestants celebrate Reformation Sunday, which marks the anniversary of the beginning of their tradition. By this time, the passing of summer and fall means that it is nearly Advent again and time to begin a new cycle of the liturgical year.

Veneration of Saints

Like the members of any group, Christians have always had their heroes. Known as **saints** ("holy ones"), they are spiritual role models who have shown how the Christian life should be lived. Without doubt, the greatest of saints is Mary, the virgin mother of Christ, who is considered the foremost example of what God can do in sanctifying a human life. Those who honor Mary point to her virtues of gentleness, humility, and submission to God's will and recall her expression of joy on learning that she had been chosen to bear the Christ: "Surely, from now on all generations will call me blessed" (Luke 1:48). According to Roman Catholic teaching, Mary was unique in being conceived without sin (the doctrine of the Immaculate Conception) and in being taken up bodily into heaven at her death (the doctrine of the Assumption). Orthodox Christians share these beliefs about Mary and honor her with the titles *Theotokos* ("God-bearer") and *Panagia* ("All-holy").

For Protestant Christians, the significance of the saints lies almost exclusively in the inspiring examples they have set for others. In Roman Catholicism and Orthodoxy, the saints have greater significance. These traditions emphasize the eternal participation of the saints in the Church, for though they now exist in heaven, they remain within the mystical communion of believers that is "the body of Christ." Catholic and Orthodox Christians believe that Paul made this point when he wrote that Christians are "citizens with the saints and also members of the household of God" (Ephesians 2:16).

This Greek icon depicts Christ holding the scriptures and raising his right hand in a sign of blessing. The Greek letters outside his halo identify him as Jesus Christ. The letters inside the halo identify him as God.

Just as the living pray for the welfare of their fellow Christians, the saints are thought to intercede for them in prayer as well. Belief in the intercession of saints is evident in early Christian literature and in epitaphs found on sarcophagi and grave markers. These implore both saints and departed family members to pray for the living. "Pray for us," says one inscription, "that we may be saved." On the sarcophagus of their little boy, his mother and father wrote: "To our son Philemon, who lived happily for two years with his parents: Pray for us, together with the saints."[6] Belief in the intercession of saints remains an important part of Roman Catholicism and Orthodoxy. Strictly speaking, one does not pray *to* the saints, but *with* them. Saints are not worshiped. Instead, they are venerated with a reverential respect that recognizes their holiness.

The veneration of saints takes a variety of forms. Most Catholic and Orthodox Christians are given a saint's name at baptism and their churches are usually named after saints. Many believers honor saints on their feast days and wear medals with their likenesses imprinted on them. In addition, the physical remains of saints, known as relics, are objects of veneration. Preserved in special containers known as reliquaries, relics can be found in many churches, where they bring a sense of the sacred to those who pray in their presence. If this practice seems a bit strange to you, it might be helpful to consider how you might be affected by a more secular "relic." For example, a photograph or keepsake from a loved you have lost can provide a sense of that person's presence. In some mysterious way, it seems, something of that person's essence remains within the item itself. So it is with the saints, whose holiness is thought to remain in the relics they have left behind.

Images of saints also produce a heightened awareness of holiness. In Roman Catholicism, images take the forms of paintings and statues whose lifelike quality is meant to underscore the experience of earthly existence that the saints share with all other believers. Meditating on a painting or statue, believers are encouraged in the spiritual life by knowing that the saint it represents once experienced the same challenges people experience now. The **icons** of the Orthodox, who make no use of statues, are meant to have just the opposite effect. These highly stylized paintings are not intended to be lifelike. Their purpose is to represent not earthly reality but the reality of transfigured and perfected humanity in heaven. Gazing intently at their observers and communicating through symbolic gestures, the saints depicted in icons offer a glimpse of the higher, spiritual realm that is the ultimate goal of every Christian.

Social and Political Activism

One of the most important features of the practice of Christianity is service to others. According to the New Testament (Acts 4:32–35), the earliest Christians took seriously the command to love one's neighbor as oneself: the wealthy gave all their money to the church, all property was held in common, and no one experienced great need. In the Middle Ages, the churches of the East and West provided important social services by supporting orphans, widows, and the disabled; seeking the release of prisoners of war; and caring for victims of plagues, earthquakes, and other disasters.

This tradition of social service continues today. Most congregations make significant contributions to support the poor, the sick, and the homeless in their communities. On a larger scale, there are hundreds of national and international Christian charities dedicated to fighting social and political injustice, bringing an end to poverty, and providing food, health services, and education to those in need. They include Habitat for Humanity, Bread for the World, International Orthodox Charities, Catholic Relief Services, the Salvation Army, and World Vision.

Christian activism has often brought important social and political change. In the nineteenth century, the British politician William Wilberforce (1759–1833) called for an end to slavery. American abolitionists such as Theodore Weld (1803–1895) and Harriet Beecher Stowe (1811–1896) played leading roles in the American antislavery movement, whose aims were realized in the Emancipation Proclamation of 1863. In the 1960s, it was a black Baptist minister, Dr. Martin Luther King, Jr. (1929–1968), who championed the civil rights movement that succeeded in outlawing discrimination against minorities and women in the Civil Rights Act of 1964. In the 1960s and 1970s, Christian activists such as the brothers Daniel and Philip Berrigan, both Catholic priests, were among the leading figures of the antiwar movement that helped to bring an end to the Vietnam War in 1975.

THE HISTORY OF CHRISTIANITY

Christianity in the Roman World

Christianity spread rapidly throughout the Roman empire. But the new religion was not welcomed by everyone. Christians met with criticism and persecution that continued until Rome's emperors became Christians themselves. Also, the rapid growth in the number of Christians and Christian groups during these early years encouraged the movement to define essential doctrines and to adopt a form of church government capable of uniting Christians and promoting uniformity of belief and practice among them.

The Church and the Roman State The Roman world was often hostile to Christians. Many suspected them of disloyalty to Rome because they refused to recognize its gods or participate in public events that involved pagan rituals. Localized persecutions began in the first century and expanded into empire-wide assaults in the third. Despite the terrors of mass arrests and executions, however, persecution failed to check the growth of the Christian movement. A dramatic turning point came in 312, when the Emperor Constantine (r. 306–337) defeated a rival after seeing a vision of a cross in the sky. Convinced that the God of the Christians had given him the victory, Constantine decreed religious freedom for Christians and began to promote Christianity by building churches and extending privileges to church leaders.

When Constantine transferred the imperial capital from Rome to Constantinople (modern Istanbul) in 330, he did so in the hope that it would be a truly Christian city free of paganism. Decades later, Theodosius I (r. 379–395) made Christianity the official state religion of the Roman empire and began the suppression of other religions and schools of philosophy.

Diversity in the Early Church During the first five centuries C.E., Christians formulated many important doctrines, thereby establishing a standard of orthodoxy, or "correct belief." However, some early Christian groups challenged the emerging mainstream Church on issues as basic as the nature of God, the humanity of Christ, salvation, and ecclesiastical (Greek *ekklesia*, "church") authority.

Three such groups are especially important. The first is Gnostic Christianity, whose unique writings, discovered in 1945, are still making news in popular magazines and television documentaries as well as in scholarly publications. Some Gnostic beliefs were strikingly different from those of most Christians. Gnostics believed that Christ's body had been a mere illusion; therefore, he could not have atoned for sin by dying a physical death upon the cross. Salvation came instead from secret knowledge (Greek *gnosis*) that Christ gave only to a select group of *gnostics* ("knowers"), who had passed it down to others.

The first Christian emperor of Rome, Constantine the Great promoted the spread of Christianity throughout the Roman empire and founded a new capital at Constantinople (modern Istanbul) in 330.

Because Gnostic Christians saw all material reality as evil, they understood salvation as the liberation of souls from their imprisonment in human bodies rather than as liberation from sin. Gnostics claimed that the Christianity preached publicly in churches was incomplete since they alone understood the higher teachings of Christ.

A second group was founded by Marcion (c. 85–160 C.E.), a theologian who had been expelled from the church at Rome for teaching that there are two Gods: the God of the Jewish scriptures, whom Marcion described as the unjust creator of an evil world, and the supremely good God revealed by Christ. According to Marcion, it was this good God who had sent Christ to rescue human souls. Seeking to cut Christianity off from its Jewish roots, Marcion rejected the Jewish scriptures and all Christian texts that seemed dependent upon them.

A third form of Christianity, known as Montanism, began with Montanus, a charismatic prophet of the late second century who claimed to be the mouthpiece of the Holy Spirit. Montanus prophesied that Christ would soon return to a "new Jerusalem" that was about to appear in southern Asia Minor. The greatest difficulty posed by Montanus was his claim that he preached a *new* prophecy. This raised two critical questions. First, would Christian teaching require ongoing revision in order to accommodate every new group and its revelations? Second, did claims of prophetic inspiration give charismatic figures like Montanus an authority greater than that of church leaders?

TIMELINE
Christianity

c. 30 C.E. Crucifixion of Jesus.

c. 46–60 Paul's missionary journeys.

70–100 Gospels of Matthew, Mark, Luke, and John written.

313 Constantine decrees religious freedom for Christians.

325 Council of Nicea declares God the Son to be "of the same substance as God the Father."

354–430 Augustine of Hippo, first great theologian of the West and author of the *Confessions* and *City of God*.

367 Contents of New Testament established.

529 Benedict of Nursia writes the *Benedictine Rule*.

c. 1000 Conversion of Russia to Orthodox Christianity begins.

1054 The Great Schism divides the churches of East and West.

1095–1272 Western Crusaders repeatedly attempt to free the Holy Land from Muslim rule.

1184 Pope Lucius III inaugurates the Inquisition.

1198–1216 Height of papal power under Innocent III.

1265–1274 Thomas Aquinas writes the *Summa Theologica*.

1517 Reformation begins when Martin Luther posts his Ninety-Five Theses.

1534 King Henry VIII establishes Church of England.

1545–1563 Council of Trent.

1647 George Fox founds the Society of Friends (Quakers).

1703–1791 John Wesley, founder of the Methodist movement.

1869–1870 First Vatican Council declares doctrine of papal infallibility.

1962–1965 Second Vatican Council.

1948 Founding of the World Council of Churches.

Defining Orthodoxy Resolving questions related to correct belief, scripture, and the authority of the Church was one of the great themes in the early history of the Church. In order to establish its authority and define orthodox belief, the Church created a canon of scripture, formulated creeds, and implemented a system of ecclesiastical government that put authority into the hands of bishops.

We have already seen that a canon of scripture consisting of the Old and New Testaments was in place by the end of the fourth century. Texts widely believed to have been written by the apostles were included, as were writings from the apostolic era that

VISUAL GUIDE
Christianity

Early Christians used the "sign of the fish" as a secret symbol to identify themselves during times of persecution. Today, many Christians identify themselves as such by mounting the symbol on their cars. The letters of the Greek word for "fish" (ΙΧΘΥΣ) are the first letters in the words that make up the phrase "Jesus Christ, Son of God, and Savior."

The cross has served as a Christian symbol since ancient times and appears in many forms. With its longer vertical and shorter horizontal arms, the Latin cross is the form favored by the Roman Catholic and Protestant churches. This one stands atop Monte Crocione in northern Italy.

Orthodox Christians use many different forms of the cross. The most common is a simple figure formed by four arms of equal length. This one decorates a small convent on the island of Mykonos, Greece.

The Celtic cross. According to legend, the Celtic cross on the left originated with St. Patrick, who brought Christianity to Ireland. This one serves as a grave marker in a cemetery in Dublin, Ireland.

(continued)

were widely used in public worship. Because the Old and New Testaments were regarded as having a unique authority, they constituted a standard against which the orthodoxy of any new teaching could be judged.

The creeds developed by the early Church were formal and concise statements of essential Christian beliefs. In fact, the word *creed* itself comes from the Latin *credo*, which means "I believe." Creeds like the Apostles' Creed and Nicene Creed served two functions. The first is that they proclaimed orthodox doctrine on the Incarnation, suffering, and death of Christ, as well as his resurrection and ascension into heaven. The second is that repeated recitation of the creeds by Christians throughout the empire promoted uniformity of belief within the Church.

Finally, the early Church established a form of government that concentrated power in the hands of bishops, who had jurisdiction over large territories called dioceses. According to the doctrine of **apostolic succession**, bishops were the successors of the apostles, who had been commissioned by Christ himself to lead the Church. Claiming to have received both their offices and correct belief through direct lines of transmission, they held an authority that Gnostics, Montanists, and Marcionite Christians found difficult to challenge. Bishops were assisted by priests, who were responsible for individual churches, and every church was served by deacons (Greek *diakonos*, "servant") who assisted priests.

Gradually, the bishops of Rome and Constantinople emerged as the leaders of the churches of the Western and Eastern halves of the empire. Known as "popes" (Latin *papa*, "father"), the bishops of Rome were said to be the successors of the Apostle Peter, the "rock" (Greek *petra*) upon whom Christ had said he would build his Church (Matthew 16:18–19). They claimed the same authority Christ had given to Peter. Other bishops—including the great patriarchs of Constantinople, Alexandria, Antioch, and Jerusalem—acknowledged the bishops of Rome as "first among equals" but without recognizing the right of popes to rule over them.

Early Christian Thought The success of the early Christian movement was due in part to the work of Christian writers who produced carefully reasoned statements of Christian belief. These texts gave Christianity intellectual respectability in a world accustomed to the high standard set by Greek philosophy.

In the second century, apologists began defending the faith in "apologies" (Greek *apologia*, "defense") often addressed to emperors. Describing Christians as loyal citizens, they called for an end to persecution. Some apologists, such as Tertullian (c. 160–220), saw Greco-Roman culture as so antithetical to Christianity that they urged Christians to resist its influence. Others, such as Justin Martyr (103–165), saw Christianity as the perfect expression of the same truths that Greek and Roman thought had always sought to grasp. They encouraged dialogue between Christians, who had seen truth fully revealed in Christ, and those who had only glimpsed it in classical philosophy and mythology.

It was this more open attitude that prevailed among the Christian writers who followed the apologists. Theologians such as Clement of Alexandria (c. 150–215) and Origen (c. 185–254) taught that God had long been at work among the Greeks and Romans, preparing them for the coming of Christ. Just as God had given the Torah to the Jews, said Clement, he had given philosophy to the Greeks as a kind of "schoolmaster" in order to "bring the Greek mind . . . to Christ."[7] Like many thinkers of his time, Clement held that all truth comes from the divine "Word," or **Logos.** Thus, truths found in scripture and philosophy were compatible. However, since the Logos had become incarnate in Jesus Christ (John 1:18), said Clement, it was only in Christ that seekers of truth would find it fully revealed.

A crucifix is a cross with an image of the crucified Christ. It is used extensively in the Roman Catholic, Orthodox, Anglican, and Lutheran traditions. A vivid reminder of Christ's suffering on behalf of humanity, it is usually displayed prominently in church interiors.

The custom of using alpha and omega, the first and last letters of the Greek alphabet, to symbolize the eternality of God is based on a verse from the book of Revelation in the New Testament (1:8): "I am the Alpha and the Omega," says the Lord God, "who is, and who was, and who is to come, the Almighty."

The Chi-Rho is a symbol of Christ. Its name is based on those of the Greek letters chi and rho, the first two letters in the Greek word Christos, or "Christ." According to one legend, the Chi-Rho was revealed in a dream to the Emperor Constantine, who won a great victory against a rival for the imperial throne after marking it on the shields of his soldiers. Today, the Chi-Rho appears on altars, plaques, priestly vestments, pendants, and other items. The symbol depicted here appears on a Christian stele from Seville in Spain and was created c. 600.

The "sign of the cross" is a ritual hand motion in which the shape of the cross of Christ is traced across the forehead and chest. It is used in both public worship and private prayer. The practice of "signing" oneself as an act of devotion goes back to ancient times. Writing c. 200, the North African theologian Tertullian noted that the Christians of his time "wore out their foreheads" making the sign of the cross.

Controversies and Councils Beginning in the third century, Christian theologians turned their attention to the concept of the Trinity and to the nature of Christ. Discussion of these issues led to ecumenical councils ("worldwide councils") of bishops at which doctrines were defined.

From the beginning, most Christians believed that God the Father, the Creator of the universe, had become present in the world in Jesus Christ, God the Son. They also believed in the Holy Spirit as the continuing expression of God's loving presence and power in the world. But how could the one God also be three? This question was taken up by early theologians such as Tertullian, who gave Latin theology its Trinitarian vocabulary by speaking of God as *tres personae, una substantia* ("three persons, one substance"). Similarly, Greek-speaking theologians described God as a single divine *ousia* ("substance" or "essence") made manifest in three *hypostases* ("subsistences").

This way of thinking about the Trinity sufficed until the early 300s when Arius, an Egyptian priest from Alexandria, began teaching that God the Son, or Logos, was of a different substance than God the Father. Going further, Arius claimed that while the Father was eternal, the Son was created in time. Arius' views alarmed other theologians, for they seemed to undermine the unity of the Trinity. If the Father and the Son were so different, they asked, how could God be truly one?

Arius' provocative teachings soon had Alexandria buzzing as people in shops and streets argued theology with the same enthusiasm we reserve for debates about sports and politics. Fearing that Arianism threatened the unity of the empire as well as the Church, the Emperor Constantine stepped in and convened an ecumenical council to settle the matter. The Council of Nicea (325) condemned Arius' views, ordered the burning of Arian texts, and formulated a creed affirming that God the Son is *homoousios* ("of the same substance or being") with God the Father. An expanded form of this creed, the Nicene Creed (see p. 411), produced by the Council of Constantinople (381) underscored the presence of the Holy Spirit within a Trinity of three distinct yet unified divine "persons."

Even as the Trinitarian controversy was being settled, another debate began over the person of Christ. Christians had long believed that Christ was both human and divine, but they differed in explaining how humanity and divinity coexisted in him. The orthodox position on this issue was determined at yet another ecumenical council at Chalcedon (451): In Christ, two complete and perfect natures, human and divine, were united without separation or fusion in a single person.

Augustine The drama of the Trinitarian and Christological controversies was played out in the Greek-speaking Eastern half of the Roman world and involved many leading theologians. The Latin West produced just one theological giant. This was Augustine (354–430), a North African bishop who laid the intellectual foundations for much of Western Christianity and Western civilization.

Central to Augustine's theology are his views on sin and human nature. Elaborating on the theology of Paul, Augustine argued that sinfulness is a fundamental flaw in human nature that clouds our moral vision and perverts the will by causing us to desire evil rather than good. In the *Confessions*, his spiritual autobiography, he illustrated this point by recalling the pleasure he and some teenage friends once found in stealing and throwing away fruit from a neighbor's pear tree. According to Augustine, the tendency to sin is so deeply ingrained that we are spiritually helpless and therefore completely dependent upon God for salvation.

But *how* did human nature become so corrupt? Augustine's answer came in his famous doctrine of **Original Sin**. All of humanity, it says, participated in the first sin: the sin of Adam and Eve, the first human beings, described in Genesis (3:1–24). At that time, Adam and Eve *were* humanity, with all future generations present in them. Thus, when they made themselves sinners by choosing to disobey God, this original sin transformed human nature in a way that was bound to affect their descendants. Every human being, said Augustine, is born with the "stain" of original sin in the form of a sinful nature.

Augustine's awareness that some people are saved from sin led him to formulate a theory of predestination. Since all human beings are sinful and therefore incapable of responding on their own to God in faith, he reasoned, God must give some people a grace that inspires faith. Divine grace is irresistible, he said, for a love that could be resisted would be incompatible with God's perfection. Thus, those whom God touches with his grace are destined to be saved. Augustine conceded that it is impossible to know *why* God extends a saving grace to some people and not to others, but he insisted that God is neither arbitrary nor unjust. Some are allowed a destiny better than they deserve, but no one receives a destiny worse than he deserves.

As you might imagine, Augustine was never entirely comfortable with his conclusions about original sin and predestination, but his reading of scripture and observation of human behavior made them inescapable. Having seen jealousy in a baby whose brother had taken his place at their mother's breast, he felt he had no choice but to conclude that sin must be something we are born with and not simply a habit everyone happens to pick up. Similarly, though predestination seemed to be the work of an unfair God, Augustine knew that scripture taught that only some would be saved and that God's justice is not always within reach of human understanding.

Augustine's masterpiece was his *City of God*, in which he formulated a Christian philosophy of history. Writing amidst the panic following the sack of Rome by a Germanic tribe in 410, he rejected the pagan claim that Rome's traditional gods allowed the city to fall because they were angry with the Romans for converting to Christianity. Augustine argued that the fall of Rome was part of God's plan for the salvation of the world. God had ordained two "cities": the earthly city, blemished by sin, and the City of God, a spiritual community grounded in love of God. Like all other manifestations of the earthly city, said Augustine, Rome must pass away so that history can move toward the full realization of the City of God on earth. This view of history as progress toward the fulfillment of God's plan for salvation soon became standard in the Christian West.

The Church in the Middle Ages

In the fifth century, Germanic tribes overran the Western half of the Roman empire. From the resulting chaos a new medieval civilization emerged that combined Christianity with Roman and Germanic culture. The Eastern half of the Roman empire survived for another thousand years. Known as the Byzantine empire, it was Greek in its language and outlook. As the gulf between West and East widened, distinctively Western and Eastern traditions within the catholic ("universal") Church began to take shape.

The Church in the West   The most powerful of the Germanic tribes were the Franks, who controlled most of Western Europe by the ninth century. The Franks supported the Roman Church and granted rich lands to bishops and monasteries. In return, the Church sanctioned the rule of the Frankish kings, supplied clergy to serve in their government, and sent missionaries to convert pagan peoples in their kingdom.

The Church's involvement in secular affairs continued after the decline of the Franks and often led to conflict between secular and spiritual rulers, and especially the popes. Early medieval popes claimed that their spiritual responsibilities gave them an authority greater than that of secular rulers, but it was not until the eleventh century that the papacy rose to the level they had imagined. The most powerful of popes was Innocent III (r. 1198–1216). Intent on unifying the Christian world under the papal banner, Innocent intervened constantly in secular matters, deposing kings and emperors whenever they displeased him.

A very ugly aspect of medieval Christianity in the West was the **Inquisition**, the Church's inquiry into allegations of heresy that began in the twelfth century. Working in partnership with secular rulers, who feared that religious diversity would undermine their authority, the inquisitors sought to eradicate false teachings they believed would endanger the salvation of those who accepted them. The Inquisition also targeted Jews and Muslims. Despite its use of torture and the execution of heretics by burning, the Inquisition could not stamp out heresy. Nevertheless, it persisted in various forms until its final and cruelest phase, the Spanish Inquisition, was abolished in 1834.

The Church in the East   In the East, the patriarchs of Constantinople governed the Church jointly with the Byzantine emperors, who were responsible for both the spiritual and material well-being of their subjects. The Byzantine ideal was a *symphonia* ("harmony") of emperor and patriarch based on their shared vision of a holy empire on earth that reflected the glory of the

Completed c. 1250, the height and soaring towers of the Gothic cathedral at Chartres in France express the medieval yearning for God. For centuries, pilgrims and secular tourists have come to experience its exquisite, light-filled interior and to see its famous relic, the tunic of the Virgin Mary.

celestial society of heaven. Clashes did occur, but only one threatened the symbiosis of emperor and patriarch. This was the controversy over iconoclasm, or "icon smashing." Icons, painted images of Christ and the saints, had long been revered by Byzantine Christians. But some saw this as idolatry. When the Emperor Leo III began removing icons from churches and other public places (726), riots erupted throughout the empire. Leo and his successors responded by deposing uncooperative patriarchs and executing monks, the leading defenders of icons. A formal end to iconoclasm came in 787, when the Second Council of Nicea determined that icons are worthy of veneration but not worship, which must be reserved for God alone.

By the twelfth century, Byzantine missionaries had brought the Slavic peoples of Russia and the Balkans into the Eastern Church. But the position of the Church became increasingly difficult in later years as the Byzantine empire gradually collapsed under pressure from the expanding Islamic world. The empire fell in 1453 with the capture of Constantinople by the Ottoman Turks. For the next four centuries, most Eastern Christians outside Russia lived in the Ottoman empire, an Islamic state in which they were tolerated but denied full religious freedom.

The Great Schism The Great Schism, the split between Western and Eastern Christianity, came after centuries of gradual separation during which the two traditions developed their distinctive forms. Some of their differences were minor: baptism, for example, was performed by a sprinkling of water in the West but by full immersion in the East, and the West urged priests to be celibate while the East preferred them to be married. Far more divisive were the attempts of popes to control Eastern bishops and Byzantine lands. In the end, it was the West's addition of the Latin word *filioque* ("and from the Son") to the Nicene Creed that brought a final break. The East rejected this move for theological reasons and because the West had acted without sanction by an ecumenical council. In 1054, angry words over the *filioque* combined with tensions over other issues to force a division of the Church into separate Roman Catholic and Orthodox traditions. Since then, both churches have sought a restoration of their original unity, but the task is immense and progress has been slow.

The Interior of the Cathedral of Hagia Sophia. Dedicated to the "holy wisdom" embodied by Christ, this sixth-century church is the supreme achievement of Byzantine architecture. After the capture of Constantinople by the Turks in 1453, the city was renamed Istanbul and the church first became a mosque, then a museum.

The Crusades Despite their differences, Eastern and Western Christians did share a common concern over the westward advance of Islamic armies. In 1095, Pope Urban II proclaimed a military crusade intended to push the Muslims back and liberate Jerusalem. Crying *Deus vult!* ("God wills it!"), armies of knights, peasants, and townspeople set out on the First Crusade. In 1099, they celebrated their capture of Jerusalem with a frenzied slaughter of Muslims and Jews. But the crusaders were unable to defend the lands they had conquered and subsequent crusades to regain them were often military or moral disasters. Participants in the infamous Fourth Crusade (1204) never made it to the Holy Land, deciding instead to plunder Constantinople. The crusades ended at the close of the thirteenth century, having failed to deliver the Holy Land permanently into Christian hands.

Monasticism and Mysticism One of the most visible features of medieval Christianity was monasticism, a movement that began in the third century when Christians seeking a deeper experience of God withdrew into the deserts of Egypt and Syria. Most early Christian monks and nuns lived solitary lives and practiced a severe asceticism. According to legend, Macarius of Alexandria (d. 395) remained standing for periods as long as forty days, subsisting on a weekly meal of cabbage. The nun Alexandra walled herself up in a tomb for ten years, never seeing another human face.

In the medieval period, monks and nuns were brought together in monasteries governed by "rules" that regularized monastic life and discouraged extreme forms of self-denial. Both the Eastern *Rule* of Basil the Great (330–379) and the Western *Rule* of Benedict of Nursia (480–547) required monks and nuns to take vows of chastity and poverty and to spend their days in communal worship, prayer, and labor. Although the monastic aim of pursuing holiness through the imitation of Christ meant that monks and nuns spent much time in prayer and contemplation, monasteries also reached out to nearby communities, providing them with spiritual guidance, education, shelter for travelers, and care for the poor and sick.

In this fresco by Giovanni Sodoma (1477–1549), Benedictine monks of the Monte Oliveto monastery in Italy eat their meal together—just as they worked and worshiped together in accordance with the Rule of St. Benedict. Note that one of the monks reads to the others from the Bible or some other holy book as they eat.

The monastic movement also encouraged mysticism, the direct and intuitive experience of God beyond the limits of mere intellect. Eastern mystics emphasized the absolute "otherness" of God, whom they regarded as so utterly unlike anything else we experience that even concepts as basic as "being" and "nonbeing" are useless in describing divinity. Though remote in his incomprehensibility, they said, God is also near, touching human beings with a love that restores the sinful nature to its original state of perfection in "the image of God" (Genesis 1:26–27). "Love, the divine gift," wrote Maximus the Confessor (c. 580–662), "perfects human nature until it makes it appear in unity and identity with the divine nature."[8] Building on these ideas, Eastern monks such as Simeon the New Theologian (949–1022) and Gregory Palamas (c. 1296–1359) practiced Hesychasm, the cultivation of an inner quietude (*hesychia*) that brings an experience of God as divine light.

Western mystics also emphasized the power of divine love. Bernard of Clairvaux (1090–1153) compared Christ to a bridegroom whose love for the soul fills her with a bliss that transcends all earthly feeling. Bonaventure (1217–1274) described how divine love lifts the mind above rational thought, allowing it to unite with God in ecstasy. Some of the greatest Western mystics were women. Catherine of Siena (1347–1380) described a dialogue between God and a human soul seeking union with the divine in her famous *Dialogue on Divine Providence*. In her *Revelations of Divine Love*, the English recluse Julian of Norwich (1342–1416) spoke of God's love as the only means to abiding joy. "Until I am substantially united to him," she wrote, "I can never have love or rest or true happiness."[9]

Theology   In the West, early medieval theology was centered in monasteries, where learned monks and nuns engaged in debates on issues such as predestination and free will, which rituals should be considered sacraments, and the means by which sacraments actually function as vehicles of divine grace. In seeking to understand how Christ can be truly present in the eucharist, for example, medieval theologians formulated a doctrine of **transubstantiation**. According to this doctrine, the bread and wine consecrated by a priest during the eucharist become the actual body and blood of Christ in substance, though their secondary qualities, such as taste, color, and texture, remain unchanged.

The growth of major universities in the twelfth century created a new setting for theological inquiry. Here, theologians applied the science of logic as developed by Aristotle to grasp the full meaning of truths revealed in the scripture. Known as **scholasticism**, this effort became the chief intellectual enterprise of the West in the Middle Ages. The greatest of the scholastic theologians was Thomas Aquinas (1226–1274), a professor at the University of Paris. In his *Summa Theologica*, Thomas argued that while some truths can be known through reason alone, others can be grasped only through faith. Ultimately, said Thomas, there is a perfect harmony between reason and faith since both come from God.

The most distinctive feature of Eastern theology was its view that all essential Christian truths had been defined once and for all by seven ecumenical councils that completed their work in the eighth century. The basic principles of Trinitarian theology were established at the Councils of Nicea (325) and Constantinople (381). The Councils of Ephesus (431), Chalcedon (451), Constantinople II (553), and Constantinople III (680–681) formulated the Church's teaching about the union of humanity and divinity in Christ. The final ecumenical council, Nicea II (787), addressed iconoclasm. After Nicea II, Orthodox theology devoted itself largely to the analysis and elaboration of the faith as articulated by the seven ecumenical councils.

The Reformation

In the sixteenth century, a religious revolution known as the Reformation rocked Western Christianity. The Reformation's first phase is known as the Protestant Reformation because of the protests of reformers against Roman Catholic doctrines and practices. Its second phase was the Catholic Reformation, which included direct responses to Protestantism as well as reforms undertaken independently of it. Ultimately, the Reformation left Europe religiously divided, destroying forever the ancient and medieval ideal of a united Christendom.

Background to the Reformation Throughout the Middle Ages, the Roman Catholic Church engaged in constant self-examination and reform. Despite this, voices calling for change grew louder and more numerous. Some complained of corruption among the clergy. Christians north of the Alps resented taxes imposed by the Church, especially since most revenues were spent in Rome. Many were angered by the luxuries enjoyed by the popes. Those who wished to emulate the simple piety of the apostles were discouraged by the example set by Church leaders more interested in wealth and power. Calls for reform were also encouraged by the revival of humanism, a deep faith in human beings and their potential that inspired the Renaissance, a cultural movement that was flourishing at the time of the Reformation. Humanists like Desiderius Erasmus (1466–1536) argued that Christians had no need to rely on the Church. Instead, they were capable of taking charge of their spiritual lives based on their own reading and interpretation of the Bible. By the dawn of the sixteenth century, the desire for religious reform was intense and widespread. The situation was volatile. In 1517, a German monk named **Martin Luther** (1483–1546) provided a spark.

The Protestant Reformation Luther had not found peace in monastic life. Despite his efforts to be an ideal monk, he was plagued by a sense of unworthiness and fear of God's judgment that followed him from his monastery to the University of Wittenberg, where he became a professor of theology. It was in Wittenberg that Luther, reading about "the righteousness of God" in Paul's letter to the Romans (1:17), suddenly understood that God's righteousness did not consist in his desire to condemn the unrighteous but in his eagerness to forgive them. God does not set before sinners the impossible task of *earning* their salvation, Luther realized. Instead, he offers salvation through Christ and asks only that it be accepted, as an expression of divine grace, by faith. For Luther, it was faith alone, and not good works or sacraments, that "justified" sinners before God.

As Luther considered the implications of "justification by faith," he identified practices of the Church that he found objectionable. Among them was the distribution of indulgences. For centuries, popes had claimed the authority to apply the surplus merits of the saints to penitent sinners, thereby releasing them from punishment otherwise due for unconfessed sin in purgatory. By Luther's time, the outright sale of indulgences (certificates of remission of punishment in purgatory) had become an important means of raising funds to finance the papal office.

In October of 1517, Luther called for public debate on indulgences and other issues by nailing his Ninety-Five Theses, a statement of his

Portrait of Martin Luther by Lucas Cranach the Elder (1529). It was Luther who set the Protestant Reformation in motion by posting his Ninety-Five Theses on the door of the All Saints' Church in Wittenberg, Germany.

theological positions, to the door of the church in Wittenberg. Supporters quickly rallied behind Luther and soon Germany teetered on the edge of religious and social chaos. When ecclesiastical and secular leaders ordered Luther to recant his views, he refused, setting the Protestant movement in motion.

Luther now began building a Protestant theology based on three principles. First, salvation is made possible by divine "grace alone." Second, it is "by faith alone" that sinners must respond to grace. Third, "scripture alone," and not papal pronouncements or church councils, is the only authority on which Christians can completely rely. In order to make the scriptures available to the people, Luther translated the Bible into German. Because he found no mandate in the Bible for an ecclesiastical hierarchy, he rejected the authority of bishops and popes as well as the traditional distinction between clergy and laity. According to Luther's doctrine of the "priesthood of all believers," the Church is a community of equals who meet God without mediation by others. Luther accepted as sacraments only the two for which he could find evidence in scripture: baptism and the eucharist. Finally, Luther rejected purgatory, the veneration of saints, monasticism, and clerical celibacy.

Luther's intention had been only to reform the Roman Catholic Church, not to create a new Christian movement, but his teachings cut too close to the heart of Catholicism to make reconciliation possible. Moreover, the rulers of many German territories saw in Luther a champion who might end the unwelcome influence of the pope and his ally, the Holy Roman Emperor, in their lands. They encouraged a break with Rome. Fighting between Catholics and Protestants broke out. By the time it ended in 1555, Lutheranism had triumphed in northern Germany and Scandinavia, where it established itself in the form of state-sponsored churches.

Luther was soon joined by other reformers who expanded the geographical scope of the Reformation. In his *Institutes of the Christian Religion*, **John Calvin** (1509–1564) articulated Protestant doctrines with a power and clarity that put his life in danger in Catholic France. Fleeing to Switzerland, he took control of the city of Geneva and made it a Protestant theocracy. Calvin accepted the essential features of Luther's thought but went beyond Luther in simplifying worship and allowing congregations to elect their own leaders. Calvin also lent dignity to all forms of honest labor by teaching that one's occupation is a "calling" given by God. Calvinism quickly took root in Switzerland in the Swiss Reformed churches, in the Dutch Netherlands as the Dutch Reformed Church, and in England and Scotland as Presbyterianism.

In Zurich, the Swiss reformer Ulrich Zwingli (1484–1531) denounced all beliefs and practices not described in the Bible. Since the Bible makes no mention of images of Christ and the saints, candles, and incense, he removed these from Zurich's churches. A space without symbolic and decorative distractions, he reasoned, would be more likely to bring worshipers into direct communion with God. In teaching that the bread and wine used in the eucharist were mere symbols, Zwingli went far beyond Luther and Calvin, who joined him in rejecting the doctrine of transubstantiation but retained a belief in the real presence of Christ in the sacrament.

The Reformation was brought to England by King Henry VIII, depicted here in a famous portrait by the sixteenth-century painter Hans Holbein the Younger.

Alongside Lutheranism, Calvinism, and Zwinglianism developed forms of Christianity that make up what some scholars call the Radical Reformation. Anabaptists ("*re*baptizers") rejected the validity of infant baptism and insisted that one must be "born again" and baptized as an adult. Refusing to recognize the authority of civil governments and their laws, Anabaptists relied exclusively on commandments in the Bible and the inner voice of the Holy Spirit for guidance. Spiritualists placed such great importance on the inner presence of the Holy Spirit that they saw no value in traditional worship or the sacraments. Anti-Trinitarians and Rationalists rejected doctrines as basic as the Trinity and the divinity of Christ because their truth was not self-evident.

In England, the Reformation began when the pope refused the request of King Henry VIII (r. 1509–1547) for an annulment of his unhappy marriage to Catherine of Aragon. Taking matters into his own hands, Henry prevailed upon Parliament to pass an Act of Supremacy (1534) that made the king of England, not the pope, the head of the Church in England. This break marked the beginning of the Church of England and of an Anglican tradition that was later exported to England's colonies. In America, the Anglican Church, as it is sometimes called, came to be known as the Episcopal Church.

Although Henry had wanted to effect only political change, the Church of England soon felt the impact of Protestant thought on the Continent. In the end, a kind of compromise was reached that left the Church of England very "Catholic" in its theology and liturgy but clearly influenced by elements of Calvinist and Lutheran theology. While this arrangement satisfied most Anglicans, there were important groups of dissenters. Calvinist Puritans wanted to "purify" the Church of England of every vestige of Catholicism. Presbyterians, also inspired by Calvinism, wanted to replace the episcopal hierarchy with assemblies of presbyters ("elders"). Quakers rejected all formal worship and all forms of church governance.

The Catholic Reformation The primary response of the Roman Catholic Church to Protestantism was the Council of Trent (1545–1563), which reaffirmed Catholic teachings but took great care to clarify them. Against Protestant belief in the authority of scripture alone, the council held that tradition is equally authoritative. Against the Protestant reduction of the sacraments to baptism and the eucharist, it reaffirmed the seven sacraments. In response to the Protestant doctrine of justification by faith, the council insisted that faith must be expressed by good works and cited the New Testament in support of this view (e.g., Romans 2:6; 2 Corinthians 5:10). The council also upheld transubstantiation, confession, priestly celibacy, monasticism, purgatory, and the intercession of saints in heaven on behalf of the living. Although it gave no ground to Protestantism on doctrinal issues, the Council of Trent did take decisive action to end corruption in the Church, to improve the quality of education received by priests, and to ensure that essential doctrines were made clear in the sermons, or homilies, that were a part of the Mass.

Although the Council of Trent left Catholics and Protestants divided, its reforms and clarification of doctrine did reinvigorate the Roman Catholic Church, especially in its efforts to spread the faith. New religious orders such as the Jesuits, founded by Ignatius Loyola (1491–1556), spearheaded the effort to reestablish Catholicism in lands where Protestantism had become popular and to bring Christianity to parts of the world where it had never been known. For example, the Spanish Jesuit missionary Francis Xavier (1506–1552) established the Church in Japan in 1549. After mastering the Chinese language and its literature, Matteo Ricci (1552–1610), an Italian Jesuit, won thousands of converts in China. Other Catholic orders sent missionaries to India, the Philippines, and Central and South America, where Catholicism remains the dominant form of Christianity today.

Christianity in the Modern World

The Reformation was only the first challenge faced by Christianity in the modern era. Dramatic scientific, social, political, and intellectual developments also forced the Church to respond to a changing world.

As early as the Reformation era, a scientific revolution was beginning to transform the traditional understanding of the universe. For centuries, the Church had endorsed the widespread belief that the universe revolves around the earth—and therefore around humanity, the supreme object of God's love. But this view was abandoned after Nicholas Copernicus (1473–1543) and Galileo Galilei (1564–1642) proved that the earth and other planets revolve around the sun. When Isaac Newton (1642–1727) demonstrated that the universe operates according to laws of nature not found in scripture, science seemed to make the Bible unnecessary to understanding the physical world. The new scientific approach also undermined old ideas about human beings. Charles Darwin's *On the Origin of Species* (1859) challenged the biblical account of the creation of humanity. Later, the work of Sigmund Freud (1856–1939) and the French sociologist Émile Durkheim (1858–1917) suggested that religion did not originate with divine revelation but in the maladjusted psyche or out of a need to create order in society.

The scientific revolution was encouraged by growing confidence in the power of human reason. This was especially evident in the Enlightenment, a philosophical movement of the eighteenth century. Encouraged by Newton's description of nature as entirely rational, Enlightenment thinkers such as Voltaire (1694–1778), Jean-Jacques Rousseau (1712–1778), and Immanuel Kant (1724–1804) believed the way to all truth was through study of the world around us. Refusing to accept as true any idea that could not stand up under rational scrutiny, they rejected traditional Christianity except for belief in God, whose existence seemed to be implied by the orderliness of nature, and ethical ideals such as honesty and kindness to others.

Divine Command Theory

In the nineteenth century, Christianity felt the effects of liberalism and secularism, Enlightenment ideals that had inspired democratic revolutions in England's North American colonies and in France in the late 1700s. Nineteenth-century liberalism held that human beings can create an ideal society if they have the freedom to think and act without interference. For this reason, liberals called for limits on the influence of both church and state. Many liberals found it difficult to reconcile Christian beliefs about the sinfulness of human nature and the revelation of truth in scripture with their own views concerning the essential goodness of human beings and the importance of independent thought. Moreover, the progress of democracy across Europe in the nineteenth century brought the implementation of liberal policies that promoted secularism, the belief that religious ideas and institutions should have no influence on the operation of the state, especially in public education. The American ideal of the separation of church and state is just one example of this new attitude toward the place of religion in society.

The Missionary Movement Despite the challenges posed by modern thought and culture, the geographical scope of Christianity grew dramatically in the modern era as European colonial powers expanded their influence into other continents. Most Westerners brought to foreign lands a confidence in the superiority of their own culture and the conviction that they had a moral obligation to share its benefits, including Christianity, with the peoples they found there. As the British poet Rudyard Kipling (1865–1936) put it, "the white man's burden" was to civilize the world's "lesser breeds." Regrettably, the "civilizing" of non-Christians sometimes involved conversions accomplished through intimidation or outright force by conquerors and colonizers.

This mosaic of the Virgin Mary and Christ Child is from the Annunciation Basilica in Nazareth, Israel. It is a wonderful example of the desire of Christians all over the world to understand Jesus in relation to themselves and their own cultures.

The first phase of the missionary movement was largely Catholic. Although missions in China and Japan in the sixteenth century had been successful at first, these countries later suppressed Catholicism out of fear of Western influence. Catholic missions were more successful in Central and South America, Africa, and Southeast Asia, where Catholic countries such as Spain and France were able to establish colonies.

In this wood carving from West Africa, an anonymous twentieth-century artist portrays Jesus as African and manages to capture the sorrow and suffering of the savior, who was about to face crucifixion.

Protestant missions became active in the eighteenth and nineteenth centuries as England, and other Protestant countries became colonial powers in North America, Africa, and Asia.

Roman Catholicism in the Modern World The Roman Catholic Church adapted slowly to the new realities of the modern era. Shaken by the Protestant Reformation and intent on resisting modern influences, it maintained the defensive posture adopted at the Council of Trent until the middle of the twentieth century.

Perhaps the greatest challenge faced by Catholicism was secularization. In France, the Emperor Napoleon (r. 1804–1815) stripped the Church of the authority it had enjoyed for centuries over important aspects of public life. Marriage and divorce became civil procedures and responsibility for education was assumed by the state, which promoted its own ideals in public schools. In Germany, the state seized vast tracts of land from bishops and monasteries and made priests public employees. Chancellor Otto von Bismarck, outraged by the loyalty of German Catholics to Rome, launched an all-out attack on Catholicism known as the *Kulturkampf* ("struggle for civilization") in the 1870s.

Bishops gathered at the Second Vatican Council (1962–1965) in St. Peter's Basilica.

During these difficult years, Catholics turned to Rome for decisive leadership. Intent on providing it, nineteenth-century popes asserted their spiritual authority even as their influence in secular affairs rapidly eroded. This trend culminated under Pius IX, whose *Syllabus of Errors* (1864) urged Catholics to reject modern evils such as civil marriage, separation of church and state, public education, and Marxism. The climax of Pius IX's reign came with the First Vatican Council (1869–1870), which increased the power of the papacy by proclaiming a doctrine of papal infallibility. According to this doctrine, the pope cannot err when defining doctrines relating to faith and morals.

Later popes upheld Pius IX's conception of papal authority but also attempted to address modernity in constructive ways. Leo XIII (r. 1878–1903), for example, decried the social inequities created by capitalism and industrialization and outlined principles by which justice might be achieved.

A major turning point came when John XXIII convened the Second Vatican Council (1962–1965), which called for recognition of the realities of modern culture. Vatican II urged an openness to dialogue with non-Catholic Christians and described the "high regard" of the Roman Catholic Church for other religions. It also reformed Catholic worship by requiring celebration of the Mass in modern languages instead of Latin and allowing laypeople greater participation in the liturgy. Moving away from the traditional tendency to set the clergy above laypeople, the council emphasized the equality of the faithful. Since Vatican II, the Roman Catholic Church has continued to make its relevance apparent in the modern world while at the same time holding fast to many of its traditions. Thus, Pope John Paul II (r. 1978–2005) was a driving force in bringing the collapse of communism in Eastern Europe at the end of the twentieth century but made no concessions to Catholics who urged a greater role for women in the Church and an end to its stand against birth control. Since 2005, Pope Benedict XVI has presided over a Roman Catholic Church that claims over a billion adherents. It is a vigorous Church with solid historical foundations, but it suffers from a shortage of priests and a concentration of power at the highest levels of the hierarchy that gives little influence to local clergy and their churches.

Protestantism in the Modern World From the beginning, Protestantism encouraged Christians to read and interpret the Bible for themselves. It also resisted the creation of any central authority capable of imposing uniformity of belief and practice. As a result, the number of Protestant denominations grew rapidly. Today, the world's 600 million Protestant Christians belong to thousands of groups. In the United States, the largest Protestant denominations are the Methodist, Lutheran, Presbyterian, Baptist, and Reformed churches.

Despite their many differences, most Protestants share basic doctrines that go back to the Reformation. Following Luther, they believe that salvation from sin is based on faith alone. They regard the Bible as the only authoritative source of revealed truth and consider it more important than sacraments or liturgy. Finally, Protestantism allows for diverse forms of church government that give great authority to laypeople and individual congregations.

Since the early 1800s, liberalism and liberal theology have had a significant influence on older and larger Protestant denominations. Interpreting Christianity in the light of modern culture, liberal Protestants have questioned the doctrine of original sin, asked whether a loving God would allow even the worst sinners to suffer in hell, and emphasized the human element in the composition of the scriptures. Embracing the liberal idea that the essential goodness of human beings makes progress toward a better world possible, they have advocated social activism based on the teachings of Jesus as a means of making the kingdom of God a reality. Liberal Protestants have played important roles in the civil rights and anti-war movements and struggled to open the Church to greater participation by women, homosexuals, and other groups.

At the other end of the Protestant spectrum are three important conservative movements: fundamentalism, evangelicalism, and Pentecostalism.

Fundamentalism emerged a century ago as a reaction against liberal theology, the theory of evolution, the academic study of the Bible, and other features of modern culture that conservatives found threatening. The movement takes its name from *The Fundamentals*, a series of booklets that identified five doctrines essential to Christianity: (1) the literal inerrancy of the Bible, (2) the divinity and virgin birth of Christ, (3) Christ's atonement for human sin on the cross, (4) the bodily resurrection of Christ, and (5) the imminent Second Coming of Christ. Seeking to defend these doctrines, leaders like the television evangelist Jerry Falwell made fundamentalism a powerful force in American culture in the 1970s and 1980s. Fundamentalists also fought to defend what they called "traditional values" against feminism, gay rights, legalized abortion, and the elimination of prayer in public schools.

Fundamentalism grew out of **evangelicalism**, a much larger movement with roots in the "Great Awakening," a revival of religious fervor that swept through England and North America in the eighteenth century. As its name suggests, evangelicalism encourages the preaching and sharing of the gospel (Greek *evangelion*). It also emphasizes the need for every Christian to have a conversion experience, often described as being "born again" (John 3:3), that leads to a personal relationship with Jesus Christ. Evangelicals regard the Bible as the sole basis of faith, though they do not always insist on its literal interpretation. Like fundamentalists, many evangelicals believe that the end of the age and Second Coming of Christ will occur in the near future. Evangelicalism is a fast-growing worldwide movement that is making its presence felt both in older Protestant denominations and in new movements. It has become a major force in Africa and Asia and is particularly strong in North America. Recent estimates suggest that more than one-fourth of the population of the United States is evangelical.[10]

Pentecostalism takes its name from the holiday of Pentecost, which commemorates the descent of the Holy Spirit upon Jesus' followers after his ascension to heaven. According to Acts 1:1–4, these Spirit-filled believers were empowered to "speak in other tongues," to prophesy, and to perform healings in the name of Christ. Since its beginnings in America in the early twentieth century, the Pentecostal movement has sought to reclaim this feature of earliest Christianity. Its most essential belief is that conversion must be followed by a "baptism in the Spirit" made evident by an ability to speak in tongues and at least one of the other "spiritual gifts" described by Paul in 1 Corinthians 12–14. The belief that the ecstatic experience of God belongs at the center of Christian life is unmistakable in Pentecostal churches, where enthusiastic worshipers raise their arms in praise, speak in tongues, and sometimes dance or weep. The phenomenal growth of Pentecostalism during the last century has made it a major force in contemporary Christianity throughout the world. Today, Pentecostalism is the most popular form of Protestantism in Latin America, where it is winning converts from Roman Catholicism. The astonishing growth of The Universal Church of the Kingdom of God is an excellent example.

Pentecostal worship at the Catedral Evangelica de Chile in Santiago, Chile.

Founded in Brazil in 1977, it has spread throughout Latin America and now claims 5,000 individual congregations served by 15,000 pastors. In Africa, Christians have combined elements of Pentecostalism with features of indigenous religions to create new forms of Christianity. Pentecostalism has also spread throughout Asia. The 700,000 members of the Korean Yoido Full Gospel Church make it the largest Christian congregation in the world.[11]

Orthodoxy in the Modern World We saw earlier that the Ottoman Turks completed their conquest of the Byzantine empire, the home of Orthodox Christianity, with their capture of Constantinople in 1453. The Ottoman state tolerated the Orthodox Church but it also brought it under government control. When Greeks, Bulgarians, Serbs, and other Orthodox peoples began declaring their independence from the declining Ottoman empire in the 1800s, they established independent national churches. Today's 225 million Orthodox Christians belong to fifteen autonomous churches, including the Church of Greece, the Russian Orthodox Church, and the Orthodox Church in America. The patriarch of Constantinople retains an honorary primacy among Orthodox bishops but has no real authority over them. Despite this, the Orthodox churches are united by a tradition of shared theology and liturgy they trace back to the time of the apostles.

Orthodox Christianity resisted the influence of Western rationalism and liberalism in the eighteenth and nineteenth centuries. But Western influence in the form of Marxism had a devastating effect on Orthodoxy after the Bolshevik Revolution in Russia (1917) and the creation of a bloc of communist states in Eastern Europe after World War II. Because these states saw all religion as an obstacle to the achievement of their social and political goals, they took drastic measures to strip the Church of its influence. Priests and monks were imprisoned, seminaries were closed, and church property was seized. The collapse of communism in the early 1990s brought a restoration of religious freedom and the revival of Orthodoxy. Since then, a dramatic rise in church attendance has testified to the commitment of millions of Russians, Ukrainians, Georgians, Bulgarians, Romanians, and Serbs to Orthodox Christianity.

Christianity Today and Tomorrow: Trends and Prospects

We live in a rapidly changing world. What the future holds for Christianity is difficult to predict, though there are signs of the directions it is likely to take. Some of the most surprising indicators are demographic. Just a century ago, 80 percent of Christians lived in Europe and North America. Today, 60 percent live in Africa, Asia, and Latin America. This trend will continue. According to some projections, by 2050 only one-fifth of Christians will be non-Hispanic Caucasians. The vast majority will live in the southern hemisphere. This global shift will bring major changes as African and South American Christians assume leadership roles in the Church and as

Christian teachings are applied in ways that address their unique social and political, as well as religious, concerns.

The beginnings of theological change along these lines became evident in the mid-twentieth century in the form of liberation theology, which grew out of the concern of Latin American priests such as Gustavo Gutiérrez and Leonardo Boff for the plight of the poor. Originating with Gutiérrez's *A Theology of Liberation* (1971), liberation theology calls for radical action to correct the social, political, and economic injustices perpetrated against impoverished Latin Americans by landowners, governments, and the Church itself. It holds that the Church must work to ensure at least the basic necessities of life for all human beings. Moreover, it finds a scriptural basis for its views in the New Testament ideal of the Church as a community of believers committed to caring for each other's material as well as spiritual needs.

The principles of liberation theology have been put to work outside Latin America. In 1970, James Cone (b. 1938) published *A Black Theology of Liberation*, in which he criticized traditional black Christianity in America, claiming that its emphasis on a better life in heaven robs blacks of dignity on earth. In another work, *Black Theology and Black Power*, Cone wrote that "the idea of heaven is irrelevant for Black Theology. The Christian cannot waste time contemplating the next world. . . . Jesus' work is essentially one of liberation."[12] In a similar way, feminist theologians have called for liberation from a Christian worldview based solely on the experience of men. In her *Beyond God the Father* (1973), Mary Daly (1928–2010) argued that the Christian habit of thinking of God as Father allows misogyny to masquerade as a spiritual norm, thereby relegating women to a secondary status in the Church. Rosemary Radford Ruether (b. 1936), another influential feminist theologian, urges a new way of thinking about God as "God/ess" and has suggested the creation of churches open only to women and men committed to the rights and equality of women. Theologies of liberation are a vibrant new voice on the theological landscape. Their insistence on taking seriously the biblical ideals of justice and righteousness will no doubt play an important role in shaping Christian thought and practice as the Church moves through the present century.

Even before the advent of feminist theology, the role of women in positions of church leadership began to expand. Isolated ordinations of women ministers in Protestant churches began in the mid-nineteenth century. Today, major Protestant denominations such

The ordination of women as pastors is becoming increasingly common in Protestant denominations.

as Lutherans, Presbyterians, and Methodists regularly ordain women. While the number of women ministers and priests within Protestantism will continue to grow, the Roman Catholic and Orthodox churches remain firmly opposed to the ordination of women. As representatives of Christ, the Orthodox say, priests must bear a "natural resemblance" to him, which includes the quality of maleness.[13] Although women have faced serious obstacles in entering the clergy, they have become a powerful force in theological scholarship. As academics specializing in biblical studies, ethics, and theology, they are communicating new ideas and insights that are bringing profound change to Christian thought.

Christians are beginning to develop a greater sense of responsibility for the health of the environment, which has been endangered by industrialization, overpopulation, and the careless exploitation of natural resources. Christian environmentalists urge their coreligionists to remember that the earth is God's creation and therefore deserving of their respect and care. They point out that the scriptural story that tells how God gave "dominion" over the earth to Adam and Eve (Genesis 1) does not imply divine permission to ravage it. Human beings do not own the earth, they say; instead, God has made them its stewards. As the theologian and environmentalist James A. Nash has put it, dominion understood in this way means a "nurturing and serving love" of the world God has made.[14]

Another important development has been the increasing number of lay movements. Traditionally, the ordained clergy have taken responsibility for determining how the mission of the Church should be carried out. The new lay movements turn this model on its head. Founded, directed, and composed mainly of laypeople, they seek to strengthen the spiritual lives of members through service to others in the form of evangelization, charitable work, or social justice advocacy. Among the larger Roman Catholic lay movements are Focolare and the Community of St. Egidio. Founded in Italy in 1943, Focolare (Italian, "hearth") has a presence in 182 countries. It seeks to foster unity among Christians and universal brotherhood among religious and nonreligious people worldwide through education, publications, and other means. The Community of St. Egidio began in 1968 through the initiative of a high school student. Taking its name from a small church in Rome, the Community is active in more than seventy countries. With the aim of alleviating the suffering caused by injustice and war, it has helped to end crises in countries such as Mozambique (1990–1992), Algeria (1994–1995), and Guatemala (1996). One of the most visible Protestant lay movements is the *Evangelische Kirchentag*, or Protestant Church Congress. The Kirchentag is a five-day event held every two years in a German city. Nearly 200,000 participants meet to address theological, social, and political issues in speeches, performances, study groups, and other events. Like most lay movements, the Kirchentag has made the solidarity and unity of all Christians worldwide one of its highest ideals. Accordingly, the 2003 and 2010 Kirchentags were jointly organized by Roman Catholic and Protestant churches.

Although the older Roman Catholic, Orthodox, and mainline Protestant churches continue to dominate the Christian scene in Europe and North America, the last century has seen an explosion of new Christian churches, most of them in the developing world. In Africa, thousands of new denominations combine elements of African cultures with features of traditional Christianity. The Nazareth Baptist Church of South Africa, for example, mixes elements of Zulu tradition with Christianity. Its 4 million members regard its founder, Isaiah Shembe, as an African messiah. In Asia, the most visible new Christian movement is the Unification Church. Founded in Korea in 1954 by Sun Myung Moon, the Unification Church has roots in both Presbyterianism and East Asian traditions. Regarded by his followers as the realization of the Second Coming of Christ, Reverend Moon is known for exercising firm control over the personal lives of church members, even to the point of selecting their marriage partners.

A final issue that will affect the future of Christianity is ecumenism. The aim of the ecumenical movement (Greek *oikoumene*, "the inhabited world") is the restoration of Christian unity. It is based on the New Testament ideal of a single, universal church. This ideal has survived throughout the course of Christian history despite the fact that cultural and historical forces have contributed to a continuing process of fragmentation. It was not until the twentieth century that organizations such as the World Council of Churches took concrete action to promote Christian unity. In the past few decades, most larger churches have declared their interest in working toward this goal, and many have established cooperative agreements with each other. It may be that further progress will occur in the twenty-first century, but a unity that truly reflects the underlying spiritual communion of all Christians is still far off.

CONCLUSION

With a history reaching back 2,000 years, Christianity has proven to be a durable religion. Like other religions that have met the test of time, much of its vitality lies in the meaning its message has had for countless adherents through the centuries. History, geography, culture, and other forces have produced many forms of Christianity, but they can all be traced back to a single figure, Jesus of Nazareth, whose teachings revolutionized the world in which he lived and continue to shape our own. Despite the differences among Christians, we can discern an essential Christianity in which they all share and which goes back to Jesus and to the New Testament texts that expound the meaning of his teachings, life, death, and resurrection: There is a single, transcendent, all-powerful, and personal God who created the universe as an expression of divine love and who seeks loving union with humanity.

In addressing the most basic questions arising from human existence, the Christian message has had an incalculable influence on individual lives. But it has also contributed to the formation of entire civilizations, shaping their political and social institutions, informing their cultural values and ideals, and inspiring some of their greatest achievements in art, architecture, and literature.

It seems that there are two great issues we must consider, however briefly, in concluding our discussion of Christianity. The first is the role Christianity will play in shaping the world of the future. How will Christians respond to the environmental, social, and political problems our world faces? What actions will they take in promoting justice? How will they apply the gospel message in acknowledging and protecting the rights of women, homosexuals, and the poor—both inside and outside the Church? The second issue is how Christianity will be affected by the rapid change we see all around us. Will its traditional forms and institutions remain solidly entrenched? As the world's Christian population becomes increasingly concentrated in Africa, South America, and Asia, how will the religious and cultural traditions of these regions influence a religion with a history that has been played out largely in Europe and North America? Of course, we cannot be certain of the answers to questions like these. We can be certain only that Christianity, the world's largest religion, will remain a major force in the world in which we live.

SEEKING ANSWERS

What Is Ultimate Reality?

Christianity teaches that there is a single, personal, transcendent, and all-powerful God— a God who is one in essence but threefold in his manifestations as Father, Son, and Holy Spirit. God created a perfect world as an expression of divine love, but it has fallen into imperfection due to human sin. Like Jews and Muslims, Christians believe that God wants to be known in and by Creation, and especially by humanity. For Christians, the supreme revelation of the divine nature is found in Jesus Christ, who was the very incarnation of God. They also believe that God has revealed himself in other ways, such as through scripture and through the immensity and beauty of the universe.

How Should We Live in This World?

For Christians, the fundamental principle on which human life in this world should be based is love. Jesus spoke of love for God and one's neighbor as the essence of scripture and described it in a radical way. Even enemies must be loved and forgiven. This demanding conception of love is one of the essential ideals in Christianity. It is also one that requires great effort. To achieve it, Christians find inspiration in study and reflection on scripture, through prayer, and in fellowship with other Christians who take love seriously. Christians find good examples of love and other virtues in the lives of the saints, whom they seek to emulate. They also believe that the sacraments offer a

(continued)

spiritual nourishment that is helpful in the cultivation of lives they attempt to live in imitation of Christ.

What Is Our Ultimate Purpose?

For Christians, the ultimate goal of human existence is union with God. As Augustine wrote in the fifth century, "You have made us for yourself, O Lord, and our hearts are restless until they find rest in you." The path to reunion with God is through Jesus Christ, whose sacrificial death, an expression of God's love, atoned for all human sin. When human beings respond in faith to God's love, or grace, they are brought into union with the divine. Christians hope to share in the resurrection of Christ, which leads to eternal blessedness in union with God. But there is also the possibility of eternal separation from God. Because the Bible offers few concrete details about these two possibilities, traditionally understood as heaven and hell, they have been interpreted in many different ways.

REVIEW QUESTIONS

For Review

1. What were the means by which the Christian movement defined orthodox belief and established ecclesiastical authority in late antiquity?

2. How did the Roman Catholic, Orthodox, and Protestant traditions within Christianity emerge from the "catholic" or "universal" Christianity of the first millennium? What were the main factors that contributed to the formation of these traditions?

3. What are the seasons and holy days of the liturgical year? What is their significance for Christians? How are they observed?

4. What is the doctrine of the Trinity? Why is this doctrine central to Christianity?

5. What are the major challenges Christianity has encountered in the modern era? How has it responded to them?

For Further Reflection

1. What are some of the more important ways in which basic Christian beliefs are expressed outwardly in worship, the sacraments, prayer, and other devotional practices?

2. If asked by a friend, how would you describe the essence of Christianity? Are there teachings embraced by all (or, at least, most) forms of Christianity?

3. How do Christian beliefs about God/ultimate reality, human nature, the world, and the ultimate goal or purpose of human existence compare with those of the closely related religions of Judaism and Islam?

4. How do Christian beliefs about these same issues compare with those of religions such as Hinduism, Buddhism, Daoism, Confucianism, Sikhism, and Jainism?

5. Do you think the Christian ecumenical movement has a realistic chance of restoring the original unity of the Christian religion?

GLOSSARY

apostle In the New Testament, Jesus' disciples, sent out to preach and baptize, are called apostles (Greek *apostolos*, "one who is sent out"). Paul of Tarsus and some other early Christian leaders also claimed this title. Because of their close association with Jesus, the apostles were accorded a place of honor in the early Church.

apostolic succession According to this Roman Catholic and Orthodox doctrine, the spiritual authority conferred by Jesus on the apostles has been transmitted through an unbroken line of bishops, who are their successors.

baptism Performed by immersion in water or a sprinkling with water, baptism is a sacrament in which an individual is cleansed of sin and admitted into the Church.

bishop Responsible for supervising other priests and their congregations within specific regions known as dioceses, bishops are regarded by Roman Catholic and Orthodox Christians as successors of the apostles.

Calvin, John (1509–1564) One of the leading figures of the Protestant Reformation, Calvin is notable for his *Institutes of the Christian Religion* and his emphasis on the absolute power of God, the absolute depravity of human nature, and the absolute dependence of human beings on divine grace for salvation.

Christmas An annual holiday commemorating the birth of Jesus, Christmas is observed by Western Christians on December 25. While many Orthodox Christians celebrate Christmas on this date, others observe the holiday on January 7.

church In the broadest sense, "church" refers to the universal community of Christians, but the term can also refer to a particular tradition within Christianity (such as the Roman Catholic Church or the Lutheran Church) or to an individual congregation of Christians.

Easter An annual holiday commemorating the resurrection of Christ, Easter is a "moveable feast" whose date changes from year to year, though it is always celebrated in spring (as early as March 22 and as late as May 8).

Epiphany An annual holiday commemorating the "manifestation" of the divinity of the infant Jesus, Epiphany is celebrated by most Western Christians on January 6. Most Eastern Christians observe it on January 19.

eucharist (*yoó-ka-rist*) Also known as the Lord's Supper and Holy Communion, the eucharist is a sacrament celebrated with consecrated bread and wine in commemoration of Jesus' Last Supper with his disciples.

evangelicalism This Protestant movement stresses the importance of the conversion experience, the Bible as the only reliable authority in matters of faith, and preaching the gospel. In recent decades, evangelicalism has become a major force in North American Christianity.

fundamentalism Originating in the early 1900s, this movement in American Protestantism was dedicated to defending doctrines it identified as fundamental to Christianity against perceived threats posed by modern culture.

Gospel In its most general sense, "gospel" means the "good news" (from Old English *godspel*, which translates the Greek *evangelion*) about Jesus Christ. The New Testament gospels of Matthew, Mark, Luke, and John are proclamations of the good news concerning the life, teachings, death, and resurrection of Jesus Christ.

grace Derived from the Latin *gratia* (a "gift" or "love"), "grace" refers to God's love for humanity, expressed in Jesus Christ and through the sacraments.

icons Painted images of Christ and the saints, icons are used extensively in the Orthodox Church.

Inquisition The investigation and suppression of heresy by the Roman Catholic Church, the Inquisition began in the twelfth century and was formally concluded in the middle of the nineteenth century.

(continued)

GLOSSARY (*continued*)

kingdom of God God's rule or dominion over the universe and human affairs. The kingdom of God is one of the primary themes in the teaching of Jesus.

liturgy The liturgy (from Greek, *leitourgia*, "a work of the people" in honor of God) is the basic order of worship in Christian churches. It consists of prescribed prayers, readings, and rituals.

Logos In its most basic sense, the Greek *logos* means "word," but it also means "rational principle," "reason," or "divine reason." The Gospel of John uses *logos* in the sense of the "divine reason" through which God created and sustains the universe when it states that "the Word became flesh" in Jesus Christ (John 1:14).

Lord's Prayer A prayer attributed to Jesus, the Lord's Prayer serves as a model of prayer for Christians. Also known as the "Our Father" (since it begins with these words), its most familiar form is found in the Gospel of Matthew (6:9–13).

Luther, Martin (1483–1536) A German monk who criticized Roman Catholic doctrines and practices in his Ninety-Five Theses (1517), Luther was the original leader and one of the seminal thinkers of the Protestant Reformation.

Messiah In the Old Testament, the Hebrew word "messiah" ("anointed one") refers to one who has been set apart by God for some special purpose and, in particular, the liberation of the Jewish people from oppression. In Christianity, Jesus of Nazareth is recognized as fulfillment of Old Testament prophecies concerning the Messiah.

Nicene Creed A profession of faith formulated by the Councils of Nicea (325) and Constantinople (381), the Nicene Creed articulates the Christian doctrine of the Trinity.

Original Sin Formulated by St. Augustine in the fourth century, the doctrine of Original Sin states that the sin of Adam and Eve affected all of humanity, so that all human beings are born with a sinful nature.

Orthodox Church Also known as the Eastern Orthodox Church and the Orthodox Catholic Church, the Orthodox Church is the Eastern branch of Christianity that separated from the Western branch (the Roman Catholic Church) in 1054.

parable According to the gospels of Matthew, Mark, and Luke, Jesus made extensive use of parables—short, fictional stories that use the language and imagery of everyday life to illustrate moral and religious truths.

Paul of Tarsus A first-century apostle who founded churches throughout Asia Minor, Macedonia, and Greece. Paul was also the author of many of the letters, or epistles, found in the New Testament.

Pentecost A holiday celebrated by Christians in commemoration of the outpouring of the Holy Spirit on the disciples of Jesus as described in the second chapter of the New Testament book of Acts.

Pentecostalism A movement that emphasizes the importance of spiritual renewal and the experience of God through baptism in the Holy Spirit, Pentecostalism is a primarily Protestant movement that has become extremely popular in recent decades.

Protestant Christianity One of the three major traditions in Christianity (along with Roman Catholicism and Orthodoxy), Protestantism began in the sixteenth century as a reaction against medieval Roman Catholic doctrines and practices.

purgatory In Roman Catholicism, purgatory is an intermediate state between earthly life and heaven in which the debt for unconfessed sin is expiated.

Roman Catholic Church One of the three major traditions within Christianity (along with Orthodoxy and Protestantism), the Roman Catholic Church, which recognizes the primacy of the bishop of Rome, or pope, has historically been the dominant church in the West.

(*continued*)

GLOSSARY (*continued*)

rosary Taking its name from the Latin *rosarium* ("garland of roses"), the rosary is a traditional form of Roman Catholic devotion in which practitioners make use of a string of beads in reciting prayers.

Sacraments The sacraments are rituals in which material elements such as bread, wine, water, and oil serve as visible symbols of an invisible grace conveyed to recipients.

saint A saint is a "holy person" (Latin *sanctus*). Veneration of the saints and belief in their intercession on behalf of the living is an important feature of Roman Catholic and Orthodox Christianity.

Scholasticism Represented by figures such as Peter Abelard, Thomas Aquinas, and William of Ockham, scholasticism was the medieval effort to reconcile faith and reason using the philosophy of Aristotle.

sin The violation of God's will in thought or action.

transubstantiation According to this Roman Catholic doctrine, the bread and wine consecrated by a priest in the eucharist become the body and blood of Christ and retain only the appearance, not the substance, of bread and wine.

Trinity According to the Christian doctrine of the Trinity, God is a single divine substance or essence consisting in three "persons."

SUGGESTIONS FOR FURTHER READING

Bowden, John. *Encyclopedia of Christianity*. New York: Oxford University Press, 2005. A one-volume collection of short scholarly articles on hundreds of topics.

Dowell, Graham. *The Heart Has Its Seasons: Travelling through the Christian Year*. Worthing, England: Churchman, 1989. A superb introduction to the significance and celebration of the "seasons" of the liturgical year.

Dowley, Tim, and Wright, David. *Introduction to the History of Christianity*. Minneapolis, MN: Fortress Press, 1995. Includes hundreds of photos, maps, charts, and articles on topics of special interest.

Ehrman, Bart. *The New Testament: A Historical Introduction to the Early Christian Writings*. New York: Oxford University Press, 2000. An excellent introduction to the New Testament texts and selected Christian texts from the second century.

Marsden, George. *Understanding Fundamentalism and Evangelicalism*. Grand Rapids, MI: William B. Eerdmans, 1991. Describes the essential features of these two movements and their involvement in politics and science.

McGrath, Alister. *Theology: The Basics*. Malden, MA: Blackwell, 2004. Individual chapters focus on specific issues such as God, Jesus, Faith, Salvation, and Heaven. Emphasis on Roman Catholic and Protestant thought.

Ware, Timothy (Kallistos). *The Orthodox Church*. New York: Penguin, 1993. A classic presentation of the history, thought, and practices of the Orthodox tradition by one of its greatest spokespersons.

White, James. *Introduction to Christian Worship*, 3rd ed. Nashville: Abingdon Press, 2001. An ideal book for beginners interested in the history and forms of Christian worship.

ONLINE SOURCES

"From Jesus to Christ: The First Christians"

pbs.org/wgbh/pages/frontline/shows/religion

From the PBS documentary series *Frontline*, this website features the full documentary as well as supplemental materials from theologians, historians, and archaeologists.

Catholic Online

catholic.org

This online resource provides access to information "on all things Catholic," including saints, holy days, Roman Catholic theology, and announcements from the Vatican.

Orthodox Wiki

orthodoxwiki.org

This online resource includes nearly 4,000 articles on all aspects of Orthodox Christianity. A great place to begin an exploration of Orthodoxy.

Theopedia

theopedia.com

An online "encyclopedia of biblical Christianity" with articles on hundreds of topics written from an evangelical Protestant perspective.

Pilgrims circumnambulate the Ka'ba in Mecca, Saudi
Arabia. The pilgrimage to Mecca, known as the *hajj*, is
a once-in-a-lifetime duty for devout Muslims.

ISLAM

FAINT TRACES OF DAWN light up the tops of tall coconut palms and lush
mango trees in a village in Zanzibar, an East African island in the Indian
Ocean. Amina, a woman in her early thirties and a devout Muslim, rises
from her bed. She was awakened by the sound of the call to prayer from
the local mosque. In the open-air courtyard of her house, she begins
her morning ablutions to prepare for the first of her daily prayers. She
takes cool water from the cistern in the courtyard and carefully washes
her face, hands, and feet, and rinses her mouth, nose, and ears. She
also wets her head and hair. Before each of the five daily prayers, Amina
performs similar ablutions. Although she occasionally wears eye makeup
and lipstick, she is careful to avoid nail polish. She explains that all such
adornment must be removed to purify herself for each prayer; makeup is
easily removed with water, but nail polish is not.

After her ablutions, Amina returns to the house, covers her head and
shoulders with a clean cotton wrap, and spreads a colorful woven prayer
mat on the floor next to her bed. She removes her sandals, steps onto
the mat, and begins the first of the five prescribed daily ritual prayers
that are expected of all devout Muslims. The prayers are called *salat*, and
consist of the recitation of verses from the **Qur'an**, the sacred text of Islam, accompanied by specific bodily movements. Together, the cycles of
prayer and movement are called *raka*. Amina has made her daily prayers

Pilgrims circumnambulate the Ka'ba in Mecca, Saudi
Arabia. The pilgrimage to Mecca, known as the *hajj*, is
a once-in-a-lifetime duty for devout Muslims.

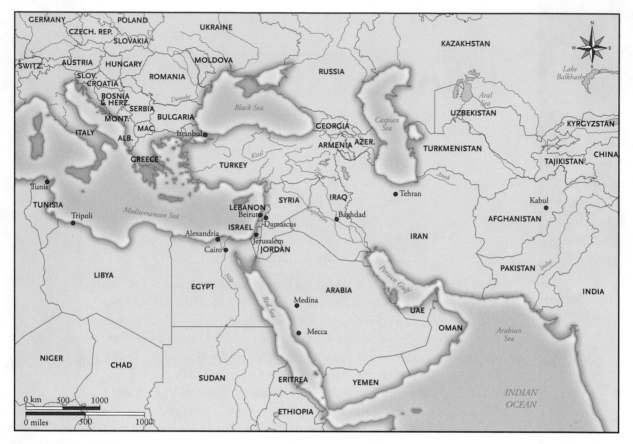

Significant sites in the history of Islam.

since she was a young girl. As a child, her mother and elder sisters taught her how to pray; eventually, she will do the same for her own children. She begins the prayer standing, then kneels, bows her forehead to the ground, and kneels again in accordance with her recitation. Hand movements accompany the bodily postures. Daily prayer is an essential part of Muslim worship. Through prayer, Amina is acknowledging to herself and her community that she is submitting herself to the will of God—an important tenet of the Islamic faith. In fact, the term Muslim means "one who submits" in Arabic.

Amina prays alone in her modest home, but men in her community typically gather at the local mosque for each of the daily prayers, which are led by a prayer leader called an **imam**. Like women, most Zanzibari men cover their heads when praying, most often with a brimless, embroidered cap. Although in some parts of the Muslim world women regularly pray in mosques, in Zanzibar, particularly in rural areas, it is uncommon for women to do so. However, women often gather together at mosques for other reasons, such as Qur'an study groups and sessions in religious instruction.

When she completes her prayers, Amina rolls up her prayer mat and sets it aside for later. She reads a few verses from the Qur'an in the early morning light, and then begins the first tasks of her day—making tea and sweeping the courtyard.

Amina is one of about 1.4 billion Muslims living in the world today; Islam is second only to Christianity in numbers of adherents. Amina lives in Africa, and most of the world's Muslims live in South and Southeast Asia, not in the Arabic-speaking countries of the Middle East. In fact, Arab Muslims make up less than 20 percent of the total Muslim population worldwide. The country with the largest Muslim population in the world is the Southeast Asian nation of Indonesia, followed closely by Pakistan, India, and Bangladesh. Many countries in Africa also have very large Muslim populations. Today, there are nearly 5 million Muslims in the United States,[1] and the number of Muslims in North America is increasing rapidly, mostly through immigration. Muslims also make up significant minority populations in many parts of Western Europe, especially in France, where they make up about 9 percent of the population.[2]

Islam developed in the Arabian Peninsula and rapidly spread through the Middle East, Asia, and Africa. Because of its global presence, Islam is practiced, understood, and interpreted in diverse ways in many different countries, cultures, and communities. However, certain beliefs and practices can be considered universal parts of

World Muslim population.

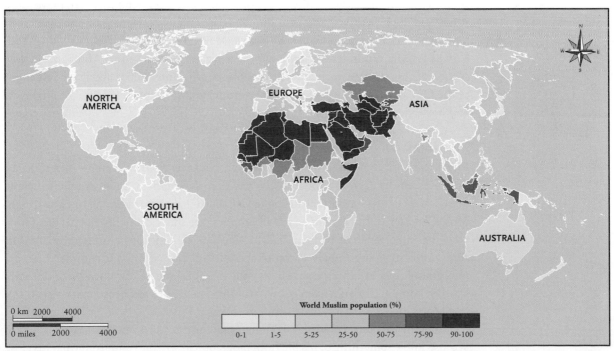

World Muslim population (%)

| 0-1 | 1-5 | 5-25 | 25-50 | 50-75 | 75-90 | 90-100 |

Muslim religious life. Most important of these is the monotheistic belief in the one-ness of **Allah**, which is the Arabic term for God. Secondly, Muslims recognize **Muhammad**, who received the message of the Qur'an from God, as the final prophet in a long line of prophets sent to humanity by God. The Qur'an is believed to be the word of God and is the holy text of Muslims. In addition, Muslims around the world share the observance of the five pillars of worship practice. The term "**Islam**" (Arabic, "submission") reflects Muslim belief in the importance of submitting to God's will.

THE TEACHINGS OF ISLAM

Islam arose in the Arabian Peninsula in the seventh century, when Muslims believe that a man called Muhammad began receiving communication from God. The primary source of Islamic teachings is the Qur'an, which Muslims believe is the word of God as revealed to Muhammad. According to Muslim belief, Islam was not introduced as a new religion. Rather, the revelations of the Qur'an to Muhammad were a reawakening or reintroduction of the original monotheistic faith of the prophet Abraham, a figure who is also important to Jews (Chapter 10) and Christians (Chapter 11). Islam is considered one of the Abrahamic religions along with Judaism and Christianity, and the three religions share a great deal. Although many people in pre-Islamic Arabia were polytheists, significant numbers of Jews and Christians also lived in the region. People in Arabia were therefore familiar with biblical stories and characters, and several of these are mentioned in the Qur'an. In the Islamic view, Abraham (or Ibrahim, as Muslims call him) was the original monotheist who received a revelation from God, a revelation that taught him the true religion centering on the oneness of God. Muslims believe that when Muhammad received the revelations of the Qur'an, he was given a reminder for humanity of what God conveyed to Abraham. In this section of this chapter, we will learn about what Muslims believe about the revelation of the Qur'an to Muhammad. In a later section, we will explore his life, his prophecy, and his leadership roles.

Muhammad and the Revelations

Muslims consider Muhammad (c. 570–632 c.e.) the final messenger in a series of prophets sent by God to humanity. In addition to Abraham, these prophets include many other figures important in the Jewish and Christian traditions, such as Noah, Moses, and Jesus. In Muslim belief, all prophets are solely human—not divine. However, the importance of Muhammad to Muslims should not be underestimated. In addition to receiving the revelation of the Qur'an, Muhammad is considered an extraordinary man in all respects. He was the religious and political leader of the early Muslim community and, even today—fourteen centuries after his death—his life is considered an example for all Muslims to follow.

Some of what we know about Muhammad and his life comes from the Qur'an. We also know something of his life from biographical writings and from what his close friends, associates, and family (who are known together as his *companions*) observed about him and passed on in reports. In addition, there are many stories and legends about the Prophet. Because most of what we know about Muhammad comes from sources that were compiled by Muslims after he became a prophet, we know very little about his early life. Muslims do not believe that Muhammad was divine, but rather consider him to be *al-insan al-kamil*, the ideal human. And although he was a prophet, in many respects he lived the life of a normal man. He had a family, earned a living, and was active in his community.

Most Muslims believe that Muhammad was a spiritual man and a religious seeker even before he began receiving the revelation of the Qur'an. He was considered a devout monotheist even at a time in which many of his contemporaries were polytheists, and it is said that he often meditated alone on the oneness of God. When he reached the age of 40, in the year 610 c.e., the angel Gabriel (known in Arabic as Jibril) visited Muhammad while he was praying in an isolated cave outside Mecca. Muhammad heard a voice that told him that he was the messenger of God and commanded him to "Recite!" Muhammad is said to have been awed and bewildered. He is thought to have hesitated three times at Jibril's command, because as an illiterate man he did not feel he was able to recite. Eventually he repeated the words the angel told him to recite, and these are considered to be the first revealed verses of the Qur'an. The rest of the Qur'an was revealed to Muhammad over the next twenty-three years.

Muhammad confided in his wife, **Khadija**, a wealthy and successful businesswoman, about the revelations. She listened carefully, and believed his message. Because she was the first to believe the truth of the message received by Muhammad, Khadija is considered to be the first convert to Islam. Other early followers were Muhammad's close friends and family members. Muhammad's young cousin 'Ali, who later became his son-in-law when he married Muhammad's daughter Fatima, was the first male convert to Islam. A friend of Muhammad's called Abu Bakr was also an early convert, and he became Muhammad's father-in-law much later in life when, after Khadija's death, Muhammad married Abu Bakr's daughter.

After the first revelations, Muhammad began a life of preaching in Mecca. The verses of the Qur'an that he received during this time emphasized the oneness of God—the central tenet of the Islamic faith. Muhammad preached this idea to the people of Mecca, and also taught about morality, social justice for the poor and downtrodden, and the inevitability of the Day of Judgment.

Muhammad was not the only prophet in the Islamic tradition. The Qur'an mentions several prophets by name and refers to the existence of many others. Muhammad, however, is known as the "seal of the prophets," which means that the door of prophecy was closed—or "sealed"—with him because he was the final prophet. Muslims believe that the revelations to Muhammad came at a time when it was necessary to reawaken understanding of God's message to humanity.

The Holy Qur'an

The Qur'an is the sacred text of Islam, and it is considered the literal word of God. The Arabic word *qur'an* means "recitation" and the book is called such because Muhammad received the Qur'an orally and taught it to his followers in the same way. When the Qur'an was eventually written down, the text was corrected by the oral knowledge of those who had committed it to memory. Even today, printed copies of the Qur'an bear the stamp of approval of a person known as *hafidh* or "keeper of the Qur'an." This is a person who knows the entire Qur'an by heart.

The Qur'an was not revealed all at once to Muhammad, but rather gradually over a period of more than twenty years until his death. The language of the Qur'an is classical Arabic, and stylistically it resembles the beauty of the Bedouin poetry of the time in which it was revealed. However, it is important to note that Muslims do not regard the Qur'an as poetry. This is because poetry is a human endeavor, and Muslims view the Qur'an as solely the word of God. Reciting, reading and studying the Qur'an are an important part of daily life for devout Muslims today, in all parts of the world.

The Qur'an is not a narrative text, which means that it does not tell a story from beginning to end (although there are some stories within the text). The Qur'an consists of 114 chapters, each of which is called a **surah**. Each *surah* consists of several verses. The *surah*s are not organized around specific topics or time periods, and they are not arranged in the order of revelation, as one might expect. Rather, they are arranged roughly from the longest to the shortest, with the exception of the opening *surah*, which is quite short. Some *surah*s are only a few verses long, and the longest has almost 300 verses. Each *surah* has a title. The titles were not revealed to Muhammad, but were rather based on a distinctive element of the *surah*. For example, the third *surah* is called "The Women" because of the many verses within it that reference the status of women.

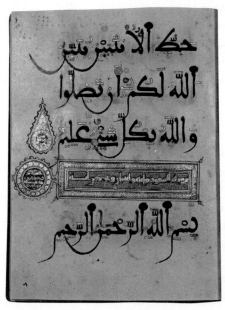

This illuminated Qur'an is from the thirteenth century.

At the time of Muhammad's death, the revelations of the Qur'an had not been collected into one book. The primary mode of teaching and learning the Qur'an was oral. During the rule of the caliph 'Uthman, however, the revelations were organized into a written text. For centuries, Muslims have considered this text standard. Today, however, some secular scholars think that a number of versions of the Qur'an originally existed, and that the written text of the Qur'an emerged gradually in the seventh and eighth centuries.

The most well known *surah* is the first one, which is called the *fatihah*, or the "opening." The *fatihah* is a common prayer used by Muslims in many different contexts. It is the first *surah* that Muslims learn when they begin studying the Qur'an as children or as adults. A devout Muslim will recite the *fatihah* several times during the day's many prayers. The *surah* evokes the oneness of God, the all-powerful nature of God, the Day of Judgment, and God's guidance for a righteous life.

THE OPENING/*AL-FATIHAH*

> In the name of Allah, most benevolent, ever-merciful
> All praise be to Allah,
> Lord of all the worlds,
> Most beneficent, ever merciful,
> King of the Day of Judgment.
> You alone we worship, and to You
> alone turn for help.
> Guide us (O Lord) to the path that is straight,
> The path of those You have blessed,
> Not of those who have earned Your anger,
> Nor those who have gone astray.[3]

Today, most Muslims consider the Qur'an both inimitable and uncreated. This means that Muslims regard the holy text as unique and eternal. Today and historically, Muslims have believed that the Qur'an's equal cannot be created by human effort, which is considered proof of its divine origins. Most contemporary Muslims also believe that the Qur'an is eternal—that it has always existed. This view has not always dominated, however. The Mutazilites, a rationalist school of Islamic thought that was prominent many centuries ago, argued that the Qur'an was not eternal but was rather created by God. The Mutazilite scholars argued that the idea of an eternal Qur'an compromised the unity of God because God alone was eternal and the creator of all things—including the Qur'an. This view had some support in the tenth century, but eventually the idea of the eternal Qur'an became dominant in the Islamic tradition.

The Teachings of the Qur'an

The major teachings of the Qur'an are found throughout the text. In any number of verses, we can find reference to the nature of God, the reality of the Day of Judgment, and guidelines for moral behavior.

The Oneness of God Like the other Abrahamic religions, Islam is a monotheistic religion, and the most important principle of Islamic belief is the oneness of God. The Qur'an teaches that God, known in Arabic as "Allah," is eternal, uncreated, all-knowing, and all-powerful, and it is God alone who created the universe and humankind. God is also merciful, just, and good. God is transcendent but also present, or immanent, in the lives of believers. A much-quoted verse of the Qur'an refers to God as closer to humanity "than the jugular vein" (50:16). Muslims believe that it is impossible for God to have a partner, consort, or family because no other being shares

God's divinity. Muslims believe that God is the same God of the Jews and Christians. However, to Muslims, the Christian doctrine of the Trinity compromises the unity of God. The Qur'an specifically comments on the impossibility of God begetting a son, as in the following verse:

> He to whom belongs the kingdom of the heavens and the earth: who
> has neither begotten a son, nor has He a partner in kingdom: (who)
> created every thing, and determined its exact measure (25:2).[4]

The Qur'an also teaches that Muslims should strive to acknowledge the oneness of God through acts of devotion. Because the unity of God is the central tenet of Islamic belief, it follows that denying or compromising this oneness is the greatest sin. This sin of associating anything or anyone else with God is called **shirk**. In the Qur'an, *shirk* is noted as the only unforgivable sin in the eyes of Allah. This is because it denies the existence of God and the true nature of God. For the believing Muslim, the worship of God should be given to God alone, and human beings should worship nothing else. Therefore, nature, idols, images, and human beings must not be worshiped.

In Muslim belief, Allah created the universe, the world, and everything in it, including the sun and the moon, the mountains and oceans, and all living things. The natural world is mentioned throughout the Qur'an, and elements of nature are referred to as *ayat*, or signs of God: "We shall show them Our signs in every region of the earth and in themselves, until it becomes clear to them that this is the truth" (41:53). Muslims view the natural world and the entire cosmos as a type of revelation from God. (The Qur'an itself, remember, is another type of revelation.) Therefore, in Muslim belief, the natural world as a whole is evidence of the existence of God, and human beings should be able to realize this simply by observing nature. Despite this, human beings cannot truly know the ultimate essence of God, God's ultimate purpose, and ultimate reality. Thus, Muslims may not be able to understand rationally why bad things happen to good people. However, they should have faith in God's purpose, even though they cannot truly know it (2:216).

Prophecy   Prophecy is also an essential component of Islamic belief, and it is mentioned several times in the Qur'an. The belief in prophecy is also important to Judaism and Christianity, and the three Abrahamic faiths share many of the same prophets. In Islam, it is through the messages revealed to prophets that humanity comes to know the desires of God and the divine laws that govern the universe and creation. The belief in revealed scripture goes hand in hand with the belief in prophecy, because Muslims believe that it is through prophets that humanity obtains scripture.

Muslims recognize many prophets since the beginning of creation. Each prophet received special words from God that were appropriate for humanity at the time in which the particular prophet lived. The prophet Abraham is mentioned several times in the Qur'an. The stories of his life resemble those told by Jews and Christians, and they serve as an important basis for the annual pilgrimage to Mecca (discussed in the next section). The Qur'an also names Jesus as an important prophet (and indeed says that Jesus will return to herald the Day of Judgment), and the Gospels are considered part of God's revelation to humanity. Muslims believe that Jesus was born of the virgin Mary, who is also mentioned in the Qur'an and is held in very high regard by Muslims. However, Muslims do not believe that Jesus was divine or the son of God. Verse 25:2, cited previously, reflects this idea.

Muslims believe that all prophets bring communication from God. The Qur'an teaches that prophets fall into different classes based on the nature of that communication. Some are said to bring simply "news" from god. Others, like Muhammad, bring a major message. In addition to Muhammad, prophets like Moses and Jesus also received major messages. Moses received the Torah as guidance for humankind, and the teachings of Jesus are regarded as a major message from God. All scriptures, including the Torah and the Gospels, are considered by Muslims to be the work of God. Although the Qur'an refers to those peoples to whom scripture was revealed as "Peoples of the Book," the Qur'an also teaches that the earlier messages have been misinterpreted or forgotten by the Christians and the Jews.

According to the Qur'an, Adam and his wife Hawa (or Eve) are regarded as the first two humans. Adam became the first prophet in the Islamic tradition. Adam and Hawa were created separately by God from a single soul (4:1), and made of dust or clay according to a divine model. Muslims believe that God blew spirit into humanity. Therefore, as in nature, the signs of God are also in humanity. The Qur'an teaches that human beings were created to worship God (51:56), and the nature of humanity is to obey God and to give thankfulness for God's blessings.

You will recall that the meaning of the term *Muslim* is "one who submits." However, as part of God's creation on earth, Muslims believe that humans should also act as responsible members of society and stewards of the natural world. The Qur'an contains a story that is similar to the one in Genesis, in which the first humans disobeyed God by tasting a forbidden fruit. In the Qur'anic story, Adam and Hawa are both to blame for this disobedience, and they are immediately forgiven for their transgressions by God (71:13–17). Most Muslims believe that, unlike other living creatures, all human beings have free choice, and thus must choose to submit to the will of God. Each individual's choices will be evaluated on the Day of Judgment.

The Day of Judgment The coming of the Day of Judgment and the reality of the afterlife is another central teaching of the Qu'ran. Many of the early *surah*s focus on God's judgment and can be read as warnings to humanity to live a righteous life or suffer the consequences when facing God at the end of days. Despite the dire warning of some of these verses, God's justice is strongly emphasized, and the Qur'an gives details about how to live a righteous life. Greed and hypocrisy are criticized, and kindness and generosity are praised. The Qur'an teaches that all believers, men and women alike, will stand alone in front of Allah, and will be judged according to their actions in life. The Qur'an teaches that after death, a person resides in the grave in a sleeplike state until the end of days, at which time the judgment will take place. The end of days is described in the Qur'an as a time when the world turns upside down in great calamity. *Surah* 99 dramatically describes Judgment Day:

> When the world is shaken up by its cataclysm
> And earth throws out its burdens,
> And man enquires: "What has come over it?"
> That day it will narrate its annals,
> For your Lord will have commanded it.
> That day people will proceed separately to be shown their deeds.
> Whosoever has done even an atom's weight of good will behold it;
> And whosoever has done even an atom's weight of evil will behold that.[5]

On Judgment Day, each person will have a book, which details the deeds of his life. The book held in the right hand indicates a righteous life, and the book held in the left hand indicates a sinner. The Qur'an teaches that each individual stands alone before God, and no one can intercede on his or her behalf. However, there is some debate about this issue, and some traditions in Islam suggest that Muhammad will be able to intercede on behalf of believers. Some Muslims believe that the Day of Judgment will be ushered in by a person known as the Mahdi, whose just rule will come to the earth at the end of days. The Mahdi is not mentioned in the Qur'an. Rather, the idea developed in Islamic thought in later centuries.

Those who are judged to be righteous will enter paradise. In the Qur'an, paradise is described in much detail as a lush garden with bountiful blessings of food, drink, and beautiful young men and women. Although some take this description to be literal, other Muslims argue that it is instead a metaphor for the beauties of paradise. Those who have led sinful lives will be cast into hell, which is often referred to simply as "the fire." Those who are doomed to hell include non-believers and Muslims who have rejected their faith by failing to live up to prescribed duties and moral standards. Some Muslims believe that sinners will eventually be forgiven and taken to paradise.

Angels and *Jinn* The existence of angels is another component of Islamic belief, and angels are mentioned throughout the Qur'an. Angels are part of God's creation, without body or gender. Humans are said to be made of clay, and angels from light. Angels serve as important messengers and assistants to God. The most well known of the angels in Islamic tradition is Gabriel, or Jibril. This angel is mentioned several times in the Qur'an, and was instrumental in bringing the revelation of the Qur'an to Muhammad from God. Islamic tradition also recognizes supernatural beings called *jinn*, which are said to be created from fire. They are also mentioned in several places in the Qur'an. *Jinn* can take various forms, and like humans they can be both good and evil and Muslim or non-Muslim. Much folklore has developed surrounding the *jinn*, and they are represented in tales like *One Thousand and One Nights* as both helping and harming humans. The English term "genie" derives from the Arabic word *jinn*.

Commentary on the Qur'an

The text of the Qur'an is ambiguous in some places and repetitive in others. This has resulted in a long tradition of commentary upon and interpretation of the meaning of the verses. The general Arabic term for commentary on the Qur'an is *tafsir*, which is translated in English as interpretation. Scholars have been engaging in *tafsir* for centuries, and their commentary takes many forms. In the first few generations following Muhammad's death, scholarly commentary on the Qur'an focused primarily on grammar, language, and explanations of inconsistencies in the text. The goal of this type of *tafsir* was to clarify the meaning of the words of the Qur'an.

Muslims have not always agreed on how the Qur'an should be interpreted and understood. Some scholars have argued that the Qur'an must only be interpreted vis-à-vis itself. In other words, verses of the Qur'an should only be explained by using other passages of the text. Other scholars think that Muslims should use their own reason and rationality as believers to interpret the meaning of the verses. This method of *tafsir* is known as speculative *tafsir*.[6] A famous eleventh-century Persian scholar called Abu Hamid al-Ghazali (1058–1111) wrote that, as rational judgment is a gift from God, people should always use it when considering the meaning of the Qur'an. However, some scholars criticized his approach as preferring human reason over the words of God. Ibn Taymiyya (1263–1328), an Arab scholar, argued that using human reason was not necessary because the entire meaning of the Qur'an could be found within the text. As we will discuss later in this chapter, Ibn Taymiyya's approach became influential to some Islamic reformist movements in the modern era.

The *Sunnah*: The Example of the Prophet

After the Qur'an, the second most important source of Islamic teachings is in the **Sunnah**, which refers to the "tradition" or way of life of the prophet Muhammad. The *Sunnah* encompasses Muhammad's actions and words. It includes the way he handled disputes in the early community, the way he dealt with his wives, friends, and children, and the way he went about the daily business of life. This extends even to such seemingly mundane matters as how the Prophet cleaned his teeth. As we discussed earlier in this chapter, to Muslims, Muhammad is considered the ideal human. He is therefore the model of the best way to live. To this day, Muhammad is an inspiration to all Muslims, who strive to follow his example of conduct in their own lives.

The *Hadith* Literature   How do Muslims know how Muhammad lived his life, how he treated his family, and how he handled problems facing members of the early Muslim community? Muslims have knowledge of Muhammad's life through a literary tradition known as the **hadith**. *Hadith* is a form of literature that records in brief reports the details of the life of the prophet, including his sayings and his deeds. The

VOICES: An Interview with Tunay Durmaz

Tunay Durmaz is a graduate student in physics at a university in the United States. He was born in Bulgaria in a Turkish family and raised a Muslim. When he was 11 years old, his family moved to Turkey. After getting his university degree, he moved to the United States to study for a Ph.D. in a scientific field.

In your view, what is the essence of Islam?

The essence of Islam is to guide humanity along the right path and bring them happiness in this world and the hereafter. It is also to teach humanity about their Creator, the purpose of creation, where we came from, and where we are going.

What is humanity's place in the world, and what does it mean to be a practicing Muslim today and also a scientist?

Humanity and all creation are the manifestation of Creator's Art. Humanity is the best of the creation. Humans differ from most of the other creation with the conscience given to them. This brings responsibility. Today, with the technology and knowledge we have it is easy to get distracted and drawn away from spirituality. This presents challenges to Muslims, because in Islam, faith (the spiritual part of religion) and worship (religious practice) go hand in hand. Fortunately, Islam does not contradict with science; in contrast, science and scientific knowledge is embraced in Islam. . . . Science is a human effort to understand Creation. And as humans we can make mistakes—this is part of doing science. If scientific knowledge seems to conflict with religion, we should think about how we have interpreted this knowledge rather than assume it falsifies religion.

How does being a Muslim shape your worldview?

Islam is a very comprehensive religion. It draws our attention to the hereafter. But . . . the rewards in the afterlife will depend on how we live this life. . . . So, everything in this life becomes an opportunity to do good deeds and gain God's good pleasure . . . it becomes important to watch for evil and to abstain from it. Thus, a Muslim lives a cautious life and it brings him awareness. Islam offers guidance in every aspect of life. Sometimes guidance is in the form of commandment, sometimes encouragement, sometimes a prohibition. So believers have responsibilities towards themselves, their families, relatives, neighbors, friends and all humanity. This is how Islam shapes my worldview. In the big picture, I have permanent and eternal life as a goal, but I can reach that goal through this temporary, short life. Islam offers all the guidance to achieve that goal. This helps me to get through difficulties and hardship I face.

From your perspective, what is it like to be a Muslim in North America today? What opportunities and challenges do you face?

I have had quite a good experience so far. Although we face the problems of maintaining a sense of spirituality in the face of many distractions of modern life, I haven't experienced any difficulties regarding my faith or practice. I can freely and comfortably perform my daily prayers anywhere. When it is time to pray I can do it in my office, I can do it in the airport. When I attend conferences, I ask the organizers for a place that I can use for a few minutes and I have been helped every time so far. Sometimes, due to the circumstances, I have to perform my prayers outside and I look for silent and calm spots to pray. In these circumstances, people see me but nobody has confronted me or threatened me or anything like that. On the contrary, I have been invited to classes, and even to church gatherings to talk about my religion and to share my faith. Those were very good experiences. It gives me hope, because I can see that people can work together regardless of their differences in faith, religion, race, or culture. Those differences are not problems. We face other common problems, real problems like poverty and warfare, which we all need to solve together.

hadith reports come from the observations of Muhammad's companions. His companions realized his importance as an example of righteous behavior. They strove to remember his actions and words, and then passed them on through the generations in *hadith* reports.

A *hadith* consists of two parts: the *isnad*, or the chain of transmission of the *hadith*; and the *matn*, the report itself. The *matn* relates Muhammad's words or deeds, and the *isnad* names those people who transmitted the *hadith* from the time of the prophet. The *isnad* always originates with one of Muhammad's close companions or a family member. Muhammad's wife Aisha was one of the most important transmitters of *hadith*: she passed on many reports about Muhammad's life. Muslims do not consider all *hadith* to be equally valid. A complex science of *hadith* developed in the centuries following the death of the Prophet to evaluate their reliability as true reports of Muhammad's life. Scholars ranked *hadith* from "solid" to "weak" based on the likelihood of authenticity. The *hadith* are compiled into collections of several thousand.

Reports known as *hadith qudsi,* or sacred sayings, are also important in the Islamic tradition. Although the name is similar, this is a very different sort of literary tradition from the regular *hadith*. The *hadith qudsi* are not reports of Muhammad's life, but are believed to be words of God. Muhammad is believed to have occasionally transmitted direct words of God that were not intended to be part of the Qur'an. Many of the *hadith qudsi* are succinct and beautiful. They focus on God's love for humanity, God's mercy, and the closeness of God to creation. The following *hadith qudsi* illustrates the quality of God's mercy:

> God says: "If my Servant intends a good deed and does not do it, I write it down for him as a good deed. Then if he does it, I write it down for him as ten good deeds, or up to seven hundred times that. And if my servant intends an evil deed and does not do it, I do not write it down against him. And if he does it, I write it down for him as [only one] evil deed."[7]

ISLAM AS A WAY OF LIFE

What does it mean to be a practicing Muslim? What does one do on a daily basis? Now that we have learned something about the major teachings of the religion, we will turn our attention to Islam as a way of life. We will learn about worship practice, the Islamic year and important holidays, and Islamic law. We will also explore gender roles and family life, and the complex concept of *jihad*. Let's begin with a discussion of what are known as the "five pillars" of Muslim religious practice.

The Five Pillars

The **five pillars** form the basis of Muslim worship practice. These pillars are

1. *Shahadah:* the declaration of faith
2. *Salat:* the daily prayer
3. *Zakat:* almsgiving
4. *Sawm:* fasting during the month of **Ramadan**
5. *Hajj:* pilgrimage to Mecca

Muslims believe that the foundation for the five pillars was set during the lifetime of Muhammad. The five pillars are carefully articulated in the *hadith* literature. All of the pillars are equally important. However, they address different elements of religious practice that must be performed at special times. For example, although prayer is a daily requirement, the Ramadan fast happens once per year, and the *hajj* must be performed only once in a lifetime. The pillars are generally required of all adult Muslims. However, individuals are sometimes excused from performing the pillars. For example, individuals who are ill, pregnant, or nursing an infant would not be required to fast. Devout Muslims generally aim to observe all of the pillars, but as with every religious tradition, there are variations in levels of observance. Furthermore, there has been some historical variation across communities and cultures in how much emphasis was placed on the pillars. Some Muslim scholars have even debated the relative necessity of the observance of the pillars, though these scholars have always been in the minority.

The Declaration of Faith

The first pillar is the declaration of faith, called the *shahadah*. This is the statement of belief: "There is no God but God and Muhammad is the messenger of God." The other four pillars all deal directly with religious practice, but the *shahadah* is different in that it is much more a statement of belief than a ritualized religious practice. To become a Muslim, all one must do is utter the *shahadah* with utmost sincerity in the presence of witnesses, rather than embarking on a complicated process of conversion. Most new Muslims will first declare the *shahadah*, and then begin a lifetime's journey of learning the Qur'an, the *Sunnah*, and other aspects of the faith. Many people in North America and elsewhere who have converted to Islam note the simplicity of the faith as something that attracted them to Islam. This simplicity is illustrated by the succinct nature of the *shahadah*.

Daily Prayer The *salat*, the mandatory daily prayers, is the second pillar. You encountered the careful preparations for the daily *salat* of Amina at the opening of this chapter. Devout Muslims perform five daily prayers at specific times of the day. Muslims cannot decide to perform all the prayers at once to get them over with for the day, week, or month. Rather, they should do them at the required times. The first prayer should be done at dawn every morning. The next prayer is performed at about noon. The remaining prayers are the late afternoon prayer, the sunset prayer, and the final prayer in the evening. Prayer is mentioned in several places in the Qur'an. However the number of prayers is established not in the Qur'an, but rather in the *hadith* literature. The *hadith* literature relates that during a miraculous journey to heaven, known as the **miraj**, Muhammad came into the presence of Allah. Allah told Muhammad he should instruct people to make fifty daily prayers. However, when Muhammad told the prophet Moses about the prayers, Moses told him to go back to God to ask for a reduction, since fifty would be too many. Eventually, the number was settled at five, although God said that every prayer would count for ten.

The *salat* are not individualized prayers requesting aid from God or giving thanks, although those personal prayers, called *dua*, are also common among Muslims. Rather, the *salat* prayers are formalized. For each prayer, specific verses of the Qur'an are recited and special body movements accompany the recitation.

Before beginning the prayers, a Muslim must enter a state of ritual purity. As you learned at the beginning of this chapter, this purification consists of ablutions, called *wudu'*, which involve cleansing the hands, head, face, and feet. The body should be covered for prayer, and most women and men also cover their heads. The prayer begins

Ablution fountains outside of a mosque.

with the *takbir*, or the declaration *Allahu Akbar*, which means "God is great." Throughout the prayer, the believer faces the direction of the Ka'ba in Mecca, the holiest site in Islam. This means that Muslims in America pray facing the east. In prayer, a Muslim stands, kneels, and bows his head to the floor. These cycles of movements along with the proper recitation are called *raka* and vary in number according to the prayer. In some parts of the world, such as parts of Indonesia, the prayer opens with a declaration of intent to indicate that the Muslim is in the right frame of mind for performing the prayer.[8] Not all Muslims declare their intent to pray, but most agree that proper intention is necessary. The intention of the believer is what validates and legitimizes the action of prayer. Many Muslims believe that the intention of the prayer is even more important than the prayer itself. After reciting verses of the Qur'an, the prayer closes with a greeting of peace.

As you recall from the interview with Tunay Dumaz earlier in this chapter, prayers may be done anywhere—even in a park or airport. However, many Muslims perform prayers at a **mosque** (this English word is taken from the Arabic term *masjid*). A mosque is a place that is designated for prayer. Many people imagine elaborate feats of architectural workmanship when they think of mosques, but a mosque can be as simple as an unadorned room in a commercial building or even a clearing in the woods. Although mosque architecture and decoration varies from the very simple to the very ornate, mosques tend to share some features. All mosques have a prayer space, and most have a fountain so people can perform the required ablutions. The direction of prayer, known as the *qibla*, is marked inside a mosque by a niche called a *mihrab*, which is sometimes beautifully decorated with botanical designs or Qur'anic verses. The floors of a mosque are often completely covered with colorful rugs or woven mats. Because Muslim prayer requires open space for bodily movement, there are usually no seats or pews. Many mosques, particularly those in the Middle East and North Africa, also have a tower called a *minaret*. The minaret is often used to broadcast the calls to prayer.

In much of the world, visitors of all faiths are welcome to enter mosques. Normally, visitors will be asked to leave their shoes outside. Sometimes, shoes are placed in a designated cabinet watched by someone who may receive a tip and even clean the shoes. By leaving shoes outside, no outside dirt will enter the mosque to violate the ritual purity of those who have made the proper ablutions for prayer. The prayer space in a mosque is open and peaceful, and people may use the mosque as a place for contemplation and rest throughout the day. When walking through the hot and dusty streets of busy Cairo, one can see men—and sometimes women—taking a break from the urban noise and bustle by resting in the serene interior of a neighborhood mosque. In many parts of the world, mosques are also used for teaching classes or for other community needs.

The beautiful Shah Mosque, in Isfahan, Iran, was built in the 1600s during the Safavid period.

Friday is designated as the day for congregational prayer, known as *salat al-jum'a*. It is incumbent upon Muslim men to attend the midday prayer together, and they may also gather at a mosque for other prayers during the day. In some areas, women also attend the communal prayer, though their attendance is not regarded as mandatory. When Muslims pray in a

This small mosque in rural Zanzibar, Tanzania, is built in an architectural style that is similar to houses in the area.

group in a mosque or elsewhere, it important that one person acts as the imam, or prayer leader. The imam regulates the prayer session and ensures that all believers are praying together. The Friday prayer often features a sermon, which may be delivered by the imam or another preacher. Friday should not be confused with the Christian or Jewish Sabbath. Rather than a day of rest, it is a day when group prayer is necessary. In some Muslim countries, Friday is a work day, and businesses are open. In others, businesses are closed.

The five daily prayers are announced in the words of the ***adhan***, or the call to prayer. The *adhan* is delivered by a person called a ***muezzin***, who calls the faithful to prayer from the door of the mosque or the minaret, sometimes using a loudspeaker. The *adhan* is usually called in a rhythmic, recitational fashion. Hearing the *adhan* several times a day from the wee hours of the morning to evening is very much a part of life in the Muslim world. Many residents and travelers miss it enormously when they move away; non-Muslim travelers often remark that hearing the *adhan* is one of the most memorable experiences of visiting a Muslim country.

ADHAN

> God is most great (repeated four times)
> I testify that there is no god but God (repeated twice)
> I testify that Muhammad is the messenger of God (repeated twice)
> Hurry to prayer (repeated twice)
> Hurry to success (repeated twice)
> Prayer is better than sleep (repeated twice before the morning prayer)
> God is most great (repeated twice)
> There is no god but God (once)[9]

Like the other pillars, the *salat* is incumbent upon all Muslims, both male and female. In much of the Muslim world, it is more common for men to pray in mosques than women, although this is not always the case. In places like urban Egypt and Indonesia, women often pray in mosques. Although females may serve as *imam* for other women, most Muslims believe that they may not do so for men. When women and men both pray in mosques, usually the genders are separated—either in separate prayer halls or with women praying in rows behind the men. Some Muslims reason that this requirement is due to modesty and concentration. They argue that women and men should not be distracted from their prayers by the presence of the opposite sex. Others argue that men's leadership in prayer is prescribed in the Qur'an. However, some Muslim feminist scholars, like the American professor Amina Wadud, are challenging this tradition by arguing that women can lead men in prayer.

The daily prayers are important for Muslims on both an individual and a communal level. Many Muslims feel closest to God during prayer. Although praying five times a day may sound very rigorous to non-Muslims, many Muslims welcome the breaks from mundane tasks to focus their attention completely on God. A believer must stop

Muslim men pray together at a mosque in Burma.

all activity to remember God five times every day. This indicates that submission to God is the most important part of life for a devout Muslim. On another level, praying the same prayers at the same time every day, and often in a group, draws the community of Muslims together in worship of God. Many Muslims report that in addition to feeling an individual closeness to God during prayer, they also feel at one with the **umma**, the global community of Muslims, in the common purpose of worship.

Almsgiving The third pillar, *zakat*, refers to required almsgiving, which is part of a believer's devotion to God and the Muslim community. The rules about *zakat* are very specific, and the amount of *zakat* is figured as a percentage (about 2.5 percent) of the value of certain types of property, including cash. *Zakat* is therefore something like a tax. The wealth on which *zakat* has been paid is considered to be pure and clean. Therefore, some Muslims describe *zakat* as a means of purifying their property. The payment of *zakat* also expresses a Muslim's commitment to improving his or her community in a real and concrete way. This is because the proceeds from *zakat* are normally distributed to the poor or are used to maintain public institutions like mosques and schools. In some countries today, such as Pakistan, the government collects and redistributes *zakat* funds.[10] Elsewhere, it is up to individuals themselves to make the *zakat* payments. All adults should pay *zakat*. However, adults who are mentally ill or unstable are exempt from the requirement.

Fasting during Ramadan The next pillar is **sawm**, which is the mandatory fast during the month of Ramadan. Ramadan is the ninth month in the Islamic calendar. Ramadan is considered a sacred month by Muslims because it was during Ramadan that the Qur'an was first revealed to Muhammad. During Ramadan, all Muslims are required to fast from dawn to sundown. When fasting, Muslims refrain from eating, drinking, and sexual activity. Muslims also strive to avoid arguing and negative thoughts during the hours of the fast.

All adult and adolescent Muslims are generally expected to fast. However, exceptions are made for those who are traveling, or women who are pregnant, nursing, or menstruating. In Pakistan, curtained food stalls are set up at train stations during Ramadan. The stalls allow travelers to eat in private, where they are respectfully out of view of those who are fasting and do not wish to be tempted by the sight of someone eating. Individuals who miss fasting days or break the fast are expected to make up the days later. However, children, the sick, the mentally ill, and the very elderly are exempt from fasting entirely. Children are usually encouraged to begin fasting when they show interest, but they are only expected to fast when they are comfortable doing so; many begin to fast early in adolescence.

The month of Ramadan is a special time. Although the fast can be challenging, many Muslims find Ramadan to be filled with religious meaning, joy, and sociability. In Muslim countries or communities, the rhythm of daily life changes significantly during Ramadan. Daily activity lessens, and streets are quiet during daylight hours. However, the world awakens at sunset, when the fast ends. Many people share the evening meal with family and friends, and streets are filled late into the evening with well-wishers. In addition to the evening meal, many families eat again around midnight, and also before dawn to give those who are fasting the strength to make it through the day.

Muslims often break the fast with dates before performing the evening prayer and eating the fast-breaking meal. This is because eating dates is *Sunnah:* Muhammad broke the fast with dates, and many Muslims seek to follow his example. In many cultures, special treats are prepared during Ramadan. Indonesian Muslims look forward to breaking the fast with a delectable drink made with coconut milk and tropical fruits. Some Indonesians say that the drink is so sweet because it represents the beauty of a day of focusing solely on God. In Iran and in Persian communities in the United States and Canada, a rice pudding flavored with saffron and rosewater is served during Ramadan.

This open-air market in Sumbawa Besar, Indonesia, is very popular during Ramadan, when people buy special delicacies to break the fast.

During Ramadan, Muslims around the world may spend time in the evenings reciting the Qur'an. Many try to achieve the goal of reciting the entire Qur'an during this special month. People may also stay up late into the night visiting friends and enjoying the celebratory and devotional atmosphere of the month. During the last few days of Ramadan, the Night of Power occurs. This is the night when Muslims believe that the Qur'an was originally revealed to Muhammad. Many Muslims believe that a wish may be granted during this special night. The end of Ramadan is marked by an important feast day called *Id al-Fitr*, the feast of fast-breaking, which we will discuss later in this chapter.

Like the preceding pillars, *sawm* is important on both personal and community levels. Fasting demonstrates an individual's dependence upon God, who provides for humanity. Also, by refraining from food and drink, Muslims become more sympathetic to the plight of the poor and the hungry, and learn to appreciate the food that they have. Like *salat* and *zakat*, fasting together also brings a sense of community to Muslims worldwide. A Muslim observing the fast in Los Angeles, for example, will know that his fellow believers thousands of miles away in Malaysia are keeping the fast. In the United States, many mosques and Muslim organizations view Ramadan as a time of outreach to non-Muslim friends and neighbors, and a way of teaching people about Islam. For example, at California State University, in Sacramento, the Muslim student organization holds a popular "fast for a day" event every year. Non-Muslims are invited to try fasting for a day, and then break the fast with a special meal prepared for the entire community. These events often include guest speakers who talk about the meaning of Ramadan and the basics of the Islamic tradition. Guests are also sometimes invited to watch the evening prayer.

Pilgrimage to Mecca   The final pillar is called the *hajj*, which is the holy pilgrimage to Mecca in Saudi Arabia. The Qur'an specifies the pilgrimage as incumbent upon humanity. Every year, millions of Muslims descend upon the city of Mecca in a spectacular display of devotion. The *hajj* is generally understood to be required of all Muslims who are physically and financially able to make it. A Muslim only needs to perform the *hajj* once in his lifetime, but many Muslims who are able to do so repeat it. Pilgrims describe the event as one of unparalleled spiritual significance, and they experience intense feelings of connection to God and humanity during the *hajj*. Muslims who returns from the *hajj* often use the title *hajj* (for men) or *hajja* (for women) before their name to indicate that they have made the journey.

The *hajj* must be undertaken at a particular time of year. This is during the second week of the month *Dhu al-Hajj*, which is the final month in the Islamic calendar. A person must be physically and financially able to make the trip, or else it is not valid. One may not borrow money to make the pilgrimage, but it is appropriate to accept financing for the trip as a gift. In addition, the money set aside for the *hajj* must be purified by paying *zakat* on it. As a means of organizing the millions of travelers who come for *hajj*, the government of Saudi Arabia today requires pilgrims to join a travel group to make the *hajj*. Planned excursions depart from every corner of the world, and tour companies arrange everything from air travel to bus transfers to accommodations. In Saudi Arabia, a great deal of planning is involved because of the sheer numbers of Muslims who arrive in Mecca and its environs during the week of *hajj*. Only Muslims may make the journey; curious tourists are not allowed to partake in the experience.

When making the *hajj*, pilgrims must leave behind indicators of their social and economic status to properly enter a state of ritual purity. This state is called *ihram*. All men must wear special clothing, also called *ihram*. This consists of two very simple pieces of white cloth—one is worn above the waist and one is worn below. Women may wear what they choose, and most dress in simple, unadorned clothing. Most women also avoid makeup, jewelry and perfume. Pilgrims should also refrain from sexual activity, arguing, and frivolous conversation while in a state of *ihram*. Ideally, these restrictions are meant to assure that the pilgrim's mind is solely on God and the *hajj*. The state of *ihram* also emphasizes the equality of all Muslims before God because all status markers, like expensive jewelry, are removed.

The pilgrimage involves a number of highly specific, ritual-ized acts. Muhammad determined the sequence of the events of the *hajj* before his death, and some events reenact moments from his life. Many of the rituals also recall the actions of Abraham and his family. In this way, the rituals connect the believer to the distant past and the origins of monotheism with Abraham.

Perhaps the most important focus of the *hajj* is the Ka'ba. As we will learn later in this chapter, the Ka'ba was a focus of pilgrimage in Arabia even before the time of Muhammad. It is a cubical building about thirty feet by thirty feet, and Muslims believe it was originally built and dedicated to Allah by Abraham and his son Ishmael. Today, the Ka'ba is covered by a cloth embroidered with gold thread that is replaced every year by the Saudi government. When a pilgrim first arrives in Mecca, he enters the Great Mosque that encircles the Ka'ba while recit-ing verses of the Qur'an. The pilgrim then circumambulates the Ka'ba seven times in a counter-clockwise direction. This is known as the *tawaf*. This ritual is an act of devotion that is be-lieved to be in imitation of the angels circling God's throne. The *tawaf* is performed three times during the course of the pilgrimage.

Muslim pilgrims prepare for prayer at the Haram mosque in Mecca.

Another important rite of the *hajj* is called the *sa'y*. This rite commemorates the story of Hagar, mother of Ishmael, who frantically searched for water in the desert by rushing seven times between two hills. During Hagar's search, God made a spring ap-pear and Hagar and Ishmael were able to quench their thirst. Pilgrims visit this spring to this day, many taking the special waters home as a symbol of Mecca. Today, the route between the two hills is enclosed as part of the Great Mosque.

Another important part of the *hajj* involves a journey to the plain of Arafat, where a tent city is established every year to house millions of pilgrims from around the world. It is here that Muslims recollect a story about Abraham that is also prominent in Jewish and Christian traditions. In all three traditions, Abraham is believed to have been commanded by God to sacrifice his son. (Most Muslims believe he intended to sacrifice Ishmael, but Jews and Christians usually regard Isaac as the object of sacrifice; the Qur'an does not mention which son was the intended sacrifice.) As Abraham pre-pared to make the sacrifice, the angel Gabriel (Jibril) appeared at the last minute and a ram was substituted for the son. Abraham's willingness to sacrifice his beloved son is regarded as a model of faith in Islam, and this is a solemn, reflective time of the *hajj*. The pilgrims perform the "standing ceremony," in which they remain standing from noon until sundown in praise of Allah.

The *hajj* ends with the most important holiday of the year, the Feast of Sacrifice, which we will discuss in the section on the Islamic year.

Together, the five pillars contain the essential beliefs and practices of the Islamic religion. However, there are many other dimensions to Muslim life.

This building in Zanzibar, Tanzania houses both Islamic and secular primary courts, as well as government offices.

The Qur'an in Daily Life

The Qur'an is an important part of the daily life of all Muslims, and the text itself is treated with great reverence and respect. To Muslims, the Qur'an is authentic only in the original Arabic. This means that a translation, like an English version of the Qur'an, is not the holy book itself, but merely an interpretation of the meaning. In many Muslim countries, children are encouraged to attend Qur'an schools, where they are often introduced to religious study through learning to memorize and recite sections of the Qur'an. In most communities, both boys and girls study the Qur'an, and people will often continue to study the Qur'an throughout adulthood. Indeed, Muhammad encouraged all Muslims to pursue a life of learning.

To Muslims, the true meaning of the Qur'an can only be understood in the original Arabic. The beauty of the language is said to lend itself to the spiritual nature of the words of God. Because of this, Muslims around the world learn to recite the Qur'an in Arabic—even if they do not speak or understand the language. (Often, a teacher will explain the meaning of the text in the local language.) Verses of the Qur'an are recited during the daily prayers, and the Qur'an is also recited at numerous other occasions, including weddings, funerals, birth celebrations, holidays, and political events.

Hearing the Qur'an recited by a talented person can be a moving experience for people of all faiths, even if they do not understand the words. Although people can achieve great fame for their ability to recite beautifully, Muslims do not normally regard recitation as entertainment or singing. In many places, children and adults recite the Qur'an in highly organized competitions that can resemble an American spelling bee. Amina, the woman you met at the beginning of the chapter, has studied the Qur'an for years, and has great skill in recitation. As a teenager, she once won a sewing machine in a recitation contest!

Jihad

The term *jihad* comes from an Arabic verb meaning to "struggle" or "strive" and has historically had complex meanings. The concept of *jihad* is often distorted in contemporary Western media. In general, the term *jihad* means exerting oneself in the name of God. *Jihad* can refer to several types of struggle on both personal and social levels. The term is used only rarely in the Qur'an, and nowhere is it explicitly linked to armed struggle. Rather, it was early in Islamic history that the term became associated with defensive military endeavors against the enemies of the growing Muslim community. There have been some Muslim groups both today and throughout history that have called for a military *jihad* against nonbelievers, even out of the context of defense of the Muslim community. You can see how the term is used in different verses of the Qur'an:

> O Believers, go out in the cause of God, (whether) light or heavy, and strive (*jihad*) in the service of God, wealth and soul. This is better for you if you understand.
> —*9:41*

> And strive (*jihad*) in the way of God with a service worthy of Him. He has chosen you and laid no hardship on you in the way of faith, the faith of your forbear Abraham. He named you Muslim earlier, and in this (Qur'an) in order that the Prophet be witness over you, and you be witness over mankind. So be firm in devotion, pay the *zakat*, and hold on firmly to God. He is your friend: How excellent a friend is He, how excellent a helper!
> —*22:78*

> So do not listen to unbelievers and strive (*jihad*) against them with greater effort.
> —*25:52*

Muslims often refer to the *greater jihad* as one's struggle to become a better person by striving against one's own sinful tendencies and to live in accordance with the will of God. Although we often see the term *jihad* translated into English as "holy war," Muslims regard the military connotations of the term as the *lesser jihad*. The idea of "greater and lesser" *jihad* comes from the *hadith* literature. Muhammad is reported to have said upon returning home from a battle "We return from the little *jihad* to the greater *jihad*."

Now that we have learned about the five pillars, the integration of the Qur'an into daily life, and the concept of *jihad*, let us turn our attention to other elements of Muslim life and practice.

The Islamic Year and Holidays

The Islamic calendar begins with the ***hijra***, the migration of Muhammad and the early community from Mecca to Medina, in 622 C.E. The Islamic calendar is lunar because the Qur'an stipulates that the moon should be the measure of time. However, in most of the Muslim world, people use both the lunar and solar calendars. The Qur'an also designates the names of the twelve months of the year. Of these, four months are considered sacred.

Several important celebrations and feast days occur throughout the Islamic year, and Muslims around the world celebrate these days in a variety of ways. The Feast of Sacrifice, or *Id al-Adha*, is the primary holiday of the Muslim year. The feast takes place at the end of the *hajj* season, and it is celebrated by all Muslims—not just those who made the pilgrimage that year. The feast commemorates Abraham's willingness to sacrifice his son at God's command. In many countries, offices and shops close for two days, and people spend time with their families and friends. In commemoration of the ram that was sacrificed instead of Ishmael, Muslims are expected to slaughter an animal to mark the holiday. However, because this is not always possible, Muslims may make charitable donations as a substitute.

The second most significant holiday in the Muslim calendar is *Id al-Fitr*, the Feast of Fast-Breaking. This holiday marks the end of the month of Ramadan. This feast is a time of joy and forgiveness, and is celebrated in many different ways around the world. Muslims mark the day by attending congregational prayers, visiting friends and family, or celebrating in public festivals and carnivals. Often, Muslims will wear elegant clothing for the holiday, and children are dressed in their finest new clothes. In some places, children are also given special treats, money, or gifts.

The Prophet's birth is also an occasion for celebration in many parts of the Muslim world, such as North Africa, East Africa, and South Asia. This celebration is known as *Mawlid al-Nabi*, and takes place around the twelfth day of the third month of the Islamic calendar. The birth of the prophet may be marked by state-sponsored ceremonies. Elsewhere, the birthday is marked by all-night recitation sessions, when participants recite the Qur'an and devotional poetry. Some Muslims criticize the celebration of the Prophet's birth. They argue that such celebration of Muhammad risks elevating the prophet to the status of God. Muslims in Saudi Arabia, for example, do not generally celebrate *Mawlid al-Nabi*.

The month of Muharram is especially significant to Shi'a Muslims. This is because the martyrdom of Muhammad's grandson **Husayn** is recalled on the tenth of the month; we will learn more about Husayn later in this chapter. This date is called **Ashura**, and the entire month of Muharram is recognized as an important and somber time. At this time of year, the death of Husayn is commemorated in many ways by Shi'a Muslims in places like Iran and Iraq. Husayn's story is retold through passion plays and street processions, called Ta'ziya. For Shi'a Muslims, the tombs of the prophet's family are sites of very important pilgrimages. Karbala, where Husayn was martyred and is said to be buried, is an important pilgrimage site in Iraq.

An Iraqi soldier stands guard as Shi'a pilgrims approach the holy city of Karbala.

The *Shari'ah*: Islamic Law

Muslims believe that God, as the creator of the universe and humanity, established a wide-ranging set of guidelines for human beings to follow. These guidelines are known as the ***shari'ah***. The literal translation of the Arabic term *shari'ah* is the "road" or "way." In English, it is most often translated as "law." However, the *shari'ah* encompasses a much broader range of law and legal activity than what is normally associated with law in the Western world. The *shari'ah* regulates almost every aspect of daily life for believers. Proper religious practice is included in the *shari'ah*, and so are areas of law that North Americans find more familiar, like marriage and divorce, inheritance, commerce, and crime. However, very few countries actually apply Islamic law in full, either today or in the past.

In Islamic belief, God is the sole legislator. In theory, this means that while humanity can interpret law, humans cannot legislate or make new laws. The *shari'ah* is drawn from several sources. The Qur'an is the primary legal source. In the early Meccan *surahs*, general legal principles are introduced. This includes the importance of generosity, of obeying God's command, and of performing prayer and religious duties with sincerity. In the later Medinan *surahs*, many technical legal matters are presented in great detail. Some of these *surahs* contain very specific laws governing community relations, marriage and family, and inheritance and commerce.

Although the Qur'an is the primary source of law, Islamic scholars throughout history have recognized that it does not address every legal situation. As a result, scholars have referenced the *Sunnah* as an additional legal source, which is second only to the Qur'an in importance. For centuries and up to the present day, Islamic jurists have consulted the *Sunnah* for answers to legal questions that are not explicitly addressed by the Qur'an. The *Sunnah* is important because Muhammad is considered the ideal human, the person closest to God, and the recipient of the revelation of the Qur'an. For that reason, his words and actions became an important legal source as a model for human behavior. Furthermore, Muhammad acted as a judge and a mediator of disputes in Medina, and the way he resolved legal conflicts is recorded in the *hadith*.

There are also other sources of Islamic law. For example, many scholars agree that if a legal matter is not addressed by the Qur'an or the *Sunnah*, then it is appropriate to use human reason to find an analogous situation. In the sections near the end of the chapter on Sunni and Shi'a Islam, we will discuss sources of law that are distinct to each.

Case files from an Islamic court in East Africa.

Today, many Muslim-majority states include Islamic law and courts in the state legal systems. However, in most countries in which Islamic law is applied, Islamic courts handle only matters of family law, and only for Muslims. Family law includes issues like marriage, divorce, child custody, and inheritance. It is only in a very few countries, like Iran and Saudi Arabia, that Islamic criminal and commercial law are recognized in the state legal system. One reason for this is that many countries that were colonized by European powers adopted European legal codes for criminal matters. Also, some countries have determined that centuries-old laws are not appropriate for modern contexts.

Many Muslims live in accordance with Islamic law in their personal lives, even if they do not live in a country with Islamic courts. As noted earlier, Islamic law informs the daily life of the believer, and regulates how a Muslim worships God. In addition, Islamic law regulates what a believer should eat and drink. For example, Muslims are prohibited from consuming pork and alcohol. Much of the legal basis for the prohibition on pork comes from the Qur'an. The prohibition on alcohol, although mentioned in the Qur'an, is more thoroughly developed in the *hadith* literature.

Marriage and Family

Marriage and family life are the cornerstones of Muslim communities. Devout Muslims, who strive to follow the example of the Prophet in their daily lives, consider Muhammad to have set the example of marriage and to have been the ideal husband and father. As a result, marriage is generally regarded as incumbent upon all Muslim men and women when they reach adulthood. Celibacy is not normally encouraged, and sexual pleasure is considered a gift from God to be enjoyed within a marriage.

Much variation exists throughout the Muslim world concerning marriage arrangements, weddings, and the organization of the family life. In some areas, marriages for young people are arranged by their parents, while in others, women and men select their own marriage partners. However, in most Muslim communities, dating is not an acceptable practice—even among Muslims living in North America. Furthermore, adult children in many Muslim families live with their parents until they marry, even if they are financially able to live on their own. Regardless of the method of arranging marriages, according to the *shari'ah*, young men and women may reject a marriage partner they deem unsuitable; the consent of both the bride and the groom is necessary for the marriage to take place. However, this legal right does not always coincide with community or cultural norms. In some cultures, a bride's silence about her parents' choice of a marriage partner is considered to indicate acceptance of the proposal.

In Islam, a marriage is considered a contractual relationship. For the marriage to be valid, the bride, the groom, and witnesses must sign a marriage contract. The contract designates the *mahr*, which is gift a bride will receive from the groom and his family.

A Muslim bride signs her marriage contract.

The gift may be cash or other property. The marriage contract may be considered invalid without the *mahr*, though the amount may vary greatly from family to family and culture to culture. The amount depends not only on the family's wealth, but also community norms. For example, urban Muslims in the Middle East might give a *mahr* of thousands of dollars, whereas the normal amount in a small African village might be only 50 dollars. According to *shari'ah*, the *mahr* is solely the property of the bride. However, in many cultures, a bride's parents may take some of the *mahr*.

On the wedding day, the bride and groom may be separated for most of the festivities. The groom usually signs the marriage contract in a mosque in the company of his male friends and relatives. The marriage official, often an imam, then takes the contract to the bride in her family's home, where she is accompanied by her female relatives and friends. Wedding celebrations are often large affairs, and feasting, Qur'an recitation, and sometimes music and dancing may accompany the signing of the contract. In many communities, men and women celebrate entirely separately. This is because some Muslims do not consider it acceptable for men and women to socialize together. In some cultures, the bride is taken to the groom's home in a big procession at the end of the day. There, the new couple shares a special meal and begins their life together.

According to most interpretations of Islamic law, Muslim men are allowed to marry up to four wives. However, this is only under certain conditions, and only if he can support all his wives and treat them equally. For example, the verses in the Qur'an concerning polygamy suggest that the practice is appropriate in times of warfare when there may be many unmarried women. Furthermore, the Qur'an states, "Marry such women as seem good to you, two, three, four; but if you fear you will not be equitable, then marry only one" (4:3). A later verse says that "You will not be equitable between your wives, even if you try" (4:129). Some thinkers, like the nineteenth-century Egyptian reformer Muhammad Abduh (1849–1905), argued that these two verses actually prohibited polygamy because the latter stated that no man could possibly treat multiple wives equitably, which is a necessary condition of polygamy. However, most Muslims have considered polygamy legal, though the occurrence of the practice varies tremendously around the world, and some countries, like Tunisia, have banned it entirely.

Several types of divorce are permitted in Islam. Guidelines for divorce come from both the Qur'an and *hadith* literature. One type is divorce by male unilateral repudiation. In this type of divorce, a man writes or pronounces the formula "I, (the man's name), divorce you, (the wife's name)." In classical Islamic law, this type of divorce does not need the approval of the wife or a legal authority. However, in many countries today, unilateral divorce is no longer permissible and men and women must both file for divorce in court. According to *shari'ah*, women may seek divorce from Islamic judges on a variety of grounds. Stipulations for divorce are occasionally written into the marriage contract. For example, a woman may specify that she can divorce her husband if he marries another wife. Divorce is very common in some Muslim countries, and uncommon in others. In some places, a divorced man or woman is dishonored and finds it difficult to remarry, while in others there is little or no stigma attached to a divorced man or woman.

Women and Islam

There is much variation in the way in which gender roles are perceived and interpreted throughout Muslim cultures. As in other religious traditions, like Judaism, Christianity, and Hinduism, patriarchal cultural norms are sometimes justified in terms of religion. When we consider the historical context in which it was revealed, the Qur'an introduced many legal rights and privileges to women that they had not previously enjoyed. For example, women were given the right to divorce their husbands on a variety of grounds; they were allowed to inherit and hold property which remained theirs even in marriage (women in England did not gain this right until the late nineteenth century); and they were given the right to refuse arranged marriages. The Qur'an also prohibited female infanticide.

According to Islamic belief, women and men are viewed as equals in the eyes of God, and will be judged on their own accord. In the Qur'an, verse 35 of *surah* 33 addresses this:

> Verily for all men and women who have come to submission,
> Men and women who are believers,
> Men and women who are devout,
> Truthful men and truthful women.
> Men and women with endurance,
> Men and women who are modest,
> Men and women who give alms,
> Men and women who observe fasting,
> Men and women who guard their private parts,
> And those men and women who remember God a great deal,
> For them God has forgiveness and a great reward.[11]

The Qur'an requires all Muslims, women and men, to live a righteous life and to seek education. Women may work outside the home, though this is still uncommon in some areas. According to religious law, all of a woman's earnings remain her property. Thus, women are not required to use their earnings to support the family and maintain the home; it is a man's legal duty to provide for his family, even if his wife is wealthier than he. Of course, in practice, many women contribute their earnings to the household.

Despite this, the place of women in Islam has occasionally been interpreted in very strict fashion. One need only consider the case of the Taliban in Afghanistan, who deny women the right to work outside the home, the right to be educated, and even the right to walk freely in the street. However, this strict interpretation of religious texts and traditions is far from mainstream. Most Muslims view the Taliban's orders as radical and even religiously unlawful.

Along these same lines, much cultural variation exists in the practices regarding interaction between Muslim men and women. In some parts of the world, men and women live very separate lives. The seclusion of women is called *purdah* in South Asia and is practiced by some Hindus and Sikhs as well as some Muslims. Elsewhere, as in many parts of Southeast Asia and Africa, Muslim men and women intermingle freely.

The Qur'an encourages both men and women to dress and behave modestly. The verses concerning dress—particularly that of women—are interpreted in many ways. Modest women's dress takes many different cultural forms. In some cultures, modest dress is interpreted as long pants and a modest top. In other contexts, Muslim women wear a type of cloak over their clothing when the leave the home. And some Muslim women choose to cover their heads and hair with a scarf. But this is not solely a Muslim practice: in the Middle East and Mediterranean, women covered their heads long before the time of Muhammad. Covering the head has also been common practice among many Christian, Jewish, Hindu, and Sikh women.

Many Muslim women dress modestly strictly out of religious commitment. For others, wearing modest dress is an important move toward gender equality in the workplace and the public sphere. Such women believe that when they are dressed modestly, they are valued by others on their merit alone, not on their appearance. To others, maintaining modest dress makes a statement of resistance to Western scholars and activists by demonstrating that feminism can be defined in myriad ways in different cultural and religious contexts. Some Muslim women say they pity Western women, who they believe must dress in way that serves men's pleasure in viewing the female form.

Three young Palestinian students in modest dress.

We should not consider the status of women in any religious tradition without also considering historical change, and this is particularly true of Islam because of the many negative stereotypes Muslim women have faced in recent years.

Reform and Women's Status Several important reformers in the nineteenth and twentieth centuries sought to improve women's status in Muslim countries and cultures. Many of these reformers have focused on proper understanding of religious sources and Islamic law concerning women.

In much of the twentieth century, particularly in the first half, Muslim feminists were upper-class women who had the time and leisure to deliberate these issues, not working-class women whose labor was necessary to support their families. One of the most famous of these early Muslim feminists was Huda Sha'rawi (1879–1947), an educated upper-class Egyptian woman who symbolically removed her face veil in an Alexandria train station in 1923. Sha'rawi was president and founder of the Egyptian Feminist Union, and did not believe that veiling was an Islamic requirement. When she removed her veil, she had just returned from a women's conference in Rome. She encouraged women to cast off their headscarves in a quest for liberation. Many Egyptian women, particularly educated and elite women, were inspired by her example and ceased wearing face veils and headscarves. Sha'rawi remained an activist and feminist leader throughout her life. She founded schools and medical facilities in Egypt, and also advocated for women's rights throughout the Arab world.

In the later years of the twentieth century, many Muslim feminists have sought paths to equality that diverge from Western models. In their view, Islam itself provides

VISUAL GUIDE
Islam

Calligraphy developed as a very important art form in Muslim. This is because of a widespread understanding that imagery is prohibited by the sacred sources of Islam. This example is the word Allah. Beautiful calligraphy decorates pages of the Qur'an, mosques, and other items.

Throughout the daily prayer, the believer faces the Ka'ba in Mecca and stands, kneels, and bows his head to the floor. These cycles of movements along with the proper recitation are called *raka* and vary in number according to the prayer.

The direction of prayer, known as the *qibla*, is marked in a mosque by a niche called a *mihrab*, which is sometimes highly decorated with designs or Qur'anic verses, like this *mihrab* at a mosque in Cairo, Egypt.

The Ka'ba, a cubical building in Mecca that measures about thirty feet by thirty feet. Many Muslims believe it was built and dedicated to the one God by Abraham and Ishmael.

the necessary means for women to achieve their rights. Many argue that the Qur'an must be reinterpreted in an attempt to eradicate cultural practices that are detrimental to women but have been justified as appropriate Islamic practice. Some have argued that women's status would be much improved only if Islamic laws were properly followed. As discussed earlier, many women in recent decades have, in a sense, reembraced modest dress as a feminist statement. In Egypt, this idea became prominent in the 1980s, and many mothers and grandmothers who had consciously decided against wearing veils or headscarves were dismayed that their daughters were wearing them, ironically with the same rationale their grandmothers used to discard it.

It is important to note that Muslim feminists differ in their approaches to Islam. Zaynab al-Ghazali (b. 1917) is an Egyptian feminist who advocates increasing women's rights and improving women's status through Islam. Nawal al-Sa'dawi (b. 1931), also Egyptian, is a woman who advocates that women can only achieve equality by rejecting what she views as the patriarchal tendencies of religion. Al-Sa'dawi is both a medical doctor and a writer, and her novels and stories have been both influential and controversial in the Arab world for her focus on feminist issues and problems facing Arab women. Recently, al-Sa'dawi was active in the 2011 Egyptian revolution that overthrew the thirty-year presidency of Hosni Mubarak.

THE HISTORY OF ISLAM

Muhammad ibn Abd Allah was born around the year 570 C.E. in the town of **Mecca**, a city in the southern Arabian Peninsula. At the time of his birth, the peninsula was not politically united, and much of the population were nomadic herders, known as Bedouins, who lived in remote desert areas. Despite this lack of political centralization, the region was by no means isolated. The peninsula was situated between the Byzantine empire to the northwest, the Persian Sassanian empire to the northeast, and the Christian Abyssinian kingdom across the Red Sea in Ethiopia. In addition, the city of Mecca was a significant trading center and place of religious pilgrimage. Although there were Christians and Jews in Arabia at the time, the majority of the people living in Arabia were polytheists who worshiped several deities. Trade fairs regularly took place in Mecca, and people passing through often left representations of deities at a temple called the Ka'ba, a large cube-shaped building in the center of town (and, as you have learned, the site to which all Muslims turn as they pray, and toward which they make a *hajj* at least once in their life). Tradition holds that at the time of Muhammad, over 300 deities and spirits were represented by idols in the Ka'ba. Muslims call this period before the revelation of the Qur'an the *jahiliyya*, or the "age of ignorance."

Muhammad was born into a tribe called Quraysh, a powerful extended family that was very influential in Mecca. His father died before he was born, and his mother died when he was a young child. After her death, Muhammad went to live with his grandfather, who was his appointed guardian. When his grandfather died, Muhammad was raised by his uncle, a man named Abu Talib. Although he spent most of his early life in the city of Mecca, as a young boy Muhammad was sent out to the desert to live with the Bedouin, who many considered to live the ideal Arab lifestyle. At the time, sending children to the Bedouin was considered an important way to impart Arab values and culture to young city dwellers.

Muhammad is known to have been a hard worker, and was active in business and trade. Indeed, he met his first wife, Khadija, while he was working for her in a trading caravan. Khadija was a widow about fifteen years older than Muhammad, and she was so taken with the integrity and dignity of the young man that she proposed to him, and they married when he was about 25 years old and she 40. Their marriage was thought to be one of close companionship and deep love, and they had several children together.

As we learned at the beginning of this chapter, Muhammad began preaching in Mecca after receiving the first revelations. His preaching was not welcomed, however, and was even controversial in some quarters of Mecca. This was because he criticized both the polytheistic beliefs held by many Meccans and the disregard that wealthy

TIMELINE
Islam

570 C.E. The birth of Muhammad.

610 The first revelations of the Qur'an to Muhammad.

622 The *hijra* (migration) from Mecca to Medina.

632 The death of Muhammad; issue of succession.

632–661 Period of the Rightly Guided Caliphs.

657 Battle of Siffin.

661 'Ali killed.

661–750 Umayyad period.

680 Battle at Karbala and martyrdom of Husayn.

750–1258 Abbasid period.

1095–1453 Crusades.

1207–1273 Jalalludin Rumi

1281–1924 Ottoman empire.

1483–1857 Mughal empire.

1501–1722 Safavid empire.

1703–1792 Ibn Abd al-Wahhab.

1849–1905 Muhammad Abduh.

1881–1938 Mustafa Kemal Ataturk.

1923 Huda Sha'rawi unveils at Egyptian train station.

1947 Partition of India and Pakistan.

1979 Iranian Revolution.

2004 France bans wearing of headscarves and other religious identifiers in schools.

2006 Keith Ellison first Muslim elected to U.S. Congress.

2009 Green Movement, Iran.

2011 "Arab Spring" pro-democracy movements spread across the Middle East.

Meccans showed toward the poor. The controversy led to persecution of the small but growing community of Muslims. Because they held much power in Mecca, Muhammad's own clan, the Quraysh, stood to lose the most with the social change that Muhammad's teachings advocated. The Quraysh were thus particularly active in ridiculing and persecuting Muhammad's followers.

This persecution inspired some Muslims to flee to Abyssinia (Ethiopia), where they were granted refuge by the Christian king. Others tried to resist. One well-known Muslim who resisted persecution was Bilal, an Abyssinian slave who had converted to Islam. The man who owned Bilal forced him to lie in the hot sun with a stone on his chest and told him to renounce his Muslim beliefs by denying the oneness of God. Bilal refused, crying out "One! One!" until he was rescued by Abu Bakr, who purchased him from his tormentor and then freed him from slavery. Bilal is remembered by Muslims to this day for his devotion and is also known as the first *muezzin*—the person who calls the faithful to prayer.

The *Hijra* and the Growth of the Muslim Community

Because of the troubles in Mecca, Muhammad eventually encouraged his followers to leave and make a new home elsewhere. The people of a little settlement north of Mecca with a small Jewish population welcomed him, and he encouraged his followers to go there. This town became known as **Medina** (from the term *medinat al-nabi*, which means "the city of the prophet"). The Muslims moved from Mecca to Medina in the year 622 C.E., and this migration is called the *hijra*. The *hijra* is a very important event in Islamic history; as we have learned, the Islamic lunar calendar begins not with Muhammad's birth, but with the *hijra*. This is because the *hijra* marked the beginning of a distinct Muslim community, or *umma*, with Muhammad as its leader.

Muhammad did not travel with the first group to go to Medina. He and some of his companions waited for a few weeks to make the trip. When they finally left for Medina, angry Meccans from the Quraysh tribe pursued them. A popular story recounts that during Muhammad's journey to Medina he hid from the Quraysh in a cave for three days. When his pursuers reached the cave, they did not look inside because a kindly spider had spun a web to hide the entrance, thus saving Muhammad. Even today, some Muslims will not kill spiders because of their appreciation for the spider's important role in protecting the Prophet from the Meccans. Stories about the *hijra* and the foundational period of Islam are well known and inform the way many Muslims live their lives. Today, Muslims around the world recall the *hijra* as a difficult but very important time.

What happened to the Muslim community with the move to Medina? With the move, the growing Muslim community took on a new political and social form. Additionally, Muhammad's role expanded over the years as he became the leader of the new community. In Mecca, Muhammad had primarily preached and taught the revelations to his followers. In Medina, however, he took on a wide variety of new roles, and oversaw political, social, and religious matters. In addition to his role as prophet of God and religious leader, Muhammad became the political head of the community. He continued to receive revelation from God for twenty more years, and reflecting these changes, the verses of the Qur'an that Muslims believe were revealed to Muhammad in Medina concern the regulation of community life.

The migration to Medina did not end the Muslim community's problems with Mecca. Muhammad and the Muslims lived a perilous existence for several years as they suffered economic hardships in Medina and threats from Mecca. With the aim of providing economically for the community, the Muslims had begun to raid trade caravans bound for Mecca, though with limited success. Although it may sound surprising to the modern reader, raiding was a common and even acceptable economic practice in Arabia at that time, especially in times of hardship. Most often, raids did not involve bloodshed.

Conflicts with the Meccans continued, primarily with the Quraysh tribe, who still viewed the Muslims as a threat. Furthermore, the raids caused many economic problems for the Meccans and increased the tension between the two cities. This resulted in one of the most famous clashes in early Muslim history, the Battle of Badr in the year 624 C.E. The Muslims had planned a raid on a Meccan caravan at a place called Badr. The Meccans learned of the plan, and sent a force of over 900 men to protect the caravan. However, the Muslims, at only 300 strong, soundly defeated the Meccan forces even though they were greatly outnumbered. The battle is mentioned in the Qur'an, which reports that angels helped the outnumbered Muslims win the battle (8:9). The Qur'an also notes this as a critical moment in the development of the spirit and destiny of the Muslims. After this dramatic battle, Muhammad's reputation as a great leader grew.

A few years later, in 628 C.E., Muhammad attempted to lead the Muslims back to Mecca for a pilgrimage. The people of Arabia had been making pilgrimages to the Ka'ba for centuries. The Meccans, expecting an attack, proposed a negotiation with the now more powerful Muslims. Muhammad agreed, and the pilgrimage was postponed through the signing of a treaty between the Meccans and the Muslims. Two years later, in 630 C.E., the Muslims returned and the Meccans surrendered when they saw Muhammad's even greater political and military strength. Muhammad accepted the surrender, and allowed the Meccan people to go free if they would convert to Islam. Muhammad and the Muslims entered Mecca. They destroyed the polytheistic idols housed at the Ka'ba, and rededicated the building to the one and only God and the religion of Abraham.

Muhammad only lived for two more years after his victorious return to Mecca. At the time of his death, he had a large family. Khadija had died several years earlier, and after her death Muhammad married several more wives. Some of his marriages were contracted for political alliances, and others to care for widowed and divorced women who had no one else. The best known of his later wives was a woman called Aisha, who was the daughter of Abu Bakr. She was much younger than Muhammad, which was not unusual in marriages at the time. Aisha was a very important early figure in

Islamic history and is thought to be one of Muhammad's most beloved wives. She was the source of much information about Muhammad's life, and was often consulted by other Muslims because of her vast knowledge of religious matters. In 632 C.E., Muhammad is believed to have died peacefully in Aisha's arms after returning from a final journey to Mecca. He was buried under her home in Medina, and to this day, some Muslims visit this site as a place of pilgrimage.

By the time of his death, Muhammad was the political and religious leader of much of Arabia. After the move to Medina, Muslim rule had spread rapidly across the Arabian Peninsula through both nonviolent political alliances and military conquests. Many people of Arabia had converted to Islam. Some did so because they believed in the truth of Muhammad's message, and others converted for political reasons, namely to form alliances with Muhammad and the powerful Muslim community.

Not all people living under Muslim rule converted to Islam, however. Significant Christian, Jewish, and other religious minority populations remained. From this early period, Muslims have considered Christians and Jews to be People of the Book, a designation that means that they are a people who have received scripture form God and are thus close to the Muslim community. Later, Hindus and Buddhists were also considered People of the Book as Muslim rule spread into South Asia. Under Muslim rule, these minority communities were governed by what are termed *dhimmi* laws; the term *dhimmi* refers to their status as protected peoples. These laws allowed non-Muslims in Muslim territories to worship how they chose, provided they paid taxes and submitted to Muslim authority. The *dhimmis* did not enjoy all the privileges of Muslims—they were not allowed to bear arms, for example—but they were entitled to the protection of the Islamic state.

The Crisis of Succession and the Rightly Guided Caliphs

At the time of Muhammad's death, communities throughout Arabia were united under Islam, but it was unclear to Muhammad's followers who should succeed him to lead the Muslims. When he died, most Muslims thought that Muhammad had not designated a successor. A minority, however, believed that Muhammad had designated his cousin 'Ali to succeed him. 'Ali was also Muhammad's son-in-law because he had married Fatima, Muhammad's daughter by Khadija. This controversy over leadership of the Muslim community is often known as the crisis of succession, and it led to the development of the two major branches of Islam: the **Sunni** and the **Shi'a**. The majority group became known as the Sunni, which remains the larger of the two major branches. The minority group became known as the Shi'a. The name comes from the term *shi'at 'Ali*, which means the "party of 'Ali"—this was the group who thought Muhammad has chosen 'Ali to lead after his death. The Shi'a is the smaller of the two major branches of Islam. Later in the chapter, we will discuss how this dispute led to other differences between the Sunni and the Shi'a.

The companions of the Prophet chose the highly respected Abu Bakr to lead the Muslim community. As you recall, Abu Bakr was one of the first converts to Islam, and was Muhammad's father-in-law. Although 'Ali was also highly regarded—even by those who did not think Muhammad had designated him to be his successor—he was also much younger than Abu Bakr. Therefore, many considered him too young to lead the community. Most Muslims in Medina agreed with the selection of Abu Bakr, but those who thought that Muhammad had designated 'Ali eventually formed a distinct community—the Shi'a. The Shi'a believed not only that Muhammad had designated 'Ali as his successor but also that the members of the family of the prophet had an intrinsic quality that made them the only appropriate leaders of the *umma*.

The leaders who came after Muhammad were not viewed as prophets. They were known rather as **caliphs**, who ruled as the representatives of God and the prophet and had both religious and political authority. This was a new form of government called a **caliphate**, and it remained the model for Islamic society for several hundred years. The designation of Abu Bakr as caliph started a historical period that came to be known as the time of the Rightly Guided Caliphs. The Rightly Guided Caliphs were Abu Bakr and his successors: Umar, 'Uthman and, finally, 'Ali.

As caliph, Abu Bakr sought to strengthen relationships with the communities and tribes of Arabia who had formed alliances with Muhammad. Abu Bakr faced the potential breakdown of Muslim unity because some of these tribes, particularly those in parts of Arabia far from Medina and Mecca, wanted to break their ties to the Muslim community when Muhammad died. After the death of Abu Bakr, which was only two years after he had been appointed caliph, the Muslims chose a man called 'Umar to lead. Like Abu Bakr, 'Umar had been close to Muhammad. Also like 'Abu Bakr, he was confronted with the problem of some communities wanting to break away from Islamic rule. However, he managed to preserve unity and expand Muslim rule, conquering the lands of Egypt, Syria, and Iraq. When 'Umar died in 644 c.e., another of the Prophet's companions, a man called 'Uthman, was selected as the new caliph.

'Uthman led the Muslims for twelve years, from 644 to 656 c.e. He continued the rapid political expansion that 'Umar had begun, but also faced many problems. Muslim rule now extended from the Mediterranean and North Africa into Central Asia. Because the *umma* now reached beyond Arabic-speaking lands, there was a great deal of cultural and linguistic diversity among the Muslims. This situation made leadership a far more complex undertaking than it had been in the time of Muhammad and Abu Bakr, when nearly all Muslims were Arabs. This eventually led to charges that the caliphs discriminated against non-Arab Muslims. Furthermore, many accused 'Uthman of nepotism when he appointed his nephew Mu'awiya as governor of Syria. He also placed other relatives in key posts, and many of them grew rich as a result. A few years into his rule, 'Uthman faced a number of rebellions in outer provinces of the empire, and in 656 c.e. he was killed by insurgents who had marched on Medina.

After 'Uthman's death, 'Ali was finally named caliph. During the time of the first three caliphs, the supporters of 'Ali's claim to leadership grew in numbers. Despite this growing support, however, 'Ali's time as caliph saw many fractures in the Muslim community. Supporters of 'Uthman were upset that 'Ali had never punished his murderers. This controversy resulted in the Battle of the Camel. This was a traumatic moment in Islamic history because it was the first to pit Muslims against Muslims. In the battle, 'Ali defeated an army led by the prophet's wife Aisha and other prominent Meccans. Aisha directed the battle from her mount on a camel, from which the battle took its name. 'Ali's forces took down her camel in order to hinder her leadership, and his forces were victorious.[12] Mu'awiya, 'Uthman's nephew, also challenged 'Ali's authority. This conflict reached a peak in the Battle of Siffin in 657 C.E. When they met on the battlefield in Syria, Mu'awiya asked 'Ali for an arbitration of their dispute, and he accepted. However, some of 'Ali's followers disapproved of the arbitration, which they viewed as a surrender to Mu'awiya. This group formed a splinter group known as the Kharijites, which means "those who seceded." In 661 C.E., 'Ali was murdered by a Kharijite.

The Umayyads and the Abbasids

After 'Ali was killed, Mu'awiya claimed the caliphate. His leadership gave birth to what is known as the **Umayyad** Dynasty. This marked the end of the period of the Rightly Guided Caliphs. The institution of the caliphate survived, but the divisions in the community of believers that had worsened under 'Ali remained.

The Umayyad period lasted over a century, from 661 until 750 C.E. Umayyad leaders ruled from the city of Damascus in Syria. Although they were considered fairly effective leaders who expanded the Muslim empire further east to India and further west to Spain, the reign of the Umayyads was controversial. For example, many Muslims thought that the Umayyads did not truly represent the diversity of the Muslim people, favoring Arab Muslims over non-Arab Muslims. Such criticism arose in part because Mu'awiya had designated his son Yazid as his successor instead of letting the community select a leader. This turned the caliphate into a dynasty.

Many Muslims who were opposed to the Umayyad Dynasty felt that the leadership of the *umma* should come from the line of Muhammad through Fatima and 'Ali. They argued that therefore their sons, Hasan and Husayn, should lead the *umma*. With the support of the Shi'a, **Husayn** eventually challenged the Umayyads for authority. However, he was slain in 680 C.E. when Yazid's armies ambushed him on the plains of Karbala, in what is now Iraq. This tragic event is referred to as the "martyrdom of Husayn." This is a moment in Shi'a history that is solemnly commemorated to the present day as Husayn's sacrifice for the Muslim people. With the death of Husayn, the number of Muslims who believed the leader of the *umma* should be from the family of the Prophet grew. It was at this point that the Shi'a formally broke away from the Sunnis and established a line of successors to the prophet that remained within Muhammad's family.

In the late seventh and early eighth centuries C.E., many more Muslims began to criticize the Umayyad Dynasty. This group included those who were critical of the Umayyads for their perceived discrimination against non-Arabs and also those who supported the family of 'Ali as rightful leaders of the *umma*. Muslims opposed to the

Umayyads became known as the **Abbasids**, taking the name of Muhammad's uncle. In 750 c.e., the Abbasid Revolution succeeded in removing the Umayyads from power.

The first caliph of the Abbasids was a man named Abu al-Abbas, and during his rule the Abbasids moved their capital from Damascus to Baghdad. Baghdad became a cultural capital of the world. Islamic arts and sciences flowered in this time, which became known as the classical period of Islamic civilization. One of the most well-known pieces of literature from this period is the *One Thousand and One Nights*. These colorful tales celebrate the reign of the most famous Abbasid caliph, Harun al-Rashid, who ruled for twenty-five years in the late eighth century.

Many of these intellectual and artistic developments had an enormous impact on world history and the cultures of Europe and Asia. Islamic scholarship in science, philosophy, and medicine built on earlier knowledge from Greek and Persian sources, and was very influential in European schools and universities for many centuries. The time of the Abbasids was also the period when many Islamic religious doctrines were developed into forms that are still accepted today. For example, it was in this period that the Islamic legal schools of thought, discussed earlier in this chapter, were formalized.

Abbasid rule continued for several centuries, but not all Muslims were united under the Abbasid Caliphate. In 950 c.e., for example, rulers in Cairo and Spain also claimed the title of caliph. Furthermore, the Abbasid period saw the influence of the Crusades in Syria and Palestine, when European Christians sought to win control of the Holy Land. Christian forces captured Jerusalem from Islamic control in 1099. The holy city was later recaptured by Salah ad-Din (also known as Saladin), a famed Muslim military leader, in 1187. The rule of the Abbasids ended in 1258 c.e. when Baghdad was sacked by a Mongol army from the east led by the grandson of Genghis Khan.

By the end of the Abbasid Caliphate and the beginning of the fourteenth century, Islam was the majority religion in a vast region stretching from Spain and the western edge of North Africa all the way to Iran in Central Asia. The religion was also gaining converts in sub-Saharan Africa, and South and Southeast Asia. Although military conquest expanded Muslim rule in some areas, it is incorrect to think that the historical spread of Islam around the globe was solely by the sword. In the earliest years of the *umma*, many tribes in Arabia joined the Muslims through political alliance. The growth of Islam throughout much of Asia and sub-Saharan Africa was gradual and peaceful. Often, Islam was introduced largely through traveling preachers and traders. The teachings of wandering **Sufis**, those who follow the mystical tradition of Islam, were key in gradually winning converts in South and Southeast Asia.

Later Islamic Empires: The Ottomans, the Mughals, and the Safavids

After the fall of the Abbasids, the Muslim world saw the rise of several powerful Islamic empires in the next few centuries. These were the Ottoman empire in the Mediterranean region, the Safavids in Iran, and the Mughal Dynasty in India.

The Ottoman empire spanned over 600 years, from the fourteenth to the twentieth centuries. The early empire was marked by rapid expansion, and at the height of

The Sultan Ahmed mosque in Istanbul, Turkey, was built in the 1600s and is a fine example of Ottoman architecture. It is also known as the Blue Mosque because of blue tiling inside.

its power, the Ottomans controlled much of the Middle East and Mediterranean, reaching into southeastern Europe and Africa. The height of the empire was the fifteenth and sixteenth centuries, and in 1453 the Turks took the city of Constantinople, the former capital of the Byzantine empire. The city, now called Istanbul, became the Ottoman capital and an important seat of Islamic learning and Islamic power. The Ottoman empire came to an end after World War I.

At the same time as the Ottoman empire reached its height, another Muslim empire arose thousands of miles away in South Asia. This dynasty, known as the Mughals, ruled much of India from the early sixteenth to the eighteenth centuries, even though the Muslim population was in the minority. The Mughal Dynasty, though not as long-lived as the Ottoman, saw a growth of literary and artistic development in South Asia, and Mughal architecture (like the Taj Mahal in Agra, India) is considered to have created some of the world's most impressive buildings. The stunningly beautiful Taj Mahal was built in the 1600s by the Mughal emperor Shah Jahan as a memorial and mausoleum for his beloved wife, Mumtaz Mahal. The Mughal empire reached its peak in the eighteenth century, and although there was a Mughal ruler until 1857 in India, Mughal power and territory saw a decline with the advent of British occupation of South Asia.

To the west of the Mughals, the Safavid empire in Iran flourished during the same period. Perhaps the most notable aspect of the Safavid rule was the establishment of Shi'a Islam as the religion of Iran; to the present day, the vast majority of Iran's Muslims are Shi'a. The Safavid period saw significant developments in Shi'a religious and philosophical thought. As with the Mughals, the period saw the development of great works of art and architecture.

Islam and Nationalism

In the twentieth century, the nation-state came to dominate the political organization of the world. Muslim leaders took different positions on the ideal relationship between religion and the nation-state. In many places, religion has served as a means to unify people across ethnic, class, and social boundaries. Some Muslim nationalists and political leaders envisioned a close link between their ideals of new states and Islam. Their vision involved a state government based on the principles of Islam and Islamic law as the basis for the legal system. Other leaders sought to distance nationalist policy from Islam, and favored European secular states as political models.

When the Ottoman empire collapsed at the end of World War I, Turkey moved toward embracing European ideals of secular nationalism. A man called Mustafa Kemal, better known as Ataturk, the founder of modern Turkey, embraced this ideal. He argued that Turkey should follow the path of the Western European nations and separate religion from politics. Ataturk disbanded the powerful Sufi brotherhoods, which had been very important in Turkey, and embraced a secular legal system that did not incorporate Islamic law at any level. He also required Turkish people to dress in a European style, which meant that women had to abandon headscarves and men had to stop wearing the traditional hat called a fez.

Although these policies were far-reaching, they did not eradicate Islam from public life in Turkey. For example, although Sufi brotherhoods had been made illegal, many Turkish people still followed the mystical path, which we will discuss later in this chapter. Though Islamic courts were no longer a part of the official legal system, Muslims still took disputes to Islamic legal authorities, particularly in rural areas. During the late twentieth and early twenty-first centuries, many Turks have re-embraced the Islamic heritage of Turkey. The Justice and Development Party, which has been supportive of re-introducing Islam into public life, has been the majority party in the governing coalition since the early 2000s.

Other Muslim countries followed a very different path. For example, in the Indian sub-continent, which was colonized by Great Britain, discussions of independence and nationalism early in the twentieth century focused a great deal on religious divisions in the region. With India's independence from Great Britain in 1947, two countries were formed: India and Pakistan. Pakistan was created as a Muslim homeland for the millions of Muslims who lived in South Asia. An important thinker behind the creation of Pakistan, Muhammad Iqbal, argued that Muslims needed a separate country to protect them from the majority Hindus in India. An organization called the Muslim League was instrumental in the early twentieth century in launching the idea of a separate state for the Muslim people of India. That ideal became a reality with independence. At first, Pakistan was divided into East and West Pakistan. In the 1970s, East Pakistan became the country that is now known as Bangladesh. Today, Pakistan and Bangladesh are among the largest Muslim-majority countries in the world, and India has a significant Muslim minority.

Iran is an important case study of Islam and nationalism in the twentieth century. Throughout much of the century, the *shah* (or king) of Iran was Reza Pahlavi. The *shah* embraced the ideals of the Western world and looked to Europe and the United States as models for development. However, Iran's Shi'a religious scholars were critical of the monarchy for marginalizing religious learning and religious authority in Iran. Iranian liberals and Marxists also criticized the *shah* as a corrupt leader who was entranced

The Taj Mahal, a mausoleum in Agra, India, was built in the 1600s by the Mughal emperor Shah Jahan as a memorial and mausoleum for his beloved wife, Mumtaz Mahal.

with the Western world and closely tied to Western governments, particularly the United States. In 1978, a coalition of clerics, intellectuals, and women's groups formed with the goal of removing the *shah* and his family from power. The revolution they staged in 1979 deposed the *shah* and ushered in the leadership of Islamic clerics. Not surprisingly, after the revolution, many of those people who had supported the overthrow of the *shah* felt neglected when the religious clerics took charge and formed an Islamic Republic.

A religious scholar known as Ayatollah Khomeini (1902–1989) headed the new government. The term *ayatollah*, which literally means "sign of God," refers to Shi'a religious scholars who have achieved a very high level of religious learning and scholarship. Khomeini had been one of the most outspoken critics of the *shah* among the religious scholars, and he argued that it was the duty of the religious scholars to build an Islamic state in Iran. This is precisely what happened in the aftermath of the revolution. The new government instituted strict reforms, which they argued reflected Islamic rules of behavior. Women were required to dress in a full-length black garment known as the *chador*. Many Iranians, among them intellectuals and professionals, left the country and made their homes abroad in places like the United States and Canada.

Today, people in Iran are divided in terms of their views on how much authority religious scholars should have in the government. In 2009, huge numbers of Iranians took to the streets to protest the disputed reelection of President Mahmoud Ahmedinajad, and many have interpreted the protests as criticism of the Islamic Republic. The protest has been called the Green Movement or Green Revolution after the color adopted by the opposition presidential candidate, Mir-Hossein Mousavi.

Islamic Reform Movements

In the last two centuries, many movements have aimed to reform local Muslim communities and the worldwide *umma*. As we discussed earlier in this chapter, in its early history, the Muslims rapidly grew into an important world power. Various Muslim empires remained powerful for many centuries, through the Abbasid period and into the later Ottoman, Mughal and Safavid sultanates. European powers were generally eclipsed by the Islamic world during this time. However, in the eighteenth century, European empires began to gain prominence as economic and political world powers. European power continued to grow with the advent of industrialization. Eventually the British, French, and Dutch empires colonized much of the Muslim world. The British and French colonized much of Muslim Africa and the Middle East, the British and the Dutch controlled Muslim lands in South and Southeast Asia.

Wahhabism During the eighteenth century, several Muslim reform movements developed. These movements were spearheaded by those who were concerned about what they viewed as a decline in Muslim communities and in Muslim power worldwide. One of the most well-known reforms was the Wahhabi movement. This was originated by a scholar named Muhammad Ibn Abd al-Wahhab (d. 1792), and it is still influential today. Ibn Abd al-Wahhab disapproved of Muslim practices that he perceived as falling outside of the Qur'an and *Sunnah*, and that had developed after the time of Muhammad. The Wahhabi movement was especially critical of saint veneration and tomb visitation. Al-Wahhab argued that these practices and others were considered innovations, and had contributed to the decline of Islam and the Muslim world. As a result, al-Wahhab's followers razed many saints' tombs and shrines, including those of Muhammad, his companions, and Husayn.

In the late eighteenth century, followers of al-Wahhab formed significant ties with the ruling family of Arabia. To this day, the movement remains influential in Saudi Arabia and in other parts of the Muslim world where it has sent teachers and established schools. Followers of the movement call themselves Muwahiddun, though they are commonly called Wahhabis in the news media.

The Wahhabi movement is often characterized as very conservative and "fundamentalist." However, we must be careful in using the latter term when discussing any religious movement. This is because not all movements called "fundamentalist" are the same. The reason the Wahhabi movement is often termed "fundamentalist" is because of its emphasis on the primacy of the Qur'an and the *Sunnah* and its criticism of later developments in Muslim thought and practice. The movement thus emphasizes the "fundamentals" of Islam—the Qur'an and the model of the Prophet. Today, the Wahhabi movement is often portrayed very negatively in the Western media. This is due to the influence of the movement on notorious extremists like Osama bin Laden, and the emphasis some Wahhabis place on bringing their version of Islam to other parts of the Muslim world. Although followers of Wahhabi Islam are generally more conservative than other Muslims, not all embrace a political version of Islam.

Resisting Colonialism During the nineteenth century, European powers increasingly dominated Muslim lands. Many Muslim thinkers lamented the loss of a cohesive and powerful *umma* and regretted the decline of several important Muslim empires. The Mughals had dominated much of South Asia for several generations, but the introduction of British rule in the nineteenth century saw the end of the Mughals. The Ottoman empire, too, had thrived in the eastern Mediterranean and North Africa, but by the early nineteenth century was threatened by increasing European power.

As a result, reformist movements developed that prioritized revitalizing the *umma*. Some focused on trying to revive the lost glory and power of the *umma*. Other movements directly resisted European imperialism and, later, American expansion and influence. And some reformers tried to deflect the criticism of the Islamic world that was coming from powerful Western governments. European leaders and scholars were often quick to criticize Islam and Muslim cultures as being "backward," and some Muslim reformers made concerted efforts to combat these developing stereotypes.

These movements took several forms. One reformer was Muhammad Ahmed ibn Abdallah (1844–1885), more commonly known as the Sudanese Mahdi. The Sudanese Mahdi organized a powerful military uprising against the Egyptian and

British forces that occupied the Sudan in the nineteenth century. Many people have claimed the title of Mahdi over the years, and Abdallah convinced people that he was indeed the Mahdi heralding the end of days. In this way, he was able to recruit a large number of followers. His movement emphasized social equality and he entirely revamped the five pillars. First, he included *jihad* as a pillar. Next, he incorporated a declaration of himself as Mahdi in the *shahadah*, and he dropped the *hajj* as a necessary duty. His revamping of the pillars was highly controversial, and many Sudanese Muslims did not support his efforts. However, his aims were more political than religious, and he successfully took the city of Khartoum in 1885 from the British and Egyptian armies.

Jamal al-din al-Afghani (1838–1897) was a reformer who sought to inspire Muslims by convincing them that the roots of revitalization were within their own faith and their own history. Born in Iran, al-Afghani traveled extensively in the Middle East and Central Asia, and advocated the idea that all Muslims worldwide should join together with the goal of revitalizing the *umma* and defeating Western imperialism. He called upon his fellow Muslims to unify against Western influence. Al-Afghani is often considered the originator of the anti-imperialist sentiment among many Muslim thinkers of the time. In addition, he argued that Islam was the religion most amenable to scientific knowledge. Al-Afghani was also well-known as an activist for the poor and downtrodden, and he called for social reform in Muslim countries to alleviate their plight.

Through calling for unification of the *umma*, al-Afghani is often considered the father of pan-Islamism, and he was a great inspiration to other reformers. Perhaps the best known of his followers is Muhammad Abduh (1849–1905), who was born in Egypt and achieved great renown as an advocate of Egyptian nationalism. Like al-Afghani, Abduh saw no conflict between religion and science, and he asserted that Islam had always embraced scientific methodologies. And like many reformers of his time, Abduh thought that the Qur'an should be interpreted in light of social changes. Abduh argued that while certain Islamic doctrines were absolute and unchangeable, some teachings should change with the times. For example, he is well known for his views of polygamy, which we discussed earlier in this chapter. One of his arguments against polygamy was that although it may have been necessary in the time of the Prophet to protect women who had no one to care for them, it was destructive in the modern context.

A third reformer of the same period was the modernist thinker Sayyid Ahmed Khan (1817–1898). Khan is best known for his educational reforms in South Asia and his support of the British. Unlike reformers such as al-Afghani, Khan admired the West, particularly the British, and attempted to bring Western ways of thought and education to India. Although he did not advocate imperial rule, he believed that the Muslims of South Asia could only move forward through embracing certain Western ways. In light of these views, it is not surprising that he was criticized by other reformers of his time as being too sympathetic with the British. He is also known for advocating interpretation of the Qur'an in a rational way in light of social changes. Like Abduh and Afghani, he embraced developments in science and argued that there was no conflict between Islam and science.

The Muslim Brotherhood The reformist spirit of the nineteenth century carried over into the twentieth. Several important and wide-reaching twentieth-century movements responded to and built on the developments of the nineteenth century. A key goal for many twentieth century reformers involved finding a path to economic development for Muslim countries that did not follow Western models. More specifically, many thinkers have sought a path that allows Muslim countries and cultures to maintain their Muslim identities and still embrace certain ideas and technologies that originated in the West. Even in the postcolonial world, Europe and the United States are criticized for cultural imperialism because Western cultural models and products are spread throughout the world, particularly through business and media.

One of the most influential contemporary movements has been the Muslim Brotherhood. The Brotherhood has been in existence for several decades. It is based in Egypt, though it has been influential all over the globe. The founder was Hassan al-Banna, who organized the movement in 1928 to revitalize Islam from within by focusing on a return to the Qur'an and the *Sunnah*. Like other reformers of his time, al-Banna was opposed to Western imperialism. He argued that encroaching Western values were contributing to the decline of Islamic societies.

Throughout its existence, the Brotherhood has had a fractured relationship with the Egyptian government. It was banned in the 1950s after members of the Brotherhood attempted to assassinate Egyptian President Gamal Abdul Nasser. Despite this, the Brotherhood remained active, and in later years made attempts to reconcile with the government under the recently-deposed President Hosni Mubarak. Sayyid Qutb, one of the more influential members of the Brotherhood, was an outspoken critic of Western influence, and he aimed to revitalize the Islamic world solely through Islamic principles. Qutb was executed in 1966 by the Egyptian government after being repeatedly accused of treason, terrorism, and a plot to kill President Nasser. Qutb's writings have continued to influence certain Islamic activists and some extremists, including those who are highly critical of Western influence on the Muslim world like Osama bin Laden and members of al-Qaeda.

Varieties of Islam

As we learned earlier in this chapter, Islam has two major branches: the Sunni and the Shi'a. Most of what we discuss in this chapter is applicable to both branches. Although the essential beliefs of the Sunnis and Shi'a are the same—including the oneness of God, the Qur'an as the word of God, and Muhammad as the messenger of God—the two branches have some important differences.

Who Are the Sunni? Sunnis make up the majority of Muslims worldwide, about 80 percent, and the Shi'a make up about 20 percent. The Sunni and Shi'a split began over the controversy surrounding leadership of the Muslim community after the death of the Prophet Muhammad. The majority of Muhammad's companions thought that he had not chosen a successor, and so supported the highly respected Abu Bakr as the next leader. However, Sunnism did not develop into a distinct branch of Islam until about 300 years later. Certain scholars emphasized that Muslims should primarily emphasize following the example of the Prophet Muhammad, the Qur'an, and the opinions of earlier scholars over engaging in rationalist thought like that of the Mutazilites, who we discussed earlier in this chapter. The word "sunni" comes from this emphasis on the *Sunnah* of the Prophet.

One of the differences between Sunni and Shi'a Islam concerns the sources of Islamic law. Both branches agree on the importance of the Qur'an and the Sunnah. In Sunni Islam, however, an additional source is the consensus of the community. This became a source of law because of a *hadith* that reported the Prophet saying, "My community will never agree upon an error." Of course, it is impossible to solicit the opinion of every Muslim on a particular legal question, so Sunnis have generally agreed that the community in question consists of the *ulama*, or legal scholars.

Because Islamic legal scholars have not always agreed on the merit of sources of law like reasoning by analogy and consensus, several schools of Islamic law developed in the centuries following the death of Muhammad. Among the Sunni, there are four schools, each named after the legal scholar who founded it. The schools were formalized by the tenth century, and all the schools recognize the validity of the others.

Who Are the Shi'a? Shi'a Muslims are in the majority in Iran and Iraq, and they form significant minorities in other countries, including Pakistan and India. In addition to believing that Muhammad designated 'Ali to be his successor, the Shi'a believe that Muhammad passed on special religious knowledge to his relatives through 'Ali. Therefore, to the Shi'a, only Muhammad's family and their descendants should lead the Muslim community. This belief in a continuing spiritual leadership of the Muslim community through the line of successors is the most significant contrast between Sunni and Shi'a Islam. For the Shi'a, the rightful leaders of the Muslim community are known as imams, the same term used for someone who leads prayer. In Shi'a Islam, the imam is both the political as well as the religious leader of the community, and he possesses the special religious knowledge that Muhammad passed on to the members of his family. 'Ali is regarded as the first imam. It is important to note that while the imam has a very prominent role in Shi'a Islam, he is not a prophet.

The authority of the Shi'a imams have a special role in Shi'a law that we do not see in Sunni approaches to Islamic law. The Shi'a schools do not recognize consensus as a source of law, but focus instead on the infallibility of the imam. Islamic scholarship is highly important in the Shi'a tradition. Also, although scholarship and learning are valued among Sunni Muslims, there is a more formal religious authority structure in Shi'ism that we do not find in Sunni Islam.

The Shi'a community itself has several branches. They differ in how they trace the line of imams down from 'Ali. The largest branch is known as the Twelvers, who make up the majority of Muslims in Iran and Iraq. The Twelvers believe that the line of imams went through several generations until the twelfth imam disappeared in the ninth century. This twelfth imam is considered to be in "occultation," or hiding. Twelvers believe that he will eventually return. In the meantime, the Islamic scholars are considered responsible for the leadership of the Muslim community. This idea was important in the new government set up in Iran after the 1979 revolution.

Another branch of Shi'ism, known as the *Ismailis*, believe that there has been an unbroken line of imams from 'Ali until the present day. They take their name from the seventh imam, a man named Ismail, whom the Twelvers do not recognize as an imam.

Sufism

Muslims have sometimes described the *shari'ah* as the "outer" way to God because it regulates a person's "outer" existence: how he should handle relationships with other people, how he should live in a community, and how he should worship. For many Muslims, however, there is also an "inner" way to God. This is the mystical tradition of Islam, which is known as Sufism. Like traditions of mysticism in other religions, the goal of a Sufi is to draw close to and personally experience God. However, unlike mystics of other religions, Sufis base this spiritual quest on the sources of Islam, namely the Qur'an and the example of Muhammad.

It is likely that Sufism arose in the years after the death of Muhammad as a response to the worldly excesses and materialism of the Umayyad Dynasty. Many early Sufis were ascetics who taught that a simple way of life was in keeping with the way Muhammad lived. One famous eighth-century Sufi was Hasan of Basra (Basra is a city in Iraq). He was known for preaching asceticism and for his constant weeping out of fear of God. A renowned early female Sufi was Rabi'a al-Adawiyya, also of Basra. Rabi'a was known for her almost giddy happiness in the love of God. There are many wonderful stories about Rabi'a. In one, she was said to have refused several offers of marriage because she claimed she was utterly devoted to God and had no time for marriage. In another popular tale, she criticized Hasan of Basra by telling him that his constant weeping and fear of God drew the focus to himself rather than God. This theme is echoed in another story, in which she walks through the streets of Basra carrying a pitcher of water and a flaming torch. When asked why she was doing this, she explained that she wanted to set paradise ablaze and put out the fires of hell so people would love God solely for the sake of God—not out of hope of paradise or fear of hell.

After Rabi'a's time, this ideal of intense love for God became a primary focus for Sufis. Love is often expressed in Sufi poetry, which is one of the premier art forms in Islamic history. The following poem, by the great thirteenth-century Sufi poet

Jalalludin Rumi, describes the beauty found in submitting to God. Those who love and submit to God are compared to a moth who is drawn to a candle's flame.

> Love whispers in my ear,
> "Better to be a prey than a hunter,
> Make yourself My fool.
> Stop trying to be the sun and become a speck!
> Dwell at My door and be homeless.
> Don't pretend to be a candle, be a moth,
> so you may taste the savor of Life
> and know the power hidden in serving."[13]

Sufis ground their belief and worship practice in the teachings of the Qur'an. Sufis believe that the study of holy texts has two dimensions—the inner and the outer. Sufi readings of the Qur'an have often searched for the inner, or hidden, meaning. This approach to interpreting the inner meaning of the Qur'an focuses on the love of God for creation and the closeness of God to humanity. Sufis often reference the *hadith qudsi*, which as you recall focus on these themes.

Like all Muslims, Sufis consider Muhammad the ideal human, and they strive to emulate the way he lived his life. Sufis emphasize the story of the miraculous night when Muhammad journeyed from Mecca to Jerusalem and from there ascended to heaven to meet God. The ascension to heaven is known as the *miraj*. Muslims believe that the angel Gabriel came to Muhammad one night while he was sleeping and took him to Jerusalem. From there, Muhammad ascended upward through the many levels of heaven. He met earlier prophets like Jesus and Moses. Eventually, Muhammad came into the presence of God. God gave him significant blessings and special spiritual knowledge that he later passed on to his companions, particularly 'Ali. Because Muhammad is believed to have personally experienced the presence of God, Sufis consider him to be the first Sufi and the source of the special spiritual knowledge they seek. Muslims around the world are very familiar with the story of the ascension. In East Africa and the Middle East, Muslims like Amina from the opening story of this chapter learn of the *miraj* through epic poems. Poems about Muhammad's life and experiences may be recited on special occasions, like *mawlid al-nabi*.

The night journey is mentioned in the Qur'an (17:1) and the *hadith* literature and is considered by many Muslims to be the greatest of all Muhammad's spiritual experiences. Because Muhammad ascended to heaven from Jerusalem, the city holds a special place in Islam, and it is one of the three Muslim holy cities, along with Mecca and Medina. In the year 691 C.E., the beautiful shrine known as the Dome of the Rock was built

The Dome of the Rock in Jerusalem.

over the spot from which Muhammad ascended to heaven. The Dome of the Rock is located on the place known as the Temple Mount, where the ancient Jewish temples were located. It is therefore easy to understand why this place in the center of Jerusalem is special to both Muslims and Jews. This is one of the primary reasons that the status of Jerusalem is so central to the Arab-Israeli conflict today: practitioners of both faiths (as well as Christians) consider the city to be holy, and long to have unfettered access to it.

Mevlevis *dhikr*; Mevlevis are sometimes known as Whirling Dervishes.

Most Sufis agree that an individual needs guidance along the spiritual path to God. As a result, a master-disciple relationship is very important in Sufism. The *shaykh,* or master, directs the spiritual training of the novices. In the early centuries of Islam, respected *shaykhs* would guide several pupils, and as a result, a number of Sufi orders, *tariqas,* developed around particular Sufi masters. Each order traces a spiritual lineage of learned leaders back to Muhammad and from Muhammad to God. This lineage is called the *silsila,* and is something like a family tree. Muhammad is believed to have passed on his special religious knowledge to his companions, who then passed it down through the generations from master to disciple.

Although members of all the orders have the same goal—personally experiencing God—they emphasize different meditation techniques and spiritual practices. Some are widespread and have members all over the world. Others are limited to a particular region. The most well-known order in the Western world is perhaps the Mevlevi order, which is based on the teachings of Jalalludin Rumi.

Sufi orders emphasize the necessity of some type of *dhikr.* The term means "recollection" and refers to Sufi meditation in which the believer strives to "recollect" God so completely that he forgets himself. *Dhikr* can take many forms and varies from order to order. Sometimes *dhikr* is as simple as the recitation of the *shahadah,* and sometimes it is much more elaborate. The Mevlevis have an elaborate *dhikr.* In the West, they are often called the "Whirling Dervishes" because their *dhikr* involves controlled whirling. For all Sufis, the goal of *dhikr* is to lose the sense of self entirely in complete remembrance of God. Eventually, the Sufi hopes to achieve spiritual union with God.

Not all Sufi practice takes place in the formal context of the orders. In many parts of the world, Muslims may participate in Sufi practice without affiliation to an order. A good example of this is the practice of saint veneration. Many Sufis venerate *shaykhs,* or saints, who were well-known and respected for their religious learning and spirituality. In some areas, like Pakistan and northern India, the tombs of deceased *shaykhs* become places of pilgrimage. At the tombs, people seek blessings from the saints. Tomb visitation is very common in South Asia, when the celebration of the

Pilgrims at the shrine of Hazrat Mu'in ud-Din Chishti in Ajmer (Rajasthan), India.

saints on the days of the death can draw thousands of pilgrims. Many pilgrims are not affiliated with a Sufi order, and some are not even Muslim; people of all faiths may recognize the power of a saint.

Throughout Islamic history, occasional tension has arisen between Sufis and other Muslims. For example, the practice of saint veneration has drawn criticism from some, who argue that the celebration of saints compromises the oneness of God by raising mere mortals to the level of the divine. Of course, those involved in saint veneration do not view saints as divine. Rather, they view saints more as close friends of God, who are filled with blessings that can be transferred to others. Historically, Sufis have sometimes been criticized by other Muslims for neglecting the five pillars in favor of more esoteric religious knowledge and practice. Some early Sufis rejected adherence to the *shari'ah* on the grounds that the technical laws merely served to veil God from the believer, not draw him or her closer. However, this was not a majority opinion among Sufism. Indeed, some Sufis have made a specific effort to reconcile the *shari'ah* and Sufism. The eleventh century scholar al-Ghazali was one of these. In his writings, he established Sufism as a branch of formal learning in the Islamic sciences.

Muslims in North America

Today, over 6 million Muslims live in the United States and about 1 million in Canada. Both populations are growing rapidly, primarily through immigration. American Muslims are making inroads and social contributions in their home communities and in regional and national politics. Many Muslims live in large urban areas, but significant populations also live in smaller towns and more rural areas. The Muslim population in the United States is not limited to one particular city or even one particular region. Muslims live everywhere from Los Angeles to Salt Lake City to Dearborn, Michigan.

The African-American Muslim population grew significantly in the twentieth century. Scholars estimate that from 10 to 30 percent of the Africans who were enslaved and brought to the United States from the seventeenth to the nineteenth centuries were Muslims. Once in the United States, however, many slaves were not permitted to freely practice their religion, although some were literate in Arabic and tried to maintain their religious practice. Many slaves were also forced to convert to Christianity or converted by choice.

In the twentieth century, African-Americans were attracted to Islam and converted for a variety of reasons. For example, many people regarded Islam as the likely religion of their African ancestors. Thus, Muslim religious leaders often stressed these ties to Africa, and some claimed that Islam was a more "authentic" religion for African-Americans. This was because Islam was not the religion of the European-American slave owners. Today, perhaps half of the Muslims in the United States are African-Americans.[14]

The Nation of Islam has played an important role in the U.S. Muslim community. However, the majority of African-American Muslims are not members of the organization. The Nation was founded by a man who was known by several different names, among them Wallace Ford and Wali D. Fard. In the 1930s, Fard established the Temple of Islam in Detroit, Michigan, and he preached that all black people were originally Muslims. Eventually, a student of his named Elijah Muhammad succeeded him as the leader of the Nation of Islam. The Nation of Islam differs significantly from mainstream Islam on several key teachings. Most significantly, followers regard Fard as God incarnate and Elijah is considered his prophet. The Nation of Islam has been controversial in the United States because of teachings that suggest the natural supremacy of black people and encourage the rejection of white society. Despite its controversial nature, the Nation has been active in improving the lives of African-Americans.

An American Muslim soldier praying.

When Elijah Muhammad died in 1975, the Nation of Islam split. One group, led by his son Warith Deen Muhammad, moved away from the teachings of the Nation toward mainstream Sunni Islam and became known as the American Muslim Mission. This is the largest organized group of African American Muslims today. Louis Farrakhan, a radical preacher who is very controversial for his espousal of black supremacist ideas and politics, has led the other group, which retained the name Nation of Islam, for many years.

Malcolm X, a leader in the black power movement of the 1960s, was perhaps the most famous American Muslim, and the most famous member of the Nation of Islam. He was raised a Christian with the name Malcolm Little and converted to Islam while serving a prison sentence. He took the name X as a statement decrying his "slave name" of Little, in reference to the historical practice of slaves being given the surname of their masters. He eventually took the name Malik al-Shabazz. Malcolm X was affiliated with the Nation of Islam for several years, and became an influential public figure. However, after he made the *hajj* to Mecca in the 1960s, he moved toward mainstream Islam and eventually separated himself from the Nation. In his autobiography, he movingly describes the sense of harmony and unity he felt while on *hajj* with Muslims of all colors, ethnicities, and cultural backgrounds.[15]

For the last century and a half, the number of Muslims in the United States and Canada has also increased dramatically due to immigration. Many American Muslims today are either immigrants or the descendants of immigrants. And like all immigrants to the United States, Muslims have come in waves from many parts of the world; most are from the Middle East, South Asia, Southeast Asia, and Iran, though others came from Eastern Europe, Africa, and elsewhere. In the late nineteenth century, people migrated from the Middle East, namely Syria, Jordan, and Lebanon, to the Americas for economic reasons. Most of them were uneducated, and most were single men. This resulted in much intermarriage between these Muslim newcomers and people of varied cultural and religious backgrounds.

In the middle of the twentieth century, Muslim immigrants began to come from other areas of the Middle East, the Soviet Union, and Eastern Europe. Many in this wave of immigrants were educated and from wealthy families, and many had a great interest in assimilating to the wider American population. In later years, Muslim peoples came to the United States from South Asia, Iran, and other parts of the world. Many in this most recent wave have had less interest in assimilating to mainstream American culture, instead hoping to preserve their cultural and religious heritage.

As the Muslim population grows in the United States and Canada, Muslims are becoming an increasingly important religious minority. In 2006, the United States saw the election of the first Muslim member of Congress, Representative Keith Ellison of Minnesota. However, as with many immigrant groups before them, immigrants from the Muslim world face challenges when moving to the United States. Not only will they be in a religious and cultural minority, but they face the added difficulty of an American population that does not know much about Islam except for unflattering stereotypes.

The tragic events of September 11, 2001, brought Islam to the forefront of many Americans' minds. Although the attackers used a religious discourse to explain their actions, American Muslims have joined other Muslims around the world in denouncing terrorist attacks as antithetical to the teachings of Islam, which prohibits the killing of innocents. Many cite the Qur'anic verse (5:32) that equates the killing of one person to be as sinful as killing all of humanity. It is perhaps best to understand terrorism as acts of political violence that perpetrators have attempted to justify with religion. Understood this way, we can see many parallels in recent and more distant world history when individuals or nations have used various religions to justify warfare, colonization, and other forms of violence.

In the aftermath of September 11, 2001, North American Muslims faced suspicion and hostility from their non-Muslim neighbors. Some non-Muslim Americans mistakenly viewed the terrorist attacks as representative of Islam and Muslims, and in turn targeted Muslim communities, breaking windows in mosques and threatening teachers at Islamic elementary schools. In 2010, a controversy about the building of an Islamic center in lower Manhattan turned especially heated. Many non-Muslim Americans were vehemently opposed to the center because it was a few blocks away from the site of the September 11, 2001, attacks on New York.

Despite these difficulties, however, many Americans have expressed increased interest in understanding other faiths and cultures—particularly Islam. Also, many

American Muslim individuals and communities have made concerted efforts to educate other Americans about their faith, beliefs, and religious practices, and to explain that the vast majority of the world's Muslims regard terrorist acts as distinctly un-Islamic with no basis in the faith. With these efforts at outreach, and the efforts of non-Muslim Americans to understand Islam and Muslim peoples and cultures, we can have great hope for meaningful religious diversity in the United States.

CONCLUSION

In this chapter, we have learned about the historical development, the beliefs, and the practices of Islam and Muslims. Islam is truly a global religion and is perhaps the fastest growing religion in the world. Many Muslim-majority counties are experiencing rapid population growth, but numbers are also increasing because of conversions. One of the most marked characteristics of the Muslim world today—its diversity—is unlikely to change. In fact, the ethnic diversity of the Muslim world is likely to increase. Muslims live in nearly every country in the world and on every inhabited continent.

Muslims everywhere, however, are responding to a rapidly changing world and increased globalization. Today, Muslims are facing questions about the role of religion in private and public life, the relationships with other religious communities in plural environments, and what it means to be a person of faith in the modern world. Some of these issues are common to many religions. Others, like the role of Islamic law in modern governments, are specific to Muslims. How will Muslims address these issues in years to come? One issue that has had much attention in the press lately is the question of Islamic dress in Western Europe. In France in 2004, schoolgirls were prohibited from wearing headscarves because officials argued it violated France's commitment to secularism. (Other religious symbols, like the yarmulke worn by Jewish boys, were also banned.) Many Muslims, however, thought this was a violation of their freedom to practice religion. In Britain, a recent controversy focused on whether or not a Muslim teacher should be allowed to wear a scarf that covered her face while teaching.

A related challenge Muslims face is the negative perceptions some Westerners hold about the nature of Islam and Muslim life. How will Muslims living in religiously plural societies grapple with this sort of challenge? In the United States, some Muslim Americans who have been invited or have volunteered visit churches, synagogues, schools, and community centers with the aim of teaching people about Islam and increasing their familiarity with Muslim ways of life. Muslim communities around the world struggle with competing interpretations of Islam's teachings. Sometimes, young Muslims who go abroad to study in places like Saudi Arabia, Indonesia, or Egypt come back to their home communities with different ideas about the way in which Islam should be practiced and taught. In many countries, as exemplified recently by some participants in the "Arab Spring" demonstrations of early 2011, Muslims are considering the relationship between Islam and democracy. While some argue that

Islam is inherently compatible with democracy because of examples like the historical emphasis on consensus, others argue that democracy is a Western concept that is not compatible with an Islamic system of government.

As we have learned, Islam is a unique religious tradition, but it also shares a great deal with Christianity and Judaism. Will these similarities lead to greater communication and cooperation between Muslim and other religious communities? Although it is difficult to predict what the future will bring, it is clear that Islam will remain a dynamic and diverse religious tradition. Throughout history, Muslim thinkers, artists, and practitioners have contributed a great deal to global human culture, and they will continue to do so in the future.

SEEKING ANSWERS

What Is Ultimate Reality?

Muslims believe that God is the creator and sustainer of the universe, the world, and all that is in it. Muslims believe that elements of the beautiful natural world are signs of God. Humans can learn something about ultimate reality through God's revelations, which are communicated to humanity through prophets. The Qur'an is the source of God's teachings about the nature of ultimate reality and the nature of the world.

How Should We Live in This World?

Muslims believe that human beings are part of God's creation. The Islamic tradition offers many guidelines concerning the right way for human beings to live. People should worship God, be generous to the needy, and live righteously. The life of the prophet Muhammad, especially as related in the *Sunnah*, serves as an example for Muslims of how to live. The "five pillars" of Muslim worship practice are the foundation for how Muslims live their faith.

What Is Our Ultimate Purpose?

Muslims believe in an afterlife and a Day of Judgment, when all humans will be judged on their actions and deeds in this life. Those who have lived righteously will enter paradise, and those who have led sinful lives will be cast in to the fire. Most Muslims think that human beings have free choice and must choose to submit to the will of God. The choices that individuals make will be evaluated on the Day of Judgment, when God will judge each person independently. Devout Muslims aim to live righteous lives by submitting to the will of God, adhering to the "five pillars," and following the example of the Prophet Muhammad.

REVIEW QUESTIONS

For Review

1. What are the essential principles of belief in the Islamic religion?

2. What are the key religious practices in Islam? How do beliefs relate to religious practice and expression?

3. What are the most important sources of spirituality for Muslims?

4. What is a prophet in the Islamic tradition? Why role does Muhammad play in Islam and in the life of Muslims today? How do Muslims know about the life of Muhammad, and how does he differ from other prophets?

5. What is Sufism, and how is it rooted in the Islamic tradition?

For Further Reflection

1. Explore the concept of scripture in Judaism, Christianity, and Islam. What important elements do these religions share? How do they differ?

2. What is the role of prophecy in each of these religious traditions? Consider the figures Abraham, Moses, and Jesus. How are they understood in each tradition?

3. What are some important challenges Muslims face in the modern world? Why do you think Islam has been so stereotyped in North America and the West?

GLOSSARY

Abbasids An important Muslim empire from 750–1258 C.E.

adhan (a-than; Arabic) The call to prayer.

Aisha A beloved wife of Muhammad who is known for transmitting many *hadith*.

Allah (a-lah; Arabic) The Arabic term for God.

caliph (ka-lif; Arabic) Leader of the Muslim community after death of Muhammad.

hadith (ha-deeth; Arabic) Literary tradition recording the sayings and deeds of the Prophet Muhammad.

hajj (hahj; Arabic) The annual pilgrimage to Mecca, one of the five pillars of Islam.

hijra (hij-rah; Arabic) The migration of the early Muslim community from Mecca to Medina in 622 C.E.; the Islamic calendar dates from this year.

Husayn Grandson of Muhammad who was killed while challenging the Umayyads.

imam (ee-mam; Arabic) Prayer leader; in the Shi'a tradition, one of the leaders of the Muslim community following the death of the Prophet Muhammad.

Islam (is-lahm; Arabic) Lit. "submission", specifically, the religious tradition based on the revealed Qur'an as Word of God.

jahiliyya (ja-hil-ee-ah; Arabic) The "age of ignorance," which refers to the time before the revelation of the Qur'an.

jihad (jee-had; Arabic) Lit. "striving"; sometimes, the greater *jihad* is the struggle with one's self to become a better person; the lesser *jihad* is associated with military conflict in defense of the faith.

Khadija Muhammad's beloved first wife.

Mecca The city in which Muhammad was born; place of pilgrimage for Muslims.

Medina The city to which Muhammad and his early followers migrated to escape persecution in Mecca.

(continued)

GLOSSARY (continued)

miraj (mir-aj; Arabic) Muhammad's Night Journey from Mecca to Jerusalem and from there to heaven, where he met with God.

mosque (mosk) Place of prayer, from the Arabic term "masjid."

muezzin (mu-ez-in; Arabic) The person who calls the *adhan*.

Muhammad The prophet who received the revelation of the Qur'an from God. The final prophet in a long line of prophets sent by God to humanity.

Qur'an (kur-an; Arabic) The holy text of Muslims; the Word of God as revealed to Muhammad.

Ramadan (rah-mah-dan; Arabic) The month in which Muslims must fast daily from dawn until dusk; the fast is one of the five pillars of Islam, the month in which the Qur'an is believed to have been revealed to Muhammad.

salat (sa-laht; Arabic) The daily prayers, which are one of the pillars of Islam.

sawm (som; Arabic) The mandatory fast during the month of Ramadan; one of the pillars of Islam.

shahadah (sha-ha-dah; Arabic) The declaration of faith: "There is no God but God and Muhammad is the Messenger of God"; the first of the five pillars.

shari'ah (sha-ree-ah; Arabic) Lit. "the way to the water hole"; specifically, Islamic law.

Shi'a (shee-ah; Arabic) One of the two major branches of Islam. The Shi'a believed that 'Ali should have succeeded as leader of the Muslim community after the death of Muhammad.

shirk (sherk; Arabic) The sin of idolatry, of worshiping anything other than God, the one unforgivable sin in Islam.

Sufi (soof-i) A follower of the mystical tradition of Islam, **Sufism**, which focuses on the believer's personal experience of God and goal of union with God.

Sunnah (sun-na; Arabic) Lit. "way of life" or "custom"; specifically refers to example of the life of the prophet Muhammad; important religious source for Muslims.

Sunni (soon-e; Arabic) One of the two main branches of Islam. The Sunnis believed that the Muslim community should decide on a successor to lead after the death of Muhammad.

surah (soor-ah; Arabic) Chapter of the Qur'an; there are 114 *surahs* in the Qur'an.

tafsir (taf-seer; Arabic) Interpretation of or commentary on the Qur'an. There are several types of *tafsir*, which aim to explain the meaning of the Qur'an.

Umayyad Dynasty Controversial Muslim dynasty from 661–750 C.E.

umma (um-mah; Arabic) The worldwide Muslim community.

zakat (za-kaht; Arabic) Regulated almsgiving; one of the five pillars of Islam.

SUGGESTIONS FOR FURTHER READING

Armstrong, Karen. *Muhammad: A Biography of the Prophet*. San Francisco: Harper San Francisco, 1993. A detailed and readable account of Muhammad's life.

Denny, Frederick M. *An Introduction to Islam*. Englewood Cliffs, NJ: Prentice Hall, 2010. A very thorough introduction to Islam aimed at college students.

Ernst, Carl W. *Following Muhammad: Rethinking Islam in the Contemporary World*. Chapel Hill: University of North Carolina Press, 2003. A readable introduction to Islam for the general public, focusing on Islam in the modern world.

Netton, Ian Richard. *A Popular Dictionary of Islam*. Chicago: NTC Publishing Group, 1997. A useful dictionary of key terms, people, and places in the Islamic tradition.

Renard, John, ed. *Windows on the House of Islam*. Berkeley: University of California Press, 1998. A collection of primary source materials from early Islamic history until the present; includes poetry, essays, philosophical writings, and more.

Schimmel, Annemarie. *Mystical Dimension of Islam*. Chapel Hill: University of North Carolina Press, 1975. A classic and comprehensive overview of Sufism.

Sells, Michael. *Approaching the Qur'an: The Early Revelations*. Ashland, OR: White Cloud Press, 2002. Translation and explanation of the earliest *surahs* of the Qur'an.

ONLINE SOURCES

Islam and Islamic Studies Resources
theislamwebsite.com
Comprehensive website from the University of Georgia with resources on all aspects of the Islamic tradition and current events.

Center for Muslim-Jewish Engagement
usc.edu/schools/college/crcc/engagement/resources/texts/muslim
Useful site from the University of Southern California with databases for searching English translations of the Qur'an and *hadith* collections.

NEW RELIGIOUS MOVEMENTS

IT IS THE EVENING of August 1, and Barbara Z. is preparing an altar for the celebration of Lughnassadh, a fall harvest festival celebrated by practitioners of Wicca. For centuries, European men and women who worshiped the forces of nature, or who believed that they could perform acts of magical power by communing with these forces, were often referred to as "witches," a term contemporary Wiccans often use to describe themselves. Unlike the witches of fairy tales and films, however, Barbara Z. is not gruesome or menacing, nor does she cast evil spells upon unsuspecting princesses; in fact, she does not even own a broomstick (or ride upon one) and has never considered keeping a black cat around her home. In reality, she is a successful businesswoman in her thirties who was raised as an Episcopalian, and who had never heard of Wicca until a close friend suggested she read *The Spiral Dance* by Miriam Simos (better known by her Wiccan name of "Starhawk").

Reading that book, and many others that described the beliefs and practices of Wicca, changed Barbara's life. She soon established a personal connection with a local coven, or witches' circle. In their company she discovered a community of like-minded men and women whose worldviews were remarkably similar to her own. For Wiccans, the natural universe is alive with sacred energy, a power that is often represented in Wiccan ritual as the worship of a specific "god," and by paying homage

An offering of wine to the Earth spirits is a common feature of Wiccan ceremonies.

to that deity, Wiccans believe they are celebrating the beauty and wonder of Nature itself. **Lughnassadh** (also known as *Lammas*), named for the Celtic god Lugh, is one such festival. Wiccans take a particular interest in pre-Christian European deities, and many of their sacred festivals are dedicated to one or another of these "pagan" gods. Like many of those who have joined a new religious movement, Barbara thinks of Wicca as a break with her Christian upbringing, and as an essential part of a journey of spiritual self-discovery.

The celebration of Lughnassadh entails several distinct ritual acts, all of them related symbolically to the Fall harvest. Part of the day was spent baking a loaf of bread, to be used later that evening during the Lughnassadh ceremony. Wiccans customarily share pieces of this bread in celebration of the harvesting of grains, and it is from this practice that the name Lammas—meaning "loaf-mass"—is derived. At dusk, Barbara will create a magic circle of lights, placing her altar at the center of this circle. On that altar Barbara will place a sheaf of wheat and several cornbread figures, representing the god Lugh and his worshipers, and a basket of star-shaped cookies. Each member of the coven will be asked, in turn, what they fear and what they desire most from the coming year, and they will then perform a dance in honor of the dying year that will soon be reborn. Having tossed the cornbread figures into a fire, the participants in this ceremony will then eat the star-shaped cookies in anticipation of a bountiful year to come. Following the conclusion of this ritual, the members of the coven will sit down to a celebratory meal, at which time the witches will address each other by their "craft" names. As a third degree Wiccan Priestess, Barbara will be addressed as Lady Sparrow, combining a title of honor with the name she chose on entering the Wiccan community.

Ritual practices will differ from one Wiccan community to another; the great constant being the underlying conviction that each act performed by the coven brings their community—and every member of that circle—closer to the indestructible source of life that is Nature itself. ☀

WHAT IS "NEW" ABOUT NEW RELIGIOUS MOVEMENTS?

Anyone who has surfed the web, using key words like "cults" and "sects,"[1] or who has ventured into a bookstore in search of works on astrology, witchcraft, or nontraditional methods of healing, must be aware of how diverse the audience for religious information has grown in our time. In fact, social scientists and historians have estimated that, globally, no less than 14,000 new religious communities have come into existence in the course of the twentieth and early twenty-first centuries. While not everyone agrees on what constitutes a "new" religious movement, most students of religion in the modern era are aware of both an exponential growth of new religious communities worldwide and of the often aggressively nontraditional (and even countercultural) character exhibited by many of these new religions. It will be useful, therefore, to begin with some general observations about the larger cultural milieu within which these new religions arose, and then to identify what is really innovative in their teachings and practices. However, it should already be evident to readers of this volume that, at some point in history, practically *every* religious movement or philosophy has been perceived as "new" by its contemporaries, and oftentimes rejected for that very reason.

Modernization, Globalization, and Secularization

In Chapter 1 we considered several interrelated phenomena that have brought about profound changes in religious thought and behavior, particularly during the last two centuries. The first, and arguably the most important, of these phenomena is the process known as **modernization**, which historians most often identify with the condition of post-industrial Europe and America in the nineteenth and twentieth centuries. Modernized societies, as we noted, exhibit higher levels of literacy and advanced technological capabilities. These societies have witnessed both the growth of scientific knowledge and a greater diffusion of political power, with a corresponding erosion of traditional authority and respect for the past, in politics as well as religion. The long-term effect of modernization, therefore, is not only a loss of influence and credibility on the part of established religious institutions, but an even more dramatic increase in the number of new religious movements that have been empowered by the very process of cultural change. This was especially true of nineteenth-century America, where "communities of dissent" (in Stephen Stein's phrase[2]) suddenly began to mushroom after the Civil War, and where a culture of religious "liberalism" and experimentation increasingly took root in American soil. Collectively, these new religious leaders (as well as their followers) often referred to themselves as "seekers," and their quest for new spiritual insights led many thousands to explore nontraditional beliefs and social ideals. The new technology of mass communications—at first books and newspapers, and much later, the digital media of our own period—ensured that the dissemination of information about any innovative teaching or social organization would be both rapid and widespread.

Globalization is yet another important factor in the growth of new religious movements. Even before the creation of the internet, the pace of cultural interaction had increased multifold as a direct result of Western imperialism and of colonialist encounters between Western and non-Western peoples. Evidence of such interactions within the religious domain can be seen in the **World's Parliament of Religions**, held in Chicago in 1893 as part of an International Trade Exposition. Representatives of such non-Western religious traditions as Vedanta, Zoroastrianism, Jainism, and Buddhism shared the stage with liberal Protestants, Reform Jews, and spokespersons for various types of Spiritualist and Theosophical belief systems, with the aim of achieving some form of global understanding of human religious diversity. When, in 1993, a second World's Parliament of Religions was held in Chicago, an even larger number of religious communities were represented, and a special effort was made to include those (like Native Americans) who had been excluded a century earlier.

These gatherings demonstrated, beyond any reasonable doubt, the exponential growth of interest in the West in religious cultures that had earlier been ignored or marginalized (or even demonized) by the West, but which were now accorded a much greater measure of respect. This movement toward a multicultural perspective on religion was enhanced significantly in the United States by the repeal of the Asian Exclusion Act in 1965, and the resulting immigration of increasing numbers of non-Western peoples to America over the following decades. But even before this demographic shift occurred, greater numbers of thoughtful, spiritually oriented persons had already come to embrace a pluralistic view of religious diversity: that is, a view of modern society that presupposes multiple forms of religious experience and expression as the *normal* condition of life in the contemporary world.

Along with these changes in outlook and socialization in the modern era, however, one more phenomenon should be discussed, and that is **secularization**. A secular society is one in which the values and methodologies of science are viewed as culturally dominant, and in which religious beliefs and worldviews are seen as largely subjective or simply lacking in intellectual authority. This subordination of religion to science is one of the immediate consequences of what historians call the Scientific Revolution, and ongoing disputes between conservative Christians and biologists who support a Darwinian model of species evolution provide ample evidence that the struggle between science and religion that began with Galileo's new astronomy in the sixteenth century is still being waged today with as much emotional intensity as in the past. However, the difference between a Galileo who challenged the prevailing geocentric view of the solar system and a contemporary biologist who challenges the biblical portrait of divine creation is profound: the weight of educated opinion in most modern societies is on the side of the scientist, whose cosmology is seen as more credible than that of his fundamentalist adversary. Moreover, the prevalence of materialist values in modern societies, and the persistent view that religious belief is a matter of personal choice, serves to reinforce the often critical perspective from which all religious ideas and institutions are regarded. It follows, therefore, that if all religious teachings are equally problematic from a radically secular point of view, then any new form of religious belief has as much, or as little, claim to credibility (in the eyes of a skeptical observer) as any more established faith. The secularization of modern societies thereby creates an opportunity for new religious ideas and social directives to develop without fear of overwhelming cultural rejection, and for many new religious communities the need to "re-enchant" the world is the most pressing spiritual need of our time.

This need is particularly evident in religious communities that have been linked to **New Age** thought, and to counterculture movements growing out of the 1960s and 1970s that embrace a belief in magic and in esoteric wisdom. New Age religious practices include (though are not limited to) the channeling of disembodied spirits, the use of crystals and magnets for healing purposes, and a reliance on astrological calculations to determine one's fate and fortune. All of these practices are commonly viewed by secularists as culturally obsolete and empirically invalid efforts at controlling the natural environment, but New Age advocates argue, in opposition, that science has neglected or suppressed ancient teachings about the human body or the physical universe that cannot be reconciled to any current model of "truth." And while it is impossible to speak of a single, coherent New Age philosophy, many groups that fall under this rubric are clearly in search of an alternative worldview that will allow a "transformation of consciousness," or at the very least a renewed sense of wonder and reverence for those hidden forces of nature, or of the human spirit, that contemporary science refuses to acknowledge.

Theoretical Models and Social Typologies

Over the past three decades, several attempts have been made to categorize the various kinds of new or "alternative" religions (as they are sometimes called) that have developed during the twentieth and early twenty-first centuries. One very popular theoretical model, formulated by J. Gordon Melton,[3] divides these new movements into eight distinctive "families" of religious thought and lifestyle. Each of these groupings exhibits its own peculiar "thought-world," though a certain amount of overlap (of outlook and social organization) can be observed throughout several of these "alternative spiritualities." The obvious advantage of this model is its ability to arrange historical data into fairly precise thematic as well as regional patterns of perception. The disadvantage of this schema, however, is that its conceptual boundaries are at times *too* precise—an obvious weakness when one is describing religions whose teachings are frequently eclectic in nature.

Another, much simpler paradigm of cultural differentiation has been proposed by Roy Wallis,[4] who classifies new religious movements in relation to their perception of the world and of human destiny. For Wallis, new religions can be understood as either "world-affirming," "world-renouncing," or "world-accommodating," though once again a certain amount of overlap and ambiguity is inevitable when attempting to situate any particular religious system within any one of these categories. Thus, a world-affirming religion is one that attributes positive value to human existence, and whose goal is to improve the conditions of life wherever it is possible to do so through human effort. Removing oneself from society or longing for self-annihilation consequently has no value for someone who has embraced this point of view. A world-renouncing religion, on the other world, takes the very opposite position, proceeding instead from the assumption that human society is irredeemably evil and that life itself is too filled with pain and futility to be worth improving. Adherents of this religious philosophy typically envision an imminent and destructive end to the world we know, and even devise strategies for bringing about an end, either to the social order or to one's individual existence. World-accommodating religions, as the term suggests, are prepared to adapt to a world that is manifestly deficient in goodness or grace, while at the same time asserting their belief in a "higher" goal for humankind (which it cannot, at present, attain). The merit of these typologies is that they focus our attention quite specifically on the relationship between a core perception of social reality and

MELTON'S EIGHT RELIGIOUS FAMILIES

1. *The Latter-Day Saint Family*. For the past century and a half, more than fifty separate Latter-day Saint communities have come into existence, each claiming some direct connection to the teachings and revelations of Joseph Smith, the chief prophet and founder of the Church of Jesus Christ of Latter-day Saints. Many of these communities have disappeared, but doctrinally they were all committed to a core belief in "restoration" of true, apostolic Christianity through the ministry and writings of Joseph Smith (and most especially *The Book of Mormon*).

2. *The Communal Family*. Any religious community that is organized around monastic ideals that entail some form of spiritual and personal discipline can be categorized as a "communal" organization. Communities like the Shakers and the Hutterites (who migrated from Russia to North America in the 1870s) are committed to principles of collective ownership and individual austerity and tend to view mainstream society as materialistic and corrupt.

3. *The New Thought Metaphysical Family*. By the late nineteenth century the phrase "New Thought" was applied to a variety of religious and philosophical views that derived from American Transcendentalism and the writings of figures like Ralph Waldo Emerson. One important line of development in this "family" can be traced through Mary Baker Eddy and the Christian Science movement she founded in the 1870s. Common to all forms of New Thought is the belief that each individual has access to spiritual forces and realities that lie behind the material world, and that this knowledge can be used to cure illnesses or end poverty and social conflict.

4. *The Spiritualist/Psychic Family*. Tracing their descent from the philosophical writings of the Swedish mystic Emanuel Swedenborg (1688–1772), these religious groups share a belief that life after death and communication with the dead are both scientifically valid and experimentally verifiable ideas. Among such "spiritualists" the practice of mediumship and "**channeling**"—that is, contacting the dead and speaking on their behalf—are widespread. In the later twentieth century, one popular variation of this paradigm can be found in **Ufology** (the belief that intelligences from other worlds are attempting to communicate with earth, and have been landing space vehicles or UFOs on our planet for centuries). Other offshoots of this family of ideas can be found in the renewed interest in astrology, reincarnation, and various forms of meditation in the later twentieth century.

5. *Ancient Wisdom Groups*. These alternative religious communities trace their beginnings back to some wisdom tradition in the ancient past. Believing in the advent of a "New Age" made possible by the release of spiritual energies that have lain dormant in the human race for many centuries, members of this family argue that they are continuing the work of ancient "masters" whose spiritual wisdom and psychic powers have been repressed by Western rationalism.

6. *The Magical Family*. These groups believe that they are empowered by "paranormal"

(continued)

MELTON'S EIGHT RELIGIOUS FAMILIES (*continued*)

forces to control both mind and matter, and like their spiritualist counterparts they assume they possess powers of healing and transformation. In the late nineteenth century, groups like the Hermetic Order of the Golden Dawn arose that claimed to have revived ancient occult practices designed to put the participant in contact with the controlling forces of consciousness and of nature. The revival of witchcraft as a form of neo-pagan nature worship (often focused on the figure of the Goddess) is one expression of this worldview.

7. *The Eastern Family.* The dissemination of various forms of Eastern religious philosophy, particularly after 1965, has led to exponential growth in the number of alternative communities that have been influenced by some form of Hinduism, Buddhism, or Daoism. Characteristically, these communities form around the personality and teachings of one (often charismatic) leader

who claims to have found the secret of spiritual enlightenment. Within these groups, social and ritual practices vary widely, with some communities leading an austere, even monastic lifestyle, while others follow a more hedonistic path. In both cases the "guru" or group leader will often attempt to represent his life-philosophy as both an experiential process and an ancient wisdom tradition.

8. *The Middle Eastern Family.* Communities deriving their inspiration from some form of Judaism or Islam fall into this category. Examples of this distinctive alternative spirituality can be found in groups espousing the beliefs and practices of Kabbalah and of Sufism (representing Jewish and Muslim mystical traditions, respectively). Offshoots of these teachings can be found in groups like the Nation of Islam, whose belief-system constitutes a radical departure from normative Muslim teachings.

a corresponding metaphysical view that surrounds it. The basic weakness of Wallis' system, however, is that it too tends to oversimplify the often eclectic teachings and social ideals of the religious movements it seeks to categorize.

Yet another theoretical overview is that of Peter Clarke,[5] who emphasizes the theme of "social transformation" that seems to run through nearly all of those religious movements commonly thought of as "new" or "alternative." Many of these new movements, Clarke notes, fix on the inner life as the primary agency of transformation, hoping that through the attainment of a "true" Self, the individual can either begin to change the conditions of life for the better, or begin the process of disengagement from life altogether. In either case, the individual who enters a new religious community is more likely than not to be searching for an ideology of change that is not to be found within existing religious cultures. Such individuals, Clarke observes, are inclined to describe themselves as "spiritual" rather than as "religious," with an implicit acknowledgment that the only personally valid religious experience these

TIMELINE
New Religious Movements

1830 C.E. Publication of the *Book of Mormon* and beginnings of the Church of Jesus Christ of Latter-day Saints.

1853 Mirza Husayn Ali Nuri (Baha'u'llah) declares himself a "Messenger of God": the beginnings of the Baha'i faith.

1875 Establishment of the Theosophical Society by Helena Blavatsky and Henry Steel Olcott.

1876 Founding of the Christian Science movement.

1881 Establishment of the Watchtower Society (Jehovah's Witnesses).

1897 Publication of Ralph Trine's *In Tune with the Infinite* (New Thought).

1933 Founding of the Worldwide Church of God.

1954 Beginnings of Wicca, The Unification Church, and the Church of Scientology.

1957 Establishment of a center for Transcendental Meditation by the Maharishi Mahesh Yogi.

1962 Creation of the Findhorn Foundation.

1965 Founding of ISKCON and Eckankar.

1966 Beginnings of the Osho Rajneesh movement.

1969 David Berg founds the Children of God community (later known as The Family).

1974 Claude Vorilhon ("Rael") creates the Raelian movement.

1975 Marshall Herff Applewhite and Bonnie Nettles found the Heaven's Gate community (collective suicide, 1997).

"seekers" are likely to find acceptable is one that lies outside the framework of established religious institutions or systems of thought.

None of these systems of classification, or several others that have been proposed, can claim to be exhaustive or universally applicable; but taken together, or employed selectively, they at least provide some insight into the social/intellectual dynamic of the innovative religious cultures that we are about to examine. What follows, then, is a series of historical vignettes of contemporary religious movements and philosophies that sociologists of religion like Melton, Wallis, and Clarke have identified as demonstrably "new" and therefore representative of the latest phase of global religious expression. We have chosen to focus on the new religions of the West, however, partly because these communities are likely to be more familiar to our readers, and partly because the sheer number of "alternative" religions worldwide is so large that no single chapter in a book could honestly claim to represent all of them.

ALTERNATIVE CHRISTIANITIES AND THEIR OFFSHOOTS

Some of the most successful new religious movements of the modern era are churches that derive their origins from recognizably Christian sources, and whose beginnings can be traced back to nineteenth-century America. Then, as now, religious culture in the United States was pluralistic, and while most Americans professed some form of Christian belief, no single Christian denomination was dominant. What historians refer to as the "**Second Great Awakening**"—a nationwide evangelical movement that evoked intense religious fervor in many communities—continued to affect Christian thought in the United States up through the mid-1800s. One manifestation of this upsurge in religious enthusiasm can be found in the formation of new Christian churches, some claiming new revelations of divine truth, and many looking forward eagerly to the imminent Second Coming of Christ. The following discussion will focus on those groups whose influence continues to be felt today: the Church of Jesus Christ of Latter-day Saints, Christian Science, Seventh-day Adventists, and Jehovah's Witnesses.

The Church of Jesus Christ of Latter-day Saints

The Church of Jesus Christ of Latter-day Saints was founded by Joseph Smith (1805–1844) in 1830 in Fayette, New York. Although its members are commonly referred to as "Mormons," they prefer to be known as Latter-day Saints. According to Joseph Smith's account, he was just 14 years old when, in 1820, he withdrew to the woods near his home and asked God which church he should join. While praying for guidance, he was approached by two figures who identified themselves as God the Father and Jesus Christ. They informed Smith that he should not join any existing church but rather establish his own, and that he had been chosen to restore the one true faith of Jesus Christ. Three years later, Smith was visited by the angel Moroni, who revealed to him the location of two thin golden plates covered with strange writing. His translation of these plates, accomplished "by the gift and power of God," resulted in the writing of the Book of Mormon, one of the principal scriptures of the Church of Latter-day Saints. Although these plates were later taken away by an angel, witnesses testified to having seen and touched them.

Published in 1830, *The Book of Mormon* tells how the prophet Lehi and his followers fled Jerusalem around the year 600 B.C.E. and migrated to America, where they founded a great civilization. During subsequent centuries, their descendants recorded their history on metal plates. These described how conflict eventually divided the people into two groups, the Nephites and the Lamanites. These plates also included prophecies of the birth and crucifixion of Jesus Christ, and described how, after his resurrection, Jesus appeared to the peoples of North America and established his church among them. In 421 C.E., the Lamanites (ancestors of the people we know as Native Americans) annihilated the Nephites, whose memory was preserved only in the history they had written. A surviving Nephite, the prophet Mormon, wrote an abridgment of that history on two golden plates and gave them to his son, the prophet Moroni, who hid them. Fourteen centuries later, Moroni—who by then had become an angel—revealed their location to Joseph Smith. Mormons believe that the Book of Mormon is divinely inspired scripture, and recognize it as having an authority equal to that of the Old and New Testaments. They also make extensive use of two other texts: *Doctrines and Covenants* (1835) and *The Pearl of Great Price* (1842), both of which consist of revelations, statements, translations and other writings, many by Joseph Smith.

The discovery of the Book of Mormon soon attracted followers to Joseph Smith and his church. At the same time, conflict with their detractors soon forced the Mormons to leave New York. After settling briefly in Kirtland, Ohio, continued

The Angel Moroni delivering the plates of the Book of Mormon to Joseph Smith.

The Mormon Temple in Salt Lake City, Utah.

opposition to Smith's teachings forced the Mormons to move on, first to Jackson County, Missouri, and then to Nauvoo, Illinois. For a time the Mormons prospered in Nauvoo, but their practice of polygamy (later abolished in 1890) aroused the animosity of their neighbors, and on June 24, 1844, Joseph Smith was killed by an angry mob opposed to the Mormon way of life. The leadership of the movement now fell to Brigham Young (1801–1877), who led the Mormons on an epic trek from Nauvoo to the Great Salt Basin of Utah, where they settled and established their church headquarters at a site known today as Salt Lake City.

Mormons accept many familiar Christian doctrines, though often with radical (and, to most Christians, unacceptable) changes. Like mainstream Christians, the Mormons believe in a Trinity, consisting of God, the Heavenly Father; his Son, Jesus Christ; and the Holy Ghost (sometimes referred to as the Holy Spirit). However, Mormons understand these figures to be three separate gods. Moreover, Mormons believe that the Heavenly Father was once a mortal man: descended from human beings who themselves had become gods, the Heavenly Father attained divinity and became the ruler of our region of the universe. Through intercourse with a celestial wife, he produced a Son, Jesus Christ, who also progressed from humanity to divinity, and finally the Holy Ghost. While the Heavenly Father and Jesus Christ possess material bodies (albeit perfect and immortal), the Holy Ghost is pure spirit.

Mormons also believe that all human beings are "spirit children" of the Heavenly Father, who sends us to earth so that we can receive physical bodies and gain both knowledge and experience that are essential for spiritual progress. We are guided in this life by the perfect example of Jesus Christ and by the Holy Ghost that dwells within believers and helps them to grasp eternal truths. Ultimately, we can return to dwell eternally with the Heavenly Father, become gods ourselves, and have spirit children of our own. Sin can prevent us from achieving this goal, but it need not do so, for Jesus Christ atoned for our sins through his suffering and death. We can therefore achieve salvation if we have faith in Christ's atonement, repent our sins, accept baptism, and receive "the gift of the Holy Ghost." The critical factor, for Mormons, in determining who can or cannot be saved from sin is the acceptance of "the Gospel of Jesus Christ in its fullness," and that form of Christian teaching can only be found within the Church of Latter-day Saints. However, it is possible for Mormons to obtain baptism (by proxy) on behalf of deceased family members who were not Latter-day Saints—and therefore insure their retroactive salvation; this explains the extraordinary interest Mormons take in genealogical research. Finally, Mormons abstain from the consumption of alcohol, tobacco, coffee, tea, caffeinated soft drinks, and illegal drugs, believing that such abstentions are not only conducive to good health but are also part of the revelation given to Joseph Smith in 1833.

Mormons are millennialists who believe that one day Christ will return to judge and rule the world for a thousand years. Though they acknowledge the existence of a hell, where some will suffer temporary punishments, Mormons are convinced that, in the end, all people will be saved. However, the final destiny of every individual will be determined by the extent of his or her obedience to God's commandments. Accordingly, there are two distinct levels of salvation: Mormons who faithfully follow the teachings of their church will attain divinity and eternal life in the presence of the Heavenly Father; Non-Mormons will receive lesser rewards and will therefore enter lesser "kingdoms" in eternity. Mormons also believe in continuing divine revelation, and more specifically that God's will is revealed through the senior leadership of their church. Its President (often referred to as "the prophet"), his two counselors, the members of the Quorum of the Twelve Apostles are all recognized as having prophetic abilities, and together they possess the same authority as the prophets and apostles described in the Bible. This link with the biblical past underlies the Mormon church's conception of itself as the *restored* church of Jesus Christ, and because other churches have corrupted the teachings of Christ, the Mormon church is therefore the only true and living church upon the earth. Needless to say, no other Christian community is prepared to accept this claim.

Christian Science and New Thought

The religious philosophy known as Christian Science has its origins in the life experiences and teachings of Mary Baker Eddy (1821–1910). As a young woman, Eddy suffered from a variety of illnesses and nervous disorders for which the physicians and hypnotists she consulted could offer no lasting relief. In 1866, however, she claimed to have been completely cured while reading an account of one of the miraculous healings effected by Jesus in the New Testament. This led her to discover the Science of Christianity, or "Christian Science," which she later described in her book *Science and Health with Key to the Scriptures* (published in 1875). A skilled organizer, Mrs. Eddy (as church members prefer to call her) established the Church of Christ, Scientist in 1879, with its headquarters in Boston. Today there are nearly 2,500 Christian Science communities throughout the world, and the newspaper she helped establish, *The Christian Science Monitor*, is a well-known and respected publication.

Like many "offshoot" Christian communities, including the Mormons, Christian Scientists regard their church as a "restored" form of primitive Christianity. Although they acknowledge the Bible as the inspired word of God, they nevertheless

Mary Baker Eddy was the founder of the Church of Christ, Scientist (Christian Science).

maintain that its full meaning can only be grasped through studying *Science and Health*, which they believe was written under divine inspiration. But what truly distinguishes Christian Science is its foundational belief that all reality is spiritual, for it derives from the purely spiritual nature of God. Matter and the body do not really exist, nor do the many evils associated with them, such as disease, deformity and death. These are nothing more than mental errors created by our limited minds. We experience pain and illness only as long as we *think* we are suffering from these things, and as long as we attribute objective reality to these illusions we will find ourselves cut off from God. To achieve salvation from this delusional state we must follow the example of Jesus Christ, the "Way-shower," whose awareness of God and God's goodness allowed him to overcome all forms of suffering and to perform miraculous healings of body and mind.

Because Christian Scientists deny the existence of material reality, they do not accept the traditional Christian doctrine of the Incarnation. Instead, they believe in Christ as the divine idea of "sonship" to God and in Jesus as the one in whom that idea was perfectly expressed. God is the Father-Mother of all, while the Holy Spirit is God's loving relationship with creation. Christian Science teaches that prayer based on a correct understanding of God and reality as spiritual existence is the key to improving human life. Prayer is therefore not so much a matter of asking God for healing as it is a yielding of the individual mind to the Divine Mind, and to the truth that whenever God's presence and loving power are recognized, health and healing are sure to follow. As a rule, Christian Scientists trust in God's love rather than in vaccinations for the prevention of diseases; when they do become ill, however, they turn to prayer for healing, often with the assistance of "practitioners," that is, church members who devote themselves full-time to teach others how to use "scientific prayer" in gaining access to God's healing love. Nevertheless, church members remain free to obtain help from medical professionals if they so choose, and they have broadened their understanding of the principle of spiritual healing to include the elimination of major social problems.

Christian Science is viewed by historians as just one of the forms taken by a larger American religious movement known as **New Thought**. Though more a philosophical current within late nineteenth-century religious thought than an actual creed, New Thought advocates tended to embrace a transcendentalist belief in the presence of the divine within nature, and especially within the human mind. This thesis was best expressed by Ralph Trine in his book *In Tune with the Infinite* (1897), and from that premise an amazing variety of related religious philosophies soon emerged. In 1914, the International New Thought Alliance was formed, dedicated to the constructive power of the mind and the "freedom of each soul as to choice and as to belief." Within that larger community of optimistic faith in the human spirit various groups took root, particularly the Unity School of Christianity. Founded by Charles Fillmore (1854–1948) and his wife Myrtle (1845–1931) in 1903, Unity was originally based on the concept of "mind-cure," or the relief from illness through the exercise of mind over matter. A prime example of this phenomenon occurred in 1886, when Myrtle Fillmore was cured of tuberculosis after repeating inwardly, for two years, "I am a child of God and therefore I do not inherit sickness." Today, Unity practitioners describe themselves as engaged in a positive and practical form of Christianity in which the daily application of the principles exemplified by Jesus Christ promotes health, prosperity, and happiness. Unity teaches that the spirit of God lived in Jesus Christ, just as it lives in everyone. By living as Christ did, we overcome sin—which Unity understands to be separation from God in our consciousnes—as well as illness, depression, and doubt. Like many New Thought churches, Unity believes that a heightened awareness of God's presence will bring peace, health and happiness to the human race.

Adventism

The Adventist movement, based on the belief that Christ would soon return to earth, represents one of the more radical tendencies of nineteenth-century Christian thought. By mid-century a number of Adventist denominations became increasingly prominent in American religious life. The first of these groups gathered around a Baptist minister named William Miller (1782–1849), whose experience at a revival meeting led him to undertake the study of biblical prophecy. In 1835, Miller announced that Christ would return to earth between March 21, 1843, and March 21, 1844, to preside over a final judgment, destroy the world, and inaugurate a new heaven and a new earth. The failure of this Second Coming to materialize prompted recalculations and predictions of new dates, but when these, too, passed without incident, many Millerites gave up their hope of seeing Christ's return. Others, sometimes scorned and ridiculed in their churches, emulated Miller by forming new ones, most of which were organized as part of the Evangelical Adventist Association.

The largest of the Adventist churches to emerge from what the Millerites called "**The Great Disappointment**" was that of the Seventh-day Adventists, founded by Ellen White (1827–1915). White became a follower of Miller in 1842, but after the Great Disappointment of 1844 White taught that the Second Coming of Christ had been delayed by the failure of Christians to obey the Ten Commandments—especially the fourth commandment, which requires observance of the Sabbath on the seventh day of the week (that is, Saturday). In addition, White believed (like her counterparts in Christian Science) that scripture contains rules for physical as well as spiritual health: "Disease," she wrote, "is the result of violating God's laws, both natural and spiritual," and would not exist if people lived "in harmony with the Creator's plan." For this reason, and because they consider the body a "temple" of the Holy Spirit, Seventh-day Adventists practice vegetarianism, abstain from alcohol and tobacco, and prefer natural remedies to drugs when ill. It was in hope of creating a health food that would meet the standards White discerned in scripture that Dr. John Kellogg, one of her disciples, invented his famous cornflakes.

Today there are more than 10 million Seventh-day Adventists worldwide, the great majority of whom live outside of North America (principally in Africa and Central and South America). Emphasizing the apocalyptic books of Daniel and Revelations in the Bible, they preach that the world must be prepared for the Second Coming, which will occur after the gospel has been spread to all parts of the world. The returning Christ will raise the faithful from their present state of unconsciousness, make them immortal, and bring them back to heaven for his millennial reign. At the conclusion of the millennium, Satan will be destroyed along with sinners who indicate they have no wish to live in Christ's presence. The saints will then descend from heaven to live forever on an earth restored to its original perfection.

Most Christian denominations consider the Seventh-day Adventist church to be a genuine Christian church, although they may not share its preoccupation with Christ's Second Coming or recognize the legitimacy of a Saturday/Sabbath worship tradition. However, some groups with roots in Seventh-day Adventism are much farther from the Christian mainstream. The Worldwide Church of God, for example, urges its members to observe the dietary laws and many of the other commandments found in the Hebrew Bible. Moreover, its leaders (Herbert Armstrong [1892–1986], and his son Garner Ted Armstrong [1930–2003]) believed that the English-speaking peoples were the literal descendants of the "lost tribes" of ancient Israel. The Davidian Seventh-day Adventists, founded in the 1930s by a Bulgarian immigrant, Victor Houteff, also observe many of the ritual requirements found in the Hebrew Bible; however, they criticize traditional Seventh-day Adventists for claiming that prophecy came to an end with the death of Ellen White. God, the Davidians say, continues to guide their church through the prophets he sends. One particular splinter group, the Branch Davidian church (founded by Benjamin Roden in the 1960s) achieved tragic notoriety in 1993 when David Koresh (born Vernon Howell in 1959), who had taken control of a Branch Davidian community located in Waco, Texas in the 1980s, convinced his followers that he was the Messiah, and that Armageddon would take place in the United States rather than in Israel. When federal agents raided the Branch Davidian compound on February 28, 1993, a shootout and fifty-one-day siege followed, culminating in an assault and fire that left 80 members of the Waco community (including Koresh himself) dead.

Jehovah's Witnesses

Another millennialist church that succeeded the Millerites was founded in 1881 by the lay preacher Charles Taze Russell (1852–1916). Officially called Zion's Watch Tower Bible and Tract Society, it is more commonly known as the Jehovah's Witnesses. Russell was only twenty years old when his study of the Bible led him to the conclusion that the Second Coming would occur in 1874, when Christ would return invisibly to prepare for the kingdom of God. This event was to be followed by the battle of Armageddon and the end of the world in 1914, after which Christ would begin his millennial reign over the earth. Russell published a more detailed account of his thought in a seven-volume work entitled *Studies in Scripture*, and in 1879 he began the publication of a magazine called *The Watchtower*. Russell's followers were at first referred to as Bible Students and Watchtower People, but once Joseph Franklin

Rutherford (1869–1942) had succeeded Russell as the head of the Watchtower organization, members of that community were officially known as Jehovah's Witnesses.

Under Rutherford's leadership both centralized control of the Watchtower organization and of its teachings increased. At the same time, its membership grew, and today there are approximately 4 million Witnesses in 200 countries. As the most "world-renouncing" of the Adventist churches of the modern era, the Witnesses continued to predict the end of history as we know it, and the imminent rule of Christ and his saints. In 1920, for example, when Rutherford published his *Millions Now Living Will Never Die*, he gave 1925 as the date by which the rule of God would be established on the earth. Rutherford's successor, Nathan Knorr (1905–1977), predicted in the October 8, 1966, issue of the Witnesses magazine *Awake* that the world would end in 1975, only to see that "prophecy" disconfirmed. More recently, however, Witnesses have become wary of fixing dates for the apocalypse, and are generally content to proclaim that Christ's return to earth will come sooner than later.

Jehovah's Witnesses take their name from the King James Bible which (erroneously) vocalized the biblical Hebrew name for God. Although they understand Jesus Christ as God's "Son," they reject the doctrine of the Trinity, and insist that the Son is simply the first of God's creations. As for the Holy Spirit, that is understood as "God's active force" within persons of true Christian faith. Witnesses continue to believe that a "great tribulation" is imminent, and that after destroying the present world system, the elect (whose "core" number is fixed at 144,000), will experience full salvation. These elect individuals, who alone have immortal souls, will ultimately be taken up into heaven. All others may be saved through obedience to God and faith in the efficacy of Christ's sacrificial death, but their reward will be eternal life on earth, which will be restored to its original, paradisiacal condition. As for the wicked, they will surely perish in the cataclysmic end-time battle (that is, Armageddon), but only after they have been given fair warning of their fate. The familiar practice of going door-to-door, which brings teams of Witnesses into thousands of neighborhoods every year, is premised on the belief that they have a responsibility to warn their fellow human beings that the world—which they believe to be under the present dominion of Satan—will soon come to an end. Witnesses also refuse military service, and will not salute the flag or hold government offices, believing these practices to be a compromise with worldly evil. Their refusal to accept blood transfusions, based on their interpretation of biblical precepts forbidding the consumption of blood (Genesis 9:4), has often placed the Witnesses in opposition to contemporary medical practice and public policy. Finally, since they regard other churches as having fallen into gross error, they have little contact with other Christian denominations and do not join in celebrating holidays such as Christmas and Easter.

The Family (Children of God)

A far less successful, and socially problematic, example of Adventist thought in the later twentieth century can be found in a community known first as the "Children of God," and subsequently as the "Family of Love," or more simply **The Family**. The

Children of God was established by David Brandt Berg (1919–1994), an evangelical minister who declared, in 1969, that he had received a revelation concerning a cataclysmic earthquake that would plunge California into the Pacific Ocean. Fearing imminent destruction, Berg led his small band of followers from California to Texas, where they proceeded to live a communal existence. Convinced that disaster loomed for the entire country, Berg moved once again, leaving the United States and ultimately relocating in London, where he established his headquarters in the 1970s.

In the decades that followed, Berg's teachings became increasingly radical, and he urged his followers to abandon their families and to renounce all allegiance to existing social and political structures, believing that the Second Advent of Christ—and all of the violent events that would precede it—was imminent. Like the Witnesses, the Children of God are millennialists, who look forward to the beginnings of Christ's 1,000-year reign. Committed to what he termed the "law of love," Father Berg (as he was called) commanded his flock to celebrate the "sacrament" of free sexuality as often, and with as many partners, as possible, and he urged his female followers to prostitute themselves for the purpose of drawing male recruits into his movement. This practice (called "flirty fishing") brought considerable notoriety to Berg's community, and by the 1980s this behavior was discontinued, partly out of fear of the AIDS epidemic. By the 1990s the movement had become somewhat more conservative in lifestyle, and it adopted a written constitution that endowed individual members with a greater measure of religious autonomy. Berg's death in 1994 left the Children of God, now renamed The Family, without a dominating prophetic personality, though he was immediately succeeded by his second wife, Karen Zerby (b. 1946, and known to members of the Family as "Maria"); nevertheless, the emphasis on charismatic gifts and an evangelical style of worship remain constants in this community. "Father David," as he is posthumously known, continues to exert considerable influence upon members of the Family from beyond the grave, however, as his spirit messages are channeled through Maria and her second husband, Steve Kelly (b. 1951; known as Peter Amsterdam).

The Unification Church

At what may be the furthest remove from traditional Christian thought, we encounter the Unification Church, officially known today as "The Family Federation for World Peace and Unification." First established in 1954 by the "Reverend" Sun Myung Moon (b. 1920), the "**Moonies**," as they are popularly called, constitute a particularly aggressive and theologically eclectic Adventist community. Within this community, the Reverend Moon occupies a position of honor and spiritual influence equal to that of Jesus, and it is therefore arguable whether the Unification Church can be considered an historically legitimate form of Christianity. Though often derided during the 1970s as a "cult," the Unification Church has consistently denied charges of brainwashing and exploitation (financial and psychological) of its members. The organization has recently sought mainstream acceptance by devoting considerable sums to the promotion of international peace gatherings and interfaith conferences, and through the purchase of major newspapers like the *Washington Times*. Still, at the heart of this movement we find both the personal presence and teachings of Sun Myung Moon, whose followers consistently think of him as the Messiah of our age.

Moon's spiritual journey began in 1936, in what is now the People's Republic of North Korea, when he received a vision of Jesus at Easter time. In that vision, Jesus informed Moon that he was to take up the mission of world-redemption where Jesus had left off, succeeding where the Christian savior had failed. Believing himself, therefore, a successor to Jesus Christ, Moon proceeded to construct a belief system that is largely based on Christian scriptures, but which also reveals a mixture of Buddhist, Daoist, and shamanistic elements. Moon's principal publication, entitled *Divine Principle*, lays out the basis for his claim to have "completed" the Testaments and to represent the next stage in the progression of Christian thought. Thus, according to Moon, God can be thought of as an invisible essence, from which all life flows. God's original plans for the biblical Adam and Eve were thwarted, however, when the Serpent (Satan) seduced Eve, inspiring her to have intercourse with Adam "prematurely," thus leading in turn to the fall of the human race. Since the sins of our first parents extend to every generation, the salvation of humankind depends on the appearance of a Messiah, who, along with his wife (who serves as a second Eve), will restore the purity of the family and reconcile the world to God's will. Moon's second wife, Hak Ja Han, whom he married in 1960, is referred to by Unificationists as the "True Mother," and through the thirteen children she has borne since then she has provided a model for the movement of authentic motherhood and spiritual guidance.

The ability to receive new revelations extends beyond the Reverend Moon himself, however, to at least one other member of his family. In 1984, Moon's second son, Heung Jin, was fatally injured in an auto accident, but almost immediately after his funeral, Moon announced that his son had become a "commander-in-chief" in the spirit world to those who had died unmarried. To insure that Heung Jin would not remain a bachelor

The Rev. Sun Myung Moon blessing a mass wedding ceremony in Madison Square Garden, New York City.

through eternity, a postmortem marriage was arranged between the daughter of one of Moon's aides and the spirit of Heung Jin, whereupon members of the Unification Church began receiving revelations from him. Perhaps the most important of these messages are those that confirm the status in heaven of both Moon and his wife, who are spoken of as the "True Parents" before whom even Jesus bows in humility and reverence. Additional testimonials from the spirit realm, celebrating Moon's cosmic preeminence, have come not only from Heung Jin but also from a deceased Unification scholar, Dr. Sang Hun Lee, who informed a Unification receptor that Buddha, Confucius, Muhammad, and Jesus all acknowledge Moon's role as the ultimate redemptive "parent" of humanity. Charles Taze Russell, Mary Baker Eddy, Joseph Smith, and no fewer than thirty-six deceased presidents of the United States have added their voices to this swelling chorus of affirmation. Not surprisingly, critics of the Unification Church have seized upon such statements as proof of a "personality cult" at the heart of Moon's gospel, and it is clear that Moon's redeemer persona is central to the salvific claims made by the Unification Church and its defenders.

THE REDISCOVERY OF EASTERN RELIGIOUS THOUGHT

As early as the 1890s, liberal intellectuals and religious "seekers" in the United States came under the spell of a charismatic Hindu reformer and writer named Swami Vivekananda (1863–1902), who was one of the more memorable speakers at the World's Parliament of Religions. Vivekananda saw himself as a cultural ambassador for Indian religion generally, and his influence in the West was felt by a number of alternative religious communities, including those attracted to "New Thought." Through his speaking tours and through the formation of the Vedanta Society, Vivekananda popularized knowledge of Hindu metaphysics, and encouraged an appreciation for Raja-Yoga and a variety of meditative disciplines. The constant theme, in fact, of his writings and lectures was the urgent need to liberate the spirit from the dead weight of the material world. In the historical vignettes that follow, we will focus on more recent religious movements that reflect the encounter between Eastern religious thought and practice and Westerners in search of an alternative and cultural disparate source of religious enlightenment.

ISKCON: The International Society for Krishna Consciousness

Better known in North America as the "Hare Krishna Movement," **ISKCON** derives its religious philosophy from the teachings of A. C. Bhaktivedanta Swami (1896–1977), a follower of the sixteenth-century Hindu reformer and mystic, Sri Chaitanya Mahaprabhu. Chaitnaya's disciples regarded him as a divine avatar, and his particular form of Hinduism stressed devotion to the god Krishna, through whom all peoples, regardless of caste or origin, could achieve spiritual fulfillment. Bhaktivedanta (referred to as Prabhupada by his closest followers) brought this message to the West in 1965 when he sailed to New York in the hopes of establishing a center for the study of Chaitnayan devotional practices. Two years later, Prabhupada was drawn to San Francisco and its emergent counterculture, where he developed a communalistic movement dedicated to both Krishna worship and an austere code of conduct. Since then, Prabhupada's disciples have established ISKCON centers in over 300 communities worldwide, and the movement appears to have survived the death of its founder in 1977.

At the heart of the ISKCON philosophy is the belief that Krishna is the sole, supreme deity in the universe, and that the highest goal of human life is to achieve "Krishna consciousness," through which the soul can return to its Creator. One of the central rituals of the movement, through which the attainment of Krishna consciousness is facilitated, is the repetitive chanting of one particular mantra—*Hare Krishna, Hare Krishna, Krishna Krishna, Hare Hare, Hare Rama, Hare Rama, Rama Rama, Hare Hare*—accompanied by the rosary-like counting of prayer beads, 16 times each day. To serve Krishna, Prabhupada taught, one must adopt a strictly vegetarian diet, and abstain from violence, gambling, alcohol, tobacco and drugs. Sexual relations outside of marriage are forbidden, and even within marriage, sexual relations are intended for procreation alone. During the early stages of the movement, ISKCON members committed themselves to selling translations of Prabhupada's commentaries on the Vedas, and the presence of Hare Krishnas (as they were called) at airports and other public locales became a familiar sight during the 1970s.

Members of a Hare Krishna community dancing on a London street.

Prabhupada's death in 1977 occasioned, at first, a crisis within the movement as the eleven gurus he had chosen to lead ISKCON proved too inexperienced (or in some cases, corrupt), and widespread criticism of the institution of the guru was voiced, both within and outside the movement. There are now approximately 100 ISKCON gurus throughout the world, and though their activities are supposed to be monitored by a Governing Body, it is clear that organizational structure within the movement is still fairly loose. Increasingly, local ISKCON temples are independent of policies established by the main Indian congregation in Mayapur (Bengal). Nevertheless, ISKCON continues to maintain a missionary outlook, and thinks of itself as an international religious movement with an appropriately global membership.

The Osho Rajneesh Movement

An even more controversial religious movement with Hindu roots that came to prominence in the 1970s bears the name of its founder, Rajneesh Chandra Mohan (1931–1990). In 1981 Rajneesh, an Indian professor of philosophy, moved from India to a ranch in central Oregon, where he and his followers established a religious commune they named Rajneeshpuram. It was there that Rajneesh hoped to establish a "Buddhafield," as he called it—a utopian community committed to his own blend of Hindu and Buddhist values   though, in fact, the outcome of this experiment in communal living was anything but utopian. The numerous critics of Rajneesh and his works regarded this movement as a fairly typical personality cult. Rajneesh changed his name at least twice during his lifetime, with each change representing a different representation of his self-defined spiritual role: in 1971, for example, he began referring to himself as "Bhagwan" Rajneesh, meaning "enlightened one," and in 1989 (after having tried and failed to convince his followers to address him as "Buddha") he settled on the title "**Osho**," a name whose precise meaning remains obscure today, but which clearly conveys the idea of spiritual master.[6] Nor was Rajneesh the only one in this movement to alter his name or identity: his disciples (known as *sannyasins*, a Hindu term denoting someone whose life was devoted to spiritual pursuits), upon entering the community, also adopted new names (often those of Hindu gods). Each *sannyasin* was required to wear a saffron robe, the traditional garb of Hindu holy men. More revealingly, members of Rajneeshpuram were also obliged to wear a necklace of prayer beads, with a locket containing Rajneesh's picture attached to it, and to perform at least one meditation every day based on Rajneesh's teachings.

Both Rajneesh and the movement had run afoul of the law by the mid-1980s, in part because of his uncertain immigration status, but mostly because his extravagant lifestyle (including a fleet of ninety-three Rolls-Royces) and political ambitions had put him in direct conflict with his neighbors. After evidence surfaced that Rajneesh's lieutenants had attempted a mass poisoning of the local population, Rajneesh was arrested (while attempting to flee the country) and subsequently deported. Upon returning to India, Rajneesh (or Osho, as he insisted on being called) resumed his career as a teacher of meditation, returning to his ashram in the city of Poona, which he renamed the Osho Commune International. His death in 1990 left the movement without its charismatic leader, but the nearly 500 books (consisting largely of his informal talks and lectures) he left behind still provide his *sannyasins* with a body of teachings that functions very much like a formal doctrine. Nevertheless, Osho International, as the movement is commonly known today, is a largely decentralized network of independent communities that draw inspiration from the variety of meditative and therapeutic ideas Rajneesh articulated during his lifetime.

Rajneesh's philosophy of life was nothing if not eclectic: he drew inspiration from practically everything he read, which included traditional tantric thought, Zen Buddhism, Hasidism, Sufism, Marxism, and the writings of Sigmund Freud. Though sometimes portrayed as an atheist, Rajneesh's ideas about the divine more often resemble a form of pantheism, and he taught his followers to search for truth and ultimate reality within themselves, as well as within nature:

> My trust is total. I trust the outer, I trust the inner—because outer and inner are both together. They cannot be separated. There is no God without this world; there is no world without God. God is the innermost core of this world. The juice flowing in the trees is God, the blood circulating in your body is God, the consciousness residing in you is God. God and the world are mixed together just like a dancer and his dance; they cannot be separated, they are inseparable. . . .
>
> I teach the whole man. I am not a materialist or a spiritualist. My approach is wholistic [sic]—and the whole man can only be holy.[7]

With superb inconsistency, Rajneesh taught the necessity of annihilating the ego to achieve final enlightenment while engaging in flamboyant self-promotion (and self-enrichment). But it was his aggressive advocacy of sexual freedom, however, that landed him in trouble with religious authorities in his native India, while at the same time attracting young people in the West to his potpourri of religious ideas. Believing, as he once said, that there were "108 paths" (the number of beads in a prayer necklace) to enlightenment, Rajneesh encouraged his *sannyasins* to plot their own journey to self-realization, while encouraging them constantly to "live wakefully." Rajneesh's defenders have long seen his avid pursuit of material goods and pleasures as, paradoxically, a demonstration of the need to reconcile (rather than oppose) spiritual and material desires, and those who still find his influence meaningful continue to heed his admonition to "live in the moment."

Transcendental Meditation

At an even further remove from traditional Hindu thought is a meditative discipline that denies it is actually a religious philosophy at all: Transcendental Meditation. "TM," as it is popularly known, was founded the Maharishi Mahesh Yogi, a figure surrounded by mystery (which includes uncertainty about his given name or actual date of birth). What is known of his personal history reveals that he was a graduate of Allahabad University (in physics) who spent thirteen years at a monastery in northern India studying under Swami Brahmananda Saraswan, commonly called Guru Dev. After Guru Dev's death in 1953, the Maharishi (a self-appointed title meaning "Great Seer") went into seclusion for a time, but when he emerged he set out to share the techniques of meditation he had learned from Guru Dev with the world. Having first established a meditation center he named the Spiritual Regeneration Movement in Madras in 1958, the Maharishi went on to open similar centers in Los Angeles and in London in 1960, which led to the founding of the International Meditation Society in 1961 and (a decade later) the opening of the Maharishi International University in Iowa in 1971. Each of these institutions was designed both to disseminate the Maharishi's teachings and to promote greater understanding among diverse peoples, all of whom, it is asserted, can benefit from the practice of meditation. In the 1990s TM renamed itself the "Maharishi Foundation," and as part of its plan to promote world peace, it sponsored the creation (in Great Britain) of the Natural Law party, whose manifesto calls for bringing existing political systems into line with "the intelligence and infinite organizing power that silently maintains and guides the evolution of everything in the universe."[8]

Those who promote TM as the solution to all human problems define it, variably, as a "technology of consciousness" and as a "Science of Creative Intelligence," though its presumed benefits to both the individual and society have been questioned by skeptical observers who find that TM's claims to enhance physical well-being and conflict resolution are simply not borne out by objective evidence. This is particularly true of the technique known as "**Yogic Flying**," during which the TM practitioner rocks back and forth with legs crossed, hoping to levitate a few inches through the air. The object of this exercise is to maximize mind-body coordination, and TM literature suggests that the key to future spiritual and moral evolution lies in this yogic form of physical transcendence. In addition, TM students are given a special mantra to recite—consisting of a sacred sound rather than a word—with the expectation that reciting this mantra will facilitate a transformation of consciousness leading to greater peace of mind. Those who have benefited from this procedure insist that it has led to significant stress reduction.

The question remains, of course, whether this is merely a therapeutic procedure of possible psychological value, or a spiritual discipline of personal growth. Unlike Christian Science and other religious philosophies influenced by New Thought, TM offers its disciples no dogmas, and its view of life is entirely "world-affirming."

THE REVIVAL OF ESOTERIC AND NEO-PAGAN THOUGHT

The religious philosophies subsumed under this heading combine many of the ideas and behaviors Melton describes as peculiar to the Wisdom, Magical, and Spiritualist "families." What all of these alternative communities share is the belief that a superior kind of spiritual knowledge—known in antiquity as *gnosis* (Greek, "knowledge")—is available to everyone in the modern world, often due to the presence of enlightened intermediaries in our midst. Once one is in possession of such knowledge, the world we presently call "real" appears very different—whether enhanced or diminished—depending on how "world-affirming" or "world-denying" one's experience of a greater reality turns out to be. The belief that the world of common, everyday perception is only a fragment (or a shadowy reflection) of something much more real is a recurrent insight of most of the world's religions. Nevertheless, the conviction that direct knowledge of that greater reality is a guarded secret that only a few initiates into the mysteries of the universe can possibly grasp is the core presumption behind all forms of esoteric thought in the West.

While it is certainly possible to trace the origins of this secretive worldview back to the Middle Ages, most new religious communities that engage in some form of metaphysical speculation have been influenced by two visionary figures of the early modern period: Jacob Boehme (1575–1624) and Emmanuel Swedenborg (1688–1772). From Boehme, a German shoemaker-turned-mystic, readers of his first published book (*Aurora*, 1612) discover the existence of a parallel world, perfect and eternal, into which each human being is destined to be reborn, but only after that individual's spiritual nature has been realized. Readers of Swedenborg, however—and especially those who survey his most often cited work, *On Heaven and Hell* (1758)—learn of the passing of successive ages, with the fifth and final age set aside for the realization of the Second Coming of Christ. With the advent of this new age, Swedenborg taught, it will suddenly be possible to converse with angels and to raise all human relationships to a higher level. Both Boehme and Swedenborg were convinced that we are surrounded by supernal intelligences, and both were equally certain that the coming Age would see a lifting of the veil that presently obscures our view of a spiritual reality that lies just beyond the horizon of "normative" experience. Echoes of these beliefs can be found in movements that have been influenced by what we have called New Age thought, and a recurrent motif in such philosophies is the realization that the "horizontal" reality of the material world is constantly intersected by a "vertical" reality of even greater power and knowledge.

Eckankar

Though first established as a distinctive religious community in 1965, Eckankar claims to be the most ancient of all faiths, and therefore the spiritual "root" from which all later religious traditions have descended. In his book *Eckankar: The Key to Secret Worlds* (1969), Eckankar's founder, Paul Twitchell (1908?–1971), endorses a belief in "**astral voyages**" (the projection of the mind or spirit onto higher levels of experience) and asserts that we can inhabit two very different planes of reality at the same time. Through the exercise of certain ancient meditational techniques, Twitchell taught, it is possible for the soul to travel outside of the body and to free itself from both the prison-world of ordinary perception and the cycle of reincarnations. These same spiritual exercises allow one to experience God's Voice as a form of light and sound, and thereby draw closer to the Source of all being. Only the *chela,* or student of Eckankar-based wisdom, can make this spiritual ascent, and a lengthy period of initiation is required before the movement of the mind to this astral plane can be accomplished successively.

Because emanative forces flowing out of God course through the consciousness of the Living Eck Master, his influence is vital if one is to experience the divine reality, whether waking or dreaming. Twitchell believed himself to be such a Master—the 971st Eck Master to be precise—which placed him in a very long line of spiritual guides going back to remote antiquity, one that included Jesus and St. Paul. Twitchell believed that they too had been influenced by Eck Masters, and that Christianity could therefore be viewed as an offshoot, or further development of Eck teachings. However, it is important to recognize that any living Eck Master can not only "channel" the thinking of deceased Masters, he can also correct any mistaken notions proclaimed by his immediate predecessors. The words of the living Master, therefore, are determinative of whatever doctrines emerge, at any given time, from the Eckankar community—an assumption that has led, as we shall see, to a measure of institutional instability.

Upon Twitchell's death in 1971, leadership of the movement fell to Darwin Gross (1928–2008), who, despite some opposition within the Eckankar community, immediately declared himself to be Living Master No. 972. That claim was later disputed, however, by his successor, Harold Klemp (b. 1942), who, as Living Master No. 973, declared that Gross was no longer an Eck Master. This power struggle within the Eckankar leadership led to a splintering of the community, and came at the culminating point of a series of public attacks on Twitchell's claims to credibility. Several critics of the movement have even demonstrated Twitchell's literal indebtedness—often in the form of outright plagiarism—to earlier writers of the Sant Mat tradition (which combines elements of Hindu and Sikh mysticism). Today, Twitchell's followers generally acknowledge similarities between his "revelations" and earlier religious texts and traditions, but insist, nevertheless, that he was merely echoing truths that have been revealed to all great religious teachers. Since the 1980s, the movement has been headquartered in Chanhassen, Minnesota, where the Temple of Eck was constructed in 1990. The number of "Eckists," as members of this community are known, is somewhat difficult to determine today, but one source speculates that the number of active members may be as high as 20,000.

The Findhorn Foundation

Like so many of the movements described previously in this chapter, the Findhorn community was the product of both the political turmoil and revolutionary expectations of the 1960s. When its founders, Peter and Eileen Caddy, withdrew to a quiet Scottish village named Findhorn in 1962, they hoped to establish there a communitarian way of life that would be open to new forms of religious experience. Their choice of this place was dictated in part by its natural beauty, but also out of a belief that it was inhabited by friendly spirits who would inspire those who lived there. Eileen Caddy had long believed that she was receiving messages from God, and that by gathering like-minded, spiritually oriented people together she might create a socially and economically viable alternative to modern urban existence.

From its beginnings, Findhorn has encouraged both the study and practice of a number of esoteric forms of religious expression, many of which have been labeled types of New Age belief: for example, the use of crystals for purposes of healing; telepathic contact with internationally renowned mediums; and attempts to contact extraterrestrials. As the community grew, the thinking of its leaders gradually moved away from a post-apocalyptic view of survival amid imminent worldwide destruction to a more adaptive, gradualist view of small-scale social change coupled with a culture of self-realization. This shift in self-understanding and political perspective—corresponding to Wallis' distinction between world-renouncing and world-accommodating ideologies—was accompanied not only by the physical expansion of the Findhorn colony (which presently consists of a Universal Hall, a hotel, a trailer park, a community center, and several smaller buildings) but also by the development of residential educational programs designed to promote "planetary cleansing." In fact, a synthesis of ecological and spiritually therapeutic concerns dominates Findhorn thinking, and its ability to sustain itself financially—Findhorn became a foundation in 1972 and has managed to remain profitable ever since—has given hope to other quasi-utopian experiments in communitarian living. Decision-making at Findhorn is arrived at by consensus, though long-term policies and major purchases fall under the purview of a management group.

Visitors to Findhorn, however, see very little of the operational structure of the community. Their encounter with Findhorn begins with a reorientation process, known as "Experience Week," during which they are encouraged to engage in rigorous self-analysis and to open themselves to the spiritual forces that are believed to permeate and sustain our world. Meditation and "sacred dancing" are among the various activities guests are invited to participate in, and everyone must share in common maintenance tasks, like cleaning up and making beds. Unlike some of the more coercive, cultlike organizations that grew out of the counterculture of the 1960s, Findhorn makes no attempt to control the lives or thought processes of those who pass through its doors. The ideal of the spiritual "seeker" who is searching for enlightenment rather than institutional affiliation is still viewed with respect in the Findhorn community, and the absence of a central authoritarian personality has helped to preserve the open, egalitarian character of this organization.

Members of Findhorn Foundation engaged in Sacred Dance.

The Raelian Movement

Another major expression of esoteric religious thought in the contemporary period can be found in movements committed to a belief in extraterrestrial beings. Popularly dubbed "UFO cults," many of these communities have assumed the concerns—and in some cases, the language—of millenarian Christian theology by projecting a visionary future in which believers will be rescued from a dying Earth by visitors from outer space, who will then transport only the chosen few to a distant planet where they will live in bliss. In addition, one recurrent article of faith among such groups is the belief that human civilization is the result of interaction with beings from another planetary system who have used our world as a laboratory for genetic and cultural experimentation. Within the context of this quasi-religious creed—which sociologists commonly refer to as "Ufology"—spiritual enlightenment consists of the realization that our collective destinies are ultimately in the hands of unearthly beings whose power and intelligence vastly exceeds our own, and whose immediate goal is to make contact with those few human beings who are capable of receiving their secret (and ultimately world-redeeming) revelations.

The Raelian movement, which was given its name and its creed by its founder, Claude "Rael" Vorilhon (b. 1946), is one of the better-known communities of UFO worshipers, and its belief system should be at once familiar and strange to anyone living within a Judeo-Christian culture. In his book *The Message Given to Me by Extraterrestrials: They Took Me to Their Planet* (1978), Rael revisits the various accounts of divine-human interaction in the Hebrew Bible, and identifies the **Elohim**—one of the principal terms used in the Hebrew Bible to identify the Creator-God—as the true creators of our planet and of the human race. However, the Elohim are not supernatural beings, Rael insists, but rather an advanced race of extraterrestrials—somewhat smaller and greener than humans, perhaps, but in no other way different (except for their superior knowledge) from the human species with whom they elected to procreate. It was the Elohim who renamed Vorilhon "Rael," and it was one of the Elohim who impregnated Mary of Nazareth and fathered Jesus centuries ago. Rael believes that he too is the result of human-extraterrestrial mating, which places him among a select group of prophets and teachers that includes, among others, Buddha, Jesus and Muhammad. Believing himself to be the Messiah of our age, Rael founded the Raelian religion in 1974 (known formally as "The Movement to Welcome the Elohim, Creators of Humanity") as a means of publicizing the presence of the Elohim within our planetary system, and as an anticipation of the day when the peoples of the Earth will be able to receive the Elohim in peace. Only then will a new world order be possible, and the global reign of men and women of superior intelligence really commence.

Rael's flair for publicity is one of the reasons why the Raelians have achieved a larger measure of public recognition than most UFO religions. In 2002, Dr. Brigitte Boisselier (b. 1956) announced that she and her fellow Raelians had successfully cloned a human baby, in fulfillment of the Raelian goal of achieving immortality through scientific means. No proof has been offered to date confirming this claim, but it did succeed in drawing international press coverage of her news conference. On a slightly more lurid plane, Rael himself has organized a conference promoting masturbation, arguing that "self-love" would stimulate the growth of new brain cells, and thereby make it possible for humans to experience sexual pleasure without guilt. And for whatever reason, Rael has repeatedly sought public confrontations with the Catholic Church, insisting, for example, that his followers address him as "Your Holiness"— a title normally reserved for the Pope. Yet even without such provocations, the Raelian movement has received so much negative publicity in France (and later in Canada where it is now headquartered) for its promotion of sexual freedom that it could not have escaped notoriety, even if it had wished to.

It should be noted, however, that many of the Raelian teachings that have provoked controversy can be found in other UFO-oriented organizations, and in esoteric religious communities generally. Critics of Vorilhon's writings have accused him of having "borrowed" Erich von Daniken's mythic account of the extraterrestrial origins of human civilization (*Chariot of the Gods* [1968]) for his own purposes, and have focused on his advocacy of various kinds of sexual "liberation" as proof of the inherently anti-social character of the movement (though a belief in "free love" is hardly unique among alternative religions). But in his own defense, Rael has pointed out that his belief in superior beings from another galaxy, or in spaceships circling the earth, is no stranger than believing in supernatural "guides" who direct the course of human history. From his perspective, all he has done is offer a more "scientific" version of a very ancient belief—a belief that, in one form or another, has been embraced by most of the world's religions. As for the Raelians' promotion of cloning (for pets as well as humans) as a legitimate response to the dilemma of mortality, it was never the desire of the Elohim, they argue, that the human race remain forever limited to a single lifespan, or that we should suffer helplessly from the ravages of incurable diseases. The Elohim, they teach, remain poised, waiting for the next evolutionary leap in human development to occur, at which time they will share with us the wealth of superior knowledge and technological expertise they have accumulated over aeons of time.

Critics insist that what is particularly disturbing about this movement (and others like it) is the potential for socially destructive behavior that resides within the core beliefs of dedicated UFO communities. Anti-cult activists point to the collective suicides of the Heaven's Gate community in 1997—whose thirty-nine members took their lives in the belief that, having shed their bodies, their spirits would ascend into the heavens and join the "mother ship"—as proof that Ufology, carried to its extreme conclusion, can generate a pathological form of world-renunciation. Still, while it is not possible to assert that the Raelian community will never adopt a radical and apocalyptic view of the human condition, Vorilhon has yet to display any sign of the psychopathology that compelled Marshall Herff Applewhite (1931–1997), the leader of the Heaven's Gate movement, and his followers to take their lives as an act of spiritual liberation.

Rael is seated in front of a model of a double helix as he announces the supposed cloning of a human child.

The Church of Scientology

Of all the new religious movements we have discussed thus far, none has aroused as much opposition, or public curiosity, as the movement founded by Lafayette Ron Hubbard (1911–1986) in 1954. Hubbard's personality, and the extraordinary claims made on his behalf by his followers, has been the focus of much of the criticism directed at the Church of Scientology over the years, but even if Hubbard had not played such a visible role in the formation of Scientology's core belief system, its teachings themselves would have stirred controversy. At its beginnings, Scientology was presented to the public as a new form of mental healing. Hubbard's best-known publication, *Dianetics: The Modern Science of Mental Health* (1950), offered its readers an alternative view of the self and the dynamic forces at work within the subconscious mind. Yet, even at this early stage in the development of his largely esoteric belief system, Hubbard was committed to a view of the "true" self—or **thetan** as it is called in his writings—that stresses the immaterial nature of what most Western religions would call the "soul." Thus, even though the thetan inhabits the body during an individual's lifespan, and even though it interacts with matter and energy, it possesses an eternal and independent reality and can therefore survive death and pass on to other bodies. To attain enlightenment, Hubbard believed, one must first acknowledge the primary reality of the thetan, or in Hubbard's language, attain "an awareness of awareness," before passing on to higher levels of spiritual understanding.

The critical moment, Scientologists believe, in this search for expanded consciousness comes when the presence of "**engrams**"—traumatic events stored as images in the "reactive" or subconscious mind—is made evident to both the subject of mental analysis and the "auditor" engaged in detecting unsettling memories and deeply irrational feelings. One of the primary purposes, then, of Scientology's form of counseling is to release the troubled individual—referred to as "pre-clear" in Scientological literature—from emotionally crippling past experiences. Indeed, once one is declared "clear" of whatever destructive engrams have accumulated in the mind, one's health (physical and mental) will improve dramatically, Hubbard believed, and those who have benefited from the process of "auditing" have testified to its liberating effects.

However, Scientology is more than the sum of its therapeutic promises and procedures. Before his death, Hubbard had evolved a complex mythology in which the "thetans"—now thought of as a race of super-beings—were seen as creators of our material universe who gradually lost their creative powers and fell victims to the reactive mind, which grew in influence as their powers waned. To recover the energy and imagination once possessed by these primordial thetans has become the mission of Scientology's elite cadres, and at the highest levels of spiritual and intellectual development within the movement, the secrets of continued progressive evolution are revealed. Such emphasis on secrecy and hidden truths, disclosed only to the initiated, is one of the persistent characteristics of esoteric movements generally, and it is only within their movement, Scientologists insist, that one can achieve the status of a spiritually evolved individual (or an "Operating Thetan," in Scientological terminology). Of course, by tightly controlling the means of progressive self-development, Scientology has, ironically, committed itself to the same kind of therapeutic monopoly that Hubbard bitterly denounced in his attacks on modern psychiatry.

Critics of Scientology[9] have attacked the movement on several fronts. The official biography of its founder, they argue, is filled with distortions of fact and outright lies, and amounts to little more than a hagiography of an almost mythical figure. In reality, they insist, L. Ron Hubbard was nothing like the hero of the mind portrayed in movement literature, but a scheming science-fiction writer whose cravings for power and wealth led him to fabricate a mock-religion of mental health. As for the E-meter— used to detect the presence of engrams in the pre-clear mind—it is no more effective, these critics charge, than an ordinary lie detector (which it resembles) in eliminating the reactive mind or in tracing the effects of negative mental energy. Counseling of practically any kind, they point out, can accomplish much of what Scientologists attribute to their methodology, and without the trappings of a science-fiction cult. Scientology's struggles with the Internal Revenue Service to have itself recognized as a legitimate religious organization were at least provisionally resolved in the Church's favor by 1993. Still, the testimonies of former Scientologists to the authoritarian nature of its leadership and to the suppression of criticism within the movement seem to indicate a fundamental discrepancy between the aspirations of the Church and its actual policies.

In response to such critics, Scientologists point out that apostates from any religious movement often bear tales of deception and mistreatment, and just as often misrepresent the very teachings they have come to reject. The ultimate goals of the Church of Scientology, its defenders insist, have not changed in the half-century or so in which the movement has existed; its goals, they claim, clearly reflect the redemptive mission of its founder: to achieve "a civilization without insanity, without criminals and without war, where the able can prosper and honest beings can have rights, and where man is free to rise to greater heights." At present there are well over 100 Scientology churches worldwide, in at least as many countries, and the influence of Scientology's teachings can be seen in a variety of public health and educational programs, most especially Narconon, a drug-treatment organization whose protocol was (according to organization literature) established by Hubbard in the 1970s. The precise number of members still actively affiliated with the Church is difficult to determine, but its presence within the contemporary religious landscape appears to be growing.

An E-meter and copies of *Dianetics*

Wicca

In the popular imagination, and in much of Western folklore, "witches" have been around forever, but the contemporary nature religion known as Wicca is a far cry from the various literary incarnations of the archetypal embodiment of evil that Shakespeare, for example, drew upon in *Macbeth*. Contemporary witches, or **Wiccans**, as they prefer to be called, do not cast harmful spells, do not communicate with spirits of the underworld, and most especially do not worship the Devil. They do claim to practice various types of magic, however, and they often worship various pre-Christian deities, particularly those associated with natural forces and phenomena. Contemporary Wiccans prefer to be thought of as pagans, though the ensemble of beliefs and practices that characterizes witchcraft today is often so eclectic that no direct link between Wicca and pre-Christian religious cultures can be said to exist.

The Wiccan movement appears to have been the brainchild of one British enthusiast, Gerald B. Gardner (1884–1964), who, after a lifetime as a civil servant in Southeast Asia, returned to England to pursue an interest in folklore and esoteric religious thought. In concert with Margaret Murray (1863–1963), an anthropologist and Egyptologist (as well as a prominent early feminist) whose book *The Witch Cult in Western Europe* (1921) argued that the witch cults of the medieval Europe were survivals of an indigenous fertility religion, Gardner sought to prove that remnants of these ancient pagan rituals could still be found in the modern world. And although professional anthropologists have rejected, decisively, both Murray's research and Gardner's more extravagant claims, the modern form of Wicca seems to have been born out of their collaboration. Following the repeal in 1954 of England's 1735 Witchcraft Act, Gardner set out to revive contemporary interest in "the Craft" by describing ancient pagan beliefs in his landmark book *Witchcraft Today* (1954), which both legitimated the pursuit of once forbidden practices and opened the door to future development of basic Wiccan principles and ritual acts. Gardner's critics have since cast doubts on the authenticity of his claims to have recovered the secrets of ancient witch cults; nevertheless, his work has inspired a generation of Wiccan writers and practitioners whose varied interpretations of Gardnerian lore have led to the proliferation of distinct schools of Wiccan thought.

At the heart of Wiccan teachings is the belief that divine magic and mystery lie within ourselves and within the natural world. The Wiccan concept of the sacred is almost entirely immanental—that is, dwelling *within* Nature rather than outside or above—and although many Wiccan communities have chosen to worship a variety of pre-Christian deities, these "gods" are generally viewed as personifications of the power and grandeur that resides within Nature and within the human imagination. When Wiccans speak of "the God" or "the Goddess" they are not referring to the transcendent Creator of the Abrahamic faiths, but rather to a creative force that lies within all existing things, to which human cultures attribute gender and personality. Wiccans are not content, however, simply to worship the powers that permeate our universe: they also seek to access those powers through ritualized acts of magic (or "magick" as most Wiccans prefer to spell that word). It is this more assertive aspect of Wicca that places it within Melton's "magical" family of new religions. The only constraint that Wiccans acknowledge upon the exercise of such power is embodied in the **Wiccan Rede**—that is, those principles of ethical behavior that virtually all modern witches accept as binding—which teaches: "An it harm none, do what you will." For Wiccan communities, however, that rule entails the use of "magick" to achieve positive ends, and many Wiccan authors urge their readers to practice deeds that will be of benefit to humanity. In addition, many versions of the Wiccan "Rede" (or "rule" in modern English) teach a belief in some form of karma; thus Wiccans are cautioned to expect that harmful acts will return to afflict the witch who inflicts them on others.

As indicated in the vignette with which this chapter began, Wiccans celebrate the change of seasons as well as the phases of the moon. Two very common ceremonies within the Wiccan community are the *Esbat* and the *Sabbat* which are designed, respectively, to pay honor to the Goddess of the Moon and the God of the Sun. Esbats most often occur when the moon is full, though custom varies from community to community. Sabbats, on the other hand, are seasonal, and mark the occurrence of equinoxes and solstices, or midpoints between them. There are eight Sabbats within the Wiccan calendar, the most familiar of which is Yule (or "Yuletide" as it is known in many

VOICES: An Interview with Mary Chapman

Mary Chapman is a teacher and high priestess of a coven in Folsom, California—one of a number of covens in the greater Sacramento area.

How would you describe Wiccan spirituality?

Wiccans seek both self-understanding and some connection to creative energies of the earth. Like Shamans in other religious cultures, we believe that it is possible to draw down the healing and transformative powers of the natural world, which, for us, is also divine.

How do you establish that connection?

By means of various ceremonial practices: dancing, singing, meditation, and feasting. We have no formal liturgy, and much of what we do is improvised, but we do form a closed circle, and within that circle we experience the presence of life forces.

Mary Chapman

Are these "life forces" gods, and do you worship them?

We are open to all forms of the sacred, and we believe that there are many ways of representing the "divine." What's most important, we believe, is to achieve balance in life, and to allow the male-female tension in nature to become a generative force in one's life. The Pentagram that I wear is a symbol of that unity and power, and when the coven forms a sacred space we connect ourselves with the creative energies of life itself. That's "Earth Magick," and you can think of it as a kind of communion with the gods.

Christian cultures). The ceremonies associated with Esbats and Sabbats differ considerably: during an Esbat celebration, for example, some attempt to "draw down the moon" (that is, draw the moon's energy into oneself) is the ritual's focus; on a Sabbat, however, it is customary to light bonfires, and to decorate an altar in a way that pays tribute to the character of the particular god who is being honored that season. In each case, Wiccans hope to align themselves with the hidden energies of Nature and to confer blessings on themselves and their loved ones through such acts of natural communion.

A Council of American Witches was held in 1974, and though it succeeded in drawing up a set of basic principles for the Wiccan movement in the United States, the council itself no longer exists, and Wicca remains today one of the most decentralized of new religious communities. Wiccans generally gather in small groups known as **covens**, though some witches prefer to practice their "Craft" in isolation. One of the more influential schools of Wiccan thought is the "Reclaiming" Movement, founded by Miriam Simos (b. 1951; better known in Wiccan circles as "Starhawk") in the 1970s. The Reclaiming philosophy is more openly political than most varieties of Wicca, and in her writings Simos blends an eclectic mix of feminist, anti-capitalist, and ecological concerns in an attempt to "reclaim" the earth from political forces that

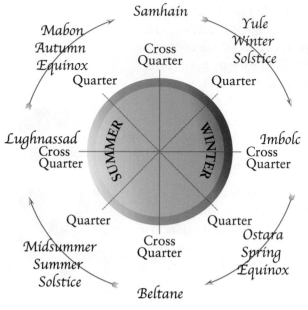

Mabon Autumn Equinox

Samhain

Cross Quarter

Quarter

Yule Winter Solstice

Quarter

SUMMER

WINTER

Lughnassad Cross Quarter

Imbolc Cross Quarter

Quarter

Quarter

Midsummer Summer Solstice

Cross Quarter

Ostara Spring Equinox

Beltane

Wicca wheel of the year.

have despoiled the planet and oppressed its population. Most Wiccans, however, prefer not to align their communities with a specific political agenda, though the formation of the Witches' League for Public Awareness in 1986 and other lobbying organizations (like the Alternative Religious Education Network) have received widespread support in the Wiccan movement. One of the more organized Wiccan communities, The Church and School of Wicca (founded in 1968), estimates the number of its adherents to be around 200,000, and while it is impossible to extrapolate the number of Wiccans worldwide, the movement has clearly benefited greatly from court decisions in the United States that conferred legal status on the practice of witchcraft, allowing individuals to claim Wicca as their legally acknowledged faith.

THE BAHA'I FAITH

As the last of the "Abrahamic" religions that traces its origins to the Middle East, Islam presents itself as the final and decisive revelation of divine truth to mankind. This belief has been challenged not only by the two Abrahamic faiths that preceded it, Judaism and Christianity, but by later monotheistic faiths as well. Perhaps the most significant challenge to Islam's belief in the finality of the Qur'an, however (at least within the context of Middle Eastern religious culture), occurred in mid-nineteenth-century Iran, in the person of a merchant-turned-religious-reformer named Sayyid Ali-Muhammad Shirazi (1819–1850) who saw himself as a successor to Muhammad, and as the recipient of new revelations from Allah. His followers called him the **Bab**—meaning the "Gate" through which the Twelfth Imam of Shi'ism would enter the world—and before long his teachings were declared heretical by Muslim authorities. His imprisonment and death failed to stifle the messianic movement he had ignited, and in 1853 one of his most devoted followers, Mirza Husayn Ali Nuri (1817–1892)—better known by the title he later bore, **Baha'u'llah**—declared himself to be a "Messenger of God," and therefore the legitimate successor to the Bab. Many of the followers of the Bab subsequently pledged their allegiance to Baha'u'llah and their adherence to his teachings, and thus began the new religious movement known as **Baha'i.**

Baha'i is both a monotheistic and a universalistic faith, based on a belief in one Creator God who is the source of all existence and goodness in the universe, and the ultimate object of worship for all peoples. Because this God is a wholly transcendent, eternal and unknowable Being, "He" cannot be described or comprehended by human minds, but his representatives or chosen "messengers" on earth can at least impart something of his will for mankind. According to Baha'u'llah, there has been a succession of such messengers in history (including Moses, Zoroaster, Buddha, Jesus, and Muhammad), each one serving as a prophet for his respective faith community. Baha'u'llah clearly saw himself as the most recent of these manifestations of divine wisdom, and for his followers no future messenger from God is expected for another thousand years. Since divine revelation for Baha'is is progressive, each of these prophets advances human understanding of the divine one step further, reaching higher and higher levels with each successive revelation. The teachings of Baha'u'llah and his successors within the Baha'i movement therefore constitute the most complete understanding of divine thought that human beings have yet attained.

The core truth that Baha'u'llah sought to impart to his followers and to the world was simply this: that since God is one, humanity must also be one. Baha'u'llah believed that all the barriers that separate people from one another (such as differences of race, nationality, gender, wealth, and religious belief) must give way to an awakened sense that the human race has at last "come of age," and that the world is ripe for political structures and cultural values that unite rather than divide our planet's population. World government (and its necessary concomitant, world peace) is finally attainable, he insisted, but only if we are willing to embrace something like the following twelve "principles" of thought and behavior:

1. The oneness of God and the common foundation of all religions
2. The oneness of humanity
3. The equality of men and women
4. The need to eliminate all types of prejudice
5. The need to eliminate all extremes of wealth and poverty
6. A belief in the harmony of science and religion
7. The need for compulsory universal education
8. The need for a common language spoken by all peoples
9. The need for independent inquiries into truth
10. The pursuit of spiritual solutions to political and social problems
11. Obedience to one's government coupled with avoidance of partisan politics
12. The establishment of a world government as the guarantor of world peace

The mission of the Baha'i community, as Baha'u'llah understood it, was to promote these teachings, and to become a role model for the world's religious communities, demonstrating in their communal life just how diverse cultures can embrace a vision of universal harmony and mutual understanding.

Over the past century and a half the Baha'i community has evolved a body of scripture, religious practices, and governing structure that have given their faith a distinctive character. Chief among the texts that Baha'is consider holy are the writings of the Bab, Baha'u'llah, Abdul-Baha (1844–1921; Baha'u'llah's eldest son), and Shoghi Effendi (1897–1957; Abdul-Baha's eldest grandson and the last individual leader of the

Referred to as the Lotus Temple, this structure borrows its design from Hindu iconography.

Baha'i community). Baha'is study these writings throughout the year and integrate readings from them in their religious services. Daily prayer is obligatory for Baha'i males over the age of 15, and because there are no Baha'i clergy, any member sufficiently familiar with the liturgy can lead these services.

The Baha'i religious calendar is made up of nineteen months, each of which has nineteen days, with an additional four days added to bring it into line with the solar year. The first day of each month is a feast day, consisting of both prayers and social events. Baha'is also celebrate eleven holy days, the most important of which are the birthday of the Bab (October 20) and his martyrdom (July 9), and three days marking the declaration of Baha'u'llah's divine mission in 1863 (April 21 and 29 and May 2). Like Muslims, Baha'is fast once a year (for nineteen days, from March 2 to March 20) and abstain from alcohol. Marriage and family life are important aspects of Baha'i life, and as in most Middle Eastern societies, parental consent is necessary for any marriage to take place and be recognized by the community.

There are eight major Baha'i Houses of Worship, the most striking of which is the temple in New Delhi—its shape is that of a lotus flower—and an administrative center in Haifa, Israel. The Universal House of Justice is also located there, and since 1963 its elected members serve as governing body for all members of the Baha'i community. At present there are over 5 million Baha'is worldwide.

THE NEW ATHEISM

Strange though it may seem to conclude a discussion of modern trends and movements in religious thought with a reference to systems of *disbelief*, any analysis of contemporary spirituality would be incomplete without some recognition of a recent groundswell of oppositional voices representing those—particularly in the West—who view any and all religious ideas as delusional and politically dangerous. And while some form of atheism—understood as the denial of belief in any supernatural being or agency—has been a fact of cultural life in both the East and the West since antiquity, the term "atheist" is most commonly applied today to those who reject the idea of a God who is presumed to be the Creator of the universe and of humankind.

Since the Enlightenment of the eighteenth century, Western cultures have seen the rise of philosophical opponents of Christianity who have sought to refute the very basis of Christian faith by denying either the validity or the rationality of any and all theistic beliefs. Baron d'Holbach's (1723–1789) *The System of Nature* (1770) is an example of this type of Enlightenment atheism in its most aggressive form. His argument against religion proceeds from the belief, supported by the science of his day, that the universe consists of nothing but matter and energy. From that premise it follows, d'Holbach insists, that there is neither a soul nor an afterlife, no heaven and no hell, and that all ideas about God are really nothing but human attributes projected onto a cosmos that obeys only the laws of physics. This argument on behalf of a materialistic anti-theism has been replicated and elaborated many times since d'Holbach's time, but it remains the essential narrative of atheism today. In the words of the modern French philosopher Jean-Paul Sartre (1905–1980), atheism has left a "God-shaped hole"[10] in the cultural consciousness of the West, and nothing, he argues, has emerged to fill that void.

That was certainly the position of a number of later twentieth-century theological skeptics—known collectively as the "Death of God" movement—who took up the cry of the nineteenth-century German philosopher Friedrich Nietzsche (1844–1900) that God was "dead," at least in the sense that it was no longer possible, in the modern world, to maintain a belief in a Deity of rewards and punishments, of Creation and of a Judgment Day. In the words of one representative voice of this movement, Thomas J. J. Altizer (b. 1927):

> "[W]e shall understand the death of God as an historical event: God has died in *our* time, in *our* history, in *our* existence. The man who chooses to live in our destiny can neither know the reality of God's presence nor understand the world as his creation; or at least he can no longer respond . . . to the classical Christian images of the Creator and the creation."[11]

In contrast to their eighteenth- and nineteenth-century counterparts, these religiously oriented "atheists" hoped that old images of a transcendent, omnipotent and benevolent deity—which, they argued, are no longer supportable in an age of scientific skepticism and mass murder—will give way to a renewed faith in creative potentialities of the human imagination. This faith-infused humanism is not Christianity, of course, nor is it really compatible with the theistic assumptions that underlie any of the Abrahamic faiths, but to its defenders it represented a response to the nihilism that followed decades of global warfare, as well as an alternative to the numbing fear that, without some form of life-affirming faith, humanity would finally succeed in exterminating itself.

More recently, a new school of polemical atheists (or "positive" atheists as they are sometimes called) have taken up d'Holbach's campaign against religion in the name of both contemporary science and enlightened political values, and unlike their Death of God predecessors, they betray no sorrow over the loss of religious conviction among their secularized contemporaries. Chief among these writers is the biologist Richard Dawkins (b. 1941), whose book *The God Delusion* (2006) offers the following critique of the claim that religious values promote human welfare:

> Religious behavior is a writ-large human equivalent of anting or bower-building. It is time-consuming, energy-consuming, often as extravagantly

> ornate as the plumage of a bird of paradise. Religion can endanger the life of the pious individual, as well as the lives of others. Thousands of people have been tortured for their loyalty to a religion, persecuted by zealots for what is in many cases a scarcely distinguishable alternative faith. Religion devours resources, sometimes on a massive scale. . . . Devout people have died for their gods and killed for them; whipped blood from their backs, sworn themselves to a lifetime of celibacy or to lonely silence, all in the service of religion. What is it all for? What is the benefit of religion?"[12]

Obviously, for Dawkins, religion has no utility at all: it is merely a divisive social force, and its very presence in society all but guarantees some form of conflict, and not infrequently, sectarian violence. For Dawkins, no religion is ultimately a religion of peace.

But on a very different level of intellectual dissent, Dawkins' objections to religion—and those of fellow atheists like Sam Harris (b. 1967) (*The End of Faith*, 2005) and Daniel Dennett (b. 1942) (*Breaking the Spell*, 2006)—spring from the perception that a religious worldview, and specifically belief in an Intelligent Designer, is simply untenable, and that science provides a truer understanding of how the universe came into existence and how humankind evolved from less complex life-forms. For centuries, Dawkins insists, religious authorities have made pronouncements on the nature of physical reality that have since been disproved, and advanced claims of inerrancy on behalf of their sacred texts that are no longer believable, and in any case mutually contradictory. And while scientists cannot answer every question the human mind can pose about the nature of reality, Dawkins concedes, they are bound by a self-correcting process of inquiry that will bring us closer to truth than any dogmatic system of beliefs that has ever been devised.

Critics of the "New Atheists," as Dawkins and those who echo his arguments have been dubbed, often observe that the zeal and certitude which this intellectual community displays is remarkably similar to the dogmatic certainty of traditional religionists; in place of God and revelation, these atheists (their critics say) substitute a materialist worldview and an empirical process of inquiry, thereby turning science into a kind of surrogate religion, with its own peculiar dogmas from which no one in the scientific community is allowed to dissent.[13] To which defenders of the atheist position reply that scientific theories are always open to disconfirmation—which religious beliefs are not, and therefore any similarities between the convictions of scientists and those of religionists are either exaggerated or mistakenly applied. Of course, the future of this debate, like the future of the global phenomenon we have termed "religion" has yet to be written.

CONCLUSION

The variety and multiplicity of religions in the modern world suggest that, despite the influence of secular thought and the challenge of scientific rationalism, religious cultures continue to be born anew, to survive, and even to flourish. Whatever needs religion may be thought to satisfy—the desire to identify oneself with some greater

Being or Power, for example, or an unsatisfied curiosity about humanity's place in the universe—the teachings and social organization of a multitude of faith communities continue to draw adherents all over the globe. Even those who are reluctant to identify themselves as persons of any particular religious faith or creed can be seen to express an interest in "spirituality" and can be numbered among readers of "New Age" publications. Certainly no one who has lived through the first decade of the twenty-first century can doubt the enduring power of religious ideas and emotions or fail to see how they continue to shape our world.

Whether future generations will see the present time as an "Age of Faith" or an Era of Disbelief cannot possibly be known, but the sheer diversity of religious expression, accompanied by a persistent and global tendency to reach outside of one's culture for spiritual stimulation, make predictions about the "Death of God" and the demise of religious experience improbable at best. As long as human beings search for a more-than-material existence, recognizably religious ideas and feelings are likely to survive as well.

SEEKING ANSWERS

What Is Ultimate Reality?

Virtually all of the new religious movements we have studied reveal a desire to move beyond the world of common, material existence, and many of them attempt to reach out to some higher plane of reality. The followers of Bhagwan Rajneesh (or "Osho"), for example, see the world as a place in which material and spiritual forces, or God and Nature, converge. We can create a utopian "Buddhafield," they believe, wherever human beings live "wakefully" through meditation and self-realization. Similarly, the followers of Paul Twitchell (the founder of Eckankar) believe that there are two distinct levels of reality and that, through techniques of spiritual ascent, we can access a higher plane of reality and release the soul from its imprisoned condition in the material world. Followers of Bhaktivedanta Prabhupada, whose teachings have their origin in Hindu mysticism, also believe that the soul can achieve release and return to its Creator—in this case the Hindu god Krishna. The Hare Krishnas, as they are commonly known, engage in devotional and meditative practices designed to raise the individual consciousness to the level of divine awareness and self-transcendence. For Christian communities, however—and especially those influenced by Adventist thought—ultimate reality is to be found in the biblical God, and the soul's deepest longing is to be united to Him. That union, for Adventists, will occur once this world has vanished or been destroyed, to be replaced at last by the Kingdom of God.

(continued)

SEEKING ANSWERS *(continued)*

How Should We Live in This World?

New religious movements emerge in response to a rapidly changing world, in which traditional certainties about society and culture are subject to swift and sometimes brutal challenges. Each of the broad categories of movements we have studied in this chapter has developed tenets by which adherents should live in this world, and with each other. Some alternative Christianities, such as Christian Scientists, hold that human life can be made better by first acknowledging that we are spirit beings rather than simply material organisms. Only then can we draw near the Divine Mind and experience God's love in the form of real healing of body and mind. For followers of the Guru Prabhupada (or Hare Krishnas), whose beliefs are based in Eastern thought, the purest life is attained only when one has achieved Krishna consciousness, which entails a strict vegetarian diet, and equally strict avoidance of such vices as alcohol, tobacco, drugs, gambling, and sexual immorality. The diversity of neo-pagan systems reflects the fractured state of contemporary society, with Wiccans emphasizing the need for humans to live in a respectful and harmonious relationship with the natural world while Scientologists believe in the power of the human mind, assisted by specific technologies, to overcome unnecessary repression of the "true" self (or thetan) and recover those creative energies which the "reactive" mind stifles or distorts. Once free from such repression, Scientologists believe, humanity can free itself from insanity, crime, and war. The Baha'i faith looks to the perfection of social and political structures in order to help all of humanity live together peacefully, while the New Atheists believe that the triumph of reason over faith would allow humans to coexist peacefully without succumbing to ancient prejudices.

What Is Our Ultimate Purpose?

Virtually all religious communities invest human existence with some ultimate end or purpose, though not all rationalize that belief by appealing to the will of a Higher Power. Scientologists, for example, believe that, as a species, we have the potential to attain enlightenment and to allow the true self (or "thetan") to grow in understanding. Similarly, practitioners of Transcendental Meditation believe that the enhancement of well-being through the meditative unification of body and mind will enable all of humanity to become one with the creative intelligence that lies behind everything in the universe. For members of the Church of Latter-day Saints (or Mormons), however, the purpose of human life is defined in more nearly Christian terms: to return to the Heavenly Father after death, and even become divine oneself, by embracing the teachings of the Mormon church. Ultimately, all people, Mormons believe, will enter one of the eternal kingdoms and enjoy immortality. Members of the Unification Church (or "Moonies"), another alternative form of Christian faith, similarly believe that the goal of life is to advance beyond our present fallen state and to enter a condition of spiritual purity, guided by the teachings of the Reverend Sun Myung Moon, whose messianic role (like that of Jesus) is to lead the world back to God.

REVIEW QUESTIONS

For Review

1. What does the term "neo-pagan" mean, and why is it applied to movements like Wicca?
2. What are "engrams," and how do Scientologists claim to be rid of them?
3. What is "New Thought," and which religious communities embody its principles?
4. Who are the "Moonies," and who does the founder of this religious community claim to be?
5. Who was the founder of the Osho Rajneesh Movement, and why did that community attract so much notoriety?

For Further Reflection

1. How sharply do Adventist churches differ in their outlook from "mainstream" Christianity? Are they more "world-renouncing" or simply closer to early Christian thought?

2. If another World Parliament of Religion were held sometime in the near future, which religious communities would you like to see invited to attend? Why?
3. What is the appeal of religious movements that focus on the personality of a powerful and charismatic leader? Are such larger-than-life figures essential to the growth of new religions?
4. Are communities that embrace some form of "Ufology" (that is, a belief in the existence of extraterrestrials) really religious organizations? Is there a difference between communicating with angels, or other spiritual beings, and talking with visitors from outer space?
5. Of all of the religious movements we have studied in this chapter, which one appears to be the most "world-accommodating"? What are the advantages in belonging to such a community?

GLOSSARY

astral voyages Any visionary experience of a mind/body projection through space and time.

The Bab (Sayyid Ali-Muhammad 1819–1850) An Iranian religious reformer.

Baha'i A monotheistic and universalist religion that first emerges in nineteenth-century Iran.

Baha'u'llah (Mirza Husayn Ali Nuri 1817–1892) A disciple of the Bab and the founder of the Baha'i faith.

channeling The ability to receive and transmit messages sent by spiritual beings not of this world.

coven A community of witches.

Elohim One of several terms used in the Hebrew Bible to identify the Creator-God; the name of alien creators responsible for the creation of the human race and culture in Raelian myths.

engrams In Scientology they are traumatic events stored as images in the subconscious mind.

The Family The revised name of the Children of God movement, led by David Berg until his death in 1994.

globalization Any movement, within commerce or culture, toward the internationalization of human interchange.

The Great Disappointment Disillusionment and shock following the failure, in 1844, of William Miller's prediction of the Second Advent.

ISKCON The official name of the "Hare Krishna" movement founded by A. C. Bhaktivedanta Swami.

(continued)

GLOSSARY (continued)

Lughnassadh (loo-nus-uh) A summer harvest festival (August 2) celebrated by Wiccans, honoring the Celtic god Lugh.

modernization Any transformation of postindustrial Western society that leads to the abandonment of traditional religious beliefs and values.

Moonies A slang term for members of the Unification Church.

New Age An umbrella term for various religious and quasi-religious practices based on a belief in the transformation of both nature and human consciousness.

New Thought A philosophical school of thought, popular in the late nineteenth century, that stressed the power of the human mind to discover the divine within nature and to control material reality.

Osho Another name for the religious movement established by Rajneesh Chandra Mohan in the 1980s.

Second Great Awakening An evangelical movement popular in the United States from the early nineteenth century to the 1880s.

Secularization Any tendency in modern society that devalues religious worldviews or seeks to substitute scientific theories for religious beliefs.

Seekers A popular term, current in the late nineteenth century, for individuals who cannot find spiritual satisfaction in "mainstream" religious institutions and who describe themselves as "spiritual" rather than "religious."

thetan A term used by Scientologists to identify the immortal Self and source of creativity in the human mind.

Ufology Any systematized belief in extraterrestrials.

Wiccan Rede A traditional set of rules and ethical values cherished by wiccans.

World's Parliament of Religions Two worldwide gatherings of religious leaders, first in Chicago in 1893 and a larger centennial gathering, also in Chicago, in 1993.

Yogic Flying A meditational practice, similar to levitation, attributed to members of the Transcendental Meditation community.

SUGGESTIONS FOR FURTHER READING

Barrett, David V. *The New Believers*. London: Cassell & Co., 2001. A comprehensive (and often polemical) overview of alternative religious movements, with extensive historical and biographical information.

Clarke, Peter B., ed. *Encyclopedia of New Religious Movements*. London: Routledge, 2006. Brief but comprehensive essays on new religious movements, arranged alphabetically.

Clifton, Chas S. *Her Hidden Children: The Rise of Wicca and Paganism in America*. Lanham, MD: AltaMira Press, 2006. A carefully documented, chronologically organized account of paganism in North America.

Hinnells, John R., ed. *A New Handbook of Living Religions*. London: Penguin Books, 1997. A popular resource work, it provides a global view of the religious landscape with essays on all of the world's principal religions, including new religious movements in Western and non-Western cultures.

Lewis, James R., ed. *The Oxford Handbook of New Religious Movements*. New York: Oxford University Press, 2004. A scholarly survey of sociological research on some of the most widely studied new religions.

Lewis, James R., and Petersen, Jesper A., eds. *Controversial New Religions*. A collection of essays

(continued)

focusing on new religions that have exhibited violent and antisocial tendencies.

Palmer, Susan. *Aliens Adored: Rael's UFO Religion.* New Brunswick, NJ: Rutgers University Press, 2004. Extensive background information on the UFO phenomenon, coupled with a largely sympathetic analysis of the Raelian movement.

Partridge, Christopher, ed. *New Religions: A Guide.* New York: Oxford University Press, 2004. The most extensive collection of brief scholarly vignettes of new religions, combined with lengthier articles of an historical and analytical nature. Cross-referenced and arranged by religious "families."

Roderick, Timothy. *Wicca: A Year and a Day.* Saint Paul, MN: Llewellyn Publications, 2005. A detailed and reliable portrait of Wiccan beliefs and practices.

Schmidt, Leigh Eric. *Restless Souls: The Making of American Spirituality.* San Francisco: Harper-Collins, 2005. In-depth biographical accounts of leading spokespersons for "liberal" religious causes and alternative spiritualities.

Stein, Steven J. *Communities of Dissent: A History of Alternative Religions in America.* New York: Oxford University Press, 2003. A readable overview of religious nonconformity in nineteenth and twentieth century America.

ONLINE SOURCES

Hartford Institute for Religion Research

hirr.hartsem.edu/denom/new_religious_movements.html

A selective website maintained by the Hartford Institute for Religion Research that provides a wide-ranging list of NRM sites and journals.

Religious Worlds

religiousworlds.com/new religions.html

An extensive list of websites and scholarly journals that discuss NRMs, with links to diverse textual and bibliographic sources.

NOTES

Chapter 1

1. Wilfred Cantwell Smith, *The Meaning and End of Religion* (San Francisco: Harper & Row, 1962).
2. See especially Immanuel Kant, *Religion within the Limits of Reason Alone*, trans. Theodore M. Greene and Hoyt H. Hudson (New York: Harper & Row, 1960).
3. Émile Durkheim, *Elementary Forms of the Religious Life*, trans. J. W. Swain (New York: Free Press, 1965 [1912]), 62.
4. William James, *The Varieties of Religious Experience* (London: Penguin Books, [1902]), 31.
5. Paul Tillich, *Theology of Culture*, ed. Robert C. Kimball (New York: Oxford University Press, 1959), 7–8.
6. Melford E. Spiro, "Religion: Problems of Definition and Explanation," in *Anthropological Approaches to the Study of Religion*, ed. Michael Banton (London: Tavistock, 1966), 96.
7. Jonathan Z. Smith, ed., *HarperCollins Dictionary of Religion* (New York: HarperCollins Publishers, 1995), 893.
8. Clifford Geertz, *The Interpretation of Cultures: Selected Essays* (New York: Basic Books, 1973), 90.
9. Gerald James Larson, "The Working Paper: Revising Graduate Education," *Soundings* 71, nos. 2–3 (1988), 418.
10. Bruce Lincoln, *Holy Terrors: Thinking about Religion after September 11* (Chicago: The University of Chicago Press, 2003), 5–7.
11. Peter Berger, *The Sacred Canopy* (New York: Doubleday, 1967), 175.
12. Clifford Geertz, *Islam Observed* (New Haven, CT: Yale University Press, 1968).
13. Sigmund Freud, *The Future of an Illusion*, trans. James Strachey (New York: W. W. Norton & Company, 1961 [1927]), 55.
14. "Contribution to the Critique of Hegel's Philosophy of Right," in *On Religion* (Chico, CA: Scholars Press, 1964), 41–42.
15. Mircea Eliade, *The Sacred and the Profane: The Nature of Religion*, trans. Willard Trask (London: Harcourt Brace Jovanovich), 11.
16. Matthew 7:12.
17. *Tremendum* literally means "causing to tremble." The English term "awesome" conveys this meaning.
18. See especially Smart's *Dimensions of the Sacred: An Anatomy of the World's Beliefs* (Berkeley: University of California Press, 1999) and his earlier and very popular *Worldviews: Crosscultural Explanations of Human Belief* (New York: Scribner's, 1983), which details six of the dimensions (Smart later separated out the material dimension as a seventh).
19. Larson, 418.
20. Ibid.
21. This analogy is drawn from Wilfred Cantwell Smith, *The Meaning and End of Religion* (San Francisco: Harper & Row, Publishers, 1964), 7.

Chapter 2

1. Denise Lardner Carmody and John Tully Carmody, *Native American Religions: An Introduction* (New York: Paulist Press, 2003).
2. Dennis Tedlock, translator, *Popol Vuh: The Definitive Edition of the Mayan Book of the Dawn of Life and the Glories of Gods and Kings* (New York: Simon and Schuster, 1985).
3. Sam Gill, *Native American Religions: An Introduction* (Belmont, CA: Wadsworth/Thomson Learning 2005).
4. Sam Gill, *Sacred Worlds: A Study of Navajo Religion and Prayer* (London: Greenwood Press, 1981), 54–55.
5. John D. Loftin, *Religion and Hopi Life* (Bloomington: Indiana University Press, 2003), 110.
6. Richard Erdoes and Alfonso Ortiz, *American Indian Myths and Legends* (New York: Pantheon Books 1984), 346.
7. Gill, *Native American Religions*, 64.
8. Ibid., 96.
9. Tedlock, *Popol Vuh*.
10. John Neihardt and Black Elk, *Black Elk Speaks: Being an Account of the Life of a Holy Man of the Oglala Sioux* (Lincoln, NE: University of Nebraska Press, 1972), 1.
11. Edoes and Ortiz, *American Indian Myths and Legends*, 85.
12. Joseph Epes Brown, *Teaching Spirits: Understanding Native American Religious Tradition* (London: Oxford University Press, 2001), 87.

13. Keith Basso, *Wisdom Sits in Places: Landscape and Language among the Western Apache* (Albuquerque: University of New Mexico Press, 1996).
14. Brown, *Teaching Spirits*, 36.
15. Ibid., 13.
16. Ibid., 15.
17. Ibid., 49.
18. Greg Sarris, *Mabel McKay: Weaving the Dream* (Berkeley: University of California Press, 1997).
19. Gill, *Native American Religions*, 98.
20. Ibid., 72.
21. Brown, *Teaching Spirits*, 17.
22. Carmody and Carmody, *Native American Religions*, 73.
23. Arlene Hirschfelder and Paulette Molin, *An Encyclopedia of Native American Religions* (New York: Facts on File Ltd., 1992), 287.
24. Loftin, *Religion and Hopi Life*, 37.
25. Gill, *Native American Religions*.
26. Thomas J. Nevins and M. Eleanor Nevins, "'We Have Always Had the Bible': Christianity and the Composition of White Mountain Apache Heritage," *Heritage Management* 2, no. 1 (2009): 11–34.
27. Ibid.
28. Helen McCarthy, "Assaulting California's Sacred Mountains: Shamans vs. New Age Merchants of Nirvana" in Jacob Olopuna, ed., *Beyond Primitivism: Indigenous Religions and Modernity* (New York: Routledge, 2004).

Chapter 3

1. Tepilit Ole Saitoti, *Worlds of a Maasai Warrior: An Autobiography* (Berkeley: University of California Press, 1988), 67.
2. Ibid., 69.
3. Ibid., 71.
4. Bilinda Straight, *Miracles and Extraordinary Experience in Northern Kenya* (Philadelphia: University of Pennsylvania Press, 2009), 56.
5. Marcel Griaule, *Conversations with Ogotemmeli* (London: Oxford University Press, 1965).
6. Rowland Abiodun, "Hidden Power: Osun, the Seventeenth Odu," in *Osun Across the Waters: A Yoruba Goddess in Africa and the Americas*, ed. Joseph M. Murphy and Mei-Mei Sanford (Bloomington: Indiana University Press, 2001), 17–18.
7. E. E. Evans-Pritchard, *Nuer Religion* (London: Oxford University Press, 1971).
8. John S. Mbiti, *African Religions and Philosophy* (New York: Frederick A. Praeger Press, 1992), 85–86.
9. Ibid., 89–90.
10. Ibid., 84–85.
11. Mbiti, *African Religions and Philosophy*, 92.
12. Benjamin Ray, *African Religions: Symbol, Ritual, and Community* (Upper Saddle River, NJ: Prentice Hall, 2000), 53.
13. Adeline Masquelier, *Prayer Has Spoiled Everything: Possession, Power and Identity in an Islamic Town of Niger* (Durham, NC: Duke University Press, 2002).
14. Ibid.
15. For example, Marion Kilson, "Women in Traditional African Religions," *Journal of Religion in Africa* 8, no. 2 (1976), 133–143.
16. Paula Girshick Ben-Amos, "The Promise of Greatness: Women and Power in a Benin Spirit Possession Cult," in *Religion in Africa: Experience and Expression*, ed. T. D. Blakely, W. E. A. Van Beek, and D. L. Thomson (James Currey, 1994).
17. E. E. Evans-Pritchard, *Witchcraft, Oracles and Magic among the Azande* (London: Oxford University Press, 1976).
18. Ray, *African Religions*, 58–59, citing Edith Turner, *Experiencing Ritual* (Philadelphia: University of Pennsylvania Press, 1992).
19. Mbiti, *African Religions and Philosophy*, 113.
20. Ibid., 114–115.
21. Ibid., 120.
22. Margaret Drewal, *Yoruba Ritual: Performers, Play, Agency* (Bloomington: Indiana University Press, 1992), 53.
23. Ellen Gruenbaum, *The Female Circumcision Controversy: An Anthropological Perspective* (Philadelphia: University of Pennsylvania Press, 2000).
24. Jack Goody, *Death, Property and the Ancestors: A Study of the Mortuary Customs of the LoDagaa of West Africa* (Palo Alto, CA: Stanford University Press, 1962), 239.
25. Ray, *African Religions*, 102–103.
26. Ibid., 170–171.
27. Ibid., 61.
28. Ibid., 171.
29. Ibid., 184–191.
30. Ibid., 85–88.
31. Ibid., 198.

Chapter 4

1. See data on adherents.com: adherents.com/largecom/com_hindu.html.
2. See Gavin Flood, *Introduction to Hinduism* (Cambridge: Cambridge University Press, 1996).
3. *Brhadaranyaka Upanishad* 3.9.1–2.
4. Ibid., 3.9.26.

5. A. K. Ramanujan, *Speaking of Shiva* (New York: Penguin, 1973), 131.

6. Diana Eck, *Darshan: Seeing the Divine Image in India* (Chambersberg: Anima Press, 1981).

7. Verse 1.2.

8. See Thomas Trautmann, *The Aryan Debate in India* (New Delhi: Oxford University Press, 2005).

9. Ibid.

10. *Rig Veda* 10.90.11–14. Cited in Bruce Lincoln, *Death, War, and Sacrifice: Studies in Ideology and Practice* (Chicago: University of Chicago Press, 1991), 7.

11. *Rig Veda* (10:129), trans. Raimundo Panikkar, Ref. 3, p. 58.

12. John Stratton Hawley and Vasudha Narayanan, *The Life of Hinduism* (Berkeley: The University of California Press, 2006), 212–213.

13. M. N. Srinivas, *Religion and Society amongst the Coorgs of South India* (Oxford: Clarendon Press, 1952).

14. An oft-quoted line from Major-General Charles Stuart's (1758–1828) *Vindication of the Hindoos*, which was published in 1808.

Chapter 5

1. Thanks to the *Upaya Institute & Zen Center* (upaya.org/about/index.php) and Roshi Joan Halifax for granting me permission to reproduce portions of the liturgy from their Tokudo ordination ceremony. And a special thanks to Jisen for sharing with me her personal thoughts and experiences in taking ordination and entering upon the Buddhist path.

2. The version told here is a condensed synthesis of some of the more widely known variants. For an accessible and excellent survey of these sources and their variants, see John S. Strong, *The Buddha: A Short Biography* (Oxford: Oneworld Publications, 2001).

3. The quotations within this retelling of the life story of the Buddha are not direct citations of translations of other sources but mark passages of dialogue that are paraphrased to adhere to the aesthetic context and narrative flow of my adaption.

4. In the Pali sources Yashodhara is depicted as the wife of the Siddhartha. In some versions he is said to have three wives (Yashodhara, Gopika, and Mrgaja) in addition to his countless royal concubines.

5. The Buddha actually achieved enlightenment through the fourth trance state. Known as "cessation," it is characterized by a profound equanimity and mindfulness. It is bypassed by the formlessness experienced in the fifth through eighth trance states. See Strong, *The Buddha*, 62.

6. It is often said that the period between death and rebirth is also forty-nine days (seven weeks).

7. Mara is one of the chief lords of the Desire Realm. He is sometimes equated with Kama, the Vedic God of Longing.

8. The four *ashravas* ("cankers" or "defilements") are desire (*kama*), clinging to existence (*bhava*), speculative views (*drishti*), and ignorance (*avidya*).

9. Translation by Thanissaro Bhikku (accesstoinsight.org/tipitaka/kn/dhp/dhp.11.than.html).

10. Most of these stories are apocryphal. He reaches Burma with 500 monks, each soaring on one of 501 flying pavilions sent by the gods. After teaching for seven days, he converts 84,000 Burmese.

11. *Mahaparinibbana Sutta*.

12. *Digha-nikaya*, 26.

13. The great *mantra* of the "Heart *Sutra*" (*Prajnaparamita-hridaya Sutra*).

14. *Majjhima-nikaya* i, 63.

15. See Stephan Batchelor, *The Awakening of the West: The Encounter of Buddhism and Western Culture* (Berkeley: Parralax Press, 1994), ch. 14.

16. *Anguttara-nikaya*. Vol. 1, III. Tika-nipata, 7 Maha-vagga and 65 Kalamasutta.

17. *Majjhima-nikaya*, i.134.

18. *Svetasvatara Upanishad*, verse 13.

19. *Majjhima-nikaya* i, 191.

20. The Upanisa Sutta of the *Samyutta-nikaya* (12.23) presents a similarly constructed system that "releases" the twelve links of the chain. It includes (1) suffering, (2) faith, (3) joy, (4) rapture, (5) tranquility, (6) happiness, (7) concentration, (8) perceiving things as they are, (9) a disenchantment with worldly life, (10) dispassion, (11) liberation, and (12) knowledge of overcoming the four mental influxes (*asava*: sensuality, views, becoming, and ignorance).

21. The first precept inspired certain texts such as the *Nirvana Sutra* & *Lankavatara Sutra* (both *Mahayana* works) that stress a strict vegetarian diet. But, for the most part, vegetarianism is only given primary importance by Chinese and Korean monks.

22. The author's retelling is adapted from Joseph Jacobs, *Indian Fairy Tales* (London: David Nutt, 1912).

23. *Majjhima-nikaya* I.46.

24. *Theravada* Buddhism is traditionally considered as emerging from the Vibhajyavadin School, a Sthavira subsect of the original eighteen branches of *Nikaya* Buddhism.

25. accesstoinsight.org/canon.

26. Thomas Byrom, trans., *The Dhammapada*.

27. Paul Williams, *Mahayana Buddhism: The Doctrinal Foundations*, 2nd ed. (New York: Routledge, 2008), 20–26.

28. For a survey of many theories on the rise of *Mahayana*, see Ibid.

29. It is interesting to note that the earliest printed book in the world is a copy of this text found at Tunhuang and dated to 868 C.E.

30. Andrew Skilton, *A Concise History of Buddhism* (Birmingham: Windhorse Pub., 1994), ch. 9.

31. Anne Bancroft, *Zen: Direct Pointing to Reality* (New York: Thames and Hudson, 1979), 5.

32. http://www.zurmangkagyud.org/zm_2006 _Chenrezig.htm; for a full form of the sadhana, see fpmt-osel.org/meditate/l4chnres.htm.

33. The earliest existent Buddhist text is a birch bark scroll found in the Gandhara region (northern Afghanistan and Pakistan) that dates from the first century C.E.

34. Some say this mendicant was Yacas or Yasheka, the monk who presided over the Second Council at Vaishali.

35. This tale is included in the various versions of *The Lives of the Eighty-four Mahasiddhas*.

36. Stephen Beyer, *The Cult of Tara: Magic and Ritual in Tibet* (Berkeley: University of California Press, 1973), 92.

37. See Stephen Batchelor, *The Awakening of the West: The Encounter of Buddhism and Western Culture* (Berkeley: Parralax Press, 1994), ch. 14.

38. coldhardflash.com/2007/07/flash-animated -philosophy-from-south.html.

39. See, for instance, Bernard Faure, "Buddhism and Violence," sangam.org/articles/view/?id=118.

Chapter 6

1. *Acarangasutra* 1.4.1.1–2; translation by Hermann Jacobi, in Friedrich Max Müller, ed., *Sacred Books of the East* Vol. 20 (Oxford: Oxford University Press, 1884).

2. Yogendra Jain, *Jain Way of Life: A Guide to Compassionate, Healthy, and Happy Living* (Boston: Federation of Jain Associations of North America, 2007), i.

3. *Tattharthadhigama Sutra*, Chapter II, 22–23; trans. J. L. Jaini, in Sarvepalli Radhakrishnan and Charles A. Moore, eds., *A Sourcebook in Indian Philosophy* (Princeton, NJ: Princeton University Press, 1957), 254.

4. This term is used of Jainism by Heinrich Zimmer, *Philosophies of India*, ed. Joseph Campbell (Princeton, NJ: Princeton University Press, 1951), 182.

5. *Avashyakasutra* 32; cited in Paul Dundas, *The Jains*, 2nd ed. (London: Routledge, 2002), 171.

6. Padmanabh S. Jaini, *The Jaina Path of Purification* (Berkeley: The University of California Press, 1979), 196–197.

7. Dundas, *The Jains*, 271.

Chapter 7

1. Gurinder Singh Mann, *Sikhism* (Upper Saddle River, NJ: Prentice Hall), 14.

2. Hew McLeod, *Sikhism* (London: Penguin, 1997), 219.

3. Adapted from a quotation in W. Owen Cole and Piara Singh Sambhi, *The Sikhs: Their Religious Beliefs and Practices* (London: Routledge & Kegan Paul, 1978), 9.

4. Quoted in Ibid., 10.

5. Quoted in Khushwant Singh, "Sikhism," *Encyclopedia of Religion*, Vol. 13 (New York: Simon & Schuster Macmillan, 1995), 316.

6. Quoted in Ibid., 316.

7. Ibid., 319.

8. Cited in McLeod, *Sikhism*, 271.

9. Cited in Ibid., 272.

10. Ibid., 98.

11. Cited in W. H. McLeod, ed. and trans., *Textual Sources for the Study of Sikhism* (Totowa, NJ: Barnes & Noble Books, 1984), 79–80.

12. Cited in McLeod, *Sikhism*, 216.

13. *Āsā ki Vār* 19:2, Adi Granth, 473. Cited in McLeod, *Textual Sources*, 109.

14. Gopal Singh, *A History of the Sikh People* (New Delhi: World Sikh University Press, 1979), 263–264.

15. Mann, *Sikhism*, 14.

16. Ibid.

Chapter 8

1. All Chinese names in this chapter are indicated in the conventional Chinese manner, namely, the family name comes first, followed by the given name. All romanization of Chinese terms and names adheres to the official Chinese pinyin system. Terms and names with an established familiar spelling in the West, such as Taoism (instead of the official pinyin rendition of Daoism) will be provided in brackets at their first occurrence.

2. Refer to the highly suggestive article of David N. Keightley, "The Religious Commitment: Shang Theology and the Genesis of Chinese Political Culture,"

History of Religions 17, no. 3–4 (Feb.–May 1978), 211–225.

3. Also translated as *Book of Songs* or *Book of Poetry*.

4. Also known as the *Book of Documents*.

5. Many Chinese books carry the name of their supposed author as their title. To distinguish between the text and its reputed author, the former will be indicated in italics.

6. See Joseph Needham, ed., *Science and Civilization in China*, Vol. 2 (Cambridge: Cambridge University Press, 1956), 55ff.

7. This term is not found in the *Book of Changes* itself but is in fact a later Daoist rendition of the idea of the primordial one.

8. The masculine pronoun is used advisedly throughout the entire discussion of Confucian teachings. Confucius and his intellectual followers after him, like many in the premodern age worldwide, did not seriously entertain the possibility that women could participate meaningfully in the exercise of virtue, pursuit of scholarship, and service in government. The masculine pronoun is adopted not as an endorsement of that view but as a faithful reflection of the Confucian assumption.

9. Wm. Theodore de Bary, *Neo-Confucian Orthodoxy and the Learning of the Mind-and-Heart* (New York: Columbia University Press, 1981), 9.

10. See his *Confucius—the Secular as Sacred* (New York: Harper Torchbooks, 1972), 7.

11. See Tu Wei-ming, "Li as a Process of Humanization," in *Philosophy East and West* 22, no. 2 (April 1972), 187–201.

12. See Xinzhong Yao, *An Introduction to Confucianism* (Cambridge: Cambridge University Press, 2000), 46.

13. See the highly nuanced discussion of the topic by Li-Hsiang Lisa Rosenlee, in her *Confucianism and Women: A Philosophical Interpretation* (Albany: SUNY Press, 2006).

14. This discussion of *feng* and *shan* rites is based on Stephen Bokenkamp's "Record of the Feng and Shan Sacrifices," in Donald S. Lopez, Jr., ed., *Religions of China in Practice* (Princeton, NJ: Princeton University Press, 1996), 251–260.

15. Summary based on Patricia Buckley Ebrey, ed., *Chinese Civilization: A Sourcebook*, 2nd ed. (New York: The Free Press, 1993), 157–163.

16. This summary of the *jiao* liturgy is based on a composite description of two separate ceremonies conducted, respectively, in 1994 and 2005 in Hong Kong. A DVD depicting the rites and explaining their religious meaning was produced in 2009 by the Center for the Study of Daoist Culture of the Department of Culture and Religion, Chinese University of Hong Kong.

Chapter 9

1. This "body" is known as the *shintai*, the physical embodiment of the deity, which is believed to contain the spirit and magical power of the deity. It will be discussed in greater detail later.

2. Quoted in H. Byron Earhart, *Religion in the Japanese Experience: Sources and Interpretations,* 2nd edition (Belmont, CA: Wadsworth Publishing Company, 1997), 10.

3. That the Japanese should regard the sun as female is most noteworthy. That this female sun goddess should serve as the primordial ancestor of the imperial line, as we shall see later, is even more noteworthy, for it is incongruent with the later patriarchal orientation of the country.

4. The *Nihongi* has a slightly different version of this episode. It asserts that the three deities are the product of the union between Izanagi and Izanami.

5. Quoted in Wm. Theodore de Bary et al., eds., *Sources of Japanese Tradition*, Vol. 1 (New York: Columbia University Press, 2001), 259.

6. Quoted in Wm. Theodore de Bary et al., eds., *Sources of Japanese Tradition*, Vol. 2 (New York: Columbia University Press, 2005), 498, 512.

7. See Evan Zuesse, *Ritual Cosmos* (Athens: Ohio University Press, 1979), 402.

Chapter 10

1. See Harold Coward, *Sacred Word and Sacred Text* (New York: Orbis Books, 1988), 4–10. See also James A Sanders, *Torah and Canon* (Eugene, OR: Wipf and Stock, 1972), 91–116.

2. See Stephen Hodge, *The Dead Sea Scrolls Rediscovered* (Berkeley, CA: Ulysses Press, 2003), 158–210.

3. See Wayne A. Meeks and Robert L. Wilken, *Jews and Christians in Antioch: In the First Four Centuries of the Common Era* (Missoula, MT: Scholars Press, 1978), 85–126.

4. Isadore Twersky, ed., *A Maimonides Reader* (New York: Behrman House, 1972), 414; also 223–224.

5. Dan Cohn-Sherbok, ed., "The Face of God after Auschwitz," in *Holocaust Theology: A Reader* (New York: NYU Press, 2002), 96–98.

6. *After Auschwitz: History, Theology, and Contemporary Judaism* (Baltimore: Johns Hopkins Press, 1992), 171–174.

7. Dan Cohn-Sherbok, ed., "Free Will and the Hidden God," in *Holocaust Theology: A Reader* (New York: New York University Press, 2002), 153–156.

8. "No Religion Is an Island," in *Moral Grandeur and Spiritual Audacity*, ed. Susannah Heschel (New York: Farrar, Straus and Giroux, 1997), 235–250.

9. Emil L. Fackenheim, *The Jewish Return into History* (New York: Schocken Books, 1978), 129–143. See also *God's Presence in History* (New York: Harper & Row, 1970), 67–79, for Fackenheim's reflections on the significance of the *Shoah* as the pivotal event in modern Jewish history.

10. "Rome and Jerusalem," in *The Zionist Idea*, ed. Arthur Hertzberg (New York: Atheneum, 1984), 117–139.

11. "The Jewish State," in *The Zionist Idea*, 204–230.

12. *The Old New Land*, trans. Lotta Levensohn (Princeton, NJ: Marcus Wiener, 2000).

13. "The Balfour Declaration," in *The Jew in the Modern World*, ed. Paul Mendes-Flohr and Jehuda Reinharz (Oxford: Oxford University Press, 1995), 582. See also Jonathan Schneer, *The Balfour Declaration* (New York: Random House, 2010).

14. See *Judaism in a Secular Age*, ed. Renee Kogel and Zev Katz (New York: KTAV Publishing, 1995), 228–234.

15. Sherwin Wine, "Secular Humanistic Jewish Ideology," in *Judaism in a Secular Age*, 235–250.

16. See Richard L. Rubenstein, *The Cunning of History* (New York: Harper and Row, 1987), 90–97.

17. See Martin Buber, *Eclipse of God: Studies in the Relation between Religion and Philosophy* (New York: Harper and Row, 1957), 13–24.

18. See Roger Kamenetz, *Stalking Elijah: Adventures with Today's Jewish Mystical Masters* (San Francisco: HarperSanFrancisco, 1998), for an engaging first-person perspective on the Renewal Movement in Judaism. A more scholarly approach to this subject can be found in George R. Wilkes, "Jewish Renewal," in *Modern Judaism: An Oxford Guide*, ed. Nicholas de Lange and Miri Freud-Kandel (Oxford: Oxford University Press, 2005).

Chapter 11

All translations from the New Testament are from the New Revised Standard Version of the Bible.

1. Augustine, *Confessions* 1.1. Author's translation.

2. Timothy (Kallistos) Ware, *The Orthodox Church* (New York: Penguin Books, 1997), 261.

3. This later view was informed by New Testament images of a "furnace of fire" (Matthew 13:42) and "lake of fire" (Revelation 21:8).

4. *Declaration on Non-Christian Religions*, no. 2. Quoted in Anthony Wilhelm, *Christ among Us*, 2nd ed. (New York: Paulist Press, 1975), 396.

5. Quoted in Ware, *The Orthodox Church*, 305.

6. See Orazio Marucchi, *Christian Epigraphy*, trans. J. Willis (Chicago: Ares Press, 1974), 153–155.

7. Clement of Alexandria, *Stromata* 1.5.28. Author's translation.

8. Maximus the Confessor, *Book of Ambiguities* 41, quoted in Vladimir Lossky, *The Mystical Theology of the Eastern Church* (London: James Clarke, 1957), 214. The idea that Christians participate in the divine nature is found in the New Testament (for example, in 2 Peter 1:4) and is supported by the doctrine that the Holy Spirit is at work in every believer (e.g., in Romans 8).

9. Julian of Norwich, *Revelations of Divine Love* 4 (short text), in *Julian of Norwich: Showings*, trans. E. Colledge and J. Walsh (New York: Paulist Press, 1978), 131.

10. Pew Forum on Religion and Public Life/ U.S. Religious Landscape Survey, at religions.pewforum.org/pdf/report-religious -landscape-study-chapter-1.pdf.

11. John Bowden, *Encyclopedia of Christianity* (New York: Oxford University Press, 2005), 910.

12. James Cone, *Black Theology and Black Power* (New York: Seabury, 1969), 35.

13. The phrase "natural resemblance" comes from an apostolic letter (*Ordinatio Sacerdotalis*) issued by Pope John Paul II in 1994.

14. James A. Nash, *Loving Nature: Ecological Integrity and Christian Responsibility* (Nashville: Abingdon Press, 1991), 105.

Chapter 12

All translations are from the *JPS Hebrew-English Tanakh* (Philadelphia, Pa.: The Jewish Publication Society, 1999).

1. Association of Religion Data Archives (thearda.com), 2011.

2. Association of Religion Data Archives (thearda.com), 2011.

3. Ahmed Ali, trans., *Al-Qur'an* (Princeton, NJ: Princeton University Press, 1993).

4. Ibid.

5. Ibid.

6. Frederick Mathewson Denny, *An Introduction to Islam* (New York: Pearson Prentice Hall, 2006), 110–111.

7. William A. Graham, *Divine Word and Prophetic Word in Early Islam* (The Hague and Paris: Mouton, 1977), 157.

8. John R. Bowen, *Muslims Through Discourse* (Princeton, NJ: Princeton University Press, 1993).

9. Denny, *An Introduction to Islam*, 110–111.

10. Aballah al-Shiekh, "Zakat," in *Oxford Encyclopedia of Islam in the Modern World* (New York: Oxford University Press, 1995).

11. Ahmed Ali translation.

12. Leila Ahmed, *Women and Gender in Islam* (New Haven, CT: Yale University Press, 1992).

13. Mathnawi V, 411–414, trans. Kabir Helminski in *The Rumi Collection* (Boston: Shambala Press, 2005).

14. Sherman A. Jackson, *Islam and the Blackamerican: Looking Toward the Third Resurrection* (New York: Oxford University Press, 2005).

15. Malcolm X, *The Autobiography of Malcolm X: As Told to Alex Haley* (New York: Ballantine Books, 1965).

Chapter 13

1. We have deliberately avoided using the terms "cult" and "sect" to describe the various religious communities discussed in this chapter, and instead have adopted the more neutral phrases "new religious movements" and "alternative religions," chiefly because of the stigma that has been associated with groups designated as "cults" since the 1970s. As employed by contemporary sociologists, however, the word "sect" commonly describes a subgroup within an established religious community, whereas a "cult" is an innovative religious organization that exists outside of any established structure. Where appropriate, however, we have noted the pejorative use of the word "cult" when it is used in criticism of a particular movement or figure.

2. *Communities of Dissent: A History of Alternative Religions in America* (Oxford: Oxford University Press, 2003).

3. J. Gordon Melton, "Modern Alternative Religions in the West," in *A New Handbook of Living Religions*, ed. John R. Hinnells (London: Penguin Books, 1997).

4. Roy Wallis, *The Elementary Forms of Religious Life* (London: Routledge and Kegan, 1984).

5. Peter B. Clarke, ed. *Encyclopedia of New Religious Movements* (London: Routledge, 2006).

6. Various etymologies for this term have been proposed, from William James' neologism "oceanic" (meaning, in this context, "One who embraces all that exists") to the Japanese term for "king" in the name of Go.

7. David V. Barrett, *The New Believers: A Survey of Sects, Cults, and Alternative Religions* (London: Cassell & Co., 2001), 293.

8. Christopher Partridge, ed., *New Religions: A Guide* (Oxford: Oxford University Press, 2004), 184.

9. See Janet Treitman, *Inside Scientology* (Boston: Houghton Mifflin Harcourt, 2011). Treitman's study of the organizational history and dynamics of Scientology is the most complete to date.

10. See Karen Armstrong, *The Battle for God* (New York: Ballantine Books, 2001), 199.

11. Thomas J. J. Altizer and William Hamilton, *Radical Theology and the Death of God* (New York: Bobbs-Merrill, 1966), 95.

12. Richard Dawkins, *The God Delusion* (Boston: Houghton Mifflin, 2006), 164–165.

13. See William A. Stahl, "One-Dimensional Rage: The Social Epistemology of the New Atheism and Fundamentalism," in *Religion and the New Atheism: A Critical Appraisal*, ed. Amarnath Amarasingam (Leiden: Brill, 2010), 97–108.

GLOSSARY

arati (aah-ra-tee; Sanskrit) A ceremony involving the waving of a lamp before one's object of worship; it is often conceived as a purificatory rite that removes *drishthi* (the evil eye or negative projections).

Abbasids An important Muslim empire from 750–1258 C.E.

adhan (a-than; Arabic) The call to prayer.

Adi Granth (ah'dee gruhnth; Punjabi, "first book") Sikhism's most important sacred text and, since the death of Guru Gobind Singh in 1708, Sikhism's primary earthly authority; traditionally known as Sri Guru Granth Sahib.

ahimsa (ah-him'suh; Sanskrit, "nonviolence," "not desiring to harm") Both the avoidance of violence toward other life forms and an active sense of compassion toward them; a basic principle of Jainism, Hinduism, and Buddhism.

Aisha A beloved wife of Muhammad who is known for transmitting many *hadith*.

ajiva (uh-jee'vuh; Sanskrit, "nonsoul") Nonliving components of the Jain universe: space, time, motion, rest, and all forms of matter.

Allah (a-lah; Arabic) The Arabic term for God.

Amaterasu (ah-mah'-te-rah'-soo) "Deity that shines in the sky," the Sun Goddess in Shinto. Enshrined at Ise, Amaterasu is the *kami* of the imperial family. As the Sun Goddess, she is the most august of all deities. Her descendants are considered the only rightful rulers of Japan.

American Indian Religious Freedom Act 1978 U.S. law to guarantee freedom of religious practice for Native Americans.

Amma (ah-ma, Dogon) The High God of the Dogon people.

amrit (ahm-reet; Punjabi, "immortalizing fluid") A special drink made from water and sugar crystals, used in the Khalsa initiation ceremony.

anatman (un-aat-mun; Sanskrit) No independent self or soul.

apostle In the New Testament, Jesus' disciples, sent out to preach and baptize, are called apostles (Greek *apostolos*, "one who is sent out"). Paul of Tarsus and some other early Christian leaders also claimed this title. Because of their close association with Jesus, the apostles were accorded a place of honor in the early Church.

apostolic succession According to this Roman Catholic and Orthodox doctrine, the spiritual authority conferred by Jesus on the apostles has been transmitted through an unbroken line of bishops, who are their successors.

Arhat (ar-haat; Sanskrit, "worthy one") One who has achieved enlightenment.

astral voyages Any visionary experience of a mind/body projection through space and time.

atheism The belief that there is no God or gods.

atman (aat-mun; Sanskrit) The self or soul; lit. "the one who breathed."

avatara (ah-vah-taah-rah; Sanskrit) A divine incarnation, God taking physical form.

axis mundi (ax-is mun-di; Latin) An academic term for the center of the world, which connects the earth with the heavens.

Baal Shem Tov (1698–1760) A charismatic faith-healer, mystic, and teacher (whose given name was Israel ben Eliezer) who is generally regarded as the founder of the Hasidic movement.

Bab (Sayyid Ali Muhammed Shirazi, 1819–1850) An Iranian religious reformer and precursor of the Baha'i movement.

Baha'i A monotheistic and universalist faith that emerges in 19th century Iran.

Baha'u'llah (Mirza Husayn Ali Nuri, 1817–1892) The founder of the Baha'i faith.

baptism Performed by immersion in water or a sprinkling with water, baptism is a sacrament in which an individual is cleansed of sin and admitted into the Church.

Bar/Bat Mitzvah A rite of passage for adolescents in Judaism, the Bar Mitzvah (for males age 13) and the Bat Mitzvah (for females age 12–13) signal their coming-of-age and the beginning of adult religious responsibility.

bhakti (bhah-k-tee; Sanskrit) Devotion.

bishop Responsible for supervising other priests and their congregations within specific regions known as dioceses, bishops are regarded by Roman Catholic and Orthodox Christians as successors of the apostles.

Black Elk Famous Lakota religious leader.

bodhicitta (bow-dhi-chit-ta; Sanskrit, "the awakening mind or heart") In *Mahayana* it is the wise intention to enlighten all beings.

bodhisattva (bow-dhi-sut-tva; Sanskrit, "an awakened being") One on the verge of awakening. In *Mahayana* it refers to an adept who has made the vow of the *bodhisattva* to remain in *samsara* until all beings are free.

bori (boh-ree; various languages) A term for West African spirits.

Brahman (Braah-mun; Sanskrit) God, ultimate reality, the all-pervasive, the ground of the universe.

brahmin (Braah-mun; Sanskrit) A member of the priestly caste.

Buddha (bood-dha; Sanskrit, "the Awakened One") A fully enlightened being.

caliph (ka-lif; Arabic) Leader of the Muslim community after death of Muhammad.

Calvin, John (1509–1564) One of the leading figures of the Protestant Reformation, Calvin is notable for his *Institutes of the Christian Religion* and his emphasis on the absolute power of God, the absolute depravity of human nature, and the absolute dependence of human beings on divine grace for salvation.

Candomblé New World religion with roots in West Africa—particularly Yoruba culture—which is prominent in Brazil.

Cha'an or Zen (chah-aahn/Zehn) Respectively, the Chinese and Japanese names for the "meditation" school of Buddhism that values meditative experience far and above doctrine.

Changing Woman Mythic ancestor of the Navajo people who created the first humans.

channeling The ability to receive and transmit messages sent by spiritual beings not of this world.

chantway The basis of Navajo ceremonial practice; includes chants, prayers, songs and other ritual practice.

Christmas An annual holiday commemorating the birth of Jesus, Christmas is observed by Western Christians on December 25. While many Orthodox Christians celebrate Christmas on this date, others observe the holiday on January 7.

church In the broadest sense, "church" refers to the universal community of Christians, but the term can also refer to a particular tradition within Christianity (such as the Roman Catholic Church or the Lutheran Church) or to an individual congregation of Christians.

cosmology Understanding of the nature of the world that typically explains its origin and how it is ordered.

coven A community of witches.

Covenant A biblical concept that describes the relationship between God and the Jews in contractual terms; often thought of as an eternal bond between the Creator and the descendants of the ancient Israelites.

dalit (daah-lit; Marathi, "oppressed") The preferred term of self-representation for people who had been traditionally branded as untouchables in the caste system.

dama (dah-ma; Dogon) A Dogon rite of passage marking the transition to adulthood and to the afterlife.

dana (dah'nuh; Sanskrit, Pali, "giving") Ritual of giving in religions of India.

dantian (dahn'-teen'ən) "Fields for the refinement of the immortal pill"; major nodal points in the human body where the "pill" of immortality can be refined through alchemical means.

dao (dow) A fundamental concept in Chinese religion, lit. "path" or the "way." In Confucianism, it specifically refers to the entire ideal human order ordained by the numinous Absolute, *Tian*. In Daoism, it is the primary source of the cosmos, the very ground of all beings.

Daodejing (dow'-duh-jing) Basic Daoist scripture, lit. "The Scripture of the Way and its Potent Manifestation"; also known as the Book of *Laozi*, the name of its purported author.

Daozang (dow' zahng) Literally "Treasury of the Dao," this is the Daoist Canon that contains the entire corpus of Daoist texts. The most complete version, still in use today, was first published in 1445.

darshan (dur-shaan; Sanskrit) "An auspicious sight." The act of seeing and being seen by a divine being or saint.

de (duh) Another fundamental concept in Chinese religions. In Confucianism, it is the charismatic power of the ruler or the man of virtue, while in Daoism it means the concrete manifestation of the *dao*.

Dead Sea Scrolls Religious literature hidden in caves near the shores of the Dead Sea (c. second–first centuries B.C.E.).

dharma (dhur-mah; Sanskrit, "that which upholds") For Hinduism: (1) religion, (2) religious prescriptions and ordinances, (3) sacred duty, (4) law, (5) moral virtue, and (6) social or caste obligation. In the Buddhist context it refers to Buddhist teaching or to Buddhism as a religious tradition.

dhikr (zik-r; Arabic) Recollection or Remembrance. In the Sufi context, the practice to recall or remember God.

Diaspora A Greek word in origin, it refers to those Jewish communities that live outside of the historical land of Israel.

Digambara (dig-ahm'buh-ruh; Sanskrit, "those whose garment is the sky") The second largest Jain sect, whose monks go about naked so as to help abolish any ties to society; generally more conservative than the Shvetambara sect.

divination The attempt to learn about events that will happen in the future through supernatural means.

Easter An annual holiday commemorating the resurrection of Christ, Easter is a "moveable feast" whose date changes from year to year, though it is always celebrated in spring (as early as March 22 and as late as May 8).

election The belief that the biblical God "chose" the people of Israel to be His "kingdom of priests" and a "holy nation." This biblical concept is logically connected to the idea of the Covenant, and it entails the belief that the Jews' relationship with God obliges them to conform to His laws and fulfill His purposes in the world.

Elohim One of several terms used in the Hebrew Bible to identify the Creator-God; the name of alien creators responsible for the creation of the human race and culture in Raelian myths.

ema (ɔ-mah') Wooden tablets expressing pleadings to *kami* for success in life.

empathy The capacity for seeing things from another's perspective, and an important methodological approach for studying religions.

engrams In Scientology they are traumatic events stored as images in the subconscious mind.

Epiphany An annual holiday commemorating the "manifestation" of the divinity of the infant Jesus, Epiphany is celebrated by most Western Christians on January 6. Most Eastern Christians observe it on January 19.

eschatological Any belief in an "End-time" of divine judgment and destruction.

ethical monotheism A core concept of Judaism: it is the belief that the world was created and is governed by only one transcendent Being, whose ethical attributes provide an ideal model for human behavior.

eucharist (yoó-ka-rist) Also known as the Lord's Supper and Holy Communion, the eucharist is a sacrament celebrated with consecrated bread and wine in commemoration of Jesus' Last Supper with his disciples.

evangelicalism This Protestant movement stresses the importance of the conversion experience, the Bible as the only reliable authority in matters of faith, and preaching the gospel. In recent decades, evangelicalism has become a major force in North American Christianity.

Exodus The escape (or departure) of Israelite slaves from Egypt, as described in the Hebrew Bible (c. 1250 B.C.E.).

The Family The revised name of the Children of God movement, led by David Berg until his death in 1994.

fangshi (fahng-shər) "Magicians" who allegedly possessed the recipe for immortality.

Five Classics The five canonical works of Confucianism designated in the Han Dynasty: *Book of Odes, Book of History, Book of Changes, Record of Rites,* and *Spring and Autumn Annals.*

Four Books The four texts identified by the Neo-Confucian Zhu Xi as fundamental in understanding the Confucian teaching: *Analects, Mencius, Great Learning,* and *Doctrine of the Mean.* Between 1313 and 1905, they made up the curriculum for the civil service examination.

fundamentalism Originating in the early 1900s, this movement in American Protestantism was dedicated to defending doctrines it identified as fundamental to Christianity against perceived threats posed by modern culture.

Ghost Dance Religious resistance movements in 1870 and 1890 that originated in Nevada among Paiute peoples.

globalization The linking and intermixing of cultures.

Gospel In its most general sense, "gospel" means the "good news" (from Old English *godspel,* which translates the Greek *evangelion*) about Jesus Christ. The New Testament gospels of Matthew, Mark, Luke, and John are proclamations of the good news concerning the life, teachings, death, and resurrection of Jesus Christ.

grace Derived from the Latin *gratia* (a "gift" or "love"), "grace" refers to God's love for humanity, expressed in Jesus Christ and through the sacraments.

The Great Disappointment Disillusionment and shock following the failure, in 1844, of William Miller's prediction of the Second Advent.

gui (gwei) Ghosts and demons; malevolent spirits.

gurdwara (goor'dwah-ruh; Punjabi, "doorway of the Guru" or "by means of the Guru's [grace]") A special building for Sikh worship that houses a copy of the Adi Granth; the central structure of any Sikh community.

Guru (goo-roo; Sanskrit, "one who is heavy" or "venerable person") A spiritual teacher and revealer of truth, common to Hinduism, Sikhism, and some forms of Buddhism. When the word *Guru* is capitalized, it refers to the ten historical leaders of Sikhism, to the sacred text (Sri Guru Granth Sahib, or Adi Granth), and to God (often as True Guru).

hadith (ha-deeth, Arabic) Literary tradition recording the sayings and deeds of the Prophet Muhammad.

halacha Authoritative formulations of traditional Jewish law.

hajj (hahj; Arabic) The annual pilgrimage to Mecca, one of the five pillars of Islam.

harae (hah-rah'-ə) Shinto purification.

Hasidism A popular movement within eighteenth-century Eastern European Judaism, Hasidism stressed the need for spiritual restoration and deepened individual piety. In the course of the nineteenth and twentieth centuries the Hasidic movement spawned a number of distinctive communities that have physically separated themselves from the rest of the Jewish and non-Jewish worlds and who are often recognized by their attire and their devotion to a dynasty of hereditary spiritual leaders.

haumai (how'may; Punjabi, "self-reliance," "pride," or "egoism") The human inclination toward being self-centered rather than God-centered, which increases the distance between the individual and God.

henotheism The belief that acknowledges a plurality of gods, but elevates one of them to special status.

hijra (hij-rah; Arabic) The migration of the early Muslim community from Mecca to Medina in 622 C.E.; the Islamic calendar dates from this year.

hindutva (hin-doot-vah; Sanskrit, "Hindu-ness") A modern term that encompasses the ideology of Hindu nationalism.

hogan (ho-gan; Pueblo) A sacred structure of Pueblo peoples.

Holocaust The genocidal destruction of approximately 6 million European Jews by the government of Nazi Germany during World War II. This mass slaughter is referred to in Hebrew as the *Shoah.*

Holy People Ancestors to the Navajo people, described in mythic narratives.

Holy Wind Navajo conception of a spiritual force that inhabits every element of creation.

hukam (huh'kahm; Punjabi, "order") The divine order of the universe.

Husayn Grandson of Muhammad who was killed while challenging the Umayyads.

icons Painted images of Christ and the saints, icons are used extensively in the Orthodox Church.

Ifa (ee-fah; Yoruba) The divination system of the Yoruba religion, believed to be revealed to humanity by the gods.

imam (ee-mam; Arabic) Prayer leader; in the Shi'a tradition, one of the leaders of the Muslim community following the death of the Prophet Muhammad.

Inquisition The investigation and suppression of heresy by the Roman Catholic Church, the Inquisition began in the twelfth century and was formally concluded in the middle of the nineteenth century.

Interdependent Origination (Sanskrit, *pratityasamutpada*, "arising on the ground of a preceding cause") The realization that our sense of "self" arises spontaneously in response to a set of conditions. These conditions are born of a vast network of relationships that are inextricably linked to all phenomena. All things are the result of antecedent causes, and our sense of independent existence is merely an illusion.

ISKCON The official name of the "Hare Krishna" movement founded by A. C. Bhaktivedanta Swami.

Islam (is-lahm; Arabic) Lit. "submission"; specifically, the religious tradition based on the revealed Qur'an as Word of God.

isnad (is-nad; Arabic) The chain of transmission of *hadith*.

Izanagi (ee-zanah'-gee) The male *kami* who is the procreator of the Japanese islands.

Izanami (ee-za-nah'-mee) The female *kami* who is the procreator of the Japanese islands.

Jahiliyya (ja-hil-ee-ah; Arabic) The "age of ignorance," which refers to the time before the revelation of the Qur'an.

jiao (jee'au) Daoist communal sacrificial offerings to signal cosmic renewal and collective cohesion.

jihad (jee-had; Arabic) Lit. "striving"; sometimes, the greater *jihad* is the struggle with one's self to become a better person; the lesser *jihad* is associated with military conflict in defense of the faith.

jina (ji'nuh; Sanskrit, "conqueror") Jain title for one who has "conquered" *samsara*; synonymous with *tirthankara*.

jinja (jin'-ja) Shinto shrine.

jiva (jee'vuh; Sanskrit, "soul") The finite and eternal soul; also the category of living, as opposed to nonliving, entities of the universe.

Jump Dance Renewal dance of Yurok people.

junzi (ju'un zee) The personality ideal in Confucianism; the noble person.

Kabbalah One of the dominant forms of Jewish mysticism, kabbalistic texts begin to appear in Europe during the twelfth and thirteenth centuries. Mystics belonging to this tradition focus on the emanative powers of God—referred to in Hebrew as *sephirot*—and on their role within the Godhead as well as within *mitzvot*, the human personality.

kachina (ka-chee-na; Hopi) Pueblo spiritual beings.

kami (kah-mee) Shinto deity and spirit with awe-inspiring power.

karma (kur-mah; Sanskrit, "activity") Action or cause; the law of causation. The moral law of cause and effect of actions; determines the nature of one's reincarnation; for Jainism, all activity (*karma*) is believed to involve various forms of matter that weigh down the soul (*jiva*) and thus hinder the quest for liberation.

kevala (kay'vuh-luh; Sanskrit) Shortened form of *kevalajnana*, lit. "isolated knowledge" (isolated from the effects of *karma*); the perfect and complete knowledge that is Jain enlightenment; marks the point at which one is free from the damaging effects of *karma* and is liberated from *samsara*.

Khadija Muhammad's beloved first wife.

Khalsa (khal'sah; Punjabi, "pure ones") An order within Sikhism to which the majority of Sikhs belong, founded by Guru Gobind Singh in 1699.

Kinaalda (kee-nal-dah) Rite of passage for young Navajo women.

kingdom of God God's rule or dominion over the universe and human affairs. The kingdom of God is one of the primary themes in the teaching of Jesus.

Kinjiketele (kin-jee-ke-te-le) The leader of the Maji Maji rebellion in Tanganyika (today's Tanzania).

Kojiki (koh'-jee-kee) *Record of Ancient Matters*, compiled in the eighth century.

lama (laah-mah; Tibetan) A teacher. But usually a degree or title reserved for one who has complete a three year retreat.

li (lee) Etiquette and proper manners; rituals and holy rites.

liturgy The liturgy (from Greek *leitourgia*, "a work of the people" in honor of God) is the basic order of worship in Christian churches. It consists of prescribed prayers, readings, and rituals.

Logos In its most basic sense, the Greek *logos* means "word," but it also means "rational principle," "reason," or "divine reason." The Gospel of John uses *logos* in the sense of the "divine reason" through which God created and sustains the universe when it states that "the Word became flesh" in Jesus Christ (John 1:14).

loka (loh'kah; Sanskrit, "world") The Jain universe, often depicted as having the shape of a giant man.

Lord's Prayer A prayer attributed to Jesus, the Lord's Prayer serves as a model of prayer for Christians. Also known as the "Our Father" (since it begins with these words), its most familiar form is found in the Gospel of Matthew (6:9–13).

Lughnassadh (loo-nus-uh) A summer harvest festival (August 2) celebrated by Wiccans, honoring the Celtic god Lugh.

Luria, Isaac A sixteenth-century mystic who settled in Safed (Israel) and gathered around him a community of disciples. Lurianic mysticism seeks to explain the mystery surrounding both the creation of the world and its redemption from sin.

Luther, Martin (1483–1536) A German monk who criticized Roman Catholic doctrines and practices in his Ninety-Five Theses (1517), Luther was the original leader and one of the seminal thinkers of the Protestant Reformation.

Mahayana (muh-haah-yaah-na; Sanskrit, "greater vehicle") Characterized by emphasizing the *bodhisattva* path and developing between 100 B.C.E. and 100 C.E.

Maimonides A twelfth-century philosopher and rabbinic scholar whose codification of Jewish beliefs and religious practices set the standard for both in subsequent centuries.

Maji Maji (mah-jee mah-jee; Swahili) A 1905 rebellion against German colonizers in Tanganyika (today's Tanzania).

mandala (muhn-daah-la; Sanskrit, "circle") Typically circular cosmological diagram used for *tantric* meditation.

mantra (mun-trah; Sanskrit) A sacred sound, name, or verse that can be used as an object of meditation, ritual adoration, magical invocation, or as a protective spell.

matsuri (mah-tsu'ree) Shinto religious festival.

McKay, Mabel A Pomo woman who was well known as healer and basket-weaver.

Mecca The city in which Muhammad was born; place of pilgrimage for Muslims.

Medina The city to which Muhammad and his early followers migrated to escape persecution in Mecca.

medium A person who is possessed by a spirit, and thus mediates between the human and spirit world.

Messiah In the Old Testament, the Hebrew word "messiah" ("anointed one") refers to one who has been set apart by God for some special purpose and, in particular, the liberation of the Jewish people from oppression. In Christianity, Jesus of Nazareth is recognized as fulfillment of Old Testament prophecies concerning the Messiah.

Middle Way Buddha's teaching on avoiding extremes, that is systematized by the eightfold path.

miko (mee'-koh) Unmarried female Shinto shrine attendants.

mikoshi (mee-koh'-shee) Portable shrine temporarily housing a Shinto deity.

mikveh A ritual bath in which married Jewish women immerse themselves each month, after the end of their menstrual cycle and before resuming sexual relation with their husbands.

ming (see *Tianming*).

miraj (mir-aj; Arabic) Muhammad's Night Journey from Mecca to Jerusalem and from there to heaven, where he met with God.

misogi (mee-soh'-gee) Shinto ritual of purification with water.

mitzvot Literally translated, the Hebrew word *mitzvot* means "commandments," and it refers to the 613 commandments that the biblical God imparted to the Israelites in the Torah (i.e., the first five books of the Hebrew Bible).

modernization The general process through which societies transform economically, socially, and culturally to become more in keeping with the standards set by industrialized Europe; also, any transformation of post-industrial Western society that leads to the abandonment of traditional religious beliefs and values.

moksha (mohk-shah; Sanskrit) enlightenment; complete liberation from the bonds of *karma* and *samsara*.

monism The belief that all reality is ultimately one.

monotheism The belief in only one god.

Moonies A slang term for members of the Unification Church.

moran (mor-an; Samburu and Maasai) A young man in Samburu or Maasai culture who has been circumcised and thus has special cultural and religious duties.

Moses The legendary leader and prophet who leads the Israelite slaves out of Egypt, Moses serves as a mediator between the people of Israel and God in the Torah and is later viewed as Israel's greatest prophet. It is to Moses that God imparts the Ten Commandments and the teachings that later became the Torah.

mosque (mosk) Place of prayer, from the Arabic term "masjid."

muezzin (mu-ez-in; Arabic) The person who calls the *adhan*.

Muhammad The prophet who received the revelation of the Qur'an from God. The final prophet in a long line of prophets sent by God to humanity.

Mul Mantra The summary of Sikh doctrine that comprises the opening lines of the *Japji*, Guru Nanak's composition that in turn comprised the opening section of the Adi Granth. (See p. 244 for an English translation of the full text.)

multiculturalism The coexistence of different peoples and their cultural ways in one time and place.

mysterium tremendum and *fascinans* The contrasting feelings of awe-inspiring mystery and of overwhelming attraction that are said by Rudolf Otto to characterize the numinous experience.

mystical experience A general category of religious experience characterized in various ways, for example, as the uniting with the divine through inward contemplation or as the dissolution of the sense of individual selfhood.

myth A story or narrative, originally conveyed orally, that sets forth basic truths of a religious tradition; myths often involve events of primordial time that describe the origin of things.

Native American Church A church founded in early twentieth century based on Peyote Religion.

neidan (nay'-dahn) Daoist "Internal" alchemy designed to attain immortality through meditation, breath control, gymnastics, dietetics, and massage.

neisheng waiwang (nay'-sheng' wī-wahng) Neo-Confucian ideal of "inner sagely moral perfection and outer political skills."

New Age An umbrella term for various religious and quasi-religious practices based on a belief in the transformation of both nature and human consciousness.

New Thought A philosophical school of thought, popular in the late nineteenth century, that stressed the power of the human mind to discover the divine within nature and to control material reality.

Nicene Creed A profession of faith formulated by the Councils of Nicea (325) and Constantinople (381), the Nicene Creed articulates the Christian doctrine of the Trinity.

Nihon shoki (nee-hohn shoh-kee) *Chronicles of [the Land where] the Sun Originates.*

Nirguna (nir-goo-nah; Sanskrit) "Without qualities." Referring to God as being beyond description.

nirvana (nihr-vaah-nah; Sanskrit, "blowing out") The ultimate goal of Buddhist practice, refers to the final liberation from the suffering of cyclic existence (*samsara*, endless cycles of death and rebirth). Lit. "to blow out or extinguish," but it might best be understood as "cooling down" or "allaying" the pain born from the unquenchable thirst of being.

nontheistic Term denoting a religion that does not maintain belief in God or gods.

norito (noh-ree'-toh) Invocational prayer offered by Shinto priests to the *kami*

numinous experience Rudolf Otto's term for describing an encounter with "the Holy"; it is characterized by the two powerful and contending forces, *mysterium tremendum* and *fascinans*.

Odu (oh-doo; Yoruba) The original prophets in Yoruba religion.

omikuji (oh'-mee-koo-jee) Paper fortunes wrapped around tree branches at shrines.

omnipotence The divine attribute of total and eternal power.

omniscience The divine attribute of total and eternal knowledge.

Original Sin Formulated by St. Augustine in the fourth century, the doctrine of Original Sin states that the sin of Adam and Eve affected all of humanity, so that all human beings are born with a sinful nature.

orisa (oh-ree-sha; Yoruba) Term for lesser deities in Yoruba religion.

Orthodox Church Also known as the Eastern Orthodox Church and the Orthodox Catholic Church, the Orthodox Church is the Eastern branch of Christianity that separated from the Western branch (the Roman Catholic Church) in 1054.

Osho Another name for the religious movement established by Rajneesh Chandra Mohan in the 1980s.

Oshun (oh-shoon; Yoruba) A Yoruba goddess.

Panth (puhnth; Punjabi, Hindi, "path") The Sikh community. In lower case, *panth* ("path") is a term applied to any number of Indian (primarily Hindu) religious traditions.

pantheism The belief that the divine reality is identical to nature or the material world.

pantheon A group of deities or spirits.

parable According to the gospels of Matthew, Mark, and Luke, Jesus made extensive use of parables—short, fictional stories that use the language and imagery of everyday life to illustrate moral and religious truths.

parinirvana (pah-ree nihr-vaah-nah; Sanskrit, "supreme release") Refers to the death of a fully enlightened being.

Paul of Tarsus A first-century apostle who founded churches throughout Asia Minor, Macedonia, and Greece. Paul was also the author of many of the letters, or epistles, found in the New Testament.

Pentecost A holiday celebrated by Christians in commemoration of the outpouring of the Holy Spirit on the disciples of Jesus as described in the second chapter of the New Testament book of Acts.

Pentecostalism A movement that emphasizes the importance of spiritual renewal and the experience of God through baptism in the Holy Spirit, Pentecostalism is a primarily Protestant movement that has become extremely popular in recent decades.

Pesach An early spring harvest festival that celebrates the liberation of the Israelites from Egypt, Pesach (better known as "Passover" in English) is celebrated for seven days in Israel and eight days in the Diaspora. The first two nights are celebrated within a family setting.

peyote Hallucinogenic cactus used in many Native American religions.

phala (puh-lah; Sanskrit) fruit, effect (as in the "fruit" of action).

polytheism The belief in many gods.

Popol Vuh (po-pol voo; Quiché Mayan, "council book") The Quiché Mayan book of creation.

prajna (prudg-naah; Sanskrit) Wisdom.

prasada (pruh-saa-dah; Sanskrit) Consecrated offering, considered to be imbued after worship with the merciful blessing of the deity.

Protestant Christianity One of the three major traditions in Christianity (along with Roman Catholicism and Orthodoxy), Protestantism began in the sixteenth century as a reaction against medieval Roman Catholic doctrines and practices.

puja (poo-jah; Sanskrit) Worship.

purana (pooh-raa-nah; Sanskrit) "Ancient"; a compendium of myth, usually with a sectarian emphasis.

puranic (pooh-raa-nik; Sanskrit) Pertaining to the *puranas*.

purgatory In Roman Catholicism, purgatory is an intermediate state between earthly life and heaven in which the debt for unconfessed sin is expiated.

qi (chee) Breath, force, power, material energy.

Quanah Parker Comanche man who called for embrace of Peyote religion.

Quetzalcoatl (ket-zal-ko-at'-l; Aztec) Aztec God and important culture hero in Mexico.

Qur'an (kur-an; Arabic) The holy text of Muslims; the Word of God as revealed to Muhammad.

Rahit (rah-hit'; Punjabi) The *rahit-nāmā*, a collection of scripture that specifies ideals of belief and conduct for members of the Khalsa and, by extension, for Sikhism generally; the current authoritative version, the *Sikh Rahit Maryādā*, was approved in 1950.

Ramadan (rah-mah-dan; Arabic) The month in which Muslims must fast daily from dawn until dusk; the fast is one of the five pillars of Islam; the month in which the Qur'an is believed to have been revealed to Muhammad.

ren (rən) Human-heartedness, benevolence, the unique moral inclination of humans.

revealed ethics Truth regarding right behavior believed to be divinely established and intentionally made known to human beings.

revelation The expression of the divine will, commonly recorded in sacred texts.

rites of passage Rituals that mark the transition from one social stage to another.

rites of renewal Rituals that seek to enhance natural processes, like rain or fertility, or enhance solidarity of a group.

ritual Formal worship practice.

Roman Catholic Church One of the three major traditions within Christianity (along with Orthodoxy and Protestantism), the Roman Catholic Church, which recognizes the primacy of the bishop of Rome, or pope, has historically been the dominant church in the West.

rosary Taking its name from the Latin, *rosarium* ("garland of roses") the rosary is a traditional form of Roman Catholic devotion in which practitioners make use of a string of beads in reciting prayers.

Rosh Hashanah The Jewish New Year, it is celebrated for two days in the fall (on the first day of the month of Tishrai) and accompanied by the blowing of a ram's horn (a *shofar*, in Hebrew). It signals the beginning of the "ten days of repentance" that culminates with Yom Kippur.

ru (rōō) Scribes and ritual performers of the Zhou period; later used exclusively to refer to Confucians.

sacraments The sacraments are rituals in which material elements such as bread, wine, water, and oil serve as visible symbols of an invisible grace conveyed to recipients.

sadhana (saah-dhah-nah; Sanskrit) Spiritual discipline or practice.

Saguna (saah-goo-nah; Sanskrit) "With qualities." Referring to God as having specific identifiable traits or characteristics.

saint A saint is a "holy person" (Latin, *sanctus*). Veneration of the saints and belief in their intercession on behalf of the living is an important feature of Roman Catholic and Orthodox Christianity.

saisei-itchi (sai-sei ik'-kee) Unity of the religious and the political realms.

salat (sa-laht; Arabic) The daily prayers that are one of the pillars of Islam.

samadhi (sah-maahd-hee; Sanskrit, "hold together") A profound state of meditative trance.

samsara (sum-saah-ra; Sanskrit, "continuous flow") This term refers to the endless cycle of life, death, and rebirth or reincarnation.

samskara (sum-skaah-rah; Sanskrit) Rite of passage.

sand painting A painting made with sand used by Navajo healers to treat ailments.

sangha (suhn-ghaah; Sanskrit/Pali) "Assemblage or community [of Buddhists]."

sannyasi (sun-nyaah-see; Sanskrit) Monk-hood; formal renunciation.

Santeria (san-teh-ree-a; Spanish) New World religion with roots in West Africa; prominent in Cuba.

sawm (som; Arabic) The mandatory fast during the month of Ramadan; one of the pillars of Islam.

scholasticism Represented by figures such as Peter Abelard, Thomas Aquinas, and William of Ockham, scholasticism was the medieval effort to reconcile faith and reason using the philosophy of Aristotle.

Second Great Awakening An evangelical movement popular in the United States from the early nineteenth century to the 1880s.

secularization The general turning away from traditional religious authority and institutions; any tendency in modern society that devalues religious worldviews or seeks to substitute scientific theories for religious beliefs.

Seder A ritualized meal, observed on the first two nights of Pesach, that recalls the Exodus from Egypt.

Seekers A popular term, current in the late nineteenth century, for individuals who cannot find spiritual satisfaction in "mainstream" religious institutions and who describe themselves as "spiritual" rather than "religious."

shahadah (sha-ha-dah; Arabic) The declaration of faith: "There is no God but God and Muhammad is the Messenger of God"; the first of the five pillars.

Shaiva (shay-vah; Sanskrit) A devotee of Shiva.

Shakta (shah-k-tah; Sanskrit) A devotee of the Great Goddess, Devi.

Shangdi (shahng'-dee) The August Lord on High of the Shang period.

shari'ah (sha-ree-ah; Arabic) Lit. "the way to the water hole"; specifically, Islamic law.

Shavuot A later spring harvest festival that is celebrated for two days and is associated with the giving of the Torah at Mt. Sinai. Along with Pesach and Sukkot it was one of the "pilgrimage" festivals in ancient times.

shaykh (shaykh; Arabic) A title sometimes used for someone with a high degree of religious learning.

shen (shən) Gods and deities; benevolent spirits.

shengren (shəng rən) (or *sheng*) The Confucian sage, the epitome of humanity.

shi (shər) Men of service; lower-ranking civil and military officials in the Zhou period.

Shi'a (shee-ah; Arabic) One of the two major branches of Islam. The Shi'a believed that Ali should have succeeded as leader of the Muslim community after the death of Muhammad.

shimenawa (shee-mə' nah-wa) Huge rope hung in front of the worship sanctuary of a shrine.

shintai (shin-tai) The "body" of a *kami* housed in a shrine or temporarily in a *mikoshi*.

Shinto (shin-toh) The Way of the Gods. Traditional Japanese religion that acknowledges the power of the *kami*.

shirk (sherk; Arabic) The sin of idolatry, of worshiping anything other than God, the one unforgivable sin in Islam.

shunyata (shoon-yah-taah; Sanskrit, "emptiness") This asserts that all phenomenon, even the momentary components of experiential reality, are devoid of ontological, independent, intrinsic existence. As with the teaching on Interdependent Origination it stresses the relational underpinnings of each and every component of existence.

Shvetambara (shvayt-ahm'buh-ruh; Sanskrit, "those whose garment is white") The largest Jain sect, whose monks and nuns wear white robes; generally more liberal than the Digambara sect.

Siddur The prayer book that is used on weekdays and on the Sabbath.

sin The violation of God's will in thought or action.

skandha (skuhn-dhaah; Sanskrit, "heaps" or "bundles") Five aggregates (form, feeling, perception, mental formations, and consciousness) that give rise to a false sense of identity through apprehending them as an integrated and autonomous whole.

Stoicism Ancient Greek and Roman pantheistic religious philosophy.

stupa (stooh-puh; Sanskrit, "heap") Reliquary mounds in which the remains or personal objects of Buddhist masters are buried and venerated.

Sufi (soof-i) A follower of the mystical tradition of Islam, **Sufism**, which focuses on the believer's personal experience of God and goal of union with God.

Sukkot A fall harvest festival that is associated with the huts (in Hebrew, *sukkot*) in which the ancient Israelites sought shelter during the Exodus. It is celebrated for seven days in Israel (eight days in the Diaspora). During that time Jews take their meals and, if possible, sleep in huts that are partly open to the sky.

Sun Dance Midsummer ritual common to many Native American religions; details vary across cultures.

Sunnah (sun-na; Arabic) Lit. "way of life" or "custom"; specifically refers to example of the life of the prophet Muhammad; important religious source for Muslims.

Sunni (soon-e; Arabic) One of the two main branches of Islam. The Sunnis believed that the Muslim community should decide on a successor to lead after the death of Muhammad.

surah (soor-ah; Arabic) Chapter of the Qur'an; there are 114 *surah*s in the Qur'an.

sutra (sooh-trah; Sanskrit, "a thread") Verses of text or scripture.

sweat lodge A structure built for ritually cleansing and purifying the body.

synagogue Jewish houses of worship. The focal point of every synagogue is the Ark, a large cabinet where scrolls of the Torah are stored.

tafsir (taf-seer; Arabic) Interpretation of or commentary on the Qur'an. There are several types of *tafsir*, which aim to explain the meaning of the Qur'an.

tallit A prayer-shawl that is worn during morning prayers (traditionally by men). The fringes of this shawl represent, symbolically, the 613 mitzvot found in the Torah.

Talmud A multi-volume work of commentary on the laws of the Torah and on the teachings of the entire Hebrew Bible, composed in two stages: the Mishnah (edited in approximately 200 C.E.) and the Gemara (edited, in its Babylonian version, around 500 C.E.). Traditionally, Jews refer to the Talmud as the "Oral Torah" and regard it as an extension of sacred scripture.

Tanakh An acronym standing for the entire Hebrew Bible: Torah (the first five books of the Hebrew Bible); Neviim (or "Prophets," which includes works of both prophecy and history); and Khetuvim (or "Writings," a miscellaneous gathering of works in poetry and prose). Taken together, the twenty-four books that make of this collection constitute the core "scriptures" of Judaism.

Tapas (tuh-pus; Sanskrit) The purifying heat of austerity.

Tathagatha (tuh-tha-gaah-tah; Sanskrit, "the Thus-gone [One]") The Buddha.

Tathagatha-garba (tuh-tha-gaah-tah gaar-bhah; Sanskrit) The Womb Matrix of the Buddhas; i.e., the inner Buddha or the potentiality for awakening found in all beings.

tefillin Taken from the word for "prayer," the term *tefillin* refers to two small boxes to which leather straps are attached. Traditionally, Jewish males from the age of 13 wear *tefillin* during weekday morning prayers. Inside each of these boxes a miniature parchment containing biblical verses can be found; while one box is placed on the forehead the other is placed on the left arm, signifying that the individual's mind and will are devoted to God.

temizuya (te mee' zoo-ya) Purification fountain at a shrine.

theistic Term denoting a religion that maintains belief in God or gods.

Theravada (t-hair-ah-vaah-duh; Pali, "the Way of the Elders") Established in 240 B.C.E. at the Mahavihara in Sri Lanka, the earliest existent school of Buddhism that is predominant in Southeast Asia.

thetan A term used by Scientologists to identify the immortal Self and source of creativity in the human mind.

Tian (tee'ən) The transcendent, numinous entity in ancient Chinese religion; the conscious Will that regulates the cosmos and intervenes in human affairs, conventionally translated as "Heaven."

Tianming The mandate or command of *Tian* that confers political legitimacy to the ruler; also understood by Confucians as the calling to morally improve oneself and to transform the world.

Tianshi (tee'ən shər) "Celestial Master"; reference to a Daoist salvational figure as well as an organized movement.

tipi A typical conical structure of the tribes of the Great Plains which is often constructed with a sacred blueprint.

tirthankaras (teert-hahn'kuhr-uhs; Sanskrit, "makers of the river crossing") The Jain spiritual heroes, such as Parshva and Mahavira, who have shown the way to salvation; synonymous with *jinas*.

Torah Literally, the word *Torah* means "teaching," and in its most restrictive sense it refers to the first five books of the Hebrew Bible. Less restrictively, it signifies the totality of God's revelations to the Jewish people, which includes not only the remaining books of the Hebrew Bible but also the writings contained in the Talmud.

torii (toh- ree' ee) Cross-bar gateway leading up to the Shinto shrine.

transcendence General category for whatever is perceived as being beyond the normal or mundane sphere of things, whether understood as external or as within the individual or world.

transubstantiation According to this Roman Catholic doctrine, the bread and wine consecrated by a priest in the eucharist become the body and blood of Christ and retain only the appearance, not the substance, of bread and wine.

trickster A common figure in North American mythologies, trickster tales often teach important moral lessons.

Trinity According to the Christian doctrine of the Trinity, God is a single divine substance or essence consisting in three "persons."

tulku (tool-kooh; Tibetan) A reincarnate lama or Tibetan teacher who often provides indications to his disciples before his death as to where he will next be reborn. Ritualized modes of testing the child are employed to ensure that he or she is the reincarnation of the lama, usually involving identifying the personal items of the lama from a group of similar objects.

Ufology Any systematized belief in extraterrestrials.

Umayyad Dynasty Controversial Muslim dynasty from 661–750 C.E.

umma (um-mah; Arabic) The worldwide Muslim community.

upaya (ooh-paah-ya; Sanskrit, "expedient means") "Skillful Means" was developed into a form of Buddhist practice that encourages imaginatively applying wisdom to whatever circumstances one is in to assist in easing suffering or cultivating insight.

urbanization The shift of population centers from rural, agricultural settings to cities.

Vaishnava (vie-sh-na-vah; Sanskrit) A devotee of Vishnu and his *avataras*.

Vajrayana (vaah-jiraah-yaah-nah; Sanskrit) The diamond or thunderbolt (*vajra*) vehicle. A kind of Esoteric Buddhism based on *tantric* teachings that mostly date back to the seventh century C.E. Considered a more dangerous but quicker means of achieving enlightenment.

Vedanta (veh-daan-tah; Sanskrit) Lit. "the end of the *Vedas*." A comprehensive term for the philosophy that originated in the *Vedas*.

Vedic (veh-dik; Sanskrit) Pertaining to the *Vedas*.

vision quest A ritual attempt by an individual to communicate with the spirit world.

Vodou (voo-doo; Fon and French) New World religion with roots in West Africa; prominent in Haiti and the Haitian diaspora.

waidan (wī dahn) Daoist "external" alchemy involving refining of "pills" with herbs and minerals for ingestion so that immortality can be attained.

Wiccan Rede A traditional set of rules and ethical values cherished by Wiccans.

witchcraft A term used by Western scholars to describe the use of supernatural powers to harm others.

World's Parliament of Religions Two worldwide gatherings of religious leaders, first in Chicago in 1893 and a larger centennial gathering, also in Chicago, in 1993.

Wovoka A Paiute man whose visions started the Ghost Dance of 1890.

wuwei (wōō way) Daoist notion of action without intention; actionless action.

wuxing (wōō shing) The five elemental phases of metal, wood, water, fire, and soil that mutually support and overcome one another.

xian (shee'ən) Daoist immortals and perfected individuals.

xiao (shee'au) Filial piety; respect and care for parents and ancestors.

xinzhai (shin jī) "Fasting of the Mind" in the *Zhuangzi*.

yang (young) Lit. the south-facing side of a mountain, representing the energy that is bright, warm, dry, and masculine.

yangsheng (young shəng) Daoist techniques of nourishing life and attaining immortality.

YHWH These four consonants constitute the most sacred of names associated with the biblical God. The exact pronunciation of this name, according to ancient Jewish tradition, was known only to the High Priest, but after the destruction of the Second Temple the precise vocalization of these letters was lost—only to be recovered in the days of the Messiah.

yin Lit. the north-facing side of a mountain, representing the energy that is dark, cold, wet, and feminine.

yoga (yoh-gah; Sanskrit) Lit. "union," from the Sanskrit root *yuj*, "to yoke." Spiritual practices oriented at controlling the mind and senses.

Yogic Flying A meditational practice, similar to levitation, attributed to members of the Transcendental Meditation community.

Yom Kippur Referred to as the "Day of Atonement," it is the most solemn fast-day in the Jewish calendar.

zakat (za-kaht, Arabic) Regulated almsgiving that is one of the five pillars of Islam.

zar (zahr, various languages) A term for spirits in East Africa.

zhai (jī) Daoist "fasts" designed to seek redemption of transgressions by the gods.

Zhuangzi (juahng-zee) A fourth-century B.C.E. Daoist figure as well as the title of the book attributed to him.

Zionism A modern political philosophy that asserts a belief in Jewish national identity and in the necessity of resuming national life within the historic Land of Israel.

ziran (zee'-rahn) Daoist notion of natural spontaneity.

Zohar A kabbalistic midrash based on the Book of Genesis (c. 1280 C.E.).

zuowang (zoh'-wahng) "Sitting and Forgetting" in the *Zhuangzi*.

CREDITS

INDEX

Page numbers in *italics* indicate photographs/illustrations.